INSURANCE PRINCIPLES AND PRACTICES

INSURANCE PRINCIPLES AND PRACTICES

FREDERICK G. CRANE

Professor of Insurance
Drake University

John Wiley & Sons
New York   Chichester   Brisbane   Toronto

Cartoon Credits:

Pages 41, 202, 236, 266, 288, and 415. Sidney Harris.
Page 88. Frank Baginski. Reprinted from The Journal of Insurance, May/June, 1978.

Library of Congress Cataloging in Publication Data:

Crane, Frederick G
  Insurance principles and practices.

  Includes indexes.
    1. Insurance. I. Title.
HG8051.C82   368   79-19510
ISBN 0-471-01763-9

Printed in the United States of America

10 9 8 7 6 5 4 3 2 1

To my family

ABOUT THE AUTHOR

Frederick G. Crane is Professor of Insurance and Chairman of the Department of Actuarial Science, Insurance and Statistics at Drake University. After receiving an undergraduate degree in liberal arts from St. Lawrence University, Dr. Crane was employed for five years as a casualty insurance underwriter. He later earned an M.A. and Ph.D. in Economics at Ohio State University. In addition to teaching at Drake University, he has served as Visiting Professor of Insurance at Indiana University. A member of the Society of CPCU, Dr. Crane's publications include articles in the Journal of Risk and Insurance and the book, Automobile Insurance Rate Regulation.

PREFACE

This book provides an introduction to insurance in a manner differing from that of other insurance texts. Its content and organization reflect the results of a survey in which I asked several dozen insurance teachers what kind of textbook they would like to use. Many teachers said they would prefer a book that is concise, stresses practical aspects of the subject from the consumer's viewpoint, emphasizes personal lines, and provides more coverage of insurance operations and vocations. I have tried to respond to those wishes.

Although the book is shorter than many insurance texts, it treats most of the material that the longer ones do. I have controlled its length by avoiding unnecessary detail. In addition, I have tried to make the book as readable as its subject matter permits. Matters of practical interest and value have taken precedence over theory, although the theoretical side is presented whenever it is important to the reader's understanding of the subject.

The book has a strong consumer orientation. It should help the reader understand how insurance can be used as an effective tool of risk management. Thus it takes the consumer's viewpoint in such topics as risk identification, selection of policies and amounts of coverage, and the use of deductibles.

The personal lines of insurance (auto, homeowners, health, and life) are emphasized because they are important to everyone. Because this is the only book on insurance that most of its readers will be exposed to, it seems appropriate to stress the kinds of protection with which they are or will be directly involved. Within the personal lines, special attention is given to auto insurance. It is an important coverage and one in which major developments are taking place. By singling out auto insurance for intensive treatment, it then can easily be compared and contrasted with other lines of coverage.

Although the commercial lines are covered in less detail here than in most other texts, they are by no means ignored. Two chapters are devoted to insurance for small business, with emphasis on the protection available under a package policy specifically designed for small firms. Concentrating upon small business avoids the encyclopedic approach that is necessary when one attempts to cover the whole range of business insurance. Also, this material will be helpful to the many students who plan to go into business for themselves or to enter an existing small business.

The operational aspects of insurance (marketing, pricing, underwriting, loss adjusting, and financial operations) are treated more fully in this book than in many longer ones. This emphasis may reflect a bias stemming from my years as an underwriter. Regardless, I have found that students are interested in learning about insurance operations—how it is sold, why insurance companies want to insure some people and not others, why one person pays more than another for the same protection, how losses are adjusted, why rates are raised, and other matters concerning the actual functioning of the business. In my view, knowledge of insurance operations is an important part of consumer education. People are wiser insurance consumers when they understand how insurance works.

This book also furnishes more vocational material than do most other insurance texts. Much of the career information is simply a consequence of the study of insurance operations. When one learns about underwriting, for instance, one learns what underwriters do. Other vocational material has been included to enhance the readers' understanding of insurance principles and practices.

The book is organized into five parts. Part I deals with basic concepts, including risk, insurance, and risk management. Risk management is presented as the context within which insurance is used, and the risk management approach is shown to be equally important in the handling of business risks and personal risks. Part II surveys the personal lines of insurance. Part III concerns employee benefit plans and social insurance. Part IV reviews insurance for small business. The operational aspects of insurance are the subject of Part V.

The book's organization differs somewhat from that of most other insurance texts. By tradition, the type of insurance introduced first is either fire or life insurance. Because many students are most interested in auto insurance, that line is introduced first in this book. I have found that starting with a topic that people are interested in builds interest in the topics that follow.

The operational aspects are placed at the end of the book because they have little meaning at the beginning of an insurance course. The study of marketing, underwriting, and other operations is more effective and more interesting when one has some knowledge of insurance principles and coverages. Organizing the book this way creates one potential difficulty, however. If the insurance functions are not introduced until late in the course, their absence may handicap both the student and teacher during the study of insurance coverages. To avoid this problem, Chapter 2 includes a section on insurance operations. This section introduces the functional side of insurance and supplies a working vocabulary, permitting the detailed study of insurance operations to be postponed until the end of the book.

I am grateful to a number of people who have assisted me in the preparation of this book, including those who reviewed the manuscript and offered suggestions: Oscar Collins, Eastern Michigan University; John Langan, North Seattle Community College; Oscar Serbein, Stanford University; and D. M. Temple, Golden Gate University. In addition, I would like to acknowledge the help of Frederick Antil, Life Office Management Association; Joseph Bonnice, Insurance Information Institute; James Chastain, Howard University; William Naverra, Insurance Services Office, New York; and Warren Adams, Donald Doudna, and Jack Manders, all of Drake University. In addition, I am grateful to Dean Richard Peebler for promoting the academic environment in which a project of this type is feasible. I also appreciate the aid of Dorothy Barnes who typed the manuscript. Finally, my wife Anne deserves a very special note of thanks for her invaluable encouragement and assistance.

Frederick G. Crane
June 1979

CONTENTS

PART I
CONCEPTS OF RISK AND INSURANCE

CHAPTER 1
FUNDAMENTALS OF RISK AND INSURANCE

RISK

LOSS, PERIL, AND HAZARD

METHODS OF HANDLING RISK

INSURANCE

HOW INSURANCE HANDLES RISK

Around 1900 the president of a large American insurance company received a request to insure something rather new and different, an automobile. He replied that this company wouldn't even insure a railroad train operated by a skilled engineer. "Then wouldn't we be nitwits," he said, to insure "an automobile travelling at breakneck speed . . . through the center of villages and cities, over railroad crossings, and driven by anybody who had enough money to buy one of the contraptions whether or not he had enough brains to operate it properly!" Over 100 million of those "contraptions" are insured in this country now, as are countless other modern developments ranging from amusement parks to computer systems, from professional football teams to communications satellites.

This chapter outlines the nature of insurance and explains how it works. It also introduces several important terms and concepts that are essential to an understanding of insurance.

RISK

Risk means uncertainty about future loss or, in other words, the inability to predict the occurrence or size of a loss. We live in a world of risk, a world in which losses of many kinds happen suddenly and unexpectedly. Insurance, as we shall see, is one method of dealing with risk.

Risk can be classified as either pure or speculative. **Pure risk** can result only in loss or in the absence of loss. A building will have a fire or it will not; a car will be stolen or it will not be. **Speculative risk** can result in either loss or gain. Gambling creates a speculative risk. A person who bets on a ball game can either win money or lose it. Business ventures involve many speculative risks. When Walt's Waterbeds opens a new store, Walt knows he is taking a risk. He makes his decision in the belief that it will result in a profit rather than a loss.

The distinction between pure and speculative risk is important because usually only pure risks, situations in which there is no chance of profit, can be insured. The possibility of loss generally cannot be insured when there is a corresponding possibility of gain, as there is in speculative risk. The owner of a valuable painting faces both pure and speculative risks. The painting could be stolen. This possibility is a pure risk, because if the painting is stolen the owner will lose, but if it is not stolen the owner's position will simply remain unchanged. The owner will not profit from the mere absence of theft. However, the market value of the painting could decline if works of its type become less popular. This risk is speculative because there is another side to the coin, the possibility that the painting will rise in value. If it does rise the owner will have a gain instead of a loss. The risk of theft is insurable but the risk of declining market value, because it is a speculative risk, is not insurable.

LOSS, PERIL, AND HAZARD

Several commonly used words have rather precise meanings when they are used in connection with insurance. It will be helpful to identify three such words: loss, peril, and hazard.

Loss

In insurance, a **loss** is an unexpected reduction or disappearance of economic value. This is a narrower definition than that frequently used. Because insured losses are unexpected, they do not include the wearing out or normal depreciation of property, nor do they include damage intentionally done to property by its owners. Also, as insured losses are confined to economic value, loss of sentimental value such as that resulting from the theft of a wedding ring is not covered by insurance.

There are four principal types of losses: loss of property, loss of income, loss associated with legal liability claims, and loss due to unexpected expenses.

1. All of us are familiar with the first type of loss, loss of property. This includes the cost of repairing or replacing things like automobiles, jewelry, or clothing that have been stolen or have been damaged by fire, collision, or vandalism.
2. For many people income loss could have more serious consequences than property loss, as the ability to work and earn an income is the most valuable asset that most of us have. The loss of this asset can be far more costly than the loss of our physical possessions. Loss of income can result from sickness, accidental injury, or death, among other causes. Business firms are exposed to this loss too. They lose income if their buildings or equipment are damaged seriously enough to force a temporary closing of the business.
3. The third type of loss stems from legal liability claims. These claims, based on the laws of negligence, are described in Chapter 4. A homeowner may be sued by someone who trips and falls over a toy left lying on the sidewalk. If such an accident happens, the owner will have to incur the costs of defending against the lawsuit and may have to pay a sum of money to the injured person. Legal liability claims can also result from automobile, boating, or hunting accidents, and from almost any

other kind of activity. Business firms are subject to liability claims from numerous sources, including people injured on their premises and customers injured by using their products. A multimillion dollar case resulting from the explosion of a Ford Pinto's fuel tank is a well-known example.

4. Unexpected expenses, primarily for medical services, are the final type of loss. Each year many families are faced with huge bills from doctors, hospitals, or nursing homes.

Peril

A **peril** is the cause of a loss. Commonly insured perils include fire, theft, explosion, and illness. A single peril can cause more than one type of loss. The explosion of a natural gas pipeline could result in damage to a building, loss of rental income to the building's owner, lawsuits against the pipeline company, and unexpected medical expenses for people injured by the explosion.

Hazard

A **hazard** is a condition that increases the likelihood of loss due to a particular peril. Poor automobile brakes are a hazard making loss due to the collision peril more likely. There are three kinds of hazard: physical, moral, and morale.

1. Physical hazards are tangible characteristics of whatever is exposed to loss. Examples include the poor brakes just mentioned, slippery floors, and dry forests.
2. A moral hazard exists when the insured person is one who may dishonestly cause or exaggerate a loss. Insurance companies try to avoid insuring situations for which there is evidence of moral hazard. A person with a record of arrests for arson would have a hard time getting fire insurance! As a matter of fact, such a person might be turned down for other kinds of insurance as well. Insurance companies figure that a person who would make one type of fraudulent insurance claim would be likely to make others too.
3. A morale hazard exists when the presence of insurance causes the insured person to be indifferent to loss. This indifference can result in extreme carelessness, such as by people who, instead of taking reasonable care of their property, say "It's insured, so why should I worry?"

The relationship between hazards, perils and losses is illustrated by Figure 1–1.

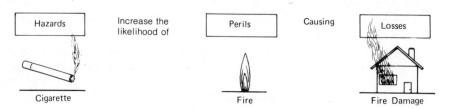

Figure 1-1   Hazards, perils, and losses.

METHODS OF HANDLING RISK

One of the interesting things about risk is the way that people react to it. If the risk is a speculative one and the amount at stake is not too high, taking a chance may be enjoyable. It may be fun to bet on a ball game or a horse race, especially if we think we have a good chance of winning. Also, we don't mind making what seem to be good business decisions, even though there is a possibility of suffering a loss. However, in the case of pure risk, because there is nothing to be gained and perhaps much to lose, the usual reaction is a feeling of uneasiness and insecurity. Generally speaking, individuals and businesses dislike pure risk and if very many dollars are involved they look for a way to minimize the risk's effects or to avoid them completely. Basically, four methods of risk handling are possible. They are risk avoidance, risk retention, loss control, and risk transfer.

Risk Avoidance

Sometimes risks can be avoided by not doing whatever produces them. People who are worried about being killed in a plane crash can practice **risk avoidance** by not flying. The obvious drawback of this approach is that it requires one to forego the convenience of air transportation. Risk avoidance sometimes is practical, though. Many people choose to avoid the risks involved in hang gliding or sky diving. We probably can think of other risks that people or businesses intentionally avoid. In most cases, however, there is no practical way of avoiding risk; it must be handled in some other way.

Risk Retention

Risk retention is practiced when risks are retained (kept) by the people or organizations exposed to them. Risks may be retained either deliberately or unintentionally.

One reason for unintentional risk retention is lack of awareness that the risk exists. Some people are not aware of the risk of legal liability claims and therefore retain that risk without really meaning to. A second reason for unintentional risk retention is underestimation of the likelihood of loss—the "it can't happen to me" attitude. The risk of income interruption due to death or disability is frequently retained for this reason. Scarcely any of us really believe we are immortal or not subject to serious illnesses or accidents. But because these are not pleasant things to think about we tend to tell ourselves that they won't happen to us. As a result, we may retain the risk without actually reaching a decision to do so, even though it would be more sensible to use one of the other risk handling methods. In other cases risks may be retained unintentionally, or at least unwillingly, because there is no other way of handling them. A family may realize that its main income supply would be cut off by the death of one of the parents, but if that person is in very poor health and is unable to obtain life insurance there may be no alternative to retaining the risk.

Intentional risk retention frequently involves losses that are too small to justify handling in any other way. If we break a comb or lose a cheap ballpoint pen, we just buy another. In other cases risk is retained intentionally because there seems to be very little chance that a loss will occur. People who live on high ground usually retain the risk of flood loss not because little flood damage is possible, but because they figure the chance of a flood is too slim to justify buying flood insurance or taking any other action.

Loss Control

The goal of those seeking **loss control** is to reduce the total amount of loss. Loss control is not an alternative to the other methods of handling risk but is used in addition to one or more of them.

The total amount of loss is a function of **loss frequency** and **loss severity.** That is, the total depends on how many losses occur and how big they are. Accordingly, there are two aspects of loss control: **loss prevention** and **loss reduction.** Loss prevention activities are aimed at reducing loss frequency; loss reduction measures are designed to limit the severity of the losses that do occur. Lightning rods are loss prevention devices. They direct lightning bolts to the ground, thus preventing fires and reducing loss frequency. Fire alarms and sprinkler systems are loss reduction devices. They do nothing to prevent fires; instead they limit the severity of fires after they begin. Some loss control measures, like automobile brakes, are aimed at both preventing losses and reducing the severity of those that occur.

Risk Transfer

A **risk transfer** occurs when risk is shifted to someone else. The usual way of doing this is to transfer the risk to an insurance company, but there are other, noninsurance transfers. A school collects a refundable $15 "breakage fee" from all students taking chemistry classes and deducts the cost of any laboratory equipment broken by each student before returning the fee at the end of the semester. The effect is to transfer part of the risk of equipment breakage from the school to the students. Notice that two other risk handling methods are also involved. First, the school retains the risk of equipment breakage in excess of $15 per student. Second, giving the students a financial stake in the matter probably motivates many of them to use the equipment more carefully. Thus, the breakage fee also serves as a loss control measure.

Risk transfer by means of insurance is the risk handling method with which this book is chiefly concerned. We shall now turn our attention to that approach.

INSURANCE

Insurance may be defined as a system of combining many loss exposures, with the costs of the losses being shared by all of the participants. The term **loss exposures** refers to the objects that are subject to loss. In auto insurance the loss exposures are autos; in life insurance they are lives.

Figure 1–2 shows how insurance operates. Imagine a group of one hundred people each of whom owns a stereo system. To simplify things let us assume that each system is worth $1,000. The owners realize that their stereos could be stolen or destroyed by fire. To eliminate the risk of losing the money they have invested in their equipment, each of them buys an **insurance policy**. An insurance policy is a legal contract under the terms of which an insurance company agrees to pay for stated losses. In this case the policies cover the stereos for the perils of theft or fire for a period of one year.

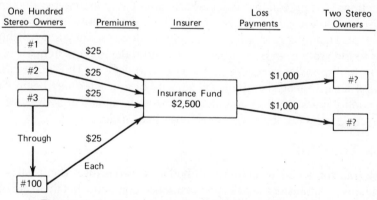

Figure 1–2 How losses are shared through insurance.

The price of an insurance policy is called a **premium**, and the premium for each of these policies is $25. That is the amount the insurance company collects from each of the participants (commonly called "policyholders" or "insureds") to pay for stolen or destroyed stereos, plus its costs of doing business. The company has been insuring stereo equipment for many years and has found that an average of two out of every one hundred of the units it insures are either stolen or destroyed by fire each year. By charging the one hundred owners $25 for the policies, the company will accumulate a fund of 100 × $25, or $2,500. If the loss experience of this group is like that of persons the company has insured in the past, there will be two losses and the company will pay 2 × $1,000, or $2,000, for them.

What about the other $500? It is an essential part of the arrangement, because it will pay the company's operating expenses. Out of the $500 difference between its income from premiums and its payment for losses the company must pay sales commissions to the people who sell the policies, salaries, office expenses, energy costs, taxes, and so forth. The $500 also includes a safety margin in case there are more than two losses or in case the company's other expenses turn out to be greater than expected. Finally, if all goes well there may be something left over as profit for the company and its owners.

What does such a system achieve? What does insurance do for the stereo owners? It relieves them of risk. That is, it removes the possibility of financial loss of the types and amount covered by their policies. It does this by a process of sharing. The losses that a few policyholders suffer are shared by all of the participants by means of the premiums that all of them pay. In other words, each stereo owner substitutes a relatively small but known expense ($25) for the possibility of incurring a much larger loss ($1,000). And this is feasible because the insurer is able to estimate the total amount of loss. Because the company can predict the amount rather accurately, it is able to calculate the premium that each owner must pay to cover his or her share of the total cost. To understand how this can be done, we shall examine the process more closely.

HOW INSURANCE HANDLES RISK

Insurance handles risk by transferring it to an insuring organization. An explanation of this process involves three other concepts: chance of loss, degree of risk, and the law of large numbers.

Chance of Loss

Chance of loss, sometimes called probability, can be defined as the probable number of losses out of a given number of loss exposures. This concept

was used in the example of insurance for stereo equipment when the
insurance company estimated that two out of every one hundred stereos
would be stolen or destroyed during the year. Another illustration of chance
of loss is betting on the flip of a coin. Because there is an equal chance of
winning or losing, the chance of loss in this case is one out of two. If we were
predicting the suit of a card to be drawn at random from a full deck, the
chance of loss would be three out of four.

Insurance companies usually have to estimate chance of loss on the basis
of what has happened in the past. Because it is important that their estimates
be as accurate as possible, the companies accumulate huge amounts of data
on the exposures they insure. In later chapters we shall see how they use
records of automobile losses, death rates, hospital costs, and so forth in
setting insurance premiums.

Degree of Risk

We should be careful not to confuse chance of loss with degree of risk.
Degree of risk is the extent of uncertainty about future losses; it is the extent
to which losses are unpredictable. If losses can be predicted quite accurately, there is a small degree of risk regardless of what the chance of loss
may be. For instance, if losses are certain *not* to happen (the chance of loss is
zero), the degree of risk is zero because there is no uncertainty. But notice
that if it is certain that a particular number of losses *will* happen, the degree
of risk again is zero because there is no uncertainty in this situation either.
The chance of loss differs in these two cases, but the degree of risk is the
same. It is the same because in both situations the outcome is known in
advance, meaning there is no uncertainty.

The following example also illustrates the two concepts. Two taxicab
companies—Red Cab Company and Blue Cab Company—have fifty cabs
apiece. The managers of both are trying to predict how many of their cabs
will be destroyed in collisions next year. Checking their records, the two
companies find the numbers of cabs destroyed during the last five years
(Table 1–1). For the five-year period, both companies have lost an average
of three cabs per year. The chance of loss for both, on the basis of past

Table 1–1 Number of Cabs Destroyed by Collision

	YEAR 1	YEAR 2	YEAR 3	YEAR 4	YEAR 5	TOTAL	AVER-AGE
Red Cab Company	2	4	2	3	4	15	3
Blue Cab Company	7	1	2	0	5	15	3

experience, is therefore 6% (3 out of 50). Both predict that they will lose three cabs next year. But what about the degree of risk? Are the managers of the two companies equally certain about their predictions? Probably not. Red Cab Company has had between two and four cabs destroyed each year. They feel quite certain that they will lose about three again next year. But Blue Cab's losses have ranged all the way from zero to seven. Its managers throw up their hands. "The number fluctuates tremendously from year to year," they say. "We'll predict three, but goodness only knows how many there actually will be!" The point is that the two firms have the same chance of loss but different degrees of risk. Red Cab's record has led its managers to be relatively certain of their prediction for next year. Blue Cab's officials, being less certain, have a greater degree of risk even though their company has the same chance of loss.

The Law of Large Numbers

The law of large numbers is the key to the functioning of insurance. Application of the law makes it possible for insurance companies to handle risks like that of the Blue Cab Company and countless other individuals and businesses. The **law of large numbers** is a mathematical principle stating that as the number of exposures is increased the actual results tend to come closer to the expected results. We can illustrate the principle by flipping a coin and predicting whether it will come up heads or tails. If we bet a dollar that it will be heads, our chance of loss is 1 in 2; we have a 50% chance of winning a dollar and a 50% chance of losing a dollar. How certain or uncertain are we of the outcome? Assuming that it is a fair flip and a properly balanced coin, we are as uncertain as we can be. Risk is at a maximum. We will either win a dollar or lose a dollar, but there is no basis for predicting which will be the case.

Now assume that the coin is going to be flipped 1,000 times. Each time we shall bet a dollar that it will land heads up. The chance of loss is unchanged; the expected result is that there will be 500 heads and 500 tails. But how certain or uncertain are we of the *total outcome*? Previously we were completely in the dark. Our prediction that the coin would land heads up was going to be either absolutely correct or dead wrong. Now the situation has changed. There is less risk because it is practically impossible that we will either win 100% or lose 100% of our 1,000 bets. We are confident that the result will not be far from the expected result, as determined by the underlying chance of loss. If, for instance, the result turns out to be 520 heads and 480 tails (or vice versa), we shall have missed our prediction of 500 by only 20, an error of only 4%. If we were to bet numerous times on fewer or more flips than 1,000 (say 100 or 10,000), we would find that the law of large numbers would continue to hold true: the greater the number of exposures, the closer the outcome is likely to be to the underlying chance of loss. In other words, the law of large numbers tells us that *increasing the number of loss exposures decreases the risk with regard to the total outcome.*

There are many other examples of the law of large numbers. Consider how it is illustrated by each of the following:

1. Which would you rather predict, the grade average of a single student chosen at random, or the grade average of the entire junior class?
2. Which can be predicted more accurately, the team batting average of the St. Louis Cardinals after the first game of the season, or the composite batting average of the entire National League at the end of the season?
3. A national organization makès predictions of the total number of traffic fatalities in the United States during a holiday weekend. The prediction is not broken down on a state-by-state or county-by-county basis. Why not?

Insurance and the Law of Large Numbers

Insurance reduces risk by combining many individual loss exposures. Because of the law of large numbers, the insurance company is then able to predict the total loss with reasonable accuracy.

The process of combining a large number of exposures and predicting aggregate rather than individual losses is essential. If an insurer covered Tom Hyde's $1,000 stereo and no others, it would be as uncertain of the outcome as Tom had been. Either it would make a $1,000 loss payment or it would make no loss payment (ignoring the possibility of partial loss as we did earlier). Tom's risk would simply have been transferred to the insurance company. But, if the company insures many other stereos in addition to Tom's, the situation is different. The company then is in a position comparable to a person who bets on 1,000 flips of a coin. Because of the law of large numbers, the insurance company's prediction of the total amount of loss payments for all the stereos it insures will be fairly close to its actual payments.

Notice that the insurer still is no better able to predict whether Tom Hyde will have a loss than Tom is. But, after Tom's risk is transferred by means of the insurance policy, the insurance company really isn't concerned about whether or not he or any other particular one of its many policyholders has a loss. It has predicted the total amount of loss and the premiums the company has charged are based on that prediction. Its only concern now is whether the total amount it pays for losses will be more or less than the total amount that it predicted.

The predictions of insurance companies are never precisely correct. Sometimes actual losses paid for a year are considerably above or below expected losses. One reason is that even the largest companies may not cover a sufficient number of exposures of a given type. The theoretical point at which predictions would become precise is when the number of exposures becomes infinitely large. If a coin were flipped an infinite number of times the outcome would be exactly that of the underlying chance of loss, half heads and half tails. But flipping a coin an infinite number of times, of course, is not possible, nor is it possible to insure an infinite number of cars or lives or houses. Another reason why combining many exposures does not completely eliminate risk (from the insurer's viewpoint) is that we live in a world of constant change. For instance, changes in the average cost of garage repairs affect future loss developments in auto insurance, as do changes in gasoline supplies, traffic law enforcement, and highway maintenance. These and many other factors influence the chance of loss in unpredictable ways. In spite of such limitations, however, insurance companies usually can predict their aggregate loss payments with reasonable accuracy. They are able to do so because of the law of large numbers.

Insurance and Gambling

Is purchasing an insurance policy the same as gambling? Is a person who insures a $1,000 stereo for a $25 premium simply betting that there will be a loss? Is the insurance company betting that there won't be?

In some ways insurance does seem like gambling. Both involve an exchange of money based on the occurrence of a future event, and in both the amount payable by one of the parties may be greater than the amount payable by the other. One difference, of course, is that insurance involves pure risk whereas gambling is a speculative risk. That is, insured exposures present a chance only of losing; in gambling one may either win or lose. Another difference, and a very important one, is that gambling creates risk, but insurance transfers an existing risk to someone else. For example, until people bet on certain horses, they have no financial stake in the outcome of a race. Placing bets puts them in a position in which they can win or lose, depending upon which horses they bet on. Gambling thus creates a risk that did not previously exist. In contrast, any person who has a loss exposure (for instance, owns an automobile or a house) already is in a position where he or she may incur financial loss. The car may crash, the house may burn, and so forth. Risk always exists *before* insurance is purchased. Insurance relieves a person of risk rather than creating a new risk. In this respect, insurance is the opposite of gambling.

Insurance and Risk

Earlier, we defined insurance as a system of combining many loss exposures so that the costs of unexpected losses are shared by all participants. We now should have a good idea of why that is done, how it is done, and what the results are.

The reason for insuring is to rid oneself of a risk, that is, uncertainty about a possible financial loss. The method used is risk transfer. The insurance buyer transfers the risk to an insurer that promises to reimburse the insured if a loss occurs. The insurer estimates its total losses and expenses and charges each policyholder a share of the total in the form of the premiums for their policies. The insurer is able to price its policies with reasonable accuracy because it is dealing with the total cost of many exposures and because, given the law of large numbers, risk decreases as the number of exposures increases. The result is that policyholders replace the possibility of a relatively large loss with the payment of a much smaller expense, the premium.

More than one hundred years ago farmers in the eastern and midwestern states established a number of organizations to insure farm properties against fire and lightning. Operating in just one or a few rural counties, many of these organizations at first covered only a few dozen farms. Losses were infrequent; one company had none at all during a three-year period and another's only payment one year was $150 for a horse killed by lightning. The usual procedure was to collect little or no premium until the need arose, and to then charge each member with his or her share of the loss. Clearly, that was a form of insurance. Risk was transferred, a number of loss exposures were grouped together, and costs were shared, even though the financing was on a pass-the-hat basis rather than through premiums paid in advance. Insurance today is essentially the same. It is still a system of handling risk by combining exposures and sharing costs.

IMPORTANT TERMS

Risk	**Loss exposure**
Pure risk	**Insurance policy**
Speculative risk	**Premium**
Loss	**Chance of loss**
Peril	**Degree of risk**
Hazard	**Law of large numbers**
Insurance	

KEY POINTS TO REMEMBER

1. Risk, meaning uncertainty about future loss, may be either pure or speculative. Pure risk can result only in loss or in no loss; speculative risk can result in either loss or gain. Ordinarily, only pure risks can be insured.
2. In insurance, a loss is an unexpected reduction or disappearance of economic value. Insured losses include loss of property, loss of income, loss associated with legal liability claims, and loss due to unexpected expenses.
3. The cause of a loss, such as fire or theft, is called a peril.
4. Hazards are conditions that increase the likelihood of loss due to a particular peril. There are three types of hazard: physical, moral, and morale.
5. There are four basic methods of handling pure risk: risk avoidance, risk retention, loss control, and risk transfer. Insurance is one type of risk transfer.
6. Insurance is a system of combining many loss exposures, with the costs of the losses being shared by all of the participants.
7. Loss exposures are units that could sustain losses.
8. An insurance policy is a legal contract by the terms of which an insurance company promises to pay for stated losses.
9. An insurance premium is the price of an insurance policy.
10. The chance of loss is the probable number of losses out of a given number of loss exposures. It should be distinguished from degree of risk, which is the extent of uncertainty about future losses.
11. The law of large numbers is a mathematical principle stating that as the number of exposures is increased the actual results tend to come closer to the expected results.
12. Insurance reduces risk by combining many loss exposures.

REVIEW QUESTIONS

1. Why is risk an important concept?
2. Give an example of each of the four methods of handling risk.
3. What is the difference between loss prevention and loss reduction?
4. Give an example of each of the four types of loss.
5. What is the difference between a peril and a hazard?
6. Give an example of each of the three types of hazard.
7. Distinguish between chance of loss and degree of risk.
8. Why is the law of large numbers vital to insurance?
9. How does insurance differ from gambling?

DISCUSSION QUESTIONS

1. Which of the following are perils and which are hazards?
   (a) Flood
   (b) Careless driving
   (c) Theft
   (d) Badly worn automobile tires

2. Some things can be either perils or hazards. (a) How could this be true of hail? (b) Of illness?

3. Several illustrations of the law of large numbers are given in this chapter. Can you think of others?

4. Changes in such things as technology, inflation, and law enforcement can affect future loss developments. How might changes in each of these affect the amount of automobile insurance loss payments?

5. Does the fact that many people enjoy gambling mean that the risk of financial loss is not undesirable after all?

6. Gambling creates risk of financial loss and insurance eliminates such risk. Can you think of instances in which the opposite would be the case?

7. In a discussion of the nature of risk and insurance, one person said that insurance eliminates risk. Another person retorted that insurance doesn't eliminate risk, but does transfer it and reduce it. A third person insisted that the first speaker was looking at insurance from the insured's viewpoint and the other was looking at it from the insurer's viewpoint. Who do you think was right?

8. A person who knows nothing at all about insurance asks how it can be possible to insure an $80,000 house for only $150 a year. Based upon what you have learned about the general nature of insurance, what would your response be?

CHAPTER 2
THE INSURANCE INDUSTRY

FEATURES OF INSURABLE RISKS

THE FIELDS OF INSURANCE

INSURANCE OPERATIONS

This chapter helps set the scene for the remainder of the book. It begins with a discussion of the characteristics that distinguish insurable risks from uninsurable risks. Next, the various fields of insurance are identified. The chapter concludes with a brief introduction to the operational side of insurance, providing a preliminary view of insurance marketing, pricing, underwriting, claims adjusting, and company management.

FEATURES OF INSURABLE RISKS

Insurance is not always available as a method of handling risk. That is, some risks are insurable but others are not. We already have seen that only pure risks can be covered by insurance. Gambling and other speculative risks are not insurable. Beyond that, what are the features distinguishing insurable from noninsurable risks?

The question is a difficult one because insurance is not an abstract science that conforms strictly to established rules and principles. It is a living, dynamic business operated by people who are capable of doing imaginative and unusual things. Therefore exceptions can be found to most generalizations about insurance, and it would be misleading to list features that insured risks "absolutely must have." At the same time, however, most insured risks have certain characteristics that risks that are generally not insured do not have. These characteristics, which can be thought of as the ideal features of insurable risks, are:

1. There are many similar loss exposures.
2. Losses are definite, measurable, and important.
3. Losses are accidental.
4. Catastrophic loss is extremely unlikely.

There Are Many Similar Loss Exposures

A large number of similar exposures is necessary. Firstly, a reasonable estimate of the chance of loss can then be made, based upon information about past experience. Premiums then can be set at the proper level. Secondly, by insuring many similar exposures it is more likely that an insurer's actual loss experience will be close to the predicted loss experience. Even if the insurance is properly priced, an insurer cannot safely cover only a few units of a given class. A fire insurance company that insures only a few buildings would be bearing too much risk; it would have less risk if it covered a great many buildings.

How many loss exposures are enough? Premiums often are based on the experience of hundreds of thousands of policies over a period of several years. Statistical agencies compile the loss data of many insurers, giving each company a broad experience base for predicting future losses. As to how many exposures a given company believes it must insure, the answer depends on how much uncertainty it is willing and able to bear. Probably many companies would not undertake to insure a new class of exposures (motorcycles or sailboats, or instance) unless they felt they could write at least several thousand policies within a year or two. Some companies would be more venturesome; others would be more conservative.

Clearly, there are exceptions, cases in which insurance is written without there being a large number of similar exposures. Lloyd's of London is well known for handling such things. A few years ago Lloyd's wrote a policy to cover the possible capture of Scotland's legendary Loch Ness monster. The policy insured a scotch whisky firm which, as an advertising gimmick, was offering $2 million if the monster was caught. The policy would reimburse the firm if it became necessary to pay the reward. Lloyd's of London wrote the policy for a premium of $6,000. Obviously, as there are not many loss exposures similar to this one (some people say there is no monster at all!), cases like this are exceptions. Lloyd's of London is both willing and able to insure certain exposures that most other organizations would regard as uninsurable. Even though there are exceptions, the existence of many similar loss exposures is generally regarded as a necessary element of insurability.

Losses Are Definite, Measurable, and Important

The second characteristic of insurable risks is that the insured losses are definite, measurable, and relatively important.

A definite loss is one that is obvious; its occurrence is unmistakable. If covered losses were not definite, too many disputes between policyholders and insurers would be likely to develop. Consider a policy that pays a weekly income if the insured person is disabled because of accident or sickness. Losses due to accident usually are definite. If an insured breaks her leg while skiing at 9:30 A.M. on January 20th, her disability begins that day. But what if the insured just doesn't feel up to par and decides not to go to work some Monday morning? Is she disabled for as long as she says she doesn't feel like working? What does disability mean? If the insured cannot return to her former job but takes a less strenuous one instead, is she still disabled? Disability due to sickness would be difficult to insure if the policies did not define the covered loss carefully. Sometimes they define it as the inability of the insured to perform his or her regular occupation. Inclusion of a waiting period also helps make this loss more definite. Payments might begin with the third week of disability, for instance. This stipulation makes it more likely that claims will be submitted for genuine disabilities only.

Losses are measurable when their dollar amount is easily determined by a method agreed upon in advance. For disability income insurance, losses are made measurable by stating in the policy the amount ($200 per week, for instance) that the company will pay. An example of a loss that is not measurable is the sentimental value that people may attach to certain property. Consider the ring that had been your great-grandmother's and that was made from gold mined by your great-grandfather during the California Gold Rush. Your family would hate to have this ring stolen or destroyed. They treasure it highly, not so much for its intrinsic worth as for its place in the family's history. In other words, the ring's value is largely a sentimental value and its insurable value may be quite small. Sentimental value is subjective and hard to measure. Unless the owners and the insurer agree upon an amount in advance and state it in the policy, sentimental value is not insurable.

Insured losses must also be important, that is, there must be the possibility of a fairly large financial loss. Insurance against damage to a cheap ballpoint pen, for instance, is not feasible. In the first place, of course, no one would buy it; it wouldn't be worth the bother. Secondly, even if it were available, it would be too expensive. The costs of selling the policy, preparing it, processing the premium, and handling claims would probably require something like a $15 annual premium to cover a 69¢ pen. Potentially large loss is necessary in order for insurance to be economically feasible.

Losses Are Accidental

Another feature of insurable risks is that the covered losses are accidental, meaning that the losses are unintended and unexpected by the policyholder. Thus fire insurance does not cover arson by the owner, and auto policies likewise exclude injury or damage caused intentionally by the insured. Also, loss that is due solely to normal depreciation of property is not insurable. If the only loss to your car is a reduced market value because of normal wear and aging, your auto insurance won't buy you a new one! In such a case the loss is unintentional, but it is not unexpected.

Catastrophic Loss Is Extremely Unlikely

Insurance companies operate on the assumption that not too many of their policyholders will suffer losses at the same time. They assume that losses will be unrelated, independent occurrences and that loss payments will be a fairly predictable and reasonable percentage of premium income. For some risks this assumption cannot safely be made. Unemployment is an example. A severe depression can put so many people out of work that an insurance company providing unemployment compensation benefits would quickly go broke. Only the government, with its power to tax and to borrow practically unlimited sums of money, can insure this risk. War damage is another source of loss that can be catastrophic. It also is generally regarded as uninsurable except by governmental agencies.

Each of the features of insurable risks, including this one, is viewed differently by different insurers. Some companies are large enough or venturesome enough to cover exposures that others would regard as catastrophic. One company might insure thousands of buildings in an area subject to severe hurricane damage, whereas another might be reluctant to cover more than a few buildings in that area.

Through the strength and ingenuity of the insurance industry, protection is now provided for a wide range of risks. For other risks, however, one or more of the features of insurability are judged to be lacking and insurance therefore either is limited or is not available at all.

THE FIELDS OF INSURANCE

This section furnishes an overview of the various kinds of insurance. It is intended to help provide a context within which the specific types of insurance will be studied in the following chapters.

In order to visualize the entire span of insurance, it is helpful to divide it into parts and then examine each part individually. There are several ways in which the various kinds of insurance can be classified for this purpose. One method is to divide insurance between that protecting individuals and that protecting businesses and other organizations. A second way is to classify insurance as either voluntary or involuntary, depending upon whether or not it is required by law. Third, insurance can be divided between the types that protect against loss of income (such as by death, disability, or unemployment) and the types that pay for damage to property. Finally, insurance can be classified on the basis of whether it is provided by private insuring organizations or by the government. Using the last of these approaches, we shall look first at private insurance and then at insurance that is provided by governmental units.

Private Insurance

Private insurance is that which is furnished by private (nongovernmental) insuring organizations. As shown by Figure 2–1, it consists of three major fields: life insurance, health insurance, and property-casualty insurance.

LIFE INSURANCE. Life insurance companies write two types of coverage, life insurance and annuities. Both types relate to people's uncertainty about

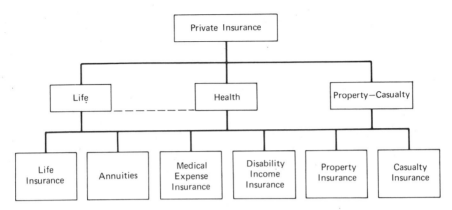

Figure 2-1 The fields of private insurance

how long they will live, and to the financial implications of that uncertainty. **Life insurance** deals primarily with the risk of dying while others are still financially dependent upon the insured person, such as while other members of a family are relying upon the earnings of a parent. Upon the death of the insured person, a life insurance policy pays a stated amount to a designated individual, called the beneficiary.

Life insurance policies deal with the financial risk associated with a short life span. **Life annuities**, on the other hand, concern the risk of living to an old age. In this case the financial problem is that of outliving one's income, as with people who retire from work and then live long enough to use up all of the funds they had saved while they were employed. A life annuity insures against this possibility by guaranteeing an income to the insured person for as long as he or she lives.

HEALTH INSURANCE. The field of **health insurance** deals with two principal types of loss. The first is the expense of medical treatment. This may include doctor and hospital bills, the cost of medicines, private nursing care, and so forth. The other loss that can be handled by health insurance is the income that an insured person is unable to earn during a period of disability.

Health insurance losses may be triggered by either of two perils, accident or illness. Some policies cover only accidents, but many health insurance contracts cover losses caused by either accident or illness.

Notice that in Figure 2–1 the fields of life and health insurance are connected by a dotted line. This indicates a close relationship between these fields. Although some insurers, including Blue Cross and Blue Shield, specialize in health insurance, a great deal of private health insurance is provided by companies whose principal business is life insurance.

PROPERTY-CASUALTY INSURANCE. The last of the three major fields of the private insurance business is **property-casualty insurance** (sometimes called property-liability insurance). It is made up of property insurance and casualty insurance. These two areas are further divided into "lines" or classes of coverage.

The distinction between property insurance and casualty insurance and the further division into more specific lines of coverage is largely due to state laws that no longer exist. Until the laws were changed (during the 1940s and 1950s) each insurance company was permitted to write only certain lines or groups of related lines of coverage. Companies licensed to write fire insurance and other property lines could not engage in the various casualty lines and vice versa. The laws now permit what are called "multiple-line" operations, enabling a single company to provide any or all lines of property-casualty insurance. In fact, it can do so in a single policy if it wishes. As a result, the old-time divisions within the property-casualty field have become less distinct. They are still used, however, to identify the various parts of this field.

Property Insurance. The **property insurance** field, as Figure 2–2 indicates, is divided into marine and nonmarine lines.

Marine insurance is a broad area divided into ocean marine and inland marine. **Ocean marine**, one of the oldest forms of insurance, covers ships and their cargo, both on the high seas and on inland waterways. **Inland marine** insurance grew out of ocean marine, originally to cover goods being carried on land to and from ocean ports. Today inland marine insurance covers cargo being shipped by air, truck, or rail. In addition, the field has expanded to include a variety of other risks that in some way relate to transportation.

The nonmarine part of the property insurance field covers damage to practically all kinds of property other than those considered to be part of the marine field. These properties range from common household articles to huge computer systems, from private residences to giant skyscrapers. At one

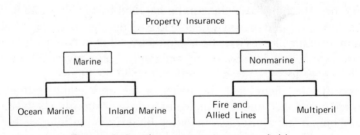

Figure 2–2   The property insurance field.

time the only damage covered was that done by fire or lightning, but over the years protection has been added for numerous other perils. Today properties can be insured for practically any peril, including wind, hail, explosion, riot, vandalism, and earthquake. The policies may cover either direct or indirect loss. **Direct loss** refers to loss that is the immediate, direct result of physical damage to the covered property. **Indirect loss** is the loss of income or the extra expenses that result from a direct loss.

The most rapidly growing part of the nonmarine property insurance field is **multi-peril insurance**, meaning policies that cover a variety of perils. Applying to either personal or business exposures, some of these policies bridge the gap between property insurance and casualty insurance by including both types of protection.

Casualty Insurance. The distinction between property insurance and casualty insurance, never very clear, has become less distinct since the advent of the multiple line laws. **Casualty insurance** can include almost any line of nonlife insurance other than those identified as part of the property insurance field. The best way to describe this field is by listing the lines of coverage that it includes, as shown in Figure 2–3.

Automobile insurance is the largest of the casualty lines in terms of total premium volume. Coverages available under automobile policies include protection against legal liability claims, payment of medical expenses, and payment for theft of or damage to insured automobiles. In states with "no-fault" laws, additional benefits including lost wages are provided.

General liability policies cover a wide variety of business and professional liability exposures. They protect people and organizations ranging from the owner of a corner hardware store to huge multinational corporations against financial loss due to legal liability claims. Also part of the general liability line are policies providing liability insurance for physicians, dentists, and other professional practitioners.

Workers' compensation insurance furnishes payments that employers are legally required to provide to employees who are injured on the job. The

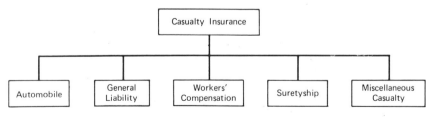

Figure 2-3 The casualty insurance field.

payments compensate for wages lost by disabled workers and for medical expenses. Because this protection is required by law and because the insurance is provided by state agencies in some states, workers' compensation might be classed as a type of social insurance. However, most of it is provided by private insurers and it is generally considered to be a form of casualty insurance.

Suretyship is a form of noninsurance risk transfer. A surety is one who guarantees to fulfill a contract if the person who is principally obligated fails to do so. An example is the co-signer of a loan agreement. If a lender isn't willing to bear the risk of default by a certain borrower, the borrower may have to provide a co-signer. The co-signer becomes the borrower's surety. That is, the co-signer promises to pay back the loan if the borrower does not do so. The lender then has transferred the risk of default to the co-signer. Although individuals can act as a surety and frequently do so as co-signers, insurance companies usually provide this service in other situations. Surety contracts are called bonds rather than policies, and a distinction is made between fidelity bonds and surety bonds. Fidelity bonds reimburse employers for loss caused by employee dishonesty. Protection is provided both for elaborate embezzlements and for simple employee theft of goods or money. Surety bonds, on the other hand, guarantee the performance of a specified act such as the construction of a building. If a building contractor fails to complete the work as specified, the insurance company protects the owner against loss resulting from the contractor's failure to comply with the contract.

Miscellaneous casualty is the name given to various other lines of casualty insurance. This includes policies covering such things as burglary, robbery, forgery, boiler explosion, glass breakage, aircraft liability, and aircraft damage.

Government Insurance

Government insurance is that which is written by governmental agencies. It may be either compulsory or voluntary.

Insurance provided by the government on a compulsory basis is called **social insurance.** In a later chapter we shall examine the nature of social insurance more closely and make some interesting comparisons between it and private insurance. The major components of social insurance in this country are social security and unemployment compensation.

SOCIAL SECURITY. The technical name for what is commonly called **social security** is the Old Age, Survivors, Disability, and Health Insurance

Program. A federal program, it is operated by the Social Security Adminis-tration and is financed by special taxes paid by employers, employees, and self-employed persons.

Since its creation in 1935, social security has expanded rapidly and now supplies an important part of the financial security of almost all Americans. The major benefits are income for retired persons, income for survivors of deceased workers, income for disabled workers and their families, and hospital and medical benefits for persons age 65 and above.

UNEMPLOYMENT COMPENSATION. In the section of this chapter that described the features of insurable risks we noted that private insurers are not in a position to furnish unemployment insurance. The government, however, can and does write this coverage. Acting upon the impetus of a federal law, each of the states has developed an **unemployment compensation** program. Workers who are laid off from their jobs receive weekly income payments, usually for a maximum of twenty-six weeks. Special taxes paid by employers finance the system.

OTHER GOVERNMENT INSURANCE. The state and federal govern-ments provide a variety of other forms of insurance in addition to social security and unemployment compensation. Most of the other forms are offered on a voluntary basis and are either the same as or similar to the kinds of protection furnished by private insurers. Examples include flood damage insurance and life insurance for military personnel.

INSURANCE OPERATIONS

Thus far we have examined the theoretical nature of insurance and have seen that it is one of several methods that can be used for handling risk. We also have learned what types of risks are insurable and have reviewed the kinds of protection that are furnished by private and government insurers. But how does the insurance system, particularly the private part of it, operate? In other words, who does what in order to make the system function? In a few short paragraphs, this section summarizes the operational side of the insurance business. It is not intended to be a complete descrip-tion; instead, it is designed to introduce some important concepts and to provide a working vocabulary that will be useful in connection with follow-ing chapters. Then, in the concluding chapters (Part V) of the book, we shall return to these topics and take a closer look at each of them: marketing, pricing, underwriting, loss adjusting, and company management.

Marketing

Marketing is the process of determining what consumers want and then directing the flow of goods and services from producer to consumer in order to satisfy those wants. Three of the factors important in marketing insurance are: (a) product design, (b) competitive pricing, and (c) customer service. An example of the first of these, product design, is the development of **package policies.** These are contracts that combine in a single policy various kinds of protection that previously had been available only through the purchase of two or more separate policies. Another example of improved product design is the recent development of shorter, easier-to-understand policies.

Competitive pricing is much more prevalent in insurance than many people realize. That is, most people believe that all companies charge about the same price for their policies, but in many cases there actually is a great range of prices. Perhaps one reason for this misconception is that few people believe they know enough about insurance to shop for it effectively, and therefore they make no effort to do so. Well-informed consumers know what forms of insurance protection they need and save money by knowing how to buy it.

Customer service is also an important aspect of insurance marketing. Insurance buyers, whether individuals or organizations, need assistance in identifying their insurable risks and determining the kinds and amounts of coverage that are appropriate. After policies are written they must be kept up to date as the policyholders' needs change; when losses occur, customer service means prompt and fair payment in accordance with the terms of the policy.

The persons most directly responsible for insurance sales and service are the agents and brokers. **Insurance agents** are men and women who are authorized to sell policies on behalf of one or more insurance companies. In life insurance, agents customarily represent a single insurer; in the property-casualty business many agents sell for a number of companies. Agents usually receive a commission, which is a percentage of the premiums that are paid for the policies they sell.

Unlike agents, who represent one or more insurance companies, **brokers** represent insurance buyers. Insurance brokers usually concentrate on serving commercial clients, arranging for business firms to be covered by one or more insurers. Although they legally represent buyers rather than insurers, brokers receive a selling commission from the insurers just as agents do. (For the sake of brevity, we customarily use the term "agent" unless it is important to distinguish between agent and broker.)

Agents are licensed by the states where they reside. Applicants for licenses must demonstrate a basic knowledge of insurance by passing a written examination. Through continuing study and experience, agents can develop the skills needed to furnish their services at a high level of professional competence.

Pricing

As we know, the price of an insurance policy is its premium. Premiums are based upon (a) rates and (b) exposure units. An **insurance rate** is a price per exposure unit. **Exposure units** are the measuring units used in insurance pricing. Premiums therefore are determined by multiplying rates by the number of exposure units. To illustrate, in life insurance the exposure unit is the number of thousands of dollars of coverage. If a policy provides $20,000 of coverage and the rate is $15 per thousand, the policy's premium is $15 × 20, or $300 per year.

$$\boxed{\text{RATE} \times \text{EXPOSURE UNITS} = \text{PREMIUM}}$$

Most insurance rates are **class rates**, meaning that the loss exposures to be insured are classified on the basis of certain characteristics and all of the loss exposures in each classification are subject to the same rate. The rating classifications in life insurance, for instance, are based on the age and sex of the insured persons. All 25-year-old males who are in good health are in the same classification. Those who are not of that age or sex are in different classifications and are subject to different rates. In automobile insurance the rating classifications are based on a number of characteristics of each driver, including age, sex, place of residence, and whether or not the car is used in business.

Insurance pricing is designed to meet two principal objectives. First, the company's premium income (together with income from other sources) must be sufficient to pay its policyholders' losses and meet company expenses. If for a particular company these total $50 million for the year, it is essential for that sum to be available. Second, the total cost must be distributed fairly among the various policyholders. Thus each insured should pay his or her fair share of the total cost. That is the reason for using rating classifications. Older people are charged higher rates for life insurance than younger people, because a higher percentage of older insureds die in any given year. For automobile insurance, teenaged drivers are charged higher rates than middle-aged drivers because a higher percentage of the former have accidents in any given year. In either case the result is believed to be a fairer sharing of the insurance company's total costs than would be the case if all persons were charged at the same rate.

Specialists professionally trained in the techniques of insurance pricing are called **actuaries.** They develop the rates and rating systems that insurers use.

Insurance pricing is regulated by the state governments. The insurance department of each state is responsible for guarding against improper or unfair pricing.

Underwriting

Perhaps you have heard of someone who has had difficulty in securing automobile insurance after a series of accidents or motor vehicle violations. Or you may know of someone who could not buy more life insurance after developing a serious health problem. Cases like these reflect **underwriting**, the process by which insurers decide which loss exposures to accept and how to insure them. Company-employed underwriters receive applications for insurance from agents and brokers, develop information about the prospective insureds, evaluate the information, and make the underwriting decisions.

The objective of the underwriting process is to select those applicants for insurance that meet the company's standards of acceptance. In other words, the underwriter's job is to avoid insuring too many below-average risks. Unless this is done, **"adverse selection"** will result, meaning that too many of the company's insureds will have losses and the company may not have enough income to cover all of its costs.

Underwriters are also responsible for seeing that the proper rate classifications and policy forms are used for each contract that is issued. In addition, they may be involved in **reinsurance**, a process by which one insurance company insures part of its risks with another company (the reinsurer). By reinsuring a portion of the insurance which it accepts, a company limits the amount it will have to pay for any one loss or group of losses.

Claims Adjusting

When insured losses are reported, policyholders are entitled to prompt and fair payment for them. It is important, however, that payment not be made for fake or exaggerated claims. Losses are paid with the premium dollars supplied by the entire group of policyholders, and if excessive loss payments are made the policyholders' premiums are wasted, requiring rates and premiums to be increased in the future.

The process of investigating, evaluating, and settling claims is called

claims adjusting. Chief responsibility for this process lies with an insurer's claims adjusting department. In many cases most of the work is done by staff adjusters employed by the company. In some situations insurance companies hire the services of independent loss adjusting organizations rather than using their own staff adjusters. In property-casualty insurance small fire, wind, and auto collision losses frequently are handled by the agents who sold the policies covering the losses.

To obtain maximum value from their insurance, consumers should acquaint themselves with their policies. They should know what losses are covered and what procedure to follow when a loss occurs.

Company Management

Several thousand insurance companies operate in the United States. Most are either stock companies (corporations) or mutual companies (a type of nonprofit organization).

Nearly 2 million people are employed in the insurance business. Of these, about one-third are engaged in insurance sales. The other two-thirds work in a great variety of occupations. These include underwriting, loss adjusting, actuarial science, investment analysis, accounting, computer programming, systems analysis, data processing, personnel administration, secretarial, clerical, and general management. The insurance work force is rather evenly divided between men and women. Although most of the women do secretarial and clerical work of various kinds, increasing numbers of management level positions are held by women.

Many of the large companies operate on a nationwide basis, with agents and offices located throughout the country. An even larger number of insurers operate in only one or a few states.

Insurance companies are subject to several forms of governmental regulation, some of which have already been referred to. In addition to licensing agents and regulating rates, the states supervise company investments and reserves. Also, insurers must submit detailed financial reports to the state insurance departments each year. Most insurance regulations are aimed at safeguarding the financial stability of insurance companies so that they will be in a position to pay the claims that their policyholders are entitled to receive.

IMPORTANT TERMS

Private insurance	Suretyship
Life insurance	Social insurance
Annuity	Social security
Health insurance	Unemployment compensation

Property-casualty insurance
Property insurance
Marine insurance
Ocean marine insurance
Inland marine insurance
Direct loss
Indirect loss
Multiperil insurance
Casualty insurance
Workers' compensation

Package policy
Agent
Broker
Insurance rate
Exposure unit
Class rate
Underwriting
Adverse selection
Reinsurance
Claims adjusting

KEY POINTS TO REMEMBER

1. Not all risks are insurable. Insurable risks generally have four characteristics: (a) There are similar loss exposures, (b) losses are definite, measurable, and important, (c) losses are accidental, and (d) catastrophic loss is extremely unlikely.
2. The three major fields of private insurance are (a) life, (b) health, and (c) property-casualty.
3. Both life insurance and annuities deal with the financial risks associated with living and dying.
4. Two types of loss can be covered by health insurance: the cost of medical treatment and income lost while insured persons are disabled.
5. Property insurance, one part of the property-casualty field, is divided into marine and nonmarine insurance. Marine insurance consists of ocean and inland marine; the rest of the property insurance field includes fire and allied lines plus multiperil insurance.
6. Property insurance can be written to cover either direct or indirect loss.
7. Included in casualty insurance are automobile, general liability, workers' compensation, suretyship, and miscellaneous casualty coverages.
8. Government insurance may be either compulsory or voluntary. Insurance written by the government on a compulsory basis is called social insurance. The principal kinds of social insurance in this country are social security and unemployment compensation.
9. Insurance is marketed on the basis of (a) product design, (b) competitive pricing, and (c) customer service. Most of the customer service is provided by agents and brokers.
10. Agents represent one or more insurance companies and sell policies on their behalf. Brokers represent insurance buyers and arrange for insurance on their behalf.
11. An insurance rate is a price per exposure unit. Premiums are determined by multiplying rates by the applicable number of exposure units.
12. Underwriting is the process by which insurers decide which applicants to accept and how to insure them. Underwriters seek to avoid adverse selection, which means insuring too many below-average risks.
13. Through the process of reinsurance one insurance company can transfer part of the insurance it has written to another insurer.

14. The goals of claims adjusting are to pay valid claims promptly and fairly and to avoid paying fake claims or exaggerated amounts.
15. Numerous occupations are involved in the operation of insurance companies and agencies. About one-third of the people employed in insurance are in sales work; the other two-thirds perform a wide variety of jobs.

REVIEW QUESTIONS

1. Why is the existence of many similar exposures a characteristic of most insurable risks?
2. (a) What is the difference between a definite loss and a measurable loss? (b) Why are these characteristics important?
3. (a) What is meant by "accidental" loss? (b) Why is it important?
4. How are life insurance and annuities related to each other?
5. In property-casualty insurance, what are multiple-line operations?
6. Distinguish between direct loss and indirect loss.
7. List the major lines of property-casualty insurance.
8. Define social insurance.
9. What are package policies?
10. What are class rates?
11. What are the principal goals of insurance pricing?
12. What is the main objective of underwriting?
13. What is the relationship between claims adjusting and rate levels?

DISCUSSION QUESTIONS

1. Do the following risks have each of the usual features of insurability?
   (a) Automobile collision
   (b) Burglary from a camera store
   (c) Shoplifting from a department store
   (c) Wind damage by hurricane
   (e) Style change that would diminish the value of a clothing store's inventory
2. In a great many cases, when people think of careers in insurance, they think only of sales work. Why do you suppose they have this attitude, given that twice as many of those who work in insurance are in jobs other than sales?
3. (a) Looking at the various fields of private and social insurance, which ones appear to affect you most directly? (b) Are there any that do not affect you at all, either directly or indirectly?

CHAPTER 3
RISK
MANAGEMENT

THE RISK MANAGEMENT CONCEPT

THE RISK MANAGEMENT PROCESS

RULES OF PERSONAL INSURANCE BUYING

The risks that large corporations face are so important and so complex that a specialized field of business management known as risk management has developed. The risk manager of General Motors Corporation, for instance, heads a forty-two person department. Although the risks of families and individuals are a tiny fraction of a big corporation's, personal insurance buyers can benefit from some of the techniques used by the professional risk managers.

This chapter describes the risk management concept and the process that is used in applying it. Consistent with our emphasis on the personal insurance consumer, the chapter concentrates on the risk management process as it applies to families and individuals. It also presents several guidelines for the personal insurance buyer.

THE RISK MANAGEMENT CONCEPT

Risk management is the systematic and efficient handling of pure risks. It deals with all pure risks, whether they are insurable or not, and uses whatever risk handling methods are most appropriate whether they include insurance or not.

Risk management is a relatively new concept, having gained little acceptance before the 1960s. Most of its development has occurred in very large corporations, some of which spend millions of dollars each year on insurance and other methods of risk handling. In several hundred of the largest firms, risk handling is now the work of specialists called **risk managers.** Although they rely heavily on insurance, they regard it as just one of several tools that are available to them. This approach, in fact, is one of the important ways in which today's corporate risk manager differs from yesterday's corporate insurance buyer. The latter's responsibility was limited to administering the corporation's insurance program, making sure that all of the conventional insurance policies were properly prepared and maintained. In contrast, the modern corporate risk manager uses insurance only as a last resort. Insurance is an important method of risk handling and is used extensively even by large corporations, but in the modern view it is not automatically presumed to be the best method.

Although the techniques of risk management were originally developed to deal with the risks of giant corporations, one does not have to employ a professional risk manager in order to use them. The risk management approach is as applicable to the Jones family or to Pete's Delicatessen as it is to General Motors.

THE RISK MANAGEMENT PROCESS

The risk management process is the set of activities that are followed in applying the risk management concept. The process, in other words, is a method of dealing with risks systematically and efficiently rather than on a hit-or-miss basis. Four activities are involved:

1. Risk identification
2. Risk evaluation
3. Selection of risk handling methods
4. Administration of the program

These four activities follow one another in logical order and can be thought of as a series of steps, but the process does not end when the fourth "step" is completed. We live in a world of risks and risk management is a continuous process.

Risk Identification

The sources of possible loss must be recognized before anything can be done about dealing with them. Accordingly, the first phase of the risk management process is identifying the risks to which one is exposed.

Families and individuals are subject to each of the four types of losses: property losses, income losses, legal liability claims, and unexpected expenses. Property losses may involve the residence and its almost limitless assortment of contents ranging from furniture and appliances to sports equipment and musical instruments. In addition, there may be a car and perhaps a boat or some other recreational vehicle. All of this property is exposed to loss from numerous perils. An effort should be made to identify all of the important categories of property and all of the perils to which they are exposed. Major income loss may befall a family because of death, disability, or unemployment. Although it is unpleasant to dwell on such possibilities, successful risk management demands that they be recognized and dealt with realistically. Legal liability claims are probably most likely to result from a family member's use of an automobile, but other possible sources of liability should also be identified. These include claims brought by people accidentally injured in the family's residence. Lawsuits also may stem from various personal activities including hunting, boating and athletics. The major risk associated with the final type of loss, unexpected expenses, is the possibility of unusually large bills for health care.

It is difficult to generalize about the risks to which families are exposed, because their possessions and activities are so varied. The important point is that a conscious effort should be made to recognize the possible sources of loss. This requires an awareness of pure risk and its importance as well as an alertness to new risks that develop as people acquire additional property and engage in new activities.

Risk Evaluation

The next step of the process is to estimate the risks' importance. Risks are evaluated on the basis of the severity and frequency of the losses associated with them. As indicated earlier, **loss severity** means the size of the potential losses; **loss frequency** refers to the probable number of losses. The two concepts, in other words, relate to the questions, How big? and How often? Of the two, loss severity is more crucial because a very large loss, although unlikely to happen, could be a financial catastrophe if it did occur.

For most families the risks with the greatest potential severity are those of long-term disability, early death of a parent, and major legal liability claims. Although such events happen only rarely, they can have a staggering financial impact. In contrast are low severity risks like the loss or destruction of inexpensive items of property. Losses of that nature can rather easily be paid for out of a family's regular income.

Selection of Risk Handling Methods

Next, the methods of risk handling must be chosen. As you may recall, there are four methods: risk avoidance, risk retention, loss control, and risk transfer.

RISK AVOIDANCE. This method is more often feasible in business situations than it is for personal risks. A corporate risk manager may recommend that the firm avoid the risks associated with selling dangerous toys or that it avoid building a plant in a country where anti-American feelings may lead to riot damage. Likewise, people may avoid airplane crashes by not flying or heart attacks from snow shovelling by moving from Michigan to Florida. Practically speaking, however, the other risk handling methods are usually more appropriate.

RISK RETENTION. As a tool of risk management, risk retention usually means retaining the risk of small losses rather than transferring the risk to an insurer. The purpose is to save money by reducing insurance costs. Some very large corporations retain "small" losses up to $100,000 or more; losses above that amount are either insured or handled in some other way. Families and individuals can practice risk retention in essentially the same way by using deductible clauses. A **deductible clause** is a policy provision stating that a specified amount will be subtracted from covered losses, the insurance paying only the amount in excess of the amount subtracted.

LOSS CONTROL. It is easy to overlook the importance of loss control, but in the management of personal risks nothing is more important than preventing unnecessary injury and damage. Loss control pays off in several ways. First, preventing losses avoids the consequences that insurance cannot pay for: inconvenience, delay, emotional strain, disruption of family plans, and other nonfinancial results of accidents, fires, illnesses, and so forth. Second, having a record of losses may increase the cost of one's future insurance protection. Third, those who don't take steps to control losses may not be able to obtain insurance. Heavy drinkers or people who are extremely overweight, for instance, may find it difficult to buy life insurance. Finally, loss control pays off in humanitarian and ecological terms. It saves lives, health, energy, and resources. Intelligent personal risk management therefore calls for reasonable care of lives, limbs, and property.

RISK TRANSFER. The usual way to transfer risk, as we know, is to buy insurance. Corporate risk managers purchase insurance only when necessary, that is, only after deciding that no other risk handling method is preferable. This does not mean that insurance is unimportant or little used by large organizations. On the contrary, it continues to be the most important and most widely used method of dealing with many major business risks. It is at least equally important in the management of personal risks.

In making a choice between insurance and the other risk handling methods, the loss frequency and loss severity of the particular risk are important. If for purposes of analysis we assume that both characteristics are either "high" or "low," there are four possible combinations, as shown in Figure 3–1.

Risks of the first type have both low loss frequency and low loss severity, meaning that losses seldom occur and when they do happen they are small. Insurance of such risks is neither necessary nor economical; risk retention is preferable. Risks with high loss frequency and low severity include the

Figure 3–1 Risk characteristics

TYPE	LOSS FREQUENCY	LOSS SEVERITY
1	Low	Low
2	High	Low
3	High	High
4	Low	High

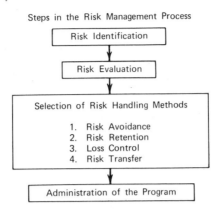

Figure 3–2 Steps in the risk management process

possibility of breaking dinnerware or small hand tools. Retention and loss control are the best methods of handling those risks. Fortunately, most people are not confronted by risks of the third type, when losses are both frequent and severe. For those who are, private insurance is extremely expensive and perhaps not available at all. An example would be the risk of early death for alcoholics or heroin addicts. Most people would agree that such risks should be dealt with by loss control or risk avoidance.

The last combination, low loss frequency and high severity, is the one for which insurance is ideally suited. The risk of legal liability is one that has these characteristics. Because loss severity is high, the risk is very important; the consequences of an uninsured loss could be severe. But because loss frequency is low, the cost of insuring the risk is not too great. Through insurance, risks with these characteristics can be shared economically by a group of policyholders.

Administration of the Program

The final step is to administer the risk management program on a continuing basis. This requires buying insurance policies, taking action to control losses, and participating in the settlement of losses. Proper administration of the program also means keeping it up to date. Our lives are in a state of constant change and as our lives change so do the risks we face. Arrangements that were made for handling our personal risks a year or two ago may be out of date today. Automobile policies, for instance, should be revised to reflect any differences in address, additional drivers, or changes of cars. Insurance of homes and personal property should be revised as property values rise or additional property is acquired. Additional life insurance should be purchased to keep pace with rising income levels and added family responsibilities. It is easy to put off making such changes or to forget them altogether. A regular review, perhaps at the beginning of each year, helps keep a program up to date.

The entire risk management process is summarized by Figure 3–2.

RULES OF PERSONAL INSURANCE BUYING

In the handling of personal risks, important decisions must be made concerning the risks to insure and how to insure them. Four basic rules can help families and individuals make these decisions in a manner that is consistent with the risk management concept:[1]

1. Insure the major risks first.
2. Don't insure small losses.
3. Shop before buying.
4. Get help from a good agent.

Insure the Major Risks First

Major risks are those with high potential loss severity—the ones that could cause serious financial harm to the persons who face them. Such risks should be insured first and only after that is done should the insuring of less important risks be considered. Less important risks never should absorb premium dollars that could be used to buy more adequate coverage for the major risks.

To illustrate, some home insurance policies cover more perils than others do. Are the broadest (and most expensive) policies always better? Not necessarily. For some people a limited and less costly policy will cover the major risks and the money saved can be used to buy more adequate life or health insurance. Another example concerns life insurance. Should parents buy life insurance to cover the lives of their children? The major risk to be handled by life insurance is loss of a family's principal source of income. If the father is the main income earner, then the family's life insurance premium dollars should be spent to insure his life first. Only if and when that major risk is adequately insured should parents consider insuring their children.

Don't Insure Small Losses

The second rule, like the first, deals with what things to insure. It tells us not to insure small losses *even if they occur frequently.* Insuring small losses is

[1]Adapted from recommendations made by E. William Alstaetter, risk manager of Rockwell International Corporation. "Buy Insurance Like the Experts and Save," *Changing Times,* January 1974.

"...AND ON MY COLLISION INSURANCE, I HAVE $25,000 DEDUCTIBLE."

Source: Sidney Harris.

unnecessary, wastes money, and drains away funds that can be spent more wisely on other insurance. Many people ignore this rule. They believe that a policy "isn't doing any good" unless covered losses occur; they think that the best insurance is that which is likely to pay for the most losses. This attitude explains the popularity of accident policies that pay a few dollars for the minor cuts and bruises that occur so frequently. It also is why many people prefer a small deductible amount on their automobile damage insurance.

Insuring small losses is uneconomical for two reasons. First, as many small injuries—collisions and so forth—are bound to happen, premiums on policies that cover them must be high simply to reimburse policyholders for them. Second, the premiums must also allow for the overhead costs of handling the numerous small claims. If it costs $20 just to process a small claim, an insurer must spend a total of $45 to pay a $25 loss. It therefore makes sense to pay small losses out of one's own pocket, perhaps by use of policy deductibles, and to buy insurance to cover large losses only.

Shop Before Buying

Many people have the mistaken impression that all insurance companies charge the same prices. Although it is true that some insurers charge "standard" prices, there is a wide range of prices in most lines of coverage. A survey of twelve automobile insurers in one city showed that for a particular policy five of them were charging $544, while the other seven offered the same policy to the same person for various prices ranging as low as $318.

Some people may be reluctant to compare prices before buying because they feel intimidated by insurance and by insurance agents. Consumers probably would shop more wisely for insurance if they had more knowledge of what it is, how it is priced, and how it is sold.

Get Help From a Good Agent

Good insurance agents provide risk management counseling and advice. They offer valuable suggestions concerning the kinds and amounts of protection that are most appropriate for their clients. In life insurance, for example, they use a process called "programming" to design a plan of protection that meets the specific needs of the particular family. Agents who use this approach are professionals in the sense that they use their expert judgment to provide the services that are in the best interests of their clients. Unfortunately, many people do not realize how valuable the services of their insurance agents can be and fail to make full use of them. The importance of this point will become more clear as we continue our study of risk and insurance.

IMPORTANT TERMS

Risk management	Loss frequency
Risk manager	Deductible clause
Loss severity	

KEY POINTS TO REMEMBER

1. Risk management is the systematic and efficient handling of pure risks.
2. Large organizations employ specialists called risk managers to handle their risks.
3. The risk management process involves four activities: (a) risk identification, (b) risk evaluation, (c) selection of risk handling methods, and (d) administration of the program.
4. Risks are evaluated with regard to their loss severity and loss frequency.
5. Loss severity is the size of the potential losses.
6. Loss frequency means the probable number of losses.
7. Modern risk management uses the most efficient and economical of the four methods of handling risks: (a) risk avoidance, (b) risk retention, (c) loss control, and (d) risk transfer.
8. A deductible clause is a policy provision stating that a specified amount will be subtracted from covered losses, the insurance paying only the amount in excess of the amount subtracted.

9. Insurance is the principal method of handling important insurable risks. Risk managers minimize costs by using other methods whenever they are appropriate.
10. Insurance is most suitable for handling risks with high loss severity and low loss frequency.
11. An important part of the administration of a risk management program is a regular review to keep it up to date.
12. Four rules of personal insurance buying which incorporate the risk management concept are: (a) insure the major risks first, (b) don't insure small losses, (c) shop before buying, and (d) get help from a good agent.

REVIEW QUESTIONS

1. (a) List the four steps of risk management. (b) Why is the order in which they are listed a logical order?
2. Name two criteria used in evaluating risks.
3. Why might it be better to retain certain risks rather than to insure them?
4. How can families and individuals practice risk retention?
5. What is the most common method of transferring risk?
6. For which of the risk characteristics shown in Figure 3–1 is insurance most appropriate and why?
7. List the benefits of personal loss control.
8. (a) The first and second rules of personal insurance buying are closely related. In what way? (b) What is the difference between these two rules?

DISCUSSION QUESTIONS

1. For which is the risk management concept more valid: large corporations or individuals?
2. How does Figure 3–1 relate to the rules of personal risk management?
3. When you buy automobile insurance the insurance company charges a premium that it estimates will cover your average losses, plus an allowance for its overhead expenses. That being the case, wouldn't you be better off if you retained the risk and paid the losses yourself? If not, why not?
4. One person says that deductible clauses are used by insurance companies to punish policyholders who have losses. Is that correct?
5. Some people say that insurance does them no good unless it actually pays them for losses. (a) Give an example that illustrates what this means. (b) Is the statement true? Explain.
6. Why do people so frequently violate the second rule of personal risk management? That is, why are they often more interested in insuring small frequent losses than in insuring rare but very large losses?
7. (a) Identify the three most important pure risks that you personally are facing today. (b) What are you (or others) doing about them?

CHAPTER 4
INSURANCE AND THE LAW

Insurance policies are legal contracts and are subject to certain legal requirements. These requirements, which may be extremely important to policy buyers, are reviewed in this chapter. The chapter also examines the nature of the liability risk and some of the laws that affect liability for automobile accidents. These topics set the stage for the study of automobile insurance, which begins with the next chapter.

THE POLICY AS A CONTRACT

"Buying insurance isn't much fun," says Sam Policyholder. "You can't slam the doors or kick the tires. It doesn't look good on you, and there's not much to be said for how it tastes or smells. It's not a very good way to impress the neighbors either. It costs a lot of money and all you have to show for it is a piece of paper!"

There is considerable truth in what Sam says, but what he says is misleading too. What his insurance gives him is financial security, and if we could talk with him about it, Sam would have to admit that is important to him and to his family. The piece of paper that he speaks of—the policy— really isn't insurance. It isn't insurance any more than a diploma is an education. Like education, insurance is intangible; it can't be seen or touched.

An insurance policy is a legal contract. It is comparable to a lease you might sign for an apartment. The lease is a contract under the terms of which you agree to pay rent to the owner and the owner agrees to provide the apartment in return. The lease is probably a rather lengthy document and includes such provisions as the date when you can occupy the apartment, the date when the rent is due, who pays for utility bills and repairs, the length of the agreement, and the conditions under which it can be cancelled. The terms of the lease are legally enforceable; that is, if the apartment owner doesn't live up to his or her promises voluntarily, the courts can force the owner to do so. Various laws directly affect the agreement, even though there is no reference to them in the document. For instance, a state law may prohibit the owner from discriminating unfairly among the tenants, and a local ordinance may forbid you as a tenant to disturb the neighborhood with your stereo.

Like a lease, an insurance policy states the terms of a contract, in this case a contract between a policyholder and an insurance company. As with the lease, many of the rights and duties of the parties are not expressed in the contract but are a matter of law. Such law, which provides the basic legal framework of insurance, is the subject of the first part of this chapter.

ESSENTIAL ELEMENTS OF CONTRACTS

To be legally enforceable, all contracts including insurance policies must have these four characteristics:

1. There must be an agreement based upon a definite offer by one party and the acceptance of that offer by the other party.
2. The two parties must be legally competent to make a contract.
3. There must be consideration; that is, both parties must give something of value and both must receive something of value.
4. The contract must have a legal purpose.

Agreement

Insurance contracts generally are made when the insurer accepts the applicant's offer to buy a policy. This is an important point and one that sometimes is misunderstood. One might assume that an insurance company offers to sell insurance and that when a person decides to buy, the contract is effective at once, but that is not correct. If Edna Lewis clips an application for an accident policy from her newspaper, completes it, and mails it to the insurance company, has a contract been made? Assume she tumbles down a stairway a few hours later and breaks a leg. Is she covered? No, because the contract had not been completed. Her submission of the application is considered by the courts to be an offer to buy. There is no agreement between the parties until and unless her offer is accepted by the company.

In the case of life insurance, applications are not valid offers to buy unless they are accompanied by the first premium payment. What if the applicant is killed after he or she applies for the policy (and pays the first premium) but before the application is received at the company's home office? The answer may be supplied by a document known as a conditional receipt. These are used by most life insurance companies today and sometimes are a part of the application form itself. A typical one might say:

If the premium on the insurance herein applied for has been paid to the Company's agent, the insurance as provided by the policy shall be effective from the date of this application PROVIDED that the Company shall approve this application at its Home Office.

Use of the conditional receipt can bring about the strange situation of a company's having either to approve or to disapprove an application for life insurance from a person who is already dead! Is it conceivable that the company nevertheless would issue the policy and pay the claim? You might suppose not, but several company officials to whom the author has put this question have said they would lean over backward to find the application acceptable. Their explanation is that, first, it is the fair thing to do and, secondly, paying the claim would probably be less costly to the company than the adverse publicity that would ensue if it were declined.

The subject of offer and acceptance is much simpler in property-casualty insurance. In that field, applications can be legal offers to buy without being accompanied by any premium payment. (As a matter of company practice, however, advance premium payment is sometimes required.)

Property-casualty insurance agents are authorized by their companies to accept offers from applicants. This point is important, because it means that agreement between an applicant and an agent fulfills a major requirement of a legal contract. Insurance coverage can be put into effect immediately without waiting for approval by the company's home office. Furthermore, in this case neither the offer nor the acceptance has to be in writing. When Jack Sanders buys a new motorboat he phones his agent, describes the boat, and discusses insurance coverage for it. When he and the agent agree on the amount and type of protection, the agent says "OK, Jack, I am binding the coverage." It is a legal, enforceable contract. In a few days, Jack will receive the written policy and a bill for the premium. In the meantime, insurance is effected through what is called a binder. A **binder** is a temporary insurance contract in effect until replaced by a formal, written policy. The binder does not have to be in writing, but it is good business practice for the agent to make a memorandum of it if the policy is not being prepared immediately. If there is likely to be a delay before the policy is delivered, the agent or the company may prepare a written binder setting forth the essentials of the contract.

Legal Competence of the Parties

Most people have legal capacity to make insurance contracts; they have the legal competence (that is, ability) to do so. Minors are the chief exception. In most states minors are now defined as those who are below age 18. Other people who are not legally competent include those who are intoxicated or insane. Note that the point here concerns the ability to make an insurance contract; it does not affect the individual's status as an insured person. Thus minors may be covered by their parents' automobile insurance policies or by life insurance policies purchased by their parents or grandparents.

The basis of an insurance company's legal competence is the charter granted to it by the state where it was organized. In states other than its home state a company operates on the basis of licenses issued by the various state insurance departments. The power to revoke a company's charter or license to operate is the source of the insurance departments' regulatory authority.

The competence of insurance agents to make contracts stems from the authority granted to them by the companies they represent. In addition, agents must be licensed by the state in order to engage lawfully in the insurance business.

Consideration

The third requisite of legal contracts is the exchange of something of value, known as consideration. The consideration given by the policyholder, of course, is the premium that he or she either pays or promises to pay. Aggressive agents have been known to deliver unsolicited policies in an effort to persuade their prospects to buy. These are not legal contracts, because there is neither agreement nor consideration.

The consideration given by the insurance company is its promise to indemnify the insured according to the terms of the policy in case of loss.

Legal Purpose

Because a contract is a private agreement, we might suppose that it could say whatever the contracting parties want it to say. However, if it is to be enforced by the courts it must have a legal purpose. The courts will not enforce agreements that are unlawful or are otherwise not in the public interest. This requirement rules out insurance to protect an individual who intentionally injures another party or who intentionally damages another's property. The legal purpose requirement does not prohibit insurance of losses caused by a policyholder's neglect, however. Indeed, a great many insured fires and accidents are due to simple carelessness on the part of insured persons.

UTMOST GOOD FAITH

Insurance originated as a means of protecting the owners of ships and their cargos. Historians have found forerunners of marine insurance in the records of ancient Greece and Rome. Insurance grew as commerce expanded around the Mediterranean during the Middle Ages and then spread into Northern Europe and the British Isles. Some of the basic legal principles applicable to insurance today—particularly the doctrine of utmost good faith—reflect this heritage.

Marine insurers often were unable to examine the property they were covering. An insurer in London perhaps would cover a cargo of wool that was being shipped from Australia to South Africa in a Dutch ship. The insurer would have to rely upon the statement of the wool merchant that his cargo was in good condition (and not already badly damaged or even at the bottom of the ocean). The insurer also would need to depend on the statement that the ship was seaworthy and properly manned (and not a leaky hulk commanded by a drunken captain). Today the insurer quickly could get information from almost anywhere in the world. But consider the situation during the times before the development of radio and telephone, or even postal service. Insurance was necessary; neither shipowners nor merchants would put to sea without it. But insurers needed a guarantee that they would not be victimized by dishonest insureds. The solution was to develop a system of insurance laws and practices which demanded a high degree of honesty and frankness from people dealing with insurance companies. This, the **doctrine of utmost good faith**, is reflected today in rules of law concerning warranty, representation, and concealment.

Warranty

A **warranty** is a policy provision making the insurer's responsibility conditional upon some fact or circumstance concerning the risk. A burglary policy on a jewelry store may contain a warranty that the policyholder will keep a burglar alarm system in operation whenever the store is not open for business. If there is a burglary loss at a time when the alarm system is not functioning the insurer has no obligation to pay.

The old common law of warranty was a very harsh doctrine; it provided that any breach of warranty would void the policy, even if it were immaterial (i.e., unimportant). This point is illustrated by a case in England (the source of American common law) in 1786. A marine insurance policy had warranted that a ship would sail from Liverpool "with 50 hands or upwards." She actually sailed with 46 but picked up 6 more from an island just off the English coast. The ship was bound for Africa and the insurance was to cover its voyage from Africa to the West Indies. She reached Africa safely but was captured and lost sometime later. The court held that the warranty had been breached and the insurer therefore did not have to pay.

In the early days of life insurance (a hundred or so years ago) policies sometimes contained a provision saying that the application was part of the policy itself and that all statements contained in the application were warranties. This provision made it possible for the companies to void the policies later on for any misstatements in the applications no matter how unintentional or inconsequential they might have been. Insurers no longer can take such action because statements by applicants for life insurance and most other forms of personal insurance protection are now construed as representations (see the next section) and not as warranties. Also, the courts and legislatures have modified the law so that warranties no longer are a trap for the unsuspecting policyholder. Warranties still are used on some forms of business insurance, such as the burglary policy mentioned earlier. Whenever they are part of an insurance contract it is essential that their terms be complied with.

Representation

Representations are statements made to an insurer to supply information or to induce it to accept a risk. Representations may be contained in formal, written applications or they may be oral. The main thrust of the law is that the facts must be as the applicant represents them to be. Misrepresentation (false statement) of a material fact makes the contract voidable at the option of the company. When Al Kopp applies for life insurance he makes representations concerning his name, age, occupation, present insurance, and marital status. He also answers questions about piloting aircraft and being treated by doctors. If Al says that the only medical treatment he has received during the past five years was for a sprained ankle, whereas he actually has been treated several times for a heart ailment, he has misrepresented a material fact. If he dies of a heart attack one year later and the company then learns the truth, Al's widow will receive only the premiums that Al paid for the policy.

Or consider the case of Ron Kerman. Ron arranges for insurance on his new car, telling the agent he has had no motor vehicle violations or accidents during the last three years. As a matter of fact he has been picked up several times for speeding and reckless driving and he lost his previous vehicle by driving it into a bridge. A policy is issued, and Ron does it again. He totally wrecks the new car and is sued for $50,000 for injuries to other people. Does Ron's insurance company have legal grounds to refuse to pay the claims? It certainly appears to. Ron lied about important facts when he applied for the policy and that is material misrepresentation.

Note that the misstatement has to be material. It must be such that if the company had known the true facts it would not have issued the policy on the same terms. Misrepresentation must also be within the knowledge of the applicant. If the applicant says he has no diseases but without knowing it actually has cancer, the statement cannot be used by the insurer as grounds to deny a claim.

Concealment

Concealment, the third aspect of the doctrine of utmost good faith, is the counterpart of misrepresentation. It is the failure to disclose material facts.

The laws pertaining to concealment, like those that relate to warranty and misrepresentation, stem from ocean marine insurance and from the insurer's need to rely upon the applicant to supply the facts.

Materiality is a requisite of concealment, as it is of misrepresentation. Also, concealment requires intentional withholding of information that the applicant knows is material. In addition, the information must be something that is not readily apparent to the company. It would not be concealment if the owner of a disco near a college campus failed to inform his fire insurance company that on Friday and Saturday nights his place is packed with students. The company is expected to realize that fact without being told. But the owner's failure to volunteer the information that he is closing the disco and converting the building to a dry cleaning shop is a concealment that could relieve the company of any obligation if the place burns down later on.

What about information secured by the insurance company? Can't it investigate and find out about the disco owner's plans? The answer is that the insurance company may secure such information or it may not. Whether or not it can and whether or not it does, the applicant has a legal responsibility to tell the truth.

Obviously, there are many borderline cases. Is it concealment in automobile insurance if an insured fails to inform the company when a 16-year-old son or daughter first starts driving? Is it misrepresentation if an applicant claims never to have had an accident when there had been a slight one four years ago? Intelligent insurance buyers do not take chances; instead, they make it a point to convey all such information to their insurers. Although the laws concerning misrepresentation and concealment are less harsh than those relating to breach of warranty, it is important to be truthful when dealing with insurance matters.

THE INDEMNITY PRINCIPLE

Insurance is strongly affected by the **indemnity principle**, a legal doctrine stating that the function of insurance is to repay (indemnify) insureds for their actual losses. Policyholders who have adequate insurance protection are to be restored to the financial position they held before the losses occurred, but they should not profit from the insurance. The intent is to avoid giving people an incentive to cause fires or other "accidents."

The indemnity principle applies most fully to property-casualty insurance. It is less applicable to health insurance and still less to life insurance. The principle is supported by several legal requirements or policy provisions:

1. Insurable interest
2. Loss measurement

3. Subrogation
4. "Other insurance" provisions

Insurable Interest

The indemnity principle requires people to have an *insurable interest* in whatever they insure. Insureds must be in a position to sustain financial loss if the event insured against occurs. Insurable interest is required for all types of coverage, including (with one exception) life insurance.

The insurable interest requirement means, for example, that Frank Mobley cannot buy insurance on John Clark's house. Without this requirement, Mobley might be tempted to insure Clark's house and then firebomb it. Clark's plight would be even worse if Mobley were able to take out life insurance covering his life! The insurable interest rule prevents the use of insurance as a speculative, profit-making device.

The sole exception to the requirement of insurable interest is when people purchase life insurance on their own lives. In spite of the fact that they will not be around to suffer financial loss when the insured event occurs, they are permitted to buy the policies. The insurable interest requirement is ignored because even without it the spirit of the indemnity principle will not be violated. In this case, the insureds will not profit from the loss even though insurable interest is absent! Incidentally, insured persons can name whomever they please as **beneficiaries**, the persons who receive the policy proceeds. Beneficiaries do not have to have an insurable interest.

There are two types of insurable interest in life insurance. In the first, insurable interest is based upon close family relationships, such as between husband and wife or parent and child. The laws of the various states are neither clear nor consistent as to what other family relationships would suffice. Probably grandparents have insurable interest in the lives of their grandchildren but it is doubtful that cousins, for instance, can legally insure one another. In any case where dispute arose the final decision would rest with the courts.

The second type of insurable interest in life insurance is based upon a specific financial interest in the insured person. A creditor has an insurable interest in the life of a debtor. If one person lends another $5,000, then the lender can take out that much insurance on the borrower's life. For the same reason, a business firm has an insurable interest in the lives of key employees who are particularly valuable to the firm. In this situation, as in the case of a loan, the party taking out the policy has a financial interest in the life of the person named in the insurance contract. Coverage of both of these risks by means of life insurance is common today.

In nonlife insurance the usual sources of insurable interest are the ownership of property and the obligation to pay debts (such as medical bills). Obviously, property owners will suffer loss if their property is destroyed. Other property relationships that can furnish insurable interest may be less apparent. For instance, a bank holding a mortgage on a house has an insurable interest in the house because the property is the security behind the mortgage. Also, people may have insurable interest in the property of others which is in their custody. Such persons are called **bailees.** A man who owns a parking garage is an example. He is responsible for damage to automobiles caused by the negligence of his employees. Because he is in a position to sustain financial loss if the property is damaged, he can insure it.

Insurable interest in life insurance must exist at the inception of the policy, but it does not have to prevail at the time of a loss. Thus, a wife who owns a policy covering the life of her husband can keep the policy even if they are divorced. In property-casualty insurance the opposite is true; insurable interest does not have to exist when the coverage is put into effect but it is required at the time of loss. You can insure today an automobile that you expect to buy tomorrow. Of course, you will be unable to recover for any damage to the car today, but setting up the policy in advance guards against delay in getting it into force tomorrow when you need the coverage.

Loss Measurement

To apply fully the indemnity principle, there must be some basis of **loss measurement**, a way to determine the amount of payment when a loss occurs. If Ben Stone insures his motorboat for $10,000 when it really is worth only $5,000, he should recover only the latter amount if the boat is destroyed.

The traditional basis of loss measurement in the property insurance field is **actual cash value.** That is, many policies state if the insured property is damaged or destroyed the amount of the payment shall be the property's actual cash value. Strangely, the policies do not say what actual cash value means; the definition is supplied by the courts and through commonly accepted insurance practices. The most frequently used definition is that actual cash value equals the cost of replacing the destroyed property with new property, minus an allowance for depreciation. **Depreciation** is the amount by which something declines in value due to its age and use. It is deducted from replacement cost so that the loss payment will be equal to the current value of the property and the insured will not profit from the loss.[1]

Assume that Barbara's Restaurant owns and occupies a twenty-year-old

---

[1] About twenty states have valued policy laws that require payment of the entire amount of insurance with no allowance for depreciation. These laws apply only to buildings and only if the building is totally destroyed.

building in a declining neighborhood. The cost of replacing the building at current prices would be $400,000. If the building has depreciated by 25%, its actual cash value is $400,000 minus 25%, or $300,000. If the building is insured on the actual cash value basis, $300,000 is the maximum payable for a loss, even if Barbara buys more than that amount of insurance.

Automobiles are insured on the same basis, but in this case actual cash value means the market value of similar cars. If an insured's two-year-old Ford is destroyed, the basis of settling the claim will be the going price of similar two-year-old Fords. As with the coverage on Barbara's Restaurant, measuring the loss in terms of the property's actual cash value helps prevent paying more than the property is worth.

Property insurance policies sometimes cover the full replacement cost of insured property, with no deduction for depreciation. The manner in which dwellings may be insured on this basis is described in a later chapter.

The indemnity principle is not always applied to the measurement of insured losses. Life insurance policies normally pay the total amount of insurance upon the death of the covered person. If a man's life is insured for $100,000, that is the amount the beneficiary will receive; there is no attempt to measure the man's "value" after he dies. Most health insurance policies use the same approach, paying a stated amount for each month of disability or each day of hospitalization, for instance.

Subrogation

Under the laws of negligence, property owners can sue those who cause damage to their property. If a suit is successful, the property owner is entitled to reimbursement by the negligent party. But let us suppose the property owner has an insurance policy covering damage to the property. To permit him or her to recover both from the lawsuit and from the insurance would clearly violate the indemnity principle. Subrogation prevents such double recovery. **Subrogation** is a legal principle that provides that to the extent an insurer has paid for a loss, the insurer obtains the right of its policyholder to recover from any third party who caused the loss. Most property insurance policies contain a provision reinforcing this principle.

Let's say that on a beautiful fall Saturday afternoon Tom Archer rakes up a pile of leaves in his backyard, starts a bonfire, and then goes into his house and turns on his television set. Becoming engrossed in a football game, he forgets his leaf burning. The fire quickly spreads along the leaf-covered ground and soon sets ablaze the garage of his next-door neighbor, Bill Carpenter. Before the fire trucks arrive, $800 worth of damage is done to the garage. In the absence of subrogation, Carpenter would be able to recover twice, once from his fire insurance and again by suing Archer. Subrogation prevents this, because after the fire insurer pays Carpenter, it can sue Archer in Carpenter's name. If the suit is successful the conclusion will be that Carpenter will be paid for his loss, his insurance company will be reimbursed, and Archer, who caused the whole problem, will be left bearing the loss.[2]

Subrogation is available to insurers only against third parties. An insurance company cannot subrogate against its own policyholders, even for losses due to their own carelessness. Subrogation usually is not applicable to health insurance and never applies to life insurance. If a man who has a large amount of life insurance is killed in a plane crash, for example, his family is entitled to any settlement that a court orders the airline to pay; the family's right of recovery is not transferred to the life insurance company.

"Other Insurance" Provisions

"Other insurance" provisions are policy clauses limiting the amount of payment if an insured has other, similar insurance protection. Without such provisions people could get around the other measures that support the indemnity principle by buying two or more policies. The most common "other insurance" provision states that if two or more policies cover the same loss they are to share in its payment on a pro-rata basis. Assume a family insures its house under two policies for a total of $90,000. Company A provides $30,000 under one policy, and Company B provides $60,000 under the other policy. The two companies will share the payment of losses in proportion to the amount of the total coverage which each one furnishes. Company A provides one-third of the coverage and will pay one-third of each loss; Company B provides two-thirds of the coverage and will pay two-thirds of each loss.

Another type of "other insurance" clause states that the coverage provided by the policy applies only in excess of any other collectable insurance. In this case, if other insurance is available to pay for the full loss, the first policy pays nothing. There are two other types of "other insurance" clauses. One states that the policy obtained earliest provides primary protection, while policies obtained at later dates furnish excess coverage. The remaining type of "other insurance" provision simply prohibits any other insurance coverage of the same kind.

Life insurance contracts never contain "other insurance" provisions. Because there is no satisfactory way to measure the loss in this case, there is no way to apportion it among policies. Each life insurance policy pays the full face amount, regardless of the number of other policies in force.

Health insurance contracts until recent years rarely contained "other

---

[2] If Archer has a Homeowners policy its liability coverage will apply. See Chapter 10.

insurance" provisions. Now, such limitations are becoming more common, especially on policies covering medical expenses. When these provisions are not included, benefits can exceed the actual loss.

THE LIABILITY RISK

The basic nature of most of the risks we face is rather obvious and uncomplicated. This is true of risks involving property loss, accident or sickness expense, and loss of income, but the liability risk is an exception. The **liability risk** is based on the laws of negligence, laws that provide that in certain situations a person may have to pay someone else for having injured them or having damaged their property. Those who have such an obligation are said to be legally liable. If they have liability insurance of the proper type and amount, it will pay the money for them. Because this risk is based on the laws of negligence, some knowledge of those laws will help clarify the nature of the risk and the function of liability insurance. We should realize that these laws are extremely complex and that the following explanation is greatly simplified.

Negligence a Form of Wrong-Doing

Under our system of laws there are two major classes of wrong-doing, criminal wrongs and civil wrongs. Criminal wrongs are public wrongs; that is, they are wrongs for which legal penalties have been established as a means of protecting the public welfare. Although they may be directed against individuals, criminal wrongs (such as theft, arson, or murder) are considered an injury to the general public. As such, they are punishable by the state.

Civil wrongs, on the other hand, involve injury to a specific party only. This class of wrong-doing is not punishable by the state. Instead, the remedy takes the form of court action ("civil action") instituted by the injured party. There are two main categories of civil wrongs: those involving contracts, and torts. Civil wrongs involving contracts are mainly breaches of contract and breaches of warranty. Torts, which are civil wrongs not relating to contracts, include such things as libel, slander, assault, trespass, false arrest, and most important, negligence. **Negligence** is failure to use the proper degree of care necessary to prevent injuring other people. (In this context the injury could be either bodily injury or property damage.) A person who negligently injures another may have a legally enforceable obligation to pay a sum of money to the injured party or, in legal terms, the negligent party may be "legally liable" to pay **damages**. Damages are sums awarded by a court to pay for injuries sustained by another party.

Elements of Negligence

Negligence is made up of four elements, all of which must exist before a court will order the payment of damages. The four elements are (a) the duty to act in a certain manner, a manner that is reasonable and prudent under the circumstances prevailing; (b) the failure to act in that manner; (c) an injury; and (d) a direct causal relationship between the defendant's carelessness and the plaintiff's injuries, that is, between (b) and (c).

Consider a negligence suit involving an automobile collision. The injured person (the "plaintiff") was parked beside a country highway at 11:30 P.M. when his car was struck from behind by a car driven by another person, the "defendant." The plaintiff, who was sitting in the parked car, claims that he is totally disabled because of the resulting injury to his back. The plaintiff's attorney is seeking to establish that all of the elements of negligence are present in the case. First, he describes to the court the defendant's duty to operate his car in a safe manner, driving at a speed within the legal limit, and keeping sober and alert. Second, he contends that the defendant failed to act in such a manner. As evidence, he points to the testimony of the investigating police officer who says there were indications that the defendant had been drinking and was exceeding the posted speed limit. Third, the plaintiff's injuries are described. Evidence is presented concerning the cost to repair his car, the expenses of treating his sore back and the amount of income which he will lose because of his disability. Finally, the plaintiff's attorney argues that the injuries were caused solely by the defendant's failure to drive safely. He says that his client was legally parked beside the highway and he contends that there would have been no collision and therefore no injuries if the defendant had kept his car under control.

As the case continues, the attorney for the defendant seeks to disprove some of these contentions. He wants to prove that his client was not negligent. He says that the defendant was neither speeding nor intoxicated. He challenges the extent of the injury, raising questions as to how sore the plaintiff's back really is. Anyway, he argues, if he really is disabled it is the result of an injury the evening prior to the collision, when the plaintiff fell off a bar stool at a neighborhood tavern. Thus the attorney for the defense contends that there is not a valid case against his client, because one or more of the elements of negligence cannot be proved.

The plaintiff's attorney, incidentally, is hired and paid by the plaintiff. The defendant's attorney, assuming the defendant carries liability insurance, is furnished by the insurance company. In addition to paying liability judgments against the insured, liability insurance provides and pays the entire cost of defending against suits alleging liability. This aspect of the coverage is important because legal expenses can be very large. If the defense is successful, the insurer may make little or no payment to the plaintiff on the policyholder's behalf, yet the cost of handling the case may be hundreds or even thousands of dollars.

Defenses Against Negligence

Defendants who are found to have been negligent may still not be legally liable. Several defenses are possible, depending upon the circumstances of the case. The most important of these defenses are contributory negligence (or comparative negligence) and assumption of risk.

According to the **contributory negligence rule**, plaintiffs cannot recover damages if they contributed to their injuries through negligence of their own. In the previous example, even if the defendant had been negligent, he might be able to avoid liability by showing that the plaintiff was partly at fault. Perhaps it could be shown that the plaintiff had not pulled his car entirely off the highway and had not kept his lights on. Another example of the contributory negligence rule would be a pedestrian who carelessly steps in front of a moving car and is unable to recover damages even though the driver of the car was also negligent.

Strict application of the contributory negligence rule can have the effect of barring payment to a seriously injured person when a minor element of carelessness by that person had contributed to the accident. The rule therefore can have harsh and apparently unfair effects. As a result, a different rule—the **comparative negligence rule**—has been substituted for contributory negligence in about half of the states. According to it, negligence by the injured party does not bar recovery but instead it reduces the amount of the damages. For instance, a person found to have been responsible for 20% of the negligence may be entitled to 80% of the damages that that person would have received if he or she had not been negligent at all. Thus a comparative negligence rule reduces the payment to a party who was partly at fault, rather than preventing any payment at all.

The **assumption of risk rule** bars recovery if the plaintiff either expressly or by implication accepted the chance of being injured by whatever caused the injury. In the earlier example the defense might argue that the plaintiff assumed the risk when he chose to remain in the parked car under hazardous conditions. The assumption of the risk rule has also been used in cases of automobile passengers who willingly accepted the risk of injury when they chose to ride with drivers who obviously were intoxicated.

LAWS AFFECTING LIABILITY FOR AUTOMOBILE ACCIDENTS

Legal liability is determined primarily by the basic rules of negligence which have just been summarized. However, various states have modified those rules as they pertain to liability for automobile accidents. Two areas in which such modifications have been made concern (a) an automobile owner's responsibility for the use of a car by others and (b) a driver's responsibility to his or her passengers. Another and more sweeping modification has been made by the states that have adopted automobile no-fault laws. Because the next chapter introduces the topic of automobile insurance, we shall conclude this chapter with a brief examination of these modifications of the laws of negligence.

Vicarious Liability

By law, there are certain situations in which one party is responsible for the actions of others; such responsibility is known as **vicarious liability.** One very common instance of this concerns employers' responsibility for the acts of their employees. For instance, if part of an employee's job is to operate a vehicle, the employer generally is responsible if other people are injured because of the employee's carelessness. In such a case, the employee is acting as the employer's agent, making the employer vicariously liable. Thus a trucking company is responsible for accidents caused by the negligence of its drivers.

Some states have adopted the "family purpose doctrine," which makes the owner of a family car responsible for its negligent operation by any member of the family. This doctrine is based on the idea that the head of a family is responsible for providing the family's necessities, including transportation. Rather similar to the family purpose doctrine are laws enacted by a number of states which make the person who signs a minor's application for a driver's license responsible for accidents caused by the minor. In those states the person signing the application (usually a parent) is vicariously liable for the minor's operation not only of the family car, but of other cars as well. About a dozen states have gone beyond the family purpose doctrine and have made the owner of an automobile responsible for its negligent operation by any other person using the car with permission, whether that person is a member of the family or not. These laws are called "permissive use" statutes.

Guest Statutes

According to the common law rules of negligence, a driver is obligated only to use reasonable care in operating the car. About half of the states have adopted laws that limit the driver's responsibility, so far as passengers in the car are concerned. Called **"guest statutes,"** these laws provide that the driver is not liable for injuries sustained by guest passengers unless gross negligence can be proved. Gross negligence is defined as willful and wanton misconduct.

The intent of the guest statutes is to make it more difficult to defraud automobile insurers. Assume that Driver and Rider are friends. If Rider is injured in Driver's car, the two may be tempted to make up a story to show that the injuries resulted from Driver's carelessness. Their purpose, of course, would be to wring a generous settlement from Driver's liability insurer. But gross negligence is harder to prove than ordinary negligence. If there is a guest statute in their state, the two friends will find their scheme much more difficult to carry off.

Guest statutes have been repealed in several states during recent years. This action is in line with a trend that has made legal liability easier to establish, a trend that also has made liability insurance more valuable and more costly.

Automobile No-Fault Laws

Since the mid-1960s, controversy has grown concerning the continued use of legal liability as a system of determining who should pay the costs of automobile accidents. As an alternative, various no-fault systems have been proposed. If a pure **no-fault system** were adopted, the concept of legal liability for auto accidents would be completely abolished. Instead, all motorists would have to carry insurance that would pay for their own injuries. Although none of the states has passed a pure no-fault law, sixteen of them have adopted partial or modified no-fault laws. In those states lawsuits are not permitted for automobile accident injuries unless the injuries are serious enough to exceed a certain "threshold" level. Less serious injuries are paid for by special no-fault or Personal Injury Protection insurance. Because the laws still permit lawsuits for serious injuries, the liability risk still prevails, even in the states that have no-fault laws, and automobile liability insurance continues to be an essential form of protection.

This brief introduction to the no-fault concept is presented at this point in order to indicate its relationship to auto liability insurance, which is the principal topic of the next chapter. A fuller analysis of no-fault, including the arguments pro and con, is presented in Chapter 7.

IMPORTANT TERMS

Insurance contract	Depreciation
Binder	Subrogation
Utmost good faith	Other insurance provisions
Warranty	Liability risk
Representation	Damages
Concealment	Negligence
Indemnity principle	Contributory negligence rule
Insurable interest	Comparative negligence rule

Loss measurement
Beneficiary
Bailee
Actual cash value

Assumption of risk rule
Vicarious liability
Guest statutes
No-fault system

KEY POINTS TO REMEMBER

1. An insurance policy is a legal contract. Some of the rights and obligations of the parties are stated in the contract; others of them are provided by laws and by court decisions.
2. Like other contracts, insurance policies require (a) agreement, (b) legal capacity, (c) consideration, and (d) legal purpose.
3. In insurance the offer is made by the applicant and acceptance is made by the company. Property-casualty agents have authority to accept offers on behalf of their companies. The temporary policies that they provide on this basis are called binders.
4. Insurance policies are contracts of utmost good faith, that is, the parties to them are held to especially high standards of fairness and honesty.
5. The doctrine of utmost good faith is supported by laws concerning warranty, representation, and concealment.
6. The indemnity principle provides that the function of insurance is to reimburse insureds for their actual losses, but is not to pay in excess of actual losses.
7. The indemnity principle is supported by laws, practices, and policy provisions pertaining to (a) insurable interest, (b) loss measurement, (c) subrogation, and (d) other insurance.
8. The insurable interest rule requires the insured to be in a position to sustain financial loss if the insured event occurs.
9. The traditional measure of property insurance loss is actual cash value, generally meaning replacement cost new minus depreciation.
10. Subrogation transfers to the insurance company that has paid for a loss the policyholder's right to recover from a negligent third party.
11. "Other insurance" provisions prevent recovery in excess of the loss when the insured has more than one property-casualty insurance policy.
12. Legal liability stems from negligence. The essential elements of negligence are (a) duty to act, (b) failure to so act, (c) injury, (d) direct cause. The most common defenses are contributory negligence and assumption of risk.

REVIEW QUESTIONS

1. In the making of insurance contracts, (a) how is agreement reached, and (b) what consideration is exchanged?
2. How does a conditional receipt affect the making of a life insurance contract?
3. What is the doctrine of utmost good faith and what laws and practices support it in insurance?
4. What is the indemnity principle? What insurance practices and policy provisions support it?

5. Give an example of subrogation and explain its function.
6. Why is insurable interest required?
7. Carson bought a new motion picture theater in 1970 for $300,000. Assuming he has sufficient insurance to cover it, what factors will determine the amount of his recovery if the theater is completely destroyed today?
8. What two principal things does liability insurance do?
9. What must a plaintiff prove in order to recover damages under the laws of negligence?
10. How do contributory negligence, comparative negligence, and assumption of risk relate to legal liability?

DISCUSSION QUESTIONS

1. Why do you suppose life insurance companies don't give their agents binding authority as property-casualty companies do? Can you think of any differences in the nature of the protection that would help explain this?
2. Liability insurance pays for injury that results from the insured's neglect. Should this be permitted? Doesn't it encourage people to be careless?
3. The chapter described how the actual cash value of a damaged restaurant and a damaged car would be determined. Why isn't the former determined in the same manner as the latter?
4. If it is not necessary to apply the indemnity principle in measuring the loss in life insurance, why must it be applied in measuring the loss in property insurance?
5. Why aren't insurance companies permitted to subrogate against their own policyholders if they cause losses through their own carelessness?
6. Why are "other insurance" clauses necessary in view of the premiums that the insurers collect? For instance, if Gloria Williams wants to pay for two $50,000 policies on her $50,000 house, why shouldn't she be able to collect $100,000 if the house is destroyed?
7. A motel guest is drowned in the motel swimming pool. How might the defenses of (a) contributory negligence or (b) assumption of risk be claimed?
8. In filling out an application for a $25,000 life insurance policy, Frank O'Connor stated that he was in good health, had seen a physician only for routine check-ups during the preceding five years, had a total of $30,000 life insurance in force, and had no other insurance application pending. O'Connor died shortly after the policy was issued. The company refused to pay the policy proceeds to the named beneficiary when it discovered that O'Connor had been treated for high blood pressure five times during the six months preceding his application. Also, at the same time that he applied for his policy, O'Connor applied for a $50,000 policy from another company.
   (a) Why do you suppose that the application form asks how much insurance the applicant has and whether or not he has applied for more?
   (b) On what legal ground will the company base its refusal to pay the proceeds?
   (c) Do you think the company's refusal can be justified legally?

PART II
PERSONAL INSURANCE

CHAPTER 5
AUTO INSURANCE COVERAGES— PART I

THE COSTS OF AUTO ACCIDENTS

THE PERSONAL AUTO POLICY

AUTO LIABILITY COVERAGE

The ownership and operation of automobiles create major risks of injury, property loss, and legal liability. For many years America has been a "society on wheels," causing these risks to be among the most obvious (and expensive) that we face. Auto insurance has become almost essential for millions of people, largely because of the importance of the risks it covers, but in some cases also because of legal requirements. For most of us, auto insurance is the first insurance purchase that we make and, except for health insurance, it is usually the first kind from which we receive payment for loss. It also is somewhat complicated and frequently is the subject of misunderstanding and dispute. For all of these reasons there is widespread interest in various aspects of auto insurance, including what it covers, how it is priced, and the laws that pertain to it. These are the subjects of this chapter and the three that follow it. Chapters 5 and 6 examine the policy coverages; Chapter 5 concentrates on liability insurance and Chapter 6 describes the other coverages. Chapter 7 examines existing and proposed modifications of the auto insurance system, including financial responsibility laws and no-fault insurance. Chapter 8 considers several aspects of insurance buying. That chapter tells how the price of a policy is determined and suggests some points to consider in selecting kinds and amounts of coverage.

THE COSTS OF AUTO ACCIDENTS

Table 5–1 shows how the cost of insurance relates to the other costs of operating an automobile. Data are from a study by the Federal Highway Administration. They are based on costs in Baltimore, Maryland, and assume that each car is driven 100,000 miles during a ten-year period.

As Table 5–1 shows, the cost of insurance averages over 10% of the total cost of operating an automobile. For some people it is less and for others it is a great deal more. Some people pay less than $200 per year for auto insurance; others pay over $2,000 per year for similar protection.

Insurance costs reflect both the number of claims that insurance companies pay and the average cost per claim. During recent years the cost of the average auto insurance claim has risen sharply. The chief reason has been rapid increases in the cost of the things that the insurance pays for, including auto repairs and medical services. Rising hospital charges have had an especially strong impact on the cost of the average auto insurance claim.

Each year there are about 25 million auto accidents in the United States. An average of about 5 million people are injured in these accidents and more than 45,000 are killed. One expert in the field of highway safety has put it this way: "Every 1,000 new vehicles during their lifetimes will be

Table 5-1   Cost of Operating an Automobile
(in cents per mile, by size of automobile)

ITEM OF EXPENSE	STANDARD SIZE	COMPACT	SUBCOMPACT
Original vehicle cost depreciated	4.9¢	3.8¢	3.2¢
Maintenance and parts	4.2	3.4	3.1
Gas and oil (excluding tax)	3.3	2.5	1.8
Parking and tolls	2.2	2.3	2.1
Insurance[a]	1.7	1.6	1.5
Taxes	1.6	1.2	.9
Total	17.9¢	14.6¢	12.6¢

[a]Cost of $50,000 liability, $2500 medical payments, uninsured motorist, and comprehensive for all 10 years, plus $100 deductible collision for the first five years only.
Source: Insurance Information Institute, *Insurance Facts 1978*, p. 34.

involved in between 2,000 and 3,000 crashes, kill an average of more than three people, and injure more than 300."[1] We should be shocked by figures like these, but we have grown accustomed to them. We accept them as normal and think very little about the human suffering they represent. The fact is that more Americans have been killed on U.S. highways than in war. The total killed in all of our wars is about 1.2 million, a figure that includes about 500,000 in the Civil War, 100,000 in World War I, 400,000 in World War II, and 57,000 in Vietnam. Since 1900, more than 2 million Americans have died in auto crashes.

Why so many traffic accidents? There are many reasons, of course. Drinking is a major cause. The National Safety Council says that it is a factor in at least half of the fatal crashes. A California study found that drinking was involved in 67% of the fatalities when a man was driving and in 56% of the cases when the driver was a woman.[2]

Whether drunk or sober most drivers who were involved in fatal accidents were driving carelessly at the time. Table 5-2 shows that three times out of four the driver either is speeding or is in some other way operating the car improperly.

Here are some other facts gathered by the National Safety Council:

1.   Deaths on rural highways outnumbered those on city streets 31,800 to 17,700 in a recent year.

[1]William Haddon, Jr., President of the Insurance Institute for Highway Safety. Quoted in *Independent Agent*, September 1978.
[2]*Accident Facts*, 1976 Edition (National Safety Council, 1976), p. 52.

Table 5–2 Causal Factors in Fatal Auto Accidents

FACTOR		PERCENT OF CASES
Improper driving		75.9
Speed too fast	30.1	
Right of way violation	14.1	
Drove left of center	10.5	
Other improper driving	21.2	
No improper driving		24.1
		100.0

Source: Accident Facts, 1978 edition (National Safety Council, 1978), p. 48.

2. Out of 100 fatalities, about 41 involve single-car crashes, 39 result from two-car crashes, and 20 are pedestrians.
3. About 45% of the fatalities occur during daytime hours; 55% happen at night. But because more driving is done during the day the death rate in relation to the number of miles driven is three times higher at night than in the day.
4. Saturday is the most dangerous day. An average of 200 people are killed every Saturday. The average is lowest (105 people) on Mondays and Tuesdays.
5. August was the most dangerous month in a recent year, with 4,760 fatalities. February was at the other extreme with 2,940 deaths.
6. Less than 20% of the fatalities occur on wet or icy roads.
7. Ten percent of all drivers are under age 20. They were driving in 17% of the fatal crashes. The 12% who are age 20 to 24 were driving in 21% of the accidents in which people were killed.

These are just a few of the facts relating to one of the most important risks which we face. For a variety of reasons, auto accidents are both frequent and costly. As a result, auto insurance is an essential form of protection for most Americans.

THE PERSONAL AUTO POLICY

The discussion of auto insurance in this and the following chapter concentrates upon what is known as the **Personal Auto Policy** (PAP). Actually, there are many different auto policies. The PAP is emphasized because it is the one most widely used for insuring individually owned private passenger cars.

Nature of the Policy

The PAP is a new policy form, having been adopted in most states during 1978 and 1979. It replaces some of the older policy forms, including the Family Auto Policy and the Special Auto Policy. The principal differences between the PAP and the older forms are noted in the next chapter. The PAP is designed to be more "readable" than the contracts it replaces. Its language, organization, and design make it more attractive and much easier to understand. Development of this policy is part of the insurance industry's response to the consumerism movement and to public interest in easy-to-read, understandable policies. Similar improvements are being made in other lines of insurance as well.

The Personal Auto Policy was developed by the Insurance Services Office, a national organization that performs various actuarial and statistical services for a large segment of the insurance industry. Although many insurers use this policy, some do not. Some companies use policies developed for them by other organizations, and a few of the largest insurers have developed policies of their own. There are minor differences among the various auto policies, but in most important respects the policies are very similar. Therefore almost all of what one learns about the PAP will be true of the others as well.

In this chapter and the next the PAP is examined in considerable detail, much more than the policies considered in later chapters. There are two reasons for this emphasis. First, auto insurance is important and knowledge of its provisions can be very useful. Second, in many respects this policy is representative of other policies. Because its terms and organization are similar to those of other insurance contracts, one who learns to read and understand this policy will become better able to read and to understand other policies also.

In the following discussion of the PAP, it is assumed that the reader will refer to a copy of the policy (see Appendix B).

The PAP is a **package policy**; it combines several kinds of protection in a single contract. Four types of protection are available. Each is designated as a specific coverage and each is furnished by a separate part of the policy. In summary form (and disregarding many of the details that are considered later), Figure 5–1 describes the protection that the Personal Auto Policy provides.

Declarations Page

The first page of the Personal Auto Policy (and of many other insurance contracts) is called the **declarations page.** It states some of the information given to the company by the policy buyer and thereby identifies the party and the risks that the policy insures. The information on the declarations

Figure 5–1 Summary of Personal Auto Policy Protection

PART	COVERAGE	PROTECTION
A.	Liability	Defends the covered persons and pays others who are injured or whose property is damaged by them if the covered persons are legally responsible.
B.	Medical Payments	Pays medical bills of covered persons and passengers.
C.	Uninsured Motorists	Pays the covered persons amounts they are entitled to recover from uninsured drivers who injure them.
D.	Damage to Your Auto	Pays for damage to the covered auto.

page includes the name and address of the policyholder and the inception and expiration (beginning and ending) dates of the policy. The auto or autos owned by the insured are also described. (We should not assume that coverage is restricted to the one or more vehicles listed here, however.)

The declarations page also states the amount of protection being provided under each of the coverages. An amount of premium is indicated for whichever of the various coverages the policyholder has purchased. Unless a premium is shown for a particular coverage, it is not in effect. At the bottom of the page the contract is signed either by the agent or by an officer of the insurance company.

AUTO LIABILITY COVERAGE

The remainder of this chapter concerns Part A, the liability coverage, of the PAP. The other Parts of the policy are analyzed in the next chapter.

Part A of the Personal Auto Policy covers about two pages of print. "Read your policy!" insurance companies frequently urge their insureds. The advice is well intentioned; people should know the terms of their contracts. But few people ever try to read an insurance policy. A glance at one is enough to persuade most policyholders that it wouldn't be worth the effort. Actually, reading a policy isn't as difficult as it may appear. The key is to know what to look for and to have some idea of where it is likely to be.

Insuring Agreement

The most important section of any insurance policy is the **insuring agreement.** It is a short, affirmative grant of insurance protection, stating the essence of what the company promises to do. Unfortunately, insurance policies seldom identify their insuring agreements by name; one simply has to learn where to find them. The PAP, because it provides four separate coverages, has four different insuring agreements. They are located at the beginning of each of the four parts of the policy. The insuring agreement for Part A, the liability coverage, reads as follows:

> We will pay damages for bodily injury or property damage for which any covered person becomes legally responsible because of an auto accident. We will settle or defend, as we consider appropriate, any claim or suit asking for these damages. Our duty to settle or defend ends when our limit of liability for this coverage has been exhausted.

This is a sweeping statement. As it reads, there are no qualifications, exclusions, limits, definitions, or conditions. These things are supplied elsewhere in the policy. The fact that the company first makes such a broad statement and then later qualifies it sometimes causes misunderstanding. "They give you coverage with one hand and take it away with the other," some people say. But consider the alternative—to use one long and complex sentence setting forth the insuring agreement and all of the definitions, exclusions, and conditions at the same time. Then the contract really would be impossible to understand! The point is that the insuring agreement states the basic nature of the coverage and it is subject to the other terms of the policy. Bearing this in mind, we can seen that Part A of the PAP is designed to meet the policyholder's need for **automobile liability coverage.**

The insuring agreement might be condensed (in the policyholder's mind) to say that "if I'm in an auto accident, the company will pay money for me that I owe because of BI or PD claims."[3] If, for instance, an insured drives through a red light and runs into another car, under this coverage the insurer will handle and, if necessary, pay for any claims brought against the insured for damaging the other car or for injuring the people in it.

It is important that the insuring agreement says that the insurer "will settle or defend . . . any claim or suit asking for these damages." The promise to defend the insured can be extremely valuable. The cost of legal defense in some cases is staggering, but defendents who have liability insurance also have what might be called "legal defense insurance." They don't have to hire attorneys to handle their cases and they don't have to pay the various costs of defending themselves. They don't even have to worry about how

---

[3]"BI" and "PD" are the usual abbreviations for bodily injury liability and property damage liability.

well they are being defended. As long as they have purchased enough liability insurance protection, any shortcomings in defending their cases will be paid for by their insurers in the form of higher settlements with the plaintiffs. Notice also that the insurance company is committed to settle or defend *any* suit covered by the terms of the policy; it must do so even if the suit is groundless or fraudulent. Thus, the company cannot turn its back on an insured who is being sued by a dishonest or foolish claimant.

Read the insuring agreement again. This time ask yourself what things it leaves unsaid. What questions are likely to arise later on during the policy period? Most of these questions have been anticipated and are answered elsewhere in the policy. For instance, who are the "covered persons?" Do they include other members of the family? What if someone else drives the insured's car? Does the policy cover them? Is the insured covered if he or she has an accident while driving someone else's car? These are some of the points we shall now consider.

Covered Persons

The insuring agreement says that the company will pay sums for which any "covered person" is legally responsible. The next paragraph of the policy tells us who the covered persons are:

> "Covered person" as used in this Part means: 1. You or any family member for the ownership, maintenance or use of any auto or trailer.

The definitions section of the policy indicates that the word "you" means the person listed as "named insured" on the declarations page. It also includes the spouse of the named insured if the spouse is a resident of the same household. Thus, if Harvey Harper is named as the insured the reference to "you" includes his wife Helen Harper, whether her name appears in the policy or not.

Any "family member" is also covered. The Definitions section says that a "family member" is "a person related to you by blood, marriage or adoption who is a resident of your household . . ." This of course will include Veronica Harper, a daughter who is a high school senior and lives at home. But what about Dustin Harper, a son who is a sophomore in college? He lives in a residence hall on a campus seventy miles from home. Is he a resident of the Harper household? Neither the word "resident" nor the word "household" is defined in the policy. The answer is supplied by insurance company practices and court interpretations. As long as Dustin considers his parents' home to be his home and treats his college dwelling quarters as a temporary residence, he probably will be considered a resident of the Harper household and therefore a covered person under his parents' policy.

Notice that the persons covered by this provision are protected for their "use of *any* auto." The protection is not limited to the use of owned autos; it also applies while the insureds are driving borrowed cars or rented cars.

The policy says that "covered person" also includes:

---

2. Any person using your covered auto.

Thus, if Harvey Harper lends the car to his friend Marvin, Marvin will become a covered person under Harvey's PAP. Harvey's policy will protect Marvin for BI or PD claims. Marvin may have auto liability insurance of his own, of course. A later section on Other Insurance indicates how Harvey's and Marvin's insurers would share the loss in such a case.

The policy also defines "covered persons" to include:

---

3. For your covered auto, any person or organization but only with respect to legal responsibility for acts or omissions of a person for whom coverage is afforded under this Part.

This clause could cover an employer for a claim involving the use of an employee's own car for business purposes. In such a case the injured party might sue both the employee and the employer. Both have protection under the employee's PAP. Another instance might concern an accident occurring while Helen Harper is using the family car to do an errand for the high school Parents Association. If the plaintiff sues the Parents Association, claiming that it is responsible for Mrs. Harper's use of the car, the Association will be protected by this section of the Harpers' policy.

The fourth and final category of covered persons is similar to the third but deals with the use of vehicles other than those defined as the "covered auto." The effect is to extend liability coverage to another person or organization drawn into a claim involving the use by the insured or a member of the insured's family of a borrowed or rented auto.

Thus, we see that a variety of interests are insured under Part A of the PAP. They include not only the named insured and spouse, but also members of the named insured's family, others using the covered auto, and people or organizations responsible for the acts of one of the other insureds. In this respect, the coverage certainly is as broad as reasonably could be expected and, in fact, is broader than many people realize. Later on, when other kinds of insurance are considered, we shall find that not all policies are as liberal in defining the insured as this kind is.

Amount of Insurance

The amount of insurance provided by Part A is indicated by the **limit of liability** stated on the declarations page. In this context, limit of liability simply means the amount of insurance. It is the maximum that the company will pay for a loss. We should not assume that a policy's limit of liability sets a limit on the amount for which the insured can be held legally liable. A person with a $25,000 limit of liability might be obligated for damages in the amount of $35,000. In such a case the insurance would fall $10,000 short of the amount needed and the individual would be personally responsible to make up the difference. Paying the additional premium required for a $50,000 limit of liability would have avoided this problem. The Personal Auto Policy's limit of liability is a single limit. It is the maximum payable for liability claims resulting from any one accident whether the claims are for bodily injury, property damage, or both.

The **basic limit** of an insurance policy is the minimum amount for which it can be written. For Part A of the PAP the basic limit is $25,000. Many policies provide only the basic limit, but it really is not an adequate amount of protection today. A much higher amount should be carried.[5] The cost of higher limits is not as great as we might expect. If $25,000 of coverage costs a particular policyholder $100, $100,000 would cost $122, and the premium for $300,000 of protection would be $140.

Other Insurance

The indemnity principle, you will recall, states that insurance loss payments are not to exceed the actual loss sustained. But what is to prevent double reimbursement to injured parties if an insured for some reason has two policies providing auto liability insurance? The answer is provided by the first portion of the Other Insurance section:

> If there is other applicable liability insurance we will pay only our share. Our share is the proportion that our limit of liability bears to the total of all applicable limits.

This is a "pro rata" other insurance clause. The company will pay its pro rata share of the loss on the basis of the total amount of insurance in force. A

[5]This point is discussed further in Chapter 7.

person might have policies with Company A and Company B providing $25,000 and $50,000 limits, respectively. Company A would pay one-third and Company B would pay two-thirds of each loss up to their limits of liability. Such instances of other insurance are rare; people do not ordinarily have more than one auto policy in their own name.

Another type of situation involving other insurance—when an insured person drives someone else's car—is more common. In an earlier example we noted that if Harvey Harper loaned his car to his friend Marvin, Harvey's policy would cover Marvin because Harvey's policy says it covers "any person using your covered auto." But if Marvin has a PAP of his own that policy will also apply, as it covers Marvin while he is using "any auto."

Assume that Harvey's policy provides $50,000 of liability coverage and Marvin's limit is $25,000. If Marvin causes an accident while driving Harvey's car and a court orders Marvin to pay $60,000 to the injured party, which policy will apply? In this case the last sentence of the Other Insurance section applies:

> However, any insurance we provide for a vehicle you do not own shall be excess over any other collectible insurance.

This is a "primary and excess" type of other insurance clause, in contrast to the pro rata arrangement provided in the first two sentences of the Other Insurance section. In the situation we have described, Marvin's policy is covering a vehicle he does not own. The policy is excess over Harvey's policy, which is covering an owned vehicle and is primary. Thus, Harvey's policy applies first and pays its full $50,000. The $10,000 excess (to pay the $60,000 loss) is paid by Marvin's policy. The rule is that insurance on an owned car is primary and insurance on a nonowned car is excess. If coverage on the owned car is sufficient, then the other policy pays nothing.

Exclusions

Insurance policies cannot cover everything; they must have limitations. Some limitations are provided by general policy provisions, definitions, or conditions and some are contained in insuring agreements. Still other limitations are shown as **exclusions**, policy provisions that specifically limit the scope of the coverage.

The number of exclusions and other limitations varies among types of insurance. Life insurance policies, for instance, have few limitations. Liability policies are at the other extreme. Part A of the PAP lists twelve exclusions. Twelve may seem like a large number, but we shall see that there are reasons for each of them.

The first exclusion pertains to an uninsurable risk, liability for intentional bodily injury or property damage. Using an auto as a weapon is no more insurable than is using a gun with intent to kill.

Exclusions 2 and 3 delete liability coverage for property that is owned by, being transported by, rented to, used by, or in the care of the person being covered. The idea is that liability insurance is intended to cover one's legal obligation for damaging someone else's property. People cannot be legally liable to themselves for damaging their own property. Also, they are expected to be personally responsible for the property of others which is in their custody or control. Damage to nonowned autos is not excluded, however, so long as they are not furnished for the regular use of the insured or a member of the insured's family.

Exclusions 4, 6, and 7 pertain to certain business exposures. Exclusion 4 bars workers' compensation claims. Exclusion 6 concerns the use of vehicles in an auto business, such as a service station or parking garage. If Dustin were working for a parking garage and had an accident while parking a customer's car, there would be no liability coverage under the Harpers' policy. The primary effect of Exclusion 7 is to exclude coverage for the use of trucks in connection with one's business or occupation. You should note that these three exclusions relating to business activities have specific and limited application. They do not exclude other claims involving business use of owned or nonowned autos. Insureds are covered while driving to and from work and while using their own or other autos in the course of their work.

The purpose of several of the exclusions is to eliminate coverage from the PAP for risks that are insured more appropriately by other policies. Excluding such risks simplifies the protection provided by this policy and reduces its cost. Exclusion 5, which eliminates coverage for the use of an auto as a taxicab, is an example. Taxi operations are insurable, but not by a policy like this one which is designed to cover the usual personal auto exposures. Exclusions 8 and 12 also exclude risks that are insured by other policies. Exclusion 8 relates to claims involving motorcycles or mopeds; Exclusion 12 concerns nuclear energy liability.

Exclusions 9 and 10 delete coverage for the use of nonowned vehicles that are not listed in the declarations but that are available for the regular use of one of the insured persons. In order to have such vehicles covered they must be brought to the company's attention so that the appropriate premium can be charged.

The remaining exclusion (Number 11) says that there is no coverage:

For any person using a vehicle without a reasonable belief that the person is entitled to do so.

This exclusion deletes coverage for the operators of stolen cars; it is necessary because of the broad terms used in defining covered persons. As defined, covered persons include family members using "any" auto, as well as "any" other person using an auto belonging to the insured. One might think that such an exclusion would be unnecessary because operation of stolen cars is illegal. However, the fact that one's actions are illegal does not prevent them from being insured. A person exceeding the speed limit or driving while intoxicated is acting illegally, but the policy still applies. Similarly, car thieves would be insured if the policy did not contain this exclusion.

Supplementary Payments

Although the basic function of liability insurance is to handle the cost of legal liability claims, liability policies customarily offer other benefits as well. The additional benefits are called **supplementary payments**.

The first of the Personal Auto Policy's supplementary payments will pay:

> 1. Up to $250 for the cost of bail bonds required because of an accident, including related traffic law violations, resulting in bodily injury or property damage covered under this policy.

People who are arrested in connection with auto accidents sometimes have to provide bail bonds guaranteeing that they will appear in court at the proper time to answer the charges against them. Posting a bond frees the person from having to wait in jail until the case is heard. If the bonded individual fails to make the required court appearance, the amount of the bond is forfeited. Harvey Harper, for instance, has an accident and is arrested for speeding, drunken driving, and refusing to stop on demand of a police officer. The police court judge sets his bail at $750. A bail bond specialist who has an office around the corner from the court house offers to post Harvey's bond for 10% for its amount, or $75. If Harvey pays the $75 his insurance company will reimburse him, as the amount is within the $250 limit applicable to this part of the PAP. Notice that the company does not say it will furnish the bond. Some insurance companies write bail bonds, but most auto insurers do not.

The second supplementary payment pays for bonds that may be required in connection with certain other legal proceedings following an auto accident. The third and fourth, paying interest on judgments and reimbursing for lost income, are self-explanatory. The fifth supplementary payment, which pays "other reasonable expenses" incurred by a covered person at the company's request, would cover the cost of traveling to another city to testify about an accident.

Other Provisions

The two remaining sections of Part A provide that the policy will meet the requirements of state laws. These are the Out of State Coverage and the Financial Responsibility Required provisions. The need for these provisions will be explained in Chapter 7, which describes financial responsibility laws and automobile no-fault laws.

IMPORTANT TERMS

Personal Auto Policy (PAP)	**Limit of liability**
Declarations page	**Basic limit**
Insuring agreement	**Exclusions**
Auto liability coverage	**Supplementary payments**

KEY POINTS TO REMEMBER

1. Automobile insurance is vital because of the great frequency and cost of automobile accidents. For the same reasons, it is a significant part of the total cost of automobile transportation.
2. The Personal Auto Policy is one of the most widely used automobile insurance contracts. It is a package policy, offering four different coverages: liability, medical payments, uninsured motorists, and damage to the owned auto.
3. The declarations page identifies the party and the risks that are insured, on the basis of information supplied by the policy buyer.
4. Part A of the PAP provides bodily injury and property damage liability protection for claims resulting from auto accidents. The company furnishes legal defense against claims for damages and pays amounts needed to settle such claims.
5. The coverage is very broad, particularly with respect to the persons insured and the automobiles which they may be operating. However, there are some important limitations.
6. The maximum amount that the company will pay for liability claims resulting from any one accident is the limit of liability stated in the declarations.
7. The indemnity principle is supported by the Other Insurance section, which prevents overpayment for losses when more than one policy is applicable.
8. In the Supplementary Payments section, the insurer agrees to make several payments in addition to payments settling liability claims. These include payment for bail bonds and the cost of attending trials.
9. Full understanding of the PAP requires knowledge of its various definitions, exclusions, and other provisions.

REVIEW QUESTIONS

Harvey and Helen Harper have a Personal Auto Policy with a $50,000 limit of liability. The Harpers' 1979 Ford is driven by son Dustin and daughter Veronica, as well as by Mr. and Mrs. Harper. Does the policy cover the following incidents? Why or why not?

1. As Harvey is rounding a curve on a wet pavement, he loses control of the auto and strikes another car. The owner of the other car sues Harvey for a total of $45,000. This sum includes claims for damage to the other car and for its owner's doctor and hospital bills, lost wages, pain, suffering, and inconvenience. After a period of negotiation, the suit is settled out of court for $12,500. In the process of defending Harvey, the insurance company incurs expenses totaling $2,100.

2. As a result of having stayed out too late one night, Veronica is "grounded"; her parents tell her that she is not to drive the car for a week. Veronica takes the car anyway and causes an accident. She is sued by the injured party.

3. The car is stolen. The thief causes an accident.
   (a) The injured party sues the thief.
   (b) The injured party sues Mr. Harper, charging that he was negligent in leaving the key in the unlocked car.

4. Harvey flies to Chicago on business. He rents a car at O'Hare Field and drives downtown. Being unaccustomed to the car, he loses control and sideswipes a taxi.
   (a) The cab company demands reimbursement from him for the cost of repairing the taxi.
   (b) The car rental company demands reimbursement from him for the cost of repairing the rented car.

5. Dustin rents a two-wheel camping trailer and together with his friend Sam drives to a state park for a weekend of camping. While Dustin is driving home from the park, the trailer breaks loose from the trailer hitch. After rolling down the road for a distance, it smashes into an approaching car, seriously damaging the car and injuring its occupants.

6. If Sam had been driving the car at the time of the above incident, would he have had liability insurance protection under the Harpers' policy?

7. Dustin's college fraternity borrows a flat-bed truck from a local lumber company to use in the Homecoming Parade. While Dustin is driving the truck, it strikes a boy riding a bicycle. The boy's parents sue Dustin, claiming that the injuries resulted from his negligence.

8. Helen Harper is driving to the grocery. She is driving within the speed limit, is in the proper lane of traffic, and has the car under control. Suddenly, a 14-year-old boy runs in front of the car. He is playing football and doesn't see the car. Mrs. Harper is able to swerve quickly so that the car only brushes the boy, bruising his left shoulder slightly. Six weeks later the Harpers are notified that a suit is being filed against Mrs. Harper in the amount of $50,000.

DISCUSSION QUESTIONS

1. (a) What is the chance of being injured or killed in an automobile accident during a 10-year period, based upon a U.S. population of 200 million, with 5 million injuries per year and 45,000 deaths per year?

   (b) Out of your class, how many probably will be injured in a 10-year period?

   (c) What are the odds that one member of your class will be killed in a traffic accident during the same period?

2. Why isn't the cost of liability insurance proportional to the amounts of protection? For instance, why doesn't a $100,000 limit of liability cost four times as much as a $25,000 limit?

3. Are any of the exclusions or other limitations of Part A of the PAP unreasonable? If so, which ones and why?

4. Auto liability insurance applies while a car is being operated illegally, such as while the driver exceeds the speed limit. Why aren't all claims stemming from illegal operations of the auto excluded?

5. Which is auto liability insurance primarily designed to protect, injured people or insured people?

CHAPTER 6
AUTO INSURANCE COVERAGES— PART II

MEDICAL PAYMENTS COVERAGE

UNINSURED MOTORISTS COVERAGE

UNDERINSURED MOTORISTS COVERAGE

COVERAGE FOR DAMAGE TO YOUR AUTO

DUTIES AFTER AN ACCIDENT OR LOSS

GENERAL PROVISIONS

THE FAMILY AUTOMOBILE POLICY

INSURING OTHER VEHICLES

This chapter continues the study of the Personal Auto Policy. Chapter 5 dealt with Part A of the policy, which provides liability protection. The remaining PAP coverages are considered in this chapter. They may provide medical payments coverage, protection against uninsured motorists, and insurance for damage to the covered auto. The other provisions of the policy are also reviewed here. In addition, the chapter describes one of the older auto policy forms that the PAP is replacing, and it concludes with a look at coverage for other types of vehicles.

MEDICAL PAYMENTS COVERAGE

Part B of the PAP provides **medical payments coverage.** This coverage pays for medical expenses required because of an auto accident. The insuring agreement reads as follows:

> We will pay reasonable expenses incurred for necessary medical and funeral services because of bodily injury caused by accident and sustained by a covered person. We will pay only those expenses incurred within three years from the date of the accident.

It is important to distinguish between the protection furnished by medical payments coverage and that which is included in Part A, the liability coverage. The term "bodily injury" appears in both insuring agreements, but the two coverages do not duplicate each other. Under the liability coverage the company promises to pay for bodily injury, but only to the extent that the insured is legally responsible for having caused the injury. In contrast, medical payments coverage provides reimbursement for "reasonable expenses incurred" without regard to legal responsibility. Matters of negligence or legal liability are not relevant to medical payments insurance.

Covered Persons

The coverage pays the medical expenses of two groups of people. First, the "covered persons" include:

> 1. You or any family member while occupying, or as a pedestrian when struck by, a motor vehicle designed for use mainly on public roads or by a trailer of any type

Thus, the named insured and members of his or her family are covered while occupying almost any vehicle, whether they own it or not and whether they are drivers or passengers. They also are covered if they are run down by a vehicle while they are on foot.

The second group for whom this coverage applies is:

2. Any other person while occupying your covered auto.

People other than the insured and family must be occupying the insured's car. The coverage does not pay their medical expenses if they are injured while occupying their own car or if they are struck as pedestrians. Occupants of another car struck by the insured or by a family member are not covered by this part of the policy. Claims brought by such people against one of the insureds are covered under Part A, of course, but on the basis of legal liability only.

The word "occupying" is important to Part B. The insured persons are covered "while occupying," the designated automobiles. Therefore, their injury does not need to have been caused by an auto accident in the usual sense of that term. The medical expenses of a person injured by horseplay or by gunshot are covered, as long as the injury happened in a car and was "caused by accident." Furthermore, "occupying" is defined to include injuries sustained while getting in or out of an automobile. If Mrs. Harper slips on some ice as she steps from a car, and she falls and breaks her arm, her medical bills will be paid (assuming that someone realizes there is coverage and submits a claim). The other definitions and most of the exclusions found in Part A of the policy also apply to Part B.

Other Provisions

The amount of medical payments protection is stated in the Declarations. The basic limit is $500 each person. The cost varies from one territory to another but is not great. For the basic $500 limit the premium is only a few dollars per year in most areas. Increased limits are available for an additional premium. In a place where $500 of medical payments cost $4 a year, $1,000 of protection would cost $6 a year. The comparable annual costs for $5,000 and $10,000 limits would be $11 and $19.

Most of the other provisions of the medical payments coverage are similar to those of the liability coverage. One exception is an exclusion of coverage for any person:

3. For bodily injury sustained while occupying any vehicle located for use as a residence or premises.

This provision, of course, excludes medical payments for injuries happening while one is occupying a house trailer or motor home while such vehicle is being used as a residence. The exclusion is necessary because without it the covered persons would be protected for accidental injuries sustained while at home, an exposure that goes beyond that intended to be covered by auto insurance.

Part B also excludes coverage for injuries sustained while using a motorcycle. The exclusion applies whether the motorcycle is owned by the insured or belongs to someone else, and whether the injured person is operating the motorcycle or riding it as a passenger.

Medical Payments as Accident Insurance

Because medical payments insures two categories of people, the insured family and other people, it really serves two different purposes. With regard to the first category, medical payments is accident insurance for the named insured and any family members. Concerning the second category, it is a means of paying other people on a "no-fault" basis.

For the named insured and family, medical payments are a specialized form of accident insurance. Whereas most accident policies pay for medical expenses resulting from almost any sort of accident, this coverage is confined to automobile accidents. It therefore is subject to the criticism that it is a piecemeal approach to the goal of adequate protection for the costs of accidental injury. In other words, it can be argued that if a family has enough accident insurance it doesn't need this coverage, and if it doesn't have enough accident insurance this coverage won't provide it. There are other points to consider, however.

Being a form of accident insurance, medical payments coverage is not fully subject to the indemnity principle. With the exception of claims involving occupancy of a nonowned car, the Other Insurance clause of Part B applies only to other auto medical payments insurance. Loss payments under this coverage therefore can duplicate payments received from other sources. Thus, it is possible for a person injured in an auto accident to receive payment for medical expenses from this coverage and also from one or more other accident policies. Furthermore, if another party were at fault the injured person might be able to secure additional payment in the form of a legal liability settlement. To illustrate this point, assume that Harvey Harper is knocked down by an automobile as he is crossing a street to go to his office. He suffers a badly bruised leg and a broken arm, and he incurs medical bills totaling $900. The full $900 is reimbursed by his auto medical payments insurance (assuming he carried $1,000 or more of this coverage). Through his job, Harvey is covered by a group accident policy. It pays $700 for the medical costs. Harvey also consults an attorney and files suit against the driver of the automobile. The suit is for pain and suffering, as well as for the actual medical costs; it demands a total payment of $10,000. The driver's auto liability insurer, after some delay, agrees to settle the case for $3,000. Of this amount, Harvey's lawyer receives $1,000. The remaining $2,000 plus the payments received earlier gives Harvey a total payment of $3,600 as reimbursement for his expenses of $1,700.

This settlement is a good deal for Harvey; he is better off financially after the accident than he was before. But it is a poor way to try to make money and is not really a desirable sort of insurance arrangement. Some people do receive more in insurance loss payments than they pay in premiums; this fact stems from the nature of insurance as a risk-handling method. On an overall basis, however, total loss payments cannot exceed total premiums, because premiums are the source of the funds with which losses are paid. The large majority of policyholders must receive less than they pay so that a few can receive more than they pay. Overpaying Harvey's loss ultimately must cause an unnecessary increase in the cost of other people's insurance.

As accident insurance, medical payments coverage has the two drawbacks described: it is a piecemeal approach to an adequate program of accident coverage, and in some cases it ignores the indemnity principle. In spite of these shortcomings, it is good protection for most families. There are three reasons why this is true. First, auto accident rates are high. Millions of people are injured on the streets and highways each year. Second, the costs of medical care are enormous. Most families do not have enough insurance to cover them. And third, the cost of this coverage is quite low.

Medical Payments for Others

Although Part B provides auto accident insurance for the named insured and family, the fact that it also pays other people's expenses gives additional reasons for buying the coverage. Bear in mind that other people are covered only "while occupying your covered auto." They are guests, in other words. Assume that Mrs. Harper gives a friend a ride to their Saturday afternoon tennis lesson. If there is an accident in which the friend is injured, the Harpers probably will want to offer to pay her medical bills. They will want to do so whether the accident was Mrs. Harper's fault or not. The Harpers have bodily injury liability protection under Part A of their PAP, but their insurer will make no payment under that coverage unless Mrs. Harper was negligent. If the Harpers have medical payments coverage it will provide payments on a voluntary basis without regard to fault.

The injured guest may be reluctant to sue the Harpers. She is a friend and doesn't want to cast herself in the role of an opponent. But if there is no medical payments coverage, suing or threatening to sue is the only way to make the auto insurance apply. This could tempt Mrs. Harper to try to cheat the company. For the sake of her friend (and to cause the company to make a settlement with her), Mrs. Harper might say that the accident was her own fault, whether or not it actually was.[1] Part B, by its prompt and voluntary payment of medical expenses, may preserve both Mrs. Harper's honesty and the friendship of her passenger. Furthermore, the expense and delay of a legal liability claim can be avoided.

UNINSURED MOTORISTS COVERAGE

Part C of the Personal Auto Policy provides uninsured motorists coverage. This coverage is designed to protect those who have legal claims against drivers from whom they are unable to collect. The fact that such situations can arise is an important shortcoming of the negligence system. In order for the system to function properly, those who are negligent must be able to compensate their victims. However, a surprisingly large number of motorists do not have liability insurance or any other means of reimbursing anyone they may injure, a lack that has created the need for this type of insurance.

Nature of the Coverage

Uninsured motorists coverage (UM) pays the covered persons damages for bodily injury which they are legally entitled to collect from the owner or operator of an uninsured motor vehicle. The coverage can be thought of as an upside-down version of bodily injury liability insurance; it pays sums that the covered persons are entitled to recover, rather than sums they are obligated to pay.

In most states, UM coverage applies to bodily injury claims only. Property damage claims which covered persons are entitled to recover, such as for damage to their car, are not paid. The basic limit of liability is governed by the state financial responsibility law and in most states is $20,000. The cost of the protection is low, only about $3 or $4 per year for the basic limit. Many states require that the coverage be included in all auto insurance policies.

The Uninsured Motorists

Who are the uninsured motorists from whom the covered persons may be entitled to recover? They are likely to be drivers who simply have failed to buy auto liability coverage, perhaps because they feel they can't afford it, but motorists can be uninsured for a variety of other reasons as well. They

---

[1] Such a scheme would be especially hard to carry off in one of the states that still have guest statutes.

can be individuals whose policies have lapsed because their premiums were not paid, or people who have policies but who were driving stolen cars. By the terms of the policy, drivers of hit-and-run cars are also considered to be uninsured motorists, as are those whose liability limits are below the amounts called for by the state financial responsibility law. Finally, persons whose auto insurers are insolvent or whose insurers refuse to pay a claim are considered to be uninsured motorists.

Uninsured motorists coverage protects the named insured and family, not the uninsured motorist. Payments to the covered persons are not made "on behalf of" the uninsured motorist. Thus, after the company pays for a claim under this part of the policy it can subrogate against the uninsured motorist.

Suppose that Dustin Harper is driving home from a date one Saturday night when a drunken driver loses control of his car and runs into Dustin head-on. Dustin is hospitalized with a broken collar bone and numerous cuts and bruises. It turns out that the drunk is unemployed, owns no property other than his wrecked car, and did not have liability insurance. Under their U.M. coverage, the Harpers' insurer is obligated to pay Dustin the amount that he would have been able to recover if the drunken driver had been insured. This could include payment for loss of income, pain and suffering, and permanent disability, as well as actual medical expenses. It may be difficult for the Harpers and their insurance company to reach an agreement on the proper amount of the payment. The Harpers may want more than the company feels they are entitled to receive. The policy provides that if the two parties cannot agree, the amount of payment will be established by arbitration. After the claim is settled the Harpers' insurer will have the right of subrogation against the other driver.

UNDERINSURED MOTORISTS COVERAGE

A newly developed form of protection, **underinsured motorists coverage** can now be added to the PAP in most states. In contrast to uninsured motorists coverage, which pertains to claims against those from whom nothing at all can be collected, underinsured motorists coverage involves claims against those who have auto liability insurance with inadequate limits. Underinsured motorists coverage pays damages for bodily injury that the covered persons are legally entitled to recover from a motorist who has auto liability insurance, when the amount of that insurance is not enough to pay the full amount of the damages. The amount paid is the difference between the amount payable by the other driver's insurance and the limit of the underinsured motorists coverage. In the case related in the preceding paragraph, assume that Dustin had been entitled to collect $40,000 and that the other driver had auto liability coverage with a limit of only $25,000. Uninsured motorists coverage would not be applicable because the other driver did have liability insurance. However, if the Harpers carried adequate limits of underinsured motorists coverage, then their policy would pay the additional $15,000.

The standard PAP does not furnish underinsured motorists protection. It can be provided, in the states where it is available, by the addition of an endorsement to the policy.[2] It generally can be purchased only if uninsured motorists coverage is also carried, and with the same limit of liability. The additional charge is small, for example, about $5 per year for a $100,000 limit. The coverage fills an important need and should always be purchased.

COVERAGE FOR DAMAGE TO YOUR AUTO

Part D of the Personal Auto Policy offers protection for damage to the insured's auto. This coverage is called "physical damage" insurance in some policies, but the PAP does not use that term. The insuring agreement of Part D reads:

> We will pay for direct and accidental loss to your covered auto, including its equipment, minus any applicable deductible shown in the Declarations. However, we will pay for loss caused by collision only if the Declarations indicate that Collision Coverage is afforded.

Note that Part D in effect provides two separate coverages, listed in the Declarations as Collision Loss and Other Than Collision Loss. As is true of the other coverages, they are in force on a particular policy only if the Declarations show amounts for them under the columns headed Limit of Liability and Premium. The policy buyer must decide whether to purchase both coverages, neither of them, or just the Other Than Collision Loss protection (collision insurance is not ordinarily written without the other coverage).

Collision Loss Coverage

Auto collision coverage pays for loss to the covered auto caused by collision. The collision may be with another vehicle or with a fixed object such

---

[2] An endorsement is a piece of paper attached to an insurance policy to alter the policy's terms. It may be a standard, printed page or a special typewritten one. In fire insurance the word "form" is commonly used for the same thing, and in life insurance it is called a "rider."

**"The heck with inventing the wheel! Then we'd
have to buy collision insurance!"**

as a utility pole. Collision also includes "upset," when an auto turns over and the impact is with the surface of the highway or ground. The coverage is confined to the insured's auto; there is no coverage for other autos or other property, nor is there coverage for bodily injury resulting from a collision. (The exact meaning of "covered auto" is examined in a later section.)

Because this is not liability insurance, collision damage is paid without regard to whose fault the collision was. The indemnity principle is applicable, however; if a collision is the fault of another driver the insurer may subrogate against that person after reimbursing the insured.

The amount of collision insurance is the actual cash value of the auto minus the deductible amount stated in the Declarations. Actual cash value means the value of the car at the time of the loss, taking into account its age, make, model, and condition. In other words, the policyholder does not purchase a stated amount of collision insurance. Instead, the amount of insurance automatically corresponds to the car's actual cash value when and if a loss occurs.

Collision coverage always is written with a deductible, an amount that is subtracted from each loss payment. If the deductible is $200 and repairs to a damaged car cost $800, the company will pay $600. If the amount of the loss is less than the deductible (less than $200 in this example) the insurance pays nothing. On the PAP the collision deductible is usually $100 or $200, although higher deductibles are available and may be desirable. Other things being equal, the higher the deductible, the lower is the cost of collision insurance. Selection of the deductible amount is considered further in Chapter 8.

Comprehensive (Other Than Collision Loss) Coverage

The word "peril," you may recall, means the cause of a loss. Collision coverage insures against just that one peril. There are many other things that can cause loss to an auto, however. Fire, theft, and flood are examples. If it is worth insuring a car against collision, the other perils should be covered too. Theoretically, at least, there are two ways in which this might be done. One method is to name each of the perils that are insured. Property insurance that uses this approach is called **named peril insurance.** The other approach is to provide **all-risk insurance**; in this case the policy is written in such a way that it covers all causes of loss except those that are explicitly excluded. (Such coverage really is "all peril," but for some reason that term is not used.)

The all-risk approach is used by the PAP in covering the auto for **other than collision loss.** This coverage pays for any direct and accidental loss to the covered auto, regardless of what peril is involved, so long as it is not collision damage and is not excluded elsewhere in the policy. This insurance customarily is called **auto comprehensive coverage**, although the term does not appear in the PAP.

A provision of this part of the policy which sometimes is misunderstood says:

> . . . the following are not considered "collision": Loss caused by missiles, falling objects, fire, theft or larceny, explosion, earthquake, windstorm, hail, water, flood, malicious mischief or vandalism, riot or civil commotion, contact with bird or animal or breakage of glass.

People who read this provision too quickly sometimes assume that it is simply a listing of the perils that Part D insures. They are not correct, as this is not a named peril type of coverage and the protection is not confined to the perils mentioned here. The provision is included because there are various kinds of loss which could be interpreted as being caused either by collision or by perils other than collision. Those that are named here will not be interpreted as caused by collision and therefore will be covered as comprehensive (noncollision) losses. Why take this approach? Paying the losses as comprehensive ones is favorable to the insured, because comprehensive coverage generally is written with a smaller deductible than is collision coverage. To illustrate, assume that Harvey Harper carries $50 deductible comprehensive and $200 deductible collision coverage. The car is parked in the driveway when a tree limb falls onto it. Repairs cost $450. Because the policy says that loss caused by falling objects is not considered to be collision loss, the company will not contend that the damage was caused by a collision between the limb and the car. It will pay $400 ($450 minus $50), rather than just $250 ($450 minus $200).

The sentence immediately following the one just quoted says:

> If breakage of glass is caused by a collision, you may elect to have it considered a loss caused by collision.

This clause prevents an insured from being subjected to a double deductible following a collision in which there was glass breakage. Without this provision the company could charge the comprehensive deductible for the glass breakage and the collision deductible for the other damage.

Covered Autos

Part D pays for loss to "your covered auto." The term, which also is used elsewhere in the PAP, is explained in the Definitions section of the policy. It includes four categories of vehicles. First, it of course includes the one or more vehicles listed in the Declarations. Second, it automatically covers vehicles acquired during the policy period, with certain limitations. If the new vehicle is an additional one (rather than a replacement for one listed in the Declarations), it is covered for 30 days, provided that within the 30-day period the insured asks the company to cover it. If, on the other hand, the new vehicle replaces one listed in the Declarations, the insured has to ask for coverage only if Part IV protection (Damage to Your Auto) is desired. That is, there are no restrictions on coverage for the use of a replacement vehicle unless the insured wants Part IV coverage for it and even then it is automatically insured for the first 30 days. The third category included as "your covered auto" is any trailer owned by the insured. Finally, a vehicle that is temporarily substituted for one that is out of service is automatically covered.

Notice that the definition of "your covered auto" does not include autos used by but not owned by the insured persons. We observed earlier that Part A of the PAP furnishes liability protection for the operation of such vehicles, those that are borrowed or rented, for instance. Part D, however, does not provide coverage if they are damaged, a fact which could leave a person who damaged a borrowed car in a difficult position, if it were not for a rather obscure provision of Part A. Exclusion 3 of Part A says there is no coverage (liability coverage, of course) for any person for damage to property rented to, used by, or in the care of that person. It is important that the exclusion also says it does not apply to vehicles not owned by the insured. Thus, if the insured is legally liable for damage to a borrowed car, such damage will be paid for under the liability coverage. Covering damage to a nonowned auto in this manner, by Part A rather than Part D, may benefit the policyholder for two reasons. First, the claim would not be subject to a deductible; and, second, the protection is available even if the policyholder has chosen not to carry Part D coverage on his or her own autos.

Insurance for Theft

Automobile theft is important enough to deserve special consideration. About one out of every one hundred and fifty autos in the United States is stolen each year. Although most of the stolen vehicles are later recovered, many of the recovered autos have been damaged or stripped of valuable parts.

Auto theft is insured as a comprehensive ("other than collision") loss. Furthermore, collision damage and other damage that occurs while a stolen car is in the hands of thieves is a comprehensive rather than a collision loss. If the Harpers' car is stolen and then is abandoned after being wrecked, the loss will be subject only to the comprehensive deductible, because the policy states that loss caused by theft is one of the types of loss not considered as collision. What about theft of items such as a coat or a camera taken from the auto? They are not covered; the insurance relates only to loss to the vehicle, not to personal effects. On the other hand, theft of a car radio or any other part of the car is covered, because Part D of the PAP pays for loss to the car, "including its equipment."

Automobile insurers have been plagued during recent years by the problem of stolen CB radios, stereo tape players, and tapes. These have been targets of thieves in many parts of the country. Also, it has been difficult to rule out fake claims, especially for equipment not built into the car. As a result, the standard Personal Auto Policy excludes all items of this nature (see Exclusions 5, 6, and 10 of Part D). Policyholders wanting to insure such equipment can request a special endorsement that is available at extra cost.

The Transportation Expenses section of Part D provides payment of transportation costs after an insured car is stolen. This helps pay necessary taxi or rental car expenses that may be incurred until the car is either recovered or replaced. Payments begin 48 hours after the theft and are subject to a maximum of $10 per day with a $300 aggregate limit. When a car is destroyed by collision or some other covered peril, the insurer usually makes prompt payment so that the car can be replaced without undue delay. But, when a car is stolen, the company is reluctant to settle the claim quickly, because of the likelihood that the car eventually will be recovered. Reimbursement of transportation expenses is designed to make the insured more willing to accept this delay.

Other Provisions

Most of the Part D exclusions, other than those relating to sound equipment, are similar to the Part A exclusions. Notice that Exclusion 2 states the company will not pay for:

> Damage due and confined to wear and tear, freezing, mechanical or electrical breakdown or failure or road damage to tires. This exclusion does not apply if the damage results from the total theft of your covered auto.

The intent of the policy is to cover unexpected accidental loss, not the deterioration and damage that normally result from use (including hard use) of a car. If a tire is damaged in a fire or collision, it is covered. There is no coverage, however, for tires damaged by puncture or for the usual blowout, even if the blowout is caused by running into a curb. If an insured forgets to put antifreeze in the radiator and the auto is damaged by freezing, comprehensive coverage will not pay for the repairs. But, if an auto is stolen and freezes before it is recovered, the exclusion does not apply.

A rather interesting provision explains Part D's limit of liability:

> Our limit of liability for losses will be the lesser of: 1. The actual cash value of the stolen or damaged property, or 2. The amount necessary to repair or replace the property.

This provision is the source of the so-called "totaled" loss, when the repair costs amount to more than an auto's actual cash value. If, for instance, an auto was worth $800 before it was damaged and repairs would cost $1,000, the company is entitled to settle for $800, that being the lesser of the two amounts.

Another provision that calls for explanation is the one headed No Benefit to Bailee:

> This insurance shall not directly or indirectly benefit any carrier or other bailee.

A bailee is a person or firm having temporary possession of someone else's property. Railroads and auto parking garages are examples. Bailees are liable for damage to property in their care if the damage is due to their negligence. Therefore, if the Harpers' car is destroyed in a parking garage fire caused by carelessness on the part of the garage, the Harpers' insurer probably would pay for the loss and then subrogate against the garage. But what if the garage states (on the receipts given to people leaving their cars there) that they accept custody of their customers' property on the condition that any insurance carried by the owners would benefit the garage as well as the owners? This approach would be an attempt to defeat any insurer's right of subrogation against the garage. The policy provision, in turn, defeats the garage's move by saying that the Harpers' insurance shall not benefit any bailee. The effect is to retain the company's right of subrogation.

DUTIES AFTER AN ACCIDENT OR LOSS

In Part E of the Personal Auto Policy, the insured's responsibilities following an accident or loss are spelled out. To understand the importance of these provisions one must be aware of the very first sentence of the contract. Under the heading Agreement, the company states:

> In return for payment of the premium and subject to all the terms of this policy, we agree with you as follows:

Thus, the insurer's promises to pay losses are conditional promises in the sense that they are "subject to all of the terms" of the policy. The terms of the policy of course include the insured's duties after an accident. Failure to fulfill these duties could relieve the company of its obligation to pay for losses. Although this point is an important one, it should not be a cause for much concern; the insured's duties are reasonable and probably are no more than one would expect them to be.

The company must be notified "promptly" of any accident or loss for which claim is made. Some other policies call for the notification to be in writing, but the PAP does not include that requirement. Notification by telephone generally is sufficient and more prompt than a written notice, although it is a good idea to make written notice also. Most insurers give claim notification forms to their policyholders. These should be carried in the car, filled out after an accident, and given to the company or agent. All accidents involving the slightest chance of a legal liability claim should be reported, even if an insured feels that he or she is not liable. The company must have the opportunity to investigate the situation promptly, while witnesses are still available and while the extent of bodily injury or property damage can best be determined.

The policyholder also is required to cooperate with the company in the handling of any claim. Cooperation includes attending hearings and trials, presenting evidence, and providing medical reports. For medical payments claims, covered persons must even submit to physical examinations by company physicians, if requested. If an insured auto is stolen the police must be notified promptly.

Another requirement is that the insured take reasonable steps after a loss to protect the auto from further loss. Leaving a damaged auto where it could be stripped by thieves rather than taking reasonable action to have it towed to a safe place would violate this condition.

GENERAL PROVISIONS

The final section of the PAP is made up of eight General Provisions. These supplement the policy's other provisions to complete the contract. We shall consider only a few of the more important General Provisions.

Territory

The policy is applicable only while the automobile is within the United States, its territories or possessions, or Canada. There is coverage for use of the car in Canada, but not in Mexico. Chapter 8 includes suggestions concerning insurance for trips to Canada and Mexico.

Changes

We have seen that the definition of "your covered auto" includes vehicles acquired while the policy is in force. General Condition 2 permits the company to adjust the premium as of the date of such acquisition (or of any other change requiring premium adjustment).

There is no statement, either in the General Provisions or elsewhere in the policy, of the method by which the premium is determined. The rating system is not stated and the company's rating manuals are not made a part of the policy; that is, rates and premiums do not affect coverage. If Dustin Harper is a member of the household he is insured, whether the company has charged extra premium for him or not (assuming that no concealment or material misrepresentation is involved). Conversely, the mere fact that extra premium is charged for Dustin does not mean that the policy covers him in any and all circumstances (such as while he is using a motorcycle). Policy coverage is determined by the provisions of the contract, not by the rating manual.

Right to Recover Payments

General Provision 5 concerns the company's subrogation rights:

> A. If we make a payment under this policy and the person to or for whom payment was made has a right to recover damages from another we shall be subrogated to that right. That person shall do whatever is necessary to enable us to exercise our rights and shall do nothing after loss to prejudice them.

Notice the prohibition in the second of these sentences. If Helen Harper's car and another slide into each other on an icy street, Helen should restrain the impulse to tell the other driver, "I'm sorry. It was all my fault; my insurance will take care of it." Depending upon the facts of the case, it is possible that the other driver was at fault. If so, the Harpers' insurer may be able to subrogate and recover its payment for the damage to the Harpers' car. An admission of fault on the part of Helen Harper might impair ("prejudice") that action.

Termination

The contract may be canceled by the named insured at any time for any reason. During the first 60 days of a new policy (not a renewal) the company also can cancel for any reason. After that period the company can cancel only if the premium has not been paid or if the driving license of one of the insureds has been suspended or revoked. Thus the company underwriters have 60 days to complete and act upon their investigation of newly insured persons. Information developed later cannot be used as grounds for cancellation. Also, the driving record of the covered persons cannot be a reason for canceling the policy, unless an insured's driving license is suspended or revoked as a result.

The foregoing provisions pertain only to the cancellation of a policy before it expires; they do not require the renewal of an expiring policy. A separate provision on nonrenewal requires the company to notify the insured 20 days in advance of the policy's expiration date if it decides not to continue the protection. There are no restrictions on the reasons for nonrenewal. The company is free to refuse to renew because of an insured's poor driving record or for any other reason. The laws of some states impose other restrictions on nonrenewal of auto policies. Those laws are considered in Chapter 7.

THE FAMILY AUTOMOBILE POLICY

Prior to the development of the Personal Auto Policy, the most commonly used auto insurance contract was the Family Automobile Policy. The Family policy is gradually being phased out as the various states approve the PAP and as existing Family policies expire. Because many people have become familiar with the Family policy, we will note a few of the most important differences between it and the PAP.

Separate Liability Coverages

The Family Automobile Policy has two separate liability coverages, one for bodily injury liability and the other for property damage liability.[3] Two limits of liability apply to the bodily injury coverage; one is a per person limit and the other per occurrence. The property damage coverage has a single per occurrence limit. The basic limits in most states are $10,000 each person and $20,00 each occurrence for bodily injury liability and $5,000 each occurrence for property damage liability. These commonly are abbreviated as 10/20 BI and 5 PD or, in an even shorter form, as 10/20/5. The limit per occurrence for bodily injury liability is subject to the per person limit; that is, if more than one person is injured in a single crash both limits apply. With a 10/20 BI limit the company would pay no more than $20,000 to all BI claimants and no more than $10,000 to any one BI claimant.

Physical Damage Coverages

Coverage similar to that provided by the Damage to Your Auto part of the PAP is furnished by what is called the Physical Damage section of the Family

[3]Although the standard Personal Auto Policy has a single liability coverage, separate coverages can be used by a particular company if it wishes to do so.

Automobile Policy. There are separate insuring agreements for Collision coverage and Comprehensive coverage. The latter covers, on the all-risk basis, "loss caused other than by collision." The protection furnished by the Collision and Comprehensive coverages combined is practically the same as that furnished by the PAP's single Part D insuring agreement.

The Comprehensive coverage of the Family policy includes payment for clothing and other personal effects that are damaged or destroyed by fire or lightning while in the owned automobile. Such losses are not covered by the PAP. This is not an important shortcoming of the newer policy form because losses of this nature are rare and, if they do occur, are ordinarily covered by the policy protecting one's home and household goods. Dropping the personal effects coverage is one of the many ways in which the Personal Auto Policy was made substantially shorter and simpler than the Family Automobile Policy.

INSURING OTHER VEHICLES

Special arrangements must be made for insuring other types of vehicles such as motorcycles and other recreational vehicles.

Motorcycles

Motorcycle owners are subject to much the same risks as automobile owners—legal liability, medical expense, and property loss. There are some differences, though, requiring the use of special policy forms.

Motorcycles cannot be insured under the Personal Auto Policy. The policy that is used differs from the PAP in several important ways. First, the insurance generally excludes protection for bodily injury claims brought by injured passengers. This protection can be added by paying an additional premium. Second, medical payments coverage, if it is available, usually is written subject to a deductible amount. Third, coverage for loss to the motorcycle itself caused other than by collision may be available only on the named peril basis rather than as the comprehensive "all-risk" coverage used for automobiles.

Many of the companies that write automobile insurance do not offer coverage for motorcycle risks. Much of the protection is provided by companies that specialize in insuring these risks.

Other Recreational Vehicles

A number of other kinds of vehicles have become popular during recent years. These include the all-terrain vehicle, dune buggy, go-cart, minibike, trail bike, moped, snowmobile, and motor home. Because there are so many types of these vehicles, ways of using them, and laws relating to them, there also are many different ways of insuring them. Depending upon the vehicle, the state in which it is located, and the company insuring it, a modified auto policy, a homeowners policy, or a specially designed policy may be appropriate. Two points are clear, however. First, ownership and operation of any of these vehicles present important risks. Second, these risks are not covered by the regular Personal Auto Policy. Owners of such vehicles should talk with their insurance agents about them and make sure that they are properly protected.

IMPORTANT TERMS

Medical payments coverage
Uninsured motorists coverage
Underinsured motorists coverage
Auto collision coverage

Comprehensive (other than collision loss) coverage
Named peril insurance
All-risk insurance

KEY POINTS TO REMEMBER

1. Auto medical payments insurance pays for medical expenses arising from auto accidents, regardless of fault.
2. Medical payments coverage applies to two groups: the named insured and any family member, and people who are passengers in the insured's auto.
3. Uninsured motorists coverage pays damages for bodily injury that the covered persons are legally entitled to collect from uninsured motorists.
4. Underinsured motorists coverage pays damages for bodily injury that the covered persons are legally entitled to collect from motorists whose liability insurance is inadequate to pay the entire amount that they owe.
5. Collision coverage pays for collision damage to the insured automobile.
6. Comprehensive (other than collision loss) coverage pays for loss or damage to the insured auto other than that caused by collision. This includes theft of the automobile and of its parts.
7. Both collision and comprehensive coverages are usually written with deductible clauses that specify amounts that are subtracted from each loss payment.
8. Named peril insurance specifies each of the perils that it covers, whereas all-risk insurance covers all causes of loss that are not explicitly excluded.
9. Collision coverage is named peril insurance. Comprehensive coverage is an example of all-risk insurance.
10. The insured has important responsibilities after a loss occurs, including notifying the company promptly and cooperating in the settlement of the claim.
11. The company's right to cancel the policy is limited but the limitations do not apply to the policy's renewal.
12. The Personal Auto Policy does not cover motorcycles and other specialized recreation vehicles. Other arrangements must be made for insuring such vehicles.

REVIEW QUESTIONS

Harvey and Helen Harper have a Personal Auto Policy that provides the following coverages: $100,000 liability, $1,000 medical payments, $100,000 uninsured motorists, $200 deductible collision, and $50 deductible comprehensive (other than collision loss). The Harpers' 1979 Ford is driven by son Dustin and daughter Veronica, as well as by Mr. and Mrs. Harper. Does the policy cover the following incidents? Why or why not? Which is the relevant coverage? (Note: Some of these questions review Chapter 5 subject matter.)

1. While driving the car, Harvey hits and injures a pedestrian, who brings suit for damages.
2. The above pedestrian suddenly had stepped from behind a parked car in the middle of the block. Harvey was not speeding or driving carelessly. There was no way he could have avoided the pedestrian. Nevertheless, he was sued.
3. When Harvey saw the pedestrian he slammed on the brakes and, as a result, struck the windshield. His forehead was badly cut and needed stitches.
4. Hitting the pedestrian put a dent in the car's fender.
5. When Harvey saw the pedestrian, he swerved the car sharply and went off the street and through the plate glass window of a gas station.
6. Before hitting the gas station, he sideswiped a gasoline tank truck that was filling the underground storage tanks. In the ensuing explosion, the truck was totally destroyed.
7. The truck driver, who had been standing by the truck, was blown to smithereens.
8. The gas station was not able to reopen until the tanks and pumps were replaced. Replacement took two weeks, during which the station operator lost $800 in profits that he normally would have earned.
9. During the confusion following the above accident, someone stole Harvey's briefcase from the car.
10. The car is repaired and some weeks later Mrs. Harper drives it to a shopping center. As she is backing out of her parking spot, she hits a man walking behind the car. He is knocked down and his right arm is fractured. The man turns out to be a friend of the Harpers. He assures Mrs. Harper that he won't sue; he says that he should have been more careful himself. "Well anyway," she replies, "our medical payments insurance will pay for your medical bills."
11. Veronica parks the car on the street before attending a movie. After the show, she finds that the car has been sideswiped by a hit-and-run driver. Repairs cost $400.
12. Dustin drives to a baseball game. He parks the car on a street near the stadium. As he is leaving the car, several boys tell him that for a dollar they will watch it for him while he is at the game. Dustin declines. After the game he finds that the car's side-view mirror is broken and the hubcaps have been stolen.
13. While driving his car, Harvey is run into by another car. He sustains a serious back injury. He is hospitalized for three months, has expensive surgery, and is

disabled for fifteen months. The driver of the other car was drunk; he is unemployed, unlicensed, and uninsured.

14. Harvey is giving his friend Gary Gilder a ride home. Gary gets into the car and slams the door on his hand, breaking two of his fingers.

DISCUSSION QUESTIONS

1. What types of automobile injury claims are not covered by automobile medical payments insurance?

2. Under the PAP, the medical payments coverage pays for expenses "incurred within three years from the date of the accident." What do you suppose is the purpose of the time limitation?

3. Occasionally people accidentally lock themselves out of their car and then intentionally break a window in order to get back in. The PAP does not pay for such glass breakage. Can you find the provision that makes the coverage inapplicable?

4. Dustin Harper is planning to buy a car of his own. The car he is considering is an old clunker that he can get for $400. He plans to buy no insurance on it. He figures that the car isn't worth insuring against collision or other physical damage. So far as liability protection is concerned, Dustin assumes that his dad's policy will cover him, because it applies while any relative residing in the household uses another car with its owner's permission. Is this good thinking on Dustin's part?

5. Is there any good reason for limiting uninsured motorists insurance to bodily injury claims? Why not include property damage claims (as is done in a few states)?

6. What is the significance of the provision in General Provision 1 that the policy applies only to accidents and losses that occur "during the policy period?"

CHAPTER 7
AUTO INSURANCE PROBLEMS AND SOLUTIONS

THE PROBLEM OF UNCOMPENSATED VICTIMS

THE PROBLEM OF INSURANCE AVAILABILITY

THE PROBLEMS OF UNFAIRNESS, DELAY, AND HIGH COST

NO-FAULT INSURANCE

About 130 million motor vehicles travel our streets and highways. Most of the time they move about their business the way they are supposed to, taking people where they want to go in relative comfort and safety. But over 20 million times a year something goes wrong and one of the vehicles smashes into something or someone. Vehicles and other property are damaged and people are injured or killed. When an accident happens, financial losses are incurred: the cost of vehicle repair or replacement, the cost of medical treatment, and the loss of wages.

Someone has to pay for each loss. This could be the person who suffers the loss, the person who caused the loss, or someone's insurance company. Clearly, there must be some sort of system to handle the costs of auto accidents. This chapter concerns that system, its problems, and some attempted solutions to the problems.

To a considerable extent, the system of paying for the costs of auto accidents in the United States is a fault system. That is, except for single-car accidents it relies on lawsuits based on the laws of negligence. As we know, motorists buy liability insurance to protect themselves against the risk of being sued. Over 60% of auto insurance premiums are for liability protection, and most of the serious auto insurance problems involve this coverage.

The problems are numerous, and various steps are being taken to cope with them. In this chapter we shall look at three problems: (a) the uncompensated victim; (b) the difficulty of obtaining insurance protection; and (c) the unfairness, slowness, and high cost of the system. We should not expect to find simple solutions to these problems. The subjects are complex and criticisms come from a variety of sources, including motorists, legislators, state insurance departments, and even the insurance industry. All agree that what is needed is a system that provides prompt, adequate, and fair payment for the costs of auto accidents and does so as inexpensively as possible. There is little or no agreement, however, as to exactly how this can be achieved.

THE PROBLEM OF UNCOMPENSATED VICTIMS

When the fault system is used to pay the victims of auto accidents, two things must be done after each accident in order for the system to work. First, the party at fault must be identified and, second, the innocent victim must be reimbursed by the party at fault. One of the problems that always has plagued this system is the fact that the second of these steps doesn't necessarily result from the first. If Harvey Harper is run into by another car, he and his attorney may be able to win a court judgment against the driver of the other car. But it could be an empty victory. The other party may not have carried auto liability insurance and may have no other financial means to pay the damages.

Various solutions to this problem have been attempted. Most of the states have financial responsibility laws, a few have set up unsatisfied judgment funds, insurance protection against uninsured motorists has been made available, and some states have made auto liability insurance compulsory for all motorists.

Financial Responsibility Laws

The purpose of financial responsibility laws is to make it more likely that innocent victims of auto accidents will be able to recover money that they are entitled to receive from those who caused their injuries. In other words, these laws are supposed to encourage all motorists to be financially responsible for the operation of their automobiles. In practical terms, **financial responsibility laws** encourage motorists to buy liability insurance by penalizing them if they fail to do so.

PROVISIONS. The laws apply (a) after a person is involved in an accident, or (b) after a person is convicted of certain motor vehicle violations. First, after there has been an accident the typical financial responsibility law requires that a written report of the accident be filed. The report must be filed with the state agency which administers the law, such as the motor vehicle department. It must be filed promptly, in some states within 24 hours after the accident. Among other things, the person filing the report must indicate whether or not auto liability insurance was in force to pay for claims arising from the accident.

For purposes of this law, "accident" is defined in a way that excludes minor incidents. For instance, it may be defined as an occurrence involving bodily injury, death, or property damage in excess of $250. The owner of a legally parked car may also be exempted from the law's requirements.

Each motorist involved in the accident must file a report, whether that person appears to have been at fault or not. The requirements of the law are fulfilled if the individual can show that he or she carried liability insurance in at least the amounts stated in the law of the particular state. These amounts appear in Table 7–1. Proof that insurance was in force is furnished by a form that is submitted by the motorist. The state agency later checks with the individual's insurer to verify that a policy was in force.

If liability insurance was not in force, the person may be able to show financial responsibility for the accident in a different way. Most of the laws offer alternatives such as posting a surety bond or depositing cash in amounts up to the state's financial responsibility limits. Persons who did not carry insurance and who also cannot fulfill any of the alternative methods of demonstrating financial responsibility have not met the law's requirements and are subject to its penalty.

The penalty for violating a financial responsibility law is suspension of the driving license and vehicle registration. The laws usually provide that the suspensions will continue either until it is determined that the person has no legal liability or until any judgment is paid (up to the amounts required by the financial responsibility law). If no suit is filed against an irresponsible driver by the end of one year, then the suspended license and registration are restored.

The provisions that have been described concern financial responsibility for accidents that happened in the past. In some situations the laws also require proof of the ability to pay for future accidents. In most states motorists who are convicted of serious traffic violations must show that they will carry liability insurance or otherwise be financially responsible in the future. The violations may include such things as reckless driving, driving while intoxicated, and unlawfully leaving the scene of an accident. Most of the laws also require proof of future financial responsibility following a judgment against a motorist and after a person's license is restored following its suspension. A motorist can satisfy the law's required proof of future financial responsibility by posting a surety bond or by depositing cash. The customary way, though, is to show that liability insurance is in force and will remain in force, by means of a certificate filed by the insurance company. The company agrees to notify the state agency if the insurance is dropped.

RELEVANT PROVISIONS OF THE PERSONAL AUTO POLICY. Two provisions of the Personal Auto Policy relate to financial responsibility laws. One, named **Out of State Coverage**, says that, if the policy covers an accident in a state whose financial responsibility law calls for higher limits than the laws of the insured's home state, the policy will provide the higher limits. Thus a resident of Texas whose policy is written for an amount barely meeting the requirements of that state might have an accident in Arizona and be required to comply with Arizona's law, which has higher limits. The Texan's policy will satisfy the Arizona law because of this provision.

The other provision, **Financial Responsibility Required**, applies when the insured is required to show proof of future financial responsibility. It states that when the policy is certified as proof of financial responsibility for the future it will "comply with the provisions of the law." In such a case the company must pay damages for which an insured is legally liable even if the insured fails to fulfill the requirements of the contract. For example, the company would have to cover a claim even though it had not been given proper notice of the accident as required by Part E of the policy. The pur-

Table 7–1   Limits of Liability Required by Financial Responsibility Laws, 1978 (in thousands of dollars)

STATE	BODILY INJURY (per person/all persons)	PROPERTY DAMAGE (per accident)
Alabama	10/20	5
Alaska	25/50	10
Arizona	15/30	10
Arkansas	10/20	5
California	15/30	5
Colorado	15/30	5
Connecticut	20/40	5
Delaware	10/20	5
District of Columbia	10/20	5
Florida	10/20	5
Georgia	10/20	5
Hawaii	25/unlimited	10
Idaho	10/20	5
Illinois	10/20	5
Indiana	15/30	10
Iowa	10/20	5
Kansas	15/30	5
Kentucky	10/20	5
Louisiana	5/10	1
Maine	20/40	10
Maryland	20/40	5
Massachusetts	5/10	5
Michigan	20/40	10
Minnesota	25/50	10
Mississippi	10/20	5
Missouri	10/20	2
Montana	25/50	5
Nebraska	15/30	10
Nevada	15/30	5
New Hampshire	20/40	5
New Jersey	15/30	5
New Mexico	15/30	5
New York	10/20	5
North Carolina	15/30	5
North Dakota	10/20	5
Ohio	12.5/25	7.5
Oklahoma	5/10	5
Oregon	15/30	5
Pennsylvania	15/30	5
Rhode Island	25/50	10

Table 7-1 (continued)

STATE	BODILY INJURY (per person/all persons)	PROPERTY DAMAGE (per accident)
South Carolina	15/30	5
South Dakota	15/30	10
Tennessee	10/20	5
Texas	10/20	5
Utah	15/30	5
Vermont	10/20	5
Virginia	25/50	5
Washington	15/30	5
West Virginia	10/20	5
Wisconsin	15/30	5
Wyoming	10/20	5

Note: Includes states with compulsory insurance laws.
Source: Insurance Information Institute, Insurance Facts, 1978, New York, p. 67.

pose of this **provision** is to carry out the law's intent to protect innocent auto accident victims.

SHORTCOMINGS. Financial Responsibility laws have an enormous loophole: They apply only after accidents and violations, not before. They do not make it illegal to drive without liability insurance or other means to pay those whom a person may injure. If you are seriously injured because Jenny Driver runs into you, it will be little comfort to you to know that she has had her driver's license revoked. That won't pay your hospital bills or repair your car! Furthermore, Jenny probably will get her license back at the end of a year. It will remain suspended longer than that only if you have sued her and the suit is still pending or if the suit has been settled but she has failed to pay you the money. But if you believe that Jenny has no liability insurance, will you go to the expense of bringing a suit against her? Probably not. So at the end of a year she will again be driving without having any way to reimburse her next victim.

Another shortcoming of financial responsibility laws is the amounts of protection which are required. Table 7-1 shows that only a few states require more than $15,000 per person for bodily injury. Some states have raised their limits in recent years, but in most cases the requirements can be met by carrying amounts of insurance that are far below the costs of serious injuries.

Financial responsibility laws are important, though. They cause many people to carry auto liability insurance in order to avoid the chance of losing their licenses after an accident. In addition, many other people do not understand the laws and carry insurance in the mistaken belief that it is illegal to drive without it. The laws therefore do make it more likely that innocent victims of auto accidents will be compensated.

Unsatisfied Judgment Funds

The purpose of an **unsatisfied judgment fund** (UJF), like that of a financial responsibility law, is to make it more likely that people will be paid the amounts they are entitled to receive as damages because of injuries sustained in auto accidents. Financial responsibility laws encourage people to buy auto liability insurance, but many drive without it anyway. To plug this loophole, several states have created unsatisfied judgment funds to compensate people injured by drivers who have no auto liability insurance and no other means to pay the damages they owe. Payments are made by a UJF after a judgment has been secured and damages have been found to be uncollectable. The funds usually apply to bodily injury damages only and are limited to the amounts specified by the state financial responsibility law. After a payment is made, the fund can subrogate against the negligent driver. If Harvey Harper sues Jenny Driver and obtains a judgment against her for $7,000, he can turn to the state UJF for payment if it turns out that Jenny has no liability insurance and no other way to satisfy the judgment. Later, the UJF will probably subrogate, perhaps forcing Jenny to repay the $7,000 in monthly instalments over a number of years.

In addition to providing a source of payment to accident victims who would otherwise receive no compensation, the funds offer a reason for pushing legal action against negligent drivers. This increases the impact of the financial responsibility laws, because if a judgment is obtained the license and registration of financially irresponsible drivers remain suspended until the UJF has been paid.

Unsatisfied judgment funds have not been popular, as is shown by the fact that only three states[1] now have them. They have been a source of confusion in people's minds. In the states that have them some motorists believe that they are a substitute for insurance and therefore fail to carry liability protection. This practice is unfortunate, as a UJF in no way relieves motorists of their legal obligations.

The methods of financing the funds have also caused problems. Money is paid into them from fees obtained from motorists and from insurance companies. To many people it seems unfair to charge insured drivers an extra fee

---

[1] Maryland, New Jersey, and North Dakota. Funds formerly existed in Michigan and New York.

to pay for a problem they are not responsible for. If the fee is paid by insurance companies instead, there is little difference. The funds still come from insured drivers, in this case in the form of higher insurance premiums.

Efforts to collect fees from uninsured drivers have not been successful. The best time to do this would be when uninsured drivers register their cars each year. The problem with doing so is that an uninsured driver can buy insurance just before registering the car, register the car as an insured driver—thus avoiding the UJF fee—and then cancel the policy.

Protection Against Uninsured and Underinsured Motorists

Uninsured motorists (UM) coverage was described in Chapter 6. When it is included in an auto policy it pays sums that the policyholder is legally entitled to recover from an uninsured driver. In most states, UM is now the principal means of handling the problem of compensating victims of auto accidents when a financially irresponsible motorist was at fault. Underinsured motorists coverage, also described in Chapter 6, is a newly developed form of protection. It serves much the same purpose as UM in cases when the other motorist has liability insurance but when the amount is insufficient to pay the damages in full.

Like unsatisfied judgment funds, both UM and underinsured motorists coverage have been criticized on the grounds that their cost is borne by their purchasers rather than by the irresponsible motorists who create the need for them.

Another criticism is that the insurance company is placed in an awkward position when claims are presented under these coverages. If the circumstances of the accident do not clearly establish both the negligence of the uninsured or underinsured driver and the amount that the insured is entitled to recover, there probably will be disagreement between the company and its policyholder. The coverages state that such disputes are to be settled by arbitration, but although arbitration can settle disputes it does not eliminate them. This problem was discussed in Chapter 2 in the context of the features of insurable risks. Satisfactory insurance arrangements are difficult unless the exact amount of covered losses can easily be agreed upon.

Compulsory Auto Liability Insurance

It might appear that a simple solution to the problem of compensating innocent victims of automobile accidents would be to enact **compulsory auto liability insurance laws** that require all motorists to carry liability protection. In other words, instead of requiring financial responsibility to be established *after* accidents occur, such laws would require it to be proved *before* the need arises. Unfortunately, experience with compulsory auto liability insurance has not proved to be successful, in the opinion of most people.

Laws requiring all motorists to have liability insurance were passed by Massachusetts in 1927, New York in 1957, North Carolina in 1958, and Louisiana in 1978. No other states have taken this step, with the exception of several that did so when they established no-fault systems during the early 1970s.

Compulsory insurance (except in connection with no-fault laws) has been strongly opposed by the insurance industry. This attitude surprises many people, as compulsory insurance would seem to give the insurance companies a guaranteed market. However, the insurance industry believes that this approach has serious drawbacks. First is the problem of "claim consciousness." When everyone knows that everyone is insured, both the number and the size of insurance loss payments increase. People injured in automobile accidents assume that the other parties have insurance and therefore press their claims more vigorously. Courts make the same assumption. Jury members are likely to say to themselves, "Oh well, the insurance company will pay the judgment; it won't come out of the defendant's own pocket." The result, of course, is that more dollars are paid out by the insurance companies. Some people argue that more dollars *should* be paid out, that loss payments are not adequate otherwise.

Another objection of the insurance companies is that, when they ask the state insurance departments to permit them to increase their rates in a state with compulsory insurance, they are likely to be turned down. The compulsory laws have tended to make insurance rate regulations a "political football"—with the insurance industry, in its opinion, on the losing side.

Another problem is that people, perhaps a majority, object to being required to buy insurance. Even though most would buy it anyway, they don't like the government telling them that they must do so.

A final difficulty is the enforcement problem. As was pointed out in connection with unsatisfied judgment funds, it is possible to require motorists to have insurance when they license their cars, but seeing to it that the policies remain in force is another matter. It is said that at one time North Carolina found it necessary to assign forty-five full-time highway patrolmen to track down drivers whose insurance had lapsed. Even if a state did overcome the enforcement problem there still would be (a) uninsured drivers from out of state, (b) hit-and-run accidents, and (c) accidents caused by drivers of stolen cars.

Experience with compulsory auto liability insurance appears to indicate that it is not a good way to solve the problem of the uncompensated victim.

Many people believe that any real solution will require drastic changes in the entire system of handling the costs of automobile accidents.

THE PROBLEM OF INSURANCE AVAILABILITY

Our system of paying the costs of auto accidents is largely a fault system. It is also an insurance system. In order for it to function properly the great majority of motorists must be insured. This requires that people both recognize the need for insurance and be able to obtain it. However, insurance companies are not always willing to make coverage available to everyone who wants it.

Insurance companies prefer not to insure some people, just as banks prefer not to lend money to some people. Banks employ loan officers to appraise loan applications. Loans are made only to those who are judged to be good risks, those who are thought likely to repay the money that they borrow. Likewise, insurance companies employ underwriters to appraise insurance applications. Insurance is provided only to those who are judged to be good risks, which in this case means those who are thought likely to drive with reasonable care and who probably will have no more accidents than the average person. The banks know that a few borrowers will default and not repay their loans. The interest rates they charge are high enough so that they can absorb a few losses. Similarly, insurance companies know that some policyholders (more than a few!) will have accidents. The insurance premiums they collect are high enough so that the expected losses can be paid. They are not high enough, though, to cover the losses if too many poor risks are insured. Thus insurance underwriters decline to insure some people.

In the case of most other types of insurance, the fact that coverage is not readily available to all who want it is not regarded as a serious problem. For example, there appears no need to make life insurance available to everyone, including those who are in poor health. In the case of auto liability, however, the general public is affected by the availability of insurance protection. If large numbers of motorists did not insure their liability risk, a great many other people would be unable to recover the costs they incur in automobile accidents. Therefore, steps have been taken to make liability insurance available to all motorists, including those whom the insurance companies would prefer not to cover.

Automobile Insurance Plans

An **Automobile Insurance Plan** (AIP) is a system that makes auto liability insurance available to motorists who are unable to obtain it in the normal manner. Each applicant is assigned to one of the participating insurers and that company must provide the insurance. Forty-two states have set up AIP's. The eight other states have slightly different systems. Countrywide, about 3% of all motorists are covered by AIPs or similar plans, but the percentage is much higher than that in some states. AIPs formerly were named "assigned risk" plans, a term that still is frequently used.

OPERATION OF THE PLANS. A motorist who is unable to obtain insurance in the regular way makes application to the state AIP. The application then is assigned to one of the companies writing auto insurance in the state. Risks are assigned on a proportional basis. For instance, an insurer that writes 5% of the auto liability premiums in the state will insure a corresponding share of AIP risks. To encourage insurers to cover youthful drivers on a voluntary basis, most of the plans give credit for such coverages as part of a company's AIP quota.

Two categories of high-risk drivers are insured through the plans. First are those whose record of accidents and violations causes them to be rejected as standard risks. These include many drivers who have had to file certificates of future financial responsibility. The second category is called "clean risks." These are drivers who have not yet developed a history of either accidents or violations but who are nevertheless regarded as high risks by insurance underwriters. Clean risks may include elderly drivers and those with physical impairments. Many of them are young drivers.

Why are young drivers regarded as high risks? Simply because of their record as a group. Remember that insurance is a pooling arrangement and that the law of large numbers makes losses predictable for groups, not for individuals. In 1977 drivers under age 30 made up one-third of all motorists, but were involved in over half of all accidents. The 10.1% of drivers who were under age 20 were in 18.1% of the accidents.[2] The traffic fatality rate (per 100,000 persons) for 18-year-olds in 1976 was 53.3, which is more than 2.5 times the national average of 21.1 for all ages. The next highest rate was 51.7 for 19-year-olds.[3] Although higher premiums are charged for insuring youthful drivers, in some cases the company underwriters believe that even the higher premiums would not be enough to cover their losses.

All AIPs provide drivers with liability insurance at least as high as the limits required by the state financial responsibility law. Thirty-two of the plans provide limits higher than those required by state law. Forty-one offer medical payments coverage and thirty-five make comprehensive and collision coverages available. Clean risks covered through an AIP are charged

---

[2]*Insurance Facts, 1978* (New York: Insurance Information Institute), p. 50.
[3]*The National Underwriter,* June 9, 1978.

standard rates. Higher rates are paid by those with a record of accidents or violations.[4]

A small number of motorists are not eligible for coverage even under an AIP. Provisions vary among the states, but the plans may exclude those who have engaged in certain illegal activities and those who have a record of frequent accidents or violations. Such individuals must either give up driving, drive without insurance, or obtain coverage from one of the companies that specialize in insuring "substandard" risks. In the latter case, premiums are usually much higher than those that the regular companies charge for AIP risks.

Automobile Insurance Plans perform an important function by making insurance available from standard insurance companies for people who otherwise would be forced into the "substandard market." The Plans seldom are appreciated by the individuals whom they insure, though. Those who are in the clean risk category are especially likely to feel that they have been unfairly discriminated against. It is difficult for them to understand the viewpoint of the insurance companies that have "rejected" them. Actually, however, the premium paid by AIP insureds as a group is not enough to cover the cost of insuring them. For the five years ending December 31, 1976, the automobile insurance industry paid out over $1 billion more in losses and expenses on AIP business than it collected in premiums.[5]

ALTERNATIVE SYSTEMS. The insurance industry and the states currently are experimenting with alternative ways to make insurance available to high-risk drivers. Florida and Missouri have established Joint Underwriting Associations. A few of the larger insurers are designated to write the policies and provide policyholder services for high-risk drivers throughout the state. Losses generated by the Joint Underwriting Association are then shared by all auto insurers in the state. This method is in contrast to that of AIPs, where there is no pooling or sharing of losses among companies, each company paying the losses on the AIP risks assigned to it. Hawaii is experimenting with a somewhat similar plan.

Massachusetts, New Hampshire, North Carolina, and South Carolina are trying what is called a **reinsurance facility**. Each insurer in those four states accepts all applicants for automobile coverage. Applicants that a company considers to be high risks are placed in a "reinsurance pool." The individual company writes the policy and provides policyholder services, but the premiums are paid into and losses are paid out of the pool. As is the case

---

[4]"Automobile Insurance Plans," *Journal of American Insurance*, Winter 1975–1976, p. 22.
[5]*Insurance Facts, 1978* (New York: Insurance Information Institute), p. 31.

with the Joint Underwriting Associations, each insurer in the state shares proportionally in the total profits or losses which result.

Maryland is using still another method. The Maryland Automobile Insurance Fund was set up by the state in 1973 to take over the insuring of high-risk drivers. The Fund is a state agency. It writes the policies and pays the losses. The insurance industry does not participate in its operation.

One of the reasons for establishing the Automobile Insurance Plans was to avoid what Maryland is doing. That is, AIPs have been seen as a way for the private insurance industry (rather than the state governments) to cover high-risk drivers. Just as most people would prefer to have their cars built by private manufacturers rather than by the government, most probably would prefer to have them insured by private companies. But the question of how insurance can be made available to high-risk drivers at a reasonable cost, and indeed whether that can be done at all, continues to be a difficult one.

Restrictions on Cancellation and Nonrenewal

Another aspect of the availability problem is the continuation of protection after a policy has been put in force. As was noted in Chapter 6, the provisions of the Personal Auto Policy restrict the right of the insurer to cancel or to refuse renewal of coverage. The limitations on cancellation during the policy term are more strict than the requirements concerning policy renewal.

The cancellation restrictions came about because of allegations that policies frequently were canceled for reasons that were not fair to the policyholder. Examples of cancellations that were said to be unfair included those due to (a) a single claim, perhaps not the fault of the insured; (b) decision by a company to stop insuring a particular class of risks, such as youthful drivers; (c) company withdrawal from a certain geographical area; and (d) a company's decision to discontinue writing policies for a particular agent. These practices never have been widespread, but there is no doubt that they have occurred from time to time.

CANCELLATION RESTRICTIONS.   Almost all of the states have laws that restrict the cancellation of automobile policies. The restrictions do not apply to cancellation of *new* insureds for the first 30 to 90 days (depending on the state) that a policy is in force. This time allowance permits a company to act on the basis of information that it develops concerning its new policyholders. If this provision were not included, company underwriters would have to refrain from writing new risks until all aspects of their investigation were completed and many applicants would have to go without coverage for a period of time.

After a new policy has been in force for the prescribed length of time, and effective immediately for a renewal, it can be canceled only for one of the reasons specified in the law. The reasons vary among the states but often include the following:

1. Nonpayment of premium
2. Suspension or revocation of the driving license of a named insured or other person who customarily operates the car
3. Fraudulent misrepresentation in obtaining the policy
4. Conviction of drunken driving
5. The making of a false or fraudulent claim

The Personal Auto Policy permits cancellation for only the first and second of the above reasons and thus is more restrictive than the laws of many states. The effect of the cancellation restrictions is to prevent unfair cancellations such as those mentioned earlier. Automobile insurers no longer can cancel policies in mid-term because of a claim or two or because of changes in the company's underwriting policy.

NONRENEWAL RESTRICTIONS. We must realize that the foregoing restrictions do not limit the right of an insurer to refuse to accept a new application or to refuse to renew a policy for another term. Insurers are free to decide whom to insure (and to cancel new policies during the first 30 to 90 days). And when existing policies expire, they may decline to renew them.

Laws have been adopted by most of the states to assure policyholders of advance notice if their auto insurance will not be renewed. In addition, many states require that, if so requested by the insured, the company shall provide a written statement of the reasons for its decision not to renew. Some of the laws go further and stipulate that an insurer may not refuse to renew a policy solely because of the age, residence, race, color, creed, or occupation of the insured.

In fairness to the insurance industry, we should understand that many companies voluntarily restricted policy cancellations and nonrenewals before the law required them to do so. Also, many insurers, including all of the ones that issue the Personal Auto Policy, offer greater policyholder protection than the law requires. Some, for instance, guarantee to renew their policies for at least five years.

The Automobile Insurance Plans and the cancellation and renewal laws appear to be solving the problem of insurance availability. Through a combination of legal requirements and voluntary action by the insurance industry, practically all motorists who want coverage, who can afford it, and who have a reasonable right to have it are now able to secure auto insurance.

THE PROBLEMS OF UNFAIRNESS, DELAY, AND HIGH COST

During the 1970s a number of states adopted no-fault auto insurance laws. These laws constitute a major revision in the system of paying the costs of automobile accidents. The laws were adopted in response to criticisms that the liability system is unfair, too slow, and too expensive. Before examining the no-fault systems, we shall consider the complaints that brought them about. We then will be able to understand why the no-fault approach was adopted and to judge whether or not it is preferable to the legal liability system.

Unfairness

The liability system (also called the negligence system, the tort system, or the fault system) is said to be unfair to the people who are injured in automobile accidents. In the first place, many injured persons are not able to recover on the basis of legal liability at all. This is usually the case when only one vehicle is involved. Also, when more than one vehicle is involved the person who is at fault usually cannot recover from the other driver. Payments based on liability are made for only 45% of the persons killed or seriously injured in auto accidents.[6]

Those who are able to recover under the liability system are not compensated in a systematic, equitable manner. Generally, the system pays too much for small losses and too little for large losses. A major research project conducted by the U.S. Department of Transportation found that, when their total loss was under $500, victims who received liability settlements were paid an average of 4.5 times their actual loss. However, those whose loss was more than $25,000 were paid only about one-third of their total loss.[7] These disproportionate payments come about basically because the liability system is based on fault; the person who caused the accident is supposed to reimburse the person who was not at fault. But in many accidents fault is not clear-cut and the parties disagree as to who was responsible. There is no systematic way to determine who is to pay and how large the payment should be. Fewer than one out of ten lawsuits for auto injuries are settled by court verdict and judgment. The rest—over 90%—are settled by negotiation

---

[6]U.S. Department of Transportation, *Motor Vehicle Crash Losses and Their Compensation in the United States*, 1971, p. 35.

[7]*Ibid.*, p. 36. The percentage recovered declines steadily as the size of the loss increases.

between the injured person's attorney and the insurance company that is defending the other party. The size of the payments therefore depends on the bargaining power and negotiating skill of the parties involved. Having a good lawyer and helpful witnesses can be extremely important.

Payments to accident victims are classified as special damages or general damages. **Special damages** repay the victim's actual expenses. They include the cost of medical treatment, car repairs, and loss of earnings. **General damages** compensate for losses that are not directly measurable in dollars, such as the injured person's pain and suffering. They may also include payment for such things as facial scars or the loss of ability to bear children. Liability insurers pay out more for general damages than they do for special damages. On the average, for every $40 paid for special damages, $60 is paid for general damages. There is, of course, no good way to put a price tag on something like pain and suffering. Sometimes large amounts are paid for it and sometimes it is ignored. The critics of the liability system say that this is unfair and that the pain and suffering "jackpot" should be eliminated.

Why do small claims so often receive generous settlements? Essentially, the reason is that they are relatively expensive for insurance companies to investigate and defend. When large sums of money are not at stake it may be cheaper for an insurer to settle claims for more than they are worth than to resist them. The Department of Transportation found that "insurance companies are usually willing, particularly with small claims where the administrative expense is greater than the economic loss, to settle a questionable claim, or in insurance parlance, to 'buy' the claim."[8]

On the other hand, the insurance companies have the bargaining advantage when the costs of an accident are great. They are in a better position to wait for a favorable compromise settlement than is a person with disabling injuries who has large medical bills to pay. Remember that a liability insurer has no direct obligation to the injured person. Its only responsibility is to defend its policyholder and to pay any amounts that the policyholder is legally obligated to pay.

Another reason for low payments for major injuries is the fact that many people are either uninsured or carry inadequate amounts of liability insurance. An Illinois case illustrates this point. The victim was a 6-year-old boy who was struck by a car. The driver of the car carried liability insurance with a $20,000 limit. The boy had severe injuries, including permanent brain damage. His medical and rehabilitation treatments cost over $100,000. The boy's family sued the driver and an out-of-court settlement of $20,000 was reached. The family's attorney advised them that because the defendant was retired and had very little money it would be useless to hold out for more

[8]*Ibid.*, p. 37.

than the liability policy would pay. (The family, incidentally, carried $300,000 of liability insurance on their own car.) After the lawyer's fee and other legal expenses were paid, the settlement received by the boy's family was $11,000.[9] We can only wonder what the settlement would have been if the car that struck the boy had been owned by a wealthy person or a large corporation; there is little doubt that it would have been much more. Cases like this further illustrate the unfairness that sometimes characterizes the legal liability system.

Delay

Whatever system is relied upon to pay accident costs should provide prompt payment of all valid claims. The automobile liability system has been severely criticized for its slowness.

The Department of Transportation study found that only half of all automobile liability claims are settled within six months. Most of the ones that are paid promptly are small claims. Seriously injured accident victims or their survivors waited an average of 16 months for final payment. The greatest delay is that experienced by the small fraction of cases that go to court. More than half of such cases took longer than two years to settle. Critics of the system say that even the claims that are settled quickly and without going to court are affected by the slowness of the system. They say that because there is such a long wait for court judgments some claimants settle for less than they could get if they waited for their cases to be tried.

The real cause of this problem is the liability system, not the insurance industry. Insurance companies are capable of paying the costs of automobile accidents promptly; they do so for medical payments and collision claims. However, the function of liability insurance is to defend the policyholder and to pay only if and only to the extent that there is legal liability. It is the nature of liability insurance that makes slow payments inevitable.

High Cost

The charge that auto liability insurance costs too much needs careful consideration. The coverage may be too expensive in one sense, but not in another. There is no doubt that the insurance costs a lot of money. Most people pay over $200 a year for their policies and many pay far more than that. In one important sense, though, auto insurance is not too expensive. It is not too expensive in relation to what it costs the insurance companies to provide it. In other words, it is not costly in the sense that the companies are making huge profits from writing it. In fact, from the viewpoint of the

[9]*Chicago Tribune*, October 6, 1976.

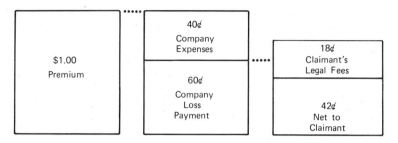

Figure 7-1   The automobile liability insurance dollar.

insurers, auto insurance has been one of their least profitable lines for many years, largely because it is underpriced! They point out that its cost hasn't gone up as fast as the cost of the things it pays for: hospital and medical care, car repairs, income replacement, and legal defense.

Looked at in another way, however, auto liability insurance is extremely expensive. It is expensive in the sense that the liability system is a very costly way to pay for automobile accidents. This fact is illustrated by Figure 7-1, which shows what happens to a dollar paid for auto liability protection.

The first thing taken out of the premium dollar is the commission the company pays the agent for selling the policy. On the average, this is about 13 cents. The company pays about 5 cents for advertising and other sales expenses, making a total of 18 cents for marketing costs. General overhead takes another 5 cents. This pays for such things as salaries, building costs, and computer systems. State premium taxes take another 3 cents, for a total operating expense of 26 cents before any claims are presented. As we know, legal defense is an important part of liability protection. It is also an expensive part, costing the company about 14 cents of the premium dollar. Added to the 26 cents for operating expenses and taxes, this gives total company expenses of 40 cents. Thus, 60 cents is left to be paid out by the company to third party claimants. However, not all of the 60 cents actually becomes available to claimants to compensate them for their injuries. Remember that they too incur legal expenses in the process of settling their claims. Their attorney fees and court costs take an estimated 18 cents out of the 60 cents paid out by the insurance companies. Only 42 cents of the premium dollar is left to pay for the injured persons' medical bills, lost wages, auto repairs and general damages.[10]

Not all insurance systems are expensive in the way that this one is. About 58 cents of the auto liability premium dollar is needed to run the insurance

[10]U.S. Senate Antitrust and Monopoly Subcommittee. Quoted in Willis Park Rokes, *No-Fault Insurance* (Santa Monica: Insurers Press, 1971), p. 148.

and legal systems in order to deliver 42 cents to the claimant. In contrast, the administrative cost for life insurance is 17 cents. For social security benefits it is only 3 cents.

The reason for these differences is not that the people employed by the life insurance companies and the Social Security Administration are smarter or work harder. And, as we have seen, it is not that the auto insurers make larger profits. The reason is that the systems differ. Life insurance is a relatively efficient system because the policies remain in force for many years and because benefits are paid quickly and routinely. Social Security is a government monopoly that has no sales or advertising expenses. Auto liability insurance is expensive in comparison with other kinds of insurance because the liability system is such a costly method of delivering insurance benefits.

NO-FAULT AUTOMOBILE INSURANCE

Because of the enormous number of automobile accidents and injuries, we need a systematic method of paying the expenses of injured people. Many people believe that this cannot be done fairly, quickly, and economically unless the liability insurance system is replaced by a no-fault insurance system. Although none of the states has completely eliminated the liability system, many of them have passed laws that move in that direction.

A pure no-fault system would abolish fault as a basis for the payment of losses. Liability insurance would be replaced by no-fault insurance. Every motorist would be required to carry a policy that would pay the motorist (and family) directly for all expenses resulting from an accident. Motorists would no longer sue or be sued for automobile accidents. Instead, they would be paid by their own insurers. Furthermore, under a pure no-fault system, there would be no specific payment for pain and suffering or other general damages.

Modified No-Fault Insurance

All of the no-fault systems that have been established so far are compromises between the liability and the pure no-fault approaches, that is, they incorporate some features of both systems. For this reason, they are called **modified no-fault systems.** Most of these laws apply only to bodily injury losses and leave property damage losses to be handled in the traditional manner. Also, they use the no-fault approach only for the smaller and more frequent injuries; lawsuits are still possible for more serious injuries. The laws creating these systems require all motorists to purchase **automobile**

no-fault insurance. It pays the insured persons' own medical expenses and lost income (up to the amounts specified in the law), regardless of who caused the accident.

Massachusetts was the first state to establish a modified no-fault system, doing so in 1971. All motorists must carry no-fault insurance, which in Massachusetts as in some of the states with similar laws is called Personal Injury Protection or PIP. The coverage is provided by means of an endorsement attached to a regular automobile policy. The Massachusetts no-fault insurance pays each insured family's medical bills, up to $2,000 per person for any accident. Loss of income up to 75% of the weekly wage is included in the $2,000 limit. In common with the other modified no-fault laws, the Massachusetts law prohibits lawsuits unless the injuries exceed a certain level. This level, or **threshold**, is the cut-off point between minor and major injuries. In Massachusetts, the threshold is any one of the following: (a) medical expenses over $500, (b) loss of sight or hearing, (c) dismemberment, (d) permanent and serious disfigurement, (e) fracture, or (f) death. If the threshold is passed, lawsuits can be filed to recover amounts in excess of the no-fault benefits. The plan also covered property damage until that part of the law was repealed in 1976.

The Michigan no-fault plan is important because it is broader than any of the others. It is the only one now covering property damage. It also is one of the few that provides unlimited no-fault insurance for bodily injury benefits. Income benefits are paid to the insured family for up to 85% of lost wages, subject to a stated maximum amount per month. The threshold for liability claims in Michigan is (a) death, (b) serious impairment of a body function, or (c) permanent serious disfigurement.

Other modified no-fault automobile insurance laws are in force in Colorado, Connecticut, Florida, Georgia, Hawaii, Kansas, Kentucky, Minnesota, Nevada, New Jersey, New York, North Dakota, Pennsylvania, and Utah. There are variations among the laws and each requires somewhat different no-fault insurance. Each state has its own threshold above which legal liability action is permitted. Many of the plans make the no-fault benefits payable to pedestrians who are struck by the insured's car. Most of them exclude coverage for certain persons, such as drunken drivers and those who are injured while avoiding arrest.

Kentucky's law is unique. It contains a provision that allows people to reject the law. The rejection, which affects only future accidents, must be written and filed with the Kentucky Insurance Department. Those who reject the law are not eligible for no-fault insurance. Thus, the individual must choose in advance between no-fault benefits and the right to sue for minor injuries (that is, those that do not exceed the no-fault threshold).

Several other states require motorists to insure medical and income losses on a no-fault basis *but do not restrict lawsuits*. Confusion is created when these are called no-fault plans. Some people call them "pseudo no-fault plans" in contrast to the modified no-fault plans that both (a) require no-fault protection and (b) prohibit lawsuits for minor injuries. South Carolina is an example. A $1,000 medical and disability income policy is required for all motorists. However, injured persons can sue for negligence, even for minor injuries. Delaware, Maryland, and Oregon have comparable laws.

Arguments Against No-Fault

Many people are opposed to the no-fault concept. Their arguments in favor of retaining the liability system include the following:

1. It is not difficult to establish blame for accidents. In most two-car crashes, one party is clearly at fault.
2. People who are seriously injured will not be compensated adequately by a no-fault system. Payment for pain and suffering must be continued. For example, attractive young people whose faces are horribly scarred or who lose arms or legs should be paid for having to bear such handicaps for the rest of their lives. Adequate compensation requires more than payment for their medical bills and lost income.
3. Most liability claims are paid without too much delay. Half of them are settled within six months, and over a third within two months.
4. The right to sue for damages on the basis of negligence is an important aspect of our personal freedom. It should be strongly defended. If this right is abandoned here, pressure will grow to eliminate the right to sue for other injuries also.
5. No-fault does not reduce the cost of auto insurance.
6. The liability system causes people to drive more carefully so that they will not be sued for negligence. No-fault systems remove the threat of suit, which results in more careless driving.

Arguments for No-Fault

The most important argument in favor of no-fault is that it is the best answer to the liability system's unfairness, slowness, and high cost. These problems have already been discussed and will not be repeated here. Those who favor the no-fault approach offer the following responses to the arguments against it:

1. Fault generally is not easy to determine. Often both drivers believe that they were innocent and that the other party caused the accident. Anyway, auto insurance should cover everyone's losses, including those

"No fault, my foot! It's your fault!"

Robert Weber © 1974 Tne New Yorker Magazine, Inc.

who are sometimes careless and those who are injured in single-car crashes.

2. Recovering for pain and suffering should be either strictly limited or completely eliminated. Doing so would hurt only the lawyers who profit from handling the jumbo cases. Actually, the liability system rarely covers serious injuries adequately. Big settlements are reached in only a handful of cases. A system that provides certain payment for actual out-of-pocket losses is better than one that offers a slight chance to win an enormous jackpot.

3. The liability system is too slow. Half of the claims are not settled within six months.

4. We should not defend a system that fails to serve people well. The present system encourages claimants and their lawyers to exaggerate the seriousness of injuries in the hope of cashing in with large settlements and large legal fees.

5. Cost savings are not the key. This is a false issue. No-fault will eliminate much of the wasted expense of determining blame for accidents. But it will also make payments to the many who now receive no payment at all. A no-fault system will pay out more dollars, but it will do so more fairly and efficiently.

6. The liability system does not really punish those who are at fault. Liability insurance pays for the losses; the people at fault don't. The liability system doesn't encourage safe driving and no-fault won't discourage it.

The Future of No-Fault

At this point the no-fault picture is a confusing one. In time it will become clearer. We should bear in mind that no-fault is in a developmental stage. The states and the insurance industry are trying out a variety of plans. The future of no-fault will depend upon which, if any, of these experiments succeed.

No-fault is being debated both in the states that have set up plans and in those that have not yet done so. It is discussed in the press, on television, among lawyers and insurance people, and in the legislatures. The opposition is led by (but by no means confined to) the attorneys who handle personal injury lawsuits. The main supporters of no-fault are those from the insurance industry and from labor and consumer organizations. Most of the insurance companies opposed the no-fault approach when the subject first began to be discussed in the 1960s. Now, however, almost all of the major companies support some sort of modified no-fault plan.

One of the issues yet to be resolved is the size of the no-fault benefits. Michigan, New Jersey, and Pennsylvania pay unlimited amounts of medical expenses; other states set a maximum, such as $2,000 or $10,000 per person. The proper amount of income reimbursement is also an issue.

Another important question concerns the threshold for liability suits. Should only minor injuries be exempt from negligence claims? Or should we move in the direction of a pure no-fault system? It appears that low thresholds ($500 of medical expenses, for example) won't work. There is evidence that they encourage people to incur unnecessary expenses or to inflate their bills artificially in order to reach the level at which they are able to sue. A threshold like Michigan's, which is not stated in dollar terms at all, may be the answer to this problem.

A major issue, and one that may decide the future of no-fault auto insurance, is whether or not the federal government should act. So far, the matter has been left up to individual states. Many of the advocates of no-fault now believe that states won't move fast enough or far enough unless the federal government forces them to do so. Since 1970 Congress has considered various bills that would establish federal guidelines and require the states to enact no-fault laws to comply with those guidelines. Opponents say that the merits of no-fault have not yet been proved and that the state-by-state experimentation should be permitted to continue.

The future of no-fault remains to be seen. It may be rejected completely, a pure no-fault system may gradually develop, or the modified no-fault approach may win out as an acceptable compromise. Whatever is done will affect not only the lawyers and the insurance industry, but also the millions of people who are injured each year in automobile accidents.

IMPORTANT TERMS

Financial responsibility law

Unsatisfied judgment fund

Compulsory auto liability insurance law

Automobile Insurance Plan

Special damages

General damages

No-fault system

Modified no-fault system

Auto no-fault insurance

Threshold

KEY POINTS TO REMEMBER

1. We rely primarily upon auto liability insurance to pay the expenses of people who are innocent victims in automobile accidents.

2. Several major problems confront the automobile insurance industry. These include uncompensated victims, unavailability of insurance, and complaints about the system's unfairness, slowness, and high cost.

3. Several steps have been taken to deal with the problem of uncompensated victims: financial responsibility laws, unsatisfied judgment funds, protection against uninsured or underinsured motorists, and compulsory auto liability insurance laws.

4. Financial responsibility laws require motorists to prove that they can pay for accidents they cause. The laws apply after accidents or major violations occur.

5. Unsatisfied judgment funds have been set up by several states. They pay auto accident victims money they are unable to collect from motorists who caused their injuries.

6. Compulsory auto liability insurance laws have not solved the uncompensated victim problem.

7. The most important steps taken to deal with the problems of automobile insurance unavailability are Automobile Insurance Plans and restrictions on policy cancellation and nonrenewal.

8. Automobile Insurance Plans make liability protection available to almost all motorists. The applications of those who cannot otherwise obtain policies are distributed among the companies writing auto insurance in the state.

9. Laws in practically every state prohibit company cancellation of auto policies except for certain stated reasons. They also impose restrictions concerning company refusal to renew policies when they expire.

10. The greatest current controversy about auto insurance stems from complaints that the liability system is unfair, too slow, and too expensive.

11. Under the laws of negligence, persons legally liable for injury to others may have to pay special damages for the injured party's actual expenses and general damages for things like pain and suffering that do not involve specific dollar expenses.

12. Under a pure no-fault system, people injured in automobile accidents would be paid for their medical expenses and lost wages by their own no-fault insurance. They would not be able to sue to obtain judgments against the party at fault.

13. Sixteen states have established modified no-fault auto insurance plans. They

permit lawsuits based on fault for injuries that are serious enough to pass a stated threshold.

14. No-fault auto insurance is controversial. Its future is uncertain.

REVIEW QUESTIONS

1. What is the purpose of financial responsibility laws? How do they attempt to achieve this purpose? What is their major shortcoming?
2. What are unsatisfied judgment funds? How are they financed?
3. How do compulsory auto insurance laws differ from financial responsibility laws?
4. Why have the state governments been concerned about the availability of automobile insurance? What have they done about the problem?
5. What is the purpose of Automobile Insurance Plans, and how do they operate?
6. What specific problems are the laws that restrict cancellation and nonrenewal designed to deal with?
7. What is the nature of the complaint that the auto liability insurance system is unfair?
8. What causes the settlement of liability claims to take so much time?
9. What is meant by the statement that auto insurance may be too expensive in one sense but not in another?
10. What would be the main features of a pure no-fault system? How do the modified no-fault plans differ from pure no-fault?
11. What are the principal arguments for and against a no-fault system?

DISCUSSION QUESTIONS

1. The only penalty for violating a financial responsibility law is loss of the right to drive. In order to help enforce this penalty, why don't auto policies exclude coverage for losses when an insured drives without a valid license?
2. The amounts of insurance protection required by the financial responsibility laws are quite low (only 10/20 BI and 5 PD in many states and not much higher in most other states). Can you think of some reason why the states don't require higher limits?
3. Who benefits from Automobile Insurance Plans?
4. Most of the states adopted Automobile Insurance Plans and financial responsibility laws at the same time. Why? What is the connection between AIPs and financial responsibility laws?
5. In some states only 1 or 2% of the motorists are insured through the AIP, while in other states as many as 10% obtain their auto insurance in that manner. Can you think of anything that might explain this difference? *Hint*: What might cause insurers either to be willing or unwilling to insure drivers on a voluntary basis?
6. Why are the auto insurance nonrenewal restrictions less strict than the cancellation restrictions?

7. In your opinion, should people who are seriously injured in automobile accidents receive large payments for their pain and suffering?
8. Do you believe that no-fault insurance is a good answer to the problems of unfairness, delay, and high cost?
9. In your judgment, is a modified no-fault plan a good compromise between the straight liability system and a pure no-fault system? If so, what should be the threshold for legal liability claims?

CHAPTER 8
BUYING AUTO INSURANCE

THE PRICING OF AUTO INSURANCE

CHOOSING THE COVERAGES

SELECTING THE AMOUNTS OF COVERAGE

SHOPPING FOR AUTO INSURANCE

OTHER CONSIDERATIONS

Because people rely so heavily upon insurance in managing the risks of auto ownership and operation, we might suppose that motorists would buy auto insurance with great care. We might logically expect that the auto owners generally would make an effort to be sure of getting the protection they need at a reasonable price. Actually, they do not. Most people are baffled by insurance. They know very little about it or how to buy it, and very few of them make any effort to learn.

We know that auto insurance is an important purchase. It is also an expensive one, an important part of the cost of owning a car. Table 5–1 in Chapter 5 shows that for compact cars, for instance, insurance costs about 1.6¢ for each mile that the car is driven. The car itself costs an average of 3.8¢ per mile. Thus insurance costs about 40% as much as the car itself.

There probably is no need for us to spend 40% as much time and effort to buy auto insurance as we spend shopping for cars. But we do need to make certain decisions about insurance protection. The purpose of this chapter is to provide the information that is needed in order to make those decisions wisely. The chapter includes a survey of the pricing of auto insurance and a discussion of the factors to consider in deciding what coverages and amounts of protection to buy.

THE PRICING OF AUTO INSURANCE

To the general public, one of the most mysterious things about insurance is how the price is determined. Almost everything else we buy has a price that is the same regardless of who the purchaser is. But the price of insurance depends upon a number of things about the particular buyer and the risks being insured. This is one of the things that complicates the purchase of insurance.

We shall not try to cover all of the details of auto insurance pricing here. The procedure is much too complicated for that. (The rating manuals used by many companies are over 100 pages long.) Furthermore, pricing systems differ from one insurance company to another. But some knowledge of pricing is important because it will help us determine the kinds and amounts of insurance to buy and the agent or company from whom to buy it. The purpose of this section is to examine the most common and the most important factors that affect the cost of a person's auto insurance policy.

The Classification System

A **classification system** is a method of establishing the price of individual insurance policies by classifying policyholders in groups, each of whose members have certain similar characteristics. From the insurer's viewpoint, the classification system distributes the total costs of insurance among its various policyholders. When auto insurance was first sold, policyholders were classified on the basis of only one factor—the horsepower of their vehicles. Those who drove the more powerful "horseless carriages" paid more and the others paid less. Today, the classification systems used by most auto insurers take into account each of the following factors:

1. The territory in which the rate applies
2. The kinds and amounts of insurance which the policy provides
3. The value of the auto (for physical damage coverages only)
4. The age, sex, and marital status of the person who drives the auto
5. The use of the auto
6. The eligibility for good student and/or driver training discounts, if there are youthful drivers
7. The eligibility for the multicar discount
8. The type of auto
9. The driving records of all operators of the auto

We shall briefly examine each of these factors, our goal being to see why (and to a lesser extent, how) each may be used. Although classification systems vary from one company to another, most are quite similar in basic respects and most incorporate each of these nine factors.

Territory

Each state is divided into rating territories. Some states have only a few territories; some have forty or fifty. The particular territory that applies is the one where the car is "principally garaged." The price can differ a great deal from one territory to another. In a high-rated territory of a given state it may be more than twice as much as in a low-rated territory of the same state. The differences depend upon the loss records of all the motorists in each territory.

Usually the large cities are the highest rated territories and the rural areas are the lowest. On the basis of their past experience, insurance companies know that they will have to pay more for losses in the big cities. There will be more accidents per policy there and the average cost per accident will be higher. Hospital care is more expensive in the large cities, car repairs cost more, and courts tend to grant higher judgments. These are the things that auto insurance pays for. The greater the average loss payments per policy in a certain territory, the higher the rates for that territory will be. Rates are revised at least once each year to reflect the most recent loss experience in the state and each of its territories.

Kinds and Amounts of Coverage

The cost of insurance of course depends upon the kinds and amounts that are purchased. The more coverages that are purchased and the higher their limits, the greater the cost. We should realize, though, that the cost does not increase in the same proportion as the amount of insurance. For instance, the cost of increased amounts of auto liability coverage is determined by factors like those shown below:

LIABILITY LIMITS	FACTOR
$ 25,000	1.00
50,000	1.13
100,000	1.22
500,000	1.48

Companies that use this table charge 13% more for $50,000 of coverage than for $25,000 and so forth. Why doesn't the cost increase proportionally? The $50,000 limit is twice as high as $25,000; why doesn't it cost twice as much? The reason is that most losses are small and are fully covered by a policy with low limits. Protection against large losses is very important, but they don't happen as frequently as small ones do, and the rates reflect this fact.

The cost of medical payments coverage also varies with the amount purchased. As with the liability coverage, the cost does not increase in proportion to the amount of protection. For instance, if $500 of medical payments costs $4 per year, $1,000 might cost $6 and $5,000 might cost $11 (depending upon the state, the territory, and the company).

The amount of comprehensive and collision insurance, you may recall, equals the actual cash value of the car at the time of a loss. Instead of selecting maximum amounts of these coverages, the purchaser chooses the size of the deductible. The higher the amount of the deductible, the lower the cost of these coverages.

Value of the Auto

Auto comprehensive and collision coverages are types of property insurance. The greater the value of the property insured (in this case, the automobile), the more these coverages will cost.

Automobiles are classified on the basis of (a) their cost when new and (b) their age. The cost of insuring a new Chrysler New Yorker, for instance, is much greater than the cost of insuring a new Chevrolet Vega. And as cars grow older the rates decline. Cars that are five or more years old take the lowest rates, often about 55% of the rates for a new car of the same model.

The fact that rates decline as a car grows older may not be apparent to the policyholder, because other factors may be pushing the total premium upward at the same time that this factor is pushing it downward. Inflationary increases in the costs of medical services and garage repairs, for instance, may overbalance the effect of a car's aging.

Age, Sex, and Marital Status

For many years insurance companies have kept track of the cost of insuring motorists according to their age, sex, and marital status. The records show that on the average more dollars have to be paid out to cover youthful drivers than those who are older. This is especially the case for young drivers who are male and unmarried. Also, losses have been found to be higher for young male drivers who own their own cars than for those who drive family cars. The classification systems used by most insurers reflect these facts. The result is that those who are most likely to have accidents (on the basis of the past experience of all drivers in the same classification) are charged higher rates. Those who are members of a class that is less likely to have accidents are charged lower rates.

Before 1965 the most commonly used classification system was based upon only six rating categories. In this system, all males below age 25 who owned their own cars were grouped together in a single classification. The rates for this group were over three times as high as the classifications that included no youthful drivers. Reaching one's twenty-fifth birthday was cause for celebration because insurance became so much cheaper at that point.

In all but a few states, most companies now use a much more detailed rating system.[1] The rates for young drivers decline gradually as they grow older, and various other characteristics of each risk are reflected in the rates. There are 161 classifications and rating factors. (Each of these factors is modified by one of 40 other factors, making a total of over 6,000 rates for each rating territory!) Table 8–1 illustrates the effects that the age, sex, and marital status of drivers may have upon the cost of insurance. The rating factors shown in Table 8–1 are used to modify the rates for a particular policy. For example, the age, sex, and marital status of persons in rating category 4 cause the price of their insurance to range from 10% to 75% higher than the persons in rating category 3. Categories 4 and 5 are also used for those who drive cars of their own. Unmarried men and women under age 25 who attend school more than 100 miles from home (and who otherwise would be

---

[1]The simpler system has been retained in Arkansas, Connecticut, Kansas, South Carolina, and Virginia.

Table 8–1 Typical Rating Categories and Factors, Based on the Age, Sex, and Marital Status of Drivers

RATING CATEGORY	RATING FACTOR
A. No Youthful Driver	
1. Only driver is female, 30–64	0.90
2. Principal driver is 65 or over	0.90
3. All other with no youthful driver	1.00
B. Youthful Drivers[a]	
4. Female, 17–24, unmarried	1.10 to 1.75[b]
5. Male, 17–24, married	1.30 to 1.95[b]
6. Male, 17–24, unmarried, not owner or principal driver	1.50 to 2.70[b]
7. Male, 17–29, unmarried, who is owner or principal driver	1.65 to 3.50[b]

[a]If not eligible for driver training discount or good student discount.
[b]These factors decline as the youthful driver approaches the maximum age for the class.

in Category 4 or 6) are rated as if they were married. The lower rate is used because so much of their driving is limited to holidays and summer vacations. Category 7 is the most expensive. Unmarried men age 17 or below who have a car of their own pay 3.5 times as much as the risks in category 3. The rates in category 7 are reduced after age 24, so that unmarried men ages 25 through 29 pay only 65% more than category 3.

Some interesting questions have been raised about the use of age, sex, and marital status in auto insurance pricing. These questions are considered in Chapter 20.

Use of the Auto

The factors shown in Table 8–1 reflect only the age, sex, and marital status of drivers. Most rating systems also take into account the purposes for which the auto is used. Autos that are used for business or that are driven to and from work generally are driven more miles and are more likely to be in accidents than those that are not. Table 8–2 shows how these and other uses of the auto may affect the price of the insurance.

Driver Training and Good Student Discounts

The cost of insurance may be reduced for young drivers who have completed driver training courses and for those who are eligible for the good student discount. The same person may receive both discounts.

Table 8-2 Typical Rating Categories and Factors, Based on Use of the Auto[a]

RATING CATEGORY	FACTOR
1. Auto not driven to work or used for business or farming	1.00
2. Auto driven to work, less than 15 miles one way	1.25
3. Auto driven to work, 15 or more miles one way	1.45
4. Auto used for business	1.45
5. Auto principally used in farming	0.90

[a]Applicable when there are no youthful drivers. Use of the car has less effect on rates in youthful driver categories.

The driver training course must be an approved one; that is, generally it has to provide 30 hours of classroom work and 6 hours of practice driving. A certificate of completion must be sent to the insurance company. The discount for driver training is about 10% but varies from one classification to another. It is available to drivers under age 21. The discount is not continued for later years because the effect of driver training "wears off" in a few years.

The good student discount is based on evidence of a correlation between the scholastic records and the driving records of full-time students, perhaps because many of them spend more time studying and less time driving. The discount is available to those who are full-time high school or college students and have a "B" average or better or are in the upper 20% of their class. A statement signed by a school official must be sent to the company to verify the grades. The statement has to be provided each time the policy is renewed. Policies are not changed during their term of coverage either to add or to delete the discount. The discount varies among classifications but usually is between 15% and 20%.

Multicar Discount

The multicar discount is usually available when more than one car is owned by the insured (or jointly owned by two or more relatives of the same household). The idea behind the discount is that a multicar family is not likely to use each of the cars as much as it would use a single car if it had only one. For instance, a family with one car might drive it 10,000 miles a year. If a second car is added, the family may then drive a total of 16,000 miles annually. The discount is usually 15% on each of the cars.

Type of Auto

Insurance companies have found that certain types of automobiles are especially costly to insure. These are the high performance or "muscle" cars and certain sports cars. Therefore, extra charges ("surcharges") are built into the rating system when such cars are insured. The surcharges are usually 30% for high performance cars and 15% for sports cars.

Driving Record

Insurers use a variety of rating systems to reflect the driving records of a car's operators. These sometimes are called merit rating or experience rating systems. The system described here, known as the **safe driver rating plan,** is one that is widely used. It classifies motorists on the basis of their driving records, so that higher rates apply to those who have had accidents or have violated the motor vehicle laws.

Risks are classified on the basis of the "driving record points" of all persons living in the insured's household. Points are assigned for convictions of motor vehicle violations and for accidents during the previous three years.

The number of driving record points charged for convictions depends on the seriousness of the violations. Three points are charged for such things as drunken driving, failure to stop after an accident, and driving without a license. Two points are charged for a series of minor convictions, such as for speeding, accumulated under a state's motor vehicle point system. One point is charged for other moving traffic violations that result in either suspension of a driver's license or the requirement that evidence of financial responsibility be filed.

One point is charged for each accident during the three-year period that results in either (a) bodily injury or death or (b) damage to property, including the insured's, in excess of $300. Also, one point is assigned if there were two or more accidents each of which did less than $300 damage to property.

No points are charged for accidents in the following situations:

1. The car is damaged while legally parked.
2. The other party or that party's insurance company pays for the loss.
3. The car is rear-ended and the insured is not convicted of a traffic violation in connection with the accident.
4. The other driver (but not the insured driver) is convicted of a moving violation.

5. The damage is caused by a hit-and-run driver and the police are notified within 24 hours.
6. The damage is caused by contact with an animal or bird (dog, deer, pheasant, etc.).
7. The loss is to property only and is caused by flying gravel or falling objects. (Falling rocks in mountainous areas are a common example of the latter.)
8. The accident happens when the operator is responding to an emergency as a policeman or fireman.

In addition to the points charged for violations and accidents, one point is assigned if the principal driver is an "inexperienced operator." This is defined as one who has had no accidents, but who has been licensed for less than three years.

The surcharges that result from driving record points are by no means minor. In fact, they can cause a tremendous increase in the cost of one's insurance, as Table 8–3 shows. For one point this particular system results in a 40% increase and each additional point brings about a greater increase (50, 60, and 70% more than the previous increase). As a result, the cost is almost doubled (a 90% increase) for two points. With four points the cost is more than three times as much as it would have been in the absence of any accidents or violations.

Rating systems such as the safe driver plan are not popular with those who have to pay additional premiums. A common reaction is, "Why should I pay for my own losses? Insurance doesn't help me if I have to repay the company!" Actually, the plan is not designed to enable insurers to recover amounts paid out for losses and it doesn't really have that result, as is indicated by the fact that the number of points charged does not depend on the size of the losses. The rate increase is the same for a $500 loss as for a $50,000 loss. Rather than being a repayment or penalty system, the safe

Table 8–3 Typical Rating Factors, Based on Driving Record

DRIVING RECORD POINTS	RATING FACTOR
0	+ 0.00
1	+ 0.40
2	+ 0.90
3	+ 1.50
4 or more	+ 2.20

driver plan actually is part of the classification system. The purpose of the classification system is to group similar policyholders together so that each will pay his or her fair share of the total. Each part of the classification system is based on a characteristic that distinguishes the persons who are more likely to have accidents from those who are less likely to have them. The age of drivers is one such characteristic. Another characteristic that indicates the likelihood of future accidents is a record of past accidents or violations. Motorists who have had accidents of violations in the past have been found to be more likely to have accidents in the future. And the greater the number of accidents they have had and the more numerous or serious their violations, the more likely it is that they will have accidents in the future. That is why the safe driver plan is part of the classification system and why those who have poor driving records are charged more.

CHOOSING THE COVERAGES

Each purchaser of auto insurance must decide which coverages to buy. In some cases, this choice may turn out to be more important than deciding what auto to buy.

Liability Coverage

Auto liability coverage is essential. It is more important than any of the other coverages, simply because the losses it protects against are far greater than the others. No one can afford to drive without protection against lawsuits and the cost of legal defense. Remember too that although liability coverage is not required by law in most states, the failure to be financially responsible can result in loss of the right to drive.

Medical Payments

Medical payments coverage is not essential, but most people should carry it. The coverage is least important in the few states that have relatively effective no-fault insurance laws. In those states the required personal injury protection provides adequate coverage for medical expenses. In Michigan, New Jersey, and Pennsylvania, for instance, the required benefits include unlimited payments for medical expenses.

Some motorists have enough accident coverage on other policies without adding medical payments coverage to their auto policies. Many are covered by group accident insurance provided by their employers; this coverage usually applies to almost any off-the-job accident. However, the amounts of protection provided by such other policies may not be enough to pay for today's high costs of medical care. Whenever this is the case, automobile medical payments coverage should be purchased.

Coverage for Damage to Your Auto

Whether or not one should buy collision and comprehensive coverages usually depends on the value of the auto, because its value determines the maximum possible loss. The question to be answered is whether or not the size of the possible loss justifies the cost of the insurance. If it does not, risk retention is preferable.

These coverages almost always are carried on relatively new cars. But as a car becomes older its value declines, and at some point it no longer is worth insuring, even though it may still be providing good service. Suppose that Warren Bowers drives a car that is worth $800 on the used car market. With $200 deductible collision coverage he would have only $600 of protection. It wouldn't take much of a crash for the cost of repairs to exceed $600. In that case, the company would treat the claim as a total loss and pay him the $600. In view of the cost of insuring it, Warren may decide to retain the risk himself.

The argument for risk retention in a case like this is strengthened by the fact that uninsured casualty losses, to the extent that they exceed $100, are deductible expenses under the federal income tax laws. If a person is taxed at a marginal rate of 40%, then a $700 deduction ($800 minus the non-deductible $100) would reduce the tax by 40% of $700, or $280. The maximum loss then would be $800 minus $280, or $520 rather than the full value of the car. If the car were worth several thousand dollars, however, the maximum after-tax loss probably would be great enough to justify buying the insurance.

Banks, finance companies, and credit unions that lend money for the purchase of vehicles usually require that coverage for damage to the auto be carried. They demand this coverage because the auto is collateral for the loan; that is, if the buyer fails to make the loan payments the lending institution will take possession of ("repossess") the auto. If the auto were stolen or destroyed and the loss was not insured, there would be nothing for the lender to repossess. This insurance requirement sometimes causes confusion. Many lending institutions and auto dealers either have insurance agencies of their own or have arrangements to insure with outside agencies. The buyer may be told that the cost of insurance is included as part of the car payments. The buyer may then assume that the lender or seller is taking complete care of his or her auto insurance needs. In such a case the buyer should determine exactly what coverages are provided and should make sure that they include liability protection.

Uninsured and Underinsured Motorists Coverages

Uninsured motorists coverage is mandatory in some states. It should also be carried in the states where it is optional. Many people are not familiar with the new underinsured motorists coverage and therefore fail to purchase it. Some agents make a point of recommending it to their clients. If that is not done, the policyholder should request that it be added. The cost of both uninsured and underinsured motorists coverages is low and the protection can be important.

SELECTING THE AMOUNTS OF COVERAGE

Selecting the proper amounts of coverage is more difficult than choosing which coverages to buy. Essentially, the decisions are personal ones, based upon the particular buyer's judgment of the importance of financial security on the one hand and the importance of saving premium dollars on the other. Each motorist must decide how much protection is enough in his or her case. In this section we shall point out some of the things that should be considered in making these decisions.

Liability Coverage

One of the toughest questions asked of insurance agents is, "How much liability insurance should I buy?" There really is no right answer, because there is no way of knowing how much protection the person will need. It is safe to say that many people have inadequate liability protection, often only enough to satisfy the requirements of their state's financial responsibility law. (See Table 7–1 in Chapter 7.) The financial responsibility limits should be thought of as the bare minimums (or better yet, disregarded when it comes to buying insurance). The size of liability settlements is increasing every day. Judgments of $50,000 and more are not unusual. Many agents and companies now advise their insureds to insure for $100,000 or more. Some people should carry even higher limits. Juries tend to assess higher damages against people who they believe can pay more. Doctors, lawyers, and wealthy businesspeople are among those who are regarded as "target risks."

In selecting the liability limits, one should realize that the extra cost of higher amounts is small, because of the infrequency of high losses. Policy buyers should ask their agents to quote the cost for several different amounts and then decide which amount to buy. Reasonably high amounts of liability protection should be thought of as essential. It is better to cut down on other coverages than to be underinsured against liability claims.

Medical Payments

If medical payments coverage is carried, it usually is a good idea to carry more than the $500 per person minimum. In most states a person buying $500 medical payments could get $5,000 for only $7 more and $10,000 for only $15 more per year.

The insurance buyer should be aware that medical payments coverage is no-fault in nature and that it covers passengers as well as the insured family. The coverage may be especially important to drivers who frequently carry a number of passengers, such as those in a car pool. Remember, though, that the limits apply to each person separately; there is no need to increase the limits to cover additional passengers.

Coverage for Damage to Your Auto

The amount of collision and comprehensive insurance equals the actual cash value of the auto at the time of a loss, minus the deductible amount. Collision coverage always is written with a deductible. Until recently, comprehensive coverage usually was written without a deductible. Now it normally has a deductible, too, but of a smaller amount than the collision deductible. Deductibles can save money. Motorists should realize, however, that the saving results from the fact that they are retaining part of the risk. With a $200 deductible, for instance, nothing will be paid for repairs that cost less than that amount. On a $700 repair job, the insured would pay $200 and the insurer would pay the remaining $500.

To illustrate how deductibles can save premium dollars, let's consider the imaginary case of Donna Murphy, who lives in a small city on the West Coast. She is paying $203 a year for $100 deductible collision coverage on her two-year-old Chevrolet Malibu. Table 8–4 shows that she could get $200 deductible coverage for $169. The difference in amount of insurance is $100; the difference in cost is $34. Thus, by carrying $100 deductible,

Table 8–4   Typical Costs to Insure an Auto, Illustrating Effect of Deductibles

COVERAGE	DEDUCTIBLE AMOUNT	PREMIUM
Collision	$100	$203
Collision	$200	$169
Comprehensive	$ 50	$ 54
Comprehensive	$100	$ 42

Note: Premiums shown are for purposes of illustration only. Their relative amounts are typical, but actual premiums depend upon numerous factors.

Donna is paying $34 for $100 more protection than she would have with $200 deductible. That is rather expensive insurance.

Comprehensive coverage (paying for noncollision loss) seldom was written with a deductible until recently; full coverage was the rule. The premium was small and the buyer couldn't save very much by using a deductible. The cost of comprehensive coverage has now increased, because of the high cost of repairing or replacing damaged or stolen cars and the rising expense of handling insurance claims. As a result, deductibles now are widely used on comprehensive coverage, just as they have been on collision. Many insurers insist on applying a deductible of at least $50 to this coverage.

Suppose that Donna Murphy has purchased $50 deductible comprehensive coverage on her Malibu. It costs her $54 a year, but if she had bought the same coverage with a $100 deductible, the cost would be $42 a year. The additional $50 of protection which the $50 deductible provides as compared with a $100 deductible is costing her $12 a year. That is 24% of the extra $50 of protection, a very high rate. Donna probably would be better off with a $100 deductible comprehensive coverage.

Uninsured and Underinsured Motorists Coverages

Uninsured motorists coverage generally is written for the same limits as those required by the state financial responsibility law. Many states require that all auto policies include the coverage for at least those limits. Higher uninsured motorists limits may not be suggested by agents or companies, but they should be requested. An accident caused by an uninsured or hit-and-run driver could easily cost the policyholder more in expenses and lost wages than the financial responsibility limits would cover.

The amount of protection of the underinsured motorists coverage should be set at the same high level as that of the uninsured motorists coverage. An exception would be the somewhat unusual situation in which the insured persons have complete medical and disability income protection under other insurance contracts. In such a case there would be little need for either of these coverages.

SHOPPING FOR AUTO INSURANCE

In the first section of this chapter we examined the factors that cause the price of auto insurance to vary from one policyholder to another. In addition to such variations, there is a wide range of prices from one insurer to another. In other words, the cost of a person's insurance depends partly upon which company writes the policy.

Comparing Prices

Various surveys have shown how auto insurance prices differ among companies. For example, the Missouri Department of Consumer Affairs and the Missouri Division of Insurance surveyed over ninety insurance companies selling auto policies in that state. The study determined how much each company would charge to insure an imaginary family consisting of mother and father, both age 45, and an 18-year-old son. Other information about the family such as its driving record (no accidents or violations) and its auto (a one-year-old Ford Granada) was the same for each insurer. Premiums were determined for a particular package of auto insurance coverages, including liability, medical payments, and damage to the auto. As might be expected, the survey found that premiums were highest in Kansas City and St. Louis, somewhat lower in the suburbs, and lowest of all in the smaller communities and rural areas of Missouri. But the range of prices within each territory was amazing. In one rating territory of St. Louis the fictitious family could pay from $405 to $2,086, depending on the company insuring them. In suburban Independence they could pay from $333 to $1,138. And in Columbia, Missouri, the prices ranged from $308 to $1,018. (In all cases still higher rates were charged by insurers specializing in substandard high-risk coverage—as high as $4442 in St. Louis, for instance!)[2] Numerous surveys in other states have found similar price ranges among companies.

Many car buyers shop around among dealers in the hope of saving money when they buy a car. Strangely, most of the people then insure the car without doing a bit of shopping. This practice hardly makes sense. A word of caution is important, though. One should not purchase insurance on the basis of price alone. Service is important too. Experienced motorists know that they can lose more than they save if they buy a car from a dealer who won't give them good service or who won't treat them fairly if problems develop later on. Insurance service is just as important. We discuss this point further in the section following this one.

How can a person find out what various companies charge? In the words of the Ohio Department of Insurance, *"Ask Questions."*[3] The yellow pages of any telephone book list names and addresses of companies and agents. A prospective buyer can contact them in person, by mail, or by phone. Asking about price is a perfectly acceptable thing to do; there is no obligation to buy.

Shopping for insurance is of course most beneficial for those who are good risks. People who have poor driving records or who were recently

---

[2]*Consumer Shopping Guide for Automobile Insurance* (State of Missouri, December 1977).
[3]*The Ohio Consumers Guide to Automobile Insurance* (Columbus: Ohio Department of Insurance), p. 6.

licensed and own their own car may have to be insured through the Automobile Insurance Plan of their state.

When price quotations are secured from different insurers, it is important that the prices be comparable. Prices can't be compared with one another if they are not applicable to identical policies. Also, the same rating information must be supplied to each insurer. Use of a simple **price quotation worksheet** such as Table 8–5 will help assure the prospective buyer that the quotations are comparable. Each insurer is given the rating information at the top of the worksheet, and each is asked to quote prices for the coverages and amounts listed on the bottom left-hand side. As the price quotations are received, they are filled in on the bottom right-hand side.

The insurance departments of several of the states have published consumer guides to auto insurance. Without exception, they advise insurance buyers to shop around among companies and agents. All of the insurance departments also point out that price should not be the only basis for choosing an insurer. Service is equally important.

Importance of Service

What kinds of service should an insurance buyer expect to receive? The list that follows is a summary of the things he or she should look for:

1. Advice concerning the kinds and amounts of insurance to buy.
2. Accurate rating, policy preparation, and premium billing.
3. Prompt, fair, and helpful handling of claims.
4. Coast-to-coast claims service.
5. Premium financing. (It is cheaper to pay in advance, but the agent should be able to arrange for premiums to be paid in installments.)
6. Prompt and accurate handling of policy changes, such as changes of address, car, or amounts of coverage.
7. Availability of other lines of insurance, including home insurance and business insurance.
8. Willingness to continue coverage after losses are paid.
9. An agent with knowledge and ability who is willing to give his or her clients the time and attention needed to handle their insurance needs properly.

The last of these points is the key to all of the others. Insurance buyers should expect their agents to provide truly professional service. Agents should be people whose advice and judgment are respected by others. They must handle routine details properly and they should be available day or

Table 8-5   Auto Insurance Price Quotation Worksheet

RATING INFORMATION

1. Drivers	Age	Sex	Marital Status	Use of Auto, %
Principal driver	___	___	___	___
Other driver	___	___	___	___
Other driver	___	___	___	___
Other driver	___	___	___	___

2. Description of accidents or moving traffic violations during last three years.

3. Autos to be insured	Make	Model	Year	Annual Milage	Miles Driven to and from Work Daily
Auto 1	___	___	___	___	___
Auto 2	___	___	___	___	___

INSURANCE INFORMATION

Annual Premiums

Coverage	Amount of Deductible	Company:	Company:	Company:
Liability	___	___	___	___
Medical Payments	___	___	___	___
Collision	___	___	___	___
Comprehensive	___	___	___	___
Uninsured motorists	___	___	___	___
Underinsured motorists	___	___	___	___
Total annual premium	___	___	___	___

Source: Adapted from *Buyers Guide to Automobile Insurance* (Department of Insurance, State of Illinois, 1974).

night if emergencies arise. Such agents can be expected to do whatever is necessary to serve their clients well.

How can a buyer find such an agent? The same way that one finds a good doctor or lawyer: by choosing carefully and by being lucky. As is the case with other professionals, good agents deserve the full confidence and cooperation of their clients as long as they provide satisfactory service. If the service is less than satisfactory, the insurance buyer should not hesitate to look for a different agent.

OTHER CONSIDERATIONS

Some people take their auto insurance for granted. They assume that as long as they pay the premiums they can forget about it. While good agents will provide important services, policyholders have to do some things themselves.

Policy Changes

Policyholders should notify their agents immediately of any developments that might affect a policy. Such developments include:

1. Change of address.
2. Marriage, divorce, or separation.
3. Purchase or sale of a car.
4. The licensing of a new driver.
5. The moving away from home of a member of the family, such as for college or military service.
6. Different use of a car, such as for a business or for driving to and from work.

In most cases the policy will continue to apply automatically, even if the company is not notified. However, there may be a change in premium and, more important, there may be something about the new situation which calls for a change in the policy. The agent will know what, if anything, should be done—but only if he or she is told what has happened.

Buying a Car

Buying a car is an exciting experience. In the process it is easy to forget all about insurance. One thing for the buyer to consider before getting carried away by it all is the cost of insuring the car. Perhaps he or she can afford the car payments, but what about the cost of insuring it? This point is especially important when a young person buys a relatively inexpensive car. The insurance may cost more than the car! The buyer should always make some inquiries about insurance costs before going ahead with the purchase.

The most important thing for the new owner to do is to make very sure that insurance is in force before driving away from the dealer's lot. And the buyer should realize that, although lenders insist that the car itself be covered, it is even more important that liability protection be carried.

Automobile buyers should also know that they have a legal right to buy their insurance wherever they choose. Auto dealers sometimes want to sell the policy. Banks may give borrowers the impression that they will finance an auto only if they also arrange for the insurance. But the laws of every state permit buyers to insure elsewhere if they wish. It is generally a good idea to check on some other insurance sources before deciding to insure with the auto dealer or bank.

Rented Cars

Many motorists from time to time rent a car from Hertz, Avis, or some other rental agency. If the agency is large and well known it is quite likely that no special insurance arrangements will be needed. But motorists should know how the rented car is insured and what options they have.

Most of the nationwide rental companies provide liability insurance with substantial limits. The renter's own policy, you may recall, applies while using a borrowed or rented car. The owner's (in this case the rental company's) insurance applies first; the renter's is available as excess insurance.

The major rental agencies provide insurance covering damage to the rented car, subject to a $250 collision deductible. Their rental contracts usually offer a "collision damage waiver" for $2 a day. The waiver relieves the renter of any responsibility for collision damage to the car. However, the agency's collision insurance applies whether the waiver is purchased or not. In other words, the extra $2 per day covers the first $250 of collision damage; the agency's insurance pays for damage above that amount. Many renters pay the extra charge without really knowing what it is for. Some people pay it in the belief that full coverage is important because they will be driving a strange car, perhaps in a city they aren't familiar with. Many other renters think that, even though $2 is a small amount, it is too much for the very small amount of protection it buys.

Most rental contracts require that all persons who drive the car be at least 21 years old. The company's insurance may be suspended if this requirement is violated. This point should be checked carefully if there is any chance that a person under 21 will drive the car.

The insurance may also be invalid if the car is not returned on time. The contract sometimes provides a 48-hour "grace period." After that the car is considered stolen property and the insurance no longer applies.

Driving in Canada and Mexico

United States motorists who vacation across the border and have accidents there may have their trips spoiled unless they have made proper insurance arrangements.

Each of the Canadian provinces has auto liability insurance requirements similar to the financial responsibility laws in the United States. The penalties are greater, however. Travelers who have accidents may have their cars impounded (that is, taken away from them) and their driving licenses suspended until they can produce evidence of their financial responsibility. Satisfactory evidence usually is easy to provide—if the motorist asks his agent for a **yellow card** before leaving home. This is the Canada Nonresident Motor Vehicle Liability Insurance Card. It is accepted in all of the provinces as evidence that the insurance required by the laws is in force. Yellow cards are supplied to their policyholders without charge by U.S. insurance companies.

The Mexican requirements are more severe. Auto liability coverage must be written by a Mexican insurance company. If it is not, the car can be impounded and the motorist may also be taken into custody.

Mexico has established a 25-mile-wide zone to encourage U.S. tourist travel to Mexican border towns. Within this zone Mexican authorities generally accept a special form known as **Endorsement 74** which some U.S. companies provide their insureds upon request. The endorsement, which is supplied without charge, extends coverage for accidents in Mexico within the border zone. Policies written in the United States do not otherwise apply in Mexico. Many U.S. insurers caution their policyholders not to rely upon Endorsement 74 and advise them to obtain short-term Mexican policies, even if they intend to travel only in the border zone. Insurance agents in the United States generally can provide the names of agents in cities bordering Mexico who sell Mexican policies. It may be possible to arrange in advance to pick up a policy from the border agent. Some U.S. agents can insure their clients with companies that have subsidiaries in Mexico. Motorists should be careful not to enter the country before the Mexican policy takes effect and to leave before it expires.[4]

[4]"When Your Client Travels," *Independent Agent*, May 1978, p. 46.

Loss Control

We have been concentrating upon insurance as a method of handling the risks of auto accidents. We should remember that loss control is important, too.

Can auto accidents be prevented? Not all of them, of course. There are over 20 million every year. But most of them involve one or more of the following: (a) improper driving, especially speeding; (b) drunken driving; (c) defective tires, brakes, or other equipment. Careful driving and proper car maintenance are the best ways to control auto accidents. Remember, too, that controlling losses is the best way to control insurance costs.

IMPORTANT TERMS

Classification system   Price quotation worksheet
Safe driver rating plan   Yellow card

KEY POINTS TO REMEMBER

1. Buying insurance is an important step and requires some careful decisions.
2. The price of an auto policy is determined by the classification system used by the particular company.
3. A classification system causes numerous factors to influence the price of each person's policy. These include the age, sex, and driving records of each of the operators. The auto and its use also affect the price.
4. The safe driver rating plan classifies insured persons on the basis of their driving records, charging higher rates to those with records of accidents or violations.
5. Insurance buyers must decide which coverages to purchase and in what amounts. They can reduce the cost of comprehensive and collision coverages by choosing sizable deductibles.
6. The purchase of liability insurance in adequate amounts is essential. The other coverages can also be very important.
7. Prices vary widely among companies. Wise insurance buyers shop for their policies, using a price quotation worksheet so that the prices of several companies can be compared.
8. Insurance agents provide valuable services. Good service can be just as important as a low price.
9. Insurance buyers should know about insuring new cars. They also should know the importance of securing a "yellow card" before driving in Canada and should make special insurance arrangements before driving in Mexico.
10. Insuring a car is important. Operating it safely is even more important.

REVIEW QUESTIONS

1. List each of the things that can affect the price of a person's auto insurance.
2. Why do rates differ from one place to another?

3. Why don't the costs of liability and medical payments insurance increase proportionately for larger amounts of coverage?
4. Why do younger drivers have to pay higher premiums?
5. Who is eligible for the good student and driver training discounts?
6. The safe driver rating plan is said to be part of the classification system, and not an attempt to penalize those who have accidents or violations. What does this mean?
7. Why is liability insurance more important than comprehensive or collision coverage?
8. If the dealer from whom you buy a car says that he will arrange for your insurance, what should you do?
9. What is the full collision waiver in rental car contracts?
10. What is a "yellow card" and why is it important?
11. What insurance arrangements should you make before driving in Mexico?

DISCUSSION QUESTIONS

1. How do the rules of personal risk management apply to the handling of automobile risks?
2. The cost of auto insurance differs among rating territories because past experience shows that insurers will have to pay more for losses per policy in one territory than in another. The text stated that the reasons for this difference include differences in the cost of medical care and auto repairs. What other factors could cause the same policy to cost more in one territory than in another?
3. In your judgment are auto insurance discounts for driver training justified? Are good student discounts justified?
4. Insurance companies have found that extra premium charges are necessary for insuring powerful, "high performance" cars. The higher charges are made for the liability and medical payments coverages, as well as for the collision and comprehensive coverages. What might explain the poor loss experience of these cars?
5. Why is selecting the proper amounts of coverage more difficult than choosing which coverages to buy?
6. How much liability insurance would be enough for you?
7. If you were in Donna Murphy's position (see page 140) which collision deductible would you choose? Which comprehensive deductible?

CHAPTER 9
INSURANCE FOR THE HOME—PART I

LOSSES COVERED BY HOME INSURANCE

HOMEOWNERS POLICIES

HOMEOWNERS BROAD FORM— SECTION I

Whether living in a house, an apartment, or a mobile home, everyone needs protection against damage to or theft of their property. People also should be protected in case they are sued for bodily injury or property damage to others. Specially designed home insurance policies that provide such coverages are the subject of this chapter and the next one. The property insurance section of the policies is examined in this chapter; Chapter 10 examines the liability insurance section. Both chapters concentrate on information that can be helpful to home insurance buyers and policyholders.

LOSSES COVERED BY HOME INSURANCE

Home insurance covers three major types of loss: damage to the home itself, loss of personal property, and the cost of liability claims.

The Home

The home is the major investment of the typical American family. Its value is often several times as much as a family's annual income. In contrast, the value of the family car is probably less than half of one year's income. Proper home insurance is essential because without it a family's major investment can be suddenly wiped out by fire, wind, explosion, or some other unexpected catastrophe.

In many cases, insurance on the home is required by the mortgage holder. Most families borrow funds to buy their homes and the lender (bank, savings and loan, or credit union, for instance) has an insurable interest because the property is security for the loan. A single policy with the owner as named insured usually is written to cover both the owner and the mortgage holder.

Personal Property

The second type of loss covered by home insurance is damage to or theft of personal property. The personal property owned by most people is worth far more than their automobile, but people typically pay more attention to auto insurance than to protection for their other possessions. Glance through the following list and try to imagine the total investment you or your family has in these items:

Beds and bedding
Books
Clothing
Collections
Dishes

Furniture
Kitchen appliances and utensils
Lamps and mirrors
Luggage
Sewing machine and supplies
Sports and hobby equipment
Television, radio, and record player
Tools and equipment
Washer and dryer
Watches and jewelry

Home insurance should protect all these items plus the thousand-and-one other things that all of us seem to accumulate. The protection should apply whether the items are in the home or elsewhere, and it should cover a wide range of perils. These should include not only the perils of fire and theft but also windstorm, water damage, explosion, vandalism, and other sources of loss.

Legal Liability

The third type of loss covered by home insurance can be even greater than the other two combined. Lawsuits of any size can stem from accidents that happen (or are claimed to have happened) in the home and elsewhere. The most common personal liability claims result from falls on residence steps or sidewalks. But there is no end to the list of things that can bring about suits for damages. For instance, they can come from hunting or golfing accidents, dog bites, fires, explosions, or bicycle collisions. Whatever their cause, the results can be costly. Protection against personal liability claims therefore is a vital part of home insurance.

HOMEOWNERS POLICIES

Until the 1950s, people who wanted adequate property-casualty insurance for the losses just reviewed had to buy three separate policies. One policy protected the home and personal property against fire and other major perils, a second policy provided protection against theft losses, and a third insured against liability claims. Separate policies were necessary because, as Chapter 2 explained, state laws divided the property-casualty insurance industry by "lines" of insurance. Property insurance was one line; casualty was another. Property insurers wrote fire insurance policies; casualty insurers wrote theft policies and liability policies. After the laws were changed it became possible for a single company to write any of the property-casualty lines.

The new laws were called multiple-line laws. After the adoption of these laws, new policies were developed which "packaged" the formerly separate lines in a single contract. These new policies were termed **multiple-line policies.** Thus, **homeowners policies** are multiple-line policies that package property, theft, and liability insurance to cover home and home-related risks.

There are seven standard homeowners policies. Four are designed to cover owners of private residences; the other three are designed for renters, condominium unit owners, and mobile home owners. The main differences concern the perils that are covered. The policies range from the Basic Form, which covers losses resulting from a limited list of perils, to the Comprehensive Form, which is written on the "all risk" basis.

In our consideration of homeowners insurance we shall concentrate on the policy called the Broad Form (also known as Form 2). It is one of the four designed to cover private residences. In both breadth of coverage and in cost it lies between the extremes of the Basic and Comprehensive forms. The next chapter explains how other homeowners policies differ from the Broad Form.

Homeowners Broad Form Policy

The policy is divided into two main sections that provide six separate coverages. Section I, the property insurance section, covers the home, other buildings on the premises, and personal property. It also provides coverage for additional living expenses and loss of rental income that result from a covered peril. Section II furnishes liability and medical payments coverages. Table 9–1 shows the coverages and limits of liability purchased by Harvey and Helen Harper. Notice that separate limits of liability apply to each of the six coverages.

Table 9–1   Harvey and Helen Harper's Broad Form Homeowners Policy

SECTION I—COVERAGES	LIMITS OF LIABILITY
A. Dwelling	$60,000
B. Other Structures	6,000
C. Personal Property	30,000
D. Loss of Use	12,000
SECTION II—COVERAGES	
A. Personal Liability	50,000
B. Medical Payments to Others	1,000

The Harpers' policy is the new, simplified version that many insurance companies started using in 1976 and 1977. (An older version is still used in some cases.) The new edition of the homeowners policy is shorter and easier to read; it uses 40% fewer words (7,000, compared to 12,000) and avoids old-fashioned words and legal terms wherever possible. A copy appears in Appendix C.

Summary of Coverages

In brief summary, here is what the Harpers' Broad Form Homeowners policy includes: Section I covers the Harpers' house, their garage, and their personal possessions. The insurance company will pay (subject to a deductible amount) for repairing or replacing any of these properties that are damaged or lost because of one of the perils listed in the policy. Seventeen perils are covered, including fire, windstorm, explosion, vandalism, theft, and falling objects. Section I also will pay for the loss of use of the Harpers' house, meaning it will cover the extra cost of their living somewhere else temporarily if the house is badly damaged by one of the covered perils. In addition, it reimburses for lost rental income if part of the dwelling is rented to others and cannot be occupied because of covered damage.

Section II of the policy furnishes legal liability protection and medical payments coverage. The liability insurance applies to most lawsuits other than those involving business or professional activities or the use of automobiles. The medical payments coverage will pay the medical expenses of anyone (other than one of the Harpers) who is injured on their premises or who is injured elsewhere as a result of something done by a member of the family.

HOMEOWNERS BROAD FORM—SECTION I

For the remainder of this chapter we shall examine the property insurance portion of the Harpers' policy. We need to know more about what property and other losses are covered, the perils for which protection is provided, and the amounts the policy will pay. The major features of the policy are summarized. One can best determine specific details by reading the policy itself.

Property Covered

Coverage A protects the Harpers' house. In addition, it covers any materials or supplies being used to alter or repair their house or garage. If the Harpers lived in a different type of residence, such as an apartment, a different policy form would be used. The Harpers have purchased $60,000 of Coverage A protection. Choosing the proper Coverage A limit is important because it sets a maximum on the amount payable for damage to the house. In addition, the limits of liability provided by the other Section I coverages usually are percentages of the Coverage A limit.

Coverage B protects the garage and other buildings. If the garage were part of the house rather than a separate building, it would be included under Coverage A. Coverage B is normally written for an amount equal to 10% of the insurance on the house. Larger amounts can be purchased if 10% is not adequate.

Coverage C provides protection for personal possessions owned or being used by any member of the family. The amount of insurance ordinarily must be at least 50% of the amount provided by Coverage A. Greater amounts can be purchased for an additional premium. Most of the items insured by Coverage C are in the house and garage, but the coverage applies anywhere in the world. It includes the baggage that Mr. and Mrs. Harper take with them on vacation trips, the things that Veronica leaves in her high school locker, and the possessions that Dustin has in his college residence hall room.

The policy states that a maximum of 10% of Coverage C can be used for personal property "usually situated" at other residences. In the Harpers' case the things Dustin usually leaves in his room at college are covered up to a maximum of $3,000. The 10% limitation applies only to property that is usually situated away from the regular residence. In other words, the entire $30,000 provided by Coverage C is available to cover property that Dustin is carrying in a car or that Mr. and Mrs. Harper have in their motel room.

Coverage C is not limited to property owned by the Harpers. It also covers items they are using but do not own. Tools that Harvey has borrowed from a neighbor, for instance, are covered. The coverage also extends to property, such as coats and hats owned by the Harpers' guests, while it is in the house.

All standard homeowners policies contain special limits for certain categories of personal property. On the Broad Form these include limits of $100 on money, $500 on securities, $500 on boats, $500 on jewelry, watches and furs, $1,000 on theft of silverware, and $1,000 on theft of guns.

Some types of property are not covered. Coverage C excludes animals, motor vehicles, aircraft, property of tenants not related to the Harpers, business property used in a business conducted on the premises, and business property located away from the premises.

Deductible Amount

Most property losses are small—about one third of those involving homes and their contents are below $100. Deductibles therefore make sense and save money on homeowners policies just as they do on auto insurance policies.

The most widely used homeowners deductible is a flat $100, applying to all Section I losses. Sometimes a higher amount is deducted from windstorm and hail losses. Higher deductibles of course reduce the premium more, and $250 or $500 deductibles are not uncommon.

In some states disappearing deductibles are used. They are arranged so that the amount deducted declines for larger losses and completely disappears for losses above a certain amount. With a $100 disappearing deductible, for instance, 125% of covered losses above $100 are paid. For a $400 loss, 125% of $300 would be paid, or $375. Losses above $500 are paid in full.

Loss of Use

Coverages A, B, and C cover direct loss to the various types of insured property caused by one of the covered perils. Coverage D provides three kinds of indirect loss protection: additional living expense, fair rental value, and prohibited use. Under the Broad Form homeowners policy, Coverage D is written for 20% of the amount of insurance on the house.

ADDITIONAL LIVING EXPENSE. If their house is seriously damaged by a fire or other peril, the Harper family may have to live in a motel for two or three weeks until it is repaired. During this period their living costs will be much higher than normal. They will have to eat all their meals in restaurants and have their laundry done commercially, they may have extra costs in order to transport Veronica to and from school, and they will have to pay for the motel in addition to the regular mortgage payments on their house. Their homeowners policy will cover the increase in their living expenses until they are able to move back home.

FAIR RENTAL VALUE. If the Harpers rented a room or an apartment in their house to a tenant, they would not be able to collect rent during the period while the house was being repaired. This part of Coverage D would reimburse them for their loss of rental income.

PROHIBITED USE. Following a major disaster such as a tornado or hurricane, the police sometimes order a section of the damaged community to be evacuated. People living in that area are unable to use their homes, even if they had been fortunate enough to escape serious direct damage. If this happens to the Harpers, their additional living expenses and fair rental value would be covered, just as if their house had been one of the ones destroyed.

Additional Coverages

Six additional Section I coverages are listed. They supplement the protection granted by the principal coverages.

DEBRIS REMOVAL.   This additional coverage pays for the cost of carrying away damaged property. An additional 5% of insurance is available if the amount payable for direct property loss plus the cost of debris removal exceeds the limit of liability. If the Harpers' garage burns down they have up to $6,000 under Coverage B to replace it and an additional 5% or $300 to clean up the remains of the old garage before building a new one.

REASONABLE REPAIRS.   Reasonable repairs are those temporary repairs that are necessary to protect damaged property from further damage. For instance, if part of the roof is torn off by a falling tree, a temporary plywood cover may be put over the opening to protect against rain damage to the interior of the house. Coverage A will pay for repairing the roof and this additional coverage will pay for the temporary cover.

TREES, SHRUBS, AND OTHER PLANTS.   Trees, shrubs, plants, and lawns are covered by this section. Payment is limited to $500 for any one tree, shrub, or plant, with an overall maximum of 5% of the amount of insurance provided by Coverage A. A limited number of perils are covered, the most important being lightning, vandalism, and damage by nonowned vehicles.

FIRE DEPARTMENT SERVICE CHARGE.   In some parts of the country, particularly in rural areas, property owners must pay for fire department services. The policy pays up to $250 for such charges if the fire department is called.

PROPERTY REMOVED.   If the house catches fire, the Harpers and their neighbors might carry out some of the furniture and other items for safekeeping. If it is a serious fire they may have to store the rescued property in a neighbor's garage for a number of days. Coverage C will, of course, protect the property wherever it is located, but only for the perils listed in the policy. This part of the additional coverage section protects the rescued property for up to 30 days against "direct loss from any cause." Furniture that is broken in the rush to get it out of the burning house, for instance, would be covered, as would property damaged by rain or dirt.

CREDIT CARD, FORGERY, AND COUNTERFEIT MONEY.   The last of the additional coverages pays the Harpers up to $500 if they lose their credit cards and other people use them to charge purchases to the Harpers' accounts. The policy says that all terms under which the credit cards were issued must be complied with; that is, the Harpers must report the loss of the cards to the companies that issued them as soon as they realize they are lost. The same $500 limit applies to loss caused by check forgery or acceptance of counterfeit money.

Perils Insured Against

The property described in Coverages A, B, and C is insured against direct loss caused by any of the 17 stated perils.

FIRE OR LIGHTNING.   In most cases it is obvious whether something has been damaged by fire or not. There are exceptions, however. For instance, what if a cigarette drops out of an ashtray and scorches a table? This probably is not a fire loss. The policy does not define fire, but the legal interpretation requires that oxidation be rapid enough to produce a flame or glow. In this case, the cigarette was glowing, but the table was not. The presence of heat, charring, or even smoke is not enough to constitute fire. For insurance purposes, it is not necessarily true that "where there's smoke there's fire"; there must also be ignition.

In addition, the law distinguishes between friendly fire and hostile fire. Only **hostile fires**—those in unintended places—are covered. A **friendly fire** is one that remains where it is intended to be: in the furnace or fireplace, or on the stove. Damage caused by heat or smoke from a friendly fire is not insured as direct loss by fire. Also, property destroyed by a friendly fire is not covered. The insurance company won't pay for the steaks that Harvey burns up on his backyard grill. But if a spark from the fireplace lands on some nearby newspapers and the fire spreads to an armchair, then the fire is no longer friendly; the chair has been damaged by a hostile fire and the policy applies. Smoke damage caused by a hostile fire is considered part of the fire loss.

In order for fire or lightning to be covered, the damage must be "direct loss caused by" one of these two perils. If a bolt of lightning hits a house, destroying part of the chimney, the loss is a direct one caused by lightning and it is covered. But let's say fire breaks out down the block from the

Harpers' house. As a fire truck goes roaring by, Dustin jumps up and dashes toward the door to follow it. In the process, he bumps into a table, knocking over and breaking a valuable antique vase. Is this a direct loss caused by fire? What about damage done in the course of fighting a fire: water damage, for instance, or windows broken by firefighters? Are these considered to be direct loss caused by fire? To answer these questions, the courts apply the **doctrine of proximate cause.** According to this doctrine, a policy covering a particular peril covers not only losses caused directly by that peril but also losses resulting from other perils that were triggered by the named peril, as long as there is an uninterrupted chain of events from the initial peril (the proximate cause) to the loss itself. Exactly how the doctrine will be applied to a particular case depends on a court's interpretation of the facts in the case. Fire generally is considered the proximate cause of damage done by firefighters. But in the case of the broken vase a court probably would rule that fire was not the proximate cause.

WINDSTORM OR HAIL.   Some of the greatest property losses result from windstorm. The largest insurance loss on record, in fact, was caused by Hurricane Betsy, which struck Florida, Louisiana, and Mississippi in 1965, causing insured damage of $715 million.

Direct damage to the exterior of buildings is the most common wind or hail loss. The policy also covers loss caused by rain, snow, sand, or dust that enter a building through an opening created by wind or hail. If hail breaks a window and the wind then drives rain through the opening, the policy will pay for water damage to the walls and draperies. But if the rain comes in through a window that Dustin left open, such damage is not covered.

EXPLOSION.   Explosions of natural gas that has leaked from defective pipelines or water heaters are among the losses covered by this peril. Furnace explosions are also covered.

RIOT OR CIVIL COMMOTION.   The laws of each state define riot. Usually the term means that at least three people are engaging in force or violence against other people or their property. Civil commotion is a large or prolonged riot. Direct loss resulting from these perils includes robbery committed during the riot or civil commotion.

AIRCRAFT.   The peril of aircraft covers damage to the insured property caused by aircraft. Because the policy does not require actual collision between the aircraft and the property, damage by sonic boom is included.

VEHICLES.   Damage to insured property caused by vehicles is covered.

The coverage even includes damage caused by members of the Harper family, other than damage to a fence, driveway, or sidewalk. If Harvey steps on the accelerator instead of the brake pedal as he is coming into the garage, the resulting damage to the garage and its contents (but not to the car) is covered. The peril also applies to personal property carried in a car and damaged by a collision.

SMOKE. Smoke damage caused by a hostile fire is considered to be part of fire loss. This peril covers smoke damage caused by friendly fires. The loss must be "sudden and accidental." If an electric oven malfunctions and burns up a roast, the resulting smoke damage to the kitchen walls is covered by this peril.

VANDALISM OR MALICIOUS MISCHIEF. Intentional damage to the Harpers' property by other people is also insured. The peril excludes loss to residential property if the dwelling has been vacant for more than 30 days. As used here, "vacant" means that a house is not occupied by either people or furniture. If the Harpers take a six-week trip to Europe, their house is not "vacant" while they are away.

THEFT. Theft is an important peril because such losses have become so frequent in many parts of the country. Possessions stolen from either the home or elsewhere are covered. Damage caused by thieves is treated as a theft loss.

The policy defines theft as "loss of property from a known location when it is likely that the property has been stolen." If Mrs. Harper's purse mysteriously disappears from the drawer that she put it in, the loss is covered. She does not have to prove that the purse was stolen as long as it seems from the circumstances that it probably was.

Theft by any insured is of course excluded. Also excluded are thefts from a dwelling under construction and theft from a room rented to others.

The coverage applies to property stolen either from the Harpers' premises or elsewhere. What about things stolen from Dustin's room at college? The policy says it covers the property in student residences away from home as long as the student has been there some time during the 45 days preceding the loss. Thus, Dustin's possessions are protected against theft while he is at school and while he is home on vacation except for the period starting 45 days after summer vacation begins.

The policy covers theft of property from the Harpers' car, but only if the car is broken into and there are "visible marks of the forcible entry." There is no coverage for things stolen from the car if the windows are left open or the doors are left unlocked (or if the thief uses a key). The forcible entry requirement can be deleted by adding the **Theft Coverage Extension** endorsement to the policy. An extra premium is charged for this endorsement. The policy does not cover theft of watercraft, trailers, or campers.

BREAKAGE OF GLASS OR SAFETY GLAZING MATERIAL. This coverage pays for the replacement of glass in windows and doors, regardless of what caused the breakage. Glass in vacant houses is not covered.

FALLING OBJECTS. Falling trees and tree limbs are the main source of loss under this peril.

WEIGHT OF ICE, SNOW, OR SLEET. This covers damage to either a building or its contents due to the weight of ice, snow, or sleet.

COLLAPSE OF A BUILDING OR ANY PART OF A BUILDING. Collapse from any cause is covered, but collapse does not include "settling, cracking, shrinking, bulging or expansion." The intent is to cover actual collapse, not gradual deterioration. Both this peril and the preceding one exclude certain items, such as fences, swimming pools, and foundations.

ACCIDENTAL DISCHARGE OR OVERFLOW OF WATER OR STEAM. This peril applies to damage caused by water or steam that escapes from the plumbing, heating, or air conditioning system or from a household appliance (such as a humidifier). If part of a wall has to be torn out to repair a leaking pipe, the cost of repairing the wall is paid. Damage caused by overflow from a bathtub or toilet is covered, but water damage due to a leaking roof is not. The intent is to cover sudden, unexpected damage; loss due to continuous or repeated seepage is excluded.

SUDDEN AND ACCIDENTAL TEARING APART, CRACKING, BURNING, OR BULGING. The main source of loss covered by this peril is damage caused by the bursting of water heaters.

FREEZING. Loss caused by the freezing of a plumbing, heating, or air conditioning system is excluded from the two preceding perils and covered under this one. There is no coverage while the house is vacant or unoccupied unless the insured either uses reasonable care to keep the house heated or shuts off the water supply and drains the system. Notice that this provision applies while the house is either vacant or "unoccupied." A house is unoccupied while its residents are away temporarily. If the Harpers go away for a few days this peril will not apply unless they take care to prevent freezing. But if they leave the thermostat set high enough to prevent freezing and the furnace for some reason goes out and causes water in the pipes to freeze, the resulting loss (bursting pipes and water damage) will be covered.

**SUDDEN AND ACCIDENTAL DAMAGE FROM ARTIFICIALLY GEN-
ERATED ELECTRICAL CURRENT.**   A sudden surge of electrical power
can cause short circuits in appliances such as television sets. There can be
enough heat to "burn out" some of the wiring, even though no fire develops.
This peril covers repair or replacement of the appliance other than its
electronic components.

Exclusions

Among the losses excluded from Section I are earthquake and other earth
movement, certain kinds of water damage, and war. The excluded water

"IT'LL BE OUT FOR A MONTH... SMITH
TRIED TO PROGRAM IT TO UNDERSTAND
HIS INSURANCE POLICY..."

Source: Reprinted from the Kemper Insurance and Financial Companies annual report.
Copyright Lumbermens Mutual Casualty Company 1978.

damage is that due to flooding, backing up of sewers or drains, and seepage of underground water, such as that into a basement.

Flood damage is excluded because of the adverse selection problem. Adverse selection, you may recall, occurs when insured risks are not an average selection of good risks and poor risks, but instead are a worse-than-average selection. In the case of flood insurance, adverse selection is certain to occur. Property owners located where floods are likely are sure to want protection, whereas those situated on high ground are not interested in it. Furthermore, those whose properties are not subject to flooding have no interest in participating in an insurance arrangement that would pay other property owners for their flood losses. Why not? Because the rates paid by everyone would have to be high enough to cover the flood losses, and the people on high ground would be subsidizing those on low ground. To overcome this problem, the federal government has established a national flood insurance program. It makes coverage available in communities that have approved flood control programs.

The war exclusion applies to insurrection, rebellion, and revolution as well as to declared or undeclared war. At the time of the riots in Los Angeles and elsewhere in the late 1960s, some news stories hinted that the insurance industry was going to say the damage was caused by insurrection or rebellion and thus excluded. (The same exclusion appears in fire insurance policies covering commercial property.) Actually, this never was an issue, except to a few imaginative news reporters. Insurrection and rebellion are attempts to overthrow the government. This was not the nature of the 1960s riots and the insurance companies never claimed that it was. Many millions of dollars in losses were paid, including $68 million for the disorders following the killing of Dr. Martin Luther King in April 1968.

Also excluded from Section I is loss resulting from the insured's neglect to use "all reasonable means to save and preserve property at and after the time of a loss, or when property is endangered by a peril insured against." Notice the word "reasonable." Harvey Harper isn't required to risk life and limb by dashing heroically into his burning house to rescue his easy chair. On the other hand, he cannot stand idly by, waiting impatiently for the property to be destroyed. He must take reasonable action to protect his property.

LOSS MEASUREMENT

The important matter of loss measurement was introduced in Chapter 4 when the indemnity principle was explained. It was pointed out that the customary measure of property loss is actual cash value, which usually is defined as the cost of replacing or repairing damaged property with new materials at current prices, minus an allowance for depreciation. The Loss Settlement provision (Condition 3) explains how losses are measured under this policy.

Losses of personal property (the items included in Coverage C) are settled on the actual cash value basis. The settlement is not to exceed "the amount necessary to repair or replace" the damaged property. If a fire in the utility room damages the Harpers' dryer, the company will pay (subject to the deductible) either (a) the depreciated value of the dryer or (b) the cost of repairing it, whichever is less.[1]

The notable function of the Loss Settlement provision is to provide that damage to the buildings (the house and garage, as distinguished from personal property) will be paid for on the basis of replacement cost without deduction for depreciation if the policyholder carries enough insurance. The amount of insurance required is 80% of the replacement cost of the building. For example, if the Harpers' house would cost $75,000 to replace, damage to it would be paid with no deduction for depreciation if they insured it for at least 80% of the $75,000, or $60,000.

How are building losses adjusted if less than 80% of the replacement cost is insured? The policy states that in that case, the larger of the following two amounts will be paid: (a) the actual cash value of the loss, or (b) the proportion of the replacement cost that the amount of insurance carried bears to 80% of the value of the building. The latter of these two amounts can be calculated by use of this formula:[2]

Loss payment =

$$\frac{\text{Insurance on building}}{80\% \text{ of replacement cost of building}} \times \text{replacement cost of loss}$$

To illustrate, let us assume that the Harpers insure their house for only $50,000 and that the value of the house has depreciated 30% because of its age and condition. The house is damaged by a large tree that is blown onto it during a windstorm. Repairs cost $6,000.

The company would pay the larger of:

    (a) $ 6,000 − 30% = 4,200 actual cash value or

    (b) $\dfrac{\$50,000}{\$60,000}$ × 6,000 = 5,000

---

[1]Replacement cost coverage is available from some companies for an additional charge.
[2]The loss payment is also limited by the replacement cost of the loss and the amount of insurance, of course.

In this case, $5,000 would be paid. However, remember that, if at least 80% of the $75,000 replacement cost of the house had been insured, the full $6,000 would have been paid.

Replacement cost coverage is granted subject to the condition that the damaged property must actually be repaired or replaced. If it is not repaired or replaced, the insurer is obligated only for the actual cash value of the damaged property. This condition does not apply, however, if the damage is either less than $1,000 or less than 5% of the amount of insurance. In that case the insurer must pay for the full cost of replacement (assuming sufficient insurance), whether the property is restored or not.

Replacement cost insurance should be thought of as an extension of coverage. Remember that the policy never pays less than the actual cash value of any loss, up to the amount of insurance carried. This provision extends the coverage beyond actual cash value if enough insurance is carried. Information about measuring the replacement cost of a particular residence is contained in the next chapter.

IMPORTANT TERMS

Multiple-line policy
Homeowners policies
Additional living expense coverage
Fair rental value coverage

Friendly fire
Hostile fire
Doctrine of proximate cause
Theft Coverage Extension

KEY POINTS TO REMEMBER

1. Homeowners policies cover three major types of loss: damage to the home, damage to or loss of personal property, and the cost of legal liability claims.
2. Section I of the Homeowners Broad Form policy covers the home, other buildings, and personal property. It also insures against loss caused by the insured's being unable to use the residence. Section II provides liability and medical payments coverage.
3. Coverages A, B, and C of Section I pay for direct loss to the home, other buildings, and personal property respectively.
4. Coverage C provides worldwide protection for personal property. It includes items that the insured persons are using but do not own. Up to 10% of the coverage applies to items usually kept at secondary residences. Some kinds of property are excluded; some are subject to special limits.
5. Coverage D insures the indirect loss that may be incurred if the insured persons are unable to use their home. It includes protection for additional living expense and loss of rental income. These are covered if they result from direct damage to the residence or from its use being prohibited.
6. Six additional coverages are included in Section I. They are: (a) debris removal; (b) reasonable repairs; (c) trees, shrubs, and other plants; (d) fire department

service charges; (e) property removal; and (f) credit card, forgery and counterfeit money.

7. Section I of the Broad Form Homeowners policy covers direct loss caused by any of 17 perils.

8. The fire peril does not insure against damage caused by smoke, heat, or charring unless there is ignition. Also, it covers neither damage caused by friendly fires nor loss that is the indirect result of a fire.

9. The theft peril covers property stolen from the home or from most other locations. It includes the disappearance of covered property from a known location "when it is likely that the property has been stolen."

10. Unless the Theft Coverage Extension is purchased, the policy covers property stolen from a car only if there are visible marks of forcible entry.

11. The policy insures the covered property for its actual cash value, with depreciation being deducted from the cost of repairing or replacing damaged property. Coverage is extended to pay for damage to buildings on the basis of replacement cost without deduction for depreciation if 80% of the building's replacement cost is insured. If less insurance is carried, a percentage of replacement cost may be paid.

REVIEW QUESTIONS

Which of the following losses would be covered by the Harpers' Broad Form homeowners policy? If a loss is covered, explain which peril or other policy provision applies. If a loss is not covered, explain why not.

1. The porch roof caves in under the weight of an accumulation of snow and ice. Some porch furniture is damaged.

2. A heavy truck runs out of control and smashes into the house. There is damage to contents as well as to the house itself.

3. While the Harpers are away someone breaks into the house. Paint is sprayed on the walls and carpets, furniture is slashed, and glassware is broken.

4. A gas main in the street explodes. The front of the house and contents of the house are damaged by flying debris.

5. As Dustin is putting a log in the fireplace, his wristwatch falls into the fire and is destroyed.

6. A short circuit causes fire in an interior wall. Fire damage is $50. Smoke damage is $200. Damage done by firefighters (water damage and breaking into the wall to get at the fire) is $500.

7. While Dustin is at home for Thanksgiving, a suit, a calculator, and a tennis racket are stolen from his college residence hall room.

8. A sudden flash flood hits the town. Water and mud cause extensive damage to property stored in the basement.

9. Helen Harper leaves a faucet running on the second floor. When the family returns from a movie, they discover that water has run down into the living room below. The walls, the drapes, and an upholstered chair are stained.

10. An antique cherry table is left standing over a hot air outlet. The table is badly warped by the heat.

11. A tornado tears off most of the roof.

12. While the roof is being repaired the Harpers live in a motel for two weeks. Motel, restaurant, and extra transportation expenses total $840.

13. A motion picture camera and a projector are stolen from the car. The car was locked, but the thief apparently had a duplicate key.

14. Harvey is away on a business trip. Walking to his hotel late at night he is held up. His billfold containing $260 is taken.

15. A big old tree in the Harpers' yard is blown down. It misses the house but falls onto their car, which was parked in the driveway.

16. A tree company charges $175 to cut up and remove the fallen tree.

17. If the replacement cost of the Harpers' house were $60,000 and it were insured for $50,000, how much would the policy pay in the event of fire damage to the house which cost $4,000 to repair?

18. How much would the policy have paid for the preceding loss if the house had been insured for $36,000?

DISCUSSION QUESTIONS

1. Can you think of any way in which Section I of the Harpers' Broad Form Homeowners policy fails to provide the property insurance protection which the family needs?

2. Homeowners policies are multiple-line policies. Is the Personal Automobile Policy a multiple-line policy?

3. The Broad Form Homeowners policy provides named peril coverage except under the Property Removed part of the Additional Coverages. Why are the companies more generous in this particular part of the policy?

4. Do homeowners policies cover damage that is caused by the negligence of the insured? For example, a fire breaks out in the Harpers' basement. The claim adjuster learns that the fire was caused by Harvey's carelessness in leaving some oily rags on a hot air duct near the furnace. Is the loss covered?

5. Homeowners policies provide replacement cost coverage on the house if enough insurance is carried. Can you think of any reason why they don't provide this coverage on personal property too?

6. What are the advantages to the policyholder of having a single, multiple-line homeowners policy rather than three separate policies covering fire and other perils, theft, and liability?

7. The amount of insurance covering personal property (Homeowners Coverage C) ordinarily must be at least 50% of the amount covering the home (Coverage A). Why? In other words, why aren't policy buyers allowed to insure their personal belongings for as small an amount as they wish?

CHAPTER 10
INSURANCE FOR THE HOME—PART II

**HOMEOWNERS BROAD FORM—
SECTION II**

OTHER HOMEOWNERS POLICIES

BUYING HOME INSURANCE

**THE PERSONAL UMBRELLA LIABILITY
POLICY**

This chapter examines Section II of the Broad Form homeowners policy. In addition, it compares the Broad Form with the other homeowners policy forms and discusses some of the things to consider when buying home insurance, including deductibles and amounts of coverage. The chapter concludes by reviewing a policy designed to protect against extremely large or very unusual liability claims: the umbrella policy.

HOMEOWNERS BROAD FORM—SECTION II

Section II provides three important coverages: personal liability, medical payments to others, and damage to property of others. They are listed as Coverage E, Coverage F, and Additional Coverage 3. Before the development of homeowners policies, those who wanted these coverages purchased a contract called the Comprehensive Personal Liability Policy. Now, Section II of all homeowners policies automatically includes the three coverages.

Personal Liability Coverage

The nature of personal liability coverage is similar to the liability coverage provided by Part A of the Personal Auto Policy. The company will defend the insured against bodily injury and property damage liability claims and make whatever payments are necessary on behalf of the insured. A major difference, of course, is that the auto policy covers liability claims arising from automobile accidents whereas the homeowners policy excludes automobile accidents.

The insuring agreement for Coverage E makes a very broad grant of coverage. It reads as follows:

> If a claim is made or a suit is brought against any insured for damages because of bodily injury or property damage to which this coverage applies, we will:
> a. pay up to our limit of liability for the damages for which the insured is legally liable; and
> b. provide a defense at our expense . . .

A single limit of liability applies to all claims, whether for bodily injury or for property damage and regardless of the number of claimants. The minimum amount is $25,000. Notice that the insuring agreement makes the limit of liability applicable to the payment of claims, but not to the cost of defending against them.

What persons are insured? The answer is supplied by the Definitions section of the policy. There it says that the word "insured" means the named insured and spouse and, if residents of the household, any relatives and anyone else under 21 who is in the care of any of the other insureds. The Harpers' policy therefore will cover liability claims against Mr. Harper, Mrs. Harper, or Veronica. What about Dustin while he is away at college? He also is covered. He is considered to be a member of the household even though he is temporarily living away from home. He still regards this as his home and returns regularly for vacations. He hasn't yet established a permanent residence elsewhere. Like the rest of the family, he has protection against lawsuits for bodily injury or property damage liability.

Medical Payments to Others

We are familiar with the nature of medical payments insurance because it is one of the coverages provided by automobile policies. We know that it pays medical expenses incurred as the result of an accident and that such expenses are paid without regard to who caused the accident. But we must be careful not to go too far in comparing auto medical payments with homeowners medical payments. There is a crucial difference. Auto medical payments covers the insured family; homeowners medical payments excludes the insured family. That is why Coverage F of the homeowners policy is called **Medical Payments To Others**.

The Coverage F insuring agreement states that coverage does not apply to the named insured, spouse, or regular residents of the household (other than residence employees). For other people, the coverage applies only:

---

a. to a person on the insured location with the permission of any insured; or
b. to a person off the insured location, if the bodily injury:
  (1) arises out of a condition of the insured location . . .
  (2) is caused by the activities of any insured;
  (3) is caused by a residence employee . . . ; or
  (4) is caused by an animal owned by or in the care of any insured.

This provision is not as complicated as it sounds. The first part of Coverage F will pay the medical expenses of other people if they are injured in or around the Harpers' house. The second part of Coverage F will pay the medical expenses of other people if they are injured somewhere else because of some condition of the premises or because of something done by one of the Harpers or by an employee or animal of theirs.

If Mrs. Harper's friend Maureen comes over for coffee and breaks a leg falling down the front steps, the policy will pay for her medical expenses. In this case the coverage applies whether there was anything wrong with the steps or not and regardless of anything that any of the Harpers did or did not do. Maureen was "on the insured location" with permission and was injured; these facts are sufficient to trigger the coverage. But let's say that Dustin and his friend Arnie are tossing a Frisbee. As Maureen is crossing the street to come to the Harpers', the Frisbee curves the wrong way and hits her in the eye. In this case Maureen was not on the Harpers' premises when she was injured. Will the coverage apply? It will if it was Dustin who tossed the Frisbee, because then the injury would have been "caused by the activities" of one of the Harpers. But if Arnie had made the toss the coverage probably would not come into play. (If Arnie's parents had a similar policy its medical payments coverage would apply.) Of course, the Harpers' personal liability coverage would protect them if Maureen sued for damages in any of these cases.

The term "insured location," as used in the Coverage F insuring agreement, is not confined to the home premises. As defined for this coverage, it would include a motel room occupied by one of the Harpers, Dustin's residence hall room, a rented campsite, or even a rented wedding hall. At any such place the medical expenses of a guest would be covered, whether or not an activity of one of the Harpers caused the injury. Remember, though, that the coverage applies anywhere in the world if someone is injured by an action of a member of the Harper family. The amount of medical payments coverage is subject to a stated limit for each person to whom benefits are paid. The minimum limit is $500.

Exclusions

The Section II insuring agreements—especially Coverage E, Personal Liability—make broad, sweeping grants of coverage. Unless they are excluded, any and all bodily injury and property damage claims are covered. Thus, the exclusions are very important, because they determine how broad the coverage really is.

Although exact wording can be obtained only by reading the policy, the following list summarizes and explains the most important of the exclusions:

- The policy excludes payment for injury or damage that is expected or intended by an insured.

    If Harvey has a fight and breaks his neighbor's nose, neither the liability nor the medical payments coverage applies.

- The policy excludes claims involving any insured's business or professional activities.

  These exposures must be insured separately.

- The policy excludes claims involving aircraft, motor vehicles, or watercraft other than small boats within stated size and power limitations.

  Insuring these exposures under this policy would require homeowners premiums to be much higher than they are.

- The policy excludes liability assumed (that is, acquired) under any unwritten contract.

  This exposure is too indefinite to insure. But notice that liability assumed under a **written** contract, such as a lease, is not excluded.

- The policy excludes liability for damage to property owned by the insured.

  Of course, people cannot be legally liable to themselves for damaging their own property. But as defined in the policy "insured" also includes some other people, such as relatives living in the same household. Because of this exclusion, the liability coverage does not cover damage to their property either.

- The policy excludes liability for damage to property rented to, occupied or used by, or in the care of the insured.

  There are two reasons for this exclusion. First, the insurers do not want to pay for losses caused by reckless disregard for other people's property. There is no coverage if Dustin borrows a friend's expensive stereo and leaves it out on the patio during a rainstorm. Nor is there coverage for broken furniture in a Fort Lauderdale motel room rented by Dustin and some of his friends during spring vacation. The second reason for excluding liability protection for property rented to, occupied or used by, or in the care of an insured is that such things may be covered by Section I of the policy. Remember that Coverage C, Personal Property, applies not only to the insured's possessions, but also to personal property "used by" any insured. Losses caused by fire, theft, and many other perils are covered there. There is a notable exception to this exclusion. It does *not* exclude damage to property if the damage is caused by fire, smoke, or explosion. If fire breaks out in a motel room rented by Dustin and he is sued by the motel owner, the personal liability coverage will protect him.

- The policy excludes payments required to be made by the insured under a workers' compensation law.

  However, coverage is provided for suits based on employers liability laws and for medical payments, so long as workers' compensation benefits are not payable. If workers' compensation benefits are to be provided this must be done separately.

The Section II exclusions are long and complicated. One might think that homeowners liability and medical payments coverages exclude many of the things that people need protection for, but that is not the case. It would be impossible to list the wide variety of losses that are covered; they can happen at any time and any place, and can result from almost any sort of activity that people engage in. The policy protects Harvey while he is golfing, Mrs. Harper while she is entertaining, and Dustin while he is camping. It even covers the activities of the family dog. The exclusions are important, but in spite of them the protection is liberal.

Damage to Property of Others

Damage to the property of others, which is shown in the policy as one of the Additional Coverages, is a rather unusual form of insurance. It is no-fault insurance on property that does not belong to the insured. It pays up to $250 for "damage to property of others caused by any insured . . ." Because the protection is automatically included, it is not listed as a separate coverage on the declarations page of the policy.

Almost any sort of damage is covered, so long as it is done by one of the insured persons and is not covered by Section I, the property insurance section of the policy. There are only a few exclusions. Intentional damage is excluded, except for damage caused by insureds under age 13. Damage to property owned by or rented to an insured and losses involving motor vehicles, aircraft, and watercraft are also excluded.

A typical covered loss would be the cost of replacing a neighbor's window broken by Dustin's Frisbee. Another example would be damage to someone's fur coat onto which Veronica spills her hot fudge sundae. Other people's property that is deliberately damaged by an insured's son or daughter under age 13 also would be paid for up to the $250 limit of this coverage. Like medical payments losses, all of these would be paid whether the insureds were legally liable for them or not.

OTHER HOMEOWNERS POLICIES

In our study of home insurance we have concentrated up to now on just one of several homeowners policies, the Broad Form. In addition to the Broad Form, three other standard policies are used to insure private residences owned and occupied by the insured. There also are policies for farmers or ranchers, renters, condominium-unit owners, and mobile home owners.

Private Residence Forms

The four homeowners policies available for owner-occupied houses are listed in Table 10–1. (The missing Form 4 is the tenants policy.) The policies are identical in most respects. Each insures buildings, personal property, and loss of use. Each includes the same coverage for personal liability, medical payments, and damage to property of others. The differences are the perils for which the property is insured.

The property coverage becomes more inclusive as one moves down the policies shown in Table 10–1. That is, the Broad Form covers everything that the Basic Form does and more, the Special Form covers everything that the Broad Form does and more, and the Comprehensive Form covers everything that the Special Form does and more.

The Basic Form provides limited named peril coverages on the buildings and personal property. Damage from the following ten causes is covered: fire or lightning; windstorm or hail; explosion; riot or civil commotion; aircraft; vehicles; smoke; vandalism or malicious mischief; theft; and glass breakage.

The Broad Form (described in Chapter 9) covers the perils just named and seven others. The additional perils are: falling objects; weight of ice, snow, or sleet; collapse; discharge or overflow of water or steam; tearing apart of a heating or air conditioning system; freezing; and damage from artificially generated electricity.

The Special Form furnishes the same property insurance on personal property as the Broad Form. That is, it protects personal property against loss caused by any of the 17 named perils. But it provides all-risk coverage on the house and other buildings. From our study of automobile comprehensive coverage we know the nature of all-risk insurance. We know that it does not literally cover each and every possible loss. Rather, all-risk insurance uses the approach of stating that all losses are covered *except* those that are

Table 10–1 Private Residence Homeowners Policy Forms

POLICY FORM		PROPERTY COVERAGE[a]	
NUMBER	NAME	BUILDINGS	PERSONAL PROPERTY
1	Basic	Limited named peril	Limited named peril
2	Broad	Broad named peril	Broad named peril
3	Special	"All-risk"	Broad named peril
5	Comprehensive	"All-risk"	"All-risk"

[a]Each policy includes personal liability and medical payments insurance.

excluded. This approach is an alternative to naming the perils that *are* covered.

The Comprehensive Form provides all-risk coverage for both the buildings and the personal property. It (and the buildings coverage of the Special Form) excludes earthquake, flood, and most of the other things that are specifically excluded from the Broad Form contract. Thus, it does not cover damage from normal wear and tear, vermin, rust, mold, war, theft of construction materials, freezing unless reasonable care is taken, and so forth. What sorts of losses, then, are paid for by the all-risk coverages that are not insured as named perils? Here are some examples:

- A cat knocks down and breaks an expensive vase.
- A can of paint is spilled, discoloring a wood floor.
- An engagement ring is mangled in a garbage disposer.
- Snow builds up on the edge of a roof, causing melting ice to back up under the shingles, damaging the interior walls and ceiling.

These losses would be covered by all-risk insurance because they involve direct physical damage to insured property and are not excluded. They would not be covered by named peril insurance, even the Broad Form, because they did not result from any of the specified perils.

COST. The cost of homeowners insurance, as might be expected, depends upon the policy form that is selected and the amount of coverage that is purchased. Several less obvious factors also influence the cost. First is the construction of the house. Houses are classified as either brick or frame. Houses constructed of brick, being more fire resistant than frame houses, have a lower rate. Second is the rating of the local fire department. Each community is rated on a scale of one to ten. The better the fire department, the lower the fire insurance rates.[1] Another factor affecting the cost of homeowners insurance is the size and type of deductible. The various types of deductibles are described later in this chapter.

Table 10–2 illustrates the differences among the costs of the four homeowners policies that are used to insure private residences. The premiums would be much higher in rural areas with poor fire protection and in coastal areas where there is greater danger of windstorm damage. Premiums also vary among insurers. Table 10–2 shows that the Comprehensive Form is about twice as expensive as the Basic Form, and that the cost of the other two forms falls between the two extremes.

[1]Pricing is more fully described in Chapter 20.

Table 10–2   Comparison of Annual Premiums for Four Homeowners Policies
Covering Frame Dwellings in One Area

POLICY FORM		AMOUNT OF INSURANCE, COVERAGE A		
NUMBER	NAME	$30,000	$40,000	$50,000
1	Basic"	$105	$149	$193
2	Broad"	133	189	245
3	Special"	148	211	273
5	Comprehensive"	215	305	396

"$50 disappearing deductible on all perils.
"$100 disappearing deductible on all perils.

SELECTION.   Because several different homeowners policies are available, policybuyers are in a position to select the one that suits them best. The choice will depend on the breadth of protection desired and the amount that the buyer is willing to pay. The Harpers chose the Broad Form, as many people do. It provides a reasonable amount of protection at a cost below that of the more liberal policies. Most people believe that the protection that the Broad Form adds as compared with the Basic Form makes the Broad Form worth the extra cost. Also, the Basic Form is not acceptable to some mortgage lenders.

The Comprehensive Form is clearly the "luxury model." It costs a great deal more than the others, more than most people are willing to spend. Buyers who are price-conscious choose one of the others. Increasing numbers of people are selecting the Special Form. It doesn't cost much more than the Broad Form, and all-risk protection on the house may be valuable. For most people, then, the choice is between the Broad Form and the Special Form. Which is the better choice? Only the individual purchaser can answer that question.

Other Residence Policies

People who do not own and occupy a one- or two-family dwelling have different loss exposures than those who do. Therefore, special homeowners policies have been designed for farmers and ranchers, tenants, condominium unit owners, and mobile home dwellers.

FARM OWNERS–RANCH OWNERS POLICY.   Farmers and ranchers can purchase package policies very similar to the Basic and Broad Form contracts used for insuring nonfarm residences. The all-risk forms are not available. Because farms and ranches involve both residential and busines exposures, the policies have some unique features.

Coverage for the farm dwelling and household personal property is practically the same as on the nonfarm residence forms. However, the insurance on the dwelling does not cover replacement cost unless a special endorsement is added. Also, the dwelling coverage does not include trees, shrubs, plants, or lawns.

Farm personal property is insured by a separate coverage. Named peril protection is provided for such things as hay, grain, fertilizer, machinery, farm vehicles, farm records, and livestock. Growing crops are not covered by this policy. An interesting feature is coverage for the electrocution of livestock.

The liability section of the Farm Owners–Ranch Owners policy covers both personal and business liability exposures, including the operation of roadside produce stands. A unique form of protection that can be added by endorsement is Animal Collision insurance. This provides physical damage coverage for cattle, horses, hogs, sheep, and goats that are struck by motor vehicles on public highways.

TENANTS POLICY.   A great many people avoid the care and expense of home ownership by living in rented houses or apartments. John and Alicia Thompson, for instance, are in their mid-twenties and live in a furnished apartment. They own an expensive stereo, a television, dishes, silverware, some kitchen equipment, and fairly extensive wardrobes. The Thompsons don't need to insure the building they live in; their landlord does that. But they do want to protect the things they own. They also want personal liability insurance.

The Thompsons carry a Tenants policy (also called Contents Broad Form or Form 4). It insures their household contents and personal possessions against the same perils that Harvey Harper's Broad Form covers. It includes coverage for additional living expenses if they have to live somewhere else temporarily because of damage to their apartment. The Tenants policy also provides liability and medical payments insurance.

CONDOMINIUM UNIT OWNERS POLICY.   A condominium is the same as an apartment building except that the individual dwelling units are owned by the residents. The rest of the building is owned by the condominium association. This includes the land, entrances, hallways, heating equipment, swimming pool, and so forth.

Although the residents own the dwelling units, the condominium association usually insures the entire building in a single policy. Handling the building insurance that way avoids disputes over whose insurance policy is responsible for which part of the building (in case of damage to the walls between dwelling units, for instance). It also prevents underinsuring or overinsuring the property.

The owner of each condominium unit is responsible for insurance of the contents of the unit. This commonly is accomplished by a special Condominium Unit Owners policy (Homeowners Form 6). The policy is basically the same as the Tenants policy just described. Because of the special nature of condominiums, the policy has some additional features that tailor it to meet the needs of the unit owner.

One special provision of the policy is the Unit Owners Building Additions and Alterations coverage. It provides $1,000 of coverage on such things as wallpaper, permanent floor covering, cabinets, fixtures, and additions within the living unit. These items are part of the building but are not owned by the association, hence the need for special insurance to cover them.

Another unique feature of the Condominium Unit Owners policy is an endorsement for loss assessment coverage. This is needed if, as is likely, the unit owner can be charged for a share of common-area losses. The condominium association agreement or by-laws will indicate whether or not this is the case. For example, if someone is injured in the swimming pool there may be a liability judgment in excess of the limit insured by the association. In that case, each unit owner may be assessed to make up the difference.

Aside from its special features the Condominium Unit Owners policy provides the same coverage as the Tenants policy. Personal property is insured for fire, theft, and other named perils. Additional living expense is covered, and liability and medical payments insurance are provided.

MOBILE HOME OWNERS POLICY.   Special policies are available for those who own and occupy a mobile home at least 10 feet wide and 40 feet long. Smaller trailers and campers are not eligible for this policy; they are insured by endorsing the automobile policy. Again, coverage is similar to that provided by the Homeowners Broad Form. That is, the policy provides broad, named peril protection for the home and contents and also additional living expense, liability, and medical payments coverages.

Coverage A includes all equipment, accessories, appliances, and furniture originally furnished by the manufacturer, as well as the mobile home itself. A collision endorsement is available to cover damage to the home while it is in transit. Incidentally, the theft coverage in homeowners policies applies to the dwelling as well as to personal property. For most insureds it covers theft of any part of their house. For owners of mobile homes, theft of the entire home is a possibility!

The cost of the Mobile Home policy is considerably higher than that for a similar policy covering a conventional house, because the size and construction of mobile homes cause them to be more readily damaged by fire, wind, and hail.

BUYING HOME INSURANCE

Many of the suggestions made in Chapter 8 about buying auto insurance also apply to the purchase of home insurance. It is an important purchase and the buyer should take care to obtain the right policy, to buy the needed amounts of protection, and to select the proper deductible. As with auto insurance, buyers are wise to compare the prices of several different insurers and to seek out an agent who will provide good service.

Additional Premises

One of the differences between homeowners insurance and auto insurance concerns the need for care in stating what property is to be covered. Auto policies are very liberal in covering replacement cars and additional cars acquired during the policy period. One should not assume that home insurance policies are equally liberal in covering different or additional premises. Homeowners policies do not provide automatic coverage for newly acquired homes. If the insured buys a new house either a new policy must be written or the seller's policy must be assigned (by the insurer) to the new owner.

What if an insured family moves to a new home but retains the old one as an investment, renting or leasing it to someone else? Because the house is no longer owner-occupied, it does not qualify for coverage under the homeowners policy forms; the family must use a different policy.

An additional dwelling such as a summer cottage owned by the insured is not automatically covered. It can and should be added to the homeowners policy by endorsement and by the payment of an additional premium.

Deductibles

Most of the states require the Section I coverages (except additional living expense) to be written subject to a deductible amount. The minimum deductible is frequently $100, either as a flat amount or as a disappearing deductible.

Policybuyers always can select a deductible amount larger than the one required in their state. In states where a disappearing deductible is standard a flat deductible can be substituted. The use of a higher deductible always should be considered, because the higher the deductible the lower the premium. For instance, if a $100 flat deductible is substituted for a $50 disappearing deductible, the premium is reduced 10%. The reduction would be 20% for a $250 flat deductible and 25% for a $500 flat deductible. These premium reductions are subject to dollar maximums of $25, $50, and $75 respectively. In other words, the saving for changing from a $50 disappearing deductible to a $100 flat deductible can be no more than $25, and so forth.

Policybuyers should ask their agents to quote premiums based on various deductibles. They should consider the option of saving premium dollars by retaining more of the risk than is required by the standard deductible clause.

The Amount of Insurance

Buying home insurance presents one question that is not involved in buying auto insurance: How much should the property be insured for? As you know, automobiles are automatically insured for their full actual cash value. Collision and comprehensive losses are paid on that basis. But a person who is insuring a home and its contents must decide how much coverage to buy. The higher the amount the more the policy will cost. No one wants to buy more than is necessary, and yet it is important to purchase enough protection so that losses will be adequately covered.

THE HOME.   Inflation and rapid increases in construction costs have caused the cost of home replacement to soar. If a home was purchased 20 years ago, was fully insured then, and is still insured for the same amount, it probably is no more than half insured today. An amazing number of families are that badly underinsured. A survey in one state showed that only one-third of the homeowners carried enough insurance to cover even one-half of the replacement value of their houses![2]

The replacement cost coverage described in Chapter 9 protects property owners against inflationary construction costs, but only if they buy and maintain adequate amounts of insurance. If a house is insured for at least 80% of its replacement value, nothing will be deducted for depreciation if a loss occurs. If less insurance is carried only part of the replacement cost will be paid.

What is replacement cost? It is the cost of replacing the home. More specifically, it is the cost of replacing it with new materials of similar kind and quality at current prices. This definition is simple enough as a concept, but in practice a precise amount may not be easy to determine. If the

[2]*A Family Guide to Property and Liability Insurance* (New York: Insurance Information Institute, 1976), p. 23.

Harpers bought their home for $35,000 five years ago, what is its replacement cost today? We can begin by identifying some things that it is *not*.

Replacement cost is not the same as the current market value of the home. If the Harpers sold their house they would also sell the land it is on, so the market value includes the price of the land. Market value also reflects the supply and demand for housing of this particular type in this particular neighborhood; these factors may be unrelated to replacement costs. The replacement cost is not the appraised tax value either. That figure also includes the value of the land and it is influenced by other things that are not related to insurable value. Nor is replacement cost indicated by the amount of insurance that the mortgage holder requires. The mortgage holder is primarily concerned with protecting its equity in the property. That will be less than full replacement value if a good part of the mortgage has been paid off.

Then how can the replacement cost be determined? There is no way of knowing precisely what it is until and unless the house is actually replaced. But there are several ways that it can be estimated. First, a construction price index can be used. The effect is to increase the original cost of the house by an inflation factor. For example, the factor today in one city and for houses of one particular type built five years ago might be 1.492. If such a house was new when purchased for $35,000 five years ago, application of the factor would indicate that current replacement cost is $35,000 × 1.492, or $52,220. A second method of estimating replacement cost is to calculate the current building cost on a square foot basis. Most insurance agents can provide booklets that indicate the current cost per square foot of various types of building construction. The booklets show how to do the calculations, taking the location and quality of construction into account. This method should give a more accurate figure than is obtained by use of a single inflation factor. The third method is to have the house appraised. It is the most accurate method, but is more expensive than the others. Insurance agents can supply the names of qualified persons who do appraisals for a fee.

The house should be insured (Coverage A) for a minimum of 80% of its estimated replacement cost. In order to maintain the proper amount of coverage the property valuation should be reviewed each year. An endorsement sometimes called the **inflation guard** can be added to the policy to help keep pace with rising costs during the policy term. One version provides an automatic increase in coverage every three months, at the rate of 1% of the original amount or 4% per year. The endorsement increases all of the Section I coverages. Its cost is 1.5% of the annual premium. The inflation guard endorsement can be written to provide a higher rate of increase in some states.

PERSONAL PROPERTY. Homeowners policies insure personal property under Coverage C for an amount equal to at least 50% of the insurance on the house. Actually, there is no reason to assume that 50% is enough. In many cases the Coverage C limit should be increased.

Estimating the value of a family's personal belongings raises two questions: What property do we have, and What is it worth? The same two questions arise after a loss: What was stolen or destroyed, and What was it worth? Both sets of questions can present major problems.

It is easy to say what *should* be done. The family should go through the house and make a careful, detailed inventory of everything that they own. Insurance agents can supply inventory forms that will make this job easier. As additional items are purchased, they should be added to the inventory. The inventory should be kept in a safe deposit box so that it won't be destroyed at the same time the property is. This procedure is what should be done—but almost no one ever does it. It is one of those unpleasant things that usually gets put off until it's too late.

More realistically, home insurance buyers should at least take a few minutes to add up the value of their major possessions: furniture, appliances, dishes, silverware, jewelry, collections, and so forth. They should realize that personal property usually is insured for its actual cash value, that is, that depreciation will be deducted. Even a quick and rough guess at the total value will convince many people of the need to increase their Coverage C protection. Another good idea is to take photographs of the property. After a major loss has occurred it can be surprisingly difficult to remember every item. Photographs taken through the house (with cabinet and closet doors open) can help jog the family's memory later. The photographs also will be helpful evidence to present to the claim adjuster.

The standard homeowners policies are designed to cover the ordinary exposures that most families have. In most cases the policies serve this purpose very well. However, many families have unusual exposures, particularly of certain kinds of personal property. For them, other insurance may be needed. It should not be assumed that only wealthy families have unusual insurance needs. Many people, for instance, have coin collections. Remember that homeowners policies limit coverage on money, including coin collections, to $100. Also, there is a $500 maximum on securities, stamps, boats, and trailers. Theft coverage is limited to $500 for jewelry, watches, and furs, and to $1,000 for silverware and guns.

Additional coverage for certain property can be provided by adding the **Scheduled Personal Property endorsement** to a homeowners policy. Insurance for nine categories of property can be written in this way: jewelry, furs, cameras and photographic equipment, musical instruments, silverware, golfer's equipment, fine arts, stamp collections, and coin collections. The

Scheduled Personal Property endorsement provides all-risk coverage and applies worldwide. It contains various provisions appropriate to each type of property. There is no coverage for the fading or creasing of postage stamps, for instance, and golf balls are insured only against fire and burglary (no coverage for losing them in the rough!). Valuable items such as furs or diamonds are scheduled; that is, they are specifically described and insured for a stated amount. The endorsement insures only those categories and items of property that the purchaser buys coverage for.

LIABILITY. The basic limit of liability provided by Coverage E is $25,000. For many people, particularly those who have substantial income and property, that is not enough. The amount should be at least as much as the limit of one's auto liability protection. The cost of higher limits is small: $2 per year for $100,000 and $6 for $300,000.

Without special endorsement, the liability and medical payments coverages do not apply to the business or profession of any insured, even if it is conducted in the home. The insured may be a doctor, lawyer, or architect and have an office in the home, or a private teacher may give piano lessons or dance lessons there. The policy can be extended by endorsement to cover such exposures.

Shopping for Home Insurance

Most of the things that Chapter 7 suggested about shopping for auto insurance also apply to home insurance. Few people shop around for their home insurance. They think that all insurers charge the same prices. They are wrong to think so and may pay more than they need to as a result. A publication of the New York Insurance Department put it this way: "The cost of homeowners insurance for any particular dwelling can vary widely from company to company. Thus, in purchasing homeowners insurance, the consumer who shops is likely to get much more value for his insurance dollars than the consumer who doesn't shop."[3]

The range of prices, although not as great as for automobile policies, is substantial. The New York Insurance Department reported the prices that each of the twenty largest insurers in that state would charge for a Homeowners Broad Form policy covering a frame dwelling for $30,000. In upstate New York localities with good fire protection, the prices ranged from $96 to $125. In Brooklyn the range was from $141 to $221.[4] More than 200 other

[3]*Competition in Homeowners Insurance in New York State* (New York: New York Department of Insurance), p. 20.
[4]*Consumers Shopping Guide for Homeowners Insurance* (New York: New York Department of Insurance, 1977).

companies write homeowners policies in New York, in addition to the 20 that were surveyed. If all of the companies were checked a greater range of prices would undoubtedly be found.

An additional factor that insurance buyers always should bear in mind is agency service. Saving a few dollars is not a good deal if the agent doesn't know enough or isn't willing to take the time to give proper advice. People who save $25 on their policies but aren't told how to insure their coin collections or motor boats properly are likely to lose money in the long run. It's a good idea to shop for a policy, but only from among good insurance agents.

THE PERSONAL UMBRELLA LIABILITY POLICY

Taken together, the liability coverages of an auto policy and a homeowners policy can provide a great deal of protection. But some people should have an additional policy—a **personal umbrella liability policy.**

General Nature

The policy is called an umbrella because it extends broad protection above that which is furnished by other policies. Actually, the umbrella does two things. First, it provides extra ("excess") amounts of coverage over the protection furnished by the insured's other liability policies. Second, it provides protection for liability claims that are not covered at all by the insured's other policies.

Umbrella policies usually have limits of $1 million or more. The companies that write them require the insured to have underlying insurance on the major exposures, including auto, homeowners, and (if the exposures exist) such things as watercraft, aircraft, and recreational vehicles.

Losses Covered

Some examples of covered losses will illustrate the value of the policy. First, the insured's car is left improperly parked on a hill. It rolls down the hill and smashes into a car filled with children. The insured, who has a $300,000 per occurence auto liability insurance limit, ends up with judgments totaling $500,000. The underlying auto policy pays its $300,000 maximum and the umbrella pays the $200,000 in excess of that amount.

In another case the insured makes derogatory statements in public about the character and competence of a well-known physician. The physician brings a $750,000 lawsuit for slander. This case illustrates the second aspect of umbrella protection because none of the insured's underlying liability policies covers slander. For this claim the umbrella coverage extends down to a deductible amount, often $250, that is stated in the contract. If the case is settled for say, $50,000, the umbrella will pay the entire amount less only the deductible. Examples of other exposures not covered by underlying liability insurance might include assault and battery, invasion of privacy, operation of automobiles outside the United States and Canada, or operation of nonowned aircraft.

Cost

Umbrella protection costs much less than one might expect, because most claims are fully covered by the underlying policies. The cost frequently is in the $50 to $100 per year range.

Although almost anyone could be hit by an enormous or unusual lawsuit, certain individuals are more likely targets than others. Well-known or wealthy persons are in that category and should seriously consider purchasing a personal umbrella liability policy.

IMPORTANT TERMS

Personal liability coverage
Medical payments to others
Damage to property of others
Inflation guard endorsement

Scheduled personal property endorsement
Personal umbrella liability policy

KEY POINTS TO REMEMBER

1. Three coverages are provided by Section II of homeowners policies: personal liability, medical payments, and damage to property of others.
2. The personal liability coverage defends against and pays the cost of liability claims. The principal exclusions are claims involving business or professional activities or automobiles.
3. The medical payments coverage pays the bills of people other than insured persons who are injured on the premises. The coverage applies away from the premises for people injured by an insured or by an insured's employee or animal.
4. The insurance for damage to the property of others pays up to $250 for other people's property damaged by one of the insureds. Payment is made regardless of fault.
5. Thorough understanding of the Section II coverages requires knowledge of the policy exclusions.
6. Four standard homeowners policies are available for insuring private residences. In order of increasing cost and breadth of protection, they are the Basic, Broad, Special, and Comprehensive Forms.

7. The Basic and Broad Forms insure both buildings and personal property against damage by named perils. The Special Form provides all-risk coverage on buildings and named peril coverage on personal property. The Comprehensive Form insures both buildings and personal property on the all-risk basis.
8. The cost of homeowners insurance depends on the policy form, the amount of insurance, the deductible, the construction of the house, the rating of the local fire department, and the company writing the policy.
9. Specially designed homeowners policies are used to insure farmers and ranchers, tenants, condomimium unit owners, and mobile home owners. Each insures the exposures that are typical of the particular type of residence.
10. Consumers should decide how much insurance to buy on the basis of careful estimates of the replacement cost of the home and the actual cash value of the personal property.
11. An inflation guard endorsement increases the amount of the Section I coverages automatically to help keep pace with inflation.
12. In shopping for homeowners insurance it is wise to make price comparisons, but consumers should also realize the value of good agency service.
13. The personal umbrella liability policy protects against extremely high liability claims in excess of the coverage provided by underlying policies. It also covers unusual liability claims that are not otherwise insured.

REVIEW QUESTIONS

Which of the following losses (Questions 1–10) would be covered by Section II of the Harpers' Broad Form homeowners policy? If a loss is covered, explain which policy provision applies. If a loss is not covered, explain why not.
1. The Harpers' dog bites the mailman.
2. The dog bites Harvey.
3. A bonfire in the back yard gets out of control and damages the neighbor's garage.
4. Veronica accidentally rips a coat that she had borrowed from a friend.
5. Veronica accidentally rips her own coat.
6. A young child of some friends who are visiting the Harpers climbs a tree in the yard. He slips and falls to the ground, breaking a leg.
7. While rabbit hunting, Dustin accidentally shoots a companion in the foot.
8. Harvey backs the car over the paper boy's bicycle, which had been left in the driveway.
9. Dustin borrows a friend's outboard motor and puts it on a rented boat. In the middle of the lake the motor works loose from the boat and sinks in 20 feet of water.
10. Mrs. Harper takes a dish of chicken salad to a church dinner. After several people suffer serious food poisoning, the cause is traced to the chicken salad.

* * * * *

11. What is the main difference between automobile medical payments coverage and homeowners medical payments coverage?
12. How does the Tenants Form differ from the regular Homeowners Broad Form?

13. Why is the Comprehensive Form called the luxury model?

14. Why do condominium dwellers need a different policy form?

15. Does the Harpers' homeowners policy automatically cover any property that they buy during the policy period?

16. With a $100 disappearing deductible, how much would be paid for an $80 loss? A $300 loss? A $600 loss?

17. High winds blow a large tree onto an insured's house. The contractor's bill for repairs is $3,000. The house cost $30,000 when it was new 10 years ago. Present market value is $50,000. Replacement cost is estimated to be $45,000. Depreciation is estimated at 20%. A homeowners policy is in force, with $40,000 applicable to Coverage A. The policy has a $100 flat deductible. How much will be paid for the tree damage?

18. How much would have been paid for the tree damage in Question 7 if the house had been insured for $30,000?

19. What are the three ways to estimate the replacement cost of a house?

DISCUSSION QUESTIONS

1. Some banks and other mortgage lenders do not accept the Basic Form of homeowners policy. Why are they interested in the type of policy purchased by the owner of a house?

2. What is the logic of disappearing deductibles? In other words, in what way do they make good sense?

3. If you were an insurance agent, would you advise your clients to use small deductibles or larger deductibles on their home insurance policies?

4. Why aren't houses simply insured for their actual cash value at the time of loss as automobiles are, so that policy buyers wouldn't have to worry about how much coverage to buy?

5. An insurance agent is explaining the "inflation guard" endorsement to a client. He says, "Of course, the endorsement by itself won't necessarily guard you against being underinsured." What does he mean? Why won't it?

6. What specific agency services are valuable to buyers of home insurance?

7. Houses are insured for their full replacement cost if enough insurance is carried, but personal property usually is insured only for its actual cash value, regardless of the amount of coverage purchased. Why isn't replacement cost coverage as widely available for personal property as it is for houses? Can you think of any reasons why insurers would hesitate to cover the full replacement cost of personal property?

8. Some examples of losses that would be covered by an all-risk policy but not by a named peril policy were given in the chapter. What are some others?

CHAPTER 11
HEALTH
INSURANCE

Private health insurance protects more than 80% of the American people and, for most of them, the protection is very important. Nevertheless, many people know very little about health insurance—even their own policies. Take Charlie Newlin, for instance. Charlie, 25 years old, works for Metro Industries as a computer programmer. His wife Ruth, who is 23, works part-time in a doctor's office. Their daughter Julie is 2 years old. It is Sunday morning. Sitting at the breakfast table, Charlie searches for the sports section of the newspaper. As he flips through the thick Sunday edition, an advertisement from an insurance company falls out. "$1,000 a Month Tax-Free Cash While You Are in the Hospital," it says. "$250,000 for Any Hospital Stay Lasting 250 Months!" Part of the ad is a letter from a famous television performer. "Dear Friend," the letter begins, "The costs of being hospitalized have probably gone way beyond your present insurance protection. I recommend this policy as a way of keeping up with today's skyrocketing hospital and medical costs." There is a "handwritten" postscript at the end of the letter: "During this Limited Enrollment Period, you can get your first month's coverage for only 25¢!"

"Hey, that might not be a bad deal," thinks Charlie. He knows he is covered by a group insurance policy at Metro Industries, and he remembers that when Julie was born the policy paid only about two-thirds of their doctor and hospital bills. Also, he recalls hearing one of the guys at work complaining that their insurance is not good enough. That evening Charlie fills out the application and sends it to the company. Since the first month he has been paying $13.55 every month to continue the policy.

Charlie's intentions are the very best. He wants adequate protection for himself and his family. But he doesn't really know what he is doing. He doesn't know what coverage he already has under the group policy, he doesn't know what additional protection he needs, and he doesn't understand what he is getting under the new policy. The chances are very good that he has done the wrong thing and that he would be better off buying a different policy.

This chapter deals with the things that Charlie should have looked into. It considers the need for health insurance, the kinds of policies that are available, and the purposes the various policies serve. In addition, it suggests some things to look for (and to look out for) when buying health insurance.

THE COSTS OF MEDICAL CARE

The advertisement that Charlie read was right about one thing. The costs of accidents and illnesses indeed have skyrocketed. Total outlays for medical care in 1965 were less than $40 billion, or about 6% of the nation's total spending for all goods and services. By 1979 the medical care bill exceeded $200 billion—over 9% of the gross national product. In 1979 this came to $920 per person or $3680 for a family of four. Table 11–1 indicates how the costs of various kinds of medical care have increased. As Table 11–2 shows, the length of the average hospital stay changed very little during recent years. As a result, the average cost per patient stay increased at about the same rate as the average cost per patient day.

The importance of the health risk and the need for health insurance stem from the fact that the actual costs of any particular family are unpredictable. Although the medical costs of all Americans average about $920 a year, in any given year many people will have far less than that. But some, of course, will have far more. Surveys show that the medical expenses of 6 families out of 100 exceed 20% of their annual income. And 1 or 2 out of 100 have expenses greater than half of their income! Expenses like these usually cannot be foreseen and few families have savings sufficient to pay them. Thus health insurance is extremely important to almost everyone.

Table 11–1 Personal Spending for Medical Care
(billions of dollars)

TYPE OF EXPENSE	1966	1971	1976
Hospital	$ 9.4	$20.4	$43.4
Physicians	8.5	14.2	26.4
Medicines	6.5	8.5	12.6
Dentists	2.9	4.9	8.9
Other	4.5	5.3	12.5
Total	$31.8	$53.4	$103.7

Note: Totals do not equal sums of items due to rounding.
Source: *Source Book of Health Insurance Data 1977–78* (New York: Health Insurance Institute), p. 52.

Table 11–2 Average Costs of Community Hospitals

	1966	1971	1976
Cost per patient day	$48.15	$92.31	$172.70
Average length of stay (days)	7.1	8.0	7.7
Cost per patient stay	$380.39	$738.48	$1330.10

Source: *Source Book of Health Insurance Data 1977–78* (New York: Health Insurance Institute), p. 60.

TYPES OF HEALTH INSURANCE

Health insurance provides benefits in the event of accident or sickness. Most policies apply to both perils, although some cover accidents only. Policies covering sickness but not accident are not widely sold.

Most health insurance benefits are provided by **group policies** covering the employees of a business or other organization. Group coverage usually applies automatically to all persons employed by organizations having group policies in force. **Individual policies** (covering one person or one family) are purchased by people not covered by group plans. They also are used by people like Charlie Newlin to supplement the coverage provided by group policies. Individual policies often are obtained from the same agents who handle the rest of a family's personal insurance needs. For reasons explained in Chapter 15, group coverage is more economical than individual policies. Over 80% of all health insurance benefits are paid by group contracts.

Two different risks are associated with illness and accident: the risk of incurring high costs of treatment, and the risk of losing income during a period of disability. Health insurance can handle both of these risks.

There are five types of health insurance protection:

1. Hospital expense insurance
2. Surgical expense insurance
3. Regular medical expense insurance
4. Major medical insurance
5. Disability income insurance

The first four of the above types deal with the costs of treatment; the fifth insures against loss of income. Each of the five can be furnished by either group or individual policies.

Hospital Expense Insurance

Hospital expense insurance is the most widespread form of health insurance protection. It pays the costs incurred while an insured person is in a hospital. It usually applies to hospitalization for either illness or accident. Benefits include the charge for room and board and for various hospital services and supplies. Physicians' and surgeons' charges are not included. The room and board benefit is provided for a stated number of days, such as 60, 120, or 180. Coverage for other hospital charges varies from one policy to another; it includes some or all of such things as drugs, laboratory services, x-ray, and use of an operating room. A separate amount often is specified for maternity benefits. Coverage usually applies to the named insured, spouse, and dependent children under age 18 or 21. Group policies exclude accidents and illnesses for which workers' compensation benefits are payable. Individual policies sometimes contain a similar exclusion.

Benefits can be provided on one of three bases: **reimbursement, valued,** or **service.** The reimbursement basis pays for actual charges up to a stated maximum. An example is a policy providing "up to $100 a day." A valued policy pays a stated amount regardless of what the actual charges were. A contract paying "at the rate of $100 a day" is a valued policy. The third benefit basis provides for certain hospital services without stating any dollar amount. Such a contract might simply pay the costs of "semiprivate accommodations" and the full cost of certain stated hospital services. This is the basis ordinarily used by Blue Cross plans.

There are about 80 **Blue Cross** plans. Each is a nonprofit association originally sponsored by a group of hospitals in its area and providing protection against the costs of hospital care. The Blue Cross plans compete with insurance companies, each system providing roughly half of the hospital expense coverage. Most Blue Cross coverage is provided by group contracts. Benefits are paid directly to the hospital on the service basis. In other words, a particular plan might furnish up to 120 days of care in a semiprivate room by a participating hospital. Persons covered by the plan would not be billed by the hospital; instead, the hospital would be reimbursed directly by Blue Cross.

Surgical Expense Insurance

Surgical expense insurance usually is furnished by a policy which also covers hospital expense; it seldom is insured separately. The amount of coverage is stated in a schedule that is part of the policy. For instance, a schedule might include the following:

Appendectomy	$240
Mastoidectomy	$300
Gall Bladder Removal	$400
Total Gastrectomy	$600
Tonsillectomy	$120

The full schedule would list 50 or more common operations. Other operations would be paid for on the basis of their difficulty relative to the ones listed. The amounts of coverage vary from one policy to another, but payment for less costly operations always is scaled down proportionally from the most expensive ones. On one policy the amount paid for the most expensive operation might be $800, payment for other operations being scaled downward from that amount; on another policy the highest payment might be $2,000.

Blue Shield plans compete with insurance companies in providing surgical benefits just as Blue Cross plans compete with them in providing hospitalization benefits. Most of the Blue Shield plans were organized by state or local medical societies. In some cases the Blue Cross and Blue Shield organizations work together in enrolling new members, handling records, and processing claims. Blue Shield benefits are provided on either the reimbursement or the service basis. In some plans the participating doctors agree to accept Blue Shield benefits as full payment for their services if the family's income is below a specified amount (such as $18,000). If the scriber's income is greater than that amount, the benefit is deducted from physician's charges. Like Blue Cross, Blue Shield plans usually operate in ingle state or part of a state. Many of them have agreements with plans in her areas so that a subscriber who needs the services of a hospital or nysician away from home is covered by the plan where the services are rovided. This problem of course does not arise when health insurance is rovided by an insurance company.

Regular   ical Expense Insurance

egu'   Medical Expense Insurance—sometimes called physicians' .se insurance—pays the fees charged by a doctor for nonsurgical care iven in a home, the doctor's office, or in a hospital. A maximum number of isits and a rate per visit are specified. For instance, coverage might be at the rate of $10 per visit for up to 30 visits per year. The usual method of providing the coverage is to add it to a group policy that furnishes hospital and surgical benefits.

Major Medical Expense Insurance

The forms of health insurance described so far have a major shortcoming: they provide limited amounts of protection. You probably know of a person who has had an extremely serious accident or illness. Following very expensive surgery this person perhaps was in the intensive care unit of a hospital, was treated with costly drugs, and required special nursing care. The cost of such treatment can be staggering and can far exceed the reimbursement available from hospital and surgical expense insurance. **Major medical expense insurance** is designed to meet the financial demands of such catastrophic illnesses and accidents. The policies have four distinguishing features:

1. Broad coverage
2. Very high limits
3. A deductible
4. Percentage participation

The broad coverage of major medical policies assures that almost any kind of medical expense is paid. In addition to hospital and physicians' charges, the policies usually cover the cost of nursing care, drugs, blood transfusions, oxygen, radiology, laboratory charges, artificial limbs, wheelchairs, and so forth.

The maximum amount payable by a major medical contract may be as low as $5,000, but generally is much higher. Many policies have limits of $100,000 or $250,000 and some have no stated maximum at all. The limit may apply either for each accident or illness, or per year.

The deductible utilizes the retention method of risk management by eliminating coverage for small, relatively frequent illnesses and accidents. It is one of the things that holds the cost of major medical insurance down to a reasonable level. The deductible may be either of two types, initial or corridor. An **initial deductible** applies to the first dollars of medical expenses. It is substantial in amount, often $250, $500, or more. The policyholder must pay this initial amount (per disability or per year, depending on how the policy is written) before the policy takes over. The **corridor deductible** is used when a group major medical policy is coordinated with group hospital and surgical coverage. In this case the major medical policy excludes whatever benefits are provided by the underlying coverage and the corridor deductible excludes an amount (frequently $100) in excess of the basic coverage. In other words, a major medical policy with a $100 corridor deductible would apply to medical costs that were greater than the underlying hospital and surgical benefit plus $100.

The percentage participation feature (sometimes called coinsurance) also utilizes the risk retention method. Under percentage participation the insured and the insurer split the costs in excess of the deductible. The insured usually pays 20 or 25%. Percentage participation is an important aspect of major medical because it gives the policyholder an incentive to avoid unnecessary expenses, which helps to hold down the amount of loss payments.

To illustrate the working of major medical, let us assume that an insured has medical expenses totaling $8,000 and is covered by a policy with a

$50,000 limit, a $250 initial deductible, and 80/20 percentage participation. Payment would be as follows:

$8,000	Expenses
250	Initial deductible
7,750	Balance after deductible
1,550	20% paid by policyholder
$6,200	80% paid by major medical

In this case the policyholder pays the $250 deductible plus $1,550, a total of $1,800.

Now let us consider a major medical policy that is coordinated with a basic hospital and surgical expense policy. If the major medical has a $100 corridor deductible and the basic insurance covers $3,000 of the $8,000 in medical expenses, payment would be computed like this:

$8,000	Expenses
3,000	Paid by hospital and surgical expense policy
5,000	Balance after basic policy
100	Corridor deductible
4,900	Balance after deductible
980	20% paid by policyholder
$3,920	80% paid by major medical

Here the policyholder pays the $100 deductible plus $980, a total of $1,080. The existence of the basic hospital and surgical expense policy reduces the amount paid by both the policyholder and the major medical policy; it also reduces the cost of the major medical policy.

In both of these examples the insured has retained substantial portions of the risk. But paying a bill of $1,080, or even $1,800, is not the immense burden that an $8,000 expense would be. And remember that the purpose of major medical insurance is to protect against unusual, very expensive accidents or illnesses. In fact, it is well to think of this coverage as one that a family would hope never to have to collect from. By arranging the contract so that (a) it does not cover the smaller cases at all and (b) the insured participates in paying the costs of the big cases, the cost of major medical insurance is held down. It is these two features that make it possible to provide high limits of coverage at a reasonable cost. The success of this approach is indicated by the fact that about 100 million Americans now have major medical insurance.

A new form of major medical called **comprehensive major medical** combines basic hospital and surgical coverage with regular major medical protection as a single coverage. Written primarily on the group basis, comprehensive major medical has the four features of major medical discussed earlier, but a very small deductible, perhaps only $25 or $50. It thus covers both the common, less expensive cases (in excess of the small deductible) and the unusual, very costly accidents and illnesses. This of course is expensive insurance. It is financially feasible for most people only on a group basis under which their employers pay part or all of the cost.

Disability Income Insurance

The types of health insurance that we have examined pay for expenses associated with illnesses and accidents. Replacement of income lost during a period of disability can be even more important than paying the expenses of medical care. The ability to work and earn an income is crucial, particularly to a person who is supporting a family. It is a sad fact, however, that this exposure is seldom insured adequately. Although about 80 million people have some disability income protection, most are covered only for short periods. Only about 18 million Americans have policies that pay for more than two years of disability. The primary reason for this is that adequate coverage for long-term disability is expensive. To hold down the cost, some policies have restrictive provisions. Therefore, it is important to examine and to understand the terms of disability income insurance.

BENEFITS.   **Disability income policies** provide weekly or monthly payments during the period that the insured is disabled. Most policies cover disability due to either accident or sickness, but some are limited to disability resulting from an accident. Accident-only policies obviously are much more restrictive; they are popular simply because they are much less expensive.

The amount payable for a period of covered disability is governed by three provisions: the amount paid per week or per month, the length of the benefit period, and the length of the waiting period. Each of the three provisions differs from one policy to another. A policy might provide for payments of $25 a week, $100 a week, $1,000 a month, or some other amount. Long-term policies sometimes pay 60% or some other portion of the insured's average monthly earnings. The benefit period can range from 13 or 26 weeks to a lifetime. Many long-term policies pay a disabled policyholder until age 65, when social security retirement benefits take over. The **waiting**

period is the length of time between the beginning of a disability and the start of the policy's benefit payments. It acts as a deductible, eliminating coverage for the frequent, less-serious disabilities. Waiting periods range all the way from three days to six months.

Each of the factors that has been mentioned affects both the cost and the adequacy of disability income protection. The factors can be combined in countless different ways. One policy might cover disability due to accidents only and pay $25 a week for up to 26 weeks following a two-week waiting period; another policy might cover disability due to either accident or sickness and pay $200 a week for life after a six-month waiting period. Company underwriting rules seek to prevent issuance of policies with benefits so high that policyholders would have as much or more income while disabled as they would have while working.

DEFINITION OF ACCIDENT. Policies may state either that they cover injury caused by "accidental means" or that they cover losses due to "accidental bodily injury." The former wording is intended to provide more limited coverage than the latter. The distinction between the two phrases is becoming less important than it previously was because some courts interpret both wordings in the more liberal sense.

In cases where the courts permit the distinction, an injury caused by **accidental means** is one the cause of which was accidental and unexpected, whereas in an **accidental bodily injury** only the result (the injury itself) has to be accidental and unexpected. To illustrate, a man is mowing his lawn with a power mower. He slips, his foot goes under the mower and is badly cut. His resulting disability would be covered by a policy using either definition of disability because both the cause of the injury (his slip) and the injury itself were accidental and unexpected. But assume that he had injured his back while lifting the mower up to a terraced section of the lawn. In this case the resulting disability would be covered by a policy written on the accidental bodily injury basis because the injury was accidental, but it would not be covered by an accidental means policy because even though the injury was accidental, the cause (lifting the mower) was not.

DEFINITION OF DISABILITY. The manner in which disability is defined is extremely important because it may determine whether or not an insured will receive income payments. Many different definitions are used, ranging from hospital confinement to the inability to perform one's regular occupation. A policy using the former definition of course would be much less valuable than one using the latter definition.

Modern long-term disability income policies frequently use two definitions of disability, one for the first two years that the insured is disabled and the other for disability extending for a greater length of time. For the first two years the disabled insured must be unable to perform the duties of his or her regular occupation. If the disability continues beyond two years, the benefits are paid only if the insured is unable to engage in *any* occupation "for which he or she is reasonably fitted by training and experience." If a policy so written covered a dentist who lost the use of one hand, benefits probably would be paid for two years only. After that period the dentist presumably would be able to do a different kind of suitable work, such as teaching or selling dental equipment and supplies. This is a reasonable provision; without a more restrictive definition of continuing disability, an insured's total income from a new occupation plus the policy benefits might be more than it was before the disability began.

Obviously, a policy using the definitions just discussed is far superior to one that defines disability as confinement to a hospital or to home. However, many policies, especially those covering short-term disabilities, contain one of the more restrictive definitions. The "$1,000 a Month" policy that Charlie Newlin bought is an example. Such a contract is called a hospital income policy.

POLICY PROVISIONS

There are no standard health insurance policies comparable to those in automobile and home insurance. State laws require certain standard provisions, but so many optional provisions are permitted and there are so many different coverages, benefits, and definitions that standardization does not really exist in the health insurance field. Thus, the only way a person buying individual health insurance can know what coverage a particular policy provides is to examine it carefully. Among the other provisions that the potential buyer should review are those concerning pre-existing conditions, other insurance, and policy continuation. Note that these are provisions of individual—not group—policies.

Pre-Existing Conditions

No one would expect to be able to buy fire insurance for a building that was on fire. Likewise, health insurance cannot pay benefits for illnesses that the insured knew about before the policy was purchased. To prevent such payments, individual policies contain **pre-existing conditions clauses** that exclude coverage for physical conditions that existed before the policy began. In the better policies the clause pertains only to illnesses and excludes only those illnesses that had manifested themselves (that is, that were known of) before the effective date of the policy. Thus, if an applicant had cancer when applying for a policy, but the cancer had not yet been discovered, the policy would cover claims arising from the cancer. The pre-existing conditions clause in more restrictive policies sometimes relates to both accident and illness and excludes coverage for any condition that the insured had before the policy's inception, whether it had manifested itself or not. Such a policy would not cover the previously undiscovered cancer, nor would it cover complications that developed after the policy began from a fall or an automobile crash if the accident had occurred before the policy began.

To reinforce the pre-existing conditions provision, many policies also include a clause called a **probationary period** or elimination period. This states that benefits will not be paid for illness that begins during a period (sometimes 30 days) starting with the effective date of the policy.

Other Insurance

In our study of property-casualty insurance, we saw several applications of the indemnity principle. Subrogation, for instance, is designed to prevent overpayment of property insurance losses. Overpayment is a potential problem in health insurance also. The problem takes the form of what is called malingering, the tendency of a person being paid as much or more while disabled as while working to prolong the "disability." "Why should I go back to work," such a person might say, "when I can make more money staying at home."

The principal method of preventing overpayment in health insurance takes the form of underwriting rules designed to prevent overinsurance. Application forms usually inquire about other policies currently in force from which the applicant could secure similar benefits. Company underwriters restrict the writing of additional coverage when the total amount would be excessive. This approach has to be relied upon because many health insurance policies do not have other insurance provisions. That is, they don't limit the total recovery to the amount of the loss. Some policies do contain other insurance clauses. These reduce the payments to the policy's pro rata share of the insured's actual expenses if other insurance is found to be available when a claim is presented. Such provisions are difficult to enforce, because insureds may be able to conceal the existence of other policies.

Because the indemnity principle is not always effectively applied, overinsurance can create two problems. The first is malingering and the resulting overutilization of medical services and exaggeration of claims. In addition to creating unnecessary demands upon doctors and hospitals, these cause higher claim payments and higher insurance costs. The second problem created by overinsurance is unwise insurance buying. People are motivated to buy the kinds of insurance that they believe they can profit from. These are not always the kinds that would provide the best protection. For example, a family might purchase a second hospital expense policy when they really would be better off buying a major medical policy instead.

Continuation Provisions

Continuation provisions, which relate to the period for which the company must continue to provide the protection, are extremely important. For instance, if an insured develops heart illness will the policy be continued? The answer depends on the continuation provision. Individual health insurance policies have one of the following five types of continuation provisions:

1. Cancelable
2. Optionally renewable
3. Conditionally renewable
4. Guaranteed renewable
5. Noncancelable

Cancelable policies can be canceled by the insurer at any time and for any reason. Such policies are rare and are prohibited by the laws of some states.

An optionally renewable policy is not much better than a cancelable one. It is written for a one-year term and the insurer can decline to renew it for another year for any reason. A person with such a policy who changed to a more hazardous occupation or developed an adverse health condition would be able to do nothing about it if the insurer refused to continue the policy.

A conditionally renewable policy is one that the company can refuse to renew, but for certain stated conditions only, such as a change in the insured's occupation. Also classed as conditionally renewable policies are those providing that renewal will not be refused solely because of a change in the insured's physical condition. The latter type has been criticized because major changes in a person's physical condition often require other changes, such as in occupation, which could be used by the company as grounds to refuse renewal.

Guaranteed renewable policies must be continued by the company until the insured is a stated age, often 65. The premium rates are not guaranteed but can be increased only for an entire class (that is, a similarly rated group) of insureds. This provision is more expensive than the previous three, but it provides superior protection. The insurer can neither cancel the policy nor refuse to renew it and an individual policyholder cannot be singled out for an increase in premium. The company's retention of the right to increase the premium for all insureds in a class is a reasonable provision. Without it, the company would have no way to handle inflationary increases in health care costs or widespread increases in disability claims.

Noncancelable policies, as the term is used in health insurance, not only cannot be canceled by the company but also are guaranteed renewable **and have a fixed premium**. The premium cannot be increased, even for an entire class of insureds. Noncancelable policies therefore are more favorable to policyholders than guaranteed renewable policies, even though their name doesn't imply that to be the case. During the 1920s many "noncan" (as they are called) disability income policies were sold. Then came the Great Depression of the 1930s. The insurers sustained huge increases in claims and heavy underwriting losses; some even went broke. The underwriters said that too many policyholders lost their jobs because of the depression, became "disabled," and stayed "disabled" until the depression ended and they again could find employment. Since then, "noncan" health insurance, when available, has been very expensive. Most companies prefer to issue guaranteed renewable policies that give them the right to increase premiums for classes of policyholders.

BUYING HEALTH INSURANCE

Remember Charlie Newlin and his $1,000 a month hospital income policy? By now it should be more clear why we suggested that he may have made a mistake in buying it. At the very least, he should have investigated his purchase more carefully. First, he should have determined exactly what protection is provided by his group coverage. He might want additional protection, but he should choose it to meet the specific needs not covered by his group contract. Then, Charlie should have examined the provisions of the hospital income policy. He was attracted by the idea of being paid $1,000 a month. Did he realize that this is only $33.33 a day? Did he know (as Table 11–2 shows) that $33.33 is less than one-fifth of the average daily hospital cost? The advertisement said the policy would pay him as much as $250,000. Did Charlie weigh the importance of insuring other losses? Did he check to see what pre-existing conditions were excluded? Did he read the advertisement closely enough to see that the policy won't cover the first five days of hospitalization for sickness? And did he consider this waiting period in relation to the fact that, as Table 11–2 also shows, the average hospital stay is less than eight days? Of course, Charlie may have done all of these things and may still have concluded that this policy was the one for him. If so, we certainly won't say that he is wrong. And if he wants to make his insurance buying decisions without weighing the alternatives, that's his business, but we would recommend a more thoughtful approach.

Applying the Rules of Personal Risk Management

Health insurance can be purchased with either of two objectives in mind, to insure small losses or to insure large losses. Few people can afford to insure

"MY POLICY COVERS A COUPLE OF ASPIRIN, SOME BAND AIDS AND A HOT WATER BOTTLE. IT'S CALLED 'MINOR MEDICAL'."

both. Most health policies pay for relatively small losses. They provide what is called **first-dollar coverage;** that is, they pay starting from the first dollar of loss incurred by the insured. First-dollar coverage is attractive to many people because they expect to get back in losses during the year much or all of what the policy costs. This goal is understandable, but it is not economical. It is very much like buying automobile collision coverage with no deductible (if that were possible). Insuring the small frequent losses is uneconomical because it is impossible for all insureds as a group to get their premium dollars back. It costs a great deal of money to operate an insurance company, and the cost of company operations comes out of premium dollars. Because minor illnesses and accidents are bound to happen, it is better to budget for them, to retain the risk and pay these costs out of regular income. Handling small losses that way avoids having to pay part of an insurance company's operating expenses.

The foregoing is of course an application of the first and second rules of personal risk management: insure the major risks first and don't insure small losses. As explained in Chapter 3, those who use these rules make efficient use of the basic insurance idea of substituting a small known expense (the premium) for the possibility of large, unpredictable losses.

Purchasing major medical coverage is consistent with the risk management concept. The large deductible eliminates first-dollar coverage and (along with the percentage participation feature) makes it possible to insure very large losses at a reasonable cost. Many wise insurance buyers base their health insurance programs on the major medical policy. They cover the big losses first and then consider supplementing their major medical insurance with other coverages. In other words, they build down toward the first dollar of protection rather than covering the first dollar first and then building their protection up to cover the large losses.

Limited Policies Versus Broad Protection

Another basic decision that health insurance buyers must make is whether to insure a wide range of losses or to cover only certain types of disabilities and expenses. Some companies issue limited coverage policies with very low premiums. These have been ridiculed as "buffalo policies," paying off only if the buyer is run over by a herd of buffalo at high noon on Main Street! Although no policies are that silly, some are extremely limited. One example is a turnpike policy. It pays for loss of life, limbs, or sight caused by an auto accident on a turnpike or interstate highway. Another limited policy applies only while the insured is a fare-paying passenger on a train, bus, taxicab, or scheduled airline. Some companies sell what are called dread disease policies. These sometimes cover only one specified sickness, such as cancer. Other dread disease policies cover a long list of unusual diseases, like typhoid fever, rabies, and diphtheria. Another type of limited policy insures against attack by 21 animals, including sharks, snakes, bears, mountain lions, alligators, and piranhas. Paying $10,000 for death, loss of limbs or sight, the policy costs $25 a year for an individual and $50 for a family.[1] Limited policies are attractive because they hold out the possibility of large loss payments and are available at low cost. The problem is that some purchasers don't understand how limited the protection is and gain a false sense of security by purchasing (or being talked into buying) such contracts. To protect the gullible public, very limited policies are now outlawed in some states.

Charlie Newlin's hospital income policy is a limited contract. The advertisement stresses that Charlie can use the $1,000 a month for any purpose—for hospital charges, medicines, or regular living costs—but the policy pays only while an insured is in the hospital. It pays nothing for long periods of nursing home care or house confinement, even following a stay in the hospital. As a result, of course, the policy costs much less than policies providing broader disability income protection.

Buying proper health insurance is not a simple matter. In an open letter to the citizens of his state, Governor John L. Gilligan of Ohio made the following recommendations:

First, look into the various types of coverage to see how they apply to your own specific requirements.

Second, remember that all policies are not the same. Coverage and rates vary from company to company.

Third, and most important, ask questions of your insurance agent. Nothing is more disheartening than to have an accident or become ill only to find your coverage doesn't really protect you.[2]

This is good advice. By following it and by dealing with reputable insurers, families and individuals can obtain the protection they need to help them manage the risks associated with accidents and illness.

---

[1]*Des Moines Register*, January 23, 1976. The author does not know whether or not the policy pays for being trampled by buffalo.
[2]*The Ohio Consumers Guide to Health Insurance* (Columbus: Ohio Department of Insurance, 1973), p. 1.

IMPORTANT TERMS

Group policies
Individual policies
Hospital expense insurance
Reimbursement basis
Valued basis
Service basis
Blue Cross
Surgical expense insurance
Blue Shield
Regular medical expense insurance
Major medical expense insurance
Initial deductible

Corridor deductible
Comprehensive major medical insurance
Disability income insurance
Waiting period
Accidental means
Accidental bodily injury
Pre-existing conditions clause
Probationary period
Continuation provisions
First-dollar coverage

KEY POINTS TO REMEMBER

1. The costs of medical care are extremely high and are continuing to rise. For individual families they are unpredictable; in a given year they may be high or low.
2. Health insurance policies cover either accidents or both accidents and sickness.
3. Accidents and sickness present two important risks, the risk of high treatment costs and the risk of losing income during a period of disability.
4. Four types of health insurance pay health care costs: hospital expense, surgical expense, regular medical expense, and major medical.
5. Hospital expense policies pay room and board charges and other specified hospital costs. Surgical expense insurance pays for operations.
6. In competition with insurance companies, Blue Cross and Blue Shield organizations cover hospital expense and surgical expense respectively.
7. Regular medical expense coverage pays a stated amount for doctor visits.
8. Major medical expense policies have broad coverage, very high limits, a deductible, and percentage participation. They insure against catastrophic illness or accidents.
9. Comprehensive major medical combines basic hospital and surgical coverage with catastrophe protection.
10. Disability income policies replace income lost because of an accident or illness.
11. Some disability income policies cover only those injuries that are caused by accidental means. Others cover any accidental bodily injury.
12. The manner in which disability income policies define disability is important. Several different definitions are in use.
13. Individual health insurance policies often contain pre-existing conditions clauses that exclude coverage for health conditions existing when the policy is purchased.

14. Many health insurance policies contain no other-insurance provision, making duplicate loss payments possible. The absence of an other-insurance provision also can lead to malingering, high insurance rates, and unwise insurance buying.
15. Policy continuation provisions determine whether or not the insurer can discontinue a person's insurance.
16. In buying health insurance, one should follow the rules of personal risk management and avoid concentrating on first-dollar coverage. Also, policies that provide broad protection are preferable to limited policies.

REVIEW QUESTIONS

1. What perils do health insurance policies cover?
2. List the five types of health insurance protection.
3. In hospital expense insurance, what is the difference between reimbursement, valued, and service benefits?
4. Which of the features of major medical insurance act to reduce its cost?
5. In major medical, what is the difference between an initial deductible and a corridor deductible?
6. A person insured by a major medical policy is badly injured in an automobile accident and incurs $6,500 of medical costs. The policy has a $75,000 limit. a $500 initial deductible and 75/25 percentage participation. How much will the policy pay?
7. How much would have been paid in the previous case if the major medical policy had a $100 corridor deductible and was coordinated with basic coverage which paid $2,500 of the expenses?
8. Adequate disability income insurance is expensive, and yet inexpensive disability income policies are available. How can that be explained? Make up two examples of disability income coverage that could be sold at a low cost.
9. What is the difference between accidental bodily injury and injury caused by accidental means?
10. Why do some disability income policies contain two different definitions of disability?
11. List five types of continuation provisions.
12. Why are guaranteed renewable policies more widely sold than noncancelable policies?

DISCUSSION QUESTIONS

1. Why do people need health insurance?
2. How do the first and second rules of personal risk management apply to health risks?
3. Which would be hit hardest by inflation, an organization providing hospital expense coverage on the reimbursement basis, the valued basis, or the service basis? Which would be least affected by inflation?

4. Some disability income policies have waiting periods of as long as six months. What are the advantages of having such a long waiting period?

5. Why do you think people buy limited policies like those described in the chapter?

6. In what ways would Charlie Newlin be better off buying a major medical policy rather than the hospital income policy?

7. Buying proper health insurance protection is not a simple matter. Why not?

CHAPTER 12
LIFE INSURANCE FUNDAMENTALS —PART I

CHARACTERISTICS OF LIFE INSURANCE

TYPES OF LIFE INSURANCE

COMBINATION POLICIES

THE BEST POLICY

Most college students aren't very interested in life insurance. And they don't see why people spend so much money for it. They can understand why during a recent year people spent $23 billion on new cars, for instance, but they don't see why people would spend $35 billion for life insurance during the same year. What would motivate people to spend that much money for something as unexciting as life insurance?

The answer is that by insuring their lives, people insure their future incomes. And future income, especially for young families, is tremendously valuable; the possibility of its being interrupted is a major risk. Consider the importance of Charlie's income to the Newlin family whom we met in the last chapter. You may recall that Charlie and Ruth have a 2-year-old daughter, Julie. They hope to have another child before long. Ruth works part-time and plans to return to a full-time job when the children are older. Until then, she and the children will rely on Charlie's income for their chief support. His income will pay for their housing, food, clothing, transportation, and education. Charlie is earning $18,000 a year now and expects substantial increases during the years ahead. He intends to retire when he reaches 65, 40 years from now. We of course don't know what his total earnings will be during that period, but let's say that they average $20,000 a year after taxes. For the 40 years, that would be a total of $800,000.[1] We don't infer that Charlie needs $800,000 of life insurance. We shall see later that a much smaller amount than that will serve the Newlins very well. The point is that families rely upon income, and the possibility of its being interrupted by death is a major risk, usually their most important one. They buy life insurance as a way of handling that risk. People insure their homes because they are valuable and because the possibility of losing them is an important risk. They insure their lives (more specifically, their earning ability) primarily for the same reason.[2]

It is not surprising that few students are interested in life insurance, especially if they are unmarried. They are concerned about how they will earn an income, not whether it may be interrupted. They are interested in buying cars and airline tickets, not life insurance. But things have a way of changing. Students graduate, find jobs, get married, and start families. Three people out of four are married by age 25. And young married people buy life insurance. Almost 60% of all life insurance purchases are made by people under age 35, 30% by those 24 or younger. Very few of these people had

---

[1] Another way of looking at this is that a sum of $343,180 invested today at a net interest rate of 5% would permit the annual withdrawal of $20,000 a year for 40 years before the fund would be exhausted. This is the "present value" concept of future income.
[2] Life insurance is also used to pay funeral expenses, provide education funds, and to make gifts or bequests. The primary function, however, is to replace income.

given a thought to life insurance while they were in school; yet just a short time later they decided that it was important to them and to their future. This chapter and the next two describe the nature and uses of life insurance. The provisions and costs of various policies are compared, with emphasis upon how they relate to the decisions that life insurance buyers must make.

CHARACTERISTICS OF LIFE INSURANCE

In several important ways, life insurance differs from other kinds of insurance. Compare it with auto insurance, which, as we know, has these characteristics: (a) policies are written for short terms (one year at the most); (b) policies have no value when they expire; (c) the events that are insured may happen numerous times to the same policyholder, and (d) the policies are contracts of indemnity. In contrast, life insurance has these features: (a) most policies are written for long terms, many for life; (b) most policies have cash values; (c) the event insured—the mortality risk—is unique; and (d) life insurance policies are not contracts of indemnity. These points are summarized by Table 12–1. We shall take a look at each of these characteristics of life insurance.

Long-Term Policies

Life insurance policies usually cover long periods, frequently from the time of purchase until the insured reaches age 65 and often longer. One implication of this is that purchase decisions are more crucial in life insurance than in other lines of coverage. It usually is easy to replace one automobile or homeowners policy with another if the insureds change their minds about the coverage they want or if they prefer a different insurer. But, as we shall see, replacement of a life insurance policy may interrupt a savings program. It also may require paying higher rates because the policyholder is older than when the original policy was purchased. Worse yet, bad health may make another policy either more costly or impossible to secure. For these reasons it is especially important to make the right choices when buying life insurance.

Table 12–1 Comparison of Auto Insurance and Life Insurance

CHARACTERISTIC	AUTO	LIFE
Long-term policies	No	Usually
Policies have cash value	No	Usually
Covers only the mortality risk	No	Yes
Contracts of Indemnity	Yes	No

Cash Value Policies

Cash values are sums payable to policy holders who choose to discontinue their insurance. The majority of individually purchased life insurance policies provide cash values; automobile policies never do. (Some life insurance policies—term policies—do not provide cash values.) Cash values increase year by year; the amounts are shown in the policies. Policyholders also can borrow any amount up to the full cash value of their policies; interest rates for such loans are stated in the policies.

Because of its accumulation of cash values, life insurance (other than term policies) can be thought of as combining savings with protection and it often is purchased with that dual purpose in mind. This is a unique characteristic of life insurance and one which must be understood in order to comprehend the ways in which life insurance can be used.

The Mortality Risk

Life insurance covers **the mortality risk,** the financial uncertainty associated with dying. Other kinds of insurance cover losses that may happen numerous times to the same policyholder; the losses usually are partial and frequently are not very serious. In contrast, the event covered by life insurance is certain to happen—but only once—to every person. The uncertainty, of course, is the time at which it will happen. Basically, life insurance protects against the risk of dying too soon. That is, the primary financial risk from the viewpoint of the family is that death may cut off their source of income while the income still is needed, especially for raising children. This is the principal risk dealt with by life insurance.[3]

Life insurance transfers the mortality risk to an insurance company. The insurance company, handling a large number of similar risks, computes the premiums it must charge on the basis of records of large groups of people. These records are compiled in **mortality tables** that show the probability of living and dying at various ages. **Actuaries,** mathematical experts who work for insurance companies, have compiled many different mortality tables. Each is based upon actual records of the number of people living and dying at various ages. Experience has shown that mortality data from the past can be relied upon to predict future mortality rates quite accurately.

Table 12–2 shows parts of one mortality table. It starts with a group of 10 million lives and shows the number dying at various ages, the mortality rate

[3]The other side of the coin—the other uncertainty associated with living, dying, and income—is living "too long" in the sense of living longer than one's savings or other source of income lasts. We shall see later that this mortality risk can be dealt with by annuity contracts that provide income for as long as a person lives.

Table 12-2 Standard Mortality Table[a]

AGE	NUMBER LIVING	NUMBER DYING	DEATHS PER 1,000	EXPECTANCY (IN YEARS)
0	10,000,000	70,800	7.08	68.30
1	9,929,200	17,475	1.76	67.78
2	9,911,725	15,066	1.52	66.90
3	9,896,659	14,449	1.46	66.00
4	9,882,210	13,835	1.40	65.10
10	9,805,870	11,865	1.21	59.58
20	9,664,994	17,300	1.79	50.37
21	9,647,694	17,655	1.83	49.46
22	9,630,039	17,912	1.86	48.55
23	9,612,127	18,167	1.89	47.64
24	9,593,960	18,324	1.91	46.73
30	9,480,358	20,193	2.13	41.25
40	9,241,359	32,622	3.53	32.18
60	7,698,698	156,592	20.34	16.12
80	2,626,372	288,848	109.98	5.85
97	37,787	18,456	488.42	1.18
98	19,331	12,916	688.15	0.83
99	6,415	6,415	1,000.00	0.50

[a]Excerpts from 1958 Commissioners Standard Ordinary Mortality Table.

per 1,000 at each age, and the number of years of life expectancy at each age. We should realize that the mortality data are averages; mortality tables are not applicable to any one individual but only to groups large enough to be subject to the law of large numbers. This table assumes that the last survivors of the group live to age 99. Of course, a few people actually live to age 100 and beyond, and some mortality tables run to a higher age, but any table must have some arbitrary limit.

We can show the use of a mortality table as a basis for life insurance premiums with a simplified example. Assume that 100,000 people, each 20 years old, are to be issued one-year $1,000 life insurance policies. The policies are to have no cash values and are simply to pay $1,000 if the insured person dies during the year. The table indicates that the insurer can expect 1.79 deaths per 1,000 persons of this age. That is the indicated **mortality rate** for 20-year-olds, the ratio of the number dying during a year to the number living at the beginning of the year. With a mortality rate of 1.79, 179 of the 100,000 insured people would die during the year. If the company charged each person $1.79 at the beginning of the year, the company's premium income would be 100,000 × $1.79, or $179,000. This amount would be sufficient to pay $1,000 for each of the policyholders who died during the year. The next year those who survived would be 21 years old and their average mortality rate would have risen to 1.83. If the policies were renewed, each person would therefore have to be charged $1.83 in order to provide $1,000 to the beneficiaries of those who died during the second year. In each succeeding year the premium rates would continue to rise along with the mortality rate.

Several important things were omitted from the preceding example. First, the fact that the company will invest the premiums it receives and will earn interest on the investment was ignored. Second, company operating expenses (such as agents' commissions, salaries, rent, and taxes) were not taken into account. The first of these would permit a reduction in the computed rates; the second would require an increase. Another factor that would have to be taken into account is the likelihood that actual mortality rates will vary somewhat from the rates predicted on the basis of past experience. Any insurer that charged exactly what the mortality table indicated would suffer if it encountered several years of worse-than-average mortality experience. Therefore a safety margin will be included in the rates that are charged.

Some policies (one-year term contracts) actually are priced in a manner similar to the one used in the example. Most are not, however, because if that system is used the cost must continue to rise as the policyholders grow older and the mortality rate climbs. And, as Table 12–2 shows, the mortality rate rises steeply after about age 30. At age 40 it is about twice as high as at age 20, and at age 60 it is more than ten times as high. If the one-year term rate system (the system just described) were used for long-term policies, rates would be very low at first but later would become so expensive that many policyholders would have to consider dropping their policies. Their decisions at this point would be affected by a crucial factor: the state of their health. Many who were in good health would let their policies lapse. But most of those who didn't expect to live much longer would keep on paying the premiums, even though they had become very high. As a result, adverse selection would develop; the group no longer would have average mortality rates. An increasing percentage of the people would be in poor health, and the mortality rate would climb higher, causing more healthy members to drop out, causing higher mortality rates, and on and on in a vicious circle. Thus, the one-year term rate system, with cost step-up year by year, cannot be relied upon for policies providing long-term protection. This has led to development of level premium life insurance.

Most life insurance today is written at a **level premium.** The premium remains the same over the term of the policy; it is the same at age 60 as it was when the policy was purchased at age 30. The level premium averages out the mortality cost; it is higher than mortality rates would indicate in the early years of the policy and much less in later years. This practice eliminates the problem of rising insurance cost for the policyholder. Also, the level premium system is the source of the savings element of cash value policies. The overpayments (relative to indicated mortality costs) that are collected during the early years are accumulated by the company and invested in bonds, mortgages, and real estate. These funds increase during the term of the policy and are the basis of the increasing cash values.

Figure 12–1 shows how a long-term policy can have a level annual premium. For a number of years at the beginning the annual cost for the level premium policy is higher than the premium for successive one-year term policies. But the cost of term policies increases to keep pace with the rising mortality rate and eventually must climb above the cost of level premium policies. The illustration also shows the source of cash values. As previously stated, the excess payments during the early years of a level premium policy (the shaded area in Figure 12–1) build a reserve. The reserve, which is used to offset the undercharge in later years when the level premium payments would be insufficient by themselves, is the source of the cash values.

Not Contracts of Indemnity

According to the indemnity principle, as outlined in Chapter 4, the function of most kinds of insurance is to repay the policyholder for the actual amount of an insured loss. The principle is supported by law and by insurance policy provisions and practices that prevent the insured from profiting from the

Figure 12–1   The level premium concept

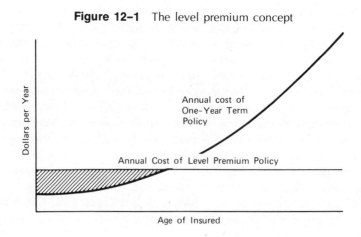

occurrence of a loss. We should realize that life insurance policies are not contracts of indemnity. Chapter 4 pointed out that several of the measures that support the indemnity principle do not apply to life insurance: (a) no attempt is made to measure the actual loss resulting from the policyholder's death; (b) a life insurance company cannot subrogate against another party responsible for an insured's death; and (c) life insurance policies do not contain other-insurance provisions. (The fourth measure which supports the indemnity principle, the insurable interest requirement, does apply to life insurance, however.)

The fact that life insurance policies are not indemnity contracts is important in another way: It makes it possible for a person to use life insurance for **estate creation.** An estate is the property that a person owns. One reason for acquiring an estate is to furnish financial security for one's dependents. By means of a will or other legal arrangement the estate can be transferred to others upon the death of the owner. By purchasing a life insurance policy the buyer immediately creates an estate in the amount of the policy.

The Newlin family can illustrate this point. Charlie's income is supporting Ruth and two-year-old Julie. One evening Charlie begins to think, "What would happen to Ruth and Julie if I should die? Would they have enough income to live decently? Would they be able to keep the house and the car?" He talks it over with Ruth. A life insurance agent named Bill Scott has been wanting to talk with them, and they decide it might be a good idea to learn what he has to say. They contact Mr. Scott and he comes to their home the next evening.

Charlie and Ruth at first are rather surprised by their conversation with Mr. Scott. They had expected him to try to sell them a policy right away. Instead, he talks with them about themselves, their plans, and their reasons for needing insurance. They discuss Charlie's job and his future prospects with Metro Industries. They talk about Ruth's part-time job and her qualifications for full-time work. Bill Scott inquires about their income and their present life insurance. Finally they discuss the family's need for protection. The most important need, all agree, is to provide adequate income while Julie is growing up. Charlie and Ruth hope that Julie will go to college, but that goal is a long way away. The first need is for income between now and her graduation from high school. If she graduates at age 18, that will be 16 years from now. "Let's concentrate on that income need first," says Bill.

Charlie does some quick calculations. He is earning $1,500 a month. Sixteen years is 192 months, and 192 times $1,500 is $288,000. "There's no way we can insure that," he thinks. But Bill's approach is different. He suggests that, if Ruth had $900 a month, that amount plus her part-time earnings might do the job. It wouldn't be easy for her, but it would be possible to lead a decent sort of life with that much income. Then Bill points out that Ruth would receive about $600 a month in social security benefits. In addition, through Metro Industries Charlie has $15,000 of group life insurance. If the proceeds of that policy were paid to Ruth in monthly instalments for the 16 years, they would provide about $100 a month. That plus the social security benefits would total $700 a month, leaving $200 to be supplied in order to reach their $900 goal. A $30,000 policy, the agent says, could provide the needed $200 a month for 16 years.

Returning to the point about estate creation, if Charlie buys the $30,000 policy, he will immediately add that much to his estate. There is no other way (short of robbing a bank!) that he could do this. Of course, he could set out to save the $30,000 from his current earnings. If he saved enough over a long enough period of time and invested it successfully, he would thereby create the $30,000 addition to his estate. But such saving would take a great deal of self-discipline and perseverance. Most of all, it would take time. And Charlie and Ruth want security for their family now, not ten years from now.

If Charlie buys the $30,000 policy and dies while it is in force, Ruth will receive that amount, even if Charlie lives to pay only the first month's premium. If that happens, the policy will have created something—an estate—that did not previously exist. Estate creation is quite different from the basic insurance function of reimbursing an insured for something like a hospital bill or a damaged car. It can be done only because life insurance is not fully subject to the indemnity principle and therefore is not confined to indemnifying for actual losses. Thus, the ability to immediately create an estate is a unique aspect of life insurance.

TYPES OF LIFE INSURANCE

To a person not familiar with the field, there would appear to be many different types of life insurance. Like auto manufacturers, life insurance companies put a variety of names on their products. But the fact is that there are only three types: All policies provide either term insurance, endowment insurance, whole life insurance, or some combination of these three. In this section we shall examine the three basic types. In the section following this one we shall look at some of the combination policies.

Term Insurance

Term life insurance provides death protection for a stated length of time. It is the simplest type of life insurance. In the case of a one-year term policy, for instance, the company promises to pay the **face amount,** the amount stated in the contract, if the insured dies during the year. If the insured survives the one-year term, the policy expires without payment. Like auto or fire insurance, term life insurance provides no savings element, no cash value. In straight term insurance there is no guarantee that the company will renew the policy. If it is renewed, a higher premium is charged.

Forms. Most term policies are written for terms longer than a single year. Five-year and ten-year term policies are common. They have level premiums during their terms; if they are renewed, the premiums for the next term are at a higher level. Term-to-65 policies provide death protection at a level premium until the insured reaches age 65.

People who are in poor health must pay higher rates for life insurance. If their condition is serious they may not be able to secure coverage at any price. Because any policyholder can develop poor health, straight term insurance is not very desirable. Most term policies therefore are either renewable, convertible, or both.

A **renewable term** policy can be renewed at the option of the insured without showing evidence of insurability or, in other words, regardless of the state of the insured's health. Thus, a five-year term policy might be renewable for three additional terms, guaranteeing a total of twenty years of protection.

Convertible term policies give the insured the option of converting the coverage to a whole life or endowment policy, again without evidence of insurability. Usually the conversion must take place prior to the last year or two of the term.

Another common form of term insurance is **decreasing term.** This policy decreases in amount each month or year. Decreasing term often is written in combination with whole life, as will be explained later.

Uses. Term insurance is appropriate when (a) the need for protection is temporary, or (b) the objective is to secure the greatest possible amount of protection for the cost of the insurance. An example of a temporary need is that in connection with a loan. A person might borrow $25,000 to start a business, the loan to be repaid in five years. A five-year term policy in the same amount would pay off the loan if the borrower died and thus would prevent the borrower's family from having to shoulder the debt.

In the case of mortgage debt, decreasing term policies frequently are used. For instance, a $50,000 thirty-year home mortgage can be protected by a $50,000 thirty-year decreasing term policy. The amount of insurance initially is the same as the amount of the mortgage. As the mortgage gradually declines, so does the amount of insurance. At any point during the 30-year period, the amount of protection is roughly equal to the amount needed to pay off the debt.

218

Table 12-3 Annual Cost of $10,000 Policies"

TYPE OF POLICY	AGE OF INSURED AT DATE OF PURCHASE				
	20	25	30	35	40
Five-year term (renewable and convertible)	$ 47.50	$ 49.50	$ 53.50	$ 62.50	$ 77.50
Straight life	115.30	133.10	158.30	187.20	228.00
Whole life paid up at 65	125.10	150.60	182.70	223.70	284.30
Twenty payment whole life	200.00	223.00	250.00	282.40	323.30
Twenty-year endowment	410.30	412.50	415.80	422.50	434.70
Endowment at 65	148.90	178.60	214.90	271.60	343.10

"Costs shown are those charged by one company for policies covering men. Rates for women are lower. For simplicity, rates for nonparticipating policies are shown; participating policies would have higher rates but would pay annual dividends. (The nature of participating insurance is explained in Chapter 13.)

Term insurance costs much less than other types of life insurance, as Table 12–3 shows. As a result, it frequently is used by people who need maximum protection at a minimum outlay in premium dollars. Charlie and Ruth Newlin may decide that they need $30,000 of insurance, but that they cannot afford a permanent form of protection (that is, a whole life or long-term endowment policy) at this time. A $30,000 five-year renewable and convertible term policy would cost them about $150 a year. Five years from now, when Charlie is 30, they may be able to convert to a straight life policy at a cost of about $475 a year.

If their sole objective is income protection while Julie is growing up, an even less expensive policy for the Newlins would be decreasing term. They need $30,000 of protection now to furnish $200 a month for the 16 years between Julie's present age of 2 and the point at which she will be 18. But, as the years go by, the $200 a month will be needed for fewer years. If Charlie dies when Julie is 10, only 8 years will remain until she is 18, and only about half as much in policy proceeds would be needed for the income payments. A $30,000 twenty-year[4] decreasing term policy would cost only about $107 a year.

Limitations.   Term insurance has three important limitations. Each of the three should be clearly understood and considered before a decision is made to purchase term protection.

First, term policies expire at the end of their terms, but the need for

[4]The shortest period for which most companies offer decreasing term.

protection may continue. The need for continuing protection is especially pressing for policyholders who have developed poor health. As explained earlier, a person who is in poor health may be unable to secure another policy. This problem can be overcome by purchasing convertible term and by exercising the option to convert to a permanent form of protection. Buyers of convertible policies should be aware, though, that many insureds fail to convert their policies while they have a chance to do so. Most of us seem to be inclined to put off until later things that we don't have to do today, particularly if they cost us money.

The second limitation of term insurance is its increasing cost. Table 12–3 shows the annual cost of renewing a $10,000 five-year term policy at successive five-year intervals. The cost would be $147.50 at age 50 and $316.50 at age 60. Somewhere along the line those who continued to renew this policy and who had a continuing need for the protection might wish that they had purchased a level premium permanent policy instead. A $10,000 straight life policy purchased at age 25 costs $133.10 a year, but the annual premium remains $133.10 for as long as the insured keeps the policy. Some people prefer term insurance in spite of its increasing cost. Their reasoning is that increases in their annual income will permit them to handle the rising cost without undue difficulty. Also, they may figure that their need for protection will decline as their children grow older and that they therefore will be able to reduce the amount of their coverage gradually and perhaps be able to hold its cost relatively constant.

The third limitation of term insurance is the absence of cash values. Other types of life insurance combine savings with protection, furnishing cash values for emergencies and for retirement income. Many people do not regard this as a shortcoming of term insurance, because they prefer to separate their savings programs from their life insurance coverage. But Table 12–4 makes it clear that most life insurance purchasers prefer policies that

Table 12–4 Types of Ordinary Life Insurance in Force, 1977
(numbers of policies in millions; amounts of insurance in billions)

TYPE OF POLICY	NUMBER OF POLICIES	AMOUNT OF INSURANCE	PERCENTAGE OF AMOUNT
Term	16.4	$429.8	33
Endowment and retirement income	14.3	$ 73.9	6
Whole life	108.8	$785.6	61
Total	139.5	$1,289.3	100

Source: *Life Insurance Fact Book 1978* (New York: American Council of Life Insurance), p. 22.

provide cash values. Less than one-third of the ordinary insurance[5] that is in force is term insurance. If the comparison were on the basis of premium volume, term insurance would comprise an even smaller part of the total, because of its lower cost per $1,000.

It sometimes is argued that many of those who buy cash value insurance do so because they fail to consider the alternative of separating their insurance and savings programs or because they are talked into buying the more expensive policies by agents who thereby earn higher commissions. There undoubtedly is some element of truth in this viewpoint. However, the majority of cash value insurance purchasers probably know what they are doing and prefer to achieve at least part of their savings through life insurance, largely because of the "forced savings" aspect of this system. Most of us are all too human when it comes to saving money. There always seems to be some excellent reason why we can't save as much out of the current paycheck as we had planned, and it is difficult to avoid drawing on long-range savings when the car breaks down or the washing machine has to be replaced. But life insurance premiums almost always get paid, because they tend to be regarded as an essential part of a family budget, much like the rent or mortgage payments. If the premiums are not paid when due, the policy may lapse, something that would threaten the future welfare of the family. Therefore, most families will go to great lengths to pay their insurance premiums regularly. In doing so, they force themselves to save money in the form of cash values. Thus, most people regard the absence of cash values in term insurance as a shortcoming of that type of coverage.[6]

Endowment Insurance

Endowment insurance pays a stated amount if the insured dies during a specified period of time or pays the same amount if the insured is living at the end of the period. Unlike term policies, endowment policies have cash value. The cash value increases gradually until at the end of the endowment period it equals the face of the policy. At that point the policy endows; that is, it pays the face amount to the policyholder. If Charlie Newlin buys a $30,000 twenty-year endowment policy, it will pay Ruth $30,000 if Charlie dies during the twenty-year period. If he is still living at the end of the period, he will receive $30,000.

An endowment policy can be thought of as a combination of an increas-

---

[5]The differences between ordinary, group, industrial, and credit insurance are explained in Chapter 13.

[6]For the report of a consumer survey supporting this viewpoint, see Beutel, Caroline, and Nuckols, Robert, "Cost Comparisons: Fact, Fiction, and Future," *Best's Review (Life-Health Edition)*, June 1978.

ing savings fund and decreasing term insurance. At the start of the policy period the term insurance equals the full amount of the policy. As the years pass and the savings part grows, the term insurance part declines. At any point, the total of the amount of term insurance and the amount of the savings fund equals the face of the policy. The policy endows at the end of its term when the savings fund has reached the face amount and the term insurance has declined to zero. Because endowment policies have high cash value (equaling the face amount of the policy at the end of the endowment period) their cost is high. The shorter the term of the policy, the higher are the premiums.

FORMS. Endowment policies are written for various periods, such as 20, 25, or 30 years. They also can be written to endow at a stated age, perhaps 65 or 70. An endowment-at-age-65 policy issued at age 25 of course would be the same thing as a 40-year endowment.

The retirement income policy is a special form of endowment that provides even more savings and less decreasing term protection than regular endowment contracts. The policy provides a retirement income of $10 per month (starting at age 65) for each $1,000 of face amount. A $10,000 retirement income policy would pay the insured $100 per month during retirement. This policy is even more expensive than other endowment contracts. A $10,000 retirement income policy purchased at age 25 from the company whose rates are shown in Table 12–3 would cost $261.11 per year.

USES. Endowment insurance really is a form of savings protected by life insurance. In effect, insureds who live until their policies endow complete their savings goals by means of their premium payments, while the protection aspect of the policy assures them that their savings goal will be completed, whether they live to complete it themselves or not.

Endowment policies sometimes are used as a means of saving money for college expenses or for other purposes. A more appropriate use is as a systematic way of accumulating a fund for retirement.

LIMITATIONS. The chief limitation of endowment insurance—particularly of short-term policies—is its high cost. In spite of the high cost, endowment contracts sometimes are bought because of the idea that "I don't have to die to win." In other words, purchasers are attracted by the idea that the policy will pay off in full whether they live or die; they also like the thought that they probably will be alive to receive the proceeds themselves. The real difficulty this creates is that the purchase of an endowment is unlikely to fill the need for income protection. Charlie and Ruth

Newlin may be tempted by the idea of buying an endowment policy so that its cash value can be used for Julie's college expenses. But, if they spend $150 a year on a 20-year endowment, they will have only about $3,600 of insurance, an amount that wouldn't go very far toward filling their income need if Charlie died.

Experts tell us that short-term endowments seldom are desirable. They caution that such policies never should be purchased until the principal need, the need for income protection, has been taken care of. Long-term endowments are another matter. A family that can afford to buy a large enough endowment-at-65, for example, can use it for both income protection and retirement savings.

Whole Life Insurance

Whole life insurance provides lifetime protection by means of level-premium, cash value policies. In terms of both cost and amount of cash value, whole life occupies the middle ground between term and endowment. That is, whole life policies are generally more expensive than term but not as expensive as endowment, and they provide some cash value but not as much as endowment contracts do. The intermediate nature of whole life is shown in Table 12–5.

A whole life policy can provide lifetime protection. It can be kept in force until the policyholder either cashes it in or dies. The cash value continues to increase as long as the policy remains in force. If the policy is still in force when the insured attains age 100, the cash value reaches the face amount and a check for that amount (along with a letter of congratulations from the company president) is sent to the insured. Note that, in effect, whole life policies endow at age 100. In one sense, therefore, whole life policies are endowments at age 100 and there are only two different types of life insurance, term and endowment. In a more practical sense, though, whole life is a separate type, because the people who buy whole life policies don't

Table 12–5 Comparison of Three $10,000 Policies Issued at Age 25"

POLICY	ANNUAL COST	CASH VALUE		
		AGE 35	AGE 45	AGE 65
Five-year term (renewable and convertible to 65)	$ 49.50	$ 0	$ 0	$ 0
Whole life (straight life)	$133.10	$ 920	$2,420	$ 5,650
Endowment at 65	$178.60	$1,410	$3,600	$10,000

"See notes, Table 12–3.

expect them to endow; whole life is neither thought of nor used as endowment insurance.

FORMS.   There are three forms of whole life insurance: single premium, limited premium, and straight life. The difference between the three forms is the length of the period during which premiums are payable.

Single premium whole life policies are paid for in one payment. A $10,000 policy can be purchased for a single premium of about $3,000 at age 25. The policy will remain in force with no further payment until it either is cashed in or pays $10,000 to the beneficiary. Single premium policies are rarely purchased; they are mentioned primarily to help explain the nature of whole life insurance.

Limited payment whole life policies provide for premiums to be paid either for a stated number of years or until the insured reaches a stated age. On a 20-payment whole life policy, premiums are payable for 20 years. (Payments could be made semiannually, quarterly, or monthly rather than annually, so there actually could be more than 20 payments; all would be made within a 20-year period, however.) A whole life paid-up at 65 is also a limited payment policy. If it were issued at age 25 it would have a 40-year premium payment period and would be the same as a 40-payment whole life policy. The longer the premium payment period, the lower are each year's premiums. Limited payment whole life policies should not be confused with endowments. At the end of the premium paying period a limited payment policy is fully paid for, but it does not endow at that point as an endowment policy would. The coverage continues after the policy is paid up; the cash value is still less than the face amount and continues to increase as long as the policy remains in force (up to age 100).

Straight life policies are the third and by far the most popular form of whole life insurance. The name of this policy is a source of confusion because it sometimes is called the whole life policy or the ordinary life policy. The most descriptive name would be continuous-premium whole life policy, but that term seldom is used. The premiums for straight life policies are payable for the lifetime of the insured. Extending the premium payment period beyond a limited number of years lowers the annual cost of the policy and makes it the least expensive form of permanent life insurance. Because the premiums are lower, the cash value of straight life policies increases more slowly than any other form of cash value insurance.

USES.   The single-premium whole life policy has very limited use except in certain tax situations or as a gift to a young person. Short-term limited payment whole life policies also have rather limited use. It usually makes little sense, for instance, for a 25-year-old to buy a 20-payment or a 30-

payment policy and thereby compress the premium payments into the period when the family's expenses are higher and its income is lower than they will be in later years.

The straight life policy and the whole life paid-up at 65, on the other hand, are well suited for the needs of many people. They offer a compromise between term and endowment insurance, combining reasonable amounts of income protection and savings at a reasonable cost. Charlie and Ruth Newlin would do well to consider filling their $30,000 income protection need with the purchase of a straight life policy. It will cost about $400 a year and will have a cash value of $1,860 in 10 years, $7,260 in 20 years, and $16,950 in 40 years when Charlie is 65. The cash value can be borrowed for emergencies, and when Charlie retires he can cash in the policy to supplement his retirement income if he wishes. In the meantime, the policy will provide the protection that Ruth and Julie need. If Charlie and Ruth want to put relatively more of their premium dollars into the savings part of a policy, they might consider a whole life paid-up at 65 or an endowment at 65. The costs would be $451.80 or $555.80 respectively.

LIMITATIONS.   Four of the policies we have been considering are seen from a different viewpoint in Table 12–6. Instead of comparing policies of equal size, this table compares policies of equal cost. Again, we see term and endowment at the extremes. For a given cost, much more term insurance can be purchased, but it of course provides no cash value. Endowment offers the greatest amount of cash value, but at a sacrifice of the amount of protection which a given premium will buy. The two whole life policies that are shown in the table provide amounts of both protection and savings that are between the extremes furnished by term and endowment.

Table 12–6 also illustrates the limitations of whole life insurance: Compared with term, whole life is expensive; compared with endowment, it provides less cash value. These, of course, are limitations only in a relative sense. Whole life avoids the more serious limitations of term (expiring

Table 12–6   What $400 a Year Will Buy at Age 25[a]

POLICY	AMOUNT	CASH VALUE AT 65
Five-Year term (renewable and convertible to age 65)	$80,800	$ 0
Straight life	30,000	16,950
Whole life paid up at 65	26,600	18,350
Endowment at 65	22,400	22,400

[a]Approximate amounts. See notes, Table 12–3.

protection, increasing cost, and absence of cash value) and of endowment (high cost).

It sometimes is suggested that a limitation or shortcoming of the straight life policy is the fact that its premiums are never paid up. This is not a valid criticism and is based on a misunderstanding of the purposes of the policy and of the reasons why it is purchased. People who buy straight life policies rarely intend to continue paying for them indefinitely, and there is no reason why they should. The company is not "cheated" if a policy is cashed in when the protection no longer is needed. In fact, this and other cash value policies offer several options that are designed to serve the best interests of policyholders if they decide to stop paying premiums and use the accumulated cash value. These options are described in the next chapter.

COMBINATION POLICIES

Although there are only three basic types of life insurance, two or more of the three can be combined in a single contract. A wide variety of combination policies is available. The most important are the family income, family maintenance, and family plan policies.

Family Income Policy

The **family income policy** is a combination of straight life and decreasing term insurance. It is designed for young families who need added income protection during the child-raising period. The use of decreasing term insurance for this purpose was discussed earlier.

The decreasing term portion of the family income policy usually covers 20 years and is sufficient to pay an income of $10 per month for each $1,000 of straight life insurance. Thus a $10,000 family income policy would pay $100 per month starting from the date of the policyholder's death within the first 20 years of the policy and ending 20 years after the policy was purchased. If a policy had been purchased at age 25, the income payments to the beneficiary would continue until the insured would have reached age 45. The $10,000 proceeds from the straight life part are paid at the end of the 20-year period. If the insured is still living when the 20-year term portion expires, the straight life part continues in the regular manner, but at a lower premium level.

Benefits similar to those provided by the family income policy can be provided by adding a family income rider to a regular whole life policy. The family income rider is simply decreasing term coverage. In this case the proceeds of the whole life policy are payable at death instead of at the end of the family income period. This arrangement generally is preferable, because the need for funds is likely to be greatest at the time of the insured's death.

Family Maintenance Policy

As Figure 12–2 shows, the **family maintenance policy** is similar to the family income policy. Both combine term and straight life insurance. However, the term portion of the family maintenance policy is level rather than a decreasing amount.

The amount of term insurance (about $15,000) again is sufficient to pay $10 per month for each $1,000 of straight life. But, because the family maintenance policy includes a level amount of term insurance, its income payments continue for a full 20 years if the insured dies at any time during the first 20 years of the policy. As explained earlier, if a family income policy is purchased at age 25 and the insured dies at age 35, the decreasing term portion pays until the insured would have been 45. But, if a family maintenance policy is purchased at the same age and the insured dies at age 35, the level term portion pays until the insured would have been 55. Again, the straight life portion continues at a lower premium level if the insured lives beyond the initial 20-year period. Because of the additional protection furnished by the family maintenance policy, it naturally is somewhat more expensive than the family income policy.

Family Plan Policy

The **family plan policy,** like the others, is sold under a variety of names. It also combines term and whole life insurance but does so by providing straight life coverage on the father and term insurance on the other members of the insured family. A typical family plan policy furnishes units of $5,000

Figure 12–2

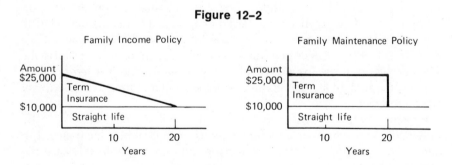

of straight life on the father, $1,000 of term-to-age-65 on the mother, and $1,000 of term-to-age-21 on each child. Additional children born to or adopted by the family are covered with no additional charge. In the event of the father's death, the coverages on the mother and children automatically become paid up for their remaining terms.

The family plan policy is attractive to many families as a way of securing relatively low-cost protection on the mother and children. To some, it appears less "selfish" than a policy insuring only the father. However, if the family relies on the income produced by the father, insuring against its interruption should always be regarded as the main objective of life insurance. In other words, the family should consider the alternative of securing a more adequate amount of income protection before diverting premium dollars for other purposes. This approach, of course, is consistent with the first rule of personal risk management.

Other Combination Policies

It should be clear to you by now that there is no limit to the ways in which the three basic types of life insurance can be combined and modified. Anyone who has a firm understanding of the basic types usually can deduce the ingredients of combination contracts. Descriptions of three other combination policies follow.

MODIFIED LIFE POLICY. This is a form of straight life policy with reduced premiums for the first few years. It is designed for young purchasers with limited incomes who expect higher earnings several years later. An example is a $10,000 straight life policy with a premium of about $85 for each of the first five years and $160 per year thereafter. After the period of reduced cost, the cost increases to a level somewhat higher than that charged for a regular level premium straight life policy. The modified life policy differs from regular whole life contracts only with regard to the premium arrangement.

MULTIPLE PROTECTION POLICY. This policy pays a multiple of the face amount if the insured dies within a specified period after the policy is purchased. An example is an endowment at age 70 offering double protection during its first 20 years. Rather obviously, this contract is simply a combination of endowment insurance and an equal amount of 20-year term insurance.

RETURN OF PREMIUM POLICY. Some combination policies are primarily marketing devices. The return of premium policy is such a contract; it seems to offer the purchaser "something for nothing." It is a policy in which the company promises that if the insured dies during the first 20 years it will pay the face amount and will also return all of the premiums that have been paid until that point. Before reading on, see if you can figure out how it can do this. How, for instance, can a company that sells a $10,000 straight life policy with an annual premium of $200, guarantee that it will pay $10,200 for death during the first year, $10,400 if the insured dies the second year, and so on up to the twentieth year when the proceeds would be $14,000? After the twentieth year, the coverage drops back to $10,000 and remains at that level.

If you have deduced that the return of premium policy is a combination of straight life and some form of term insurance, you are right. If you have decided that it is increasing term insurance, you are exactly right. The term insurance portion of the contract simply equals the cumulative premiums for the first 20 years, increasing from $200 the first year to $4,000 the twentieth year. The cost of the policy is enough higher than regular straight life to pay the added cost of the increasing term insurance. Therefore, the purchaser doesn't really get something for nothing. As with any other kind of insurance, one pays for what he or she gets. The trouble is that (a) those who buy this policy probably don't understand what they are paying for, and (b) they usually would be better off with decreasing term rather than increasing term, because the need for income protection is generally a decreasing need rather than an increasing one.

THE BEST POLICY

Our discussion of the kinds, uses, and limitations of life insurance policies leads to a very important conclusion: The best policy is the one that best serves the needs of the purchaser. There is no single "best" policy, because one that serves the needs of one family very well will not necessarily suit the needs of another. Well-informed life insurance buyers understand that the primary differences among various policies are the relative amounts of protection and savings which they provide. They also know that the costs of the policies reflect these differences. Knowing these facts, each purchaser must decide what balance of protection, savings, and cost is proper for his or her particular situation.

IMPORTANT TERMS

Cash value
Mortality risk
Mortality table
Mortality rate
Actuary
Level premium
Estate creation
Term life insurance
Face amount
Renewable term insurance
Convertible term insurance
Decreasing term insurance

Endowment insurance
Whole life insurance
Single premium whole life
Limited payment whole life
Straight life
Family income policy
Family maintenance policy
Family plan policy
Modified life policy
Multiple protection policy
Return of premium policy

KEY POINTS TO REMEMBER

1. Life insurance covers the mortality risk. Rates are based on data compiled in the form of mortality tables.

2. With the exception of the insurable interest requirement, the indemnity principle does not apply to life insurance. Because it does not, life insurance can be used to create or add to an estate.

3. There are three basic types of life insurance: term, endowment, and whole life.

4. Term policies provide pure protection for a stated length of time. Most term policies provide options to renew for additional terms or to convert to a permanent form of life insurance.

5. Term insurance is appropriate when the need for protection is temporary. Because it is the least expensive type of life insurance, it also can be used to secure the greatest possible amount of protection for a given cost.

6. Term policies have three limitations: They may expire while protection is still needed, their cost increases at each renewal, and they do not provide cash values.

7. Endowment insurance combines income protection with a relatively large element of savings. An endowment policy pays the face amount if the insured dies during the endowment period *or* pays the same amount if the insured is still living at the end of that period.

8. Short-term endowments are very expensive and seldom are desirable purchases. Long-term endowments can be used as a combined income protection and retirement savings program.

9. Whole life insurance consists of several forms of level premium, cash value policies that provide lifetime protection.

10. The premiums for whole life policies are payable either all at once (single premium policy), for a stated period (limited payment policies), or for the lifetime of the insured (straight life policy).

11. In both cost and amount of cash value, whole life policies are a compromise between term and endowment policies.
12. The family income policy combines straight life with decreasing term insurance to furnish additional income protection during the first 20 years. The family maintenance policy is similar but uses a level amount of 20-year term insurance.
13. The family plan policy covers all members of the insured family, providing straight life insurance on the father and term insurance on the mother and children.
14. There is no one "best" policy. The policy that is best for a particular family depends upon the balance of protection, savings, and cost that is most appropriate for their needs.

REVIEW QUESTIONS

1. Why do people buy life insurance?
2. List four ways in which life insurance differs from most other kinds of insurance.
3. What is a mortality table? What are mortality tables used for?
4. How do term, endowment, and whole life insurance differ from one another?
5. Why are the renewability and convertibility options desirable on term policies?
6. For what special uses can decreasing term insurance be used?
7. How does the concept of "forced savings" apply to life insurance?
8. Explain the nature of a $10,000 endowment at 65.
9. Why is an endowment at 65 more expensive than a whole life policy paid up at 65?
10. What is the difference between a limited payment whole life policy and a straight life policy? In what ways are these two policies similar?
11. How does the protection furnished by a family maintenance policy differ from the protection furnished by a family income policy?
12. What is a modified life policy?
13. What is a multiple protection policy?

DISCUSSION QUESTIONS

1. The chapter indicates that the only legitimate way in which one can immediately create an estate is that through the purchase of life insurance. Couldn't this also be done by borrowing the money?
2. Term policies that are either renewable or convertible are more expensive than those that are not. Why?
3. In view of the fact that endowment and whole life policies accumulate cash values, is the absence of cash values in term insurance unfair?
4. Why are straight life policies, for which premiums are payable for the insured's lifetime, more popular than other whole life policies for which premiums are payable for only a limited number of years?
5. Which would be more appropriate for a family like the Newlins, a family income policy or a family maintenance policy?

6. If you were visited by a life insurance agent who immediately told you that he had a policy that was just the thing for you, what would your reaction be?
7. Many people purchase cash value life insurance because of its forced savings aspect. Do you agree with them that this is a good reason for preferring cash value insurance to term insurance?

CHAPTER 13
LIFE INSURANCE FUNDAMENTALS —PART II

CLASSES OF LIFE INSURANCE

POLICY PROVISIONS

ANNUITIES

The preceding chapter described the basic nature of life insurance and identified the various kinds of policies. This chapter deals with several other aspects of life insurance, beginning with the ways that it is marketed. It then describes the important policy provisions and options and concludes with an explanation of annuity contracts.

CLASSES OF LIFE INSURANCE

Life insurance is classified on the basis of how it is marketed. Basically, there are two different marketing systems, individual and group. Both are divided into two classes, making four classes in all. The individual marketing system involves the sale of policies to individual persons and families. The two classes using the individual marketing system are **ordinary insurance** and **industrial insurance.** The group marketing system uses the technique of insuring a number of people under a single policy. The two classes that use this system are called **group insurance** and **credit insurance.**

Individual Marketing

ORDINARY.   Ordinary is the oldest and largest class of life insurance. The policies generally cover multiples of $1,000. Only the first premium is collected by the agent; later premiums are sent directly to the company and are paid either annually, semiannually, quarterly, or monthly. The policies may be any of the types described in Chapter 12. This is now the principal way of marketing individual policies and, unless otherwise indicated, the policies discussed later in this chapter are those marketed as ordinary insurance.

INDUSTRIAL.   Industrial life insurance was developed to serve the needs of low-income families who could not afford large policies and who were unable to save money for large, infrequent premium payments. The policies are generally in amounts of $1,000 or less. They may be either whole life or endowment insurance. The premiums (perhaps 25¢ or 50¢) are collected by the agent each week or month at the insured's home. For this reason, industrial is sometimes called "home service" life insurance. During the first 60 years of this century, more Americans were covered by industrial than by any other class of life insurance. As people have become better able to afford ordinary insurance and as group insurance and social security have grown, the volume of industrial has declined relative to the other classes. But, as Table 13–1 shows, many people still rely on industrial life insurance.

Table 13-1 Classes of Life Insurance in Force, United States, 1967 and 1977 (numbers of persons insured in millions; amounts of insurance in billions)

CLASS	1967		1977	
	NUMBER OF PERSONS	AMOUNT OF INSURANCE	NUMBER OF PERSONS	AMOUNT OF INSURANCE
Ordinary	113	$ 585	139	$1,289
Industrial	84	39	66	39
Group	69	395	106	1,115
Credit	70	62	79	139
Total	336	$1,080	390	$2,583

Note: Inconsistencies in totals are due to rounding.
Source: Life Insurance Fact Book 1978 (New York: American Council of Life Insurance), p. 19.

Group Marketing

GROUP. Most insurance is sold to employers to cover groups of employees. The coverage is paid for either by employers alone or by both employers and their employees. Other group policies cover members of unions or of associations. Most group life coverage is term insurance. As Table 13–1 shows, group is the fastest growing class. The nature of group insurance is described more fully in Chapter 15.

CREDIT. Credit life insurance covers the lives of people who owe instalment debt. The insurance pays off the debt if the borrower dies before completing the payments. Some credit life insurance is sold on the individual basis, but most is provided by group contracts arranged by banks, finance companies, credit unions, and retail stores. The coverage is term insurance, usually decreasing term.

Credit life insurance frequently is encountered in connection with the purchase of an automobile. The bank or other financing institution may require the borrower to furnish life insurance in the amount of the loan, with the lender named as beneficiary. In fact, the bank loan officer may simply quote instalment loan payments that include the insurance. It is worth knowing that in most states the financing institution cannot legally require that it be the source of the insurance. That is, borrowers may assign existing insurance to the lender or may purchase additional coverage on their own; they do not have to buy it from the lender. Buying the insurance elsewhere may be more economical. In some cases, credit life insurance is expensive because the insurers pay large commissions to the lenders. Some states recently have adopted consumer protection legislation in this field.

POLICY PROVISIONS

There are no standard life insurance policies, but all policies contain certain standard provisions, some of which are required by law. A knowledge of the more important policy provisions gives one a fuller understanding of how life insurance operates.

Beneficiary and Assignment

Beneficiary Clause. The **beneficiary** is the person (or other entity) named by the policyholder to receive the proceeds of the policy after the death of the insured. Note that the policyholder (who owns the policy) is not necessarily the person whose life is insured. The policyholder might, for instance, be a father who had purchased a policy insuring the life of a son or daughter. More typically, though, the policyholder owns a policy covering his or her own life. The beneficiary's name is stated in the application, which later is attached to and made a part of the policy.

The insurable interest requirement does not apply to the beneficiary. The policyholder must have an insurable interest in the life of the person whom the policy insures, but the policyholder can select whomever he or she chooses to be the beneficiary.

The policyholder also elects whether or not to retain the right to change the beneficiary. If this right is retained, the beneficiary is said to be revocable. If the policyholder does not retain the right to make a change, the beneficiary is irrevocable. The distinction can be an important one. A revocable beneficiary can be changed by the policyholder at any time without the beneficiary's permission. But a policyholder who names an irrevocable beneficiary gives up the right to make a change later, even if there is a divorce or some other reason for change. In this case the policyholder also may not assign the policy, surrender it for its cash value, or borrow on it without the beneficiary's consent.

A contingent beneficiary frequently is named. This person receives the policy proceeds if the primary beneficiary is no longer living when the insured dies. In many cases the spouse of the policyholder is primary beneficiary and the couple's children are named as contingent beneficiaries.

The naming of life insurance beneficiaries is similar to writing a will and should be done with equal care and precision. At the time when policies are written the policyholders know whom they intend to receive the benefits,

"THAT'S JUST IT — IF I HAD ANY BENEFICIARIES,
I WOULDN'T BE A HERMIT."

but many years later this may be subject to dispute. Misunderstandings are particularly likely to develop when there has been a divorce or when additional children have been born or adopted. For this reason, policies should be reviewed occasionally to make sure that beneficiary designations still are appropriate.

ASSIGNMENT PROVISION.   If an irrevocable beneficiary has not been named, the policyholder retains not only the right to change the beneficiary but also the right to **assign** (that is, transfer) the policy to another party. The usual purpose of assigning a policy is to provide collateral for a bank loan. When this is done, the owner of the policy instructs the insurer to pay death claims to the bank to the extent of the balance of the loan.

Life insurance policies can be assigned without the insurer's consent. However, the assignment provision states that the company is not legally bound by an assignment unless it has received a copy of the assignment document. This wording protects the company from being notified of an assignment after it has paid the policy proceeds to the named beneficiary.

Grace Period and Reinstatement

Grace Period. The **grace period** is one of the provisions that is required by law. The policy states the amount of the premium payments and the dates when they are due. The grace period allows a number of days, usually 31, to elapse after the due date. If the premium is paid during this period, the policy remains in force. If the premium is not paid by the last day of the grace period, the policy lapses.

REINSTATEMENT. The **reinstatement provision** provides that a lapsed policy may be put back in force within a stated period, usually three or five years. Before reinstating the policy the company can require evidence that the insured still is in good health. Also, all overdue premiums must be paid plus interest. Reinstating a lapsed policy may be preferable to replacing it with a new one if the old policy has favorable provisions that are not otherwise available.

Incontestability, Suicide, and Misstatement of Age

INCONTESTABLE CLAUSE. In Chapter 4 we learned that insurance policies are contracts of utmost good faith. If a person misrepresents important facts when applying for a policy, the contract can later be voided by the company, which would suggest that, if a man lied about the state of his health when applying for life insurance and the misrepresentation was discovered after his death ten years later, the beneficiary would not be entitled to receive the policy proceeds. Actually, that would not happen. The **incontestable clause** gives the insurer a period of time, two years on most policies, to check the information supplied by the applicant. Only during that period can the company contest a death claim or seek to void the contract. After the contract has been in force for two years it cannot be contested by the insurer, even if it discovers that material misrepresentations were made by the applicant.

The incontestable clause is a rather surprising provision, in that it appears to condone fraud. Nothing like it is contained in other insurance policies. It is required by law in life insurance because of the long-term nature of most policies and because of the difficulty of proving or disproving statements many years after they are made. The clause forces insurers to investigate applications carefully. It also enhances the value of life insurance by assuring beneficiaries that they will receive the benefits stated in the policy.

SUICIDE CLAUSE.   If an insured dies by suicide during the first two years of policy coverage, the beneficiary receives only the premiums that had been paid until that time. After the policy has been in force for two years, it applies to suicide just as it does to death resulting from other causes.

The purpose of the **suicide clause** is to prevent the insuring of people who plan to kill themselves. According to some estimates, nearly 2% of the deaths in this country result from suicide. Psychologists tell us that many of those who commit suicide threaten to do so for a period of time beforehand. If such people were able to insure their lives, life insurance rates would have to be raised; other insureds would be forced to help pay the death benefits of those who had purchased policies with the intent of killing themselves. This clearly would be a case of adverse selection, with a disproportionate number of policies being purchased by persons who would die shortly thereafter. Interestingly, the suicide clause apparently assumes that suicide-prone people will not buy policies with the intention of taking their lives more than two years later.

MISSTATEMENT OF AGE.   A 30-year-old applicant for life insurance who stated that he was only 25 would be charged a lower rate. Such **misstatement of age** is treated as a special form of misrepresentation to which the incontestable clause does not apply. Instead, the policy provides that the amount of insurance will be reduced to the amount that would have been purchased if the age had been stated correctly. If a 30-year-old man who said he was only 25 had purchased a $10,000 straight life policy, the amount would be reduced to $8,408 when the truth was discovered (based upon the rates used in Table 12 3). It is quite likely that the insured's true age would be discovered when his death certificate was submitted to the company, if not before.

Dividend Provisions

PARTICIPATING AND NONPARTICIPATING INSURANCE.   Life insurance policies are either participating or nonparticipating. A **participating policy** is one on which annual dividends are payable to the policyholder.

Holders of **nonparticipating policies** do not receive dividends. Although the percentage of nonparticipating insurance is rising, the majority (about 60%) of the ordinary life insurance now in force is participating.

The participating basis is occasionally used in other lines, but it is especially well suited to life insurance because of the long-term nature of the policies. Rates for life insurance are based on mortality, interest earnings, and company expenses. At the time a policy is issued, there is no way of knowing what any of these three elements actually will be during the years or decades ahead. In making the rates for a participating policy, actuaries make conservative estimates. They assume rather high mortality rates, low company interest earnings, and high company expenses. These assumptions cause the policy to be priced higher than it would be if more realistic estimates were used, and it gives the company a margin of safety if things don't turn out as well as expected. During the life of the participating policy, dividends are computed and paid to the policyholder. The dividends are based on the company's actual experience in mortality, interest, and expenses. The result is that the net premiums (after the dividends are paid) reflect the company's actual cost of providing the insurance.

Rates for nonparticipating policies are based on more realistic assumptions. They also include an allowance for the possibility that mortality or expenses will be higher or that interest earnings will be lower than expected. If any of these things happens with regard to participating policies, the company can reduce the dividend payments. When the insurance is nonparticipating, however, the price is fixed and cannot be adjusted to reflect either adverse or favorable developments.

Table 13–2 illustrates the differences between typical participating and nonparticipating policies. The rate for the participating policy is higher; that is, for a given amount of premium the purchaser of a nonparticipating policy

Table 13–2 Comparison of Participating and Non-participating Straight Life Policies Purchased from One Company for $100 by a 25-Year-Old Man

	PARTICIPATING POLICY	NON-PARTICIPATING POLICY
Rate per $1,000	$ 18.60	$ 13.85
Size of policy for $100 premium	5,380.00	7,220.00
Gross premium for 20 years	2,000.00	2,000.00
Dividends for 20 years (projected)	576.41	0
Net premium for 20 years (gross premium minus projected dividends)	1,423.59	2,000.00
Cash value at the end of 20 years	1,490.26	1,848.32

will get more coverage. However, the annual dividends reduce the net premium for the participating policy. The dividends can only be estimated (projected); they cannot be guaranteed. But, on the basis of the dividends that this company estimates it will pay during the first 20 years, the net premium for that period will be less for the participating than for the nonparticipating policy. You should bear in mind, though, that the nonparticipating policy is larger.

The two systems are actuarially equivalent, meaning that a participating policy costing $100 theoretically should be worth exactly as much as a nonparticipating policy costing $100 (if they are otherwise identical policies). Choosing between the two is similar to choosing between an endowment at 65 and a whole life policy paid up at 65. That is, purchasers shouldn't base their decisions upon which of the two they think is the better "bargain"; instead, they should decide which is more suitable for their particular needs.

DIVIDEND OPTIONS.   Participating policies allow the policyholder to choose from among at least four different **dividend options.** First, dividends may be taken in cash; the company will mail the policyholder a dividend check each year. Second, the policyholder may choose to use the dividends to reduce the premium payments. If this option is selected, the premium notice from the company will show the dividend subtracted from the premium and will bill the policyholder for the difference.

The third option permits dividends to be left on deposit with the company. Using this option is similar to putting the dividends into a savings account. The company pays interest on the accumulated amount. A guaranteed interest rate is stated in the policy; a higher rate is paid if, as normally is the case, the company's interest earnings permit. Dividends accumulated at interest by using this option can be withdrawn at the policyholder's request. If not withdrawn, they are added to the amount paid when the policy endows or when the insured dies. Over an extended period of time dividend accumulations can add up to a surprising amount. For instance, based on the recent dividend scale and interest rate paid by one company, dividend accumulations would total $9,920 at age 65 on a $10,000 straight life policy issued at age 25.

The fourth dividend option uses each year's dividend as a single premium to buy a paid-up addition to the policy. For example, a $25 dividend at age 35 could be used to add about $60 to the amount of a straight life policy. If the dividends were used this way every year on a $10,000 straight life policy purchased at age 25 (again, using the present dividend scale of the company in the previous example) the paid-up additions at age 65 would total $11,150, more than doubling the amount of the policy. The paid-up additions themselves have a cash value that always is at least as large as the amount of the dividends that were used to purchase the additions. The use of this option thus increases the cash and loan value as well as the death protection that the policy provides.

Some companies offer other dividend options. These may include paying up a limited payment policy in fewer years, shortening the period of an endowment policy, or purchasing one-year term insurance additions.

Nonforfeiture Provisions

Cash value policies that have been in force for at least a year or two cannot expire without value. In other words, a policyholder who stops paying the premiums does not thereby forfeit the policy's cash value. For this reason, the cash value is sometimes called the nonforfeiture value.

Cash value policies provide three **nonforfeiture options.** If the policyholder decides to stop paying the premiums he or she can take the cash value as cash, use it to buy a reduced amount of paid-up insurance, or use it to buy extended term insurance. The policyholder may also borrow the cash value while keeping the policy in force. The cash value and the amounts of the other nonforfeiture options are specified in a table in each policy. Table 13–3 is an example.

CASH OR LOAN VALUE.   There is little or no cash value for the first year or two because the company's expenses are concentrated in that period. The agent is paid half or more of the first year's premium as sales commission and there are other initial expenses, such as underwriting the application, preparing the policy, and setting up necessary accounting records. After the first year or so the cash value increases at a rate determined by the company and stated in the contract.

Cash values are an important element of competition among companies. Because of this, policies that are alike in other respects may have different cash values at different times. One company may increase the values rapidly in the early years; another may increase the values more slowly so that they can reach a higher point at age 65. Also, some companies may furnish higher cash values but provide lower policy dividends or less generous settlement options than others.

The policyholder has a contractual right to the cash value. Assume Ken Harris owns a $10,000 straight life policy that provides the nonforfeiture values shown in Table 13–3. If he decides to cash in the policy at the end of the fifth year, the company will send him a check for $650 ($65 × 10, the policy being for $10,000). If Ken waits until he is 65, the cash value will be $5,480.

If a policyholder needs to use some or all of the cash value but wants to

Table 13-3 Table of Nonforfeiture Values from One Straight Life Policy, Issued to Male, Age 35

POLICY ANNI-VERSARY	AGE ON ANNI-VERSARY	CASH OR LOAN VALUE PER $1,000 FACE AMOUNT	PAID-UP LIFE INSURANCE PER $1,000 FACE AMOUNT	EXTENDED TERM INSURANCE	
				YEARS	DAYS
1	36	$ —	$ —	—	—
2	37	8	19	2	61
3	38	27	60	6	34
4	39	46	100	8	311
5	40	65	138	10	311
6	41	85	177	12	161
7	42	105	213	13	236
8	43	125	249	14	208
9	44	146	285	15	127
10	45	166	317	15	319
11	46	188	352	16	139
12	47	209	384	16	257
13	48	228	411	16	301
14	49	246	435	16	300
15	50	265	459	16	297
16	51	284	483	16	275
17	52	303	506	16	236
18	53	322	528	16	184
19	54	342	551	16	134
20	55	361	571	16	60
27	62	493	696	14	130
30	65	548	741	13	175

continue the policy, a **policy loan** can be made. That is, the company will lend the policyholder part or all of the cash value. This also is a contractual right; the company will send the amount requested without asking the reason for the loan or when it will be repaid. The interest rate charged on policy loans is stated in the policy. On policies issued in past years the rate usually is 5 or 6%. Because interest rates have climbed recently, many policies currently being issued permit the company to increase the policy loan interest rate to as much as 8%. The amount of any unpaid loan and any unpaid interest is deducted from the proceeds otherwise payable at the death of the insured. If Ken Harris should die while a $2,000 loan is outstanding on his $10,000 policy, his beneficiary would receive $8,000 instead of the full face amount.

Policyholders frequently ask why they have to pay interest when they borrow their own cash value. The reason is that in computing premium rates company actuaries assume that the funds held by the company will be invested and will earn interest. You may recall that interest earnings are one of three components of life insurance rates. (Mortality rates and company expenses are the other two.) Thus, from the company's viewpoint, lending cash values to policyholders is not really different than lending the funds to an industrial firm or some other borrower; the company must earn interest on the funds however they are used.

The availability of policy loans is a valuable aspect of cash value life insurance. Cash values can be borrowed for emergencies, for making the down payment on a house, or for any purpose that the policyholder wishes. There is no repayment schedule. In fact, the loan never has to be repaid unless the policyholder wishes to do so. This possibility creates a potential danger, however. Although most people intend to repay their policy loans, the absence of any repayment requirement makes it very easy to put off or avoid repaying. And, when loans are not repaid, the protection provided by the policy is reduced. If the interest on the loan is paid each year the amount of the loan will remain constant, but interest that is not paid when due is added to the principal of the loan. In the case of a $2,000 loan on a policy with a 5% loan interest rate, the interest is $100 the first year. If no payment is made, the amount of the loan becomes $2,100 the second year and the interest payable for that year is $105 (5 percent of $2,100). By the end of only the sixth year, still assuming no payment of either interest or principal, the loan would be $2,552.56. The point is that, although policy loans are valuable and convenient, those who utilize them will drain away their protection if they don't discipline themselves to follow a repayment schedule.

A policyholder of course has the right to borrow from the cash value to pay premiums. When the **automatic premium loan** provision is in force, this borrowing is done automatically whenever the premium is not paid by the end of the grace period. That is, if a premium is not paid, the company will deduct the amount of the premium from the cash value (as a policy loan) in order to prevent the policy from lapsing.

Some policies provide automatic premium loan payments without request. In other cases the provision will be included (without extra charge) if it is requested when the policy is applied for. Because it prevents unintended policy lapses, the provision is a desirable one. Like regular policy loans, the automatic premium loan can be abused, however. Life insurance purchasers might do well to make sure the provision is included—and then forget that it exists.

PAID-UP INSURANCE OPTION.   The second nonforfeiture option permits the policyholder to use the cash value to purchase a reduced amount of **paid-up insurance.** The amount is indicated in the policy's table of nonforfeiture values.

To illustrate, if Ken Harris elects to stop paying for his $10,000 straight life policy at age 45 (and again using the values in Table 13–3), he can convert the policy to a fully paid-up straight life policy in the amount of $3,170. If he chooses this option, at age 65 the amount of the paid-up insurance will be $7,410. The paid-up insurance has cash and loan values and it pays dividends if the insurance was originally provided by a participating policy.

This option is particularly useful at retirement age. For the typical policyholder, the need for life insurance has diminished by then, but a limited amount to pay for funeral costs and other final expenses is desirable. The retired person therefore may elect to stop paying premiums, put some of the insurance on the reduced amount paid-up option, and use the remaining cash value to supplement retirement income.

EXTENDED TERM INSURANCE OPTION.   When the third nonforfeiture option is used, the cash value buys **extended term insurance.** The amount is not reduced; it is the full face amount of the policy (assuming there is no policy loan outstanding). The length of time the term insurance covers is shown in the table of nonforfeiture values.

Again referring to Table 13–3, at age 45 Ken Harris can convert his $10,000 straight life policy to $10,000 of term insurance that will remain in force for the next 15 years and 319 days or, in other words, until he is almost 61 years old. If he exercises this option at age 65, the term insurance will run for 13 years and 175 days.

Settlement Options

The main purpose of life insurance is to replace income that is cut off by retirement or death. Accordingly, life insurance benefits can be paid in the form of monthly income. The payments are made to either the policyholder or the beneficiary, depending upon whether they represent cash value or endowment proceeds in the one case or death proceeds in the other.

The policy proceeds can also be taken in a single lump sum cash payment. In fact, the great majority of proceeds are paid that way. However, because what the recipient usually needs is more income, use of one of the **settlement options** may be preferable. The options that may be chosen are:

interest income, installments for a fixed period, installments in a fixed amount, or life income.

INTEREST INCOME.   Under this option the company holds the proceeds and the payee (the policyholder or beneficiary) receives interest earnings. A minimum rate of interest is guaranteed in the policy; a higher rate is paid if the company's earnings permit.

This option can be used temporarily until a beneficiary decides upon a more permanent arrangement. It also is used if the proceeds are to be paid to children when they reach a certain age and the primary beneficiary is to receive interest income until that time.

INSTALLMENTS FOR A FIXED PERIOD.   This settlement option pays out the principal and interest in a fixed number of monthly or yearly payments. An example was given in Chapter 12 when Charlie Newlin considered buying a $30,000 policy in order to provide income for Ruth while Julie is growing up. The $30,000 would pay about $200 a month if payments are spread over a 16-year period.

If this option is chosen, payments continue for the stated period whether or not the initial payee survives. If that person dies before the end of the period, the remaining installments will be paid to his or her estate or to a contingent beneficiary if one was named.

INSTALLMENTS IN A FIXED AMOUNT. This option is similar to the fixed period option. The difference is that in this case a fixed amount per payment is specified, rather than the length of the payment period. For instance, the company might be instructed to make payments in the exact amount of $200 per month for as long as the money lasted (as the previous example suggests, this would be about 16 years). Again, the payments will continue after the death of the initial recipient if that person dies before receiving the full amount.

LIFE INCOME.   This settlement option guarantees an income for the remaining lifetime of the recipient. In effect, the proceeds of the policy are used to purchase a life annuity.

Life annuities.   A **life annuity** is a series of payments that continue for as long as the payee (the annuitant) lives. It is the opposite of life insurance. A life insurance policy guarantees that a fund equaling the face amount of the policy will be created, even if the person who buys the policy lives only a short period of time. In contrast, a life annuity guarantees that an existing fund (such as the proceeds of a life insurance policy) will provide a lifetime income, even if the person who buys the annuity lives for a very long time. Both the life insurance policy and the annuity transfer a risk to the insurance company. In the case of the life insurance policy, the risk is dying too soon (before a sum of money can be saved). In the case of the annuity, the risk is living too long; that is, the risk is living beyond the time when the fund would have been used up. Both are based on the law of large numbers, both are insurance, and the rates for both are based on average mortality rates. People who live to pay life insurance premiums for a longer than average length of time help pay for the policies of those who die sooner. In contrast, annuity purchasers who die sooner help pay for the income of those annuitants who live longer than average lives.

Life income options. Most life insurance policies offer three **life income options:** life only, life annuity with period certain, and refund annuity. Each guarantees a lifetime income to the annuitant.

The **life only** option pays a stated amount per month as long as the annuitant lives. The payments end with the death of the annuitant, regardless of how many (or how few) payments the annuitant has received at that time. If the annuitant dies after only two years, the payments stop at that time.

A **life annuity with a period certain** pays as long as the annuitant lives and also guarantees to pay for a certain minimum length of time. For instance, a life annuity with five years certain will pay as long as the annuitant lives, but will pay for a minimum of five years. If the annuitant dies at the end of the second year, payments will be made to the contingent beneficiary for three more years. Life annuities with 10 or 20 years certain are also available. Naturally, the longer the guaranteed period, the less each payment will be. This is seen in Table 13–4.

The other life income option, the **refund annuity,** also includes a minimum guarantee. In this case the company promises to pay out in installments at least the full amount of the purchase price. Table 13–4 shows that a widow, age 70, who is the beneficiary of a $50,000 life insurance

Table 13–4 Monthly Life Income Payments Offered by One Company to Females, Age 70

LIFE INCOME OPTION	PAYMENT PER $1,000 OF PROCEEDS	PAYMENT PER $50,000 OF PROCEEDS
Life only	$8.51	$425.50
Life, 5 years certain	8.40	420.00
Life, 10 years certain	8.11	405.00
Life, 20 years certain	6.86	343.00
Instalment refund	8.09	404.50

policy and who chooses this option will receive a lifetime monthly income of $404.50. If she dies before receiving $50,000 in monthly installments, the company will continue the $404.50 payments to the contingent beneficiary until the full $50,000 has been paid out.

All policies contain tables showing the amounts payable under each of the settlement options. These usually are minimums, the amounts that the company will pay even if it has extremely low interest earnings. Normally, interest earnings are sufficient to pay substantially more. The payments shown in Table 13–4 are amounts that were actually being paid by a particular company during a recent year; they are much higher than the payments guaranteed in the policies issued by this company.

Guaranteed Insurability

Guaranteed insurability is an optional provision that many companies will add for an additional premium. It permits the policyholder to purchase specified additional amounts of coverage at stated times. The value of the provision lies in the fact that the additional insurance is available whether or not the insured is in good health when the option is exercised. Thus, it literally does guarantee the insured person's continued insurability.

A typical guaranteed insurability rider on a $10,000 policy issued at age 25 permits the purchase of additional $10,000 amounts at ages 28, 31, 34, 37, and 40. If the policyholder elects to add the coverage, standard rates at the attained ages apply. Because people who are in poor health are very likely to take advantage of the option to buy more coverage, insurers anticipate adverse selection and price the rider accordingly.

Health Insurance Benefits

Three types of health insurance benefits can be added to life insurance policies: **accidental death benefit, waiver of premium,** and **disability income.** These are optional benefits for which additional charges are made.

ACCIDENTAL DEATH BENEFIT. The accidental death benefit is an agreement to pay the beneficiary a multiple of the face amount of the policy if the insured is killed by accident before reaching age 65. In effect, it is the same as a separate accidental death policy. The amount paid is usually the same as the face amount, the policy thus providing "double indemnity" in the event of accidental death. Triple indemnity is offered by some companies. Accidental death typically is defined as being caused by "solely external, violent, and accidental means." The limitations of "accidental means" were described in connection with disability income insurance in Chapter 11. Death caused by suicide, war, or drugs is often excluded.

Most life insurance experts frown upon the accidental death benefit feature. They believe that it gives policyholders an exaggerated idea of their life insurance protection, causing them for instance to think of a $25,000 policy as providing $50,000 of protection. Also, the logic of the accidental death benefit is questionable. After all, survivors need the same amount of income replacement whether an insured's death is caused by cancer or by an automobile accident. It probably would be better to use the money that could be spent for double indemnity to buy a larger face amount of insurance instead.

WAIVER OF PREMIUM.   This provision states that future premiums will not have to be paid if the insured becomes totally and permanently disabled before a stated age, usually 60 or 65. All benefits and values provided by the policy, including dividends if the policy is participating, continue just as if premiums were being paid.

This is a desirable benefit. Its cost is quite low, and it prevents a disabled insured from having to let a policy lapse at a time when it may be especially needed.

DISABILITY INCOME.   This provision is not as commonly used as the preceding two, because of the availability of disability income protection under separate health insurance policies. When it is added to a life insurance policy, the disability income rider usually provides $10 per month for each $1,000 of face amount. The benefit is paid if the insured becomes totally and permanently disabled before age 55 or 60. If the insured is still disabled at age 65, the disability income payments stop and the face amount of the policy is paid.

ANNUITIES

We have seen that life annuities are a form of insurance providing a lifetime income, and that they are available as life insurance settlement options. Annuities are more frequently purchased as separate contracts. They are the basis of either individual or group pension plans. In this section we shall consider annuities with regard to the various features shown in Figure 13–1.

Ways of Buying Annuities

Annuities can be purchased in any of four ways. First, they can be obtained with the proceeds of a life insurance policy. One of the life income settlement options can be used to liquidate either the cash value (the annuitant in this case being the insured) or the face amount of the policy after the death of

Figure 13-1 Features of annuities

1. *How purchased?*
   Lump sum: From life insurance proceeds
   Lump sum: From savings
   Installments: Group pension
   Installments: Individual contract

2. *When will income payments begin?*
   Immediately
   Deferred

3. *How long are payments guaranteed?*
   Life income only
   Life income with minimum number of years guaranteed
   Life income with refund of purchase price guaranteed

4. *How many lives are covered?*
   One
   Two or more

5. *How many dollars will be paid?*
   Fixed amount
   Variable amount

the insured (the annuitant in this case being the beneficiary). Annuities can also be purchased with a cash lump-sum payment the source of which is not life insurance. A person who has accumulated investments in securities or real estate may choose to sell some of the investment at retirement and use the proceeds to buy an annuity. The third method of buying an annuity is through a group pension plan. Many workers are covered by group annuities that provide income after retirement. These arrangements are described in Chapter 15. Fourth, annuities can be purchased by individuals, with pre-miums being paid in installments during the person's working years.

Time When Payments to the Annuitant Begin

Annuities are either immediate or deferred, depending upon when payments to the annuitant begin. **Immediate annuities** begin making income payments the first month after they are purchased. An annuity purchased at age 70 with the cash value of an endowment policy probably would provide immediate payments. Most annuities are **deferred annuities,** paid for an installments and with income payments postponed until the purchaser reaches retirement age. Pension plans and individually purchased retirement annuities are usually written on the deferred payment basis.

Guarantee of Payments

Life annuities guarantee income payments to the annuitant either (a) for life only, (b) for life with at least a minimum number of payments, or (c) for life with at least the full amount being refunded. These alternatives were described in the earlier discussion of life insurance settlement options.

Number of Lives Covered

Most annuities are **single life annuities,** covering the lifetime of one person. Subject to the minimum guarantees furnished by period certain annuities and refund annuities, payments end with the death of the single annuitant.

The **joint and survivor annuity** covers the lives of more than one person. This arrangement is frequently chosen by retired couples who need income payments as long as either spouse lives. The joint and survivor annuity will pay the surviving spouse the same amount that was paid while both persons were living. Under this plan the insurer of course expects to continue to pay for a longer period than it would under a single life annuity. Each monthly payment therefore is considerably smaller. A compromise is available in the form of a joint and survivor annuity that pays a reduced benefit to the survivor. For example, the joint-and-two-thirds-survivor annuity reduces the payments by one-third upon the death of the first spouse. If payments had been $900 a month, they will continue in the amount of $600 a month for the rest of the survivor's life.

For people who are about to retire, choosing among these options can be a tough decision. On the one hand, the single life annuity will provide the highest income. On the other hand, the joint and survivor annuity will provide greater security, but with lower income. The joint and survivor annuity with two-thirds benefit to the survivor frequently is selected as a reasonable compromise.

Fixed or Variable Payments

Most annuities are designed to provide a fixed amount of monthly income, $1,000 a month, for instance (subject to dividend additions, if the contract is participating). During periods when general price levels are rising, this creates a major problem. People living on fixed incomes find that their purchasing power is declining, because for the same number of dollars they can buy less and less in goods and services. Inflation is especially hard on purchasers of deferred annuities, due to the length of the period that such contracts cover. There may be 50 or 60 years between the time when dollars are first paid toward the purchase of a deferred annuity and the time when the last monthly retirement income check is received. Even a small rate of inflation will destroy much of the buying power of a fixed number of dollars over that length of time. In an attempt to cope with this problem, the variable annuity was devised.

A **variable annuity** is one that does not guarantee to pay a fixed number of dollars of monthly retirement income. Instead, it pays an income that is based upon the fluctuating value of the common stocks in which the insurance company has invested. The theory is that over a long period of time, common stock prices will move in the same direction as the cost of living. If living costs rise, says the theory, common stock prices will rise also; annuitants will then receive more dollars to pay for the higher costs of food, housing, energy, and so forth.[1]

An example of a variable annuity is the one that is available to the employees of most colleges and universities through the College Retirement Equities Fund (CREF). Employees may divide their premium payments (and their employer's payments) between CREF and a regular fixed-dollar annuity plan. The CREF variable annuity is divided into an accumulation period and a liquidation period. During the employee's working years a number of "accumulation units" are purchased. At retirement, these are converted into "annuity units" that then become the basis of the individual's retirement income.

Let's assume that Professor Long and his college put $100 into CREF each month. Each payment buys a number of accumulation units. The number of units credited to Professor Long each month depends on the current value of the accumulation unit. The value of the accumulation unit is determined each month by dividing the current market value of CREF's diversified common stock holdings by the total number of accumulation units. Each unit thus represents a small fraction of CREF's investment portfolio. If the current value of the stock is $60 million and there are 3 million accumulation units, then the value of each unit is $20. In this case, Professor Long's $100 will buy 5 accumulation units. He will buy fewer units for his $100 when the accumulation unit value is higher and more units when it is lower. As the months and years go by, the number of his accumulation units grows. The total value of these units continues to fluctuate with the monthly calculation of the accumulation unit's value.

When he reaches retirement age, Professor Long will have acquired a certain number of accumulation units. If he has, say, 2,000 units and they

[1]Alternatively, variable annuity payments can be based directly on a cost of living index.

are then valued at $40 each, their total value will be $80,000. As we know, the $80,000 could be used to purchase a regular, fixed-dollar annuity at that point. Instead of doing that, however, CREF will convert the 2,000 accumulation units into annuity units. Using a mortality table, CREF will then calculate the number of annuity units that can be allocated each month for Professor Long's retirement income. For instance, this might be 20 units. The dollar value of the annuity units, like the dollar value of the accumulation units, depends on the value of CREF's common stock investments. It is computed each year to reflect the changing value of the investments. The year when Professor Long retires the annuity units might be worth $30 each, giving him an income of 20 × $30, or $600 a month for that year. If stock prices advance, the annuity units may be valued at $31 the next year. If so, Professor Long will receive 20 × $31, or $620 per month that year.

As we have seen, both the accumulation unit and the annuity unit are variable. The units are different because they perform different functions. The accumulation unit measures the current market value of Professor Long's share in CREF's investments during the years before he retires. The annuity unit is used to spread out the payments to Professor Long during his retirement years.

The variable annuity is designed to deal with the risk of inflation, but it is not without risks of its own. It is based upon a number of studies that appear to show a correlation between long-run changes in stock prices and long-run changes in the cost of living. Some financial experts say that this correlation does not exist; many say that although it may exist over a long number of years it should not be expected to hold for shorter periods. During the mid-1970s, for instance, stock prices declined while living costs continued to rise. If Professor Long had retired in 1972, his income would have dropped for several years thereafter, while the prices of the things he needed to buy rose each year. The future will reveal whether the variable annuity is based on sound principles or not. In the meantime, many people are following a middle course and are dividing their retirement dollars between fixed and variable annuities.

IMPORTANT TERMS

Ordinary life insurance	Incontestable clause
Industrial life insurance	Suicide clause
Group life insurance	Misstatement of age clause
Credit life insurance	Participating insurance
Beneficiary	Dividend
Assignment	Dividend options
Grace period	Nonforfeiture provisions
Reinstatement provision	Policy loan

Automatic premium loan	Waiver of premium
Paid-up insurance option	Disability income benefit
Extended term insurance option	Immediate annuity
Settlement options	Deferred annuity
Life annuity	Single life annuity
Life income options	Joint and survivor annuity
Guaranteed insurability	Variable annuity
Accidental death benefit	

KEY POINTS TO REMEMBER

1. Life insurance is classified as either ordinary, industrial, group, or credit. The first two classes are individually marketed; the last two use the group marketing system.
2. The life insurance policyholder names the beneficiary, who receives the policy proceeds after the insured's death. Beneficiaries may be either revocable or irrevocable. Contingent beneficiaries are usually named also.
3. Life insurance policies can be assigned as collateral for loans, but assignments are not binding on the company unless it receives a copy of the assignment.
4. If the premium is not paid by the end of the grace period (usually 31 days after the due date), a policy will lapse.
5. The reinstatement provision permits a lapsed policy to be put back in force within a stated number of years. The person insured must be in good health and overdue premiums must be paid.
6. A life insurance company can void a policy if it finds that the applicant made a false statement that was important to the acceptance of the application. The incontestability clause imposes a time limit of two years for the company to do this. After two years the policy cannot be contested by the company.
7. Suicide is not covered during the first two years of a policy. The purpose of the suicide clause is to avoid adverse selection.
8. If the insured's age is misstated, the amount of insurance becomes the amount that the premiums paid would have purchased if the proper rate had been used.
9. Participating policies pay policyholder dividends; nonparticipating policies do not.
10. Participating policies provide at least four dividend options, permitting dividends to be (a) taken in cash, (b) used to reduce premiums, (c) left with the company to earn interest, or (d) used to buy paid-up additions to the policy.
11. Nonforfeiture options state three ways in which the cash value of a policy can be used if the policyholder stops paying premiums. The three options are: (a) cash payment, (b) purchase of a reduced amount of paid-up insurance, or (c) purchase of extended term insurance.
12. The policyholder can borrow the cash value at an interest rate stated in the policy. Unpaid loans and interest are deducted from the policy proceeds that otherwise would be paid.
13. If the automatic premium loan provision is included, unpaid premiums are automatically paid by means of policy loans.

14. Life insurance policies offer four settlement options in addition to lump sum cash payment: (a) interest income, (b) installments for a fixed period, (c) installments in a fixed amount, or (d) life income.
15. The life income settlement option is a life annuity, a form of insurance that guarantees an income for the lifetime of the annuitant.
16. Most policies offer three life income options: (a) life only, (b) life annuity with period certain, and (c) refund annuity.
17. The guaranteed insurability rider permits the purchase of additional amounts of insurance at stated times regardless of the condition of the insured's health.
18. Accidental death benefit, waiver of premium, and disability income are three kinds of health insurance benefits that can be added to life insurance contracts.
19. Life annuities often are purchased separately, rather than as a life insurance settlement option. They can be classified on the basis of (a) how they are purchased, (b) whether they are immediate or deferred, (c) what guarantees other than life income they provide, (d) whether they are single or joint and survivor, and (e) whether payments are fixed or variable.
20. The variable annuity is designed to reduce the impact of inflation. The annuitant's income depends on the value of the insurer's common stock investments.

REVIEW QUESTIONS

1. Distinguish among the four classes of life insurance.
2. What is the difference between a revocable and an irrevocable beneficiary?
3. In what circumstances can a life insurance company contest the payment of a policy's proceeds?
4. Are policy proceeds paid if the insured commits suicide?
5. Can an insurer void a policy if it discovers that the applicant's age was misstated?
6. Explain the "paid-up additions" dividend option.
7. Why do policyholders have to pay interest if they borrow their cash value?
8. Explain the difference between the paid-up insurance and the extended term nonforfeiture options.
9. What is the difference between the fixed period and the fixed amount settlement options?
10. How do the three life income options differ from one another?
11. Upon what grounds is the accidental death benefit criticized?
12. What is the waiver of premium rider?
13. In what ways can life annuities be purchased?
14. What is the difference between immediate and deferred annuities?
15. Why might an annuity be written to cover the lives of more than one person?
16. Upon what theory is the variable annuity based?

DISCUSSION QUESTIONS

1. It sometimes is said that cash value life insurance policies are "flexible in filling the needs of their owners." In what ways is this true?

2. Why does the length of time covered by the extended term option (see Table 13–3) at first increase and then decrease?

3. Why is it suggested that people make sure their life insurance policies include the automatic premium loan provision and then forget that the provision exists?

4. Which is more expensive, participating or nonparticipating life insurance?

5. Does the two-year suicide clause seem to you to be a reasonable policy provision?

6. (a) Applicants for life insurance often must pass a medical examination. Why?
   (b) Applicants for annuities don't have to take a medical examination. Why not?

7. Why would anyone in their right mind buy an immediate life annuity, when they could instead invest the money, use the interest income, and leave the principal to their heirs?

8. On refund annuities, the insurance company promises to pay out at least the full purchase price, and if the annuitant lives long enough, it will pay out much more than that. Isn't this a money-losing proposition for the insurance company? How can it afford to do this?

9. Does it seem to you that the variable annuity is based on sound principles? Would you advise your parents to buy one?

CHAPTER 14
BUYING LIFE INSURANCE

LIFE INSURANCE PROGRAMMING

ESTATE PLANNING AND BUSINESS USES

THE COST OF LIFE INSURANCE

LIFE INSURANCE FOR COLLEGE STUDENTS

From the consumer's viewpoint, life insurance is one of the most important of all purchases. A life insurance program is a lifetime plan; it is a major bulwark of a family's financial security; and it costs a lot of money. Life insurance therefore confronts consumers with some important questions, including the purposes for which it should be used, and the kinds and amounts that should be purchased. This chapter provides information that can help life insurance buyers deal with those questions.

LIFE INSURANCE PROGRAMMING

Life insurance programming is a process of arranging a plan of life insurance to serve the needs of a particular family. In effect, it uses the risk management concept to handle a family's risk of income loss. Four steps are involved. The first step is to analyze the family's needs and to decide which of them are most important. Second, goals are set for the amounts of protection that the family will try to provide. Third, resources presently available to help meet the goals are reviewed. Finally, a plan of action is decided upon with regard to both the kinds and the amounts of insurance that will be purchased.

Analyzing the Family's Needs

No two families are alike. Each has unique circumstances, and each is made up of individuals who have their own ideas about what things are important and what things are unimportant. To some families, future financial security is more important than having a new car or taking a vacation trip. Other families live for the here and now—perhaps because they believe they can't afford to prepare for the future, or because they haven't really considered what the future may bring. But for any family an analysis of the financial needs that would arise with the death of a family member can be helpful. It can help them decide what steps to take now in order to provide for their future financial security. Seven specific needs should be considered:

1. Cash for immediate expenses
2. Income for the child-raising period
3. Insurance for the mother
4. Life income for the widow
5. Mortgage payment
6. Educational funds
7. Retirement income

CASH FOR IMMEDIATE EXPENSES.   The death of a family member is always followed by bills that must be paid. These include funeral expenses, doctor and hospital bills, unpaid taxes, and personal debts. Cash for the payment of these bills is an immediate and pressing need. In some cases, extra funds may also be needed for the first weeks or months while the family is adjusting to its changed circumstances and learning how to cut back its living expenses.

INCOME FOR THE CHILD-RAISING PERIOD.   For families with young children, the greatest need in the event of the death of a major income earner is income while the children are growing up. Unfortunately, this need is greatest at the very time when a family is in the poorest position to deal with it. The younger the children, the longer the period until they will be self-sufficient. At the same time, when there are young children a family's income usually is limited and its expenses are high.

   Many families assume that if the father dies the mother will then support the family; frequently, there is no other choice. However, the problem should be considered realistically. Does the mother have training and experience that would enable her to earn a good income? How much would she net after allowing for extra transportation, clothing, food, and child care costs? If she works full time, how much would she have to give up in social security benefits?[1] Would relatives be available to help care for the children? How important is it to the parents to make it possible for the mother to spend her time with the children instead of at work?

INSURANCE FOR THE MOTHER.   Because fathers are the major income earners in most families, insuring their lives usually has the highest priority. In fact, until recent years, insuring the mother's life often was not even considered. Table 14–1 shows that this practice is changing. Of the policies purchased during 1977, 36% covered females.

   One reason for the growth of insurance for women is their increased activity in the business and professional world. More and more wives are employed outside the home and supply major portions of their families' total incomes. When a working wife's family depends on her earnings for its standard of living, insurance is needed to replace her income in the event of her death. This need of course is crucial when a woman is the family's sole financial support.

   Increasing amounts of insurance are also being written on the lives of women who do not have outside jobs. Their economic contribution is harder to measure than that of working wives (and husbands), but it is no less

---

[1]This amount is based upon the social security "earnings test." See Chapter 16.

Table 14-1 Purchases of Ordinary Life Insurance, by Age and Sex of the Insured

PERSON INSURED	PERCENTAGE OF POLICIES		PERCENTAGE OF AMOUNT	
	1967	1977	1967	1977
Male under 15	9%	7%	3%	2%
Female under 15	8	7	2	2
Male adult	61	57	85	77
Female adult	22	29	10	19
	100%	100%	100%	100%

Source: Life Insurance Fact Book 1978 (New York: American Council of Life Insurance), p. 14.

real. The increased recognition of this fact is another reason for the growth of insurance for women.

LIFE INCOME FOR THE WIDOW. Income provided for the child-raising period will end when the children are grown. Although the widow may then obtain full-time employment, she may not be in a position to earn a large income. Many families rely on life insurance proceeds to continue to protect the widow's standard of living.

This need may be greatest during what is called the social security blackout period. This is the period between the end of social security benefits when the children are grown and the time when the widow reaches age 60 and becomes eligible for social security retirement benefits. (Higher benefits are paid if the widow waits until a later age to begin receiving them.)

MORTGAGE PAYMENT. The family's insurance program can include provision for paying off the balance of the home mortgage. Paying off the mortgage will reduce family expenses and thereby reduce the need for income replacement. However, this is not always the best thing to do. Instead of paying off the mortgage, it may be better in some cases to provide an income sufficient to continue to make the house payments; doing this will give the family more flexibility in deciding whether to stay in the present home or to move to a different one.

EDUCATIONAL FUNDS. Most parents hope that their children will be able to go to college, and supplying funds for college expenses is frequently a major reason for buying life insurance. Educational funds are only one of several needs, however, and when each of the various needs is examined realistically, it sometimes is found that others must be given higher priority than this one. For instance, if a family cannot afford to cover all of its needs, should it concentrate on providing college funds before making sure that there will be enough income while the children are still in elementary and high school? How does the first rule of personal risk management apply in this situation? Facing up to questions like this and setting realistic priorities are two of the purposes of this step in the life insurance programming process.

If educational funds are to be provided, another question is how this is to be done. Should a family purchase an endowment policy on the life of a child? Many families do so, with the very best intentions. However, endowments on children are seldom the best approach. The policy should cover the father instead (if he is the major source of family income), and it probably should not be a short-term endowment. Table 14–2 shows us why. It shows that $500 a year would buy an $8,400 endowment at age 18 covering the life of a boy who was 3 years old when the policy was issued. The policy, of course, would have a cash value of $8,400 when the boy reaches 18, and this sum could then be used to help pay his college expenses. The same $500 could be used to buy a 20-year endowment covering the life of a 25-year-old father. This would buy a $12,100 endowment, having a cash value of $6,830 when the boy is 18. The cash value would be somewhat less than in the other case, but this policy would have the important advantage of providing $12,100 of income protection. But wouldn't an even better approach be to buy straight life insurance on the father? For the same cost, a $37,600 straight life policy can be obtained. In 15 years it will have $6,350 of cash value that can be used for college expenses. And, while the child is growing up, this policy will furnish $37,600 of income protection. Also,

Table 14-2 Comparison of Policies Purchased for $500 Premium[a]

POLICY	RATE PER $1,000	ANNUAL PREMIUM	AMOUNT OF INSURANCE	CASH VALUE AFTER 15 YEARS
		COVERING BOY, AGE 3		
Endowment at age 18	$59.66	$500	$ 8,400	$8,400
		COVERING FATHER, AGE 25		
20-year endowment	41.25	500	12,100	6,830
Straight life	13.31	500	37,600	6,350

[a]Nonparticipating policies. Approximate amounts.

remember that the cash value can be borrowed. If this is done the policy will remain in force and continue to provide over $30,000 of coverage.

The point is that too many families buy endowments on children to finance college expenses. It generally is better to buy some form of whole life insurance on the life of the major income earner. This approach helps meet two objectives: It accumulates a fund for educational expenses and at the same time it provides a substantial amount of income protection during the child-raising period.

RETIREMENT INCOME.   When we are young we don't think much about retirement. When we are in our twenties and thirties our parents are still working and we associate retirement with our grandparents. Retirement worries are two generations away, and we are safely insulated from them by our parents' generation. In a way, this approach is a healthy one. Getting an education, getting a good job, and perhaps starting a family present enough worries. Yet, those who have the most enjoyable retirement years often are the ones who did look ahead and make plans for their future many years earlier. Therefore, in setting up a program of life insurance, one of the needs that we should consider is that of retirement income.

Most people will receive social security benefits when they retire and many will also receive income from their employer's pension program. The question to consider is whether or not these benefits will be large enough to pay for the travel, recreational activities, and other things that can make retirement enjoyable, rather than merely possible. Additional income from cash value life insurance may make the difference. However, providing for retirement income again raises the issue of priorities. Few families can afford to cover all of their needs. The problem here is the same as the one involving educational funds: first things must come first. Highest priority usually must be given to the first two needs on our list, cash for immediate expenses and income for the child-raising period. Some of the other needs that we have considered may also have a higher priority than retirement income.

As we pointed out previously, the problem is most difficult for young families. Their needs are the greatest, and their ability to handle them is usually the least. Many young families are hard pressed to deal with even high priority income protection needs. They may have to confine themselves to term insurance, at least temporarily, and thus do without the advantages of cash value policies. Practically all families must make compromises, often in the form of relying upon a combination of term and whole life insurance. Such a combination may permit them to cover their highest priority needs fairly well and also make a start toward such needs as educational funds and retirement income. Then, as time goes along, they may be able to add cash value policies or make other provisions for long-term savings.

Setting Goals

The second step of the programming process, after deciding what the various needs are, is to set goals. In other words, the family must decide how much protection it needs.

At this point one must use some common sense. If Charlie and Ruth Newlin or any other young couple were to go through the list of seven needs and put a figure on each one, the result could be staggering. They probably would come up with a total need of several hundred thousand dollars. At that point they might conclude that there was no way they could afford so much insurance and that the whole programming effort had been a waste of time. However, if we compare building a program of life insurance with furnishing a house, it might seem more reasonable.

When Charlie and Ruth got married, they had very little money, certainly not enough to buy a house and equip it with fine furniture and appliances. Actually, they couldn't even afford to furnish an apartment, let alone buy a house. So they moved into a furnished apartment. Gradually, they began to acquire some things of their own. A while later they moved to an unfurnished apartment. They recently have rented a house, and they hope some day to be able to buy and furnish a house of their own. In the same way, building an ideal life insurance program, like furnishing a home, is a process that takes both money and time. The fact that it can't be acquired right away doesn't mean that it isn't worth working toward. But first things must come first. The Newlins started out with a furnished apartment, not an $80,000 house. They also began their life insurance program by concentrating upon a need that was vitally important to them and yet was within their range financially.

You may recall that it was the need for income protection while their daughter Julie is growing up that first aroused the Newlins' interest in life insurance. Charlie was earning $1,500 a month. He and Ruth decided that their goal would be to make $900 a month available in the event of his death. Bill Scott, their life insurance agent, knew that they would need more protection later, but he felt that providing for $900 a month for the 16 years until Julie would be 18 would be a good beginning. He decided to wait until next year to talk with them about developing their program further.

Reviewing Present Resources

The next step in programming is to find out what resources are available to meet the family's objectives. These frequently turn out to be much more than it had realized. For a young family, usually the most important existing resource is social security. It furnishes income to survivors and to retired workers. Other resources may include group life insurance, individual life

Figure 14–1 Newlin family protection plan I.

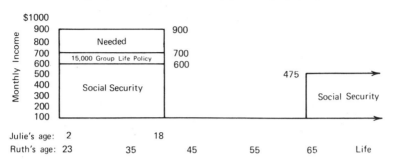

insurance policies already in force, real estate, investments, and the potential earning power of survivors.

When Bill Scott first met with Charlie and Ruth, he drew the diagram shown in Figure 14–1. This made it easy for them to see what their situation was at the time. The diagram shows how much monthly income would be available if Charlie were not alive to provide it. The vertical axis measures the amounts; the horizontal axis indicates, in terms of the survivors' ages, the periods during which the income would be paid. If Charlie died, Ruth would receive about $600 a month in social security benefits until Julie reached 18.[2] She would again be eligible for benefits at retirement age; this would provide about $475 a month starting at age 65.[3] Charlie had $15,000 of group life insurance. Bill showed them that it could be used to provide an additional $100 a month for the 16-year period. Because their goal was to provide $900 a month, they were left with an unfilled need of $200 a month.

Adopting a Plan of Action

Acting on Bill Scott's advice, the Newlins decided to buy a $30,000 straight life policy. Since the time of that purchase, their situation has changed and so has their insurance program.

It is now three years later and Charlie and Ruth have a son, Chad, aged two. Julie is five. Ruth has given up her part-time job. Charlie is doing well with Metro Industries and is earning $2,000 a month. During the three years since their first meeting, the Newlins have developed a good relationship with Bill. They believe that he understands their needs, and they have grown

---

[2]After age 18, social security benefits for children of deceased workers who are in college continue at a reduced level until age 22.
[3]Social security benefits are set by Congress and are changed frequently. Although the figures used here are realistic estimates, they are approximations only.

to trust his judgment, even though they haven't been able to buy as much insurance as he has recommended. However, they have added to their program, as Figure 14–2 illustrates. This diagram is more complicated than the previous one because the family now has more policies. Also, social security benefits would be higher as long as both children were under age 18; after the older child reached that age benefits would continue at a lesser level until the younger child reached age 18.

The Newlins have purchased three more policies. The first was a 20-year term policy covering Ruth. In addition, they bought a $5,000 20-year term policy covering Charlie; its purpose is to provide funds for immediate expenses in case of his death. Recently, they purchased a $20,000 straight

Figure 14–2 Newlin family protection plan II

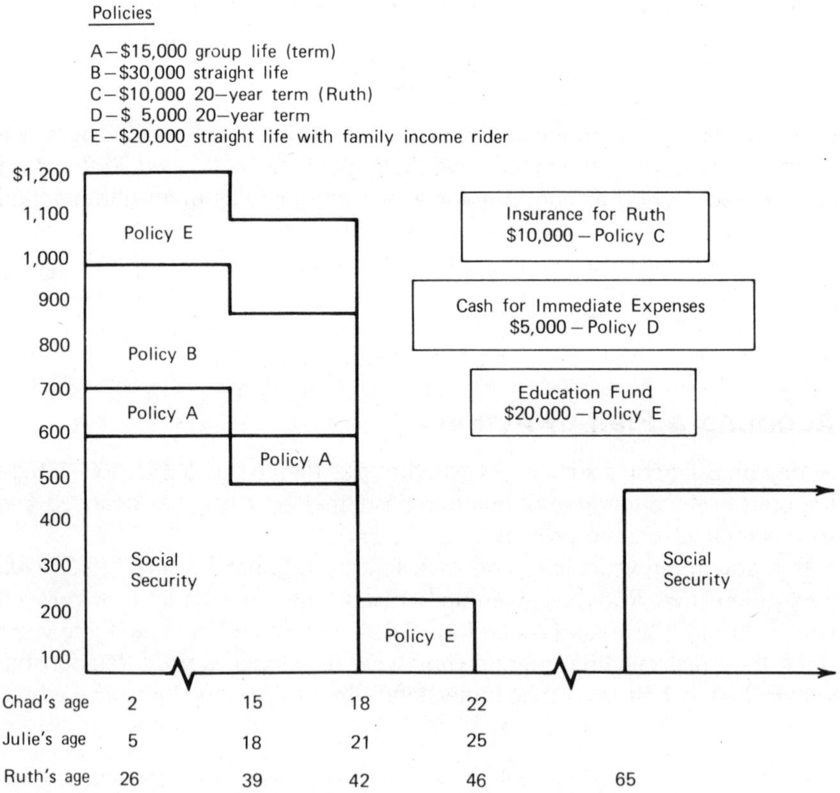

Policies

A—$15,000 group life (term)
B—$30,000 straight life
C—$10,000 20—year term (Ruth)
D—$ 5,000 20—year term
E—$20,000 straight life with family income rider

Note: Income from Social Security would be reduced when Julie reached age 18. Continuation of benefits for college years is not shown.

life policy with a family income rider. This was a tough decision for them. Ruth calls their living room furniture "Salvation Army Modern" and they would have liked to replace it this year. But they decided (at Bill's urging) to put up with it for another year or two and buy the additional insurance instead.

As we can see, the Newlins' insurance program still has some large gaps. They have concentrated on the need for income protection while the children are growing up. Until their most recent purchase, they hadn't earmarked anything for college expenses. The new policy gives them a $20,000 fund for that purpose, while its family income rider provides an additional $200 of monthly income protection for the next 20 years. If Charlie is living when the children go to college he will be able to borrow the cash value of that and the other straight life policy to help cover expenses. They have done very little about income for Ruth during the social security blackout period. Also, the need for retirement income has been given a rather low priority. It hasn't been completely neglected, though. They will have a total cash value of about $28,000 in the two straight life policies when Charlie reaches retirement age. This won't be very much if inflation continues at its current pace, but it will help.

The Newlins have made a good start on their life insurance program. With future increases in income, they may be able to include other types of saving in their program, such as investment in a home or a mutual fund. They realize that their needs will change in the future as their family responsibilities change. Life insurance programming is not something that they can do just once and forget. In two or three years Charlie and Ruth will again sit down with Bill Scott to analyze their needs, set new goals, review their resources, and decide what course of action is most appropriate at that point in their lives.

ESTATE PLANNING AND BUSINESS USES

We have concentrated on the uses of life insurance in typical family situations. In this section we shall briefly summarize some of the other ways in which life insurance is used.

Estate Planning

Making arrangements to conserve the value of a person's property is called **estate planning.** The estate planning process goes beyond life insurance programming to include a variety of measures designed to help create an estate and to transfer it to others economically after its owner dies. The methods used may include wills, trusts, gifts, and life insurance.

"MY FINAL REQUEST IS THAT YOU MAIL
THIS INSURANCE PREMIUM FOR ME."

The importance of estate planning stems largely from the state and federal taxes that are levied when property is transferred from one person to another—and from the size and complexity of those taxes. In years past estate planning was important only to a very small segment of the population—persons who had enormous investments and other assets and who therefore were subject to high estate tax rates. Today inflation has pushed up salaries, home values, and the worth of other property so that millions of people who do not consider themselves wealthy find that they have taxable estates of significant size. Because estate taxes are high (the rate ranges from 18 to 70%) it is important to take whatever actions the laws allow in order to avoid unnecessary taxation.

Estate planning may require the joint efforts of several specialists: a lawyer, an accountant, and the trust officer of a bank, in addition to an expert life insurance agent. The lawyer gives legal advice and draws up wills and other legal documents. The accountant handles tax, business valuation, and other accounting matters. The trust officer provides investment and financial services. The life insurance agent frequently is the one who initiates the estate planning process by explaining its potential value and encouraging families to seek legal and other technical assistance.

One use of life insurance in estate planning is to provide cash for the debts, taxes, and administrative costs that must be paid soon after a property owner's death. In the absence of life insurance it may be necessary to sell off some of the property immediately in order to make these payments. When such "forced sales" are necessary, the selling price frequently is below the real worth of the property. But if the owner had sufficient life insurance its proceeds can be used to make the required payments, thus permitting a more orderly and economical disposition of the estate's assets.

The details of estate planning are far too complex to describe here. Our purpose is simply to point out that proper planning can minimize the tax and other costs of estate creation and transferral, thus maximizing the benefit of an estate to its present and future owners. It is important to realize that a skillful life insurance agent can play a key role in the estate planning process.

Business Uses of Life Insurance

Two of the important uses of life insurance in business are to fund buy-and-sell agreements and to insure the value of key employees.

BUY-AND-SELL AGREEMENTS. Three men named Allen, Bailey, and Cook are the managers and principal owners of ABC Manufacturing, Incorporated. The business is worth about $3 million. What will happen if one of the three, say Cook, dies? Will Allen and Bailey pay Mrs. Cook $1 million? Will Mrs. Cook be forced to take over Mr. Cook's duties at the plant? These can be serious questions. Mrs. Cook may have neither the desire nor the ability to do the work that her husband had been doing. But, if she wants to withdraw her husband's share of the firm's value, that may not be easy either. What would force Allen and Bailey to pay Mrs. Cook her husband's share? Where would they get $1 million in cash? Would they have to sell the business? Could Mrs. Cook sell her interest in the firm? Who would buy it? If the firm pays out its earnings primarily in salaries, rather than in stock dividends (and even if it hadn't done this in the past, it could start doing so now), why would anyone pay $1 million for Mrs. Cook's shares of stock?

Life insurance, together with a **buy-and-sell agreement,** can help overcome these problems. Allen, Bailey, and Cook can enter into a contractual agreement under the terms of which the heirs of any of the three will be paid $1 million. Term life insurance policies will be purchased covering each man for that amount. The agreement can take either of two forms. One would be a "cross-purchase plan," under which the three men would individually insure one another (each buying $500,000 policies on the lives of the other two) and use the policy proceeds to buy out the share of the deceased owner from his heirs. The other way is an "entity plan" under which the corporation would pay for the insurance and would acquire the interest of the one who died. Under either method, life insurance automatically provides the funds needed to carry out the terms of the buy and sell agreement.

Similar problems exist in other forms of business. The situation in a partnership may resemble the one just described. The owner of an individual proprietorship also should make plans for transferring the value of the business. If the business has debts, cash will be needed to pay them at the owner's death. Life insurance can provide these funds and thus a forced sale of the business will be avoided. Also, it may be desirable to arrange in advance for the sale of the business at an agreed price so that the owner's heirs will receive its fair value. Again, a buy-and-sell agreement can be arranged, perhaps with an employee of the proprietorship; the person who contracts to buy the business purchases insurance on the owner to provide the purchase price at the owner's death.

KEY EMPLOYEE INSURANCE.   A business firm obviously has an insurable interest in the buildings and equipment that it owns. It carries insurance to pay for the cost of replacing them if they are destroyed. Perhaps less obviously, a business also has an insurable interest in the lives of its key employees. If an important manager, engineer, or salesperson dies, the firm will suffer a loss. It will take time and money to locate and train a replacement, and in some cases the loss can be substantial. Key employee life insurance, again usually term, is purchased and paid for by some businesses to insure against such loss.

In any of these situations, loss can also result from disability. That is, the permanent and total disability of an owner, partner, or key employee can create problems similar to the death of such persons. Disability income insurance therefore has uses in business situations comparable to those described for life insurance.

It is important to realize that arranging for estate planning and business uses of life and health insurance are very technical matters. The drafting of a proper buy-and-sell agreement, for instance, requires the services of an experienced attorney. Such arrangements also call for knowledge and skill on the part of the insurance agent. These, in fact, are typical of the challenges of professional life insurance sales work. Life insurance agents sometimes are thought of simply as salespeople who spend their time trying to pressure others into buying something they really don't want. Some of them are. But the work of most of the men and women who make professional life insurance sales their career is quite different from the image of the high-pressure salesperson. They face a never-ending challenge not only to learn the intricacies of life insurance and the skills of sales work, but also to acquire the ability to serve those clients who can benefit from estate planning or from the use of life insurance in their businesses. The men and women who have developed these abilities are properly regarded as professionals and are compensated for their services accordingly.

THE COST OF LIFE INSURANCE

In the entire range of insurance topics, few are more complicated and difficult to understand than the cost of life insurance. To begin with, the various types of term, whole life, and endowment policies have different premium rates. These differences were discussed in Chapter 12. Next, there are differences in the rates charged for participating and nonparticipating policies. These were discussed in Chapter 13. In addition, there are differences in the rates which various companies charge for policies of the same type. A 25-year-old man might find that he could buy a $50,000 participating whole life policy from one company for $900 a year and an apparently identical policy from another company for $800 a year. The real difficulty arises from the fact that the $900 policy may be the better buy; its true cost to the buyer may be less than the $800 policy! Why? Because the $900 policy may pay larger dividends or may have a more rapidly increasing cash value.[4] On the other hand, the dividends and cash value of the $800 policy might be just as good and thus it really may be the lower cost policy.

One might assume that competition among insurers would prevent cost inequalities so that differences in premiums would reflect actuarial dif-

---

[4]As we know, both policies would have cash values of $50,000 at age 100. But if two policies are alike in all other respects except that the cash value of one rises more rapidly than the other, then the value of the former is greater and its true cost (if the premiums and dividends are alike) is less.

ferences and buyers would in one way or another get exactly what they pay for. Recent studies indicate that such an assumption should not be made. Research by the Federal Trade Commission led to the following conclusions.

Policies with the same annual premium often differ substantially in cost, depending primarily on their dividend scales and the growth of their cash value. The apparently large variation in cost for similar insurance policies may be the result of inadequate cost-comparison information being furnished to prospective purchasers and a tendency on the part of buyers in the absence of adequate cost information to equate "premium" and "cost."[5]

Because higher premium policies are not always worth more than those with lower premiums, consumers need a way to compute the true cost of life insurance.

Traditional Net Cost Method

The most common method of computing the cost of participating cash value life insurance—the **net cost method**—is rather simple and easy to understand. Unfortunately, it also is misleading. In fact, life insurance companies have been severely criticized because so many of their agents have used this method in their sales presentations. Reacting to this criticism, the major company associations appointed a committee of experts to look into the problem. Here is an example of the net cost method taken from the committee's report. The example is based on a $10,000 straight life policy purchased at age 35. The policy has a $240 annual premium, projected dividends totaling $1,500 for the first 20 years, and a cash value of $3,610 at the end of 20 years. The illustration assumes that the policy is cashed in at the end of the twentieth year:

Total premiums for 20 years	$4,800
Subtract dividends for 20 years	1,500
Net premiums for 20 years	$3,300
Subtract cash value at end of 20 years	3,610
Insurance cost	−$ 310
For average cost per year, divide by 20	−$ 15.50
For cost per year per $1000, divide by number of thousands of face amount (10)	−$ 1.55

[5]*The National Underwriter,* December 18, 1976, p. 1.

Notice that by using these figures the agent can "prove" that the policy will cost the prospective purchaser nothing. In fact, the net cost is shown to be *negative!* The figures make it appear that if the policy is cashed in at the end of 20 years, the buyer will have had two decades of free protection and, indeed, will be $310 ahead.

Although the net cost method may provide good sales ammunition for agents, and although the analysis does take dividends and cash values into account, it is deceptive. The trouble with the method is that it ignores the interest that money can earn over a period of time. This oversight becomes clear if we consider that an alternative to buying the policy for $240 a year would be to put $240 a year into a savings account in a bank. If a person did this, and if he earned interest at the rate of 4% a year, he would be able to withdraw $7,433 at the end of 20 years ($4,800 in deposits plus $2,633 in interest earnings). The net cost approach ignores these alternative interest earnings. The insurance industry study committee concluded that the interest factor is "too important to ignore" and recommended another method (the interest adjusted method) of computing life insurance costs.

Interest Adjusted Method

The **interest adjusted method** method works much like the traditional net cost method except that it includes adjustments for interest earnings. The industry study committee recommended that a 4% interest rate be assumed. For the sake of uniformity, most analyses use that rate. Thus, 4 percent is added to the first year's premium; that sum is added to the second year's premium and the total is increased by 4%, and so on for the 20-year period.

The same interest adjustment is applied to the annual dividends. Then the interest adjusted dividends and the cash value are subtracted from the interest adjusted premiums. The result is similar to the "insurance cost" figure shown in the traditional cost method. With the interest adjusted method, the "insurance cost" is not simply divided by 20 to get the average cost per year, however. Instead, it is divided by the amount to which $1 deposited annually at 4% would increase in 20 years. The result is the amount that the policyholder would need to deposit every year at 4% in order to end up with an amount equal to the "insurance cost." This method is considerably more complicated than the net cost method, but it gives a much more accurate estimate of the policy's true cost.

Applying the interest adjusted method to the same policy that was analyzed earlier gives the following results:

Total premiums for 20 years, each accumulated at 4%	$7,433
Subtract dividends for 20 years, each accumulated at 4%	2,003
Net premiums for 20 years	$5,430
Subtract cash value at end of 20 years	3,610
Insurance cost	$1,820
Amount to which $1 deposited annually will increase in 20 years at 4%	$ 30.969
For interest adjusted cost per year, divide $1820 by $30.96	$ 58.77
For cost per year per $1000, divide by number of thousands of face amount (10)	$ 5.88

One way to understand these figures is to compare the policy with a 4% savings account. If a man put $240 a year into such an account, at the end of 20 years he could withdraw $7,433. This amount would be the total of the deposits plus interest earnings.

Instead of depositing the money in a bank account, the man could purchase a life insurance policy for $240 a year. If he did and if he instructed the insurance company to hold all the dividends and invest them at 4%, what would he have at the end of 20 years? That is, if he cashed in the policy at the end of 20 years, how would the results compare with the savings account alternative?

To begin with, if bank deposits of $240 a year are worth $7,433 at the end of 20 years, it is reasonable to say that the same amount paid for life insurance would also be worth $7,433. If the annual dividends are accumulated at 4%, they will total $2,003 in 20 years. The policy's 20 year cash value is $3,610. The policyholder therefore could cash in the policy and collect $2,003 plus $3,610. Subtracting both of these amounts from the $7,433 leaves $1,820. This amount is the cost to own the policy instead of putting the money into a savings account. It is what the policyholder pays for 20 years of protection.

The rest of the analysis applies the interest adjustment concept to the $1,820 insurance cost. This step is taken because the insurance cost, like the premiums and the dividends, applies to a 20-year period. How much would one have to put away each year at 4% in order to have $1,820 to spend at the end of 20 years? The answer is $58.77. Therefore, the average annual cost of the $10,000 policy, adjusted for interest, is $58.77, which is $5.88 for each $1,000 of insurance. These figures ($58.77 or $5.88) are used as a basis for comparing the cost of this particular policy with other similar policies or, in other words, with other $10,000 straight life policies available to a male purchaser at age 35.

The National Association of Insurance Commissioners has recommended that states adopt laws requiring life insurance companies to issue buyer's guides showing the cost of each company's policies computed on the interest-adjusted basis. Some companies are doing this voluntarily. Persons considering policies offered by several different companies should ask each one for interest-adjusted cost data. Another source of the data is a volume called Life Rates and Data, published annually by the National Underwriter Company.[6] It can be found in many libraries.

The interest adjusted method is superior to the traditional net cost method as a basis for comparing the costs of similar policies, but several other factors should be kept in mind:

1. It is essential that similar policies be compared. It would be misleading, for instance, to compare a policy that includes a guaranteed insurability rider with one that does not.
2. The comparisons are published for 10- and 20-year periods and assume that the policies will be cashed in at one of those times. A particular policy might rank higher or lower if kept for a longer or shorter period.
3. The costs of participating policies are based on estimated dividends. Actual dividends may be higher or lower than the estimates.
4. For some buyers, the immediate out-of-pocket premium may be more important than the interest adjusted cost. Nonparticipating policies usually have a lower cost in the early years, permitting the purchase of a larger amount of protection for a given outlay.
5. The company selected should have a reputation for integrity and unquestioned financial strength. See Chapter 22 for information about Best's Insurance Reports as a guide in this regard.
6. The services of reliable agents who help their clients obtain the right kinds and amounts of coverage can easily justify a somewhat higher policy cost.

The last two points emphasize that cost is not the only factor to consider when one selects an insurance company and that it may not even be the most important one. There are significant differences in costs, though, and they should not be ignored. The best available means of checking these differences is to compare interest adjusted costs.

[6]What we have termed the interest adjusted cost per year is shown there as "surrender cost index." Also shown there is a "payment index", which is the average annual outlay (premiums less dividends) adjusted for interest.

Life Insurance as an Investment

If we assume that one selects a reasonably priced cash value policy, how will the return on the money invested in it compare with the return from other investments? This might seem an easy question to answer, but it is not. Even the experts are unable to tell us exactly what rate of interest one can expect to earn on the savings element of a life insurance policy.[7] The best answer probably is that the return will average somewhere between 3 and 5%.

There are several reasons why a more precise interest rate cannot be stated. In the first place, the return will depend upon when the policy is cashed in. Cash values are low during the early years because the company's expenses (which include the agent's commission) are highest then. Cash values and interest earnings are higher on policies that are kept for longer periods. Second, the interest rate varies from one company to another and even varies among different policies issued by the same company. A third factor is that the rate earned by the policyholder depends on the earnings rate of the company, and the latter rate varies from year to year. The majority of ordinary life insurance is participating; company earnings on invested funds are reflected in the annual dividends paid to policyholders. During 1977 the net rate of investment earnings of all U.S. life insurance companies was 6.89%. However, in 1965 it had been 4.6% and in 1955 the companies earned an average of only 3.51%.[8] These rates of course are indicative of the general level of interest rates prevailing throughout the economy at the particular times. Higher interest rates during recent years have permitted the companies to earn more on their investments. They in turn have increased their dividend scales, giving their policyholders greater returns.

Given the fact that the earnings rate on funds invested in cash value life insurance can only be approximated, and assuming it to be in the 3 to 5% range, is it a reasonable rate? Most financial experts say that it is, even though higher rates are available elsewhere. Their reasoning for this takes into account the following four points.

1. The yield must be compared with other conservative investments. These include savings accounts, government bonds, and certain high-grade securities. More speculative investments naturally offer higher returns.

2. Evaluation of life insurance as an investment must include considera-

---

[7]Note that the question relates only to the savings element and not to the protection element of life insurance. If an insured dies shortly after buying a policy, the company will pay out a large sum relative to the premiums paid. However, this is payment for an insured loss, not interest that is paid for the use of invested funds.

[8]*Life Insurance Fact Book 1978* (New York: American Council of Life Insurance), p. 61.

tion of its tax advantages. Policyholder dividends are not subject to federal income tax. In addition, increases in cash value are not taxed until the policy is cashed in and at that time only the excess of the cash value over premium payments is taxed. It sometimes is argued that instead of buying cash value insurance, one should "buy term and invest the difference." According to this advice, if a cash value policy costs $150 a year and the same amount of term insurance costs only $50, one should buy the term policy and invest $100 in some other manner to earn a higher yield. Consumers should realize, however, that depending upon the tax bracket of the individual, the tax advantage of life insurance can mean that the investor would have to earn 2 or 3% more on the alternative investment in order to equal the earnings on the policy. For instance, a 7.5% yield that is taxed at 40% is equal to a 4.5% tax-free yield.

3. Investments in life insurance can be liquidated in the form of income payments (including life income) by using policy settlement options. Also, policy loans are available.

4. Life insurance has an important psychological impact because of its connection with the family's financial security. For this reason, most purchasers are very reluctant to let their policies lapse, and as a result they tend to carry through with their savings plans. Those who pay $150 for cash value policies may not earn a high rate of interest, but at least they do save and invest regularly. Those who buy $50 term policies may sometimes find it easy to skip the annual $100 outside investment and thus may fail to accumulate a larger amount after all.

We should realize that the desirability of any type of investment depends upon the financial position and needs of the particular investor. For some people, "buy term and invest the difference" is good advice; for others, it is not. When all things are considered, life insurance is a reasonable investment for many people. There are, of course, numerous other reasonable investments. For many people, the best answer is some combination of term life insurance, cash value life insurance, and other investments offering · greater yield and growth potential. The latter may be especially important as hedges against continued inflatrion.

LIFE INSURANCE FOR COLLEGE STUDENTS

Here's a riddle: What group of otherwise intelligent people often buy a product they don't need from salesmen using high-pressure tactics to convince them that they should borrow money to pay for? The answer: college students. The product: life insurance.

Right away, let's make it clear that some college students do need life insurance. Also, some agents who specialize in selling on campus do not use high-pressure tactics. However, the fact remains that billions of dollars worth of life insurance are purchased every year by students who would be better off either buying other policies or buying none at all. Three problems are involved: the question of need, the sales method, and the nature of the policy.

The Question of Need

Most college students don't need life insurance. One magazine article put it bluntly: "From a hardheaded, purely economic standpoint, the death of a young person with no dependents (and no obligation to repay those who have financed his education) creates relatively little hardship for anyone."[9] There are exceptions, of course. Some students do have dependents and some have debts that would have to be paid by others. Also, it may be desirable to have a small amount of coverage to pay for burial expenses. But the main reason for buying life insurance, as we know, is to replace income. And few students earn enough to even cover all of their living expenses. A more valid reason for a young person to buy insurance is to protect his or her future insurability, so if a student does buy a policy, it should provide options to purchase additional amounts at later dates.

Sales Methods

A few life insurance companies (out of the approximately 1,800 operating in the United States) concentrate on the campus market. Some of these companies offer specialized policies and use specialized marketing methods. Frequently, their agents are young; sometimes they are students themselves. When a student is first contacted, the agent may offer a free road atlas or bottle of perfume in exchange for permitting the agent to discuss a "savings and investment proposal." Ideally, such a discussion would give the student an opportunity to learn something about life insurance, a subject that most students know very little about. Most of these particular agents don't see it that way, though. "After all, their job is to sell as much as possible, not to waste time educating people."[10] One study of campus life insurance sales had this to say about the marketing techniques: "An absence of professionalism is characteristic of many agents who sell insurance on campus.

[9]"They're Selling College Kids Bad Buys in Insurance," *Changing Times,* March 1974, p. 28.
[10]*A Shopper's Guide to Life Insurance for College Students* (Washington, D.C.: Consumer News Inc., 1975), p. 11.

The use of high pressure and fear tactics is the rule."[11] Tactics that have been used include:

1. Pressure to buy "before the price goes up."
2. Pressure to buy while the "specially designed" policy is still available.
3. Backing of the policy by a campus organization or star athlete.
4. Urging of the prospect to sign a document to permit the company to check medical records, when the document actually is a policy application.
5. Belittling of the student who wants to talk with his or her parents before buying.

One result of such tactics is that they frequently become the basis of students' impression of the entire insurance business. This is unfortunate because *these methods are not representative of the business; they are not typical of life insurance sales or of any other insurance activities.*

The Contracts

In Chapter 12 we learned that many different policies are available, each appropriate for specific needs. We also have learned that the professional approach to life insurance sales begins with analyzing the needs of the individuals in order to determine what amounts of protection and which policies would be suitable. Some agents who sell on campus use the professional approach. But you shouldn't expect it from those who use the sales tactics that have just been described. They will "know" what policy is best without finding out anything about the person, and it is certain to be a policy with high cash values, extra frills, and high cost. In the typical case the contract will be some form of whole life policy and will include:

1. Waiver of premium
2. Guaranteed insurability
3. Double, triple, or quadruple indemnity
4. Return of premium provision
5. Financing of the first year's premium

The first two of these, the waiver of premium and guaranteed insurability provisions, are desirable features. The extra indemnity provision is of questionable value for reasons that were stated in Chapter 13. The return of premium feature also was described in Chapter 13. It is a sales gimmick designed to appeal to those who believe you can get something for nothing and to help wear down the sales resistance of those who know better.

[11]Gary K. Stone, "Life Insurance Sales Practices on the College Campus," *Journal of Risk and Insurance,* June 1973, p. 168.

Needless to say, all of these features increase the policy's cost (and the agent's commission) to a level considerably above that of many otherwise similar policies.

The most troublesome part of the contract is the premium financing provision. It is included in order to overcome the objections of students who can't afford (or say they can't afford) to pay the premium. "Don't worry," says the agent, "this policy won't cost you a cent this year. We'll lend you the first year's premium." The loan requires the signing of a promissory note. The note typically is due in five years, at which time it, interest on it, and that year's premium all must be paid. (Sometimes the policy even includes a small 5-year endowment portion, the proceeds of which automatically repay the loan, the premium for the policy of course being increased accordingly.) But what happens if the student later lets the policy lapse, as a rather high percentage of those who buy these policies do? If one of the premiums is not paid during the initial five-year period, the note becomes due and payable immediately. If it is not paid, the company can initiate a lawsuit to recover its amount plus interest and plus the expenses that are incurred in collecting it.

State insurance departments, reputable insurance people, and college administrators all are concerned about this situation. It is a difficult matter to deal with because it involves an extremely small minority of the insurance industry. As in so many other instances, it is difficult to control the actions of an irresponsible minority without at the same time limiting the rights of those who operate in a responsible manner.

In summary, here are some things you should keep in mind:

1.   College students usually have little or no need for life insurance.
2.   Beware of "free" insurance and low-cost "deals."
3.   Refuse to do business with any insurance agent you don't like or respect. (See Chapter 19 for more on agents' qualifications.)
4.   Don't feel obligated for the time that an agent spends talking with you (or for the free atlas or whatever).
5.   Don't be pressured. At the very least, discuss any life insurance proposal with an agent of another company, with your parents, or with your insurance teacher.
6.   If you run into high-pressure tactics, don't get the idea that insurance always is sold that way and that all insurance people favor such methods. *It isn't and they don't!*

IMPORTANT TERMS

Life insurance programming	**Key employee insurance**
Estate planning	**Net cost method**
Buy-and-sell agreements	**Interest adjusted method**

KEY POINTS TO REMEMBER

1. Programming is a systematic process of developing a plan of insurance designed to serve the needs of a particular family.
2. The four steps of the programming process are (a) analyzing the needs, (b) setting goals, (c) reviewing present resources, and (d) adopting a plan of action.
3. Possible needs for life insurance include cash for immediate expenses, income for the child-raising period, insurance for the mother, life income for the widow, mortgage payments, educational funds, and retirement income.
4. In the goal-setting step of life insurance programming, both short-range and long-range goals are considered. Because of the cost of building a complete program, long-range goals sometimes must be given lower priority until short-range goals are achieved.
5. The programming process should be repeated every few years in order to adapt the program to the family's changing life cycle.
6. Estate planning provides arrangements to conserve property during the owner's lifetime and to distribute it at his or her death without unnecessary taxation or other costs. It is performed by a team of experts which includes a skilled life insurance agent.
7. Life insurance can be used to fund buy-and-sell agreements. In this way, a person's ownership share in a going business can systematically be transferred after the owner's death.
8. Business firms sometimes purchase key employee insurance. This covers the firms' losses resulting from the death or disability of important employees.
9. The traditional method of showing the cost of cash value life insurance, the net cost method, is misleading because it ignores the interest that buyers could earn by investing their money elsewhere.
10. The interest adjusted method is a much more accurate basis for comparing policy costs. It takes the time value of money into account.
11. Funds invested in life insurance earn a moderate rate of return. But, if all things are considered, life insurance is judged to be a reasonable investment for many people.
12. Most college students have little or no need to purchase life insurance. They should be cautious about dealing with one of the small number of irresponsible companies that operate on some campuses.

REVIEW QUESTIONS

1. What is the purpose of life insurance programming?
2. (a) Which of the seven needs for life insurance are usually most important for young families? (b) Which are most important for middle-aged couples with grown children?
3. For what reasons is more life insurance being purchased to cover the lives of women?
4. For families with young children, why wouldn't providing funds for college always get top priority?

5. Why shouldn't families with young children buy short-term endowments on them to accumulate funds for college?
6. Who are the members of an estate planning team?
7. In the example of ABC Manufacturing, Inc., how can life insurance help the principal owners and their families?
8. In the example of the traditional net cost method, why is it misleading to say that the 20-year cost of the policy is −$310?
9. (a) In the example of the interest adjusted method, why is the premium for 20 years shown as $7,433 when the policyholder actually pays 20 × $240, or $4,800? (b) Why are the dividends shown as $2,003, when the amount actually paid out by the company is $1,500? (c) To get the cost per year, why is the $1,820 divided by 30.969 rather than by 20?
10. In comparing the earnings on funds invested in life insurance with earnings available from other investments, what four points should you take into account?
11. Explain the premium financing arrangement that sometimes is involved in policies sold to college students.

DISCUSSION QUESTIONS

1. How do the rules of personal insurance buying apply to the handling of the mortality risk?
2. At the end of 1977 Americans carried a total of $2.6 trillion of life insurance protection. This averages out to about $36,900 per family, which is equal to about 27 months of disposable personal income per family. Does the typical family have enough insurance?
3. The need for income during the child-raising period is said to be a decreasing need. Why?
4. In life insurance programming, how should the possibility of remarriage by the widow or widower be taken into account?
5. The Newlins have $10,000 of insurance covering Ruth's life, far less than that of Charlie's policy. They recently purchased another policy on Charlie. Should they have bought more to cover Ruth instead?
6. Why can't an all-purpose life insurance program be devised that would be appropriate for any family?
7. How will the Newlin family's life insurance needs probably change during the years ahead?
8. (a) Does it appear to you that Bill Scott has helped Charlie and Ruth Newlin? (b) Do you suppose that he has used high-pressure tactics with them?
9. Why isn't the question of interest earnings raised in connection with automobile or fire insurance as it is in connection with life insurance?
10. Do you agree with the statement that most college students don't need life insurance?
11. If shady insurance marketing practices are not the rule elsewhere, why are they used on the college campus?

PART III
EMPLOYEE BENEFIT PLANS AND SOCIAL INSURANCE

CHAPTER 15
EMPLOYEE BENEFIT PLANS

GROUP INSURANCE

GROUP LIFE INSURANCE

GROUP HEALTH INSURANCE

PENSION PLANS

OTHER EMPLOYEE BENEFIT PLANS

GROUP AUTO INSURANCE

Insured protection against the financial losses that are caused by death, old age, and poor health comes from three sources: individually purchased insurance, employee benefit plans, and social insurance. Many American families, in effect, have three layers of protection from these sources (see Figure 15–1).

Social insurance is provided by the government, chiefly in the form of the social security program. It can be thought of as the basic layer, providing a minimum amount or "floor" of protection. **Employee benefit plans** are furnished through employment, in the form of group insurance and pensions. They provide the second layer of protection. The top layer, supplementing the other two, is insurance purchased in the form of individual policies. Until this chapter, we have concentrated on the top layer. In this chapter and the next one we shall examine the other two layers.

Employee benefit plans provide what used to be called fringe benefits. This term is no longer appropriate, because these benefits today are far more than incidental frills. They are important parts of the total employee compensation package. They consist chiefly of group life insurance, group health insurance, and group pensions. Other insured employee benefits include dental care, visual care, and legal services. An idea of the magnitude of employee benefits can be gained from their cost to a large employer. In 1977 General Motors Corporation paid an average of $9.64 per hour for wages (including vacation pay). The company incurred more than 30% of additional costs ($2.86 per hour) for employee benefit programs, chiefly pensions and health insurance.

GROUP INSURANCE

Over 40% of the life insurance in force in the United States is written on the group basis. A large majority, over 80%, of the health insurance is group coverage. In both areas, group protection is growing more rapidly than individually purchased coverage. Much of the growth of group insurance has resulted from collective bargaining; in many major industries labor union contracts include group insurance and pension benefits.

Figure 15–1

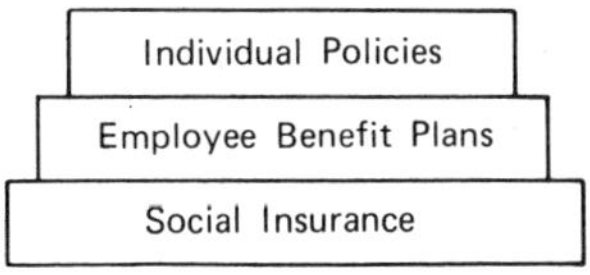

The Nature of Group Insurance

Group insurance covers a number of persons under a single contract. The size of the group can range anywhere from a few people to several hundred thousand. In some states a minimum number is required by law. The members of the group usually are employed by the same organization, although some policies insure other groups, such as members of professional associations. Multi–employer plans are another exception. The United Mine Workers Welfare and Retirement Fund, for instance, covers miners employed by various companies. Our discussion of group insurance will concentrate on the more typical single-employer plans.

A single master policy is written. The members of the group receive certificates or booklets that summarize and explain their protection. In **noncontributory plans,** the entire cost is paid by the employer. In **contributory plans,** the cost is shared by the employer and the employees.

The contract designates what categories of employees are eligible to be covered and for what amounts. It is not necessary to insure all employees, nor do the amounts of protection have to be identical for all who are insured. However, unless the benefits are the same for all employees, they must be determined on a stated basis such as salary, position, or length of employment. Individual employees cannot choose the amounts of their protection; they receive the same amount as all other employees in the same category. This requirement prevents the adverse selection that would occur if individuals in poor health were able to select high amounts.

From the standpoint of the insurer, the entire group is underwritten as a single unit. There are no medical examinations, because the insurer is not in a position to accept or to reject individual employees. If it decides to write a group policy, it insures all of the covered employees, whether they would be acceptable for individually underwritten policies or not.

The Cost of Group Insurance

For several reasons, group insurance generally costs less than that furnished by individual policies:

1. The cost to the employee is less, because the employer pays either all or part of the premium.
2. The cost of investigating the insurability of individuals, including the cost of medical examinations, is avoided.
3. Some of the administrative costs are borne by the employer. These may include the handling of claims, as well as routine record keeping.
4. There is an income tax advantage, in that the cost to the employer is

deductible as a business expense, while normally neither premiums paid by the employer nor benefits received by an employee are taxable as employee income.

5. Marketing costs are reduced. Agents who sell policies covering 100 employees receive far less than 100 times the commission that they would earn for selling that many individual policies.

Some of these factors simply transfer the costs from one party to another, such as from employee to employer or from employer to the government. In other instances the savings are real, reflecting the efficiencies that are inherent in the group method of marketing and handling insurance.

GROUP LIFE INSURANCE

The principal differences between group life insurance and ordinary life insurance stem from the unique methods of underwriting, marketing, and administering group policies.

Coverage

Group life insurance almost always is one-year renewable term coverage. The policies are renewed from year to year as long as the premium is paid and enough persons are insured. In a very small fraction (about 2%) of the cases, cash value insurance is written rather than term, the cash values being used either for pension payments or to give employees paid-up policies when they retire.

All of the states require contributory plans to insure at least 75% of all eligible employees; in noncontributory plans all eligible employees must be covered. As new workers become eligible during the year (perhaps after three or six months of employment), the employer reports their names and the amounts of their coverage to the insurer. Each covered worker designates a beneficiary and can change this designation at any time.

Amounts

The amount of each person's coverage is determined by a schedule; usually the amount cannot be increased or decreased for any individual. The simplest approach is to provide the same amount, $15,000 for instance, for everyone. A more common method is to relate the amount of coverage to the employee's earnings, for example, by setting payroll brackets. For instance, the policy might provide $10,000 coverage for everyone earning less than $10,000 a year, $15,000 for those earning between $10,000 and

$20,000, and $25,000 for those whose earnings are above $20,000 a year. Other methods are to base the amounts upon job classifications or the length of service with the employer. In plans established through collective bargaining, changes in the amounts of coverage or in the method of determining them are frequently subjects of negotiation between union and management.

Cost

In contributory group life plans, the cost to the employee is typically 60 cents per month per $1,000 of insurance. Each employee pays the same amount per $1,000, regardless of age. Thus, young employees pay a higher percentage of the total cost of their coverage than older employees do. In fact, for young workers the cost may be slightly greater than the cost of an ordinary term policy. Should young workers refuse to participate in contributory group life insurance plans? No. For one thing, $7.20 per $1,000 (60 cents per month) is not an exorbitant price. More important, workers who choose not to participate when they become eligible will have to pass a medical examination if they decide to join the group later; at that time they may not be insurable.

The cost to the employer depends largely upon the number of people insured and the amounts of their coverage. The employer pays part (usually half) of the cost of contributory plans and all of the cost of noncontributory plans. In either case, the policies usually are participating, the insurer returning any excess premium to the employer in the form of a policyholder dividend. The employer's final cost therefore is influenced by changes in the three factors that determine the insurer's cost: mortality, company expenses, and interest earnings. The last of these is relatively unimportant in group insurance, because of the absence of reserve accumulations to fund cash values.

The insurance company's expenses for a group policy depend partly upon the amount of administrative work that is done by the employer. Company expenses also depend on the size of the policy; large policies normally can be handled more economically than small ones. The factor that usually has the greatest impact on the employer's dividend is mortality. The better the mortality experience, the higher the dividend and the less the cost to the employer. Two of the identifiable elements that affect a group's mortality rate are the nature of the industry and the age distribution of the group. Some industries have higher mortality rates than others. Mining and lumbering companies, for instance, generally have higher mortality rates than average.

The age distribution of the group also is a major determinant of mortality experience. A group with a relatively high percentage of older workers is likely to have a higher mortality rate than a younger group. This can have a great impact on the cost of insuring the group, even if all workers have the same amount of coverage. The impact is magnified when the amounts of protection depend upon salary, job classification, or length of service. Then older workers will typically have more coverage than younger ones. The cost of insuring an aging group therefore can increase rather rapidly. However, if sufficient numbers of young workers join the group each year, the mortality cost will probably remain relatively constant.

Conversion

Group life insurance contracts ordinarily include a **conversion clause.** This gives workers who leave their jobs an option to convert to an individual policy that provides the same amount of coverage. The converted policy must be either endowment or whole life insurance. Conversion is permitted regardless of the state of the worker's health.

The conversion option is exercised by only a small fraction of departing employees, partly because of the cost of doing so. Continuing the same coverage under a converted policy is much more expensive because: (a) the employee must pay the entire cost of the converted policy, (b) the converted policy must provide a type of cash value insurance, and (c) for the reasons already explained, group insurance is less expensive than ordinary insurance. It is possible that the option would be exercised more often if more terminating employees understood its value. It is especially important for workers who leave their jobs because of disability or poor health. They may find it difficult or impossible to secure protection at standard rates unless they take advantage of the option to convert their group coverage.

Limitations

During recent decades, group life insurance has replaced former methods of providing funds for the families of deceased workers. In earlier times, employers often felt obligated to make charitable donations for this purpose. In addition, employees customarily "passed the hat" for the benefit of a coworker's widow and children. Group insurance has now largely replaced those methods. Group insurance is also replacing industrial life insurance as the form of protection relied upon by low-income workers. Group coverage certainly is a preferable system: It is more equitable and more reliable than charity, and it is more economical than industrial life insurance.

The principal drawback of group life insurance is that it may give a false sense of security. Too many families believe they need no additional protection. The fact is that the average group life certificate provides only about $11,000 of protection, which is less than the average family's disposable income for one year. Not only is the amount of protection minimal, but there are no cash or loan values and insureds have no option to purchase additional coverage. Also, the covered persons do not have the benefits of an agent's service and advice. Although group coverage furnishes valuable protection, it never should be thought of as replacing the need for a well-planned program of individual life insurance.

GROUP HEALTH INSURANCE

Group coverage dominates the health insurance field. Over 80% of all health protection (and more than 90% of the hospital expense insurance) is written on the group basis. Both the insurance companies and the Blue Cross and Blue Shield organizations write group coverage.

"WE'D LIKE TO SEE SOMEONE ABOUT GROUP INSURANCE."

Coverage

All of the various health coverages described in Chapter 11 are available on the group basis. Hospital and surgical expense are the most common coverages. Large amounts of regular medical expense, major medical, and disability income are also written.

Ordinarily, the same coverages and benefits are provided for all employees, regardless of their earnings, job classification, or length of service. Disability income benefits are an exception; they often are a percentage (frequently 50%) of the employee's monthly earnings. Another instance of nonuniformity of benefits is coverage for dependents. Many policies give employees who have dependents the option of adding health expense coverage for them; the cost to the employee is increased when this is done. Because occupational injuries and diseases are covered by workers' compensation insurance, group health insurance usually does not cover on-the-job accidents and illnesses.

Other Characteristics

Group health insurance is more economical than individual policy coverage. The reasons for this are much the same as with life insurance, although the absorption of administrative costs is a more important factor in the case of health insurance, because of the greater frequency of health insurance claims and the greater expense of processing them.

Group health policies often include a **coordination of benefits** provision. This is designed to prevent duplication of benefits when an individual or family is covered by more than one group health contract, such as when the worker has more than one job or when both husband and wife have group coverage. The coordination of benefits clause usually does not apply to individually purchased health policies.

Although group life insurance almost never is adequate without being supplemented by individual policies, group health insurance sometimes is sufficient by itself. There is no way to generalize about this point, because there are wide variations among group health policies. Each of the larger ones is tailor-made, reflecting the wishes of the employer and employees. Some provide very liberal benefits for almost all kinds of accidents and illnesses; others are more limited. Some group policies cover only basic hospital and surgical expenses. In such cases, the addition of an individual major medical policy may be important. Frequently, group contracts that are liberal in other respects provide little or no long-term disability income protection.

Some insurers make a real effort to provide employees with booklets that explain their protection as clearly as possible. This is an important service. The policies usually are rather complicated, and it is difficult for workers who are not familiar with insurance to understand what is covered and what is not. Unless they do understand, they may not take full advantage of the protection. Also, unless the policy's limitations are understood, employees will not be in a position to consider the need for individual contracts to supplement their group coverage.

Health Maintenance Organizations

As an alternative to conventional group health insurance, many large employers are supporting the development of **health maintenance organizations** (HMOs). Unlike insurance companies or Blue Cross–Blue Shield organizations, HMOs both finance and furnish medical care. Most HMOs employ salaried physicians and other professionals who provide comprehensive health care services to a specific group of subscribers. The services range all the way from treating the flu to performing heart surgery and include hospital charges as well as doctor bills.

The HMO receives a fixed periodic payment from each subscriber (or, more often, from the subscriber's employer or the employer's insurer). This is a key feature of this system and one that, in the opinion of many people, brings about major reductions in health care costs. Charging a flat periodic fee rather than a fee for each service as it is rendered controls costs in two ways. First, it encourages preventive care because the HMO has a financial incentive to keep its subscribers healthy. The HMO has an incentive to encourage flu shots, for instance, so that its subscribers won't end up with penumonia and force the HMO to pay unnecessary hospital bills. Second, the flat fee system encourages HMO doctors to avoid hospitalizing their patients unless necessary or for longer periods than necessary. One study showed that a group of employees enrolled in an HMO used about half as many hospital days per year as a similar group covered by Blue Cross.

The Health Maintenance Organization Act of 1973 supports the development of HMOs. One of its provisions requires employers that have group health insurance programs and that employ 25 or more persons to give their workers the option of joining an HMO if one is available in their area. Thus far, only a small fraction of all covered employees are participating in HMOs. For many, no HMO is available; in the late 1970s only about 200 plans were operating, most of them in large cities. A contributing factor is that many potential HMO members have elected to stay with their private-practice doctors, perhaps feeling that an HMO would be too impersonal and bureaucratic.

Various kinds of organizations are assisting the development of new HMOs. These include insurance companies, Blue Cross–Blue Shield organizations, and labor unions, in addition to many large corporations. There appears to be little doubt that within the next few years many more American workers will be able to choose whether to continue with their regular group health insurance or to join a health maintenance organization.

PENSION PLANS

Pensions, providing income payments to retired workers, are the third major part of our system of employee benefit plans. As with group life and group health insurance, pension plans are voluntary; they are not required by law. But, as is the case with life and health benefits, pension plans have grown rapidly during the period since World War II. They are now furnished by most large employers and by many smaller ones as well. Pension plans that meet federal requirements qualify for favorable tax treatment. Employer contributions to qualified plans are tax deductible as a business expense and are not taxable income for employees until received by them as retirement benefits.

Employee Retirement and Income Security Act

The Employment Retirement and Income Security Act, called ERISA, was adopted by Congress in 1974 to establish federal regulation of private pension plans. The law does not require employers to provide pension plans, but it makes those who do provide them subject to federal supervision. Prior to the enactment of ERISA, employers had no legal responsibility to provide the pension benefits that their employees expected to receive. Most pension plans were properly financed and managed, but there were numerous exceptions. Also, even well-run plans often depended upon the continued prosperity of the corporation that furnished them. A famous case in point was the Studebaker Company. When it folded in 1964, the pension expectations of 4,500 workers were ruined. The company was able to pay only a fraction of the benefits that it had promised. ERISA was adopted primarily for the purpose of preventing further episodes of that kind. Much of the description of pension plans which follows reflects the requirements of the 1974 law.

Funding Agencies

Pension funds can be administered by the trust department of a bank or trust company or by a life insurance company. When a bank or trust company is the funding agency, the plan is not insured. Such plans are called trust fund plans; plans handled by life insurance companies are called insured plans.

Trust fund plans cover more than half of the employees who have formal pensions. The employer periodically transfers funds to the trustee (the bank). The trustee, acting with the advice of a consulting actuarial firm, invests the funds and sends pension checks to retired workers. ERISA imposes certain restrictions upon the manner in which the funds are invested; however, the risk of reductions in the value of the investments is retained by the employer. The employer also retains the risk of unexpected increases in the longevity (length of life) of retired workers. Because the plan is not insured, neither the trustee nor the consulting actuary assumes these risks.

Insured plans cover less than half of the employees. But, because most smaller plans are insured rather than trusteed, insured plans constitute well over half of all formal pension plans. Life insurance companies offer a variety of different types of plans. Some plans are fully insured; that is, the insurer guarantees that pension payments will be made regardless of fluctuations in longevity or declines in investment values. Other plans offered by insurance companies offer differing degrees of insurance guarantees and more flexibility in both investment and benefit arrangements.

As we might imagine, competition between the life insurance companies and the large bank and trust companies is intense. Enormous amounts of money are at stake, the assets of all private pension plans totaling about $250 billion. At one time, the banks had a distinct advantage because they could tailor plans to suit the wishes of large clients and were able to make more lucrative investments. The insurance companies now offer a variety of plans; because both kinds of funding agencies must meet the requirements of ERISA, the differences between trust fund plans and insured plans have diminished and the competition is stronger than ever.

Retirement Benefits

Pension plans often are designed so that retirees will receive an income, including social security benefits, equal to about half of their earnings during their last five or ten years of employment. The income that a particular retiree receives is determined by a **benefit formula.** An example is a formula basing the retirement income on the worker's average earnings and length of service. Such a plan might pay 1.5% of the worker's average earnings during the five years before retirement for each year of his or her employment. A worker retiring after 30 years who earned an average of $1,200 a month for the last five years would receive .015 $\times$ $1,200 $\times$ 30, or $540 per month.

Other Benefits

In addition to retirement income, pension plans commonly include other benefits as well.

DEATH AND DISABILITY BENEFITS. If a worker dies before reaching retirement age a beneficiary always is paid the amount that the worker had contributed to the pension fund, usually plus interest. In some cases, additional death benefits are payable if the worker dies shortly before reaching retirement age. Spouses of workers who die after retiring will continue to receive income payments from the pension plan if the worker had elected a joint and survivorship annuity. ERISA requires that retiring workers be given the option of choosing this form of payment.

Disability benefits are included in some pension plans. These provide all or part of the normal retirement benefits to workers who become totally and permanently disabled before retirement age. These benefits are expensive, and many plans either do not include them or provide them in limited amounts.

VESTING. When an employee receives a permanent, irrevocable right to receive pension benefits, that right is said to be vested. In the case of contributory plans, workers who leave their jobs before reaching retirement age always are entitled to take with them the contributions they themselves have made to the pension fund. To the extent that a departing employee's rights are **vested,** he or she is also entitled to receive the contributions made by the employer.

One of the most important things about ERISA is that it requires all plans to include some type of vesting arrangement. Before ERISA was adopted, a Treasury Department study found that two-thirds of all workers covered by private pension plans had no vested rights; slightly more than half of the covered workers aged 60 and above did not have vested rights. Thus, in view of the mobility of American workers, many people would qualify for very limited pensions because of their having given up pension rights when they changed jobs. Even more serious, elderly workers who lost their jobs, perhaps because of recession cutbacks, would have no private pension income at all.

ERISA requires that employees be granted certain vested rights to their employers' pension contributions. The rules are complex but, in general, they permit the vesting to be for an increasing percentage, reaching 100% after a certain length of employment.

Plan Termination Insurance

One of the principal purposes of ERISA is to protect the pension rights of workers whose employers go out of business. To this end, the law includes detailed requirements concerning the funding of pensions or, in other words, the way in which employers budget their pension costs. As further protection, ERISA established a system of plan termination insurance. The insurance is furnished by the **Pension Benefit Guarantee Corporation** (PBGC). PBGC is comparable to the Federal Deposit Insurance Corporation, which protects bank depositors in the event of a bank's failure. It protects employees in the event a pension plan fails and is unable to pay the intended retirement benefits. The termination insurance is funded by premiums paid by all employers having pension plans.

Disclosure Requirements

To help assure the proper handling of pension funds, ERISA requires that detailed annual reports be filed with the Internal Revenue Service and the Department of Labor. Also, an actuarial evaluation of each plan must be submitted every three years. Employees must be given a description of the plan and any changes in it. In addition, they are entitled to receive information concerning their own benefits.

Deferred Profit-Sharing Plans

Some employers provide **deferred profit-sharing plans** instead of or in addition to regular pension plans. The contributions to a profit-sharing plan are a percentage of the firm's annual profits. Because profits fluctuate from year to year, contributions to such a plan also fluctuate; if there are no profits, nothing is added to the profit-sharing fund.

These plans have the advantage of giving employees an additional incentive to contribute to their firm's success, because the higher the firm's profits are, the greater will be their own retirement income. In order to be eligible for favorable tax treatment, profit-sharing plans must meet most of the standards that ERISA imposes upon regular pension plans.

Individual Retirement Plans

Individuals who are self-employed or who work for firms that don't offer pension plans can set up retirement plans of their own and receive tax benefits similar to those granted to group pension plans. Federal law provides two arrangements: the Keogh Plan for self-employed persons, and the Individual Retirement Account, which is primarily for employees who are not covered by a group pension plan. In either case the individual puts part of his or her income into a retirement fund each year. The money may be invested in several ways, including a bank savings account, special government retirement bonds, or an individual insured annuity.

OTHER EMPLOYEE BENEFIT PLANS

Group insurance has proved to be an effective way of providing life and health insurance and pensions. Because of the success in those areas, interest in using the group insurance method to provide other kinds of employee benefits has grown.

Group Dental Insurance

Dental expense insurance was slow to develop but now is one of the fastest growing forms of coverage. Because of the problem of adverse selection, almost all dental insurance is provided on the group basis, rather than by individual policies. The coverage ordinarily applies to the spouse and dependent children, as well as to the covered worker.

Because it is a new form of protection, various types of contracts are in use. Some incorporate dental coverage into major medical expense protection, but most use separate policies. Sometimes a schedule of benefits is provided, similar to those found in surgical expense policies; more often, the contracts cover "reasonable and customary charges," subject to deductibles, contribution clauses, and annual maximums. One example is a plan covering a large cosmetics firm. This policy pays 80% of the cost of basic dental services, such as simple fillings, subject to a $25 annual deductible per person. For major dental services, such as the construction of bridges, it pays 50% of the cost, subject to another $25 annual deductible. There is a $500 annual maximum for basic services and a similar maximum for major services. Although some plans cover orthodontia, this one does not. The cost is shared by the firm and the employees, with the employees each paying $13.77 per month.

Nonprofit dental service corporations, the counterpart of Blue Cross and Blue Shield, now are competing with the insurance companies in most of the states. Often called Delta plans, they are sponsored by the state dental societies. Most of these plans reimburse participating dentists directly for the services provided to members of insured groups. The HMOs are another source of dental insurance; some of them provide dental care in addition to other health services.

Group Visual Care Insurance

The cost of eye care necessitated by accident or disease is commonly covered by major medical insurance. In contrast, group visual care insurance covers the cost of regular eye examinations and glasses. This type of insurance is not widely carried and perhaps never will become popular.

Because the maximum expense resulting from normal eye care is moderate, higher priority should be given to other kinds of employee benefit plans.

Group Legal Expense Insurance

This is another relatively new type of insurance. It pays for legal services used by the covered employees. There is as yet no uniformity of coverage. Some plans permit the insured persons to choose their own lawyers; others offer the services of a particular group of lawyers only. Some plans cover only unexpected legal services; others cover such predictable costs as the preparation of wills. The types of legal services most commonly paid for include those involving automobile accidents, divorce, unemployment compensation claims, and real estate transactions. Until recently, legal expense insurance did not have the tax advantages that have been given to the more popular kinds of employee benefit plans, but now they do. The Tax Reform Act of 1976 established tax exemption for employers' contributions to group legal expense plans and for the benefits received by covered workers. As a result, this kind of insurance may expand rapidly in the future.

Group Property-Casualty Insurance

A small amount of auto and homeowners insurance is being written on a modified group insurance basis. This is an interesting development and could bring about an important addition to employee benefit plans. The nature of group auto insurance is examined in the next section.

GROUP AUTO INSURANCE

Will the employee benefit plans of the future include auto insurance? Will group auto insurance develop along the same lines as group life and health insurance? There are reasons to believe that these things could happen, but on the other hand, several factors may prevent them from coming about. The subject is worth examining because it illustrates an important characteristic of insurance—its adaptability. Insurance is not static and unchanging; on the contrary, it changes constantly to fill new needs and to respond to new opportunities.

The Nature of Group Auto Insurance

In its present form, group auto differs significantly from other group insurance. Group life and health insurance utilize a single master policy, group rating, and group underwriting. In contrast, group auto uses individual policies, individual rating, and individual risk selection. Another difference is that employers pay at least part of the cost of other group coverages, but the entire cost of group auto is borne by the insured workers. Finally, there is no requirement that a certain percentage of employees participate; because they pay the entire cost, their participation is completely voluntary. (Given these differences, some people prefer not to call this group insurance and refer to it as "mass merchandising" instead.)

The similarity between group auto and other group insurance is that it, like the other kinds, provides insurance and insurance services to a group of people who usually are employees of the same firm. The employer participates in establishing the plan, and premiums are deducted from the employees' paychecks. Also like other group insurance, group auto is designed to reduce administrative and sales expenses, thereby making protection available to employees at a cost below that of individually purchased policies.

The reduction in the cost of group automobile insurance is frequently estimated to be about 15%. The economies stem from reduced sales commissions, from payment through payroll deduction, and from the more efficient use of computerized accounting systems. Other advantages for employees include the convenience of payroll deduction and the receipt of policyholder service at the place where they work. Also, because the employer oversees the choice of the insurer and the functioning of the plan, workers can be assured that they have good protection and will receive proper service. The primary disadvantage is that employees give up the benefit of receiving personal service from companies and agents of their own individual choosing. To many, this is a major drawback.

What are the reasons for the special treatment of group automobile insurance? Why isn't it set up in the same manner as group life, health, and pensions? There are several reasons, one of which relates to federal tax laws. Premiums paid by an employer for group life or health insurance are deductible as a business expense and are not taxable income to the employee. In contrast, group auto premiums paid by an employer are considered to be part of the employee's taxable income. As a result, there is little incentive for employers to pay group auto premiums and in almost all cases the employees bear the entire cost themselves.

Another reason for the special treatment of group auto insurance is that there are such great differences among the risks to be covered. Workers drive various kinds of cars and want various kinds and amounts of protection. Perhaps a system of handling these differences will be developed, but at present they seem to justify the issuance of individual, separately rated policies. Another complicating factor is the differences in loss experience among various drivers. Most of the insurers have retained the right to decline to insure workers who have poor records of motor vehicle accidents and violations.

The Future of Group Automobile Insurance

If we assume that it continues to have certain unique characteristics, what is likely to be the future of group auto insurance? Will it grow to become as widespread as other employee benefits? The answer probably will depend upon several things: insurance regulations and tax laws, the attitudes of employees and employers, the positions taken by insurers and agents, and the further development of no-fault auto insurance.

INSURANCE REGULATIONS AND TAX LAWS.   The insurance laws and regulations of many states presently discourage the sale of auto insurance on the group basis. These controls are said to have been adopted largely because of pressures brought by insurance agents who feared that their income would be reduced if the system becomes widespread.[1] Some of the states have dropped such restrictions; others are likely to do so in the future.

The federal tax laws, as stated earlier, do not extend to group auto the same favorable treatment that group life and health insurance receive. Changing these laws is one of the keys to the future of the coverage.

ATTITUDES OF EMPLOYEES AND EMPLOYERS.   Employees rarely consider auto insurance to be an important part of their benefits package. A few labor unions have bargained for the coverage, but most have not given it high priority. Furthermore, when group plans have been established, a relatively small number of employees have taken advantage of them. In the typical case, only 10 or 20% of the workers have signed up; the majority have preferred to continue to buy policies from their own insurance agents. Employee interest no doubt would increase if the cost were further reduced through employer contributions.

Many employers oppose the broadening of employee benefits and do not favor changing the tax laws to permit the deduction of group auto insurance costs. They point out that life and health insurance and pensions are logical employee benefits because they replace income provided by employment. But they say that there is no direct connection between employment and auto insurance. In addition, they don't like the idea of becoming involved in their employees' auto insurance underwriting, rating, and loss adjustment problems.

POSITIONS OF INSURANCE COMPANIES AND AGENTS.   No kind of insurance can develop and grow without the efforts of those who sell it. Thus far, few insurers have worked very hard to promote group auto; some

[1]Willis Rokes, "Impetus for Group Property Coverage," *Insurance Field,* December 15, 1971, p. 11.

who did so a few years ago have since dropped the effort completely. A recent and potentially important development is the entry into this field of several large life and health insurance companies. Because they already are providing other employee benefit plans, they see this as a way to increase their share of the family insurance market.

The position taken by insurance agents is mixed. Much of the reduction in the cost of group insurance comes about by reducing sales commissions; thus some agents naturally fear that their incomes will decline if group auto catches on. They also point out that, although group life and health insurance often stimulate the sale of individual policies to provide a more complete program of protection, group auto insurance completely replaces individual sales. Not all agents oppose development of the group method, however. Many large and successful agencies already are handling group life and health policies and pension plans; they would be glad to write auto coverages for the same groups.

RELATIONSHIP TO THE NO-FAULT SYSTEM. The future of group auto insurance may also depend upon the future of no-fault auto plans. A nationwide, compulsory plan of insuring each family's own losses on the no-fault basis would adapt itself to the group insurance system much more readily than does insurance based on the legal liability system. In fact, some group health insurers (including Blue Cross) argue that it would be a logical extension of the protection they are now providing. They say that they should be permitted to extend their policies to pay no-fault auto accident benefits in addition to the accident benefits they are already paying.[2] Not surprisingly, the auto insurance companies disagree. They argue that they, not the health insurers, have the expertise needed to handle auto accident insurance. Regardless of whether this debate is won by the auto insurers or the health insurers, it does seem that continued development of the no-fault system would be likely to encourage further growth of group auto insurance.

IMPORTANT TERMS

Employee benefit plans	Pension plan
Group insurance	Employee Retirement Income Security
Contributory plan	Act
Noncontributory plan	Benefit formula
Conversion clause	Vesting
Coordination of benefits	Pension Benefit Guarantee Corporation
Health maintenance organization	Deferred profit-sharing plans

---

[2]In some states this already can be done. Michigan auto insurers, for instance, must offer no-fault benefits—at reduced rates—with deductibles and exclusions that relate to separate health insurance policies covering the insured persons.

KEY POINTS TO REMEMBER

1. Three separate layers of insurance protection are provided by: social insurance, employee benefit plans, and individual policies.
2. Employee benefit plans consist mainly of group life insurance, group health insurance, and pensions.
3. Group insurance covers a number of persons, usually employees of the same employer, under a single policy.
4. Group insurance is economical because of savings in sales and administrative expenses. The employer pays part or all of the cost and the premiums generally are not subject to income tax.
5. Group life insurance usually is term coverage. The amounts are determined by a schedule; all workers in the same category usually have the same amount. In contributory plans the employer and employees share the cost, all employees paying the same rate per $1,000 of coverage. In noncontributory plans the employer pays the entire cost.
6. Group health insurance covers nonoccupational illnesses and injuries. Except for disability income, all covered workers usually receive the same coverage.
7. Health maintenance organizations provide comprehensive health care services to their subscribers for a fixed periodic payment.
8. Group pension plans provide lifetime incomes for retired persons. Some of the plans are handled by noninsured trust funds, others by life insurance companies.
9. Employees who leave their jobs always can withdraw whatever amounts they have contributed toward their pension. To the extent that their pension rights are vested, they also can withdraw their employers' contributions.
10. Among the important provisions of the Employee Retirement and Income Security Act are requirements concerning pension funding, vesting, termination insurance, and disclosure.
11. Retirement benefits sometimes are provided by deferred profit-sharing plans, rather than by regular pension plans.
12. Dental insurance and legal expense insurance now are being added to numerous employee benefit packages.
13. A limited amount of auto insurance is being written on a modified group basis, using individual policies, individual rating, and individual underwriting.
14. The future of group auto insurance will be determined by several factors, including possible changes in the tax laws and developments in the no-fault system.

REVIEW QUESTIONS

1. What are employee benefit plans?
2. What is group insurance? In what ways does it differ from individual insurance?
3. For what reasons is group insurance less expensive than individual insurance?
4. Regarding group life insurance:
   (a) What is the nature of the protection?

    (b) How is the amount of an individual's coverage determined?

    (c) What is the conversion option?

5. Regarding group health insurance:

    (a) What kinds of coverage are provided?

    (b) What accidents and illnesses are usually covered?

    (c) What is the coordination of benefits provision?

6. What organizations furnish group health insurance?

7. Regarding group pensions:

    (a) What are the two funding agencies?

    (b) How is the amount of an individual's pension determined?

    (c) What is meant by vesting?

8. How does the Employee Retirement and Income Security Act protect workers' pension rights?

9. How does a deferred profit-sharing plan differ from a regular pension plan?

10. What other forms of insurance may employee benefit plans include?

11. Why aren't group auto policies written, rated, and underwritten in the same manner as group life and health policies?

DISCUSSION QUESTIONS

1. Why is group life insurance usually term rather than whole life or endowment?

2. The text says that because of the adverse selection problem, almost all dental insurance is provided on the group basis rather than by individual policies. Why isn't adverse selection as great a problem with group dental policies?

3. Insured employee benefit plans have grown rapidly during the last 30 years. There are a number of reasons. What are some of them?

4. Although group health insurance contracts sometimes furnish adequate protection, group life insurance contracts almost never are sufficient without being supplemented by individual policies. Why is this the case?

5. In order for a group life insurance plan to qualify for tax deduction under the rules of the Internal Revenue Service, the amount of each employee's coverage must be determined by a schedule or formula; ordinarily the amount cannot be increased or decreased for any one employee. What are the reasons for this rule?

6. In many of the cases where group auto insurance is available to them, only 10 or 20% of the employees have elected to take advantage of it. Why don't more employees participate? If such a plan were available to you, would you sign up for it?

CHAPTER 16
SOCIAL INSURANCE

THE NATURE OF SOCIAL INSURANCE

THE DEVELOPMENT OF SOCIAL INSURANCE

OLD AGE, SURVIVORS, DISABILITY, AND
  HEALTH INSURANCE

PROPOSALS FOR NATIONAL HEALTH
  INSURANCE

UNEMPLOYMENT INSURANCE

Our study of insurance emphasizes private insurance, that which is written by private insuring organizations. Insurance provided by the government is another major source of financial security. We saw an indication of its importance when we looked at Charlie and Ruth Newlin's life insurance program in Chapter 14. Their largest single source of income protection was social security. In addition to income for survivors of deceased workers, social insurance furnishes disability income protection, retirement pensions, health care coverages, and unemployment compensation.

In this chapter we shall examine the nature and development of social insurance, with emphasis on the U.S. social security program. We also shall consider proposals for adding national health insurance to the American social insurance system.

THE NATURE OF SOCIAL INSURANCE

Social insurance is provided by the government on a compulsory basis. A more precise definition is difficult, because the government can use its power and resources to apply the insurance method or modifications of it in a wide variety of ways. In the United States, there has been a tendency to look first to the private insurance industry for coverage of the risks that society deems important. When such risks have not been handled adequately by private insurance, social insurance plans have been established.

Characteristics of Social Insurance

A closer look at social insurance reveals several ways in which it differs from private insurance:

1. Social insurance is based on law, rather than on contract. Both the cost and the benefits are established by and can be changed by government units.
2. Coverage is compulsory for all persons to whom the law applies. They cannot choose to decline to participate, nor can they select the coverage or the amounts of the benefits.
3. Social objectives are primary. The purpose is to provide some minimum level of economic security for large portions of the population. This is called the **floor of protection concept.** The philosophy is that, in an economic system that stresses free enterprise and individual initiative, people should not rely entirely upon governmental programs. Social insurance is designed to guarantee economic security at minimal levels; those who want more adequate benefits obtain them through personal savings and private insurance.

4. The benefits of social insurance are weighted in favor of certain groups, usually those with low income. This approach is necessary in order to carry out the social objectives. Unless low-income groups are subsidized by high-income groups, the payments of the former will not be large enough to furnish the minimum levels of protection that are desired. At the same time, however, each person's benefits generally are somewhat related to his or her contributions.
5. Social insurance usually covers only those who are or who have been employed. Most social insurance plans concern the interruption of income (by death, disability, unemployment, or retirement) earned through employment. Covering employed persons also facilitates the collection of premiums, often by means of payroll taxes.

Social Insurance and Public Assistance

Social insurance should not be confused with public assistance programs. The latter include federal-state aid to families with dependent children; the federal Supplementary Security Income program for the aged, blind, and disabled; and the state Medicaid programs that pay medical and hospital charges that Medicare does not cover.

The difference between social insurance and public assistance is that public assistance payments are given to those who show that they need them, whereas social insurance payments go to all who are eligible for them, regardless of need. A further distinction is that public assistance programs are financed by the general revenues of the government, whereas most social insurance programs are financed by specific payroll taxes paid by participating individuals and their employers.

THE DEVELOPMENT OF SOCIAL INSURANCE

The United States has not been a leader in the development of social insurance programs. Several European countries established programs before 1900; ours did not get under way until 1935. Today, numerous countries have more extensive programs than we do. The U.S. program is expanding rapidly, however. Table 16–1 shows how payments have grown since 1950. Notice that they increased from about 3% of the total national income in 1950 to over 11% in 1977.

The development of our social insurance program is closely associated with several changes in U.S. society, including: industrialization and urbanization, a rising standard of living, an increasing percentage of elderly persons, and growing concern for the well-being of others.

Table 16–1 Social Insurance Payments and Personal Income
(amounts in billions)

YEAR	TOTAL PERSONAL INCOME	SOCIAL INSURANCE PAYMENTS[a]	
		AMOUNT	PERCENT OF PERSONAL INCOME
1950	$ 226.1	$ 7.0	3.1
1955	308.8	13.1	4.2
1960	399.7	23.9	6.0
1965	537.0	34.2	6.4
1970	801.3	65.4	8.2
1975	1,255.5	143.6	11.4
1977	1,529.0	177.0	11.6

[a]Includes OASDHI, railroad retirement, unemployment insurance, veterans pensions, workers' compensation, temporary disability insurance, and related programs.
Source: Social Security Bulletin, January 1979, p. 85.

Until this century, U.S. society was chiefly agricultural. Most people were members of large, virtually self-sufficient farm families. Economic security was provided by the family and by the farm itself. With growing industrialization, population gradually shifted to the cities, and employment changed from farm to factory. This movement continued until the mid-1900s. For the bulk of the population, self-sufficiency became a thing of the past; almost everyone now depended upon wages earned from outside employment. If the family wage earner was laid off, died, or became disabled, the family was threatened with destitution. Although some families were very well off indeed, many found it difficult or impossible to provide for their financial security through savings or insurance. The demands upon private charity, religious and ethnic organizations, and local poor relief programs soon exceeded their ability to respond. Increasingly, people turned to the state and federal governments. Until this time, most people had believed that the government's role was to provide a stable and secure environment within which individuals could work to achieve their own well-being. But many Americans adopted the view that government was directly responsible for guaranteeing at least a minimum level of welfare for all.

As the nation prospered and living standards rose, attitudes about the minimum acceptable level of well-being changed. The floor of protection concept developed. The economy seemed capable of furnishing subsistence for all, and social insurance was regarded as an appropriate means of providing it.

Another factor accounting for the growth of social insurance is the increasing percentage of older persons in the U.S. population. Today nearly 10% of all Americans (over 20 million persons) are age 65 or above. This percentage has about doubled during the last two generations. Not only are there many more elderly persons, but thanks to better health care and improved living conditions, they are living longer than ever before. Thus, the elderly have more years of retirement, a longer period during which they cannot depend upon their current earnings to supply the necessities of life.

Finally, there has been growing concern for the welfare of others, an increase in the feeling that society as a whole has some responsibility for all of its members. To some extent, this philosophy seems to be replacing the concept that responsibility rests with the individual, the family, and the local community. We should realize, however, that social insurance is only one part of our system; it is but one of the things that contributes to our economic security. Government programs have by no means replaced individual responsibility. Although social insurance can be relied upon to provide a minimum floor of protection, really satisfactory levels of protection require that it be supplemented by group insurance and by individual savings and insurance.

OLD AGE, SURVIVORS, DISABILITY, AND HEALTH INSURANCE

Almost all of the U.S. social insurance program is based upon the Social Security Act of 1935. This Act originated during the administration of President Franklin Roosevelt and was part of what came to be known as the New Deal program. Since then, it has been amended and expanded in a variety of ways. Today 9 out of 10 Americans are protected by social security; nearly 1 out of 7 receive monthly social security income checks.

Originally, social security provided only retirement benefits. In 1939 the Act was amended to pay income to the survivors of deceased workers. Disability income coverage was added in 1954, providing benefits to workers who become totally disabled. In 1965 the program was expanded to include Medicare, furnishing hospital and medical protection for persons age 65 and over.

Although the Social Security Act includes programs of public assistance as well, our concern is its social insurance coverages. These constitute the Old Age, Survivors, Disability, and Health Insurance (OASDHI) program, which is commonly referred to as **social security.** We shall review each of the four

Table 16-2 Examples of Monthly Social Security Retirement Payments[a]

COVERED PERSON	AVERAGE YEARLY EARNINGS AFTER 1950			
	$4,000	$6,000	$8,000	$10,000
Retired worker at 65	$296.20	$388.20	$482.60	$534.70
Retired worker at 62	237.00	310.60	386.10	427.80
Wife or dependent husband at 65	148.10	194.10	241.30	267.40
Wife or dependent husband at 62	111.10	145.60	181.00	200.60
Widow or widower with one child	444.40	582.40	724.00	802.20

[a]Effective June 1978. The higher amounts are not yet payable, as explained in the text.
Source: Your Social Security, Social Security Administration, August 1978.

coverages and see who is protected by them. We also shall consider how the program is financed. Because OASDHI rules and benefits frequently are changed by Congress, detailed descriptions are impractical. Local offices of the Social Security Administration can supply the latest detailed information.

Retirement Benefits

The basic **retirement benefit** is paid to those who retire at age 65. Workers can retire as early as age 62, but their payments are permanently reduced if they do. Slightly higher benefits are paid to those who delay their retirement beyond age 65. An additional 1% is added for each year that a person continues working from age 65 to age 72.[1] The retirement benefit is increased for those who have dependents.

The amount of the monthly retirement income checks is also related to the retiree's average earnings while employed. The formula used to compute this amount favors those with low incomes. Furthermore, it does not take into account wages above a certain maximum and it provides that all eligible persons will receive at least a certain minimum even if their earnings were extremely low. An idea of the size of the retirement benefits is indicated by Table 16–2. Notice that benefits are based on a worker's average earnings since 1950 and therefore are affected by lower wages earned in the 1950s and 1960s. Furthermore, only those earnings that were subject to the social security tax are counted. This amount is less than many workers' total earnings, a factor that further limits the average upon which retirement benefits are based. For instance, the maximum annual earnings that were taxed (and included in the average) for the years 1959 to 1965 was $4,800.[2] Because some of the earnings upon which retirement benefits are based are

[1]For workers reaching 65 after 1981, the credit will be increased to 3% for each year.
[2]For 1979 the limit was $22,900, with further increases scheduled for future years.

quite low, the amounts shown in the last two columns of Table 16–2 will not actually be payable until future years. The maximum benefit generally payable to workers retiring at age 65 in 1978, for instance, was $489.70 per month.

Since 1972, social security benefit payments have been tied to the cost of living. The law provides that, if living costs increase by 3% or more in any year, payments will be increased by the same amount starting with the checks issued for the following July.

To be eligible for retirement benefits, a person must have credit for a certain amount of employment under social security. The length of employment required depends on the worker's age and the date of his or her retirement. For instance, persons reaching age 62 in 1981 need 7.5 years of employment. Those who reach 62 in 1991 or later will need 10 years.

Survivor Benefits

Survivor benefits are payable to the families of deceased workers. These benefits, which are comparable to life insurance, include:

1. A small lump sum payment (usually $225).
2. Income for widows or widowers with children under age 18. The payments continue until the children are 22 if they are still in school.
3. Income for dependent children (under 18 or 22).
4. Income for widows or dependent widowers age 60 or above.

To illustrate, if a man dies at age 40, leaving a widow and a ten-year-old child, monthly income payments will be made to the survivors until the child reaches age 18. (Payments to the child will continue until age 22 if he or she remains in school.) The payments to the widow stop (during the so-called blackout period) from the time the child becomes 18 until the widow reaches age 60. At that time she becomes eligible for a lifetime pension. Her pension payments will be larger if she delays receiving them until she is older than 60.

To be eligible for survivor benefits, a certain amount of covered employment is required, as it is for retirement benefits. However, in this case a shorter period may be sufficient, depending on the age at which the worker dies. A worker who dies at age 28 or younger needs to have been working only 1.5 years. Those who are older at the time of their death need longer periods of employment, the maximum being 10 years.

Both survivor benefits and retirement benefits are subject to an **earnings test**. Survivors and retirees who earn no more than a certain limit per year from current wages receive full benefits. Those who earn more than that amount lose $1 in benefits for each $2 they earn above the limit. The limit in 1979 for people under 65 was $4,000 (a higher limit applies for those 65 or over). To illustrate, assume that a young widow with children qualifies for survivor benefits of $600 a month, or $7,200 a year. If she works and earns $10,000 a year, her earnings exceed the $4,000 limit by $6,000. As a result, her benefits will be reduced by half of the $6,000, or $3,000, and will be $4,200 rather than $7,200. Thus, her total income will be $10,000 from her employment plus $4,200 from social security, or a total of $14,200.

The earnings test applies only to current wages. Income from savings, investments, or other pensions is not counted. The test does not apply to persons age 72 or above.

Disability Benefits

Workers who become totally disabled before they retire and who are expected to remain disabled for at least 12 months receive disability income payments. The amount is the same as the person would receive for retirement; it is increased when there are dependents. Payments begin after a five-month waiting period and continue until age 65, at which time they become pension payments in the same amount. Notice that the disability benefits provide monthly income only; they do not specifically pay for the costs of medical treatment.

The eligibility requirements for disability benefits are rather similar to those for survivor benefits, again ranging from 1.5 to 10 years, depending upon the worker's age.

Medicare

Medicare is a health insurance program for people over 65. It also covers certain disabled persons below that age. The program has two parts. The first is a basic hospital insurance program; the second is a voluntary program of medical insurance. The hospital insurance helps pay for in-patient hospital care and for follow-up care after a patient leaves the hospital. The medical insurance pays for doctors' services, outpatient hospital services, and certain other medical items and services not covered by the hospital insurance.

It is difficult to summarize Medicare benefits because they are determined by a tangle of complex rules and regulations. Furthermore, the deductible amounts are changed rather frequently. The brief summaries that follow indicate the benefits effective in 1979.

MEDICARE HOSPITAL BENEFITS. The hospital insurance part of Medicare provides the following benefits:

1. Up to 90 days of in-patient hospital care for each benefit period. (A benefit period begins when a patient enters a hospital; it ends when the patient has been out of the hospital or nursing home for 60 days.) The patient pays a deductible amount ($160 in 1979) for the first 60-day period of hospitalization. After that, there is a daily deductible ($40 in 1979).

2. An extra 60 days of in-patient hospital care, subject to a daily deductible ($80 in 1979). These are called "reserve days." They can be used anytime during a person's lifetime when he or she is hospitalized for more than 90 days in a single benefit period.

3. Up to 100 days of nursing home care. After the first 20 days, the patient pays a stated amount per day ($20 in 1979) for the remaining 80 days. The nursing home care must begin within 14 days after being hospitalized for at least 3 days.

4. Up to 100 days of home health visits by nurses or other health workers (but not by doctors). These visits must come within one year after leaving a hospital or nursing home.

Medicare hospital insurance pays for semiprivate hospital and nursing home rooms, regular nursing services, and special care units such as a hospital's intensive care facility. It also pays for drugs furnished to in-patients of a hospital or nursing home. It does not cover doctor bills or the cost of private nurses.

This part of Medicare is compulsory, being financed by a payroll tax that is paid by employers and employees. Practically everyone at least 65 years old is eligible, whether they have retired or not.

MEDICARE MEDICAL BENEFITS.   This part of the Medicare program is available on a voluntary basis to anyone age 65 or above. Those who want the protection pay a monthly premium ($8.20 in 1979); the government matches that amount out of its general funds. Coverage must be applied for at a local social security office. It provides the following benefits:

1. Doctors' services (including surgery) at home, in a doctor's office, in a hospital, or elsewhere. These include all physicians' services, and drugs that are not self-administered.

2. Outpatient hospital services.

3. Up to 100 home health visits (in addition to those covered by Medicare hospital insurance).

4. Certain other medical and health services that are prescribed by a physician, including diagnostic services, x-ray treatment, and medical equipment.

There is an annual $60 deductible, after which the medical insurance pays 80% of the patient's expenses. The benefits do not include routine physical checkups, prescription drugs, glasses, hearing aids, or full-time nursing care in the patient's home.

It is clear that, although Medicare provides significant protection, its benefits are limited. It has been estimated that the program pays only about half of the health care costs of the nation's elderly. It is important, therefore, that older people make plans to supplement this protection, perhaps by purchasing individual health insurance policies.

ADMINISTRATION OF MEDICARE. Although Medicare is a part of the social security program, much of its administration is handled by private organizations. These organizations, including Blue Cross, Blue Shield, and commercial insurance companies, operate under contracts with the Social Security Administration. They determine the reasonableness of the charges for services and disburse the funds to health agencies and physicians.

Financing the OASDHI Program

The OASDHI program (except Medicare medical insurance) is financed by a special payroll tax paid by employers and employees. When the program began in 1935 the tax was 1% on the first $3,000 of a worker's annual income. As the benefits have grown, both the tax rate and the amount of annual income subject to the tax have been raised.

In 1979 the tax for employed persons was 6.13%. As of then, the law called for rates of 6.65% in 1981 and 6.70% in 1982, and for further increases that would bring the tax to 7.65% in 1990. The maximum amount of income subject to the tax in 1979 was $22,900. This amount is increased automatically as average income levels rise. The full tax is paid by both employee and employer. Workers earning $22,900 or more in 1979 paid over $1,400 in social security taxes, with an equal amount being paid by their employers.

The taxes are collected by the Internal Revenue Service and deposited in social security trust funds. Both benefit payments and administrative costs come from the trust funds. Amounts not currently needed are invested in U.S. government securities.

THE FUNDING ISSUE. The funding of OASDHI differs from that of life insurance, a point that sometimes causes confusion. A life insurance company must be "fully funded;" that is, the funds on hand always must be enough so that they, together with future income from premiums and investments, will be sufficient to meet all of the company's future obligations.

Because of this requirement, life insurance companies set aside a large part of their revenues each year to pay policy benefits during the years ahead. Over a period of many years the amounts set aside in this manner reach enormous proportions. (One company alone has over $50 billion.)

The social security program is funded differently. Since 1939 it has been on a "pay as you go" basis; the benefits it pays each year come almost entirely from that year's revenues. Because benefits are paid from current revenues rather than from those of previous years, the social security system does not accumulate vast funds. In a recent year its trust funds totaled "only" $30 billion.

Confusion arises when OASDHI funding is compared with life insurance funding. If they are judged on the same basis, it may appear that the social security program is practically broke, because its funds are so limited. But such a comparison is incorrect and the conclusion is unjustified. Life insurance companies are private organizations; they are required to be fully funded to protect policyholders and beneficiaries. Social security, on the other hand, is based upon the taxing power of the federal government. If it is assumed that the program will be continued indefinitely, there is no need for it to be funded the way that private insurance companies are and to have the enormous funds that they do.

RATE LEVEL QUESTIONS.   Another issue involving OASDHI financing concerns the tax rates. Are they set at the proper level? Sometimes it is said that they are too high and that the system will accumulate a large surplus. At other times it is claimed that the rates are too low and that bankruptcy is just around the corner. The latter was the theme of numerous newspaper stories during the late 1970s.

The setting of social security tax levels, like the setting of rates for insurance policies, is based on prediction of future events. In the case of social security, this is an especially difficult task because of the large number of variables that it involves. Tax revenues, for instance, are influenced by future wage levels and by unemployment rates. Claim costs are affected not only by mortality and disability rates, but also by changes in average family size, average retirement age, and remarriage rates (the latter because widows who remarry lose their survivorship benefits). All of this makes precision in the setting of social security tax rates extremely difficult and there is plenty of room for differences in opinion among various actuaries and other experts. However, the government has always intended the program to be financially sound and no one questions that intent or suggests that it has been changed. Furthermore, OASDHI financing is under constant review by government actuaries and by a panel of thirteen independent actuaries and economists who are members of the Advisory Council on Social Security.

Dramatic news stories notwithstanding, there is no apparent reason for the public to fear that the benefits that have been promised will not be paid. The cost will be great, and benefits certainly cannot continue to be expanded indefinitely, but these are separate issues. The point being made here is that neither the lack of full funding nor temporary maladjustments of tax levels seriously threaten the long-range stability of the social security system.

PROPOSALS FOR NATIONAL HEALTH INSURANCE

We have reviewed three different methods that are used for insuring the costs of health care: privately insured individual policies, privately insured group policies, and the government's Medicare program. Actually, these are not the only means of paying for medical costs. Others include public assistance, charities, personal savings, borrowing, workers' compensation, bodily injury liability settlements, and medical payments insurance. Dissatisfaction with this unsystematic, multifaceted approach has stimulated a search for alternatives.

Most Americans want the government to develop a better system. Opinion polls show that a majority of the public favors the adoption of some sort of **national health insurance** program. As a result, about twenty different proposals have been considered by the Congress during the last few years. In one way or another, each would extend health insurance protection to all or almost all of the population. We shall review the reasons for the interest in national health insurance and then take a look at some of the specific proposals.

Criticisms of the Present System

Complaints about the current health insurance set-up are based upon its costs, the unevenness of its protection, and its apparent failure to promote excellence of care.

The cost problem has two aspects. First is simply the extremely high and rapidly rising level of expense. Personal spending for medical care has skyrocketed during recent years, rising more rapidly than practically every other component of the total cost of living. President Carter pointed out that the typical family spends about one month's earnings each year for health care. The second aspect of the cost problem is the belief that the methods of paying for medical care are themselves contributing to the rising costs. About two-thirds of the total bill is paid by private and social insurance; only one-third comes directly from personal funds. Many people believe that this practice leads patients to demand unnecessarily expensive care and encourages doctors and hospitals to boost their charges. The federal programs have been criticized most strongly on this point. One author stated his opinion this way:

What seems chiefly at fault is Medicare's and Medicaid's peculiar method of reimbursement, whereby they pay whatever the doctor or the hospital claims to be "reasonable" and "customary." In effect, the Congress has handed a blank check to the health-care industry, with predictable results. [3]

The second criticism concerns the unevenness of protection that current arrangements provide. Some people have excellent health insurance protection, while others have little or none. This situation runs counter to the majority opinion that Americans should be able to obtain high-quality health care regardless of their income, age, or employment. Although about four out of five people have some form of health insurance, the quality of the protection varies: One person out of five has none at all; the elderly have Medicare; group insurance protects those who happen to work where such plans are provided; some of those who are not eligible for group coverage can afford individual policies, but many cannot; some who are not otherwise protected are poor enough to qualify for Medicaid and others are not; and some medical costs are paid by workers' compensation or by lawsuits. In effect, what we have is a patchwork system that provides uneven amounts of protection for the various segments of society.

The third criticism is that, in spite of its great expense, the system does not appear to promote the general health of the population. No nation spends as much per person for health care as ours does; yet we are lagging behind in some of the statistics that measure the health of a nation's people. The United States ranks 13th among all nations in infant mortality, 11th in female life expectancy at birth, and 18th in male life expectancy. These statistics of course reflect numerous economic, social, and environmental factors, but included among them is the fact that too many Americans cannot pay for the medical services they need. An efficient means of paying for proper medical care is vital to any nation's general level of health.

The Major Proposals

The United States is the only industrialized nation that does not have a national health insurance program. The many proposals to establish such a program have come from a variety of sources and offer a wide range of approaches. Several of the proposals have come from organizations that are

[3]Richard J. Margolis, "National Health Insurance—The Dream Whose Time Has Come?" *The New York Times Magazine*, January 9, 1977, p. 13.

directly involved in furnishing and insuring health care. Associations of hospitals, doctors, and health insurance companies each are supporting their own plans. Labor unions and consumer organizations also are involved in the political infighting.

Each of the proposals differs from the others with regard to the benefits it would provide, its cost, how it would be paid for, and how it would be administered. Rather confusingly, several of the proposals go beyond establishing national health insurance and also include measures designed to control the cost and to improve the quality of the nation's health care. We shall not try to cover all of the details but shall summarize three of the most important plans.

THE KENNEDY PLAN. This plan, whose chief sponsor is Senator Edward Kennedy, is the most far-reaching—and expensive—of the current proposals. The bill is co-sponsored by Representative Henry Waxman and is supported by many labor, civil rights, and consumer organizations.

All residents of the United States would be covered, regardless of age, employment status, or ability to pay. A complete range of benefits would be furnished, including full coverage for hospital care, physician services in or out of the hospital, laboratory services, and medical equipment. There would be no deductibles; insurance protection would begin with the "first dollar" of expense. Catastrophic illnesses would be fully covered, with no limit on the number of hospital days or physician visits.

For most people the coverage would be in the form of group insurance provided by private insurance companies or Blue Cross-Blue Shield organizations. Employers would pay most of the cost, although they could (subject to negotiation with employee groups) require workers to provide up to 35% of the premium. The federal government would shoulder the cost of Medicare for elderly patients, as it does now. Most of the poor, who now are covered by public assistance (Medicaid) programs, would be covered by the new national health insurance plan, but at public expense.

The Kennedy plan, which would be administered by a newly-created National Health Insurance Board, also would place strict controls on hospital and physician fees and would add new regulations governing the quality of health care. Supporters of the plan see these measures as essential to the reforms they favor; opponents believe the cost controls and quality controls could lead to the development of an expensive and burdensome federal bureaucracy.

Although it is a far-reaching proposal, the Kennedy plan would not nationalize the health care system; hospitals still would be privately operated (subject to increased federal and state controls) and doctors still would be self-employed, although group practice and health maintenance organizations would be encouraged.

The plan also would leave the private health insurance business intact. In contrast, under an earlier proposal by Senator Kennedy all benefits were to have been paid directly by the government, thus eliminating the need for private insurers. Under the new Kennedy plan, insurance companies would pay most of the benefits and would compete with one another to handle mandatory group health insurance protection much as they now compete to handle voluntary group health insurance protection.

THE LONG PLAN.   The plan proposed by Senator Russell Long is in one sense at the opposite extreme from the Kennedy proposal. It takes the major medical approach, being designed to cover only catastrophic illnesses and accidents. All employed or self-employed persons, their spouses, and their dependents below age 26 would be covered. The program would pay for hospital costs after the first 60 days of hospitalization and for other medical expenses exceeding $2,000 a year. The plan also would expand the Medicaid public assistance program for low-income persons.

Employers could elect to buy the catastrophe coverage either from the government or from a private insurer. Existing health insurance (other than major medical plans) would not be affected. Expenses recovered from either individual or group policies would count toward the 60-day and $2,000 deductibles.

The Long plan has the merits of being simple, easy to establish, and relatively inexpensive. It would cost about one-fourth as much as the Kennedy proposal. The plan has been criticized on the grounds that it would not be of equal benefit to all, as what is a financial catastrophe for a family with a low or moderate income would not be equally burdensome for a wealthy family. The plan has the further advantage of not creating a new federal bureaucracy; on the other hand, it would do little to control the rising costs of medical care.

THE CARTER PLAN.   The Carter Administration's proposal is a compromise. Its estimated cost is roughly twice that of the Long plan, but only about half as much as the Kennedy plan.

The Carter plan would cover everyone and would provide a full range of medical services, as would the Kennedy bill. However, like the Long plan, it follows the major medical approach; benefits would be payable only after a family or individual has incurred $2,500 a year in medical expenses. Standard medical services in excess of that amount would be paid in full. Full coverage with no deductible would be provided for pregnant women and infants less than a year old.

Most of the benefit payments would be handled by private group insurers. Employers would bear at least 75% of the cost; employees would pay no more than 25%.

For the unemployed and for low-income families, all basic health costs would be financed by federal and state revenues. Medicare for the aged and Medicaid assistance for the poor would be merged into a single, more generous Healthcare program. For Medicare patients, the annual deductible would become $1,250 per person.

The Carter plan's cost controls would be concentrated on the new Healthcare program. Doctors' fees to Healthcare patients would be set by the government; doctors' fees to other patients would not be controlled. A separate law would be aimed at controlling hospital costs.

Healthcare would be administered by a new federal agency. The rest of the Carter program would be handled by insurance companies, health maintenance organizations, and self-insured employers.

The Outlook for National Health Insurance

National Health insurance has been receiving serious consideration by the Congress and the public since the 1940's and on several occasions passage of a plan has seemed likely. However, the proponents never have been able to concentrate their support upon a single bill and the opponents (including most doctors, hospitals, and insurers) have prevailed.

Over the years many of the issues which formerly split the advocates of national health insurance have been resolved. The role to be played by private insurers is such an issue. Some of the strongest advocates previously favored plans which in effect would have eliminated the private health insurance industry. But as we have seen, each of the three major proposals now being considered relies upon private insurers to provide the protection and distribute insurance benefits to the public. One of the major remaining issues is that of "first-dollar" coverage (the Kennedy plan) versus the major medical approach (the Long and Carter plans). Another important issue which must be resolved is the kind and extent of controls which a national health insurance plan should impose upon the cost and quality of health care. These are important issues which demand careful consideration; however, public dissatisfaction with the status quo is continuing to mount and it appears that some action will have to be taken in the near future.

UNEMPLOYMENT INSURANCE

Unemployment insurance is designed to provide short-term protection for regularly employed persons who lose their jobs and who are willing and able to work. Each state has its own unemployment insurance program. The state programs came about because of one of the provisions of the federal Social Security Act. That Act provided for a federal unemployment insurance program to be financed by a special payroll tax. Because the intent really was to encourage the states to establish programs of their own, the federal law said that 90% of the tax revenues would be returned to each state that set up an acceptable unemployment insurance plan. Nor surprisingly, all of the states established such plans. The tax, which in 1977 was set at 3.4% of payrolls up to $6,000 per person, is paid by employers. The federal government's portion of the revenues is used to pay federal and state administrative costs.

Eligibility and Benefits

The federal law sets minimum standards for eligibility and benefits. As long as they meet the federal standards, the states can set their own eligibility rules and benefit patterns.

Eligibility rules normally require that the worker (a) has been regularly employed, (b) is unemployed through no fault of his or her own, such as quitting or being discharged for misconduct, (c) is willing to work, and (d) is able to work. All of the states require persons receiving unemployment compensation to register for work with the state employment service and most require further evidence that they are actively seeking jobs.

Weekly benefit payments are based on the worker's past earnings in all but a few states. Usually the person must have been out of work for a week before payments begin. In most states the normal maximum benefit period is 26 weeks. During periods of high general unemployment the Congress frequently has adopted legislation permitting the states to set longer benefit periods, with part or all of the extra cost being financed by the federal government.

Disabled workers are not eligible for unemployment insurance benefits in most states. If their disability was caused by an occupational injury or illness, they of course receive workers' compensation benefits. If their disability is due to other causes, they may be eligible for payments from group or individual nonoccupational disability income policies. Five states (California, Hawaii, New Jersey, New York, and Rhode Island) have separate temporary disability insurance laws. These laws furnish income for unemployed workers who are disabled. The benefits are similar to those provided by unemployment insurance.

Problems

Scarcely anyone is satisfied with the unemployment insurance programs. Workers and labor unions complain that the payments are too small, the benefit periods too short, and administrative standards too strict. At the same time, employers say that the costs are too high because benefits are paid to many people who should not receive them. They point to cases when strikers and seasonal workers have been paid and instances when unemployed persons have refused to accept jobs that appeared to be suitable.

Private insurance companies never have written unemployment insurance, largely because of the catastrophe exposure associated with high unemployment rates during recessions. In view of the problems they have avoided, they probably are fortunate!

IMPORTANT TERMS

Social insurance	Medicare
Floor of protection concept	Medicare hospital benefits
Retirement benefits	Medicare medical benefits
Survivor benefits	National health insurance
Earnings test	Unemployment insurance
Disability benefits	

KEY POINTS TO REMEMBER

1. Social insurance is provided by the government on a compulsory basis. It has social objectives, including the provision of a minimum level of economic security for a large part of the working population. Benefits usually are weighted in favor of low-income groups.
2. Social insurance differs from public assistance in that payments are made to all eligible persons as a matter of right, rather than only to those who are in need. Also, social insurance is financed by special payroll taxes instead of from the government's general revenues.
3. After a slow beginning, the social insurance program of the United States is expanding rapidly. It is designed to furnish only a floor of protection; more adequate protection requires group or individual insurance.
4. The U.S. social security program primarily consists of the coverages provided by the Social Security Act: retirement pensions, survivor benefits, disability income benefits, and health insurance for persons over 65.
5. Eligibility rules for retirement, survivor, and disability benefits require credit for certain periods of work in covered employment.
6. Medicare, the health insurance portion of social security, consists of two parts: a compulsory hospital insurance program and a voluntary medical insurance program.
7. Social security (except medical insurance) is financed by special payroll taxes paid by employers and employees. Contrary to frequent criticisms and in spite of rising costs, the program is financially sound.
8. The unsystematic arrangement through which medical costs are paid in the United States is being severely criticized for its high cost, unevenness of protection, and failure to promote excellence of health care.
9. Numerous proposals to create a system of national health insurance are being

considered. The proposals vary with regard to their benefits, costs, financing, and administration.

10. State unemployment insurance programs provide short-term income protection for people who lose their jobs and who are willing and able to work.

REVIEW QUESTIONS

1. In what ways does social insurance differ from private insurance?
2. What changes in U.S. society were associated with the development of social insurance?
3. List the types of protection provided by the U.S. social insurance program.
4. What factors determine the amounts of social security retirement benefits that a person receives?
5. What is the black-out period?
6. What is the earnings test?
7. What major benefits are provided by the two parts of Medicare?
8. How is social security paid for?
9. Describe two of the major national health insurance proposals.
10. What roles might private health insurers have if national health insurance is enacted?
11. What are the usual eligibility requirements for unemployment insurance?

DISCUSSION QUESTIONS

1. Certain changes in U.S. society have been associated with the development and growth of social insurance. Do you believe that the changes mentioned in the text justify the social insurance system that now exists?
2. Social insurance benefits are weighted in favor of low-income groups; that is, to some extent their benefits are subsidized by higher income workers. Is this fair?
3. Social insurance programs are designed to furnish only a floor of protection. Is this the right objective, or should the goal be to provide a comfortable level of living?
4. How can it be logical to fund social security on a "pay as you go" basis when life insurance companies must be fully funded?
5. Would it be desirable to expand social insurance enough to eliminate the need for private insurance?
6. In your opinion, should the United States adopt a national health program? If so, which of the proposals described in the text should it be most similar to?
7. Some people say that social security (OASDHI) actually is not insurance at all; others say that it is. What arguments can be presented pro and con?

PART IV
INSURANCE FOR SMALL BUSINESS

CHAPTER 17
PROPERTY INSURANCE FOR SMALL BUSINESS

**PROPERTY INSURANCE
AGAINST DIRECT LOSS**

LOSS OF INCOME

BURGLARY AND ROBBERY

EMPLOYEE DISHONESTY

Stereo City has just opened for business. The store is located in a large new shopping center. It handles high-quality stereo and high fidelity equipment—receivers, amplifiers, speakers, and so forth. The store has a large stock of parts and it services the brands of equipment that it sells. Stereo City is actually a partnership; it is jointly owned by Ted Polito and Gary Harmish. Ted has had several years of experience in stereo sales management. Gary is new to the business, having just finished college. Gary's father, a doctor, loaned the partners most of the funds they needed to start the business; a local bank provided the rest.

Ted and Gary began making plans for Stereo City over one year ago. One of the first things they discovered was that they were going to need insurance. There was no way they were going to have that big investment wiped out by a fire or theft! Besides, the loan officer at the bank told them the bank would insist that they be insured. As they proceeded with their plans, the partners found that they would need other kinds of insurance, too, including liability and workers' compensation. This chapter and the next one are concerned with the kinds of insurance protection needed by Stereo City and similar small business firms.

The insurance of business risks is a very complex topic. Even small firms can have unusual risk management problems that call for specialized handling. Therefore, we must realize that the scope of these two chapters is limited. They deal only with "typical" small business risks like those of Stereo City. They do not attempt to survey all of the risks to which businesses—even small ones—are exposed, nor to review all of the various ways in which business risks can be insured. The chapters will identify the common insurable risks and the customary forms of business insurance. Business managers who have this information will not be insurance experts, but they will be in a position to recognize their major insurance needs and the importance of obtaining good risk management advice.

To simplify the study of property-casualty insurance for small business, we shall focus on the coverages available in the **Businessowners Policy.** It is a package policy designed for insuring small stores, office buildings, and apartment buildings. This policy is well suited for Stereo City and for many other small businesses. In summary form, here is what the Businessowners Policy covers:

1. **Buildings and Contents** are covered on the replacement cost basis. Coverage can be either for named perils or for all risks.
2. **Loss of Income** pays for income lost and extra expenses incurred while the insured is out of business because of damage caused by an insured peril.

3. **Optional Coverages** include burglary and robbery, and employee crime.
4. **Liability** furnishes comprehensive protection, including liability claims involving premises, operations, and products.
5. **Medical Payments** pays for medical expenses of others who are injured because of the insured business operations.

The first three kinds of protection are reviewed in this chapter. The other two, along with workers' compensation insurance, are discussed in Chapter 18.

First used in 1976, the Businessowners Policy does for small business firms what homeowners policies do for individuals. That is, it packages in a single contract a number of coverages which previously were available as separate policies. Package policies offer advantages in cost, coverage, and convenience. They cost less because they can be marketed and handled more efficiently by the agents and insurers. The coverage is superior to that of separate policies because gaps and overlaps of protection are avoided. The policies are more convenient because they avoid the need for numerous contracts, expiration dates, and premiums.

PROPERTY INSURANCE AGAINST DIRECT LOSS

Like all businessowners, Ted Polito and Gary Harmish need insurance that will pay for direct damage to their firm's property. This section examines the property and perils insured by the Businessowners Policy, as well as the basis and amounts of the coverage.

Property Covered

The first two parts of the Businessowners Policy are Coverage A, Buildings, and Coverage B, Business Personal Property. If Ted and Gary were owners of the building where Stereo City is located, they would need both coverages. Because they are tenants, they of course will not need Coverage A.

The property insured by Coverage B, Business Personal Property, is primarily the store's inventory of stereo equipment. However, the owners need additional protection for personal property, and the policy provides it through several important extensions:

1. Business personal property is defined to include "similar property held by the insured and belonging in whole or in part to others." This includes customers' stereos that are on the premises for repairs.

2. Property coverage is extended to include "tenant's improvements and betterments." This encompasses fixtures and alterations permanently installed in the building by Stereo City. It protects the firm's investment in such improvements even though they are permanently attached to the building and therefore now belong to the building owner.
3. Personal property coverage also includes items that are temporarily away from the store, including property in transit. This would pay for goods (including customers' equipment in the insured's custody) that are damaged while being transported to or from the store. Coverage under this extension is limited to $1,000 per occurrence.
4. Property located at any new Stereo City location is covered for up to $10,000 for a 30-day period. This gives automatic protection until the policy can be endorsed to add the new location.

Among the optional coverages available under the Businessowners Policy is one providing insurance on exterior signs. If the partners purchase an expensive advertising sign for the outside of their store, they may want to consider buying coverage for it.

Perils Covered

Two Businessowners Policy forms are available. One, the Standard Form, covers named perils; the other, the Special Form, provides all-risk coverage. We observed the difference between these two approaches in the discussion of auto and homeowners policies. Assuming that the owners of Stereo City have chosen the Standard (named peril) Form, let us review the perils that it covers. They are: fire and lightning, the extended coverage perils, vandalism and malicious mischief, sprinkler leakage, and transportation.

FIRE AND LIGHTNING. The products handled by Stereo City make use of the latest technological advances in the field of sound reproduction, but they can be destroyed by at least two things older than mankind: fire and lightning.

EXTENDED COVERAGE PERILS. For many years, most property insurance policies have covered numerous perils in addition to fire and lightning. A certain group of the other perils is called the **extended coverage** perils; the name stems from an endorsement that can be used to insure them. The extended coverage perils are:

1. Windstorm or hail
2. Explosion

3. Smoke
4. Aircraft or vehicles
5. Riot or civil commotion

These perils are also covered by homeowners policies and were described in Chapter 9.

VANDALISM AND MALICIOUS MISCHIEF. These perils cover "wilful and malicious damage to or destruction of the property covered."

SPRINKLER LEAKAGE. This peril is important for businesses located in buildings with automatic sprinkler systems. The protection is for damage caused by leakage or discharge from the system or collapse of a tank that is part of the system.

TRANSPORTATION. As we noted earlier, the policy provides $1,000 of coverage for business personal property that is temporarily away from the premises. This peril pertains to that extension and provides that while property is in transit it is covered for these additional perils:

1. Collision, derailment, or overturn of a vehicle
2. Stranding or sinking of a ship
3. Collapse of a bridge or wharf

Basis and Amount of Coverage

Several provisions of the Businessowners Policy simplify the insurance (in comparison with other business policies) to make the contract suitable for small firms. Three such provisions are those providing replacement cost coverage, seasonal automatic increase of coverage, and inflation protection.

REPLACEMENT COST COVERAGE. One of the notable features of the Businessowners Policy is that it pays for the full replacement cost—rather than the actual cash value—of damaged property. This is another concept that we discussed in connection with homeowners insurance. You may recall that, in computing actual cash value, the amount that property has depreciated is deducted from the cost of replacing it with new property. If the replacement cost is $10,000 and if, because of its age and condition, the property is considered to have depreciated 30% before it was damaged, the actual cash value is $7,000 and this amount would be the maximum paid by a policy insuring on the actual cash value basis. But, if the policy were written on the replacement cost basis, the full $10,000 would be covered.

Although business properties traditionally have been insured on the actual cash value basis, the Businessowners Policy covers full replacement cost.

FULL INSURANCE REQUIRED. Purchasers of this policy are required to insure the full value of their properties. If Stereo City's inventory and other covered personal property would cost $80,000 to replace, they will be required to buy that amount of insurance. The reason for this requirement is that the rates (per $100 of insurance) are computed on the assumption that properties will be insured for their full value. Most fire and other property losses are small, causing only a few hundred or a few thousand dollars of damage. Therefore, if policyholders were permitted to insure their properties for smaller amounts (say 50% of their value), they would be protected for the great majority of all losses. Only a relatively small number of large losses (those damaging over 50% of the value in this case) would not be fully covered. As a result, the insurance companies would be forced to raise the rates. By requiring all buyers of the Businessowners Policy to insure their property for full value, the rates can be held at a lower level.[1]

DEDUCTIBLE. A $100 deductible applies to most property losses. It applies separately to each building; that is, if properties in two buildings were damaged, the deductible amount would be $200.

SEASONAL AUTOMATIC INCREASE. This feature of the Businessowners Policy is designed to benefit firms that have seasonal peaks in inventory values. If the amount of insurance under Coverage B, Business Personal Property, is at least 100% of the firm's average monthly values for the preceding 12 months, the amount of protection can be increased by 25% if it is needed to cover a loss during the peak season. If Stereo City's values averaged $80,000 for the previous 12 months but increase to $100,000 during November, the owners will be eligible for this increase, assuming they have purchased $80,000 of Coverage B protection. Then they will have coverage for 125% of $80,000, or $100,000 of peak season losses.[2]

INFLATION PROTECTION. The insurance on the buildings covered by the Businessowners Policy automatically increases by 2% at the end of each

[1] In place of the requirement for insuring full value, some policies contain a coinsurance clause. A coinsurance clause limits the amount payable for losses if less than a stated percentage (usually 80%) of the value is insured. The Businessowners Policy does not have a coinsurance clause.

[2] This feature of the policy substitutes for the use of a "reporting form" that many other policies include. A reporting form requires the insured to send monthly reports of property values to the insurer and adjusts the amount of insurance to correspond to the values reported.

"Considering your route and the length of time you'll be away, I'm sure you'll want to protect your loved ones with our blanket coverage that includes storms at sea, shipwreck, demons of both the land and the deep, sirens and monsters, in addition to all acts of the gods."

Charles Saxon © 1971 The New Yorker Magazine, Inc.

three months. (A greater rate of increase can be chosen at a higher cost.) This protection is intended to help keep pace with inflation and to maintain full coverage without endorsing the policy frequently. Note that this pertains only to Coverage A and does not affect Coverage B, Business Personal Property.

LOSS OF INCOME

A unique feature of the Businessowners Policy is its automatic coverage of income lost by the firm following damage by an insured peril. Two types of income loss are covered: earnings lost due to interruption of the business and loss of rental income. Both are examples of indirect loss that stems from the occurrence of direct damage to the insured property.

Business Interruption

When Ted and Gary got together with an insurance agent to discuss property insurance for Stereo City, the agent pointed out a risk they hadn't considered. "If your store gets hit by a good sized loss because of fire, explosion, or something like that," he said, "there really will be two losses. First, there will be the cost of repairing or replacing whatever is damaged. Your property insurance will cover that. Second, while the store is closed you will lose the income that you otherwise would have earned. That can be covered by **business interruption insurance.**"

The agent told the two partners not to underestimate their possible business interruption loss. He said that many small businesses that have a serious direct loss become bankrupt, even if their insurance pays for the damage, because they don't carry business interruption insurance. They go broke when they can't pay the expenses of the business while it is closed.

The first reaction of Ted and Gary was that they wouldn't have to worry about this, because if Stereo City were closed they wouldn't have any expenses. But they soon realized that would not be the case. They would have to pay rent even if they couldn't open for business. They would have to make the regular payments on their loans. If they employed a repairman they would want to continue paying his salary so that he wouldn't quit and take a job somewhere else. The agent showed them a list of continuing expenses that they might have. The list included the costs of salaries, rent, telephone, advertising, bookkeeping, property taxes, association dues, legal fees, and insurance.

Business interruption insurance reimburses the insured firm for (a) lost profit and (b) continuing expenses when the business is closed because of direct loss by an insured peril. Of course, profits and expenses can be recovered only if they were lost because of the interruption. In other words, the business must have been earning these amounts before the loss. The insurance is designed to do for the firm what it would have done for itself if there had been no interruption.

Rental Income

If Stereo City subleased part of their premises to a tenant, they probably would lose their regular rental income if the rented premises were damaged and could not be used. The Businessowners Policy automatically covers such a loss.

BURGLARY AND ROBBERY

Crime is a risk that the owners of Stereo City are certain to be aware of. It is estimated that crime costs American business firms as much as $100 billion a year. A major crime is committed every 68 seconds, and the number of crimes has been increasing at a rate of about 10% every year.

The great majority of crime loss is not insured. According to one estimate, only 10% is covered. One reason is that crime insurance is quite expensive. It is especially costly for businesses that have the greatest loss exposure and therefore have the greatest need for insurance protection. Stereo City is a good example. It is a small business, and small firms have relatively more crime losses than large ones. Also, the kind of merchandise handled by Stereo City is attractive to thieves; it is valuable relative to its size and weight, and it can be disposed of illegally at a profit.

When Ted and Gary discussed crime insurance with their agent, they found that it can be a rather complicated topic. Several different forms of coverage are available, each covering specific types of loss. A basic distinction is made between employee crime and nonemployee crime. Loss caused by the former usually is covered by fidelity bonds. Loss caused by people who are not employees of the insured business is covered by insuring against burglary, robbery, or other named perils.

The Standard Form of the Businessowners Policy offers both (a) burglary and robbery and (b) employee dishonesty protection as optional coverages. That is, they are available at extra cost but are not automatically included as the loss of income coverages are. Both coverages are subject to $250 deductibles.

Perils Covered

Many of us tend to use the words burglary, robbery, and theft as if they mean the same thing. Actually each has a legal meaning of its own. This is an important fact, because a policy covering one crime does not necessarily cover the others. **Burglary** means the taking of property by breaking into the place where it is kept. Policies that cover burglary usually require that there be visible signs of forcible entry, such as a broken window or a blown safe. **Robbery** means the taking of property by violence or threat of violence, or in other words, hold-up. **Theft** is a broader term meaning the taking of property by burglary, robbery, or any other act of stealing. Property taken by someone with a key to a building or by someone who knows the combination of a safe would be a theft. Shoplifting is also a theft loss, but it is rarely insured.

The burglary and robbery coverage of the Businessowners Policy applies to those two perils only. Both are carefully defined in the policy.

BURGLARY. This peril is defined as follows:

> Burglary means the abstraction of insured property from within the premises by a person making felonious entry or exit therein or therefrom by actual force and violence, evidenced by visible marks made by tools, explosives, electricity, chemicals, or physical damage to the exterior of the premises at the place of such entry or exit.

The burglar must have either broken into or broken out of the premises. If a person hides in the store at closing time, gathers up a load of expensive stereo equipment, and leaves by simply unlatching a door, there is no burglary within the terms of the policy; there is no coverage because there are no signs of forced entry or exit.

ROBBERY. The definition of robbery is also interesting:

> Robbery means the taking of insured property:
> 1. by violence inflicted upon a messenger or custodian;
> 2. by putting him in fear of violence;
> 3. by any other overt felonious act committed in his presence and of which he was actually cognizant, provided such other act is not committed by an officer, partner, or employee of the insured;
> 4. from the person of a messenger or custodian who has been killed or rendered unconscious when such property is in his direct care and custody.

This definition covers a broad range of hold-ups, but notice that some kinds of crime loss do not fall within the definitions of either burglary or robbery. There is no coverage for shoplifting, for instance, nor for forgery or shortages revealed by checking inventory. Also, loss resulting from confidence games or trickery is not covered. To be sure of the latter, the policy specifically excludes loss "caused by voluntary parting with title or possession of any property by the insured or others to whom the property may be entrusted if induced to do so by any fraudulent scheme, trick, device, or false pretense."

Property Covered

When burglary and robbery protection is purchased as part of the Businessowners Policy, the categories and amounts of property covered are as follows:

1. Business personal property (other than money and securities) located on the insured premises. Maximum amount is 25% of the limit for Coverage B, Business Personal Property.
2. Money and securities on the insured premises—$5,000 maximum.
3. Money and securities away from the insured premises—$2,000 maximum.

EMPLOYEE DISHONESTY

Employee crime is excluded from burglary and robbery insurance coverages. Actually, employee theft seldom takes the form of simple burglary or robbery, as the following examples illustrate:

- A branch of a large supermarket company had seven cash registers. Every night the register stubs checked out with the day's receipts. There was only one thing wrong. The company had equipped the store with only six registers. The seventh was the idea and property of the store manager and his assistant. Their own check-out counter netted them thousands of dollars during the 27 months until they were found out.
- The janitor of a wholesale tobacco firm dropped cases of cigarettes out of a storeroom window to a friend in an alley below. In a three-year period their take was $65,000.
- By overstating the refunds to customers for the return of empty pop bottles, employees of a soft drink manufacturer netted $90,000.
- During a period of over 20 years, a trusted employee of a small-town bank embezzled in excess of $200,000 before she was discovered.

No one knows the extent of employee crime. Much of it goes undiscovered for long periods and some cases are hushed up when they are found. Computers offer a new means of stealing from employers. Several huge cases have been publicized; other examples of computer crime will no doubt come to light in the future.

The contracts that are customarily used to cover employee crime are called **fidelity bonds.** Years ago, a separate fidelity bond was issued for each employee who was bonded and it was the employee's responsibility to secure and pay for the bond. That is seldom done now. Instead, employers who want the protection usually purchase a fidelity bond that covers either (a) employees listed by name, (b) specified positions (such as accountants and cashiers), or (c) all employees without naming them or their positions. The last of these is called a blanket bond.

The employee dishonesty coverage available under the Businessowners Policy is a simplified version of a blanket fidelity bond. We shall examine the protection with regard to the amount and the losses that it covers.

Amount Covered

The employee dishonesty coverage of the Businessowners Policy has a basic limit of $5,000 per occurrence. To judge the amount of protection needed, if any, one should understand the following policy provisions:

> Dishonest or fraudulent acts or a series of similar or related acts of any employee acting alone or in collusion with others during the policy period shall be deemed to be one occurrence for the purpose of applying the deductible and the limit of liability.
>
> Regardless of the number of years this policy shall continue in force, the limit of liability shown in the Declarations shall not be cumulative from year to year.

According to the first of these provisions, if the coverage is written for, say $10,000, that is the maximum payable for a series of employee thefts, even if more than one employee is involved. Under the second quoted provision the stated limit is the maximum payable for a series of thefts occurring over a number of years. If the coverage has a $10,000 limit and it is discovered that a bookkeeper has stolen $8,000 each year for 10 years, only $10,000 will be paid. Many employers overlook the possibility of such a cumulative loss and find themselves badly underinsured when one comes to light. Many other employers convince themselves that their employees are trustworthy and that they have no need for this protection. "I know my workers and I trust every one of them," many employers have said, to their later regret. That attitude is another reason why only a small fraction of employee theft losses are covered by insurance.

An insurance company writing this coverage has the right of subrogation against an employee for whose dishonest acts a loss is paid. The employer is entitled to receive any uninsured loss before the insurer is reimbursed, however. For example, if a $35,000 fidelity loss is covered by a policy with a

$20,000 limit, the employer would receive $20,000 from the insurance company and then would be entitled to receive up to $15,000 of any amount later obtained from the employee. The insurer would get any recovery from the employee in excess of $15,000.

Losses Covered

Employee dishonesty insurance protects against loss of merchandise or other property as well as loss of money or securities. The insured is protected against losses ranging from cigarettes or pop bottle refunds, as in the examples cited earlier, to stereo equipment, as in the case of Stereo City.

There is no coverage for loss caused by the owner or any partner, officer, or director of the insured firm. If Ted or Gary steals from his own business, the loss will not be covered.

Another limitation pertains to additional thefts by a particular employee after a loss is discovered. The insurance is canceled with respect to further losses caused by such a person. Thus, lenient employers who continue to employ workers known to be dishonest do so at their own risk.

IMPORTANT TERMS

Businessowners Policy	Robbery
Extended coverage	Theft
Business interruption insurance	Fidelity bonds
Burglary	

KEY POINTS TO REMEMBER

1. The Businessowners Policy is one example of the property-casualty insurance protection available to small businesses.
2. Buildings and business personal property can be insured either for named perils or for all risks.
3. Covered personal property includes (a) property of others held by the insured, (b) tenant's improvements and betterments, (c) items temporarily away from the insured location, and (d) property at new locations.
4. The named perils insured are fire and lightning, the extended coverage perils, vandalism and malicious mischief, sprinkler leakage, and transportation.
5. The Businessowners Policy covers the full replacement cost of the property that it insures. The policy also provides automatic increases for (a) seasonal peaks in inventories and (b) rises in the value of insured buildings.
6. Income lost by business interruption or by stoppage of rental income is covered.
7. Insurance for burglary and robbery is optional. It covers merchandise on the premises, and money and securities on or away from the premises.
8. Employee dishonesty is a separate optional coverage. It pays for employee theft of money and other property owned by the insured business firm.

REVIEW QUESTIONS

1. What are the principal coverages of the Businessowners Policy?
2. What are "tenant's improvements and betterments" and how can they be insured?
3. What is extended coverage?
4. Why are the purchasers of the Businessowners Policy required to insure the full value of their property?
5. What protection is furnished by business interruption insurance?
6. In crime insurance, what are the general meanings of (a) burglary and (b) robbery?
7. A section of the employee dishonesty coverage of the Businessowners Policy says that its limit of liability is not cumulative. What does that mean?
8. How does subrogation apply to employee dishonesty insurance?

DISCUSSION QUESTIONS

1. "The insurance of business risks is a very complex topic." Why is that statement true? In other words, why is insuring business risks any more complicated than insuring personal risks?
2. With regard to the risks discussed in this chapter, how might the owners of Stereo City use the risk management methods of (a) risk avoidance, (b) risk retention, and (c) loss control?
3. If you were in the position of Ted Polito or Gary Harmish as owner of a business like Stereo City, could an insurance agent's advice and assistance be helpful to you? If so, how?
4. Would Stereo City be likely to benefit from the Seasonal Automatic Increase feature of the Businessowners Policy?
5. Can you think of any explanation for the requirement in burglary insurance of visible signs of force by the burglar?
6. Can you think of any reasons why shoplifting is seldom insured?

CHAPTER 18
LIABILITY INSURANCE FOR SMALL BUSINESS

GENERAL LIABILITY

AUTO LIABILITY

PROFESSIONAL LIABILITY

WORKERS' COMPENSATION

This chapter continues the discussion of insurance for small business. The preceding chapter dealt with property coverages; this one concerns liability coverages. For business firms, the area of legal liability is one of a limitless variety of potential claims. Consider the following incidents:

- A clothing manufacturer is sued by the parents of a child who was severely burned when her sweater caught fire.
- A customer in a department store falls into an open elevator shaft.
- The roof of a grocery store is being repaired by a roofing contractor. The store is sued when an employee of the contractor drops a bucket onto a customer entering the store.
- A widow sues a heating contractor. Her husband was killed by the explosion of a furnace that the contractor had installed.
- An employee of a manufacturing firm loses a hand when it is caught in a punch press.
- Three employees of an excavation contractor are killed by the collapse of a sewer they are constructing.

The co-owners of Stereo City don't expect to be hit by losses like these, but they realize that thousands of such incidents occur every day. They know they need protection for themselves and their business. This chapter deals with the kinds of insurance that can protect Stereo City and other small business firms against losses like the ones listed. It will consider two major areas of insurance: general liability and workers' compensation (including employers liability). In addition, although it technically is not a business coverage, it will briefly review professional liability insurance.

GENERAL LIABILITY

General liability refers to the legal liability of business firms other than liability for automobile or aviation accidents or for employee injuries.

General Liability Exposures

The field of general liability traditionally has been divided into the following six exposures:

1. Premises
2. Operations
3. Products

4. Completed operations
5. Independent contractors
6. Contractual

Business liability insurance can be written to cover either (a) one or a few of the six traditional exposures, (b) all six, or (c) all six plus some others. The liability insurance section of the Businessowners Policy is the third type, providing extremely broad protection. Before examining its provisions, we will identify the general liability exposures.

PREMISES.   The first category of business liability—**the premises exposure**—stems from the ownership or control of the place where a business is conducted. Whether a firm owns its premises or is a tenant, it may be held legally liable for injury to people or damage to property resulting from conditions or defects of the premises.

The law defines three categories of visitors to premises and indicates the degree of care owed to each. The three categories are invitees, licensees, and trespassers. Property owners (and tenants) owe the greatest care to **invitees,** persons whom they invite onto the premises. Customers in a store, for instance, are invitees; there has been an implied invitation for them to come there. The law provides that invitees are entitled to expect the premises to be in a reasonably safe condition. If they are injured because of an unsafe condition, such as a loose stair tread, the owner probably can be held legally liable.

People who are on the premises for business purposes of their own usually are distinguished from invitees and classified as **licensees.** Firemen or deliverymen are examples. Licensees are entitled to a somewhat lesser degree of care than invitees.

Trespassers, those who have neither express nor implied permission to be on the premises, are the third category. To them the property owner has little or no obligation. If a burglar trips on a loose stair tread, his injuries are his own problem! An exception to the rule concerning trespassers is the **attractive nuisance doctrine.** It provides that trespassing children are owed a degree of care similar to that owed to invitees if the children are attracted onto the premises by some dangerous object or condition. Examples of attractive nuisances include ladders, construction machinery, and excavations. If such things attract children onto the premises and cause them to be injured, the property owner may be held liable, even though the children were trespassers.

In sum, the premises liability hazard is one that no business can afford to overlook. Although steps can and should be taken to reduce the likelihood of injury to the public, hazard is always there; it cannot be eliminated.

People are injured on business premises in countless ways. In addition, property damage claims arise when customers' possessions are damaged or when fire or explosion at one location causes damage to other properties nearby. Some types of business have particularly serious premises exposures. These include carnivals, skating rinks, swimming pools, theaters, and auto race tracks.

OPERATIONS.   Claims may arise from **operations** being conducted away from a firm's premises. To illustrate, let us consider a firm named the Capital Construction Company. It builds houses and small commercial structures. Capital Construction has very little premises liability exposure, because its office and garage are located in an industrial section of town and are seldom visited by the public. But a variety of liability claims may arise at its job sites. Capital Construction may be sued by the owner of an adjacent building for damage done by a careless bulldozer operator, by parents of children injured while playing in a house under construction, or by someone who falls into an open excavation. Among the most serious operations exposures are those of contractors doing road construction, tunneling, wrecking, or blasting work.

PRODUCTS.   Manufacturers and retailers may be held responsible for injuries caused by the **products** they make or sell. Products liability claims can involve literally any kind of product. Beverage manufacturers sometimes are sued by people who claim they were made ill by an insect in a bottle. Shampoo manufacturers have been sued by people claiming that the product caused their hair to fall out. Claims are not confined to obviously hazardous products. The manufacturer of a part used in making heaters and air conditioners paid damages of $247,000 when a defective heater caused a fire in a television station. A furniture polish manufacturer was sued by the parents of a boy who died after drinking the polish.

Products liability claims can be based on any of three legal grounds: negligence, breach of warranty, or strict liability. Claims based on **negligence** seek to show that the plaintiff's injuries were directly caused by the negligence of the seller. In such cases it must be proved that the seller failed to use reasonable care in designing, making, or handling the product, or failed to warn the user of its potential hazards. Because it often is difficult to prove that the seller was negligent, claims usually are based on one of the other grounds.

The second basis for products claims is **breach of warranty.** A warranty is a statement or promise made by the seller concerning the product being sold. Warranties may be either express (meaning actually stated) or implied. Claims frequently allege breach (that is, breaking) of the implied warranty that products are fit for their intended use. For instance, the seller of a camp stove implies that the stove is fit for use as a camp stove. In other words, by offering this particular item for sale as a device that can be used as a heat source for cooking, the seller implicitly warrants that, when properly used for that purpose, the stove will not blow up and injure the user. If such an injury does occur, the seller may be sued for breaching the implied warranty. Historically, the courts did not permit buyers of products to sue manufacturers for breach of warranty because of the "privity of contract" rule. According to it, a buyer's contract was made with the retailer, not with the manufacturer. Therefore, the buyer's only course of action was against the retailer (and, of course, the retailer was seldom responsible for any warranty of the manufacturer). The privity of contract rule now has been changed so that in most states breach of contract can be used as the basis of products claims against manufacturers. This development is important, because claims based on contract generally are not as difficult to establish as those based on negligence. Dropping the privity of contract rule thus has led to an increase in the number of products claims and in the average payment for them.

The third legal basis of products claims is **strict liability.** Also a new development, it too is contributing to the number and size of products liability payments. Interpretations of strict liability vary from state to state, but in general the plaintiff has to show only (a) that the injury was caused by a defect in the product and (b) that the defect existed when the product left the hands of the manufacturer. This could be the basis of a lawsuit by a person injured while using a power saw. If the strict liability rule applies, the manufacturer would be legally liable if the injury is proved to have been due to the manufacturer's failure to provide the saw with a proper safety guard.

Before the 1960s it was rather difficult for injured consumers to recover damages. Among the effects of the consumerism movement of the 1960s and 1970s were legal changes that have made products claims easier to establish. Now news stories of multimillion dollar settlements are not unusual; even more important may be the large and increasing number of cases that are settled for a few hundred or a few thousand dollars. One result has been a great increase in the cost of products liability insurance. For some businesses the cost now is several times as great as it was just a few years ago.

Stereo City does not appear to have a major products liability exposure, but claims can come from unexpected sources. For instance, they could be sued for fire damage to a house alleged to have been caused by a short circuit in a unit they sold. While the manufacturer might be held responsible in such a case, one of the current trends is to sue retailers as well as manufacturers. Other claims against Stereo City could range from a customer whose finger was cut on a broken knob to a person alleging severe electrical shock from a faulty component.

COMPLETED OPERATIONS. The completed operations exposure is very similar to the products exposure. It applies to liability claims arising from construction, installation, servicing, or repair work done by the firm. While such work is in progress it is part of the operations exposure; after it is done it becomes a completed operations exposure. An example is a lawsuit by a person who slipped on a highly polished floor in an office building. The injured person sued the building maintenance company that had polished the floor the night before the accident. Capital City Construction Company might have a completed operations claim from nearby residents if its construction of a house caused a change in the runoff of rainwater in the area, flooding the basements of other houses.

INDEPENDENT CONTRACTORS. This exposure applies to claims brought against a firm in connection with work being done for it by an **independent contractor.** Assume Capital Construction is building an addition to the Discount Drug Store. In the process, a scaffold falls, injuring a Discount customer. The customer sues both Discount and Capital Construction. To the construction company this is an operations exposure; to the store it is an independent contractors exposure. It is likely that the court will hold Capital Construction responsible for the injury; but it is possible that Discount Drug will be found negligent for not selecting a more careful contractor. Regardless, Discount will have to defend itself against the lawsuit.

CONTRACTUAL LIABILITY. Contractual liability arises from contracts that require one party to assume another party's legal liability. Stereo City's lease agreement may contain a clause under which it agrees to be responsible for some of the legal liability the owner of the building otherwise would have to people injured on the premises. That is, by signing the lease, Stereo City assumes certain of the building owner's potential liability.

OTHER GENERAL LIABILITY EXPOSURES. There are other general liability exposures in addition to the six we have reviewed. They include personal injury liability, host liquor liability, and fire legal liability. Each of these is covered by the Businessowners Policy and will be identified in the next section.

Comprehensive Business Liability Insurance

Continuing in the manner of the preceding chapter, our survey of liability insurance for small business will focus on the coverage provided by the Businessowners Policy. The reader should bear in mind that this policy can be used only for small stores, for office buildings, and for apartment buildings. Other policies must be used for insuring other kinds of business.

The liability insurance furnished by the Businessowners Policy is extremely broad. Called Comprehensive Business Liability Insurance, it breaks away from the traditional method of covering one or more specified liability exposures and covers all liability exposures unless they are excluded by the policy. Among the excluded exposures are most claims involving automobiles, aircraft, watercraft, workers' compensation, and professional liability.

The policy has a single limit of liability. To simplify the policy's marketing and rating, purchasers are given a choice of only two limits: $300,000 or $1 million per occurrence.

COVERAGE OF TRADITIONAL EXPOSURES.   Although it does not specify them by name, the Businessowners Policy of course includes coverage for liability claims in the six traditional areas that were identified in the preceding section: premises, operations, products, completed operations, independent contractors, and contractual liability. For Stereo City and most other retail stores, the greatest number of claims are brought by customers and other people injured on the store premises. Claims frequently stem from slippery sidewalks or interior floors, loose handrails or stair treads, and sharp or broken display counters. Like the liability insurance included in automobile and homeowners policies, the Businessowners Policy provides legal defense for policyholders who are sued, and pays on their behalf any sums (up to the policy limit) that they are legally obligated to pay.

For products and completed operations claims, the policy's single limit also serves as an aggregate limit for the year covered by the policy. If, for instance, the limit is $300,000, no more than that amount will be paid for any one case, and no more than that will be paid for the total of all products claims during the year. Another point concerning products liability insurance is that the policy will not pay for replacing faulty products. If certain equipment sold by Stereo City does not work properly, products insurance will not pay for its replacement. But, if a customer claims to have been injured by a short-circuit in the equipment, the insurance will protect Stereo City.

PERSONAL INJURY LIABILITY. The insuring agreement of the Businessowners Policy's liability section reads as follows:

> The Company will pay on behalf of the Insured all sums which the Insured shall become legally obligated to pay as damages because of bodily injury, property damage or personal injury caused by an occurrence to which this insurance applies.

Notice that the insured is protected for **personal injury** claims as well as those resulting from bodily injury or property damage. This is one of the ways in which the liability coverage of this policy exceeds that of most other policies.

Personal injury claims allege other kinds of harm than physical injury or damage. For example, assume that one of Stereo City's owners or employees accuses a customer of shoplifting. The customer, guilty or otherwise, may sue for false arrest, slander, or defamation of character. Such a suit would not be for bodily injury or for property damage and therefore would not be covered unless the policy also covered suits for personal injury. Other covered personal injuries include libel and violation of privacy.[1]

HOST LIQUOR LIABILITY. A number of states have **liquor liability** (or "dramshop") laws that make bars, restaurants, or taverns legally responsible for injuries caused by intoxicated patrons. Business liability policies, including the Businessowners Policy, exclude liquor liability claims. This policy, however, contains an unusual exception to the exclusion. It says the exclusion does not apply to liability resulting from serving alcoholic beverages "at functions incidental to the insured's business." If, for instance, Stereo City has an anniversary party at which drinks are served, they are protected for liquor liability claims. The protection applies only to incidental exposures like this one. Bars, restaurants, and taverns (which are not eligible for the Businessowners Policy anyway) can purchase liquor liability coverage from certain insurers specializing in covering "high risks."[2]

FIRE LEGAL LIABILITY. A business lilke Stereo City could become legally liable for fire damage to other people's property in three different ways. First, they could be liable for a fire that started in their store and spread to other properties nearby. Their regular property damage liability insurance

---

[1]Claims stemming from advertising are excluded. Advertisers liability is available from specialty insurers.
[2]In this context, "high" means "extreme."

covers such a situation. Second, Stereo City could be responsible for fire damage to customers' stereos in their custody for repair. The property insurance section of the Businessowners Policy, you may recall, pays for such losses whether the insured is legally liable or not. Third, Stereo City could become liable for damage to the premises they occupy as tenants. Although the building owner probably carries fire insurance on the building, the owner's insurer could subrogate against Stereo City if the damage had been their fault. In situations like this, tenants frequently do not have insurance protection, because most liability policies exclude coverage for damage to property rented to or in the "care, custody or control" of the insured.

Again, the Businessowners Policy comes to the rescue. It specifically insures claims of the type just described. This coverage, called **Fire Legal Liability,** has a separate $50,000 limit of liability. It applies to liability for damage to structures rented to or occupied by the insured when the damage is caused by fire or explosion.

MEDICAL PAYMENTS.   A separate part of the policy's liability section provides medical payments coverage. It pays up to $1,000 for the medical expenses of any person other than an employee of the insured firm, subject to a limit of $10,000 for all medical expenses resulting from a single accident.

Like the medical payments coverage provided by auto or homeowners policies, this coverage is a form of accident insurance. Payments are made for accidents involving the insured's business operations. If a man falls and breaks his arm while shopping at Stereo City, his medical expenses will be covered (up to $1,000), whether the fall was due to the store's negligence or to the man's own carelessness.

AUTO LIABILITY

Because personal auto insurance was covered rather thoroughly in earlier chapters, auto insurance for business firms will not be described here in detail. With few exceptions, business auto risks and the manner of insuring them differ very little from personal auto risks. In either case, the major exposures are legal liability and damage to vehicles. Of course, in states that require it, no-fault coverage must also be included.

If the business is a proprietorship owned by an individual or by husband and wife and the only vehicles are private passenger autos, the Personal Auto Policy or a similar contract can be used. If the business is a partnership or corporation or if other types of vehicles are to be insured, a different policy must be used.

Two exposures calling for special attention involve hired autos and employers' nonownership liability. **Hired autos** are those that are rented or leased. Business managers should make sure that their policies cover this exposure, as they may not automatically do so. **Employers' nonownership liability** stems from the fact that employers can be held liable for the negligence of employees who use their own autos in connection with their work. You may recall that the definition of "covered person" in the Personal Auto Policy includes organizations legally responsible for the acts of the named insured or any member of his or her family. Thus, the employer is covered by the employee's policy. However, the employee may not have adequate limits or may have no coverage at all. Employers' nonownership liability insurance, covering nonowned autos for claims in excess of the employee's insurance, furnishes the needed protection.

PROFESSIONAL LIABILITY

When a physician or dentist fails to use the proper degree of care in treating a patient, the result may be **professional liability** or, as it is also called, **malpractice.** Other professionals such as accountants and lawyers also have a professional liability exposure.

Medical Malpractice Liability

The number and size of medical malpractice cases increased rapidly during the 1970s. In 1969 one out of 23 doctors covered by one large insurer was sued. In 1974, only five years later, one out of 10 was sued. From 1970 to 1976 the size of the average award nearly doubled, increasing from $14,281 to $27,708. Some malpractice settlements have been enormous. Several have exceeded $1 million. The record may be a California case involving a three-year-old boy who suffered brain damage and became a quadriplegic following a delay in his treatment. The case was settled with the purchase of an annuity that will pay the boy over $21 million if he lives to age 68.

Naturally, the cost of medical malpractice insurance has skyrocketed. A group policy insuring 18,000 members of the New York Medical Society cost $4.4 million in 1965. Ten years later the policy covered 20,000 doctors and cost $64 million. The American Medical Association reports that in 1975 doctors paid an average of $4,533 for malpractice coverage, as compared with $610 in 1968. Obstetricians, neurosurgeons, and some other specialists pay much more.

MEDICAL MALPRACTICE INSURANCE.   Policies that insure the malpractice exposure of physicians, surgeons, dentists, and other medical practitioners are essentially the same as other liability policies. They pay on behalf of the doctor sums that he or she is legally obligated to pay because of "injury arising out of the rendering of or failure to render . . . professional services . . . ." They also cover claims involving the activities of persons for whom the insured doctor is responsible, such as nurses or other assistants.

Defense against malpractice claims is especially important. With other kinds of liability insurance, claims are usually settled by the company through negotiation with the claimant. If the company believes an out-of-court compromise settlement would be less expensive than fighting the claim in court, the company is free to make such a settlement. This is not always the case with malpractice insurance. A compromise settlement of a malpractice claim could be taken by the public to be evidence of improper professional conduct, even if the claim were groundless and the insurer had made a small payment just to get rid of it. Some policies therefore require the insurer to obtain the policyholder's written consent before settling a claim. Not all malpractice policies contain that provision, however. Because defending malpractice claims in court can be extremely expensive, many policies now provide that claims can be settled by an arbitration procedure, even without the insured's consent.

Other Professional Liability

Professional liability insurance also is written for accountants, architects, lawyers, insurance agents, funeral directors, and others. In these cases the coverage sometimes is called "errors and omissions insurance."

A wide variety of claims may be involved. An architect was sued for the design of a bowling alley which resulted in the alley's being six feet too short. Accountants have been sued for failing to spot the theft of funds by employees of businesses that they audited. Insurance agents have paid damages for failing to arrange proper insurance protection for their clients. A New York City funeral director was sued for pain, suffering, and humiliation. His hearse had moved ahead of the funeral procession because of a traffic jam. The driver took advantage of the situation by stopping at a bar. Discovering that the procession had passed him by, the driver made a frantic effort to catch up. The hearse hit a bridge abutment, turned over, and spilled the casket onto the street. The family sued for $100,000.

WORKERS' COMPENSATION

Workers' compensation is a governmentally required no-fault system that pays for employee injuries. The benefits, which include both medical expense and income replacement, are provided by the injured worker's employer. The amounts of the benefits are specified by state law. Most employers purchase **workers' compensation insurance** policies under the terms of which the insurer pays the benefits on the employer's behalf.

Employers' Liability

It is interesting to compare the adoption of the workers' compensation system with the current movement toward a no-fault system for auto insurance. In some respects it seems that history is being repeated, although in other ways the two events are not alike.

Under common law an employer may be held legally liable if a worker is injured because of the employer's negligence. Before the workers' compensation laws were passed, such **employers' liability** was the only basis for injured workers' claims. Workers had to sue their employers in the hope of collecting damages. They weren't likely to do this because their chances of winning were slim. The burden of proof rested with the workers—they had to prove that their employers were negligent—and the law was on the side of the employers.

COMMON LAW DEFENSES. Imagine that it is 100 years ago. A team of horses is pulling a wagon loaded with kegs of beer through a city's streets. For some reason, the driver loses control of the horses and the team runs wild. Rounding a corner, the wagon hits the side of a building and tips over. The driver's helper is thrown off the wagon and one of his legs is crushed by the weight of several kegs of beer. The helper is crippled. No longer able to carry kegs in and out of taverns, he loses his job.

It is possible that the brewery can be held legally liable for its employee's injuries, but it is not likely. The common law provides three defenses for employers: contributory negligence, assumption of risk, and the fellow servant rule. Because of the first of these, the helper cannot recover if his own carelessness in any way contributed to the accident. The second of the common law defenses provides that when the worker took the job he voluntarily assumed the risks that go with it. The pay rate he agreed to includes compensation for the chance of his being injured. Therefore, he is not entitled to any additional compensation now that he has been injured. The third defense, the fellow servant rule, says that if the injury was caused by the negligence of a fellow worker, the employer is relieved of liability. Thus, if the brewery can show that the driver was responsible for the runaway, the helper will lose his case.

It would be difficult for the injured helper to overcome the brewery's three common law defenses. Furthermore, a lawsuit would be expensive and there could be a long delay before it was finally settled. In the meantime, who would hire a crippled man who is known to be suing his previous employer? The future for the injured helper is bleak indeed.

MODIFICATION OF THE COMMON LAW.   The common law was so obviously harsh that the courts and the state legislatures eventually took steps to change it. Various court decisions reduced the strength of the employers' defenses. For instance, one decision held that the fellow servant rule could not be used in cases of negligence by an injured worker's foreman.

Employers' liability laws were adopted by most of the states during the period between 1885 and 1910. These laws required employers to provide (a) a safe place to work, (b) safe tools and equipment, and (c) competent supervision. Failure to do any of these things provided grounds for lawsuits by injured workers. Gradually, the employers' liability system began to provide payments for occupational injuries. However, the system did not prove to be satisfactory.

Adoption of Workers' Compensation

Beginning in 1910, one state after another abandoned employers' liability as the primary system of paying for occupational injuries. In its place the states adopted the workers' compensation system.

FAULTS OF THE EMPLOYERS' LIABILITY SYSTEM.   The employers' liability system was unsatisfactory for several reasons. First, it continued to be difficult for workers to prove that their employers were negligent. Employees still were saddled with the burden of proof. Second, the employers' liability system was very expensive because of the high legal costs incurred by both employers and employees. Third, the system worked slowly. Cases were delayed by court congestion and legal procedures. Fourth, awards were unsystematic and unpredictable. In many cases it was difficult to determine who really was to blame for an accident. Some workers were able to recover substantial amounts; others were not. Fifth, many accidents really were not the employer's fault. Maybe the brewery worker fell off the wagon because he had sampled too much beer. Or maybe the horses had been frightened by someone's dog. But if that were the case and the employer didn't pay for the injury, who would? Someone had to. With the growth of population and industrialization following the Civil War, thousands of work injuries were happening every day. One way or another medical expenses had to be paid for, and one way or another disabled workers and their families had to be supported.

RATIONALE FOR WORKERS' COMPENSATION. The workers' compensation system is based on the principle that industrial injuries are one of the costs of an industrial society and therefore should be paid for by society. In an industrial society many employees will be injured. Some accidents will be the employer's fault and some will be the worker's fault, but the real responsibility lies with society as a whole. Society enjoys the benefits of the industrial system and it should pay for all of its expenses, including the cost of industrial injuries.

This philosophy is carried out by the workers' compensation laws. Employers are required to pay for job-connected injuries, not because they caused them, but because of social policy. The cost of the injuries is not to rest with the workers who are injured but is to be considered a cost of production. Therefore the prices that consumers pay for the things they buy include the cost. Brewery workers are still injured (though seldom by runaway horses), but the price we pay for a bottle of beer now includes the cost of their injuries.

Workers' Compensation Laws

There are many differences among the compensation laws of the various states, but they all have the same purpose: to provide an efficient, fair, and inexpensive system for paying the cost of work injuries. We shall briefly examine who the laws cover, what they cover, the benefits that are paid, and how the benefits are provided.

PERSONS COVERED. Initially the laws applied only to those who were employed in hazardous occupations. Over the years coverage has been extended to other kinds of employment. Now the great majority of all workers are protected. The main exceptions are agricultural, domestic, and casual workers,[3] although even they are now covered by the laws of some states. Small employers, those with only a few employees, also are sometimes exempt.

INJURIES COVERED. The laws apply to injuries "arising out of and in the course of employment." The application of this provision is clear in most cases; most injuries are either obviously job-connected or they are not. There are borderline cases, though. These include workers injured while going to and from work and salesmen injured while away from home. Cases where a heart attack, nervous disorder, or loss of hearing is alleged to have

---

[3]The definition of "casual" employment varies among the states, but it usually means temporary employment that is not within the usual course of the employer's business. A person hired to shovel snow would be an example.

resulted from employment also present problems. Such cases are resolved by the state courts. The trend has been in the direction of interpreting the laws in favor of injured workers.

The laws also cover "occupational disease," such as silicosis, lead poisoning, or radiation sickness.

BENEFITS.   Four categories of benefits are provided: medical expense, disability income, death benefits, and rehabilitation benefits.

Medical expense.   Payments for medical services constitute about one-third of the total amount paid out as workers' compensation benefits. In most of the states unlimited medical expenses are paid. A few states still have a dollar maximum on this benefit, but the trend is to remove such limitations.

Disability income.   Cash weekly income benefits are paid to workers who are totally disabled (whether temporarily or permanently) and to those who are permanently partially disabled. These payments begin after a waiting period of two to seven days. If the disability continues, the worker is compensated for the income lost during the waiting period.

The amount of the disability income payments is critically important to injured workers and their families. The national average is now about 75% of the worker's take-home pay. In earlier years the laws were far less generous. As recently as 1960 the national average was only 54%. Many states now pay 80% of the injured employee's weekly spendable earnings,[4] up to a stated maximum amount. The maximum is also a key provision, as it can be set so low that it, rather than the percentage of spendable earnings, determines the amount of the benefit for most workers. Some of the laws provide that the dollar maximum will be determined annually and will be equal to the statewide average weekly earnings for the previous year. Thus a state might provide for disability income benefits of 80% of the worker's spendable earnings but no more than $195 per week (if that were the average earnings figure for the previous year).

The length of time during which disability income will be paid is also critical and is another point of difference among the states. For total disability, some states have no time limit and will pay benefits as long as the disability continues. Other states set either a time limit (such as 10 years) or a maximum amount (such as $50,000). Here again the trend has been to liberalize the laws by increasing or eliminating the limits.

Payment for permanent partial disability is a complicated process. It depends upon whether or not the disability is a type scheduled in the law.

[4]Spendable weekly earnings is defined as the amount remaining after deduction of payroll taxes.

For scheduled disabilities, such as the loss of a thumb or an eye, payments are made for the number of weeks stated in the law. This varies from state to state but might be 60 weeks for the loss of a thumb, 140 weeks for the loss of an eye, and so forth. These payments are made regardless of how long the employee actually is unable to work. Compensation for permanent partial disabilities that are not scheduled in the law (such as back injuries) is based on the extent of the disability in relation to permanent total disability.

Death benefits. Widows (or widowers) and children of workers whose death was due to a covered injury or disease also receive income payments. Like the benefits for total disability, these are a percentage of the worker's wages and are subject to a dollar maximum. In many states a widow's benefits continue for her lifetime or until she remarries. Some states limit the widow's benefits to a stated number of years. Children's benefits usually are paid until age 18. In addition to the income benefits, the laws provide an amount, typically $1,000, for funeral expenses.

Rehabilitation benefits. The laws of most states include some provision for paying the costs of rehabilitation. The goal of rehabilitation is to return disabled workers to their jobs. If a physical impairment is such that the worker cannot resume his or her previous employment, the goal is to train the person for another suitable job. Unfortunately, rehabilitation activities are extremely limited in all but a few states. In the absence of effective state programs, some of the insurance companies have developed rehabilitation programs of their own.

SECOND INJURY FUNDS. **Second injury funds** are designed to help overcome the reluctance of employers to hire handicapped workers. Specifically, they deal with the fact that a second injury could cause a worker who already is partially disabled to become totally disabled. A worker who is blind in one eye, for example, will become totally disabled if the other eye is lost. Total disability benefits of course are much more costly than those for partial disability; therefore employers who hired handicapped workers would be assuming an added workers' compensation loss exposure.

To meet this problem the laws of all but a few states provide that employers are responsible for only the benefits that would have been payable to nondisabled workers. The additional payments (such as for the loss of a second eye) are paid by the second injury fund. The fund is supported by assessments paid by all employers or by their insurers.

PROVISION OF BENEFITS. Adoption of the workers' compensation laws would have been an empty gesture for many injured workers if the states had not also taken steps to see that the benefits actually would be paid.

The laws provide that benefits must be paid from one of three sources: a state fund, an insurance company, or an approved self-insurance program.

Six states have monopolistic state funds. In these states (Nevada, North Dakota, Ohio, Washington, West Virginia, and Wyoming) all workers' compensation insurance is provided by an agency of the state government. Twelve other states have state funds that compete with commercial insurance companies. The remaining states do not have state funds. There, benefits are provided either by insurance companies or by those large employers that have qualified as self-insurers.

Workers' compensation continues to be a state system, even though many other programs concerned with economic security are operated by the federal government.[5] From time to time the establishment of a federal compensation system has been proposed. In recent years the Congress has considered a bill that would require the state laws to meet federal standards concerning coverage and benefits. The bill provides that a federal compensation act would replace the law of any state that did not meet the federal standards. One effect of this proposal has been that many of the states have amended their laws to provide broader coverage and more adequate benefits. This action might well forestall further action by the Congress.

Workers' Compensation Insurance

Most employers provide for the payment of workers' compensation benefits by purchasing an insurance policy. A standard workers' compensation and employers' liability policy is used in all states where insurance by private companies is permitted.

COVERAGE. There are two separate coverages, one for workers' compensation and the other for employers' liability. Coverage A, workers' compensation, is very simple. Under it the insurance company agrees "to pay promptly when due all compensation and other benefits required of the insured by the workers' compensation law." The policy does not say what the benefits are; the insurer simply pays whatever is required by the law of the particular state.

Coverage B provides employers' liability insurance. Employers who are sued for employee injuries that are not covered by the compensation law have legal liability protection under Coverage B. The coverage usually is written with a $100,000 limit of liability. Because the workers' compensation laws are very broad, employers' liability claims are uncommon.

---

[5]Federal programs do provide occupational injury benefits for federal employees, railroad workers, and longshoremen.

COST. Workers' compensation premiums are based on rates that apply per $100 of payroll. There are over 500 classifications. The rate for each classification reflects the loss experience for that particular type of work. For nonhazardous occupations the rates are low. To illustrate, the rate for clerical workers in one state is 11¢ per $100 of payroll. At the other extreme are window cleaning ($24.10), logging and lumbering ($25.02), and aerial crop dusting ($28.56). In the latter types of business, compensation premiums obviously are an important part of the employers' total costs. The rates for most types of work are much less, but insurance still can be a significant expense. For instance, Stereo City's rate in the same state is 65¢ and the rate for Capital Construction's carpenters is $3.47 per $100 of payroll. The rates for each classification vary considerably from state to state, reflecting the different levels of benefits provided by the various states.

LOSS CONTROL. It is far better to prevent injuries than to pay for their costs. One of the fortunate effects of the workers' compensation system is that it provides both employers and insurers with an incentive to reduce industrial accidents. For employers, the incentive is based on the cost of insurance. The rating systems offer substantial premium savings to employers that have good safety records.

Insurance companies have two principal reasons for wanting to reduce injuries. First, an insurer's profit depends largely upon the amount of its claim payments. Controlling accidents increases the company's profits. Second, insurers compete with one another on the basis of the services that they offer their policyholders. Many employers, particularly larger ones, select workers' compensation insurers that they believe provide superior loss control service. Workers' compensation insurers employ safety engineers who work with their insureds to reduce work injuries. They inspect factories, stores, and construction sites. Hazardous conditions are brought to the attention of employers, and recommendations for improvement are made. Safety engineers also conduct training courses for foremen and help organize safety contests in insured firms. The larger insurers have research departments that work on such things as industrial pollution, safe handling of dangerous chemicals, and the design of safety devices for hazardous equipment.

IMPORTANT TERMS

General liability	Attractive nuisance doctrine
Premises liability exposure	Operations liability exposure
Invitee	Products liability exposure
Licensee	Breach of warranty
Trespasser	Strict liability

Completed operations exposure	Employers' nonownership liability
Independent contractors exposure	Professional liability
Contractual liability	Malpractice
Personal injury	Workers' compensation laws
Host liquor liability	Workers' compensation insurance
Fire legal liability	Employers' liability
Hired autos	Second injury fund

KEY POINTS TO REMEMBER

1. General liability insurance covers the legal liability of business firms except for automobile or aviation accidents or employee injuries.
2. The general liability exposures most commonly insured are: premises, operations, products, completed operations, independent contractors, and contractual.
3. Businesses owe the highest degree of care to customers and others whom they invite onto their premises. Less care is owed to licensees and still less to trespassers.
4. Products liability claims can be based on negligence, breach of contract, or strict liability.
5. There has been a great increase in products liability awards during recent years, partly due to changes in the privity of contract rule and acceptance of strict liability as a basis of legal action.
6. The Businessowners Policy covers the traditional general liability exposures plus personal injury, host liquor liability, and fire legal liability.
7. Business auto insurance is similar to personal auto insurance. Policies should specifically cover the hired car and employers' nonownership liability exposures.
8. Professional liability policies cover malpractice claims against physicians, surgeons, and dentists. They also insure against professional liability in other fields, such as accounting and architecture.
9. Workers' compensation insurance pays state-required benefits to injured workers on behalf of their employers. The principal benefits are medical expense and disability income.
10. Before the workers' compensation laws were adopted, the only legal recourse for injured workers was on the basis of employers' liability. Employers had three common law defenses: contributory negligence, assumption of risk, and the fellow servant rule.
11. Workers' compensation laws are based on the idea that the members of society, as consumers, should pay for the costs of industrial injuries.

REVIEW QUESTIONS

1. Explain the difference between an invitee, a licensee, and a trespasser.
2. What is an attractive nuisance, and how does it relate to the premises liability exposure?

3. What is privity of contract, and how does it relate to the products liability exposure?
4. Why is the adoption of strict liability as a basis for products claims an important development?
5. Explain the independent contractors liability exposure.
6. How does the contractual liability exposure arise?
7. What are personal injury liability claims?
8. Do all businesses have a liquor law liability exposure?
9. What does fire legal liability insurance cover?
10. What is professional liability insurance? Whom does it insure?
11. What system for the reinbursement of injured workers preceded the workers' compensation system? What were the faults of that system?
12. What injuries do the workers' compensation laws cover? What benefits do they provide?
13. What are second injury funds?
14. How can workers' compensation benefits be provided?

DISCUSSION QUESTIONS

1. Capital Construction Company builds houses and small commercial structures. How do its general liability exposures differ from those of Stereo City?
2. Does the inclusion of medical payments coverage in the Businessowners Policy serve any useful purpose from the standpoint of the insured business? In other words, why should the firm pay for insuring injuries that it isn't responsible for?
3. How has the consumerism movement affected business and professional liability insurance?
4. What are the similarities between the adoption of the workers' compensation system and the recent adoption by many states of no-fault auto systems? What are the differences?
5. Workers' compensation benefits differ from state to state. They are quite generous in some states and rather limited in some states. What factors might explain these differences? That is, what would account for the high benefits in one state and the low benefits in another?
6. Why do workers' compensation policies specify no maximum limit for the amount of workers' compensation coverage?
7. What types of injuries would result in the greatest workers' compensation benefits?

PART V
OPERATIONAL ASPECTS OF INSURANCE

CHAPTER 19
INSURANCE MARKETING

AGENTS AND BROKERS

MARKETING SYSTEMS

SUPERVISORY ORGANIZATIONS

SUPPORTING FORCES

PROFESSIONALISM IN INSURANCE MARKETING

PRODUCT DEVELOPMENT

We now have reached a major dividing line in our study of insurance principles and practices. We started out by examining the nature of risk and insurance. We then studied risk management and saw that insurance actually is one of several methods of handling risk. After considering the legal background of insurance, we surveyed the personal lines: automobile, homeowners, health, life, and social insurance plus employee benefit plans. Following that came a review of insurance for small business.

Now we are ready to look at insurance from a different viewpoint. This is called the operational viewpoint, because it is concerned with operations, the things that are done to make insurance work. In our review of insurance operations we will consider how insurance is marketed and how it is priced. We also will examine the underwriting and claim adjusting processes. Finally, we will learn how insurance companies are organized and why and how they are regulated by the state insurance departments.

The first operation that we shall study is marketing. This chapter concerns the people who sell insurance and the ways in which insurers organize, supervise, and support their marketing systems.

AGENTS AND BROKERS

People need insurance. Insurance companies exist to provide insurance. Agents and brokers provide the necessary linkage; they are the connection between the potential customers and the insurers.

The marketing function in insurance is of unique importance because an insurance company can succeed only if it sells a large number of policies and spreads its risk among many insureds. To accomplish this, it must rely on its marketing organization. No matter how efficiently an insurer manages all of its other functions, its sales force is the key to the company's success. In fact, private insurance literally cannot exist without sales. The role of the salesperson is so important that insurance agents often are called "producers," a term that draws attention to the fact that in this business the functions of creating the product and selling it are combined. Insurance policies do not exist until they are sold; the act of selling, in effect, produces the insurance.

Furthermore, few buyers are familiar with their exact needs or with the various contracts that are available to meet their needs. They rely upon agents to give them the appropriate advice and service. Insurance marketing therefore is essential to both companies and policyholders.

Agents

Insurance agents sell insurance for one or more companies. They are paid a commission, which is a percentage of each policy's premium. Legally, insurance agents have two kinds of authority. First, they have the authority stated in the contracts between them and the companies they represent. This is **express authority;** it is what is expressed by the terms of the agency contract. The second type is **implied authority.** It arises because the law says the public is entitled to believe that insurance agents will act in accordance with their express authority. To illustrate, agents ordinarily have express authority to accept auto insurance for their companies. Agent Smith is told by his company to accept no more applications from teenage drivers. In spite of this, he sells a policy to 18-year-old Jenny Driver and tells her the insurance is now in force. If Jenny promptly smashes her car into a tree, can Agent Smith say "Sorry, Jenny. I exceeded my authority, so you weren't insured after all?" The law of implied authority says he cannot. Smith has the authority that Jenny could reasonably expect him to have. Because agents can be expected to be authorized to sell auto policies, coverage was in force and Smith's company will have to pay Jenny's claim.

As Chapter 4 explained, a binder is a temporary insurance contract, written or oral, that is in force until it is either canceled or replaced by a regular policy. Property-casualty agents normally are granted authority to bind certain kinds and amounts of coverage; this is the express authority that Jenny Driver assumed Agent Smith had. One of the differences between property-casualty agents and life insurance agents is that the latter do not have **binding authority.** Life insurance agents are authorized to solicit applications from prospective clients and to accept initial premium payments, but they cannot bind coverage on their companies' behalf.

Brokers

Whereas agents legally represent companies and sell insurance on their behalf, **brokers** represent policyholders and arrange insurance for them. In other words, brokers sell their services to clients and place their clients' insurance protection with various insurers. Most of them work primarily with business clients, rather than with individuals and families. Although brokers are agents of the insureds, they receive a commission from the insurers with whom the policies are placed. Because they are not legal agents of insurance companies, brokers do not have binding authority.[1]

Brokers are most important in the fields of property-casualty insurance

[1]Although they do not have binding authority as brokers, they may have agency contracts with certain companies and be able to bind coverage in their capacity as agents.

and employee benefit plans. Some are very large and have offices in many cities. The largest is Marsh & McLennan, which has over 9,000 employees. The firm has about 80 offices in the United States and almost that many in other countries throughout the world. It handles insurance placement for more than 100,000 commercial clients. The second and third largest (Johnson & Higgins and Alexander & Alexander) are each about half the size of Marsh & McLennan.

MARKETING SYSTEMS

Insurance companies use various systems to market their services. Basically there are three different systems, although there are many modifications of the three. In two of the systems insurance is marketed by agents; in the third the company sells directly to the public. The agency systems are, first, the **exclusive agency system** and, second, the **independent agency system.** Exclusive agents represent only one company; independent agents represent more than one. In the third marketing system, **direct selling,** policies are sold either by company employees or through the mail. The exclusive agency system dominates in life insurance; all three marketing systems are widely used in the property-casualty business.

Life Insurance Exclusive Agency System

Life insurance marketing relies primarily upon the exclusive agency system. That is, most life insurance agents represent a single life insurance company. The agents identify themselves with their companies. Agent Jones, instead of calling his business the Jones Insurance Agency, says that he is a Prudential Life Insurance agent, Agent Williams says that she is a Metropolitan Life Insurance agent, and so forth.

The exclusive agency system has been found to be very well suited to life insurance marketing. There is little need for an agent to represent more than one company because most life insurers offer an ample variety of policies. Agents who work exclusively for one company are able to become familiar with that company's policies and procedures. Also, when its agents represent it exclusively, the company is able to establish a closer relationship with its sales force. This is particularly important in life insurance because in this field the emphasis is upon selling.

It frequently is said that "life insurance isn't bought; it has to be sold." The statement means that even though many people realize the value of life insurance, most put off doing anything about it until they are contacted by an agent and persuaded to buy a policy. Customers rarely come to life insurance agents (although they frequently contact property-casualty agents); instead, the agents have to seek them out and induce them to buy. In this situation, life insurance companies must use great skill in developing and guiding the activities of their sales forces. They work hard to recruit new agents who have high potential for success in sales work. They conduct extensive sales training programs. And for established agents the companies have programs designed to provide continuing education and motivation. All of these sales-oriented activities are most likely to succeed when agents represent one company exclusively and rely upon it for sales training and supervision. Equally important, when an insurer's agents don't represent other companies it is willing to spend more money to assist them than it would if they worked for several companies.

The commission arrangements used in life insurance reflect the emphasis upon sales. A variety of arrangements exist, but the commission is always highest for a policy's first year. For instance, an agent might receive 55% of the first year's premium, 5% for each of the next 9 years, and 2% of the premium thereafter. The high first-year commission motivates and compensates the life insurance agent for his or her chief and most difficult task, that of selling new policies.

Established agents are compensated solely on the basis of commissions. Because new life insurance agents may at first make few sales and earn very little commission, the companies must provide some other source of income until they can develop a reasonable volume of business. Various financing plans are used for this purpose. The effect is to subsidize new agents during their first two or three years. As their sales and commission income gradually increase, the subsidy diminishes until finally it is replaced entirely by commission income.

Life insurance sales work is not easy, particularly for the first few years. After that, an increasing percentage of an agent's income usually comes from repeat sales to clients who are adding to their existing insurance programs; correspondingly less income has to be from sales to brand-new clients. Also, as their businesses grow, agents receive an increasing amount of income from renewal commissions for policies sold in previous years. However, becoming established is difficult, and many who try do not succeed. Some companies report that as many as half of their newly appointed agents drop out during their first year and another quarter fail before the end of the second year.

For those who do succeed, the financial rewards can be very great. In fact, of all kinds of insurance careers, none offers more potential income than life insurance sales. To illustrate, the Million Dollar Round Table is an organization composed of agents who consistently sell at least $1.25 million of life insurance a year. There are about 15,000 members, representing over 350 companies. It is estimated that the average member earns more than $40,000 a year—and many earn in excess of $100,000 a year. Many members of the Million Dollar Round Table are young. More than 40% are under age 40. One out of four first have qualified for membership in the group before reaching age 30. Over half have qualified during their first five years in business.[2]

We should emphasize, though, that most people in life insurance sales work do not have such spectacular success. Figures of the more typical earnings are reported by one manager whose agency force is composed of eleven women and one man. The average annual income for the women with only one year of experience was $11,500. The women who had sold for two years averaged $15,000; those with three or more years of experience earned an average of $17,000.

Property-Casualty Agency Systems

Although one agency system prevails throughout most of the life insurance industry, both the exclusive agency system and the independent agency system are found in property-casualty insurance. One might assume that there would be little difference between the two systems and that it wouldn't matter whether agents represented only one or more than one company. The distinction is important, however, and it is one that insurance buyers should be aware of.

INDEPENDENT AGENCY SYSTEM. This method, the traditional one for marketing property-casualty insurance,[3] is used by the great majority of property-casualty companies. The agents are independent businessmen (or women) who have contracts with several insurance companies. Independent agents usually do not identify themselves with any one company. Instead, they run the Jones Insurance Agency (or whatever) and sell their own services as insurance advisors. When they talk with clients about writing policies they frequently do not even mention any one company's name.

Independent agents function as middlemen between their companies and their clients. The policies sometimes are typed in their offices (on forms that the companies supply). They send out policy renewal notices and collect premiums; retaining their commissions, they remit the balance of the premiums to the companies.

Independent agencies vary in size and form of organization. They may be individual proprietorships, partnerships, or corporations. Some are one-

[2]Data from Life Insurance Marketing and Research Association and Million Dollar Round Table.
[3]It is so traditional that it sometimes is called the American Agency System.

Table 19–1   How Independent Agents Obtain New Personal Lines Business

HOW OBTAINED	PERCENTAGE OF NEW BUSINESS
Referrals from present clients	35.7%
Solicitation of present clients for additional coverages	14.3
Social contacts	13.9
Walk-ins	13.5
Telephone	9.2
Yellow pages advertising	6.2
Other advertising	5.8
Direct mail solicitation of new prospects	1.4
	100.0%

Source: Stuart d'Adolph "Who is the Independent Agent?" *Independent Agent,* January 1977, p. 15.

person operations; some have dozens of employees. The typical agency today handles an annual premium volume of about $500,000.[4] It employs two agents and has an office staff consisting of two other persons. The latter are a vital part of the agency. The members of the office staff maintain the agency's books and records. They also furnish many of the services that are important to an agency's clients, such as handling requests for policy changes, assisting with the submission of claims, and providing information about rates, premiums, and policy coverage.

Independent agents usually devote most of their time to servicing existing accounts: amending or adding policies to meet new needs, explaining coverages, handling claims, arranging for renewal policies, and supervising the activities of their agency staffs. Most of them spend very little time in developing new accounts. Table 19–1 shows how their new personal lines business is developed. Notice that little of it comes from the direct solicitation of prospective clients other than those referred to the agency by present clients.

A final important characteristic of independent agents is that they "own their expirations." They, not the companies they represent, decide what companies will renew expiring policies. This practice is significant for two reasons. First, it gives the agents bargaining power with their companies. If they are dissatisfied with a company's underwriting or claim settlement practices, for instance, they can transfer the business to other companies.

---

[4]In property-casualty insurance the quantity of business generally is measured by total annual premium. In life insurance the usual measure is total face amount of insurance.

Table 19–2 The Ten Leading Automobile Insurance Company Groups and Their Marketing Systems[a]

COMPANY GROUP	AUTOMOBILE INSURANCE PREMIUM, 1978 (in millions)	PRINCIPAL MARKETING SYSTEM
1. State Farm	$4,450	Exclusive agency
2. Allstate	2,893	Exclusive agency
3. Farmers of Los Angeles	1,461	Exclusive agency
4. Aetna Life and Casualty	1,152	Independent agency
5. Nationwide	1,037	Exclusive agency
6. Travelers	779	Independent agency
7. Liberty Mutual	752	Direct selling
8. Hartford Fire	693	Independent agency
9. Kemper	644	Independent agency
10. Continental of New York	624	Independent agency

[a]Company groups include subsidiary companies.
Source: National Underwriter, May 4, 1979, p. 37.

Second, ownership of expirations is a valuable property right, a right that agents can sell or transfer when they retire. (Thus, the present Mr. Jones of the Jones Insurance Agency is often the son or grandson of the agency's founder.)

EXCLUSIVE AGENCY SYSTEM. One of the great success stories in the whole world of business has been written by a small number of property-casualty insurers that use the exclusive agency system. The success of these companies is said to have had an impact on the insurance industry "greater than any other change in the history of insurance marketing."[5]

Until the 1920s, practically all of the coverage in this field was written by independent agents and the companies they represented. By 1953 exclusive agency insurers were writing 20% of the automobile insurance. Today they handle about 45% of the automobile business, a large but somewhat smaller percentage of homeowners insurance, and a small but rapidly increasing share of the commercial lines business.

Exclusive agents in property-casualty insurance represent a single company, as they do in life insurance. As Table 19–2 shows, four of the ten largest automobile insurers use this system. (The great majority of the ap-

[5]George Nordhaus and Stephen Brown, *Marketing of Property & Casualty Insurance* (Santa Monica: Insurance Marketing Services, Inc. of California, 1976), p. 131.

proximately 600 other automobile insurers are independent agency companies.)

The success of the exclusive agency insurers can be attributed to several factors. First, they have concentrated on the personal lines market. Initially, these companies sold little but automobile insurance. They later expanded into home insurance and more recently into life and health protection. In these lines many millions of similar policies are purchased and the companies are able to use methods comparable to the mass production techniques of large manufacturing concerns. Most of the independent agency insurers, on the other hand, have offered a wide variety of coverages in both the personal and commercial lines. And they have devoted much of their talent and resources to insuring the high values and complex exposures of business risks.

Second, the exclusive agency companies developed new and efficient methods of handling personal lines policies. Instead of relying upon their agents to write policies, collect premiums, and keep records, these activities are performed in company offices where maximum use is made of the latest computerized data processing systems. As a result, the agents do not have to employ and supervise office staffs; instead, they are free to concentrate upon increasing their sales volume. During the 1950s and 1960s these techniques gave the exclusive agency companies a big price advantage. Offering coverage at lower rates, they were able to expand their sales at the expense of the independent agency insurers.

The independent agency companies have responded by modernizing their own methods. Among the moves they made was adoption of the direct billing technique that had been pioneered by the exclusive agency companies. **Direct billing** means that bills for renewal premiums are sent directly to the policyholder by the company and the policyholder makes payment directly to the company. By bypassing the agent, the independent agency companies can realize the same savings that the exclusive agency companies had obtained. Because the agent no longer has to handle the premiums, commissions (and premiums) can be reduced. By using direct billing and other modern business management methods, many independent agents and insurers have cut their costs and now offer personal lines policies at prices that are competitive with the exclusive agency insurers.[6]

A third characteristic of the exclusive agency system in the property-casualty field is that the system emphasizes new sales production, just as it

[6]Adoption of direct billing was at first strongly resisted by many independent agents. They feared that it would lessen their bargaining power with the companies and weaken their independence. A majority now have accepted it as a necessary means of reducing costs and prices in order to remain competitive in the market for private passenger automobile insurance. Most independent agents are not using direct billing for other coverages, however.

does in life insurance. The sales management staffs of the companies work closely with their agents. Training and supervision are geared to the generation of new business. The commission structure also encourages the sale of new policies. Allstate agents, for instance, generally receive 15% of the premium for new business (just as many independent agents do), but only 6.5% for renewals.

A fourth and final factor that helps explain the success of the exclusive agency insurers concerns advertising. National advertising of insurance is more effective when agents are associated directly and exclusively with one company. All of the 14,000 State Farm agents identify themselves with the company's "good neighbor" advertisements, and all 10,000 Allstate agents benefit from their company's "good hands" image. The independent agency companies advertise, too, of course. Many people are familiar with Travelers' red umbrella, Hartford Fire's stag, and the firefighter's helmet of Fireman's Fund American. But, as mentioned previously, Mr. Jones identifies himself primarily with the Jones Insurance Agency, rather than with any particular one of the companies he represents. At least in the personal lines market, this aspect of his independence appears to diminish the effectiveness of his companies' national advertising.

The independent agents themselves also advertise nationally through a trade association, the Independent Insurance Agents of America. It uses the slogan, "Your Independent Insurance Agent Serves You First."[7]

The impact of national advertising campaigns cannot be determined with any precision. However, it appears to be of greater advantage to the exclusive agency system because of the close ties between its agents and companies.

Direct Selling Systems

In the early days of insurance in this country there were no insurance agents. Companies advertised that they would sell policies, and people wanting to buy made application at a company office. Insurance is rarely sold that way today but some companies do sell directly to the public without using agents. Companies using the direct selling system either market their policies through company employees or sell them by mail. (This approach is sometimes called "direct writing," a term that also may be used to refer to any property-casualty marketing system other than the independent agency system.)

COMPANY-EMPLOYED PRODUCERS. In this system the sales people legally are employees of the company, not independent contractors as

[7]Many independent agents belong to another association, the Professional Insurance Agents. Both associations have state as well as national organizations.

agents are. They often are paid both a salary and sales commissions. A point of confusion is the fact that all insurance salespeople, company-employed producers included, must have a state license to sell insurance, and they are licensed as "agents." That, however, is simply a different usage of the same word and does not affect the status of these individuals as company employees.

Many of the insurers that sell through company-employed producers specialize in specific services or markets. Liberty Mutual is an example. It is one of the countrry's largest property-casualty companies and is the largest private insurer of workers' compensation. Its sales people emphasize the company's outstanding industrial accident prevention services. Another example is Federated Mutual. It specializes in serving specific types of accounts. Its producers sell all lines of insurance to automobile dealers, farm implement dealers, and certain other small business organizations.

MAIL ORDER. Several companies have had remarkable success in selling insurance by mail.[8] One of the largest auto insurers, Government Employees Insurance Company, uses this method. It originally sold only to employees of the government, but later broadened its market to include people employed elsewhere. Another large mail order insurer is United States Automobile Association. It sells only to active and retired officers of the United States armed services.

Substantial amounts of health insurance are sold by mail also. Two approaches are used: direct mail advertising sent to lists of prospects, and newspaper or magazine advertising. Companies like Mutual of Omaha and American Republic sell much of their health insurance in this manner.

Little life insurance is sold by mail, although numerous companies have tried to do so. As was stated previously, few people purchase life insurance on their own initiative; personal contact by an agent seems to be necessary. There is an exception, though. Numerous professional and trade associations offer group life insurance to their members through advertisements in the organizations' publications and by direct mail. Many people are persuaded to buy on this basis because the group rates are low and because the sponsoring association endorses the plan and the insurer.

SUPERVISORY ORGANIZATIONS

Most insurance is sold by companies that use one of the agency systems, and most of the companies operate over a large area, often countrywide. As a

[8]In this case too, some company employees must be licensed insurance agents.

result, some kind of decentralized system of supervision is needed. Two types of supervisory organizations are widely used: managing general agencies and branch offices. Less commonly, a direct reporting system is used instead.

Managing General Agencies

When an insurance company is first established, the easiest and most economical way for it to set up a marketing system is to appoint **managing general agents,** assigning a certain territory (perhaps a city or a state) to each. To illustrate, let's say that John Jones is made managing general agent for the state of Oregon. Jones is an independent businessman operating under contract with the company. He hires and supervises the activities of his own sales force throughout Oregon. The company pays him a commission for all of the business that his organization produces. He, in turn, pays part of the commission to his agents. The balance of the commission, after General Agent Jones pays the other costs of running the organization, is his profit.

This type of organization is still widespread in the life insurance business, although the trend is toward the use of branch offices instead. In the property-casualty business most of the managing general agencies have been converted to branch offices. Managing general agencies today often are corporations or partnerships and may represent several companies.

Branch Offices

A **branch office** performs the same functions as a managing general agency. However, instead of being privately owned, it is part of the company and is run by a branch manager who is a company employee. The branch manager, with the help of the branch office staff (who also are company employees), appoints agents in the territory that the office serves. To illustrate, picture a large property-casualty insurer with its home office in Hartford, Connecticut. The company sells through independent agents and operates from coast to coast. As a means of decentralizing its operations, the company has 40 branch offices. A typical branch office has about 100 employees. These consist of a manager, an assistant manager, sales management personnel, claim adjusters, underwriters, loss control specialists, auditors, and clerical staff. In the territory served by this office the company might have 200 agents. The job of the branch office staff is to work with these agents in a variety of ways and to handle the insurance that they produce for the company.

Direct Reporting

Some companies have neither general agencies nor branch offices. Instead, their agents report directly to the company's home office. This **direct reporting** system is used primarily by small insurers operating within a limited territory. A company writing insurance in only one state, for instance, wouldn't need to decentralize its marketing organization.

SUPPORTING FORCES

Although insurance marketing ordinarily relies upon the work of agents and brokers, one shouldn't think that they are the only persons engaged in the marketing process. Although they are the ones out on the firing line, so to speak, they are backed by a small army of supporting forces.

Life Insurance Supporting Forces

Life insurance agents are assisted by field managers, group representatives, and advanced underwriting specialists.

FIELD MANAGERS. Life insurance agents ordinarily work under the direction of a **field manager** or supervisor. Large managing general agencies and branch offices sometimes have assistant managers or training supervisors whose principal duties are the training and supervision of newly appointed agents.

Because sales production is of such great importance in life insurance, the agencies and companies provide extensive training programs for new agents. One of the first steps in the training process is to help the person prepare to take the state insurance agents' licensing examination. Study manuals designed specifically for this purpose often are used. After the new agent has passed the state examination, training continues using various books and other specialized educational materials. Each field manager tries to choose training methods and materials that will help the new agents get off to a good start.

The training of new agents covers two main areas. First, agents must learn about the products that they will sell, the technical aspects of insurance. They are instructed in the principles of insurance, kinds of life insurance and their uses, policy provisions, application forms, use of the company's rate manuals, and company procedures. Second, new agents are carefully trained in the field of salesmanship. They learn how to develop new sales prospects, conduct sales interviews, and handle prospective clients' objections. They are instructed in how to manage their time in order to maximize their sales, and they go with other agents to call on prospects and watch them conduct sales interviews.

The development of an agent's knowledge and ability is a continuing process. Successful agents never stop studying and learning. There always is more to know about insurance and how it can be used to help individual and business clients. And there always are new marketing skills and techniques to develop in order to increase an agent's effectiveness and income. As their experience grows, agents accomplish more of these things on their own, but the assistance, encouragement, and support of the field manager continue.

GROUP REPRESENTATIVES. Because of the complex nature of group insurance and pensions, companies assist their agents in handling them. The assistance is provided by **group representatives,** salaried company employees who are specialists in the employee benefits field. They help the agents sell and establish group insurance and pension plans, and they also aid employers in administering the plans.

ADVANCED UNDERWRITING SPECIALISTS. Other company employees called **advanced underwriting specialists** assist agents with complicated nongroup insurance matters. These persons are particularly helpful in dealing with estate planning problems. They also prepare educational materials and conduct special courses dealing with life insurance programing and estate planning.

Property-Casualty Insurance Supporting Forces

Company supporting forces also assist agents in the property-casualty field. Training programs similar to those in life insurance are conducted by exclusive agency and direct selling companies. Some independent agency companies also offer educational programs to their agents. Of course they are offered on a voluntary basis; participation in them is optional.

In this field, as in life insurance, the companies employ technical experts who assist agents in working with large commercial accounts.

To promote good relationships with their agents, many independent agency companies employ **field representatives.** (Other terms sometimes used include field supervisor, fieldman, special representative, or special agent.) The job of the field representative is to serve as liaison between the company and its agents and to encourage the agents to submit a large amount of their best business to this particular company. For an illustration we might return to the example of the Hartford-based company and its typical branch office. Among the 100 branch office employees are four field representatives. They work under the direction of a field supervisor who in turn reports to the branch manager. In the territory served by this particular office the company has 200 agents. The field supervisor and each of the four field representatives are assigned a part of the territory; each has an area in which there are about 40 agents.

The field representatives spend most of their time in the field, calling on and working with agents. Much of their work is educational—explaining changes in the company's coverages and procedures, assisting in the development of efficient methods of agency management, and suggesting ways to increase sales through advertising or other techniques. Field representatives also must explain company underwriting and loss settlement policies. Often they work as trouble shooters, smoothing out relationships between agent and company. For instance, a company underwriter may have declined an important application for what the agent believes to be inadequate reasons. In this situation the field representative is in the middle and must try either to persuade the underwriter to reconsider or to convince the agent that the underwriter's decision was proper. At other times, field representatives are called upon to help agents with sales, especially those presenting difficult technical problems. Another task is to locate and to appoint new agents, and for this purpose field representatives call on agents who do not yet represent their company.

Because field representatives are a company's link with its agents, they are carefully chosen and well trained. Many companies send them to a formal training school at their home office. This usually is a four- to six-week period of intensive education and training. The new field representatives then are assigned to branch offices where they observe underwriting, loss settlement, and other processes before going into the field, at first with the field supervisor and then on their own.

One of the attractive things about the position of field representative is the opportunities it provides for advancement into other kinds of work. Because of their training and their unique connecting role between the companies and the agency forces, field representatives soon acquire a great deal of knowledge about the actual workings of the property-casualty business. They become valuable persons to their companies and may advance within the corporate structure. A path sometimes followed begins with promotion to the position of field supervisor, directing the activities of the field representatives in a branch office. The individual later may become assistant branch manager, then branch manager, and then perhaps will move into an executive position in the company's home office. Many top level company executives started their careers as field representatives.

Many individuals prefer an alternative career path. Because field representatives get to know the agents in their territories, they are likely to learn about opportunities in agency work. One may, for instance, develop a friendship with an older man who runs a growing agency by himself. The agent may be interested in bringing a young person in to become his partner, with the idea of eventually selling the agency to the newcomer. Actually, the companies know that a good number of their field representatives will find opportunities of this kind. They are not really distressed when it happens, because frequently some of a company's best agents started out as field representatives.

PROFESSIONALISM IN INSURANCE MARKETING

It is clear that insurance agents need a certain amount of technical skill in order to perform their jobs effectively. The concept of professionalism in insurance marketing goes well beyond this minimum level of technical competence in two respects. First, professionalism requires advanced study in order to achieve a high level of knowledge in a particular field of insurance. Second, professionalism involves a desire to use that knowledge not only to advance the position of the particular agent but at the same time to serve the best interests of his or her clients. Are all insurance agents professionals in this sense? Of course they are not. Is there any reason why insurance agents cannot be professionals? There is not, and indeed many of them are; many agents have engaged in the required study and have adopted the concept of professional service to others.

Several organizations promote academic and professional competence in insurance. Two of the leading ones are the Chartered Life Underwriter and the Chartered Property Casualty Underwriter programs.

The Chartered Life Underwriter Program

The **Chartered Life Underwriter (CLU)** program was established in 1927. About 40,000 people have completed the program and are entitled to use the letters "CLU" after their names. The letters signify completion of an educational program conducted by the American College of Life Underwriters, which has headquarters in Bryn Mawr, Pennsylvania. A minimum of three years experience in life insurance is also required. Candidates must pass written examinations in each of the following subjects:

1. Economic Security and Individual Life Insurance
2. Life Insurance Law and Mathematics
3. Group Insurance and Social Insurance
4. Economics

5. Accounting and Finance
6. Investments and Family Financial Management
7. Income Taxation
8. Pension Planning
9. Business Insurance
10. Estate Planning and Taxation

Courses in the ten subjects are conducted in 300 cities across the country. Candidates who prefer to study on their own can take the examinations without enrolling in formal classes. The national examinations are given twice each year, and the goal of many agents is to pass two examinations a year, thus completing the program in five years. Graduates can join the American Society of Chartered Life Underwriters, an organization that seeks to maintain professional standards in life insurance marketing. The Society also promotes continuing education for its members by publishing a professional journal and by sponsoring institutes and meetings.

Every CLU accepts responsibility to uphold the following pledge:

In all my relations with the insuring public I agree to observe the following rule of professional conduct—I shall, in the light of all the circumstances surrounding my client, which I shall make every conscientious effort to ascertain and to understand, give that service which, had I been in the same circumstances, I would have applied to myself.

A rather small percentage of life insurance agents have achieved the CLU designation. More than 200,000 people earn at least half their income from life insurance sales but there are only about 40,000 CLUs, many of whom are in executive or academic positions rather than sales. The CLU program is an admirable one and the persons who complete it deserve special recognition.

The Chartered Property Casualty Underwriter Program

The objectives and format of the **Chartered Property Casualty Underwriter (CPCU)** program are comparable to those of the CLU program. Started in 1941, it also promotes high standards of knowledge and conduct, but in the property-casualty side of the business. The program is sponsored by the American Institute for Property and Liability Underwriters of Malvern, Pennsylvania. Candidates for the CPCU designation must pass examinations in the following subjects:

1. Principles of Risk Management and Insurance
2. Personal Risk Management and Insurance

3. Commercial Property Risk Management and Insurance
4. Commercial Liability Risk Management and Insurance
5. Insurance Company Operations
6. The Legal Environment of Insurance
7. Management
8. Accounting and Finance
9. Economics
10. Insurance Issues and Professional Ethics

Over 10,000 property-casualty agents and company employees have completed this program. Through their professional organization, the Society of Property and Casualty Underwriters, they publish a journal and conduct seminars and workshops to promote continuing educational development in their field. Persons holding the CPCU designation also pledge to uphold a strict code of professional ethics.

We should not infer that the only competent and ethical persons in the insurance business are those with CLU or CPCU following their names, nor is it implied that each and every such person is a paragon of knowledge and conduct. Nevertheless, insurance buyers should know that agents and others who have earned one or both of these designations are strongly enough committed to their work to have completed a rigorous educational program in their special field.

PRODUCT DEVELOPMENT

According to the modern view, marketing is more than just selling a product. Its purposes are (a) to offer the products that the public wants, and (b) to help earn a profit for the seller. Thus, the marketing process should include the development of products designed to meet buyers' needs.

In the past, the insurance industry was not noted for flexibility and innovation. To much of the public it appeared that insurance products were offered on a "take it or leave it" basis with little concern for the needs or wishes of individual purchasers. Fortunately, this approach has changed and in numerous ways insurance marketing now is strongly oriented toward the consumer's viewpoint.

Examples of product development in property-casualty insurance include homeowners policies, a profusion of new package policies for business risks, and the development of shorter and more readable editions of auto and homeowners contracts. Product developments in life and health insurance include a number of combination life insurance policies; the variable annuity; major medical; and the growth of an unlimited variety of group life, health, and pension contracts.

Closely related to the development of new products is the growth of professionalism in insurance marketing, with its emphasis on designing programs of protection which suit the needs of particular clients. This approach, which is consistent with the risk management concept, is found in the activities of property-casualty agents who survey the needs of their business clients and recommend total packages of business risk protection. It also is found in life insurance programing and estate planning.

All of these developments are relatively recent. They appear to indicate an increased desire on the part of the insurance industry to offer products and services that are designed to meet the needs of the public.

IMPORTANT TERMS

Insurance agent	Managing general agent
Express authority	Branch office
Implied authority	Direct reporting
Binding authority	Field manager
Broker	Group representative
Exclusive agency system	Advanced underwriting specialist
Independent agency system	Field representative
Direct selling system	CLU
Direct billing	CPCU

KEY POINTS TO REMEMBER

1. Marketing is of particular importance in insurance because sales, in effect, produce insurance protection.
2. Insurance agents sell on behalf of the insurance companies they represent. Insurance brokers represent buyers and make insurance arrangements for them.
3. Property-casualty agents normally have binding authority. Brokers and life insurance agents do not.
4. Exclusive agents represent a single insurer. Independent agents represent several insurers. The exclusive agency system predominates in life insurance. Both systems are used in the property-casualty field.
5. In life insurance marketing the major emphasis is that of producing new business. In property-casualty insurance relatively more emphasis is placed on the servicing of existing accounts.
6. Independent agencies are private business organizations. Their owners select the companies that write their policies, and they have the right to sell their agencies.
7. Several companies that use the exclusive agency system have become major property-casualty insurers in recent decades. Concentrating on personal lines, they have developed effective methods of handling, selling, and advertising the coverages.

8. Insurance is also marketed through direct selling systems by which policies are sold and serviced by company employees or by mail.
9. Most agency companies decentralize their organizations by means of either managing general agencies or branch offices. Some of the smaller companies use a direct reporting system.
10. The activities of life insurance agents are supported by field managers, group representatives, and advanced underwriting specialists.
11. Independent agents are assisted by field representatives who serve as liaison between the companies and their agents.
12. Persons who hold the CLU or CPCU professional designation have completed a program of advanced study in life insurance or property-casualty insurance and have pledged to uphold high standards of professional conduct.
13. As part of the marketing process, insurers today are seeking to design products and services that meet the needs and desires of the insuring public.

REVIEW QUESTIONS

1. Why are insurance agents called "producers?"
2. What two kinds of legal authority do insurance agents have?
3. What is binding authority?
4. What are the two principal kinds of agency systems and how do they differ from each other?
5. How do sales commissions in life insurance differ from those in property-casualty insurance? What is the reason for this difference?
6. Independent agents "own their expirations." What does this phrase mean? Why is it important?
7. How has the marketing strategy of companies like State Farm and Allstate differed from that of the independent agency companies?
8. What is direct billing?
9. What is direct selling? Name two examples of it.
10. What is the difference between a managing general agency and a branch office?
11. What are the duties of a field representative?
12. Why is product development regarded as part of the insurance marketing function?

DISCUSSION QUESTIONS

1. Why don't insurance brokers have binding authority?
2. Why is it that "life insurance isn't bought; it has to be sold?" Why isn't this equally true of property-casualty insurance?
3. Why is the exclusive agency system particularly suitable for the marketing of life insurance?
4. Why are field representatives used in the independent agency system but not in the exclusive agency system?
5. In life insurance marketing great emphasis is placed on sales and relatively less

importance is attached to the servicing of existing policies. The opposite is true in property-casualty insurance. What differences in the two fields of insurance explain this difference?

6. There is a trend toward the use of the branch office type of supervisory organization in preference to general agencies. Can you think of any reasons why insurance companies would prefer to use branch offices?

7. The CLU pledge of professional conduct is quoted in this chapter. If such a pledge were followed, would a high standard of professional conduct result? What sorts of nonprofessional conduct would it rule out?

8. Has the insurance industry utilized the marketing concept? That is, are insurance products and services really designed to meet the needs and wishes of insurance buyers? What suggestions do you have for improvement in insurance products and services?

CHAPTER 20
INSURANCE PRICING

WHAT INSURANCE PREMIUMS PAY FOR

PREMIUMS, RATES, AND EXPOSURE UNITS

PRICING OBJECTIVES

TYPES OF INSURANCE RATING

INSURANCE PRICING: LIFE INSURANCE VS.
PROPERTY-CASUALTY

THE RATEMAKERS

To most people, some of the greatest mysteries about insurance concern its pricing. Compare it with the pricing of clothing, for instance. If you buy a coat for $80 you probably figure that the price is $80 because that is about what all of the things that went into it cost—the labor, material, transportation, energy, advertising, and so forth. In other words, you believe that the price is reasonable and that the coat is worth $80 to you. In addition, you assume that anyone else who buys a coat like this from the same store on the same day will pay exactly the same price for it that you did.

But the pricing of insurance appears to be different. To most people, there seems to be no relationship between what they pay for a policy and what they get out of it. They may pay $300 for an auto policy, for instance. They receive a piece of paper which they take home and put in a drawer. Unless they receive payment for claims, most people are not at all sure that the policy is worth $300 to them. And if they have no claims, they still have to pay for a new policy when the old one expires, even though they never used the old one! Furthermore, and again unlike the pricing of other things, different purchasers are charged different prices for identical policies.

In spite of these apparent distinctions, the pricing of clothing and the pricing of insurance policies are basically the same. In either case the seller must charge enough to cover all of the costs that it incurs to make the product available. But beyond this basic similarity there are some major differences. Two of them are particularly important: First, when an insurer sells a policy it has no way of knowing what its costs for that particular policy will be. It cannot just add up the costs of labor, materials, rent, and so forth. Instead, the insurer must estimate the cost, basing its estimate upon what it has cost to provide similar policies in the past. The second difference between the pricing of insurance and the pricing of most other products is that the cost to the seller depends partly on who the buyer is. The clothing manufacturer's costs are the same regardless of who buys the coat. Therefore it charges everyone the same price. But the insurer's costs depend largely upon whether or not the policy buyer has losses and, if so, how many and how large they are. Of course, this is the reason that different people are charged different prices for policies providing the same kinds and amounts of insurance.

This chapter examines the unique characteristics of insurance pricing. It explains how insurers set prices for their policies even though their costs are not known and it describes why and how various buyers are charged different prices for the same policies. It gives special attention to the pricing of fire and life insurance. The chapter concludes with a brief look at the organizations and people who handle the insurance pricing function.

WHAT INSURANCE PREMIUMS PAY FOR

We shall begin our examination of insurance pricing by identifying the three things that premiums must cover: the pure premium, operating expenses, and margin.

Pure Premium

The first component, the amount needed to pay policyholders' losses, is the **pure premium.** If a company expects to pay 1,000 losses averaging $500 each, it should collect at least $500,000 of pure premium. The pure premium allows for loss payments only; it does not cover any of the other things included in the price of the insurance.

Operating Expenses

The second part of the premium pays for the insurance company's **operating expenses.** These include the sales commission and other marketing costs, home office and branch office administrative costs, taxes, and the cost of handling claims.

The relative size of this part of the premium varies from one line of insurance to another, largely depending upon the extent and variety of policyholder services that the insurer provides. For instance, a large component of liability insurance premiums pays for defending policyholders against lawsuits. Workers' compensation premiums include the cost of loss control services. Operating expenses average less than 17% of the premium for life insurance, but they are about twice that amount for liability and workers' compensation insurance.

Margin

The third part of the premium is called the **margin.** The margin includes an allowance for (a) contingencies, and (b) underwriting gain or profit. The first of these provides the funds needed in case of an unexpected increase in the number or size of benefit payments. The second finances the future growth and expansion of the company.

PREMIUMS, RATES, AND EXPOSURE UNITS

As we know, insurance prices are called premiums; premiums are based on rates; and rates are prices per unit of exposure. We can compare insurance pricing with gasoline pricing. When you fill your gas tank you are charged a certain price per gallon. The total price is determined by multiplying the price per gallon times the number of gallons you buy. The price per gallon is comparable to the insurance rate; the total price is comparable to the insurance premium.

Exposure units are the quantitative units used in insurance pricing. In other words, they are what the rates apply to. In gasoline pricing the quantitative units are gallons. In automobile insurance the quantitative units are cars; the rates apply on a per car basis. A variety of other exposure units are used in other kinds of insurance. Some of them are shown in Table 20–1. Ideally, the exposure unit should be an accurate measure of the loss-producing characteristics of the particular risk. That is, if one policy is likely to produce more loss payment than another, its premium should be accordingly higher. In most lines of insurance the exposure unit does measure the probable loss quite accurately. In life insurance, for instance, the rates apply per $1,000 of insurance. This is logical, because a policy twice as large as another is likely to yield twice the benefits of the other.

In some lines of insurance the ideal measure is not practical for use as an exposure unit, and some other basis must be used. In workers' compensation, for example, the rates apply per $100 of payroll. This is a fairly good measure of the loss exposure. Workers' compensation insurance pays for employee injuries, and firms with larger payrolls generally have more employees and therefore are likely to have more injury claims. But it also means that if one employer pays higher wage rates than similar employers in the same business, it will have a higher workers' compensation premium even if it does not have more workers. The number of employee-hours worked would be a better measure of exposure in this case. Payroll is used instead of hours because payroll records are readily available, whereas many employers do not keep complete records of employee-hours worked.

What about automobile insurance? Is the number of cars insured the ideal exposure unit? A two-car family ordinarily does have more loss exposure than a family with only one car, but the number of miles actually driven would measure the exposure more accurately. The number of cars is used as the rating basis by almost all companies because it is easy to use and avoids

Table 20–1 Exposure Units Used in Several Kinds of Insurance

KIND OF INSURANCE	EXPOSURE UNIT
Automobile	Automobiles insured
Fire	$100 of insurance
Products liability	$1,000 of sales
Workers' compensation	$100 of payroll
Life	$1,000 of insurance

the expense that would be required to determine the number of miles actually driven.

PRICING OBJECTIVES

In setting insurance rates, actuaries have several objectives. In the first place, rates must be high enough so that the company will receive sufficient income to pay its claims and expenses, but low enough so that the company will be able to sell its policies in competition with other insurers. In addition, insurance pricing has several more specific objectives.

Statutory Standards

The laws of most of the states specify that property-casualty rates must not be "excessive, inadequate, or unfairly discriminatory." In other words, they say that rates must be reasonable, adequate, and fair. These therefore are called the three **statutory rate standards.** Although legally required only of property-casualty insurers, the three statutory standards are pricing objectives in other lines as well.

ADEQUACY. Adequacy must always be considered the primary objective of insurance pricing. It is essential that rates be adequate to generate the premium income the insurer needs to pay its claims and expenses. In addition, the company must have enough income to do two other things. First, those who have invested their funds in the company's operation must be paid a fair rate of return. Second, the company must have sufficient earnings to finance its continuing growth and expansion.

Another reason why insurance rates must be adequate is sometimes not understood by the general public. Unless insurers are able to charge adequate rates, they will not be willing to make insurance available to those who need it. State officials frequently are pressured to keep the companies from raising their rates, particularly for auto insurance. The governor and the state insurance commissioner may be told that further rate increases would be too much of a burden for the people who would have to pay more for their policies. But when insurers are unable to charge what they believe to be adequate rates, the public is harmed in another and perhaps more serious way. The insurance companies then refuse to renew many of their policies, and people must either obtain limited coverage through the state Automobile Insurance Plan or go without the protection. Thus, there is a direct connection between rate adequacy and insurance availability.

REASONABLENESS. Insurance rates must be reasonable; that is, they must not be too high. Most of the efforts of the states in regulating property-casualty rates have focused upon this standard.

Historically, the reasonableness standard was established because insurance companies are not subject to certain antitrust laws. The Sherman Antitrust Act, among others, makes it illegal for companies in other kinds of business to cooperate in setting prices. Insurance companies are specifically exempt from this restriction; they are permitted to work together in making their rates. This practice recognizes the fact that insurance is based on the law of large numbers; the greater the amount of data that rates are based upon, the more accurate the rates can be. In many cases individual companies do not have a large enough volume of business to rely upon as a basis for their rates. Companies therefore are allowed to join together to pool their records of past premiums and losses and make rates on the basis of the combined data. Because insurance companies are permitted to engage in such joint pricing, the reasonableness standard has been made a legal requirement. Its purpose is to prevent the companies from using joint pricing as a means of creating a monopoly and charging excessive prices.

When insurers want to change the rates they are using for automobile, homeowners, and other property-casualty coverages, they must (in most states) file the new rates with the state insurance department. The department will not approve the filing if it judges the rates to be excessive. Thus, one of the objectives of the property-casualty ratemaker has to be reasonableness.

FAIRNESS. The third statutory rate standard provides that rates must not be "unfairly discriminatory." In other words, insurance rates must be fair; they must discriminate fairly. This concept is an interesting one, because in many other instances discrimination is frowned upon altogether. How can discrimination be fair?

As it is applied to insurance pricing, fair discrimination means that proper distinctions should be made among various insureds. Those who are alike should be charged the same rates; those who are different should be charged different rates. Two women age 30 and in good health who buy the same kind and amount of life insurance from a particular company should pay the same price. But if one of the women is 30 and the other is 40, they should not pay the same price. Proper discrimination requires the older woman to pay more because the average life expectancy of women her age is shorter. If older women were not charged more, the rates for younger women would have to be increased, and that would discriminate unfairly against the younger ones.

The same reasoning explains the different classifications and rates in other lines of insurance. It is why fire insurance rates are higher for frame buildings (those made of wood) than for those made of fire-resistant materials, why products liability rates are higher for trampolines than for less hazardous products, and why automobile rates are higher for young drivers than for more experienced ones.

Other Pricing Objectives

Actuaries usually are guided by several other objectives, in addition to the three that have been described.

First, the pricing system should be relatively simple, easy to understand, and inexpensive to use. Second, rates should be stable and yet flexible. That is, they should not fluctuate widely from year to year, yet they should be responsive to changes in the expected number and cost of claims. Third, whenever possible, insurance pricing should encourage the reduction of losses. This cannot be done in all lines of insurance, but in some it is rather effective. Fire insurance rating, for example, encourages the use of sprinkler systems and other protective devices. In auto insurance the safe driver rating plan probably has some impact on driving habits. Workers' compensation rating gives employers an incentive to reduce employee injuries.

TYPES OF INSURANCE RATING

Insurance rating determines how much each policy will cost. There are three different types of rating: judgment rating, class rating, and merit rating. Depending on which of these three types is used, the price that a particular policyholder pays may be (a) entirely different from that paid by anyone else; (b) the same as that paid by many other policyholders; or (c) similar to that paid by others, but more or less than that amount for one reason or another.

Judgment Rating

Judgment rating is used when the risk being insured is so unusual that little or no statistical information about similar risks is available. The cost to insure against finding the Loch Ness monster, for instance, must be based entirely on judgment, because records showing the probability of discovering legendary creatures of the deep simply do not exist. Judgment must also be relied upon when insuring new exposures. Protection for the operation of nuclear power plants is an example of this.

When judgment rating is used, each premium is unique and is based primarily upon the opinion of the person making it. Obviously, this method is quite unscientific. It is used only when information for constructing class rates is not available.

Class Rating

Most insurance rates are **class rates.** Insured risks are classified on the basis of one or several important characteristics and all that are in the same class take the same rate per unit of exposure. This sometimes is termed manual rating, because the various classifications and rates are printed in books called rating manuals.

Life insurance is one of the lines for which class rating is used. Insured persons are classified on the basis of their age and sex. All 30-year-old women who are in good health and who buy the same policy from the same company pay the same rate per $1,000 of insurance.[1] The rate, as explained in Chapter 12, is based on the average mortality of 30-year-old women; it also reflects expected company expenses and investment earnings. Class rating is also used for automobile, general liability, homeowners, workers' compensation, and health insurance.

How Many Classifications? How many different classifications and rates should there be? How many characteristics of the covered risks should class rating take into account? These two questions go together because the number of classifications depends upon the number of rating factors that are considered; the more the factors, the more the classifications.

In some lines of insurance only a few rating factors are used. Rates for property insurance on private dwellings, for instance, depend only upon whether the house is made of brick or wood and the community's fire protection rating. Thus, all one-family frame houses in a particular community are charged the same rate per $100 of coverage. In contrast, over 500 classifications are used for workers' compensation insurance. As for automobile insurance, you may recall that the class rating system used by many companies is based on a long list of factors and includes over 6,000 rates for each territory.

When rates are based on just a few factors, many other characteristics of each risk are ignored. Residential property rating, for example, disregards such things as the age of the house, its type of heating system, the number of occupants, and the general condition of the property. What factors are ignored in life insurance rating? You probably can list a number of things, starting with the insured's income and marital status.

---

[1]Extra premium charges for poor health or hazardous occupations are made on about 5% of all life insurance policies.

In deciding upon the number of rating classes to use, the ratemaker faces a dilemma. The greater the number of classes, the more the factors that can be taken into account and therefore the more similar the risks in any given class will be. Thus the persons in each automobile rating class are not only of the same sex and age (if below 30), but also drive similar cars, have similar driving records, and so forth. On the other hand, increasing the number of classes reduces the number of insureds in each one. And the law of large numbers tells us that the greater the number of exposures in each class, the more reliable will be the prediction of future loss experience. Thus there are reasons for having many classes and there are equally strong reasons for having only a few. Increasing the number of classes causes the risks in each class to be more nearly alike, but reducing the number of classes causes the rates to be based on a larger body of data and to be more reliable.

ARE CLASS RATES FAIR?   Class rates relate to the questions of fairness in insurance pricing that were discussed earlier. For instance, is it fair or unfair for life insurance rates to differentiate among insureds on the basis of age and sex? Is it fair for auto insurance rates to differentiate on the same basis? Most actuaries and underwriters say that it is fair, because age and sex significantly affect the average probability of loss in those lines of insurance. Therefore, they say, taking such factors into account is proper differentiation; to ignore them would create unfair discrimination because various groups of insureds would then pay either more or less than their fair share of the total costs.

This subject recently has become rather controversial. Auto insurance rating in particular has been criticized, and several states have banned the use of auto classifications based on age or sex. The insurers argue that the record justifies the use of such factors. They support their position with insurance loss data and with statements like this one from the 1976 Fact Book of the California Department of Motor Vehicles: "Teenage drivers average twice as many accidents as adult drivers. Teenage drivers drive only half as many miles an adult drivers, so that the teenage accident rate per mile is four times as great as that of adult drivers."

Territorial rate classifications for auto insurance also have come under attack. Not surprisingly, the objections in this case have come largely from cities where rates are much above those in nearby towns and rural areas. Again, insurers defend the rate differentials as being designed to help create a reasonable match in each territory between the premiums they receive and the losses they pay for. If single statewide rates were used, they say, the cost of policies of course would be lowered in the high-rated territories, but this would require an equivalent increase in the presently low-rated territories. Motorists in the low-cost areas (primarily smaller communities) would then be forced to help pay for the insurance of those living in the high-cost (primarily metropolitan) areas.

Thus there appear to be good reasons for distinguishing among different groups of people in insurance pricing; it can logically be shown that class rates result in reasonable differentiation rather than in unfair discrimination. But the matter does not necessarily end here. Important social values are involved. If society demands that class rating be dropped, it will be dropped. As the subject is debated, however, we should be aware of the trade-offs that this would require. If the costs of auto accidents are to be insured, policyholders as a group must pay the necessary total premium. While dropping class rates would give cheaper insurance to some people, it also would force others to pay more.

Merit Rating

The third type of rating (in addition to judgment rating and class rating) is **merit rating.** In one sense, merit rating is a modification of class rating. It modifies the class rates (or premium) of a particular insured. In doing so, it reflects the extent to which a specific risk differs from the others in the same class.

From the ratemaker's viewpoint, a particular risk[2] might differ from the others in its rating class in any of three ways: its expected experience, its past experience, or its actual experience during the current policy year. There are three corresponding forms of merit rating: schedule rating, experience rating, and retrospective rating. **Schedule rating** modifies the rates for a particular insured on the basis of the expected experience of that insured; **experience rating** modifies the rates on the basis of the insured's past experience; **retrospective rating** modifies the premium on the basis of the insured's actual experience during the policy year. These and the other types of insurance rating are summarized in Table 20–2.

SCHEDULE RATING. In the use of schedule rating, the first step is to examine the risk (the person or object insured) in order to identify the features that are likely either to cause losses or to prevent them. Next, the risk is compared with the average or standard risk of its type. Finally, deductions are made from the standard rate for this risk's desirable features and additions are made for its undesirable features. The result is a rate that is tailored to reflect the characteristics of the risk for which it is used.

---

[2]As used here, "risk" means the person or object being insured. The word is used this way in the insurance business. Underwriters, for instance, speak of rating or investigating a "risk." See Launie, J. J., et al., *Principles of Property and Liability Underwriting* (Malvern, Pa.: Insurance Institute of America, 1977), p. 2.

Table 20–2   The Basis of Insurance Rates

TYPE OF RATING	BASIS OF RATING
Judgment rating	Judgment of the ratemaker
Class rating	Loss experience of all insureds in the same classification
Merit rating:	The particular insured's:
Schedule rating	Expected experience
Experience rating	Past experience
Retrospective rating	Current experience

Schedule rating in fire insurance.   A good illustration of schedule rating is found in fire insurance covering industrial and large commercial properties.

Class rating is used in fire insurance for some kinds of property. Owner-occupied dwellings, for instance, are classified according to (a) their construction (brick or frame), (b) the number of families using them, and (c) the fire protection rating of the community. No further distinctions are made among the individual dwellings in each class.

In contrast, schedule rating is used for factories, large apartment buildings, large stores, and most other expensive structures and their contents. By means of schedule rating, a separate rate is established for each such property. The schedule rating process is handled by a national organization, the Insurance Services Office and its state branches. A fire protection engineer first makes a careful inspection of each building. The engineer then develops the rates for that building and its contents using a detailed system of charges and credits. Starting with a basic rate that depends upon the effectiveness of the community's fire protection, additional charges are made for undesirable features and reductions are allowed for desirable features. The schedule rating system takes into account five major factors: occupancy, construction, location, protection, and maintenance. Each is summarized below:

1.   *Occupancy.* This term refers to how the building is used. Buildings used for manufacturing purposes present different hazards than those used as theaters or retail stores. The occupancy of a particular building affects the likelihood that a fire will start and, if one does start, how quickly it will spread.

2.   *Construction.* Building construction is a major factor. It relates partly to whether the building is made of frame, brick, or "fire-resistive" mate-

rials. Construction also concerns things like open stairways, the amount of undivided area that can make fire-fighting more difficult, and the use of unprotected steel beams. (Fire protection engineers tell us that the fact that steel is incombustible can be misleading. They point to countless cases where fire has warped and twisted uninsulated steel beams, causing entire buildings to collapse.)

3. *Location.* This factor considers the exposures from fires originating in nearby buildings and spreading to the one being rated. The rating of one building therefore has to take into account the nature of adjacent structures and their occupancy, construction, and so forth.

4. *Protection.* Protection includes the availability of fire-fighting equipment and personnel. The rating system gives credits for fire extinguishers, sprinkler systems, automatic fire alarms, fire doors, and watchman service.

5. *Maintenance.* Clean well-maintained properties are better fire insurance risks than those that are not kept in good condition. Additional charges are made if the engineer sees evidence of poor maintenance.

The various additions to and subtractions from the basic rate are based upon the judgment of the persons who develop the overall schedule rating system. For instance, the system may give a 20% charge for an open stairway and allow a 5% reduction for fire extinguishers. These percentages are based upon judgment rather than upon statistical data, which is one of the differences between this rating system and the class rating system. For fire insurance on dwellings, the rates in Milwaukee or Phoenix, for example, reflect the actual loss experience in the particular locality. But, for insurance on nonresidential properties, the countless variations in occupancy, construction, location, protection, and maintenance (plus the low frequency of losses) make the gathering of detailed statistical data very difficult. Therefore, fire insurance schedule rating is primarily a reflection of the best judgment of actuaries, underwriters, and fire protection engineers.

One of the merits of this system is that it identifies the factors entering into an insured's rate. Property owners can secure a copy of their rating from the Insurance Services Office and may be able to take steps, such as adding protective measures or improving maintenance, that will lower their rates. Also, architects can design buildings in ways that will minimize fire insurance costs for their owners.

EXPERIENCE RATING. This type of merit rating modifies the class rate on the basis of the loss experience of a particular risk. The risk's losses for the experience period (usually two or three years) are compared with the average for other risks in the same class. The rate is reduced if the risk has a better record than the average; it is increased if the record is worse than average.

Experience rating can properly be used only for rather sizable risks. They must be large enough to have many losses each year. Usually their loss record will then show a pattern that tends to be repeated year after year. An example is the record of employee injuries in a factory employing several hundred workers. There will be many injuries each year, some serious, but most of them minor. Because there are many loss exposures in such a case, the law of large numbers causes the total cost of the firm's workers' compensation losses to be fairly predictable. Therefore, experience rating is used to modify the workers' compensation insurance rate. The manual rate for similar factories might be $2.00 per $100 of payroll. If this particular firm's loss record for the last three years is good, the experience rating formula might result in a 25% reduction, lowering the rate to $1.50 for the coming year. If the firm had a $1 million annual payroll, the effect would be to reduce its workers' compensation premium from $20,000 to $15,000. Such a potential saving gives the employer an incentive to work toward reducing the injury rate.

This type of rate modification cannot be used for small risks or for kinds of insurance having low loss frequency rates. It is not suitable for fire insurance, for instance. The fact that a building has been standing for 20 years and hasn't burned down yet is not a reliable indication that it won't burn down next year!

RETROSPECTIVE RATING. This is the third form of merit rating. It is available for large liability and workers' compensation policies; it seldom is used on policies with less than $10,000 annual premium. A modified form of retrospective rating is used for group life and health insurance.

In contrast to experience rating, which modifies insurance cost on the basis of past experience, retrospective rating modifies the cost on the basis of current experience. When it is used, an endorsement is attached to the policy stating that the final premium will be determined by means of a retrospective rating formula. The formula provides that the final premium will be no less than a stated minimum and no more than a stated maximum. For example, these might be $25,000 and $50,000, respectively. The final premium is determined after the policy expires and depends upon the amount of losses incurred during the year. If the losses are very small, the insured will pay the minimum premium; if they are very large, the insured will be charged the maximum premium. Usually the losses will be such that the actual premium will be somewhere between the minimum and the maximum. Retrospective rating increases the insured's incentive to control losses, because the pay-off in premium savings can be substantial.

INSURANCE PRICING: LIFE INSURANCE VERSUS PROPERTY-CASUALTY

Even though we have not delved into the complex mechanics of ratemaking, we have learned a number of things about insurance pricing and about the differences between the pricing of life insurance and property-casualty insurance. Specifically, we can see that the life insurance pricing system is simpler and that life insurance rates are more stable and more precise.

Simplicity

Life insurance pricing is relatively simple. The class rating system based on the insured's age and sex is logical, uncomplicated, and easy to understand. About 95% of the policies are issued at standard rates and, except in group insurance, neither experience nor retrospective rating is used.

The pricing systems used for property-casualty insurance are much more complicated. Several different rating systems are used, employing various exposure units and thousands of rating classes and territories. And for commercial risks in this field, schedule, experience, and retrospective rating are widely used.

Stability

In comparison with property-casualty rates, life insurance rates are more stable; they change very little from one year to another. Of course, for a particular level-premium policy they remain fixed for the life of the contract. But, in addition, there is little change from year to year in the cost of newly issued policies—basically, because there is little fluctuation in the three components of life insurance rates: mortality, overhead expense, and company investment earnings. Average mortality rates change scarcely at all from year to year. The changes that have occurred generally have resulted from gradual improvements in nutrition, sanitation, and health care. There also is little fluctuation in the level of company overhead costs. The third component of life insurance costs—investment earnings—is subject to more change than mortality or expense. Table 20–3 shows how interest rates earned by U.S. life insurers have varied since 1930.

In contrast to the stability of life insurance rates, consider the fluctuation of auto insurance rates. Total insurance costs in this case vary with the frequency of accidents and injuries and their average cost. Frequency is affected by such factors as changes in speed laws, licensing requirements, gas shortages, automobile safety features, law enforcement, and traffic conges-

Table 20–3   Net Interest Rates Earned
by U.S. Life Insurance Companies

YEAR	RATE
1930	5.05%
1935	3.70
1940	3.45
1945	3.11
1950	3.13
1955	3.51
1960	4.11
1965	4.61
1970	5.30
1975	6.36
1977	6.89

Source: Life Insurance Fact Book 1978
(New York: American Council of
Life Insurance), p. 61.

tion. Average claim costs are influenced, among other things, by changes in
the level of medical and hospital charges, by garage repair costs and jury
awards, and by legal changes such as the adoption or modification of
no-fault laws. To keep pace with such changes, actuaries calculate new
property-casualty rates frequently, usually each year. As policies in this field
customarily are written for one-year terms, renewal premiums normally are
below or (as is more likely the case in times of inflation) above the cost of
expiring policies.

Precision

Life insurance rates are more precisely calculated—more exact—than
property-casualty rates. They are more exact partly because, as we have
seen, (a) mortality, company expenses, and investment earnings are quite
stable, and (b) the rating system lumps large numbers of insureds together in
a small number of rating classes. They also are more precise because (c) life
insurance policies cover an event that is certain to occur to each person, and
(d) the amount that will be paid when the event occurs is known in advance.

   A life insurance company knows that, except for term policies, it ultimately will have to pay either the face amount or the cash value of every
contract it issues. If a $50,000 policy is sold today, the insurer must be in a
position to pay $50,000 to the beneficiary when the insured dies, whether
that is next week or 70 years from now. And it must pay precisely $50,000

regardless of wars, epidemics, stock market crashes, legal and political changes, inflation, deflation, or whatever else happens in the meantime. There are no "ifs, ands, or buts" in life insurance.

In property-casualty insurance the rating is less precise partly because both the losses and their amounts are uncertain. Here, the insurer promises to pay for damaged or stolen property, medical bills, the cost of lawsuits, and so forth. The number of losses depends upon the number of fires, explosions, collisions, lawsuits, or whatever. In addition, the amount of each loss depends upon the circumstances of each incident. In contrast to the case with life insurance, almost all property-casualty losses are partial losses. The amount of insurance is the maximum that the company will pay, but only rarely does the size of the policy determine the amount of a loss payment. In fire insurance, for instance, the size of a loss depends upon how fast the fire spreads, how quickly it is put out, the cost of lumber, the wage rate of carpenters, and countless other factors; almost always the amount of the loss is less than the total amount of insurance.

Thus property-casualty insurance covers events that may or may not occur and pays amounts that cannot be determined in advance. Life insurance, on the other hand, covers events that are certain to happen and pays amounts that are known in advance. These differences, combined with the stability and simplicity of life insurance pricing, explain why life insurance rates are more precise than those for other lines of coverage.

THE RATEMAKERS

Insurance rates are made by individual companies and by rate-making organizations. In either case, actuaries are in charge of the rate-making process.

Rate-Making Organizations

In the discussion of rate reasonableness we noted that insurance companies are permitted to cooperate in making their rates. The main reason for doing so is that many companies do not have sufficient rating data of their own. By working together and pooling their premium and loss data, they can develop more reliable rating information. In addition, cooperative ratemaking is economical, especially for the smaller companies. By participating in rating organizations, companies avoid unnecessary costs of employing actuaries, processing data, printing rate manuals, and handling rate filings with state insurance departments.

There are numerous rating organizations in the property-casualty insurance industry. One is the Insurance Services Office (ISO), whose making of fire insurance schedule rates was mentioned previously. The ISO employs about 20 actuaries, 15 attorneys, and 50 professional engineers. It collects insurance statistics from many companies and classifies and processes the data for use by the companies that pay for its service. In some cases ISO actually makes rates for the insurers; in other cases it provides data for the companies to use in making their own rates. In addition, ISO helps develop standard policy forms, does actuarial research, and assists the companies in filing new rates with the state insurance departments.

Until recent years, most property-casualty rates were made by rating organizations like ISO. Almost all of the companies belonged to what then were called rating bureaus and used the standard bureau rates. Today price competition is much stronger. Although most insurers still use the services of rating organizations, increasing numbers of them either modify the standard rates or combine the rating organizations' statistics with their data to make rates that more closely reflect the experience of their own policyholders. Also, many of the larger companies now employ actuaries and rely entirely upon their own statistics, particularly for auto insurance.

Rate-making organizations like ISO do not exist in the life insurance industry. The companies either have their own actuarial departments or use the services of consulting actuarial firms. The life companies do cooperate in compiling and analyzing mortality data, however. Much of this work is done through the Society of Actuaries. It conducts a continuing study of mortality, using data supplied by a number of companies. The published findings are available for use by any company.

Actuaries

Actuaries are specialists in the mathematics of insurance; they have chief responsibility for the rate-making process. Their work is by no means confined to rate-making, though. Other activities of actuaries may include:

- Developing new forms of insurance to meet the changing needs of consumers.
- Determining the financial reserves needed to meet their company's future obligations.
- Analyzing company expenses and earnings.
- Developing the data needed to determine the company's annual dividend scale.
- Conducting studies of claim experience.

- Projecting future claims, expenses, and earnings.
- Communicating with company officials, agents, policyholders, and regulatory authorities about company policies and practices.

To become a fully qualified actuary, one must become a member of either the Society of Actuaries or (for work in the property-casualty area) the Casualty Actuarial Society. Membership requires passing a series of very rigorous examinations, nine for the Society of Actuaries or ten for the Casualty Actuarial Society. After passing the first five examinations, candidates for the Society of Actuaries become Associate members and can use the letters A.S.A. after their names. For the Casualty Actuarial Society, Associate membership and the A.C.A.S. designation follow the first seven examinations. Those who pass the remaining examinations in their field become full members or Fellows; their status is indicated as F.S.A. or F.C.A.S.

What sort of persons become actuaries? Many have majored in actuarial science or mathematics in college. Although such majors are not required, the person must have a strong aptitude in mathematics and a solid background in the field at least through calculus. Courses in probability and statistics are helpful, as are courses in English, accounting, economics, finance, business law, and computers.

Those who set out to become actuaries must be prepared for long hours of study. Many candidates study 500 or more hours for each of the examinations—in most cases at least 6 or 8 years of study after graduation from college. To reduce the amount of study that must be done at home, companies employing actuarial candidates often provide study programs during working hours. Also, they usually furnish books and pay for evening courses taken at local universities.

Actuaries have been in short supply for many years. There are scarcely enough at present to fill the needs of the life insurance companies, and demand in the fields of property-casualty insurance, social insurance, and employee benefits is growing rapidly. As a result, salaries have risen to levels comparable to those in better known professions, such as law and accounting. The work is demanding, but the field offers unlimited opportunities. Many actuaries eventually become senior executive officers in their companies. Students with outstanding mathematical ability and an appetite for continued study would do well to consider careers in the actuarial field.[3]

---

[3]More information can be obtained from mathematics teachers, or from one of the professional societies: Society of Actuaries, 208 South LaSalle Street, Chicago, Illinois 60604, or Casualty Actuarial Society, 200 East 42nd Street, New York, New York 10017.

IMPORTANT TERMS

Pure premium
Operating expenses
Margin
Exposure unit
Statutory rate standards
Judgment rating

Class rating
Merit rating
Schedule rating
Experience rating
Retrospective rating
Actuary

KEY POINTS TO REMEMBER

1. The three components of all insurance prices are pure premium, operating expenses, and margin.
2. Insurance prices are based upon rates that apply per unit of exposure.
3. Various exposure units are used as measures of the probable losses of insured risks.
4. Most states have three statutory rate standards: adequacy, reasonableness, and fairness.
5. Rates must be adequate to cover the insurer's claims and expenses, to compensate investors, and to finance future growth of the company.
6. Rates must be reasonable so that the company can sell its policies. In property-casualty insurance, reasonableness is required by law because an exemption from the antitrust laws permits cooperative pricing.
7. Fairness in insurance pricing requires that proper distinctions be made; that is, higher prices are charged for policies covering greater loss exposures.
8. There are three types of insurance rating: judgment rating, class rating, and merit rating.
9. Most policies are class rated; all risks in the same class are charged the same rates.
10. Merit rating modifies class rates or premiums to reflect differences between a particular risk and others in its class.
11. There are three forms of merit rating: schedule, experience, and retrospective. They modify the rates or premium on the basis of expected experience, past experience, or current experience.
12. In comparison to property-casualty insurance, life insurance pricing is simpler and life insurance rates are more stable and more precise.
13. The insurance rate-making process is handled by actuaries who are employed by insurance companies, rate-making organizations, or independent consulting firms.

REVIEW QUESTIONS

1. What is a pure premium?
2. Why must insurance premiums include a margin?
3. What is the exposure unit in auto insurance? In life insurance?

4. Among the various objectives of insurance pricing, which one is primary?
5. What is the connection between rate adequacy and the availability of insurance?
6. What is the difference between judgment rating and class rating?
7. How does merit rating differ from class rating?
8. What dilemmas do ratemakers face in deciding how many rating classes to establish?
9. Why is schedule rating particularly suitable for fire insurance on commercial properties?
10. Why is experience rating particularly suitable for workers' compensation insurance?
11. List the five factors to be considered in fire insurance schedule rating.
12. What general comparisons can be made between life insurance pricing and property-casualty insurance pricing?

DISCUSSION QUESTIONS

1. (a) In what major ways does the pricing of insurance differ from the pricing of other things?
   (b) In what essential way is insurance pricing the same as the pricing of other things?
2. Auto insurance rates apply per car. It has been suggested that basing the rates upon the number of miles that insured cars are driven would measure the loss exposure more accurately. If one insurance company adopted "each 100 miles actually driven" as the exposure unit:
   (a) What problems would be created?
   (b) How might these problems be handled?
   (c) How might policyholders be benefited?
   (d) How might policyholders be harmed?
   (e) How might the company benefit?
   (f) How might the company be harmed?
3. "In order for insurance rates to be fair, they must discriminate fairly among various policyholders."
   (a) What does this statement mean?
   (b) Do you agree?
4. What factors does the class rating system used in life insurance ignore? (Three such factors mentioned in the chapter are income, occupation, and marital status. What other factors might life insurance rates conceivably be based upon?)
5. Why isn't schedule rating used for homeowners policies?
6. Why isn't experience rating used in fire insurance?
7. "Whenever possible, insurance pricing should encourage the reduction of losses." In which lines of insurance does the rating system have this effect?

CHAPTER 21
UNDERWRITING AND CLAIMS ADJUSTING

UNDERWRITING

REINSURANCE

CLAIMS ADJUSTING

This chapter considers two of the most important functions of insurance companies—underwriting and claims adjusting. It also examines reinsurance, a technique that is closely related to underwriting.

UNDERWRITING

In Chapter 20 we compared the pricing of insurance with the pricing of things like clothing. We discovered that one of the rather unusual things about insurance is the fact that different buyers frequently are charged different prices for the same policy. Something else about insurance is even more unusual: Anyone who wants to buy a coat or a car or a ton of steel and who has the money to pay for it can buy it, but not everyone who wants insurance can get it, regardless of their ability to pay the premium. To understand the reasons for this we shall examine the underwriting function. We shall learn what it is, why it is necessary, and what things underwriting decisions are based upon. We shall consider some of the problems that underwriters deal with and shall also take a look at underwriting as a career.

The Definition of Underwriting

Underwriting is the process of determining what risks to accept and how to insure them. The process is handled by company employees called **underwriters.** (In an entirely different usage of the word, insurance agents sometimes are also called underwriters.) Underwriters receive the applications from a company's agents. They conduct any necessary fact-finding and then decide whether or not the company will write the insurance that has been requested and, if so, exactly how it will be written.

RISK SELECTION. Deciding which applications to accept and which to reject is by no means the only thing that underwriters do, but it is their most important responsibility. Consider the importance of deciding whether or not a company will write these policies:

- $100,000 term insurance policy on the life of a stockbroker. Annual premium $560.
- Automobile insurance, including $50,000 of liability protection, for a young driver. Annual premium $630.
- $60,000 of burglary coverage for a camera store. Annual premium $460.
- $300,000 of multiple peril property insurance on an apartment building. Annual premium $1,850.

- $500,000 of general liability insurance for a building contractor. Annual premium $7,200.

Risk selection is absolutely essential to the success of a company's operation. If it is not done properly, the number and size of the company's loss payments will be too great relative to its income and the company may be ruined. Risk selection is not strictly a negative function, however. That is, its purpose is not simply to avoid writing unacceptable risks. Instead, the goal is to increase the volume and profitability of the insurer's operation by accepting a proper selection of risks.

Risk selection is necessary in order to avoid **adverse selection,** the insuring of too many poor risks. Adverse selection must be guarded against because of the nature of class rating. Class rates are averages; they are proper for the average of the many, many risks in each class. But in each class are risks that are better than the average and others that are worse than the average. The class rates actually are excessive for the former group and inadequate for the latter. The underwriter's task is to select a balanced group of risks so that the class rates will be adequate for the total. Most important, the underwriter must avoid writing too many below-average risks.

"But," someone may say, "if the rates for each class are adequate for the class as a whole, why not go ahead and accept all applicants on the assumption that the poor risks will average out with the good ones? If that is done, won't the total premium be adequate for the total amount of insurance written?" The answer is that, without risk selection, the good and the poor risks would in fact not average out. Instead, the company would find itself with an adverse selection of risks. To illustrate this point, assume that all life insurers require medical examinations of all applicants over age 45. What would happen if one company (without increasing its rates) started requiring medical examinations only of applicants above age 60? It is very easy to predict what would happen. Many people between ages 45 and 60 would continue to be turned down by the other companies. As they and their agents looked for companies willing to insure them, many of them would apply to the company with lower underwriting standards. Because it was less careful in selecting its risks, the average quality of this company's insureds would gradually worsen. Without intending to do so, it would be insuring more and more people who were in poor health, a group of people whose average mortality rate was higher than the average of all insured persons in their age group. The result, of course, would be that the company's income would not be large enough to pay for its claims. The company would go broke, perhaps destroying the savings and protection of its other policyholders.

Underwriters have a saying, "Select or be selected against." In the example, one company stopped selecting its risks as carefully as its competitors.

But when it stopped selecting applicants, applicants began selecting it and the company ended up with an adverse selection of risks. That is why risk selection is necessary.

OTHER UNDERWRITING ACTIVITIES. Other duties of the underwriting department (in addition to risk selection) include rating, policy preparation, answering questions about coverage, and furnishing information for quotations to prospective clients.

Rating means the assignment of rates to specific risks. Actuaries make the rates; underwriters apply them. To illustrate, the rating manuals for workers' compensation insurance include six different classifications for carpentry payroll. The underwriter must know that there are six carpentry classifications, must know the differences between them, and must see to it that the proper ones are used. Improper classification can result in the use of rates that are either too high or too low. If the rates are too high, the business may be taken away by a competing agent; if they are too low, the company won't receive enough premium to cover expected costs. Rating also includes the application of schedule, experience, and retrospective rates to specific risks.

Policy preparation is supervised by the underwriters. Much of this function is handled by data processing equipment, particularly the renewal of auto and homeowners policies. Preparation of policies for commercial accounts often requires individual treatment in order to see that proper forms and endorsements are used.

Underwriters also respond to countless questions about policy coverage. Because they prepare the policies, they are expected to be able to interpret them. When agents or field representatives find policy provisions to be unclear on a particular point, they turn to the underwriters for answers. Underwriters generally deal with hypothetical coverage questions. ("Would this be covered if it happened?") Questions about coverage for actual losses are the responsibility of the claim department. Underwriters and claim adjusters sometimes confer with each other about especially tough questions.

Another underwriting function is the supplying of information to agents who are bidding for new accounts. For large commercial accounts underwriters frequently work with agents in preparing bids involving special experience and retrospective rating arrangements or modifications of standard policy forms.

The Underwriter's Options

The risk selection aspect of underwriting would be simple (and perhaps rather dull) if the only alternatives were to accept or reject the applications.

However, there are several other options. The underwriter uses his or her judgment and experience to decide which of the several options, or which combination of them, is most appropriate.

ACCEPTANCE WITHOUT OTHER ACTION.   More often than not, the underwriter is able to accept an application with nothing other than routine action. This is usually the case with policy renewals and with most of the personal lines such as auto insurance. Efficient operation of an underwriting department requires that this part of the company's business be handled smoothly and systematically so that the underwriters can concentrate their efforts on the more unusual and more difficult cases.

HAZARD REDUCTION.   Sometimes risks that otherwise would be declined can be accepted if action is taken to reduce the hazard. Burglary coverage for a jewelry store, for instance, was written after the owner agreed to keep valuable items in a safe at night. Liability insurance was provided for a theater after a new emergency power generator was installed. In cases like these, the underwriter's action is often based upon investigations made by the company's loss control department.

COVERAGE LIMITATION.   If the company is not willing to provide as much insurance as a particular application requests, the underwriter may offer to write a smaller amount of coverage. Instead of writing auto liability at the requested $100,000 limit, for instance, the underwriter may offer to provide protection for basic limits only. Deductibles also can be used to reduce the coverage.

USE OF MERIT RATES.   Merit rating is another of the underwriter's options. In life insurance, 92% of the individual applications are accepted at standard rates. About 3% are declined, and the remaining 5% are insured at higher rates. Table 21–1 shows the reasons for charging higher rates.

As we know, merit rating is widely used on property-casualty policies also. Many business firms are able to secure general liability and workers' compensation insurance only because their policies are issued at above-standard rates. In other cases rate reductions are granted, both for fairness and as a means of competition.

REINSURANCE.   By making special reinsurance arrangements, underwriters sometimes are able to insure risks that they otherwise would have to decline. Reinsurance is described later in this chapter.

SUPPORTING LINES.   Another of the underwriter's tools is the require-

Table 21–1 Reasons for Extra Rating of Life Insurance

REASON	PERCENTAGE OF RATED POLICIES
Heart disease or its symptoms	30%
Weight problems	19
Other medical reasons	31
Occupation or other reasons	20
	100%

Source: *Life Insurance Fact Book 1978* (New York: American Council for Life Insurance), p. 100.

ment of what are called supporting lines. Supporting lines are desirable forms of coverage that an underwriter asks to write in addition to less desirable ones. For instance, products liability coverage seldom is written by itself. Because the premium is small relative to the potential loss, underwriters commonly insist on writing the firm's general liability coverages and perhaps its workers' compensation insurance as well. Sometimes young drivers find it difficult to get auto insurance except from the company that insures their parents' car and home. From the underwriting viewpoint, the parents' insurance is desirable business and "supports" the young driver's coverage.

REJECTION. The underwriter's last resort is to reject requests for coverage. Applications usually are declined only when the underwriter judges it to be absolutely necessary. Rejection deprives the insurer of income and potential profit. It also deprives the agent of a sale that perhaps has required considerable time and effort to make. Maintaining good relationships between a company and its agents therefore demands that applications be turned down only when there is no way that the business can be written profitably.

Basis of Underwriting

Underwriters seldom have direct contact with the risks they are considering. They don't interview prospective clients personally, nor do they usually see the properties they insure. Thus, they must gather information from other sources. Various kinds and amounts of information are important, depending upon the type of coverage and the nature of the particular risk. Among the keys to good underwriting are recognizing what information is needed and knowing how to get it.

The chances of making good underwriting decisions would be increased by conducting very thorough investigations of each and every risk, but this approach isn't feasible. Underwriters always must weigh the desirability of having more information against the time and cost that would be required to obtain it. In other words, they always must act on the basis of incomplete information. Thus, they customarily insure private residences and automobiles without having them inspected, because the cost of inspections would be too great relative to the premium received.

We shall review the various things that underwriting decisions are based upon. These are:

1. The application
2. Recent experience of the risk
3. Other information from the agent
4. Company underwriting policy
5. Examination or inspection reports
6. Reports from investigation services
7. The underwriter's judgment

THE APPLICATION. The **application** is a printed form that is filled out by the agent and submitted to the company underwriting department. Many different application forms are used, each designed to supply the information that the underwriters will need for the particular kind of coverage. A typical application for auto insurance would include:

1. Name and address of the named insured and all other drivers living in the same household
2. Age, sex, occupation, and marital status of all drivers
3. Information about driver training and good student discounts
4. Description of all cars to be insured
5. Information about use of the car in business and the number of miles driven to work
6. Name of previous insurer
7. Complete information about accidents and motor vehicle violations during the last three years

RECENT EXPERIENCE. To the underwriter, no single piece of information is more important than the last item just listed, a risk's recent loss experience. Take the case of a homeowners application for a family living in a house that is 35 years old. The agent reports that the family bought the house six years ago and had submitted no claims to the previous insurer for the first four years. Last year there was a $300 water damage claim and the year before that a $200 fire loss caused by electrical wiring. Before approving the application, the underwriter will look into the possibility that these two small losses are the tip of an iceberg. They may be evidence of deteriorating plumbing and electrical systems. If this is true, the next loss could be a large one, or there could be a continuing series of small claims. After investigating, the underwriter might conclude that the recent losses were isolated events and that the risk is still a good one. If not, the application may be declined.

People sometimes have the idea that the premiums they pay to a company over a period of years build up an account that they are entitled to draw upon for loss payments in later years. But, as we know, insurance doesn't work that way. It is essentially a loss-sharing arrangement; each person's losses are paid not by his or her own premiums but by the total pool of premiums paid by all policyholders. Therefore, the renewal of a risk that has gone bad after a number of loss-free years would not be in the best interest of either the company or the other policyholders. Suppose a company has written Peter Gunn's auto insurance for 12 years. During all of that time, Peter never has submitted a single claim. But recently he has had a speeding violation and two small accidents totaling $450. One happened when he was backing into a parking space; the other was a minor parking lot collision. The fact that Peter has been a good risk for many years is certainly a point in his favor. But the underwriter must make a judgment about the likelihood of future losses. Peter's premiums have given him security in the past, and they have helped the company pay other people's losses. They are not an account that can be "cashed in" for future losses. The underwriter will look into the circumstances of the case. Is there a reasonable explanation? Has there been a change in Peter's behavior? If there was a problem, has it been corrected? If this is no longer a good risk, the underwriter must refuse to renew the policy.

OTHER INFORMATION FROM AGENTS. Underwriters rely heavily upon agents for information. They expect them to act as field underwriters and to screen their business before submitting applications. Experienced agents understand the importance of underwriting and are familiar with their companies' underwriting rules. Whenever possible, they avoid the wasted time and money as well as the bad feelings that are involved in submitting applications that will not be accepted. They also are a major source of whatever information an underwriter needs in addition to that contained in the application.

The relationships between underwriters and agents are very important. Ideally, they should be based on mutual respect and understanding, but that is not always the case. Because of the nature of their duties, there is naturally an element of conflict. Agents are producers; they create business for the company, and that is the source of their income. It is easy for them to become convinced that underwriters are hatchetmen who want to deprive them of their best accounts. For their part, underwriters can easily be carried away by the negative side of underwriting and sometimes they do appear to be seeking reasons to decline applications, rather than looking for ways to approve them.

Consider the case of Sam Spade, an agent who has been trying for several years to get the property-casualty account of a large automobile dealer. Sam presently is insuring the dealer's airplane and is writing his fidelity bond. He has been promised a chance to offer a quotation (that is, make a bid) for the auto, general liability, and workers' compensation coverages next year. Sam's commission on these lines would be several thousand dollars a year. The automobile dealer has a 17-year-old son who has just started to drive an expensive, high-powered car of his own. Guess who is asked to insure the son and his car! Our friend, Sam, of course. And, unless he handles this request to the dealer's satisfaction, he won't have much chance of writing the other lines. Sam fills out an application, writes a long letter of explanation, and sends them in. From Sam's viewpoint, it makes no sense at all for the underwriter to think twice before writing the auto policy. After all, it can be the key to lots of additional business, both for him and for the company. But the underwriter has an entirely different point of view and perhaps is even bound by the company's underwriting policy to decline the submission. Unless both parties approach the matter with a great deal of calm good sense, there may be an explosion!

Submissions like this one sometimes are written as so-called "accommodation business." Very likely, the decision will not be made by a junior underwriter, but instead will be handled by a supervising underwriter and the branch office manager. If Sam Spade is a valuable and trustworthy agent, they may agree to accommodate him by writing the policy. To repeat, relationships between underwriters and agents can be sensitive. Normally, however, the individuals learn to respect one another's points of view and develop good working relationships. This point is important because, although their opinions sometimes may differ, neither can succeed without the other.

COMPANY UNDERWRITING POLICY. One of the first assignments given to newly employed underwriters is to familiarize themselves with their company's underwriting policy. The policy is established by top company officials, including the Underwriting Vice President. It is the framework within which underwriting decisions always are made. The underwriting policy usually is printed in a manual, a copy of which is kept at each underwriter's desk. It indicates the kinds of coverage that the company writes and does not write, the amounts that can be written without approval of a home office official, the states in which the company operates, and so forth. The rules differ from one insurer to another. For instance, one company may not write fire insurance on lumber yards, liability insurance on excavation contractors, or auto insurance on long-haul truckers. Another company may welcome such business.

As part of or in addition to a company's underwriting policy, there may be a lengthy underwriting guide. Written by top members of the home office underwriting department, the guide deals with the underwriting of various kinds of risks. It might include several pages on resort hotels, for example, indicating the liability limits that can be written, special endorsements that should be used, and suggestions concerning supporting lines. It also would alert the underwriters to special hazards sometimes connected with resort hotels, such as swimming pools, elevators, boats, horses, and ski lifts.

EXAMINATION OR INSPECTION REPORTS. Depending upon the type of risk and the amount of insurance, the underwriter may ask for a physical examination or inspection. Life insurance application forms furnish a limited amount of medical data; additional information can be supplied by a doctor's examination of the applicant. In property-casualty insurance, the company's loss-control department can inspect the premises and operations of applicants. Examination and inspection reports are valuable sources of information but they are expensive. Their use therefore is confined to cases where the potential premium is high enough to justify the cost.

To be able to evaluate the reports properly, underwriters must become familiar with the technical terms and practices in the fields they are dealing with. Life insurance underwriters must understand the meaning and implication of medical terms, conditions, and procedures. Property-casualty underwriters must learn about things like building construction, elevator safety devices, and motor vehicle fleet maintenance.

INVESTIGATION SERVICES. The reports of independent investigation services are another source of underwriting information. Several organizations provide such reports for use in connection with employment, credit, and insurance. The largest such organization is Equifax Service (formerly the Retail Credit Company). It has offices across the country in thousands of cities and towns.

Insurance underwriters can use these reports to verify information received from other sources. For instance, an applicant for auto insurance tells an agent that, although he has three cars, his children no longer live at home and the cars normally are driven only by himself and by his wife. The underwriter who receives the application can (a) assume the applicant is telling the truth and issue the policy without charging for youthful drivers, (b) assume the applicant is lying and reject the application, or (c) ask an investigation service to check out the facts. If a report is requested, an investigator will talk with the applicant's neighbors, employer, or other associates and inform the underwriter of the findings.

Investigation services sometimes are asked to look for moral or morale hazards; that is, evidence of conduct by the applicant which could produce excessive insurance claims. Such conduct may include dishonesty, deception, fraud, or extreme carelessness and utter disregard for preventing losses. Although applicants sometimes object to having their character and reputation investigated, such conduct is of legitimate concern to underwriters. Policyholders can defraud insurance companies in many ways, such as by faking thefts, fires, or injuries, by padding medical or garage repair bills, and by concealing information about previous claims. Because all losses must ultimately be paid by the entire group of policyholders, avoiding unnecessary and fraudulent loss payments prevents needless increases in everyone's insurance bills.

Even so, is it right for insurance companies to seek information from an applicant's friends and neighbors? Most underwriters believe that it is. As they see it, the applicant is asking them to provide thousands of dollars of protection for a relatively small premium. From the underwriter's viewpoint, investigation reports are just one of several sources of information, each of which must be carefully weighed and evaluated.

Consumers' rights in connection with this type of investigation are protected by the Federal Fair Credit Reporting Act. The Act requires investigation services to show those who request it the information that has been supplied concerning them. People who believe that the information is incorrect can insist that corrected reports be sent to the insurance companies or other organizations that received them. In addition, insurers must inform applicants in advance whenever an investigative report is to be prepared. The law also provides that, if insurance is denied or a premium is increased on the basis of a report, the company must inform the person and supply the name and address of the investigation agency.

JUDGMENT. Finally, underwriters rely upon judgment. It sometimes is suggested that underwriters could be replaced by computers that would analyze data from the same sources and reach the same decisions that human underwriters do. Using computers would have the advantage of avoiding personal bias. But most observers believe that sound underwriting requires human judgment in order to appraise the various kinds of information that are involved.

In evaluating a particular application for workers' compensation, for instance, an underwriter may need to consider (a) the technical information contained in the loss control department's report, (b) the company underwriting policy, (c) the importance to the company of the agency submitting the application, (d) the current trends in the loss experience of this type of business, (e) the past experience of this risk, (f) the competition from other insurers, and (g) the current or potential supporting lines. It is difficult to imagine that a computer could be programmed to evaluate combinations of factors like these. Remember too that the underwriter's task is not simply to accept or to reject the application; in addition, measures like merit rating and hazard reduction should be used when appropriate.

In dealing with a case like the one just referred to, it may appear that the underwriter's decision is largely a matter of guesswork or intuition (and there may be a bit of both). But the decision really reflects the underwriter's judgment, based upon experience gained from working with many other cases, each with its own particular combination of relevant factors.[1]

Underwriting Departments

In life insurance, practically all underwriting is done in home offices. Property-casualty underwriting is done in both home offices and branch offices; considerable authority is granted to branch office underwriters. To illustrate, picture again the typical branch office that was mentioned in Chapter 19. It is an office of a large property-casualty insurer that sells through independent agents. There are about one hundred employees. In addition to the four field representatives whose work was described in Chapter 19, there are ten underwriters. Four work in personal lines (auto and homeowners), three in commercial lines (mostly workers' compensation and general liability), and one supervises the personal and commercial lines underwriting. There also is one accident and health underwriter and one surety bond underwriter. The starting position in the department is as underwriting trainee. Trainees generally become underwriters at the end of one year. Later promotions are to senior underwriter, to supervising underwriter, and then perhaps to more generalized administrative work, such as assistant branch manager and manager.

Several of the larger property-casualty insurers recently have changed the organization of their branch offices by combining the functions of their

---

[1]While being interviewed for an underwriting job, a college senior once asked an old-time underwriter what risk selections are based upon. "Well," he was told, "when I leaf through a stack of applications, some of them just feel hot when I touch them." The young man took the job and worked as an underwriter for five years. Eventually he came to understand what the old-timer had meant: that through experience one learns what to look for and spots danger signals almost subconsciously. The author attests to this story. He was the young man.

underwriters and field representatives. In these companies, account analysts engage in risk selection and other underwriting duties and also do agency development and sales promotion work. This arrangement may be adopted by other companies in the future.

Underwriting as a Career

As we have seen, underwriters appraise and select the risks that their companies insure. Dealing with anything from simple accident policies to complex business insurance packages, their decisions may literally be worth millions of dollars.

It is estimated that 60,000 people are employed as underwriters. Their backgrounds are varied. Newly employed underwriters ordinarily are college graduates with degrees in business administration or liberal arts. No specific academic background is required. Employers look for people with broad interests, good judgment, and ability to learn. Underwriters should be able to communicate effectively, perhaps with an agent who is unhappy about having an application turned down or with a safety engineer who is discussing a firm's loss control program. Above all, underwriters must function well as decisionmakers within a framework of company policies and procedures. Underwriters have a greal deal of responsibility but they cannot be free-wheelers. They must be able to develop and evaluate the information that is needed to apply general underwriting guidelines to specific situations.

REINSURANCE

From what we have learned about insurance so far, it should not be difficult to see how an automobile or a house can be insured. The maximum loss is not large from the insurer's viewpoint and because many similar risks are insured the insurer can predict the total amount of loss payments with reasonable accuracy. But how can really large exposures be insured? How can a company write a policy covering a $2 million products liability claim or a $50 million office building? How can a small life insurance company dare to write a $100,000 life insurance policy? How can hurricanes that destroy thousands of homes and other structures be covered? In particular, how can such losses be paid without threatening to bankrupt the insurance companies and to undermine the security of their policyholders? The answer, or at least an essential part of the answer, is **reinsurance.**

The Nature of Reinsurance

Reinsurance is the insurance of insurance. It is an arrangement whereby an insurance company transfers part of its risk to another organization. For instance, a company writing a $300,000 liability policy might keep $50,000 of the risk and reinsure the remaining $250,000. The company that writes the policy is called the **ceding company** (because it "cedes" or hands over part of the insurance). The part of the risk it keeps is the retention. The company to which the balance is transferred is the reinsurer. It, of course, also receives part of the premium that the policyholder paid the ceding company. The reinsurer probably will retain only part of the risk it has accepted from the ceding company and will transfer the rest to one or more other companies, a process that is called **retrocession.**

Policyholders usually are not aware that their risks are being spread among several companies. There is no need to notify them, because reinsurance does not affect a company's obligations to its insureds. That is, the company writing the policy remains obligated to pay the full amount of all covered losses. After paying the losses, it is reimbursed by its reinsurers.

Purposes of Reinsurance

Looking at reinsurance more closely, we can see that it serves three different purposes. It provides capacity, protects against catastrophe losses, and furnishes stability.

CAPACITY. By capacity is meant the ability of a company to provide insurance. Through reinsurance, companies obtain additional capacity and are able to write more coverage than they could if they had to retain all of the risk themselves. All insurers, even mammoth ones, have limited resources and must set maximums on the amounts of coverage that they will retain. A moderate-sized life insurer might set its maximum retention on the life of any one person at $50,000. Without reinsurance, it would have to decline all submissions for policies larger than that amount. This limitation would force it to turn down a lot of good business and would also make it difficult for the company to recruit and retain good agents.

CATASTROPHE. In considering their need for reinsurance, insurers must also protect against catastrophes in which many separate policies could be involved. A fire insurance company might be able to handle up to $100,000 on any one property, but it must consider the possibility that a single hurricane, tornado, brush fire, or riot could destroy many of its insured properties. Some kinds of reinsurance are specially designed to protect insurers against such catastrophes.

STABILITY. A slightly different purpose of reinsurance is to provide stability in year-to-year underwriting results. Insurance companies like to avoid large fluctuations in their profits (or losses), just as other organizations do. In this respect, reinsurance serves a purpose similar to that of insurance itself, avoiding large, unexpected losses and making aggregate loss ratios more predictable.

Reinsurance Methods

Either of two methods can be used to arrange reinsurance contracts. The first, called **facultative reinsurance,** is used to reinsure a specific policy that the ceding company is issuing. The policy might provide a form of coverage or amounts of protection that the company does not normally handle. Therefore, it would not be covered by the company's usual reinsurance program. To arrange facultative reinsurance, an underwriter would phone or write a reinsurer and negotiate terms of coverage for reinsuring the particular policy.

The other method of arranging for reinsurance is by treaty. A **reinsurance treaty** is a standing contract between an insurance company and a reinsurer. Under the terms of the treaty the insurance company automatically cedes and the reinsurer automatically reinsures stated portions of certain types of risks. For the kinds and amounts of insurance that a company normally writes, the treaty method is more efficient and economical then facultative reinsurance, as it avoids having to reinsure each policy separately.

Reinsurance and Underwriting

A person who knows about reinsurance might wonder why underwriters have to decline poor risks. Why not assume that the company's reinsurance treaties will take care of large losses and, if they wouldn't, why not buy facultative reinsurance that would? Any company whose underwriters adopted this attitude, however, would soon be in big trouble. It would be in a position like that of an agent who dumped poor risks on unsuspecting insurers. Just as insurers expect their agents to do a certain amount of underwriting and not to conceal unfavorable information, reinsurers expect each insurance company to underwrite the risks it submits for reinsurance. If this practice is not followed, it soon will become apparent (as the reinsurer's losses mount) and the company will find itself having difficulty locating reinsurers that are willing to take its business. Thus, although reinsurance is essential to underwriting, it must not be misused; it does not relieve underwriters of the need to engage in careful risk selection.

CLAIMS ADJUSTING

Claims adjusting is the process of investigating, evaluating, and settling claims for insured losses. From the policyholder's viewpoint, the payment of claims is what insurance is all about. When a loss has occurred, the policyholder expects to find out if insurance really "works." This is not an unreasonable position; claimants (insureds presenting claims for losses) have every right to expect insurance companies to live up to their end of the bargain. Unfortunately, some people have mistaken ideas about the claim settlement process. First are those who assume they will not be treated fairly; they expect the company to take advantage of them and pay less than they are entitled to. Another group has an entirely different attitude. They figure that the occurrence of a loss is a golden opportunity to get back at the corporate monster that has been swallowing their premium dollars. They don't ask for a fair settlement; they want to make money on the loss. Most

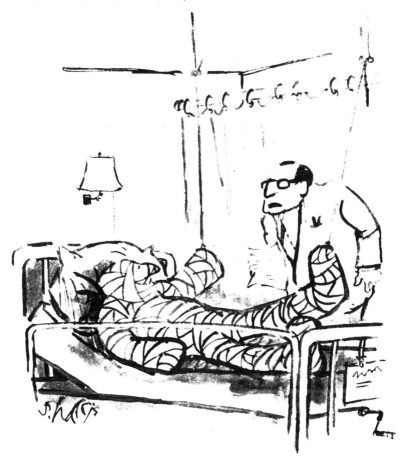

*"I have some bad news. Your health
plan doesn't cover bandages."*

claimants fall into neither of those categories. They expect to be treated fairly and ask for nothing more than a reasonable payment for their losses.

Objectives of Claims Adjusting

In their handling of claims, insurers have two main objectives. First, they try to settle claims promptly and fairly. Second, they must resist the payment of unjust or exaggerated claims.

FAIR SETTLEMENTS. Surveys show that the great majority of claimants are satisfied with their loss settlements. This finding is not surprising. Adjusters are instructed to be fair with claimants and pay them exactly as much as they are entitled to receive—no more and no less. The companies realize that losses give them a chance to cement good relationships with their policyholders. And they know that dissatisfied claimants become "walking billboards," telling and retelling of their mistreatment.

RESISTING UNJUST CLAIMS. The making of fair loss settlements also requires that excessive payments be avoided. As we know, all loss payments ultimately come from premiums. Payment of more than the fair value of losses is, in effect, an indirect tax on other policyholders.

Some kinds of claims can be handled quite routinely. Most health insurance claims, for instance, present no problems at all. Hospital and medical bills usually are paid as soon as it is determined that coverage was in force and the bills are for reasonable amounts. But the nature of some kinds of insurance is such that claims must be investigated carefully. Liability insurance is the most obvious example. The insurer must defend the policyholder, but it has no obligation to pay unjust or inflated liability claims. Property insurance also can present problems, largely because of the difficulty of setting an exact dollar value on the damaged or destroyed property. Sometimes there are sincere differences of opinion between the insured and the company. For instance, how much should be paid under a homeowners policy for a cigarette burn in a living room carpet? The insured may really believe that the entire carpet must be replaced. The adjuster probably will have a different opinion.

In addition, and unfortunately, claim adjusters cannot assume that all insureds are honest. Fraud has plagued the insurance industry at least since 1730, when a London woman faked her own death three times in order to collect the insurance money. More recently, a California man reported his $1,600 camera lost or stolen 16 different times—to 16 different insurance companies. The man claimed that the camera had been stolen from an apartment, taken from an automobile, dropped off a cliff, lost in a river.

He finally was brought to trial and sentenced 10 to 20 years for each count of grand theft. Another claimant attempted to collect from his insurer for a knee injury that he said prevented him from kneeling at Catholic Mass, thus depriving him of full participation and enjoyment of his religious life. His fraud was discovered when he turned out to be a Methodist.

Probably the most prevalent kind of insurance fraud is **arson,** the intentional burning of property. Arson fires include those started by vandals and other fires set for the purpose of defrauding insurance companies. There are about 150,000 arson fires each year. They result in about 1,000 deaths and cost insurance companies over $1 billion in claims. Fire investigation experts estimate that 30% of all fires are caused by arson. They say that during summer months a large majority of fires in major cities are deliberately started.

The insurance industry works hard to combat fraud. Over 300 companies support the Insurance Crime Prevention Institute. It searches out evidence of criminal claims and turns its findings over to the police. A similar organization, the National Automobile Theft Bureau, works for the prosecution of auto theft rings. Other organizations concentrate on other aspects of insurance fraud.

The vast majority of claimants are average, honest people. They may be inclined to overestimate the value of their stolen overcoats or demolished automobiles, but claim adjusters don't expect the typical claimant to be a con artist. Adjusters must however be prepared to identify and resist dishonest or unreasonable claims.

Claims Adjusters

The people who handle the payment of insurance losses are called **claims adjusters,** loss adjusters, or claims representatives. There are several different types: staff adjusters, independent adjusters, and public adjusters. Insurance agents also handle some loss adjustments.

AGENTS AS ADJUSTERS. Insurance agents frequently are authorized to settle small claims for their companies. Their authority is limited to a stated maximum payment, often $250 or $500. This permits them to settle directly with their insureds for routine fire, wind, auto damage, and medical payments losses. Agents also help their insureds with other losses, seeing that proper notice is sent to the company claim department or to an independent adjuster.

STAFF ADJUSTERS. **Staff adjusters** are salaried company employees. They may work in a company home office, branch office, or local claim office. The large property-casualty companies have sizable claim departments. In the "typical" branch office that we have previously described, nearly half of the total number of employees may be in the claim department. In areas where a company does a lot of business it may also have local claim offices in a number of other communities, each staffed by one or a few adjusters.

INDEPENDENT ADJUSTERS. **Independent adjusters** are employed by organizations that sell claim adjusting services to various insurance companies. They are used in three situations. First, they handle claims for companies that do not have enough business in a given area to justify the staffing of a company claim office. Second, they are used when several insurers cover the same loss, as often is the case with commercial property insurance. Third, independent adjusters play an important role in handling catastrophe losses. When a hurricane or tornado strikes, for example, hundreds of properties may be damaged. Teams of independent adjusters are rushed to the scene, where they work for days or weeks, inspecting the damaged properties and settling the claims. The largest independent adjusting organization is the General Adjustment Bureau. It employs 3,300 adjusters, who are located in more than 650 offices throughout the country.

PUBLIC ADJUSTERS. In contrast to the adjusters who handle claims for insurance companies, **public adjusters** work on behalf of claimants. Dealing primarily with property insurance losses, they prepare and present claims and negotiate with the adjusters who represent the insurance companies. (People with liability claims, which of course must be collected from other persons or their liability insurers, usually hire attorneys for this purpose.) A public adjuster charges the claimant 10 or 15% of the amount the loss is settled for. Competent public adjusters can be helpful in connection with large, complicated property losses, particularly those involving business firms; they seldom are needed for personal auto or homeowners claims.

The Adjustment of Property Losses

It is difficult to make general statements about the loss adjustment process, because there are such great differences in the handling of various types of losses. To illustrate, consider the difference between settling a $40 claim for medical treatment under an accident policy and settling a $40,000 medical malpractice claim. Or compare a claim from the named beneficiary for the proceeds of a life insurance policy with a claim from an airline whose plane has collided with another on a runway. Insurance claims are just about as varied as human activity itself. To illustrate the loss adjustment process, we shall consider the handling of ordinary property losses, such as those covered by homeowners and auto policies.

We must realize that when a loss occurs the policyholder cannot just sit back and wait for the company to pay. Property insurance contracts require claimants to take several steps themselves. These include: notifying the insurer of the loss, protecting the property from further damage, and assisting in the settlement of the loss. Failure to do any of these things may relieve the insurer of its obligation to pay for the loss.

NOTIFICATION OF LOSS.   The insured must notify the company of the loss. The Personal Auto Policy requires notice "promptly." Homeowners policies call for "immediate" notice, but this is interpreted to mean as soon as is reasonably possible. The company must be informed right away so that it can begin its investigation of the loss without delay. The insured is not permitted to wait until a number of small losses have been accumulated, nor can the insured have the property repaired before notifying the company. Notification is usually by means of a phone call to the agent or company. The policies say that the notice is to be in writing, but this requirement is usually waived.

PROTECTION OF THE PROPERTY.   The insured property must be protected from further damage. It is not to be abandoned to damage by weather or vandals. Insureds are required to take reasonable steps to care for their property after a loss just as they would if they were not insured.

ASSISTANCE IN SETTLING THE CLAIM.   Cooperation with the company in settling the loss is explicitly required. The insured must assist the adjuster, such as by showing the damaged property, furnishing purchase records, supplying detailed information about the circumstances of the loss, and getting estimates of repair costs.

ADJUSTMENT PROCEDURES.   Upon receiving notice of the claim, the adjuster will make sure that a policy was in force at the time of the loss, that the damaged property was insured, and that the policy covers the particular peril and location that the loss involves. The adjuster must also make sure that the claimant is the insured and is the owner of the property. These points usually can be established quickly and easily, but each must be verified.

Property insurance policies, including both auto and homeowners, may require the claimant to submit a sworn Proof of Loss. That is, the insured may be required to fill out a form detailing the loss and swear that the information supplied is true. In routine cases the adjuster draws up the Proof of Loss and the form is then signed by the claimant. In unusual cases, such as when the facts of the loss are suspicious, the adjuster may require the claimant to fill out the Proof of Loss and supply supporting evidence. If the claim is one for stolen property, for instance, and the adjuster is not convinced it is a valid loss, the claimant may be asked to show purchase receipts or other evidence of ownership. The adjuster will also check with the police to get their version of the loss.

Reaching agreement on the amount to be paid is a smaller problem than many insureds expect it to be. Because most losses are small, the amount paid usually is the cost of repairing the property. For automobile damage the adjuster may estimate the costs, the company may have a drive-in claim service where estimates are made, or the insured may be asked to submit estimates from local repair garages. The cost of homeowners repairs is usually estimated either by the adjuster or by the contractor who will do the work. One of the responsibilities of adjusters is to know what various repairs should cost and to avoid paying unnecessarily high amounts if garages or contractors inflate their estimates.

What happens if the adjuster and the insured cannot agree on the amount of the loss? This impasse rarely occurs, but if it does the policies provide that both parties shall appoint appraisers. The two appraisers then try to settle the dispute. If they cannot, an umpire is chosen to settle the difference between the two appraisers. This process obviously is cumbersome and expensive. Fortunately, it almost never has to be used; the adjuster and the insured usually reach agreement with little difficulty.

Loss Adjusting as a Career

Three things characterize the job of a loss adjuster: variety, independence, and responsibility.

Every claim is different. Much of the adjuster's work takes place in the homes and offices of claimants or at the scenes of fires, windstorms, or accidents. Adjusters deal with people of all types: insureds, third party claimants, witnesses, police, doctors, lawyers, repairmen, and contractors. Each situation is new; each must be dealt with differently.

Adjusters have a great deal of independence; they negotiate claim settlements with a minimum of supervision. Along with their independence goes an equal amount of responsibility. The decisions they make are important to their companies' reputations and success. They need to act fairly and promptly and at the same time to be on the lookout for padded or fraudulent claims.

To perform their duties, loss adjusters have to develop a variety of skills, perhaps more than those of anyone else in insurance. They of course must be familiar with policy coverages and know how they apply to specific losses. Also, they need to understand human nature. Claimants may be angry, injured, or distraught. Their homes may have gone up in smoke or have been swept away by high winds. Adjusters must be diplomatic and understanding; they must try to gain people's respect and confidence. In addition, claim adjusting requires knowledge of a variety of subjects, including law, medicine, property values, and the costs and methods of repairing and replacing all kinds of property.

Its great variety of skills and challenges makes loss adjusting a fascinating type of work. One property loss adjuster says that the fact that "new, interesting and different claims and claimants always lie ahead is probably what causes most adjusters, once adjusting is 'in their blood,' to remain in that vocation all their lives and forget the long and irregular hours, the lingering smell of burned timbers and damp stock, the basements full of dirty water, the cold chill of frozen and dripping water in winter and the hot humidity of steaming merchandise in summer."[2]

What sort of people qualify for loss adjusting? Most of the 130,000 adjusters are college graduates. Over 45% are women (up from only about 10% in 1962). No specific type of academic training is required, nor are newly hired adjusters expected to have any particular knowledge of insurance. Training is supplied at company offices and by experience on the job. What is required is the ability to learn how to handle the variety, independence, and responsibility that loss adjusting involves.

IMPORTANT TERMS

Underwriting	Reinsurance treaty
Underwriter	Claims adjusting
Adverse selection	Arson
Application	Claims adjuster
Reinsurance	Staff adjuster
Ceding company	Independent adjuster
Retrocession	Public adjuster
Facultative reinsurance	

KEY POINTS TO REMEMBER

1. Underwriting is the process of determining what risks to accept and how to insure them.
2. The most important aspect of underwriting is risk selection. Risks must be selected by the company in order to avoid adverse selection, the insuring of too many poor risks.

[2]Walter D. Swift, *A Primer on Adjustments* (Indianapolis: The Rough Notes Company, 1972), p. 57.

3. The underwriter's options, in addition to accepting or rejecting risks, are to (a) reduce the hazard, (b) limit the coverage, (c) use merit rates, (d) make special reinsurance arrangements, and (e) require supporting lines.
4. Reinsurance is the insurance of insurance. It transfers part of the risk assumed by an insurer to another insuring organization.
5. Reinsurance serves three purposes. It increases the capacity of insurance companies, protects against catastrophe losses involving many policies, and stabilizes underwriting results.
6. Facultative reinsurance contracts pertain to one specific policy. Reinsurance treaties automatically reinsure all policies of a certain type.
7. The loss adjuster's responsibility is to settle claims promptly and fairly, and to resist the payment of unjust or inflated claims.
8. Loss adjustments are handled by agents, staff adjusters, independent adjusters, and public adjusters.
9. Property insurance claimants must notify the insurer promptly, protect the property from further damage, and assist the company in settling the claim.

REVIEW QUESTIONS

1. What is the most important thing that underwriters do? What else do they do?
2. What is adverse selection?
3. What are supporting lines?
4. List five things that underwriting decisions are based upon.
5. Why is there naturally an element of conflict between underwriters and agents?
6. What is meant by capacity, catastrophe, and stability as they relate to reinsurance?
7. How do independent adjusters differ from staff adjusters?
8. What is a Proof of Loss?
9. What procedure might be followed if a company and an insured cannot agree on the amount of a property loss?

DISCUSSION QUESTIONS

1. Why can't everyone who wants it obtain insurance?
2. Why must underwriters make decisions without having complete information?
3. (a) If you were to apply for an automobile insurance policy, would you resent it if the company hired an investigating agency to ask your friends and neighbors about your character and reputation? (b) Do you believe that insurance companies are justified in having such investigations made?
4. Chapter 20 mentions that one of the objectives of insurance pricing is rate adequacy. Can you see any way in which rate adequacy or inadequacy would affect the risk selection aspect of insurance underwriting?
5. The Social Security Administration doesn't employ underwriters. Why isn't underwriting needed for the OASDHI program?
6. Automobile and homeowners policies require the policyholder to protect the

insured property from further damage after a loss. Give an example of a situation in which this requirement might be important.

7. What problems can you think of that the settlement of life insurance claims might involve?

8. Which would you rather be, an underwriter or a claim adjuster? Why?

CHAPTER 22
INSURANCE ORGANIZATIONS

This chapter concerns the organizations that provide insurance. It describes the various types of insurers and examines their financial operations. The chapter also discusses the things to consider when one selects an insurer. It concludes with a look at training and education for insurance careers.

TYPES OF INSURERS

Insuring organizations can be classified in several ways. First, they can be classified according to the lines of coverage that they write: life, health, property-casualty, and so forth. Second, they can be classified on the basis of their agency system: exclusive agency, independent agency, or direct selling. In this section we examine a third basis of classification, legal organization. Under this classification, most American insurers are either stock companies or mutual companies. Other kinds of insurers include reciprocals, Lloyds associations, health associations, government agencies, and self-insurers.

Stock Companies

A **stock insurance company** is simply a corporation engaged in the business of insurance. Like any other corporation, it is owned by stockholders. The stockholders elect a board of directors that, in turn, appoints officers who are responsible for running the company. The stockholders hope to profit from their investment in the company through stock dividends and through increases in the value of their stock.

The policies issued by stock companies usually are nonparticipating. That is, dividends usually are not payable to the policyholders. There are exceptions, though. Stock life insurance companies sometimes do sell participating policies. There are two types of dividends—stock dividends and policy dividends. Dividends on stock are paid only to stockholders. Policy dividends are paid to the buyers of participating policies. Most policyholders are not stockholders, although it is possible for a person to be both and to receive both kinds of dividends.

Most of the large property-casualty insurers are stock companies. Among the largest are Allstate, Travelers, Hartford Fire, Aetna Life and Casualty, Continental, INA, and Fireman's Fund American.

Mutual Companies

Mutual insurance companies (commonly called "mutuals") are nonprofit organizations owned by their policyholders. There are no stockholders. Any excess earnings are returned to the policyholders, either by means of policyholder dividends (if participating policies are sold) or by reducing the cost of renewal policies (in the case of short-term nonparticipating policies).

Legally, mutuals are controlled by their policyholders. Each policyholder is entitled to attend the company's annual meeting and cast a vote in the election of the board of directors. In practice, scarcely any policyholders attend the meetings and the companies are controlled by their directors and officers. A similar situation prevails with stock companies (and other corporations), as few stockholders bother to cast votes either.

Most mutuals operate in the same manner as stock companies. They sell the same forms of coverage, provide the same services, and have comparable financial strength. Many of the largest life insurers are mutuals. These include Prudential, Metropolitan, Equitable Society, New York Life, John Hancock, and Bankers Life of Iowa. Among the large mutual property-casualty insurers are State Farm, Nationwide, Liberty Mutual, and the Kemper Group. Life insurance policies sold by mutuals usually are participating. A few mutuals issue participating property-casualty policies, but most do not.

ASSESSMENT MUTUALS. In some parts of the country there are many small mutuals that specialize in insuring farm properties. Depending on the area, they are called farm mutuals, county mutuals, town mutuals, or local mutuals. Often they operate in only one or a few counties.

Many of these companies are **assessment mutuals**; that is, they issue assessable policies. The insureds are charged a small fee in advance, enough to pay for operating expenses and a normal number of small claims. If more funds are needed later, the insureds are charged ("assessed") additional amounts. Many years ago most mutuals in the property-casualty field operated on this basis. Now only some of these small companies issue assessable policies.

FRATERNAL INSURERS. Many fraternal benefit societies write life insurance for their members. These **fraternal insurers** are primarily social organizations, most of which were organized to serve particular religious, nationality, or labor groups. Examples are Aid Association for Lutherans, Knights of Columbus, Brotherhood of Railroad Trainmen, and Polish National Alliance.

In their role as insurers, fraternal societies are similar to mutual insurance companies: they are nonprofit organizations owned by and operated for the benefit of their members. Until recent decades many of them were not subject to state regulation, and some issued assessable policies. Today most of the larger fraternal insurers issue nonassessable policies and operate on a sound financial basis.

Reciprocal Exchanges

Reciprocal exchanges sometimes are called interinsurance exchanges. This is an appropriate term, because it helps describe the way they operate. A reciprocal is an association the members of which exchange insurance. In other words, the members insure one another.

To illustrate, assume each of ten business firms owns a building valued at $1 million. The ten firms could form an association and agree that each member would insure (and be insured by) each of the others in the amount of $100,000. If any of the buildings were damaged or destroyed the loss would be shared by all of the association members, each paying 10% of the loss. The advantage of this arrangement would be that each firm's loss exposure would be spread among the ten locations. Instead of standing to lose $1 million in a single loss, each would be exposed to a maximum $100,000 loss at each of the various locations. If the association grew to include 100 members the exposure of each would be lowered to $10,000 at each of 100 locations.

Some reciprocals started out exactly that way, organized by a group of similar businesses such as bakeries or nursing homes. Some continue to operate on a small scale, maintaining separate accounts for each member. Each account is credited with the premium paid by the member and is charged a share of all losses incurred by the group. Other reciprocals have expanded to the point where they operate like stock or mutual companies, charging regular premiums and paying losses and expenses from general funds rather than from individual members' accounts.

Another important characteristic of reciprocal exchanges concerns their management. All administrative duties, including sales and underwriting, are handled by an attorney-in-fact. The attorney-in-fact (which may be an individual or a corporation) receives a percentage of the premiums. Any part of this percentage which remains after the administrative costs are paid becomes profit for the attorney-in-fact. Thus, a reciprocal is a profit-making venture from the standpoint of the attorney-in-fact.

There are only about 50 reciprocal exchanges, but some of these are quite large. The biggest is Farmers Insurance Exchange. Located in Los Angeles, it is one of the largest automobile insurers in the country. Several other reciprocals write substantial amounts of property-casualty insurance. None of them sells life insurance.

Lloyd's of London

Lloyd's of London is the most famous insurer in the world. It is also one of the oldest, having been formed over 200 years ago. Lloyd's is not the largest insurer in terms of premium volume, but it probably is the most important, because of the major risks that it insures throughout the world.

The first thing to understand about Lloyd's of London is that it is not an insurance company. It is an association, the individual members of which engage in insurance. In this respect, Lloyd's can be compared with the New York Stock Exchange. The Stock Exchange as such does not buy and sell securities. Instead, it provides the facilities or marketplace where its members engage in the securities business. Likewise, Lloyd's does not itself write insurance, but its members do. The members of Lloyd's are called "names." There are about 15,000 of them, including several hundred Americans. The names operate through syndicates that are managed by other members called underwriters.

The word "underwriter" originated at Lloyd's. In the late 1600s, a man named Edward Lloyd ran a coffeehouse in London. Lloyd's coffeehouse came to be known as a place where shipowners could go to find men interested in insuring ships and cargoes. The shipowners would go from table to table at the coffeehouse and various men would agree to insure part of the shipowners' risks. They did so by writing their names underneath a description of the risks being insured. (Thus, they were "underwriting" the risks.) Sometimes an underwriter would add the names of friends who didn't have time to go to the coffeehouse themselves but who wanted to invest some of their funds in the hope of earning a profit. These "names" would have given the underwriter permission to accept risks on their behalf. The business is conducted in essentially the same way today. The insurance is written by syndicates, which are groups of names organized under the heading of an underwriter who is authorized to conduct the business. There are about 350 syndicates, ranging in size from just a few names to several hundred. Each syndicate specializes in a certain form of insurance, either marine, aviation, automobile, or other property-casualty lines. Incidentally, an extremely small part of the business handled by Lloyd's covers the odd types of risk that we so often hear about. It is true that Lloyd's insures things like pianists' fingers, movie stars' anatomy, and prizes offered for holes-in-one, but the great bulk of their business is conventional property-casualty insurance and reinsurance. (To be technically correct, we of course should say that the insurance is written by "the underwriters at Lloyd's" or by Lloyd's syndicates.)

Lloyd's of London is distinguished from other insuring organizations by the fact that the insurance is provided by its individual members (the names) and not by a corporation or association. The security of Lloyd's policies rests on the financial strength of its members. If it became necessary, an individual name would be personally responsible for insured losses right down to his or her last penny. Because of this, applicants for membership are carefully screened with regard to their financial resources and moral integrity. They must have substantial assets and a clear record of good conduct in their business affairs. In addition, each name must deposit a certain amount of money with Lloyd's to guarantee the payment of losses. A separate trust fund of over $1.3 billion is deposited in the First National City Bank of New York to guarantee the payment of claims to American policyholders.

PLACING A RISK AT LLOYD'S. To illustrate the working of Lloyd's of London, let us imagine that you are going into the business of manufacturing skateboards. Naturally, you want products insurance to protect you against bodily injury liability claims. A large insurance agency in your hometown contacts several insurance companies and finally locates one that is willing to write a $25,000 policy with a $10,000 deductible. Because you want more protection, the agent then contacts a surplus lines broker, an organization that specializes in placing risks that are hard to insure. Your agent gives the surplus lines broker complete information about your skateboard business and asks him to see if he can arrange for $500,000 of products liability insurance in excess of the $25,000 policy.

The surplus lines broker may be able to place the coverage with an American company specializing in "high-risk" business. If he cannot, the next step is that he transmits the information to a Lloyd's broker. There are about 200 Lloyd's brokers and all Lloyd's business must go through one of them. They have offices in London near Lloyd's and elsewhere around the world. The Lloyd's broker who receives the information about your products liability risk summarizes it on a form called a "slip." The slip contains all of the relevant details in abbreviated form, so that when the broker carries it into Lloyd's he or she can show it to the underwriters.

Next, the Lloyd's broker takes the slip to Lloyd's and enters "The Room." The Room, which houses all of the Lloyd's underwriters, is said to be the largest single room used for business purposes in the world. As a carryover from the old coffeehouse days, the underwriters sit at separate tables (or "boxes") throughout the Room. The Lloyd's broker first goes to an underwriter who heads a syndicate that specializes in high-risk liability insurance and asks this underwriter to lead the writing of your risk. This is a crucial stage in the placing of your coverage, because if the right person agrees to be the "lead underwriter," the underwriters for other syndicates probably will be willing to follow. Also, the lead underwriter sets the premium rate at which the risk is written.

If all goes well, the first underwriter agrees that his syndicate will take part of your risk. He initials the broker's slip and writes on it the amount that his syndicate will insure. The Lloyd's broker then goes to various other underwriters in The Room to complete the placement of your risk. If the effort is successful, the slip will be initialed on behalf of a number of syndicates who together agree to provide the $500,000 of coverage for claims in excess of your $25,000 policy. Finally, the policy will be prepared by members of the 2,000-person staff that handles policywriting, claims, data processing, and other services for the Lloyd's organization.

AMERICAN LLOYDS.   There have been a number of attempts to establish American insurance organizations along the lines of Lloyd's of London. About 30 so-called Lloyds associations are operating in this country. None of them is very large and none has any connection with Lloyd's of London.

Most of the **American Lloyds** associations have limited resources. Several of them have failed and some states refuse to license additional ones. The lack of success on the part of these organizations points up the unique nature of Lloyd's of London and the importance of its centuries-old reputation for stability and integrity.

In 1978 the State of New York passed a law permitting the creation of the New York Insurance Exchange, an organization conceived of as being similar to Lloyd's of London. At the time this text was written, the Exchange had not yet begun operating.

Health Associations

Several different types of organizations have been established to provide for the payment of health care costs. The best known are Blue Cross and Blue Shield associations. In most states these organizations operate under special laws as unique nonprofit, nontaxable associations. They are not mutual insurance companies, because they are not owned by policyholders. Instead, they usually are governed by boards of directors that represent the hospitals, doctors, and general public of the particular area.

Another characteristic of Blue Cross and Blue Shield is that they provide health care services rather than reimbursement for health care expenses. That is, they offer "service contracts" for hospital or doctor care. The persons who subscribe to the contracts receive the described care (semiprivate hospital accommodations, for instance) and the plan reimburses the hospital or doctor furnishing the care. Therefore, Blue Cross and Blue Shield are considered to be providing for the prepayment of health care, rather than reimbursing the subscribers for their health care expenses as insurance companies do.

Health maintenance organizations (described in Chapter 15) are a new development. In addition to financing health care services on a prepayment basis, as Blue Cross and Blue Shield do, they also provide the services themselves.

Government

Agencies of the federal and state governments have become major insurers during recent years. Most of the governmental insurance programs were established because private insurers were either unable or unwilling to provide coverage. In some instances, though, government agencies compete with private insurance organizations.

FEDERAL INSURANCE PROGRAMS. Numerous agencies of the federal government provide insurance. A summary of some of the major federal programs follows.

1. The Social Security Administration, which operates the Old Age, Survivors, Disability, and Health Insurance program, is the country's largest insurer. This program was described in Chapter 16.
2. The Federal Deposit Insurance Corporation insures bank depositors against loss of their funds due to bank failure. A similar agency, the Federal Savings and Loan Insurance Corporation, insures depositors in savings and loan associations.
3. The Federal Crop Insurance Corporation provides all-risk coverage for farm crops. It competes with private insurers that offer coverage for the perils of hail and fire.
4. Several programs of life insurance for members and veterans of the armed forces are provided by the Veterans Administration.
5. Several agencies of the federal government insure mortgage loans.
6. A program known as FAIR (Fair Access to Insurance Requirements) is designed to make property insurance available to those who are not otherwise able to obtain it. This program was set up in the 1960s when urban riots caused private insurers to be reluctant to cover properties in some areas. The coverage is written by insurance companies that pool their premiums and losses for these risks. Riot losses sustained by the company pools (which are set up on a state-by-state basis) are reinsured by an agency of the federal government.
7. A similar program was created in 1971 to provide burglary and robbery insurance in areas where high crime rates made those coverages hard to secure. The policies are written by private insurance companies but are insured by the Federal Insurance Administration. In this case the government assumes the entire risk, in contrast to the FAIR plan where the government reinsures the excess above an amount retained by the insurance companies.
8. A national flood insurance program was established in 1968. At first the coverage was written by a pool of about 130 private property-casualty insurers and was reinsured by the federal government. In 1978 the

private insurers withdrew from the program and the government took over completely. Administration is handled under contract by a private corporation, Electronic Data Systems Federal Corporation of Dallas, Texas. The policies are sold by private insurance agents in those communities whose flood control measures have received government approval.

STATE INSURANCE PROGRAMS.   All of the states administer unemployment insurance programs. Eighteen states provide workers' compensation insurance, six on a monopolistic basis, and twelve in competition with private insurers. Additional state insurance programs are varied. One or a few states provide the following: automobile, crop hail, life, medical malpractice, temporary non-occupational disability, and title insurance.

One of the most interesting of the state-run insurance programs is the Maryland Automobile Insurance Fund (MAIF). It was created in 1973 to provide auto liability insurance for Maryland motorists who are unable to obtain coverage from private insurance companies. This is the first time that any of the states have entered the auto insurance business. MAIF was established in response to complaints that the rates charged by the insurance companies were too high and that too many motorists were unable to obtain coverage except through the state's automobile insurance (assigned risk) plan. Maryland law provides that MAIF will insure all persons who have been denied coverage by at least two private insurers or have had their policies canceled or nonrenewed for any reason other than failing to pay the premium.

When it was first established, MAIF charged rates that were 34% lower than the auto insurance plan which it replaced. Since then, the rates have been increased substantially and the number of persons insured by MAIF has declined. By 1977, MAIF had lost so much money that it was threatened with bankruptcy; it was rescued by a $9 million assessment paid by the private insurers operating in the state. As might be expected, the insurance industry claims that Maryland's experience proves that government cannot provide auto insurance as efficiently as the private enterprise system can. Whether or not this claim is true, the establishment of MAIF demonstrates once again that government is willing and able to move into the business of insurance. It can either replace or compete with private insurers if the public becomes sufficiently dissatisfied with their services. Can the government actually do a better job than the insurance companies in coping with problems like inflation and high accident rates? Probably not. Regardless, the threat of additional governmental intervention gives the insurance companies an extra reason to serve the public as well as they possibly can.

Self-Insurance

The final type of insurance organization is the self-insurer. **Self-insurance** is a type of risk retention in which an organization with many similar loss exposures sets aside a fund for the payment of future losses. In effect, a self-insurer charges itself insurance premiums; it pays them into a special fund rather than to an insurance company. The two risks most frequently self-insured are vehicle damage and workers' compensation. Many organizations that have large fleets of vehicles and hundreds or thousands of employees self-insure both of these risks.

INSURANCE COMPANY ORGANIZATION

Most insurance that is obtained on a voluntary basis is obtained from either stock or mutual companies. In this section we shall briefly examine the internal organization of such companies.

Board of Directors and Officers

Authority for a company's management theoretically stems from its stockholders (in the case of a stock company) or policyholders (in the case of a mutual company). These groups elect the board of directors.

The board of directors is responsible for the overall direction of the company and for selecting officers to manage it. There usually are between ten and twenty members of the board, including the company president and several other senior officers. The majority of the directors generally are outsiders: bankers, lawyers, and heads of other organizations. They are selected for their knowledge and judgment and perhaps because they have contacts that are important to the company. The full board may meet only a few times a year, but committees of the board usually meet more frequently. The board ordinarily does not concern itself with day-to-day company operations; instead, it concentrates on general policies and long range plans.

One of the most important duties of the board of directors is to select the company's chief executive officer. This may be either the chairman of the board or the company president. This person is responsible to the board for the conduct of the company's operations. Large companies have many other officers, all appointed by the board of directors. These may include an executive vice president, other vice presidents, treasurer, secretary, general counsel, controller, actuaries, assistant treasurers, and assistant secretaries. (The title "assistant secretary" doesn't sound very impressive. But one of the first things a new employee may learn is that his or her supervisor reports to a department manager who in turn reports to an officer of the company whose title is assistant secretary!)

Departments

One of the key responsibilities of top management is to establish a workable and efficient system of company organization. There is little uniformity among companies in this regard; each is organized somewhat differently from the others.

Most companies are divided into numerous departments. The departments frequently are based upon (a) function, (b) kind of insurance, and/or (c) territory. Departments organized according to function include the agency, underwriting, claim, actuarial, investment, accounting, and personnel departments. Departments based on kind of insurance may be found in life insurance companies having separate departments to handle ordinary, industrial, health, and group insurance. Property-casualty insurers may be similarly divided into personal and commercial lines departments. Territorial departmentalization is used to divide operations among geographical areas.

FINANCIAL OPERATIONS OF INSURANCE COMPANIES

Thus far, our discussion of insurance functions has concentrated upon those that relate to risk handling: marketing, pricing, underwriting, and loss adjusting. There is another side of insurance, the financial side. It deals with the handling of funds between the time they are received by the insurer and the time they are used to pay for losses and company expenses.

The financial side of insurance is more or less hidden from the view of most insurance buyers, not because it is intentionally concealed from them but simply because they usually are not interested in finding out about it. However, to have a firm understanding of insurance and how it works, we must have some idea of its financial operations. Therefore, we shall consider insurance company assets, where they come from, and how they are invested. We shall also examine insurance reserves and surplus and determine the source and nature of insurance company profits.

Assets

Insurance companies have enormous assets. The largest life insurer, Prudential, has over $50 billion. At the end of 1977 all U.S. life insurers had $351 billion; assets of property-casualty insurers totaled $127 billion.

SOURCES OF ASSETS.   These assets come from three sources: original capital and surplus, premium income, and retained earnings.

The original capital and surplus are the funds supplied by investors or lenders when an insurance company is first established. The laws of the various states require that these be at least a certain size; the minimum amounts depend upon the type of company and the lines of insurance that it intends to engage in. In most cases the minimums are $1 million or less.

Premium income is the major source of the assets. As we know, premiums usually are collected at the beginning of the periods for which insurance policies apply. Expenses, including commissions paid to agents, are deducted and most of the remainder is held for the payment of claims. This practice is obviously the sensible thing to do; if the funds were not set aside the companies would not be able to pay claims when they developed. We shall see later that insurance companies actually have no choice in the matter; they are legally required to maintain reserves for this purpose. From our knowledge of the difference between life and property-casualty insurance we now can understand why life insurers accumulate larger assets than property-casualty companies. Their policies cover much longer periods of time and funds must be built up over the years in order to handle rising cash values and the payment of death claims. Property-casualty policies, usually being written for only one year (and not all incurring claims), do not require as large a build-up of funds as do life policies.

Retained earnings, the third source of company assets, are the profits from past years that have been kept by the companies and plowed back into the business. Some of the profits are paid out as dividends to stockholders or policyholders and some are retained by the companies in order to strengthen their financial position and support future growth.

INVESTMENT OF ASSETS.   Insurance company assets do not stand idle. They are invested in a variety of ways to earn income. The earnings on the invested assets make the cost of insurance protection less than it otherwise would be.

The major types of investments are shown in Table 22–1. Notice the difference between the investments of the two types of insurers. Life insurers invest heavily in mortgages, which generally are long-term investments providing a fixed rate of return. This practice reflects the nature of the life insurance companies' obligations to their policyholders. As we know, these obligations are mostly for long terms and for stated amounts; the beneficiary of a $10,000 policy will have to be paid $10,000—no more and no less. The investments of life insurers therefore are conservative; they emphasize safety and certainty of return. In contrast, property-casualty companies invest

Table 22-1 How Insurance Company Assets Are Invested

TYPE OF INVESTMENT	LIFE INSURERS	STOCK PROPERTY-CASUALTY INSURERS
Government securities	6.8%	21.0%
Corporate bonds	39.2	38.2
Corporate stocks	9.6	23.9
Mortgages	27.5	0.3
Real estate	3.2	0.9
Policy loans	7.8	—
Premium balances	—	7.9
Miscellaneous	6.0	7.8
	100.0%	100.0%

Source: *Life Insurance Fact Book 1978* (New York: American Council of Life Insurance), p. 68. *Best's Aggregates and Averages 1978* (Oldwick, N.J.: A. M. Best Co.), p. 70.

relatively more in common stocks. Again, this practice is consistent with the nature of the companies' obligations to their policyholders. Property-casualty policies are short-term contracts and are not used as a means of savings and investment. Moreover, claim payments are not fixed; they fluctuate as economic conditions affect such things as repair bills, medical costs, and liability judgments. It therefore is appropriate for property-casualty insurers to invest more of their assets in the stock market. The government securities held by these companies include short-term notes that can readily be liquidated if catastrophes suddenly require large loss payments.

Insurance company funds are invested in an even greater variety of ways than Table 22-1 reveals. For instance, the mortgage loans help build homes, apartment buildings, office buildings, shopping centers, and motels. The corporate stocks and bonds provide funds to finance all kinds of industry, from airlines and television networks to steel, utilities, and computer companies.

The larger insurance companies have investment departments that select and oversee the investment of their funds. In these departments security analysts often specialize in a particular field of investment, such as the transportation industry or public utilities. They evaluate current investments in those fields, analyze new issues, and negotiate loans. Most of the persons employed as analysts have graduate degrees in business or economics. The investments of small companies usually are handled for them by banks or consulting firms.

Liabilities

One might wonder if insurance companies need such large assets. Are those enormous investments really necessary? The answer is that they indeed are necessary. The reason they are needed is that the companies have almost equally large liabilities. Each policy that is issued and much of each premium that is received represent a potential obligation of the companies to their policyholders. Most insurance company assets are funds held to pay future claims and expenses on policies currently in force.

Insurance companies are required by law to maintain reserves. Although a reserve is ordinarily thought of as a fund of money (an asset), in insurance **legal reserves** are liabilities. They are not funds; instead they are the reason that funds must be held. That is, an insurance company is legally required to estimate its future obligations and to show this amount on the liability side of its balance sheet. In order to avoid bankruptcy, the company of course must balance its liabilities with an equal amount of assets. Thus the assets are required indirectly—to balance against the required legal reserves.

LIFE INSURANCE RESERVES. The nature of insurance reserves will be made clearer if we refer to Table 22–2. ABC Life Insurance Company has $1 billion of assets. Of this amount, 80% represents its legally required policy reserve, 4% represents policyholders' dividend accumulations and 10% represents other liabilities. The company's liabilities thus equal 94% of its assets. The remaining 6% is surplus, the amount by which the company's assets exceed its liabilities.

The policy reserve is the principal liability of ABC Life and other life insurance companies. It comes about because most life insurance policies are long-term level premium contracts. Because the mortality rate rises as policyholders become older, the premiums collected in the early years of each policy are greater than the amounts needed to pay death claims at that time. However, the excess premiums (plus income from investments) will be

Table 22–2 ABC Life Insurance Company Balance Sheet (December 31, 1980)

ASSETS		LIABILITIES AND SURPLUS	
Bonds	$ 400,000,000	Policy reserve	$ 800,000,000
Stocks	100,000,000	Dividend accumulations	40,000,000
Morgages	350,000,000	Other liabilities	100,000,000
Other assets	150,000,000	Total liabilities	940,000,000
	$1,000,000,000	Surplus	60,000,000
			$1,000,000,000

needed in the later years when the mortality rate is higher. Thus, the collection of excess funds creates an obligation on the part of the company, an obligation to make payments to policyholders and beneficiaries at a later time. The policy reserve represents this obligation.

Calculation of the policy reserve for a company insuring hundreds of thousands of people is of course a big undertaking. One way of expressing its size is as follows: It is the amount that, together with all future premium collections and future interest earnings, will enable the company to pay all future benefits on all policies currently in force. In the case of ABC Life Insurance Company, this is $800 million. That amount must be shown on the balance sheet as a liability, and the company must have assets of at least the same amount.

Ownership of assets equal to the policy reserve and the company's other liabilities is the test of a company's solvency. It indicates the company's ability to meet its present and future obligations.

PROPERTY-CASUALTY RESERVES. Property-casualty insurers have two principal reserves, the unearned premium reserve and the loss reserve. Both are required by law. They are illustrated in Table 22–3.

XYZ Casualty writes automobile and other kinds of property-casualty insurance. Notice that it is a stock company. The $5 million capital stock item represents the initial investment by the company's stockholders.

Unearned premium reserve. The **unearned premium reserve** corresponds to the portion of the premiums received by the company that it has not yet earned. For example, a one-year homeowners policy might have a $120 premium. At the end of the first month the company will have earned 1/12 or $10 of the premium; the remaining 11/12 or $110 will be unearned and will have to be allowed for in the unearned premium reserve. As the

Table 22–3 XYZ Casualty Insurance Company Balance Sheet (December 31, 1980)

ASSETS		LIABILITIES, CAPITAL, AND SURPLUS	
Bonds	$ 50,000,000	Unearned premium reserve	$ 25,000,000
Stocks	40,000,000	Loss reserve	45,000,000
Other assets	10,000,000	Other liabilities	5,000,000
	$100,000,000	Total liabilities	75,000,000
		Capital stock	5,000,000
		Surplus	20,000,000
			$100,000,000

year goes by the unearned premium will gradually decline as more and more of the premium is earned by the company.

The unearned premium reserve has two purposes. First, it assures that the company will be able to return the unused portion of the premium to the insured if the policy is cancelled. The second purpose is to protect the company's solvency. The unearned premium reserve does this by recognizing that the company will incur further losses and expenses on policies now in force. By requiring that assets equal to the unearned premiums be held by the company, it helps assure that future losses and expenses will be paid.

Loss reserve. The **loss reserve** is a liability representing the estimated cost to the company of settling all of the claims for losses that already have occurred but have not yet been paid. As of December 31, 1980, XYZ Casualty estimated that all of its currently unpaid loss claims would eventually cost it a total of $45 million. Most of this amount is probably for bodily injury liability claims. Some of these, especially the larger ones, take a long time to settle. Property insurance claims, such as for fire, wind, and auto collision, are settled more quickly and therefore do not bulk as large in the loss reserve.

Both the loss reserve and the unearned premium reserve represent the company's future obligations. The loss reserve is for losses that already have occurred but have not yet been paid for. The unearned premium reserve is for losses and expenses that will occur in the future.

Surplus

An insurance company's **surplus** is the amount by which its assets exceed its liabilities. In other words, the surplus is the amount by which the company's assets could decline (or its liabilities could increase) before it went broke. Sometimes it is called "policyholders' surplus" because the portion of the assets equal to it furnishes additional financial strength for the company and therefore provides extra security for the company's policyholders.

LIFE INSURANCE SURPLUS. As we know, life insurance rates have three components: mortality, interest, and expense. A life insurance company's earnings increase when the mortality rate of its insureds improves, when its expenses decline, or when its investment income rises. If the insurer is a stock company, part of the earnings are paid to stockholders; if the policies are participating, some of the earnings are paid to policyholders. The earnings that remain are retained as additions to surplus, providing an extra safeguard against such things as an unexpected rise in death rates or a drop in the value of the company's investments.

PROPERTY-CASUALTY INSURANCE SURPLUS.   You may have no-
ticed that Table 22–3 shows the XYZ Casualty Insurance Company has
$20 million in surplus. This amount is equal to 20% of its assets, which is
relatively much more than ABC Life Insurance Company's $60 million
surplus (which is only 6% of its assets). In both cases the figures are typical of
actual companies of the two kinds. Does this mean that property-casualty
insurers have more money than they need? Does it show, as some people
believe, that the companies have plenty of funds to pay for claims, no matter
how large or how many? It does not. The surplus is needed. Contrary to what
its name implies, the surplus is not excess or unnecessary. Property-casualty
insurers need relatively more surplus than life insurers because the business
is much more volatile and unpredictable. What can go wrong? What can
create an unexpected need for extra funds? Here are some of the things:

1.   Investment earnings can drop. This is more likely for property-casualty
     companies because, as we have seen, their investments are usually not
     as conservative as those of life insurers. (We also have noted that it is
     appropriate that they not be as conservative.)
2.   Underwriting selection can turn out to be unfavorable. Adverse selec-
     tion is difficult to avoid in the property-casualty business, especially if a
     company is seeking to grow by writing more policies. Furthermore, loss
     ratios can climb because of rising auto accident rates, or hurricanes,
     tornadoes, major fires or explosions, and the like. Such unexpected
     developments are almost unheard of in life insurance.
3.   Loss reserves can be underestimated, perhaps because of rising price
     levels. The loss reserve of XYZ Casualty is equal to almost half of its total
     assets. If it finds that it has misjudged the cost of settling its outstanding
     claims and they cost 10 or 15% more than expected, the company will
     have a real need for its surplus.
4.   Premium rates can be too low. This danger is probably the factor that is
     most likely to cause the company's surplus to be needed. If the rates are
     too low, premiums are too low and the unearned premium reserve is too
     low. We observed in Chapter 20 that property-casualty rates are less
     stable and less precise than life insurance rates. In the property-casualty
     field, both the number of losses and their size are uncertain. If either the
     number or the size exceeds predictions, rate levels will turn out to be
     too low. Remember also that rates are based on past experience, not
     present experience. This fact, coupled with inflationary increases in the
     cost of claim payments, can cause major problems. Consider, for in-
     stance, automobile policies in force during 1980, issued in 1979 at rates
     that were based on price levels during 1978, 1977, and 1976. Bear in

mind that these policies will pay for liability claims that are not settled until 1981, 1982, or later. If inflation pushes the cost of average loss settlements upward during these years, the companies' premium income may easily prove to be inadequate.

Because of factors like these, property-casualty insurance is an unpredictable business and the companies need large amounts of surplus. The fact that the problems can be real ones is proved by the record of company insolvencies. During the period from 1969 to 1978 at least 50 property-casualty insurers failed (out of a total of approximately 2,900). In other words, those 50 companies did not have enough surplus to protect their policyholders. (Fortunately, the industry's system of guaranty funds protected most of the policyholders. See Chapter 23.)

Underwriting capacity. An insurer's **underwriting capacity** is its financial ability to provide insurance. In the property-casualty field a company's capacity is limited by the amount of its surplus. Many experts say that a company's premium volume should be no more than three times as much as its surplus. In other words, surplus should be at least one-third the size of the company's total annual premiums. A company writing $100 million in premiums should have at least $33 million in surplus to protect its policyholders. Thus, if a company (or the entire industry) is to expand it must increase its surplus. And, if inflation requires rates and premiums to increase, it must increase its surplus even if it writes no more policies than it did previously.

Sources of surplus. The final point to consider is how property-casualty insurers can increase their surplus. As population and the economy grow, the companies are being asked to insure more cars, more houses, and more businesses. And as price levels rise they must pay for more expensive repairs, medical bills, and so forth. In order to do these things without threatening the security of their policyholders, they must accumulate more surplus.

The principal way in which insurance companies add to their surplus is by earning money, by taking in more than they pay out. They have two potential types of earnings, underwriting earnings and investment earnings. **Underwriting earnings** come from insurance operations; **investment earnings** come from the investment of funds. To illustrate the nature of underwriting earnings, let us say that for a particular year XYZ Casualty has earned premiums totaling $50 million. During the same year it incurs $33 million in policyholders' losses and has $15 million in expenses, for a total of $48 million in losses and expenses. Subtracting the latter figure from the $50 million of premiums leaves $2 million in underwriting earnings. (This is a simplification; insurance accounting is much more complicated than this. The example is realistic in its essentials, however.)

If insurers regularly have underwriting earnings of this sort, they have no problem in building up the surpluses they need. But sometimes they earn little or nothing from their insurance operations. If claim costs rise because of disasters, increased claim frequency, or inflation, underwriting earnings may disappear and underwriting losses may develop. For the two-year period 1974–1975, for instance, the property-casualty insurance industry as a whole had underwriting losses of more than $7 billion. During periods like this, company surplus and company underwriting capacity may be sharply reduced and (as happened in 1974 and 1975) some companies may be forced into bankruptcy.[1]

SELECTING AN INSURER

There are literally thousands of insurance companies operating in the United States. How can purchasers make intelligent choices among them? What are the characteristics of a good company?

Ideally, an insurer should be chosen on the basis of three characteristics: service, cost, and financial strength. These factors are far more important than whether the company is a stock company, a mutual, or a reciprocal exchange.

Service

We noted the importance of policyholder service in our study of auto, homeowners, and life insurance and in connection with insurance marketing, underwriting, and claims adjusting. Good service is important to all policyholders, whether they are individuals or business organizations. For individual insureds, agency service is the major factor and finding a good agent should take precedence over selecting the company. However, consideration of cost and the company's financial strength should not be ignored.

Cost

As we have learned, all companies do not charge the same premiums. There are substantial differences in the cost of similar auto, homeowners, life, and

---

[1]Serious problems may be avoided if investment earnings are available to make up for the underwriting losses, but that is not always the case.

other policies. It therefore is wise to shop around before one buys. This advice does not suggest that one should buy on the basis of price alone, jumping from one company to another at each renewal, however. Purchasers should also consider service and the insurer's financial strength.

Financial Strength

The value of an insurance policy rests upon the ability of the insurer to pay its claims. But how can a purchaser judge the financial strength of the company? In particular, how can one predict what its financial condition will be at some unknown time in the future when a claim may be made? Very few insurance buyers are in a position to evaluate the financial strength of insurance companies. The subject is far too complex. There is a way, though, that one can easily find out how impartial experts have rated the financial condition of many companies—by consulting the publications of the Alfred M. Best Company.

Two volumes of *Best's Insurance Reports* are published each year, one reporting on property-casualty companies and the other on life and health companies. They are available in most large libraries. Both volumes give information about the history, operations, investments, and financial condition of insurance companies. In addition to this purely factual information, Best's Reports includes ratings of the individual companies, based upon the analysis and judgment of the publisher. The Reports have been published every year for over 70 years and are highly respected in the insurance industry. Best's ratings are based upon an evaluation of: (a) underwriting results, (b) expense control, (c) adequacy of reserves for liabilities, (d) adequacy of resources to handle unusual needs, and (e) soundness of investments. With some exceptions, each company is given one of the following Policyholders' Ratings:

A+ or A	Excellent
B+	Very Good
B	Good
C+	Fairly Good
C	Fair

Some companies are not rated. The reasons for omitting ratings are stated in the introductory section of the books. Minor differences in Best's ratings probably can be ignored. However, consumers should think twice before buying from insurers that are given extremely low ratings.

INSURANCE TRAINING AND EDUCATION

Because so many insurance operations are of a specialized nature—
underwriting, claims, investment, and so forth—the insurance industry has
unique educational needs. To fill these needs, several types of insurance
training and education have developed.

Notice that there is a difference between training and education. Training
means developing the skills and abilities that are required to do a specific
job. Training programs are conducted by companies for their own employees. Education is a broader concept that is more concerned with general
knowledge and understanding. Professional education involves advanced
study in specialized fields. Programs of professional insurance education are
sponsored by industry-wide organizations and by colleges and universities.

Company Training Programs

All of the major insurance companies have carefully planned training programs. Combining on-the-job training with classroom study, they furnish
rather complete technical training for a variety of jobs. One of the larger
companies, for instance, devotes an entire wing of its new headquarters
building to classroom and instruction facilities. Eight classrooms, some
seating as many as 35 students, are located in the wing. This company has
19 instructors who teach courses in such subjects as underwriting, claims,
sales, typing, data processing, communications, and management. In addition to organized classes, the company makes self-study courses available to
all of its employees. Employee training is equally important to the smaller
companies that cannot afford such extensive facilities. These companies rely
mainly upon on-the-job training. Many of them also use correspondence
courses supplied by industry trade associations.

Professional Insurance Education

There are two types of professional insurance education programs, those
sponsored by the insurance industry and those sponsored by colleges and
universities.

INDUSTRY SPONSORED PROGRAMS.   In previous chapters two of the
industry sponsored programs of professional insurance education were
identified. These are the Chartered Life Underwriters (CLU) and the Chartered Property Casualty Underwriter (CPCU) programs.

COLLEGE AND UNIVERSITY PROGRAMS. Professional insurance
education is also offered at many colleges and universities. Approximately

600 schools offer at least one specialized insurance course and about 65 offer undergraduate majors in the field.

In the colleges and universities that offer the insurance major, students in the school or department of business can elect to specialize in insurance. Like those who major in other business fields, students majoring in insurance have most of their coursework in subjects outside of their specialty. These generally include other business courses (such as accounting, finance, management, and marketing), and courses in the arts and sciences. Students majoring in the field usually take four to six insurance courses (out of about 40 required for graduation). These courses cover such topics as insurance principles, property-casualty insurance, life and health insurance, group insurance and pensions, social insurance, and risk management.

College programs approach the subject of insurance from a broad, academic point of view. They generally are not thought of as providing training to handle a particular job; that is provided by the students' future employers. But those who take insurance courses often find that they are one step ahead of other students when it comes to getting jobs. A survey of large insurance companies showed that the great majority (83%) prefer to hire graduating students who have taken insurance courses.[2]

IMPORTANT TERMS

Stock insurance company

Mutual insurance company

Assessment mutual

Fraternal insurer

Reciprocal exchange

Lloyd's of London

American Lloyds

Self-insurance

Legal reserve

Unearned premium reserve

Loss reserve

Surplus

Underwriting capacity

Underwriting earnings

Investment earnings

Best's Insurance Reports

KEY POINTS TO REMEMBER

1. Stock insurance companies are corporations owned by stockholders and engaged in the insurance business.
2. Mutual insurance companies are nonprofit organizations owned by their policyholders.
3. Reciprocal exchanges are associations whose members insure one another. They are managed by an attorney-in-fact.
4. Lloyd's of London is an association whose members provide insurance. The business is conducted through syndicates headed by underwriters who accept insurance risks on behalf of the syndicate members.

[2]Leonard L. Berekson and William R. Randall, "The Campus Recruitment Position of Insurance Companies," *Best's Review*, October 1976.

5. Other insurance organizations are health associations, government agencies, and self-insurers.
6. The board of directors of a stock or mutual company is responsible for setting the company's general policies and objectives and for selecting officers to manage the company.
7. Most insurance companies are divided into departments that are responsible for certain functions, kinds of insurance, or territories.
8. There are three sources of company assets: original capital and surplus, premium income, and retained earnings.
9. Assets are invested to provide income and reduce the cost of insurance protection to policyholders.
10. Insurance companies are required to maintain reserves, which are liability accounts representing their future obligations.
11. Life insurers have a single legal reserve, the policy reserve. Property-casualty companies must maintain both an unearned premium reserve and a loss reserve.
12. A company's surplus is the amount by which its assets exceed its liabilities. It is needed in case the company's assets decline or its liabilities increase.
13. There are two major sources of surplus: underwriting earnings and investment earnings.
14. Insurers should be selected on the basis of their service, cost, and financial strength.
15. Best's Insurance Reports are a useful source of information about the financial condition of insurance companies.
16. Company training programs provide instruction in how to do specific jobs. Professional insurance education is offered by industry associations and universities.

REVIEW QUESTIONS

1. What are the differences between stock and mutual companies?
2. What are assessment mutuals?
3. What is the difference between a large reciprocal exchange and a large mutual insurance company?
4. How does Lloyd's of London differ from other insuring organizations?
5. What are the "names," syndicates, and underwriters at Lloyd's of London?
6. How do Blue Cross and Blue Shield differ from mutual insurance companies?
7. List eight insurance programs of the federal government.
8. What is the principal source of insurance company assets?
9. Why do insurance companies have large assets? What do they do with them? Why?
10. What are reserves? Why are insurers required to have them?
11. Property-casualty insurers have two legal reserves. What are they and what is the difference between them?
12. What is surplus? What purposes does it serve?

13. Why do property-casualty insurers need relatively more surplus than life insurers?
14. Why do insurers need to keep increasing their surpluses?
15. How do professional insurance education programs differ from company training programs?

DISCUSSION QUESTIONS

1. Both the people who own stock in stock insurance companies and the members of the syndicates at Lloyd's of London hope to earn a profit. How do the positions of the two groups of investors differ?
2. Many years ago most mutuals issued assessable policies. Most no longer do. Why do you suppose they stopped?
3. Explain why the assets of life insurance companies are so much larger than the assets of property-casualty companies, even though their total premium volume is roughly equal.
4. Explain why the investments of life insurers differ from those of property-casualty insurers.
5. Upon which would inflation have the most serious effect: life insurance companies or property-casualty companies?
6. What would be the likely result if automobile insurance companies were unable to earn money and increase their surpluses over a period of time (say five years)?
7. What do you believe is the most important factor to consider when choosing an insurer?
8. If you were to work for one or the other, which would you prefer, a life insurance company or a property-casualty company?

CHAPTER 23
GOVERNMENT REGULATION OF INSURANCE

Until now, we have concentrated upon how insurance handles many of the insurable risks of individuals and small business firms. In this concluding chapter we shall consider an entirely different aspect of insurance, its regulation by government. Government regulation of insurance is unique. Few other businesses are subject to such strict controls as insurance is, and none is controlled in exactly the same ways or for the same reasons. In this chapter we shall look into such questions as what aspects of insurance are regulated, why they are regulated, and how they are regulated. Studying questions like these can provide insights not only about insurance itself, but also about the U.S. economic system and the relationships between government and other types of business.

Governmental agencies in one way or another influence almost all kinds of business activity. Business firms of all types are subject to regulations concerning such things as employment practices, employee safety, pollution control, and minimum wage rates. However, a few kinds of business are supervised much more strictly than others are. These are called "regulated industries." Regulated industries include public utilities (such as power companies and telephone companies), transportation companies (airlines, railroads, and truckers), banks and insurance companies.

To illustrate the extent of insurance regulation, insurance companies cannot start operating unless they have the funds (capital and surplus) required by law; few other businesses must meet such a requirement. Although most other businesses can have their products sold by whomever they choose, insurance can be marketed only through agents or brokers officially licensed by the state. Most other goods and services can be designed and priced as the manufacturers and retailers wish, but insurance policy forms and premium rates commonly are subject to state approval. Although most other businesses can spend their income in whatever ways they wish, insurance companies are required to maintain large reserves to protect their policyholders. Why is insurance regulated so strictly? To answer that question, let us look at the goals of insurance regulation.

GOALS OF INSURANCE REGULATION

Insurance regulation has four main goals: (a) to prevent insurer insolvency, (b) to prevent fraud, (c) to make sure that policies are reasonably priced, and (d) to make insurance protection widely available.

Prevention of Insolvency

Guarding against the bankruptcy of insurance companies is the most important goal of insurance regulation. Several forms of government control, including capital and surplus rules and reserve requirements, are specifically designed to help prevent company insolvencies. This is interesting, because the government makes no attempt to keep most other kinds of business from going broke. If a restaurant or a gas station fails to make a profit and must close, we figure that probably there wasn't enough demand for its services or that it wasn't being run efficiently. In either case, this is the way a competitive free enterprise system is supposed to work. The companies that are not filling an important need or that are not able to compete successfully drop out and leave those that are most needed and best run. The people who had invested in the bankrupt businesses lose their money and the people who had worked for them lose their jobs, but the general public benefits because it presumably gets the goods and services it wants and gets them at reasonable prices. This is a simplified explanation and is based on the assumption that the businesses are competitive. However, it explains why competition, rather than government, is chiefly relied upon to protect the consumer and why company failures usually are considered to be a normal and necessary part of the business system.

What is different about insurance companies that causes government to want to prevent insolvencies? The difference is that the value of insurance to the purchaser depends upon the continued solvency of the insurer. If we buy a television set and the manufacturer later goes broke, we still have the set; it doesn't stop working when the company goes out of business. But if an insurer becomes bankrupt and stops paying benefits, its policies become worthless, because insurance policies are contracts calling for future services by the insurer. The premium is paid in advance and claims, if any, are paid later. If the company becomes insolvent, not only do the investors lose their money and the employees lose their jobs, but the policyholders (plus beneficiaries and third-party claimants) lose their protection.

We should also note a closely related point. Because insurance policies are contracts for the provision of future services, the cost to the insurer is not known at the time of the sale; it has to be estimated. If a company underestimates the number of its future losses or their cost, it will set its rates too low. This point was illustrated during the early 1970s. Many property-casualty insurers at that time misjudged the speed at which the cost of liability claim settlements was rising. As a result, their policies were underpriced, which was one of the factors leading to enormous underwriting losses a few years later. This is a problem which most other businesses do not have. When a television manufacturer sets it prices, it knows exactly what its labor, materials, and other costs are. The fact that insurers do not know the cost of their products at the time they are sold means there always is a chance that rates will be set too low, thus endangering the companies' solvency. This is an added reason for government supervision of insurance.

Prevention of Fraud

The second goal of insurance regulation, protecting policy buyers against being cheated by their insurers, stems from the technical nature of insurance. There are two aspects of this point. First, the policies themselves are complicated legal documents that few buyers are able to understand. In the absence of regulation, their complicated nature would make it easy for insurers to use tricky or misleading wording to avoid paying claims. Second, the worth of a policy depends upon the insurer's continued solvency, as we have seen. Of course, each company will say that it is strong and well managed, that its surplus and reserves are adequate, and that its funds are safely invested. But how can a buyer know whether or not these things are true? The fact is that without regulation very few consumers would have any way to tell a strong, well-managed company from one that was teetering on the brink of bankruptcy. State regulators, however, can examine company records to make sure that reserves, investments, and so forth are exactly as the company claims them to be.

Reasonableness of Rates

The third of the major objectives of insurance regulation is to keep rates and premiums at reasonable levels or, in other words, to prevent them from being too high. An insurer wanting to raise the rates it charges for auto or homeowners policies, for instance, must (in most states) file the new rates with the state insurance department. If the department objects to the increase, the company cannot make the change.

As with regulations aimed at preventing insurer insolvency, this is an unusual type of control. Most U.S. business organizations, from neighborhood lemonade stands to General Motors, are free to offer their products for as high a price as they wish. They are free to do this because it is assumed that competition among sellers will prevent any one of them from being able to charge unreasonably high prices. Furthermore, and very importantly, antitrust laws prevent the sellers from getting together and agreeing not to undercut each other's prices.

Insurance is an exception. Insurance prices are controlled by the government. The reason (as explained in Chapter 20) is the law of large numbers. Insurance rates are based upon statistical records of past experience and upon the assumption that future experience will be similar to that of the past. Generally speaking, the broader the record of past experience, the more accurate the predictions drawn from it will be. Therefore, rates based upon the combined experience of many insurers will tend to be more reliable than rates based upon the experience of a single insurer, especially if it is a small one. Thus, insurance companies are not subject to the price-fixing prohibitions of the antitrust laws. Instead, lawmakers have permitted the companies in this particular industry to set their prices on the basis of their combined experience. In most states sixty insurance companies can combine the data of their past premiums and losses and, if they wish, all sixty can charge the same prices. To the extent that this is done, price competition is eliminated and does not function to keep prices down to reasonable levels. Government regulation then takes the place of price competition to prevent prices from going too high.

Most of the states began regulating insurance rates in the late 1940s.[1] At that time there was very little price competition among property-casualty insurers. There is much more today, especially in auto insurance, and it can be argued that the need for rate regulation has declined.

Availability of Protection

The final goal of insurance regulation is to make insurance protection available to all persons who need it. The state Automobile Insurance Plans, for instance, were established to make auto liability insurance available to many drivers who would not otherwise be able to obtain it. In addition, the laws of many states restrict mid-term cancellation of auto policies and bar unfair discrimination among applicants for coverage. Other measures aimed at making protection more widely available include federal programs that reinsure private compaines writing high-risk property and crime insurance. Government agencies have also taken steps to preserve the availability of medical malpractice and products liability protection.

This is a relatively new goal of insurance regulation. It presents some difficult problems because, on the one hand, insurance companies are private organizations and their managers argue that they should have the right to decide whom to insure or not to insure. On the other hand, some kinds of insurance are practically essential in modern society and there is a growing belief that they should be available to all persons who need them. Workers who must drive to their jobs need auto insurance; doctors need malpractice liability coverage; manufacturers need products insurance. The real difficulty arises when insurers believe they cannot furnish the protection profitably. In extreme cases, two courses of action may then have to be considered. First, insurers may be forced to write the coverage at a loss. This is being done in the operation of some of the state Automobile Insurance Plans and some of the FAIR plans for high-risk property insurance. Second, the government can step in and furnish the protection. The establishment of the Maryland Automobile Insurance Fund and of the Medicare program are instances where this was done.

[1] New York and a few other states started earlier.

THE DEVELOPMENT OF REGULATION

Over the years, government has established more and more regulations concerning the operation of various kinds of business. Many of these controls were at first imposed by the states, but with the passage of time most regulation has become concentrated in the hands of the federal government. One of the interesting things about insurance regulation is that even though it could be centralized in Washington most of it continues to be handled by the state governments instead. To understand why, we must see how insurance regulation came about.

Establishment of State Insurance Departments

Until shortly before the Civil War, scarcely any efforts were made to supervise the insurance business. The states encouraged the establishment of companies and at the same time imposed taxes upon their premium income. Some of the states required the companies to publish annual reports, but beyond this insurers were free to operate as they wished, just as other kinds of business were. Gradually, the need for regulation became apparent. Unfair policy provisions were being used; many companies lacked adequate reserves; company funds were invested recklessly; insurers frequently became bankrupt. It was clear that the public needed protection. Less obviously, the companies also would benefit from controls that stabilized the business and prevented deceptive, cut-throat competition.

In 1850, New Hampshire became the first state to appoint a commissioner of insurance. The first state department of insurance was created in Massachusetts in 1855; three years later Elizur Wright was appointed Massachusetts insurance commissioner. Wright, a mathematics professor, did more than any other person to shape the future direction of insurance supervision. Through his efforts the concept of regulation to preserve insurer solvency became established. During the years that followed, additional states set up departments to oversee the activities of the companies operating within their borders.

Paul vs. *Virginia*

A Supreme Court case decided in 1869 established the legal right of the state governments to regulate insurance. The case involved Samuel Paul, a Virginia insurance agent who sold fire insurance policies on behalf of several New York companies. The Virginia law imposed special requirements upon agents representing out-of-state insurers. Paul refused to comply with those requirements and as a result was fined $50. He appealed his case to the federal courts. Paul argued that the insurance business was commerce and in this case was interstate commerce. Because the United States Constitution reserves control over interstate commerce to the federal government, Paul claimed that the Virginia law was unconstitutional.

The Supreme Court rejected Paul's argument, saying that the issuance of an insurance policy was not commerce. Insurance policies are personal contracts, the Court said, and "not commodities to be shipped . . . from one State to another and then put up for sale."[2] On the basis of the **Paul v. Virginia** decision, insurance was not subject to the commerce clause of the Constitution and could not be controlled by the federal government. Therefore, state regulations like Virginia's were upheld.

The *Paul* v. *Virginia* case is important, not because Mr. Paul had to pay the $50 fine, but because it established the right of the state governments to regulate insurance. The doctrine that insurance was not commerce stood for the following 75 years. During that period, the states continued to develop the laws, departments, staffs, and other apparatus needed for regulating insurance.

The Rating Bureaus

The most troublesome aspect of insurance regulation was controlling fire insurance rate levels. The companies had found that important benefits could be gained by joining together in associations (later called "**rating bureaus**") and agreeing not to undercut one another's rates. This practice prevented what they called "cut-throat competition" and reduced the number of company insolvencies. It also made the business more profitable.

At first, many of the states tried to prevent such cooperative pricing arrangements. Then, in 1911, a committee of the New York State Legislature (the Merritt Committee) published the results of an investigation it had made. After studying the matter at length, the Committee had decided that it would be best to let the companies form rating bureaus and establish their rates jointly. Rates based upon the combined experience of a group of companies would be more reliable, the Committee said, and the companies would be stronger. However, in exchange for permitting the companies to do this, the State must approve of the rates. In other words, the Merritt Committee proposed that cooperative rate-making be legalized in New York and that the jointly made rates be controlled by the State.

The New York legislature adopted the Merritt Committee's plan, and most of the other states followed New York's lead. This action set the pattern, both for state regulation and for industry organization. The property-casualty

[2]*Paul* v. *Virginia,* 8 Wall. 183 (1869).

insurance industry expanded rapidly with the enactment of the workers' compensation laws and the development of automotive transportation. And, as the industry grew, the rating bureaus gained strength. Almost all of the hundreds of insurers belonged to the bureaus and used the same bureau-made rates. The state laws and insurance departments supported and encouraged this system on the grounds that price competition would weaken the industry and undermine the public's insurance protection.

The South-Eastern Underwriters Association Case

In the South-Eastern Underwriters Association case, which was decided in 1944, the Supreme Court reversed the *Paul* v. *Virginia* doctrine. The South-Eastern Underwriters Association (SEUA) was a fire insurance rating bureau with headquarters in Atlanta, Georgia. About 200 stock insurance companies were members. The SEUA was charged with violating the federal Sherman Antitrust Act by monopolizing the fire insurance business in a six-state area and by "fixing and maintaining arbitrary and non-competitive premium rates."[3]

The SEUA based its defense on the *Paul* v. *Virginia* doctrine that insurance was not commerce and that because the Sherman Antitrust Act pertained only to commerce it did not apply to insurance rating bureaus. However, the Supreme Court reversed its earlier position, saying that insurance is commerce and therefore is subject to federal control when conducted between states. This ruling thus meant that the Sherman Antitrust Act prohibited cooperative pricing by insurance companies, just as it prohibits such action by the companies in any other industry.

The McCarran Act

For the insurance industry, the SEUA decision was a shocking development. It implied that from now on each individual insurer would have to determine its rates on the basis of its own experience, no matter how limited that experience was. State officials were also distressed. It appeared that they were going to lose their control over this business and be forced to lay off many of the people employed by their insurance departments.

The Congress quickly came to the rescue, passing the **McCarran Act** the following year (1945). This Act says that continued regulation by the states is in the public interest. It also says that the federal antitrust acts apply to insurance only "to the extent that such business is not regulated by state law." Therefore, if state regulation is strong and effective, the federal antitrust laws will continue to be inapplicable to insurance.

[3]*U.S.* v. *SEUA*, et al., 322 U.S. 533 (1944).

This legal philosophy applies today. The Supreme Court has said that the Congress can regulate insurance (when transacted across state lines, as most of it is), and the Congress has said that it chooses not to do so. Thus, regulation is left in the hands of the states, but the federal government can take over when and if it elects to repeal the McCarran Act.

THE MACHINERY OF STATE REGULATION

We have examined the reasons for insurance regulation and have seen why it developed at the state level. In this section and the next we shall discover how the regulations are carried out and what they control.

The State Insurance Departments

Each of the state legislatures has adopted numerous laws relating to insurance. Many of the laws are long and detailed; in many states they total several hundred pages in length. To administer these laws, each state has established an **insurance department** as part of the executive branch of the government.

Each insurance department is headed by an **insurance commissioner** (in some states called superintendent or director). In a few states the commissioner is elected, but in most he or she is appointed by the governor. The commissioner has chief responsibility for administering the insurance laws of the state. Assisting the commissioner is the department staff, which in most the states numbers between 50 and 100 persons.

The National Association of Insurance Commissioners

The **National Association of Insurance Commissioners** (NAIC) is an interesting organization. There is little doubt that state insurance regulation could not succeed without it; yet it is not a governmental body and can neither enact nor enforce legislation. It is essential, because it prevents the confusion and expense that would result if each of the 50 states developed its own laws and regulations without regard to what the others were doing.

The full membership of the NAIC meets twice each year. Between the dates of the national meetings, regional meetings are held. In addition, various committees work on specific topics throughout the year. To illustrate, one of the committees is in charge of deciding what information is to be included in the financial statements that the companies must submit to the insurance departments each year. The committee has developed a standard form (or "blank") that is used by all of the states. Although some states require additional information, the use of a single standard form saves a great deal of time and expense on the part of the companies' accounting departments.

Much of the work of the NAIC concerns the development of legislative proposals. When it appears to the members that a new law may be needed, the appropriate committee studies the matter. If a majority of the committee agrees upon what is needed, a proposed statute is drawn up and is presented to the entire membership at one of the semiannual meetings. Adoption of such a proposal by the full membership has no legal effect, since the NAIC does not have authority to enact laws. But it is an important step, because the organization has approved a "model bill" and is recommending its enactment by the various states. Although some of the states may reject the model bill completely and others may adopt it in modified form, out of this process comes substantial uniformity among the state laws pertaining to insurance regulation.

WHAT IS REGULATED?

Three aspects of insurance are regulated: (a) company financial strength, (b) rates and forms, and (c) sales and sales practices. The major regulations in each category can be summarized as follows:

1. *Company Financial Strength*
   a. *Capital and surplus requirements.* The laws of each state specify minimum financial requirements for newly organized insurers of various types. Also, regulators expect established insurers to have enough surplus to serve as a cushion in the event of unexpected claim costs or declines in the value of company investments.
   b. *Investments.* Regulations guard against high-risk, speculative investments. Control of life insurers' investments is especially strict, severely limiting the percentage of their assets that can be invested in common stocks or in the ownership of real estate.
   c. *Reserves.* All insurance companies are required to have reserves that represent their future obligations. As explained in Chapter 22, life insurers must maintain large policy reserves, whereas property-casualty companies must have unearned premium reserves and loss reserves. The method of calculating the reserves is specified by the states.
2. *Rates and Forms*
   a. *Rates.* Property-casualty rates are controlled by state laws that prohibit "excessive, inadequate, or unfairly discriminatory" rates. Life insurance rates must not discriminate unfairly but are not otherwise

controlled directly. They are controlled indirectly by the policy reserve requirement in the sense that rates must be at the level necessary to generate the assets needed to offset the reserve.

b. *Forms.* The state insurance departments have authority to forbid the use of deceptive, unfair, or ambiguous policy forms.

3. *Sales and Sales Methods*

   a. *Licensing of agents.* Insurance companies are permitted to do business only through agents or brokers holding licenses issued by the state insurance department.

   b. *Sales methods.* The laws of most states forbid unfair selling methods, including misrepresentation, twisting, and rebating. "Misrepresentation" includes making untrue statements about the policy coverage or financial condition of an insurer. "Twisting" is expressing unfair comparisons of policies in order to induce a policyholder to drop an existing policy and replace it with a new one. "Rebating" is giving a policybuyer part of the agent's selling commission.

METHODS OF REGULATION

In this section we shall review the chief methods that are used to carry out the regulations just summarized.

Company Financial Strength

The regulations concerning capital and surplus, investments, and reserves are enforced through a system of annual reports and company examination.

Each company must submit an **annual statement** to each of the states in which it operates. These reports use the standard NAIC form referred to earlier. The form, over 50 pages long, is designed to reveal complete information about the reporting company's financial operations and condition. It includes detailed exhibits of such things as the company's income, disbursements, investments, and reserves.

How do the insurance commissioners know that the information contained in the annual statement is correct? The answer is that they verify it periodically with an **examination** of company records by state-employed auditors. Each company's home office records are physically examined every few years (three or five, usually). The department auditors make a thorough investigation, verifying the information submitted in the annual statements and confirming that all legal requirements are being met. They make sure that the company has the assets reported in its annual statement and that its investments are worth as much as the company says they are.

The auditors review the company's reserves to see that they have been computed properly and represent the company's future obligations in the manner that the law requires. Such an examination is a time-consuming process. Depending upon the size of the company, it may take many weeks or months to complete.

Without cooperation among the states, the examination process would be extremely wasteful and expensive. Each state would need to employ a huge staff of auditors and, at the larger companies, numerous examinations would be under way at any given time. To avoid this, a system of zone examinations has been devised by the NAIC. The country is divided into six zones, each containing about eight or nine states. Examinations are conducted by teams of auditors. A typical team consists of one auditor from the company's home state and one from one of the states in each of the other zones where the company operates. The auditing teams submit reports of their examinations to each of the states where the company does business. This system minimizes both the number of examinations and the number of auditors conducting them.

Rates and Forms

Insurance rates and policy forms are regulated in various ways, depending upon the kind of insurance and the particular state that is involved. In most states, property-casualty rates and forms must be filed with the insurance department before they are put into use.

When rate filings are made, the companies must also submit the loss and expense data that the proposed rates are based on and they must show exactly how the rates were calculated. The insurance departments evaluate the filings in terms of the three statutory rate standards that prohibit excessive, inadequate, and unfairly discriminatory rates. If a department disapproves a filing, the company cannot use the rates.

The strictness of property-casualty rate regulation varies among the states. At one extreme are the states whose laws require explicit approval by the insurance commissioner prior to the use of the new rates. At the other extreme are a number of states that have adopted "open competition" rate laws. In the latter states there is an assumption that competition, when it is effective, regulates prices fully as well as the government can. The insurance commissioner in these states has authority to prevent the use of rates that violate any of the rate standards, just as the commissioners in the other states do. But here the rates do not have to be filed and approved before they are put into use, and the insurance department usually does not interfere with the rate-setting process.

As noted earlier, life insurance rates are not regulated in the manner that property-casualty rates are. The control in this case is indirect and is based upon supervision of mortality tables, dividends, and the interest rates used in computing reserves. In addition, one important state (New York) sets a limit on the percentage of a premium that can be paid as commission to the agent selling the policy. In combination with reserve requirements, these various controls indirectly help prevent life insurance rates from being inadequate and thereby endangering the companies' ability to pay their claims.

State regulation of rate levels is a controversial topic, particularly in auto and life insurance. In auto insurance, the companies complain that the insurance departments of some states force them to use inadequate rates. By repeatedly turning down requests for needed rate increases, they say, the regulators are forcing them to use rates so low that they lose money on the auto coverage they write in those states. The companies insist that, if this practice goes on for a long period, either they will have to stop writing auto insurance in those states or else their policyholders in other states will have to make up for the losses in the low-rate states.

In life insurance, the controversy concerns "cost disclosure," a topic that we considered in Chapter 14. As we noted there, life insurance rates and premiums often do not reflect the true cost of the policies. Because of the complications of cash values and policy dividends, a policy having a low price (premium) may actually have a high cost and vice versa. The interest-adjusted method of computing policy costs was designed to give consumers a better method to compare the costs of various life insurance policies. The NAIC has recommended that the states require life insurers to give policy-buyers detailed cost information. Several states have responded to this recommendation. In those states, buyers must receive written statements containing interest-adjusted cost indexes and other information about any policy at the time it is purchased. Some life insurance agents and company people oppose these requirements. They say that the interest-adjusted method is too difficult to understand, and that it leads buyers to over-emphasize minor differences in policy costs.

Policy form regulation includes such things as requiring property insurance on homes to include deductibles, and forbidding the sale of accident policies that provide very limited protection. (Both examples prevail in some states, but not all.)

Sales and Sales Methods

Regulation in this area is based on the licensing of agents and brokers. The states issue licenses only after prospective agents or brokers pass written examinations covering insurance policy provisions and state laws relating to insurance. Until recent years, the examinations in some states proved little except that the applicants could read, write, and pay the required fee. The requirements are changing, however; in a number of states the examinations now are rigorous enough to guarantee that those who pass them have a good, basic knowledge of insurance.

The regulations concerning sales methods include those forbidding misrepresentation, twisting, and rebating. They are enforced by the investigation of complaints brought to insurance departments by the public, and by fining agents who use such methods. In extreme cases, agents' licenses may be suspended or revoked. Taking away an agent's license is a severe penalty, because it deprives the person of his or her livelihood. It seldom has to be done, but an insurance department's power to take this step strengthens its ability to enforce the law.

GUARANTY FUNDS

Earlier in this chapter, we noted the serious impact that insolvency of an insurance company can have for insureds, beneficiaries, and third party claimants. We also have seen that preventing insurer insolvency is the primary goal of insurance regulation. In spite of the efforts of insurance regulators to prevent them, a few insolvencies do occur. Most of the companies that fail are small and many of them are specialists in high-risk protection. Regardless, for a person relying on it for financial security, the failure of any insurer could be a serious blow.

Responding to this problem, almost all of the states have established **insurance guaranty funds**[4] to protect policyholders and claimants from heavy financial loss when a company fails. The funds apply only to property-casualty companies, as bankruptcy of other insurers has not been a widespread problem. With a few exceptions, the guaranty funds operate on the "post-solvency assessment" basis; that is, they do not build up reserves in advance as insurance companies usually do. Instead, they assess the state's other property-casualty insurers after a particular company fails. The maximum assessment in most states is 2% of the assessed companies' total premium volume. The funds assure the payment of covered losses up to a stated maximum, typically $300,000. In most states there is a $100 deductible per claim. If your auto insurer went bankrupt and it owed you $3,000 for covered medical expenses, the state's guaranty fund would see to it that you got your money, subject to the $100 deductible.

The money used by these funds comes indirectly from other insurance

---

[4]As of August, 1977, only Alabama and Oklahoma had not established funds. The laws setting up funds in Arizona and Utah had been ruled unconstitutional.

consumers. That is, the money is obtained by assessing solvent insurers, and the basic source of those companies' funds is the premiums they receive from their policyholders. Thus, the money paid by the guaranty funds to some policyholders comes indirectly from other policyholders. During the period 1969–1979, these payments totaled in excess of $200 million.

CONSUMER SERVICES

Broadly speaking, all of the activities of the state insurance departments are intended to serve consumers. In a more limited sense, two of the services are furnished directly to consumers. These are complaint handling and shoppers' guides.

Complaint Handling

The following is an excerpt from a letter to the Iowa Insurance Department, dated September 14:

I bought two policies from [named] Insurance Co. on July 22. One was a skilled nursing home policy and I paid $232.50 in premiums. The other was a Medicare supplement and I paid $205.25 for it. I have never received either policy, and sent into the company to refund my money. I am 84 years old and think this agent is trying to take my money.

Another letter to the department from the same woman, dated October 7, said:

Why don't I hear from someone? I don't hear from the agent or company or you. What has gone wrong? Did I do something wrong? Would like to hear from you or the company soon, as this sure worries me. I was told if I mailed the policies back right away, they would have to pay me. I only had them one day. [5]

Actually, the department had contacted the insurance company shortly after it received the first letter. On October 6 the company wrote the department, promising to refund the two premiums. The department then passed this word along to the woman and the problem was solved.

Handling consumer complaints is one of the important services performed by the state insurance departments. Illustrating the diversity of this service,

[5] *Des Moines Register,* March 20, 1978.

the Illinois Insurance Department in a recent year investigated over 12,000 complaints. The largest number (44%) involved automobile insurance. The next most heavily represented areas were health and life insurance, with 33% and 11%, respectively, of the total complaints. Over three-fourths of the complaints concerned the handling of claims.

Many of the departments have individuals or divisions whose main duty is dealing with questions and complaints. Consumers should be aware of this service and should phone or write their insurance department if they believe their companies or agents are treating them unfairly.

Shoppers' Guides

Several of the states have published booklets furnishing information about the personal lines of insurance. These usually are called "shoppers' guides" or "consumers' guides." They are designed to help buyers choose policies and insurers more intelligently. The guides describe insurance coverages, give tips on how much to buy, explain what to do after a loss, and so forth. A few states have gone beyond offering descriptive information and have included tables comparing the costs of various companies' policies. For auto and homeowners, such a list generally compares premiums for several typical combinations of coverage, at several locations in the state. For life insurance, interest-adjusted cost indexes may be shown.

Everyone seems to agree that the objective of the shoppers' guides is a proper one, but many have serious doubts about their true value. Critics have come down especially hard on the inclusion of cost data. A Wisconsin Insurance Commissioner even called the guides "deceptive and misleading to the consumer."[6] One of the objections is that cost data become obsolete too soon to be worthwhile—particularly auto and homeowners rates, most of which are revised every year. If a consumer consults a homeowners insurance guide in November and the guide shows rates that were being used in March, most of the information can already be out of date. A second objection is that in a line like auto insurance it is dangerous to generalize about high-cost or low-cost companies. A company whose rates are low for one set of classification factors in one locality may have high rates for other drivers or for other rating territories. And even lengthy shoppers' guides cannot show all of the thousands of different rates.

Critics also say that shoppers' guides that compare prices cause consumers to overemphasize that particular factor. The guides usually caution their readers to consider other things in addition to price, such as company claims practices and agency service. However, the guides do not quantify anything

---

[6]*National Underwriter,* December 18, 1972.

but prices, a fact that makes it easy—probably too easy—for users to base their buying decisions on price alone.

Because of the criticisms of shoppers' guides (and the cost of preparing and distributing them), they have been issued by only a few of the states. Several that issued them in response to strong consumer interest during the early 1970s have since either dropped them completely or have stopped including cost data.

STATE VERSUS FEDERAL REGULATION

Since 1944, when the South-Eastern Underwriters Association case was decided, the federal government has had constitutional authority to regulate insurance. As we know, the Congress permitted state regulation to continue by adopting the McCarran Act in 1945. Should the Congress repeal the McCarran Act and create a system of federal regulation? This question has been discussed since 1945. Recently the sentiment in favor of federal control seems to have been growing. Let us review the principal arguments, both pro and con.

The Case for Federal Regulation

Arguments for federal control stress two main points: uniformity and effectiveness. Uniformity, of course, refers to the replacement of fifty separate state regulatory systems (plus Puerto Rico and the District of Columbia) with a single federal agency. The idea of exchanging the present variety of laws, rules, forms, and procedures for a single set of controls is especially appealing to some of the companies that operate throughout the country and therefore work under the supervision of many different insurance departments. In addition, it is argued that federal control would be more effective. Some of the small states whose insurance departments operate with small budgets are particularly vulnerable on this point. Although a few states (most notably New York and California) have large, well-staffed departments, those at the other end of the financial scale have to get along on very limited resources. Federal regulation, its supporters argue, would be more effective because it would be conducted with an adequate budget and would be handled by a sufficient number of well-qualified persons.

The Case for State Regulation

The supporters of state regulation, who at least until now have been on the winning side of this debate, base their case on flexibility and workability. The flexibility of state control is very important, they say. The state governments are more aware of local needs and can adapt to them, whereas a centralized bureaucracy would be bogged down by red tape. This point is particularly important to agents and to the smaller companies; many of them feel that their voice is heard in the state capitals but is ignored in Washington. Those who oppose federal control also argue that state regulation has been shown to be workable. It is a going system, they say, that is doing the job it is supposed to do. Therefore, it would be foolish to tear it down to substitute a system that would be no better and might be worse. According to this view, one reason that state regulation functions well is the work of the National Association of Insurance Commissioners; the NAIC has brought to state regulation the advantages that federal regulation theoretically is supposed to have, so state regulation should be retained.

Dual Regulation

It is possible that a compromise, dual state-federal system will be established some day. Former Senator Edward Brooke of Massachusetts proposed such a system for property-casualty companies. They would be given the option of taking part in a new Federal Insurance Fund instead of participating in the state guaranty funds that were described earlier. In contrast to the post-solvency assessment by the state funds, the federal fund would be operated on a presolvency assessment basis, building up reserves in advance for the protection of policyholders and claimants. The companies would be assessed a known amount by a single federal guaranty fund instead of being subject to numerous state postsolvency assessments. Thus, the companies would be relieved of the risk of multiple assessments in the event that a number of insurers became bankrupt in various states during the same year. If this proposal were adopted, insurers also would be able to operate under federal charters and federal regulation if they chose to do so. In return, they would be freed from state rate regulation. The proposal has received little support in the Congress so far. However, changes like this frequently occur only after a proposal has been considered, debated, and revised over a period of several years. It therefore appears that the issue of state versus federal regulation will exist for some time to come.

CHALLENGES AND OPPORTUNITIES

Insurance exists in a world of change, a world that is a constant source of new challenges and opportunities. This currently is illustrated by the new field of space insurance that is being developed to cover communications satellites, space shuttles, and other ventures into "the final frontier." The list of changes to which insurance must respond is practically endless. It includes: the rising cost of medical care and the likelihood that some type of national health insurance will be adopted; changes in the traditional family structure and their uncertain impact on financial planning, including life insurance; continuing threats to our physical environment, raising questions about the desirability of pollution insurance; internationalization of business activity and the corresponding need for insurance in a multitude of social and political systems; international terrorism and resulting demands for kidnap and ransom insurance; deterioration of the cities, creating difficult problems for the suppliers of property insurance and crime insurance. We shall briefly review three other areas of challenge and opportunity, those of inflation, affordability, and education.

Inflation

We all are aware of inflation, the continuing increase in price and wage levels and the resulting decline in the purchasing power of the dollar. Inflation has an especially strong impact on insurance.

For property-casualty insurance, rising price levels mean rising loss payments; when medical costs, repair bills and negligence awards go up, so do payments for auto accidents, employee injuries and other losses in this field. The result, of course, is necessary increases in premium levels. But beyond that obvious consequence are unresolved questions: Can rates based on past loss experience produce adequate premiums when prices are rising? Can insurers meet the public's need for protection when losses are rising at a rapid rate? Will the state insurance regulators permit necessary rate increases—particularly if the voting public does not understand why they are needed?

Inflation has an entirely different impact upon life insurance. Here it does not cause an increase in benefit payments, because they are fixed. The beneficiary of a $50,000 policy still gets $50,000 and the cash value of a $50,000 endowment at 65 is still $50,000. The problem is that $50,000 is worth far less when it is received than it was when the policies were being paid for, a fact which may discourage potential life insurance buyers in the future, particularly those considering the use of cash value policies for long-term savings. The life insurance industry is developing new contracts that are designed to help purchasers meet this problem, but to adapt life insurance successfully to a world of inflation will be a continuing challenge and opportunity.

Affordability

Affordability means the ability to pay. Earlier in this chapter we noted that one of the goals of insurance regulation is to make protection available to all who need it. That is a new goal; only in recent years has government taken responsibility for the **availability** of insurance. The concept of affordability is closely related to the goal of availability. It is argued that if some people cannot afford to buy insurance then it is not really available to everyone. The unanswered question is whether or not it *should* be made available for everyone. That is, should the government see to it that insurance costs are kept low enough so everyone can afford to buy it? When liability insurance costs skyrocketed during the late 1970s some manufacturers went out of business, saying they could not afford products liability insurance and did not want to stay in business without it. Some doctors retired early, expressing similar complaints about the cost of professional liability protection. For some motorists, auto insurance is not really affordable. Young drivers in large cities face staggering premiums, especially if they drive powerful cars or have poor driving records. The insurance companies of course point to the frequency and severity of covered losses as the reason for these high premiums. Although these are proper explanations, they do not eliminate the affordability issue.

One way to make insurance more affordable concerns class rating, which was discussed in Chapter 20. Eliminating rating classifications would lower the cost for those in the high cost classifications. However, this would be achieved at the expense of those in the lower cost classifications, because their premiums would have to be increased to avoid a reduction in the insurance companies' total premium income—income that is needed to pay for losses and expenses. Should rating classifications be changed to make insurance more affordable? Which insureds should pay less and which should pay more? Who should decide? Finding answers to those questions is another of the challenges facing insurers today.

Education

To understand how problems such as inflation and the affordability issue affect policyholders and insurance companies, one must have some knowledge of insurance and how it operates. Unfortunately, the general public is very poorly informed in this regard. This lack of understanding is illustrated by a survey in which people were asked how many cents of each premium dollar auto insurers keep as profit and how many cents they should keep. The consensus of those questioned was that the companies retain an average of 39 cents of each dollar and that they should keep 22 cents. The average amount auto insurers actually do keep is less than 5 cents! Such an exaggerated idea of profits probably helps explain why many people think insurance prices are too high and why they are insisting that policies be made more affordable. On a related point, the same survey found that only one person in four knows that auto insurance prices are regulated by the government.

Perhaps even more important is the public's lack of awareness of the basic nature of insurance as a system of handling risk by combining loss exposures and sharing costs. Without a knowledge of this concept, it is easy to think that an insurance policy is worthless unless it pays for a loss and that insurance companies somehow are sources of unlimited sums of money waiting to be tapped at no cost to anyone.

Educating the public about insurance principles and practices certainly is a major challenge; it cannot be accomplished quickly or easily. It also is an important opportunity for both the public and the insurance industry. Those who understand what insurance is and how it operates are able to act as responsible citizens in helping shape the goals of insurance regulation. In addition, people who understand insurance are able to use it wisely as an effective method of business and personal risk management.

IMPORTANT TERMS

Paul v. *Virginia*
Rating Bureau
South-Eastern Underwriters Association
   case
McCarran Act
Insurance department
Insurance guaranty funds

National Association of Insurance
   Commissioners
Annual statement
Company examination
Affordability
Availability

KEY POINTS TO REMEMBER

1. The principal goals of insurance regulation are (a) to prevent insurer insolvency, (b) to prevent fraud, (c) to make sure that policies are reasonably priced, and (d) to make insurance protection widely available.
2. The legal right of the states to regulate insurance was established by the *Paul* v. *Virginia* case of 1869.
3. The South-Eastern Underwriters Association case of 1944 established the right of the federal government to regulate insurance.
4. The McCarran Act of 1945 permitted the states to continue their regulation of insurance.
5. Uniformity of insurance regulation among the states is promoted by the National Association of Insurance Commissioners.
6. The main aspects of insurance which are regulated are (a) company financial strength, (b) rates and forms, and (c) sales and sales practices.
7. State guaranty funds are designed to protect insureds and claimants from serious financial loss following the insolvency of a property-casualty insurer.
8. Critics of state regulation cite uniformity and effectiveness as advantages of federal regulation. Those who support state regulation emphasize its flexibility and workability.

9. Inflation has a strong impact on insurance, although it affects life insurance and property-casualty insurance in different ways.
10. Some people are urging that affordability be added to the goals of insurance regulation.
11. There is a great need to educate the public about the nature and use of insurance.

REVIEW QUESTIONS

1. What is there about insurer insolvencies that justifies government regulation designed to prevent them?
2. What are the chief methods of safeguarding the financial strength of insurance companies?
3. What are the main issues relative to insurance rate regulation?
4. What are insurance guaranty funds, and how do they operate?
5. What services do the state insurance departments furnish directly to insurance consumers?
6. Why are insurance shoppers' guides controversial?
7. What does dual regulation mean?
8. How does the affordability of insurance relate to its availability?

DISCUSSION QUESTIONS

1. The Sherman Antitrust Act of 1890 prohibits monopolistic price fixing by various firms within an industry. Why didn't it prevent the use of rating bureaus in the property-casualty insurance industry?
2. In most states, the insurance commissioner is appointed by the governor. Some people say that instead of being a political appointee, the commissioner should be part of the civil service and should be promoted to the commissioner's job solely on the basis of merit. Do you agree?
3. With few exceptions, government does not regulate the prices charged by U.S. business firms. As this is the case, do you think that insurance rates (auto insurance, for instance) should be regulated?
4. (a) Do you think the state insurance departments should publish shoppers' guides? (b) If so, should the guides compare the prices charged by various insurers?
5. The future of insurance shoppers' guides may depend upon the extent of public interest in them. Why and how would public interest have such an influence?
6. Would federal insurance regulation be preferable to state regulation?
7. Chapter 23 noted that some of the state Automobile Insurance Plans are operated at a loss. That is, auto insurers are required to make insurance available through the AIP's, even if they lose money in doing so. When this happens, who pays for the loss?

APPEN-
DICES

APPENDIX A
GLOSSARY

Accident insurance. A form of health insurance covering accidental injuries.

Accidental bodily injury. In health insurance, an injury to the insured person that is unintended and unexpected. See also accidental means.

Accidental death benefit. A life insurance policy provision that pays the beneficiary an extra amount if the insured is killed by accidental means. If the benefit equals the face amount it is commonly called double indemnity.

Accidental means. In health insurance, an unintended and unexpected occurrence that causes injury to the insured person. When this term is applied, both the injury and its cause must be accidental. See also accidental bodily injury.

Actual cash value. The traditional measure of property insurance loss. Usually defined as the cost of replacing the destroyed property with new property, minus an allowance for depreciation.

Actuary. A person professionally trained in the technical aspects of insurance and related fields, particularly in the mathematics of insurance.

Additional living expense coverage. Insurance for the increase in living costs incurred as a result of damage to an insured residence.

Adjuster. See claims adjuster.

Advanced underwriting specialist. An insurance company employee who is a specialist in the technical aspects of life insurance and estate planning.

Adverse selection. The insuring of too many below-average risks; a predictable result of ineffective underwriting.

Affordability. The ability of the public to pay for needed insurance protection. See also availability.

Agent. A person authorized to sell policies on behalf of one or more insurance companies. Agents legally represent insurance companies.

All-lines insurance. A combination of several lines of insurance, including life and health as well as property-casualty. See also multiple-line insurance.

All-risk insurance. Any insurance that covers all perils that are not explicitly excluded. See also named peril insurance.

American agency system. See independent agency system.

American Lloyds. American insuring organizations that operate in a manner similar to that of Lloyd's of London.

Annual statement. A detailed financial report that insurance companies must submit each year to the insurance department of the states in which they operate.

Annuitant. The person during whose life an annuity is payable.

Annuity. A contract that provides an income for a stated period or for a person's lifetime.

Application. A form on which persons seeking insurance provide information to an insurance company about the risk to be insured.

Appraisal. A survey of property to determine the amount of value or loss.

Arson. The intentional burning of property.

Assessment mutual. A type of mutual insurance company that can charge its policyholders additional amounts to pay for claims and expenses.

Assigned risk plan. See Automobile Insurance Plan.

Assignment. The transfer of one person's legal interest in an insurance policy to another person.

Assumption of risk rule. A legal defense that bars recovery of damages if the injured person consented to the chance of being injured by whatever caused the injury.

Attractive nuisance doctrine. The legal rule concerning the degree of care owed by property owners to children who are attracted onto the premises by some dangerous condition.

Auto collision coverage. A form of auto insurance that pays for collision damage to the insured auto.

Auto comprehensive coverage. A form of auto insurance that pays for loss or damage to the insured auto other than that caused by collision.

Auto liability coverage. A form of auto insurance that protects against claims for legal liability.

Auto no-fault insurance. Insurance written in connection with an auto no-fault law and paying the insured persons' own medical expenses and income loss up to the amounts stated in the law.

Automatic premium loan. A life insurance policy provision authorizing the company to use the policy's loan value to pay any premium not paid by the end of the grace period.

Automobile Insurance Plan. A state program that makes auto insurance available to persons who cannot otherwise obtain it. Formerly known as assigned risk plan.

Availability. The ability of the public to obtain needed insurance protection. See also affordability.

Bailee. A person having temporary possession of property that belongs to another.

Basic limit. Minimum limit of liability.

Beneficiary. The person who receives the proceeds of a life insurance policy after the death of the insured.

Benefit formula. The provision of a pension plan that determines the amount of income payable to retirees.

Best's Insurance Reports. Annual publications that present information about the history, operations, investments, and financial condition of specific insurance companies.

Binder. A temporary insurance contract (written or oral) that is in effect until replaced by a regular policy.

Binding authority. The legal right to issue binders.

Blue Cross. A nonprofit hospital expense protection plan operating in a given geographic area.

Blue Shield. A nonprofit plan providing protection against the cost of surgical and medical care in a given geographic area.

Bodily injury liability. The legal liability that may arise from injury or death of another person.

Bond. See fidelity bond and surety bond.

Branch office. A unit of an insurance company that supervises the company's marketing and other operations within a given territory. Branch office managers are company employees. See also general agent.

Breach of warranty. Failure of a seller to abide by the terms of a guarantee. One of the legal grounds for products liability.

Broker. A person authorized to make insurance arrangements on behalf of insurance buyers. Brokers legally represent buyers.

Burglary. The taking of property by breaking into the place where it is kept. See also robbery and theft.

Business interruption insurance. Covers lost profit and continuing expenses when a firm is closed because of direct loss by an insured peril.

Businessowners policy. A package policy providing property-casualty insurance for small stores, office buildings, and apartment buildings.

Buy and sell agreement. A contractual arrangement under which a property owner agrees to sell and another party agrees to buy an item of property. If the sale is to occur after the death of the seller, funds to pay for the property can be provided by insuring the seller's life.

Cancellation. Termination of an insurance policy before its scheduled expiration date.

Cash value. The amount of money payable to a policyholder who discontinues a life insurance policy.

Casualty insurance. A broad field of insurance which includes most kinds of nonlife insurance other than those considered part of the property insurance field. Includes auto, general liability, workers' compensation, and suretyship.

Ceding company. An insurance company that is being reinsured.

Chance of loss. The probable number of losses out of a given number of loss exposures.

Claim. A request to an insurance company for the provision of a policy's benefits.

Claimant. One who makes a claim for payment of a loss or benefit.

Claims adjuster. A person who performs the claims adjusting process.

Claims adjusting. The process of investigating, evaluating, and settling insurance claims.

Class rate. A rate that applies to a group of policyholders having certain similar characteristics.

Class rating. A method of establishing rates by grouping together all risks having certain similar characteristics. See also judgment rating and merit rating.

Classification system. See class rating.

CLU. Chartered Life Underwriter. A professional designation granted by the American College of Life Underwriters to persons who meet experience requirements and pass a series of written examinations.

Commercial lines. Kinds of insurance covering business firms and other organizations rather than individuals and families. See also personal lines.

Commission. The payment made by insurance companies to agents for the sale and servicing of policies.

Company examination. An audit of an insurer's records, assets, and methods, conducted by a state insurance department.

Comparative negligence rule. The legal doctrine effective in some states that negligence by the injured party reduces the amount of recoverable damages but does not bar recovery. See also contributory negligence rule.

Completed operations exposure. The legal liability exposure connected with finished construction, installation, servicing, or repair work.

Comprehensive major medical insurance. A form of major medical expense insurance that includes basic hospital and surgical expense coverage.

Compulsory auto liability insurance law. A statute requiring all motorists to carry auto liability insurance.

Concealment. The failure to disclose important information relating to an insurance policy.

Continuation provisions. Policy provisions, especially in health insurance, which relate to cancellation or renewal.

Contract. See insurance contract.

Contractual liability. Liability assumed under any contract or agreement.

Contributory negligence rule. The legal doctrine effective in some states that injured persons cannot recover damages if their injuries were partly due to negligence of their own. See also comparative negligence rule.

Contributory plan. A group insurance plan for which the insured persons pay at least part of the cost. See also noncontributory plan.

Conversion clause. A provision in a group insurance policy giving employees who leave their jobs an option to purchase individual policies providing the same coverage.

Convertible term insurance. Can be exchanged for another plan of life insurance at the option of the policyholder and without evidence of insurability.

Coordination of benefits provision. A group health insurance policy provision designed to prevent duplication of benefits when an individual or family is covered by more than one such policy.

Corridor deductible. On major medical expense policies, a deductible that applies between the benefits paid by underlying hospital and surgical expense coverage and the start of the major medical benefits.

Coverage. The protection provided by insurance.

CPCU. Chartered Property Casualty Underwriter. A professional designation granted by the Institute for Property and Liability Underwriters to persons who meet experience requirements and pass a series of written examinations.

Credit life insurance. Term life insurance issued through a lender to cover payment of a loan if the borrower dies.

Damage to property of others. A form of no-fault insurance included in home-owners policies. It pays up to $250 for damage to other people's property caused by an insured person.

Damages. A sum of money awarded by a court as payment for injuries sustained or property damaged by another party. See also general damages and special damages.

Declarations page. The page of an insurance policy that identifies the party and the risks that the policy covers.

Decreasing term insurance. Term insurance that decreases in amount each month or year.

Deductible clause. A policy provision stating that a specified amount will be subtracted from covered losses.

Defendant. A person who is sued by a plaintiff.

Deferred annuity. An annuity that postpones the beginning of income payments to the annuitant, usually until he or she reaches retirement age. See also immediate annuity.

Deferred profit sharing plan. A pension plan funded by a predetermined share of an employer's annual profits.

Degree of risk. The extent of uncertainty about future losses.

Depreciation. Decrease in the value of property due to age, use, and obsolescence.

Direct billing. A system under which insurers send bills for renewal policies directly to the policyholders and premiums are paid directly to the insurers rather than to the agents.

Direct loss. Loss that is the immediate and direct result of an occurrence. In property insurance, the cost of repairing or replacing the property. See also indirect loss.

Direct reporting. A system of supervising an insurer's marketing and other operations directly from the home office, rather than by means of managing general agencies or branch offices.

Direct selling. A marketing system in which insurance is sold by company employees or by mail.

Direct writing. In general, any marketing system in property-casualty insurance other than the independent agency system.

Disability income insurance. A form of health insurance that provides periodic payments when the insured person is disabled as a result of an accident or sickness.

Dividend. See policy dividend.

Dividend options. Alternative ways in which owners of participating policies can elect to receive dividends.

Double indemnity. See accidental death benefit.

Earnings test. A provision of the Social Security program that reduces the retirement or survivors benefits payable to persons whose annual earnings exceed a certain amount.

Effective date. The date when an insurance policy begins.

Employee benefit plans. Programs of assistance, other than wages or salary, provided for employees by employers and including group insurance and pensions.

Employee Retirement Income Security Act. A law adopted in 1974 to establish federal regulation of private pension plans. It includes requirements for funding, vesting, termination insurance, and disclosure.

Employers' liability. The legal liability of employers to employees who have been injured due to the employers' negligence. In general, adoption of the workers' compensation laws established a no-fault system in place of employers' liability.

Employer's nonownership liability. Liability of an employer for the operation of autos owned by employees and used in connection with the employer's business.

Endorsement. A form attached to and changing the provisions of an insurance policy. Also called rider.

Endowment insurance. Life insurance payable to the insured if he or she is living on the maturity date stated in the policy, or to a beneficiary if the insured dies before that date.

Estate creation. Adding to one's assets; a major function of life insurance.

Estate planning. The process of arranging to conserve property during the owner's lifetime and to distribute it at his or her death without unnecessary taxation or other costs.

Exclusions. Provisions that explicitly limit the coverage provided by a policy.

Exclusive agency system. A marketing system in which insurance agents represent a single insurer.

Expense ratio. An expression of an insurance company's operating costs as a percentage of premiums. See also loss ratio.

Experience. Record of losses.

Experience rating. A type of merit rating in which the class rates for a particular insured are modified on the basis of that insured's past loss experience. See also schedule rating and retrospective rating.

Expiration date. The date when an insurance policy ends.

Exposure. The state of being subject to loss.

Exposure unit. The measuring unit used in insurance pricing.

Extended coverage. Property insurance covering the perils of windstorm, hail, explosion, smoke, aircraft, vehicles, riot, or civil commotion.

Extended term insurance option. A nonforfeiture option permitting the policyholder to use the cash value to purchase term insurance equal to the policy's face amount.

Face amount. The death benefit of a life insurance policy. It usually is stated on the face or first page of the policy.

Facultative reinsurance. The reinsurance of an individual policy as opposed to reinsurance by means of a treaty.

Fair rental value coverage. Insurance for the loss of rental income resulting from damage to an insured residence.

Family income policy. A combination of straight life insurance and decreasing term insurance.

Family maintenance policy. A combination of straight life insurance and a level amount of term insurance.

Family plan policy. A life insurance policy providing coverage on all or several family members.

Fidelity bond. A contract that reimburses an employer for loss caused by employee crime.

Field manager. A supervisor, particularly of life insurance agents.

Field representative. In companies using the independent agency system, a company employee who provides direct contact with the company's agents in a particular territory.

Financial responsibility law. A statute that requires motorists to prove they can pay for accidents they cause.

Fire insurance. Insurance covering loss caused by fire or lightning. Also a general term for property insurance.

Fire legal liability. Liability for fire damage to a structure rented to or occupied by the liable party.

First dollar coverage. The insurance of very minor losses, a practice that may contradict proper risk management principles.

Floater. A policy covering movable property wherever the property is located.

Form. An insurance policy, endorsement, or rider.

Fraternal insurer. A social organization that provides insurance for its members.

Friendly fire. A fire that remains where it is intended to be, such as in a furnace or fireplace. See also hostile fire.

General agent. An independent business person or firm that supervises marketing and other operations for one or more insurance companies within a given territory. See also branch office.

General damages. Payment for an injured party's losses that do not involve specific expenses, such as pain and suffering. See also special damages.

General liability. The liability of business firms other than liability for automobile or aviation accidents or for employee injuries.

Grace period. A period of time following the date the premium is due, during which a policy remains in force even though the premium has not been paid.

Group insurance. Any insurance plan that covers a number of individuals under a single contract. It is typically issued to an employer for the benefit of employees.

Group policies. Those issued on the group insurance basis.

Group representative. An insurance company employee who is a specialist in the field of group insurance and pensions.

Guaranteed insurability. A life insurance policy provision permitting the purchase of additional insurance at stated times regardless of the condition of the insured person's health.

Guest statutes. Laws providing that automobile drivers are not legally liable for injury to guest passengers unless gross negligence is proved.

Hazard. A condition that increases the likelihood of loss due to a particular peril.

Health insurance. Insurance that pays for medical treatment or provides income payments to a disabled person.

Health maintenance organization. An organization of physicians that provides comprehensive health care services to its subscribers for a fixed periodic fee.

Hired autos. Autos that are rented or leased.

Home office. An insurance company's central headquarters.

Homeowners policies. Policies that combine property, theft and liability insurance on home and home-related risks.

Hospital expense insurance. Pays some or all of the costs of being in a hospital, including room and board and various hospital services and supplies.

Host liquor liability. Liability for injuries caused by intoxicated persons to whom liquor was served by the liable party.

Hostile fire. A fire that is not confined to an intended place. See also friendly fire.

Immediate annuity. An annuity that begins making monthly payments to the annuitant the month after it is purchased. See also deferred annuity.

Incontestable clause. A policy provision that prevents the insurer from challenging or contesting claims after a stated period of coverage, regardless of misstatements made by the applicant.

Indemnify. To pay for a loss.

Indemnity principle. A legal doctrine stating that payment for property-casualty losses is to equal but not exceed the losses actually sustained.

Independent adjuster. A claims adjuster who operates as or for an independent contractor, adjusting claims for various insurers on a fee basis. See also staff adjuster.

Independent agency system. A marketing system in which insurance agents represent more than one property-casualty insurer.

Independent contractors exposure. The legal liability exposure connected with operations being performed for a party by an independent contractor.

Indirect loss. The loss of income or the extra expenses that result from a direct loss.

Individual policies. Those sold to particular individuals or families in contrast with those sold on the group insurance basis.

Industrial life insurance. Individually marketed life insurance issued in amounts less than $1000 with premiums collected weekly or monthly by an agent of the company.

Inflation guard endorsement. When added to a homeowners policy, automatically increases the amounts of property insurance by a stated percentage every three months.

Initial deductible. On major medical expense policies, a deductible that applies to the first dollars of medical expenses incurred.

Inland marine insurance. A broad field of insurance covering cargo being shipped by air, truck, or rail. Also includes various policies on movable property and property which relates to transportation.

Insurable interest rule. The requirement that insureds be in a position to sustain financial loss if the insured event occurs.

Insurance. A system of combining many loss exposures, with the costs of the losses being shared by all participants.

Insurance agent. See agent.

Insurance commissioner. In most states the title of the person heading the state insurance department.

Insurance contract. An insurance policy. As with other legal contracts, agreement, legal capacity, consideration, and legal purpose are required.

Insurance department. The agency of state government responsible for administering the state insurance laws.

Insurance guaranty funds. State assessment funds designed to protect policyholders and claimants from serious financial loss in the event a property-casualty insurance company becomes insolvent.

Insurance policy.   A legal contract under the terms of which an insurance company agrees to pay for stated losses.

Insurance rate.   The price of insurance per exposure unit.

Insured.   A person or organization that is protected by insurance.

Insurer.   An insurance company or other organization that provides insurance.

Insuring agreement.   The section of an insurance policy that states the essence of what the insurer agrees to do.

Interest adjusted cost.   A concept of the cost of life insurance that takes the time value of money into account. See also net cost of life insurance.

Investment earnings.   The portion of an insurance company's earnings that comes from the investment of funds. See also underwriting earnings.

Invitee.   A business visitor whose presence on the premises is encouraged by the owner. See also licensee and trespasser.

Joint and survivor annuity.   An annuity that provides income payments as long as either of two or more persons lives. See also single life annuity.

Judgment rating.   A method of establishing rates for unusual risks, based primarily upon the judgment of the ratemaker. See also class rating and merit rating.

Key employee insurance.   Life or health insurance written to protect an organization against financial loss resulting from the death or disability of important employees.

Lapse.   Termination of a policy because the premium has not been paid.

Law of large numbers.   A mathematical principle, which states that as the number of exposures is increased the actual results tend to come closer to the expected results.

Legal reserve.   A liability that an insurance company is legally required to maintain. It is offset by assets and represents the company's obligation to pay future losses and expenses.

Level premium.   In life insurance, a premium that remains the same from year to year even though the insured is growing older.

Liability insurance.   Covers the liability risk. Provides legal defense and pays sums necessary to settle claims against the insured.

Liability risk.   The possibility of financial loss resulting from negligence or alleged negligence.

Licensee.   A person who is on the premises with the owner's permission, but for his or her own benefit or convenience. See also invitee and trespasser.

Life annuity.   An insurance contract that provides an income for the lifetime of the annuitant.

Life insurance.   Insurance that provides a payment upon the death of the insured person.

Life insurance programming. A systematic process of developing a plan of life insurance designed to serve the needs of a particular family.

Limit of liability. The maximum amount an insurer will pay in case of a covered loss.

Limited payment whole life. Whole life insurance on which premiums are payable for a specified number of years.

Line. A type or class of insurance.

Lloyd's of London. A famous insuring organization located in London, England. It is an association, the individual members of which engage in insurance.

Loading. The part of an insurance rate that is intended to pay for operating expenses and margin, as contrasted with the pure premium.

Loss. An unexpected reduction or disappearance of economic value.

Loss control. Activities intended to reduce loss frequency and loss severity. Includes both loss prevention and loss reduction.

Loss exposures. Objects or persons that are subject to loss. See also insurance.

Loss frequency. The rate at which losses occur. The number of losses.

Loss measurement. Way of determining the amount of an insured loss.

Loss prevention. Activities that are intended to reduce the frequency of losses.

Loss reduction. Activities that are intended to reduce the severity of losses.

Loss reserve. A legal reserve in property-casualty insurance representing the estimated cost of settling all claims for losses that have occurred but have not yet been paid.

Loss severity. The size of losses.

Major medical expense insurance. Pays for a broad range of medical services up to a very high maximum amount, subject to a deductible amount and percentage participation.

Malpractice. Alleged professional misconduct or lack of ordinary skill in the performance of a professional act.

Malpractice insurance. Covers professional practitioners such as doctors or lawyers against liability claims for damages resulting from alleged misconduct or lack of skill in the performance of their professional duties.

Manual. A book of insurance rates, classifications, and rating rules.

Margin. The part of an insurance premium that is intended to provide for contingencies and for underwriting profit.

Marine insurance. A field of insurance consisting of inland marine and ocean marine.

McCarran Act. A federal law adopted in 1945 permitting the states to continue to regulate the insurance business. See also South-Eastern Underwriters Association case.

Medical payments coverage. A form of insurance that pays for medical and funeral expenses without regard to liability. It is available in auto policies and other policies providing liability coverage.

Medical payments to others. Medical payments insurance that is included in homeowners policies. Residents of the insured household are excluded.

Medicare. The social security health insurance program for persons age 65 and older.

Merit rating. A method of establishing rates by modifying the class rates for risks which differ in important ways from other risks in the same rating class. See also judgment rating and class rating.

Misstatement of age clause. A life insurance policy provision stating that if the insured's age has been misstated, the amount of insurance will be adjusted to the amount the premium would have paid for if the age had been stated correctly.

Modified life policy. A form of straight life insurance with reduced premiums for the first few (usually 3, 5, or 10) years.

Modified no-fault system. A system that partially uses the no-fault principle by limiting but not abolishing recovery based on tort liability. See also threshold.

Moral hazard. The possibility of loss due to the insured's dishonesty. Frequently used as a more general term including morale hazard. See also physical hazard.

Morale hazard. The possibility of loss due to the insured's carelessness or indifference to loss resulting from the existence of insurance.

Mortality rate. The ratio of the number of persons dying during a year to the number living at the beginning of the year.

Mortality risk. The financial uncertainty associated with dying.

Mortality table. A statistical table showing the mortality rate at each age.

Multiperil insurance. Policies that cover various perils. Some multiperil policies include both property and casualty coverages.

Multiple-line insurance. A combination of several lines of property-casualty insurance. See also all-lines insurance.

Multiple protection policy. Any life insurance policy that pays a multiple of the face amount if the insured dies within a specified period after the policy is issued.

Mutual insurance company. A nonprofit insuring organization that is owned by its policyholders.

Named peril insurance. Any insurance that specifies the perils it covers. See also all-risk insurance.

National Association of Insurance Commissioners. An association of state insurance commissioners. Its activities enhance the effectiveness of state insurance regulation.

National health insurance. Any system or proposed system of health insurance for all or almost all persons either provided by or required by the government.

Negligence. Failure to use proper care to prevent injury to other people or damage to their property.

Net cost of life insurance. A concept of the cost of life insurance, computed by subtracting from a policy's premiums the cash value and dividends as of a certain time. See also interest adjusted cost.

No-fault system. A system in which reimbursement for injuries on the basis of fault (tort liability) is not legally available. See also modified no-fault system and auto no-fault insurance.

Noncontributory plan. A group insurance plan for which the employer pays the entire cost. See also contributory plan.

Nonforfeiture options. Alternative choices available to a policyholder who discontinues premium payments on a policy that has a cash value.

Nonparticipating insurance. Insurance provided by policies on which policy dividends are not payable. Called nonpar.

OASDHI. The Old Age, Survivors, Disability and Health Insurance program, commonly referred to as social security.

Ocean marine insurance. Insurance covering vessels and their cargoes. Also includes liability coverage in connection with them.

Operating expenses. In insurance, the costs of running an insurance company. Includes sales and administrative expenses but not the amounts paid for losses or benefits.

Operations liability exposure. The legal liability exposure connected with the conduct of a business, especially those activities conducted away from the firm's own premises.

Ordinary life insurance. Individually marketed life insurance issued in amounts of $1000 or more with premiums payable annually, semiannually, quarterly, or monthly. The term is also used to mean straight life insurance.

Other insurance provision. A policy clause limiting the amount of payment if the insured has other, similar insurance.

Package policy. An insurance contract that includes several different kinds of protection.

Paid-up insurance option. A nonforfeiture option permitting the policyholder to use the cash value to purchase a reduced amount of paid-up insurance of the same type.

Participating insurance. Insurance provided by policies on which dividends are payable to the policyholders. See also dividend.

***Paul* v. *Virginia*.** A U.S. Supreme Court case of 1869 that established the right of the states to regulate the insurance business. See also South-Eastern Underwriters Association case.

Pension Benefit Guarantee Corporation. The federal agency that administers the pension plan termination insurance program established by the Employee Retirement Income Security Act.

Pension plan. A retirement income program for employees.

Peril. The cause of a possible loss. See also hazard.

Permanent life insurance. Loosely, any form of cash value individual life insurance.

Personal Auto Policy. A widely used auto insurance policy that includes coverage for liability claims, medical payments, claims against uninsured motorists, and damage to the insured's auto.

Personal injury liability. Liability for kinds of harm other than physical injury or damage. Includes liability for libel and slander.

Personal liability coverage. Liability insurance that is included in homeowners policies. Among the principal exclusions are claims involving business or professional activities or autos.

Personal lines. Kinds of insurance covering individuals and families rather than businesses and other organizations. See also commercial lines.

Physical hazard. The possibility of loss due to tangible characteristics of the insured property or person. See also moral hazard.

Plaintiff. A person who brings a lawsuit against a defendant.

Policy. See insurance policy.

Policy dividend. A partial return of premium, reflecting the difference between the premium charged and the amount needed in view of the company's experience. See also participating insurance.

Policy loan. A loan made by a life insurance company to a policyholder on the security of the cash value of his or her policy.

Policy period. The term for which a policy is in force, beginning with the effective date and ending with the expiration date.

Policy reserve. A legal reserve in life insurance, representing the funds held by the company to fulfill its policy obligations.

Policyholder. A nontechnical term commonly used to mean the insured.

Preexisting conditions clause. A provision of a health insurance policy that excludes coverage for physical conditions that existed before the policy began.

Premises liability exposure. The legal liability exposure connected with the ownership or control of land or buildings.

Premium. The price of an insurance policy.

Price quotation worksheet. A form used for recording and comparing the prices of two or more insurers.

Private insurance. That which is furnished by nongovernmental insuring organizations. See also social insurance.

Probationary period. In health insurance, a period of time between the beginning of the policy and the date that coverage becomes effective for certain conditions such as illness.

Proceeds. The amount payable by a life insurance policy at the death of the insured.

Producer. Insurance agent.

Products liability exposure. The legal liability exposure connected with the manufacture, distribution, or sale of products.

Professional liability. Liability of doctors, lawyers, architects, and other professionals resulting from claim alleging malpractice, error, or mistake in connection with their professional duties.

Programming. See life insurance programming.

Property insurance. Insurance paying for loss of or damage to property. Divided into marine and nonmarine lines. Includes coverage for both direct and indirect loss.

Property-casualty insurance. A major field of insurance consisting of property insurance and casualty insurance.

Property damage liability. The legal liability that may arise from damaging the property of others.

Protection. The coverage provided by insurance.

Provisions. The terms of a policy.

Proximate cause. The immediate or direct cause of a loss.

Public adjuster. A claims adjuster who handles claims on behalf of claimants rather than on behalf of insurance companies.

Public liability insurance. A general term referring to bodily injury and property damage liability insurance.

Pure premium. The part of an insurance premium that is intended to pay for losses, as contrasted with the part that is intended to cover operating expenses and margin.

Pure risk. Risk that can result only in loss or absence of loss, there being no possibility of gain. See also speculative risk.

Rate. See insurance rate.

Rating bureau. An organization that gathers statistical data, calculates rates, and files rates with state insurance departments.

Reciprocal exchange. An association, the members of which insure one another.

Regular medical expense insurance. Pays for the cost of nonsurgical treatment by a physician, usually on a per visit basis.

Reimbursement basis. Refers to insurance benefits that are based on the dollar amount of loss actually sustained up to a stated maximum. See also service basis and valued basis.

Reinstatement provision. A policy clause permitting the restoration of a lapsed policy under stated conditions.

Reinsurance. A process by which one insurance company insures part of its risks with another company (the reinsurer).

Reinsurance treaty. A contract, usually annual, under which a reinsurance company agrees to reinsure stated kinds and amounts of insurance written by a ceding company. See also facultative reinsurance.

Release. To give up or abandon a claim against another party. Also, a document that is evidence of such action.

Renewable term insurance. Can be renewed at the end of the term at the option of the policyholder and without evidence of insurability.

Renewal policy. One that continues insurance coverage upon the expiration of a previous policy.

Replacement cost. The cost of replacing with new property without deducting for depreciation.

Representation. A statement made to an insurer to supply information or to induce it to accept a risk.

Reserve. See legal reserve.

Retrocession. The transfer of risk from one reinsurer to another.

Retrospective rating. A type of merit rating in which the premium for a particular policy is modified on the basis of the loss experience under that particular policy. See also schedule rating and experience rating.

Return of premium policy. A life insurance policy which upon the death of the insured pays the face amount plus an amount equal to all of the premiums that have been paid.

Rider. See endorsement.

Risk. Uncertainty about future loss. The term is also used to indicate the person or object being insured.

Risk management. The systematic and efficient handling of pure risks.

Risk manager. A person responsible for risk management.

Robbery. The taking of property by violence or threat of violence. Holdup. See also burglary and theft.

Safe driver rating plan. A method of classifying motorists on the basis of their driving records, with higher rates applying to those who have had accidents or have violated the motor vehicle laws.

Schedule. A list of covered property or amounts of insurance.

Schedule rating. A type of merit rating in which the class rates for a particular insured are modified on the basis of that insured's expected loss experience. See also experience rating and retrospective rating.

Scheduled personal property endorsement. Can be added to homeowners policies to provide increased protection for certain items or categories of property.

Second injury funds. Established in connection with workers' compensation laws, to avoid discouraging the hiring of disabled workers. Employers must pay only the benefits payable to nondisabled workers, the fund paying any additional benefits.

Self-insurance. A type of risk retention in which an organization with many similar loss exposures sets aside a fund for the payment of future losses.

Service basis. Refers to insurance benefits in the form of services described in the policy, with the insurer's payment being made directly to the provider of the services such as a hospital or physician. The customary basis of Blue Cross and Blue Shield benefits. See also reimbursement basis and valued basis.

Settlement options. The ways, other than immediate payment in cash, in which a life insurance policyholder or beneficiary may choose to have policy benefits paid.

Single life annuity. An annuity covering the life of one person. See also joint and survivor annuity.

Single premium whole life. Whole life insurance that is fully paid for by a single payment.

Social insurance. Insurance provided by the government on a compulsory basis.

Social security. The term commonly used for the Old Age, Survivors, Disability, and Health Insurance program.

South-Eastern Underwriters Association case. A U. S. Supreme Court case of 1944, which superseded the *Paul* v. *Virginia* case of 1869 and established the right of the federal government to regulate the insurance business.

Special agent. See field representative.

Special damages. Payment for an injured party's actual expenses, such as medical bills and repair costs. See also general damages.

Speculative risk. Risk that can result in either loss or gain. See also pure risk.

Staff adjuster. A claims adjuster who is employed by an insurance company. See also independent adjuster.

Statutory rate standards. Charcteristics of insurance rates that are required by law. The usual standards are that rates not be excessive, inadequate, or unfairly discriminatory.

Stock insurance company. An insuring organization of the corporate type, owned by its stockholders.

Straight life. Whole life insurance on which premiums are payable for life.

Strict liability. Liability without fault, based on a legal rule that sometimes is applied in cases of hazardous activities or defective and dangerous products.

Subrogation. A legal principle that provides that to the extent an insurer has paid for a loss, the insurer obtains the policyholder's right to recover from any third party who caused the loss.

Suicide clause. A life insurance policy provision restricting the insurer's liability to the return of premiums in the event the insured dies by suicide during an initial period of coverage.

Supplementary payments.   Benefits (such as the cost of bail bonds) that are provided by liability insurance in addition to the cost of legal liability claims.

Surety bond.   A contract of suretyship.

Suretyship.   A form of risk transfer in which one party is responsible for the fulfillment of an obligation by another party. Includes fidelity bonding and surety bonding.

Surgical expense insurance.   A form of health insurance that pays for the cost of surgery.

Surplus.   The amount by which an insurance company's assets exceed its liabilities.

Term life insurance.   Life insurance payable to a beneficiary when the insured dies within a specified period. If the insured is living at the end of the period, the policy expires without value.

Theft.   The taking of property by burglary, robbery, or any other act of stealing.

Theft coverage extension.   An endorsement that adds coverage to a homeowners policy for items stolen from an unlocked auto.

Threshold.   Under modified no-fault laws, the degree of seriousness of injuries that permits legal action based on tort liability. Under such laws there is no tort liability for less serious injuries.

Tort.   Legally, a civil wrong not associated with a contract. Negligence is a tort.

Trespasser.   A person who is on the premises without the express or implied permission of the owner. See also invitee and licensee.

Umbrella liability insurance.   Covers losses in excess of amounts covered by the insured's other liability policies; also protects for types of liability claims not covered by the usual liability policies.

Underinsured motorists coverage.   A form of auto insurance that pays the covered persons damages they are legally entitled to collect from motorists whose liability insurance is inadequate to pay the entire amount they owe. See also uninsured motorists coverage.

Underwriter.   A person who performs the underwriting process.

Underwriting.   The process by which insurers decide which loss exposures to insure and how to insure them.

Underwriting capacity.   An insurance company's financial ability to provide insurance.

Underwriting earnings.   The portion of an insurance company's earnings that comes from insurance operations. See also investment earnings.

Unearned premium reserve.   A legal reserve in property-casualty insurance, representing the part of the premiums received by the company that it has not yet earned.

Unemployment insurance.   A type of social insurance providing income benefits for unemployed persons.

Uninsured motorists coverage. A form of auto insurance that pays the covered persons damages they are legally entitled to collect from uninsured motorists. See also underinsured motorists coverage.

Unsatisfied judgment fund. A state fund to pay auto accident victims money they are legally entitled to but cannot collect from motorists who caused their injuries.

Utmost good faith. A legal doctrine stating that insurers are entitled to rely upon the information given by applicants. The doctrine is supported by laws relating to warranty, representation, and concealment.

Valued basis. Insurance benefits in amounts specified in the policy, such as a health insurance policy providing a flat amount for each day an insured is hospitalized. See also reimbursement basis and service basis.

Variable annuity. An annuity contract in which the amount of each periodic income payment fluctuates. The fluctuation is usually related to security market values.

Vesting. The rights that departing employees have to funds provided by their employers' contributions to a pension plan.

Vicarious liability. The responsibility of one party for the negligent action of another party.

Waiting period. In disability income insurance, the period of time between the beginning of a disability and the date that the policy's income payments begin.

Waiver of premium. A life or health insurance policy provision stating that premiums will not be charged if the insured becomes totally and permanently disabled.

Warranty. A policy provision that makes the insurer's obligation conditional upon some fact or circumstance concerning the risk.

Whole life insurance. Life insurance payable to a beneficiary at the death of the policyholder whenever that occurs. Premiums may be payable for a specified number of years (limited payment life) or for life (straight life).

Workers' compensation insurance. Pays, on behalf of the employer, for the workers' compensation benefits required by law.

Workers' compensation laws. State laws that are the basis of a system of required benefits for employee injuries. The benefits are furnished by employers, regardless of fault.

Write. In insurance, to insure, to underwrite or to sell.

Yellow card. The Canada Non-Resident Motor Vehicle Liability Insurance Card. It shows that auto insurance required by the Canadian provinces is in force.

APPENDIX B
PERSONAL AUTO POLICY

NAME OF COMPANY

PERSONAL AUTO POLICY
DECLARATIONS

Renewal of Number

No. PA
Named Insured and Mailing Address (No., Street, Apt., Town or City, County, State, Zip Code)

Policy Period:
From: To: 12:01 A.M. Standard Time

Description of Auto(s) or Trailer(s)

AUTO	Year	Trade Name — Model	VIN	Symbol	Age
1					
2					
3					
4					

The Auto(s) or Trailer(s) described in this policy is principally garaged at the above address unless otherwise stated:
(No., Street, Apt., Town or City, County, State, Zip Code)

Coverage is provided where a premium and a limit of liability are shown for the coverage.

Coverages	Limit of Liability		Premium			
			Auto 1	Auto 2	Auto 3	Auto 4
A. Liability	$ each accident	$	$	$	$	
A. Liability						
Bodily Injury	$ each person / $ each accident	$	$	$	$	
Property Damage	$ each accident	$	$	$	$	
B. Medical Payments	$ each person	$	$	$	$	
C. Uninsured Motorists	$ each accident	$	$	$	$	
C. Uninsured Motorists	$ each person / $ each accident	$	$	$	$	
D. Damage to your Auto — Actual Cash Value minus						
1. Collision Loss	$ Deductible	$	$	$	$	
2. Other than Collision Loss	$ Deductible	$	$	$	$	
Towing and Labor Costs	$ each disablement	$	$	$	$	
		$	$	$	$	

Endorsements made part of this Policy at time of issue:

Endorsement Premium $

Total Premium Per Auto $ $ $ $
Total Premium $

Loss Payee (Name and address)

Countersigned:

By_____
Authorized Representative

JDL 8054-2 (Ed. 1-77)

AGREEMENT

In return for payment of the premium and subject to all the terms of this policy, we agree with you as follows:

DEFINITIONS

Throughout this policy, "you" and "your" refer to the "named insured" shown in the Declarations and the spouse if a resident of the same household. "We", "us" and "our" refer to the Company providing this insurance. For purposes of this policy any private passenger type auto leased under a written agreement to any person for a continuous period of at least six months shall be deemed to be owned by that person.

Other words and phrases are defined. They are boldfaced when used.

"Your covered auto" means:

(a) Any vehicle shown in the Declarations.

(b) Any of the following types of vehicles of which you acquire ownership during the policy period, provided that you ask us to insure it within thirty days after you become the owner:

(1) a private passenger auto.

(2) if not used in any business or occupation, a pick-up, sedan delivery or panel truck.

If the vehicle replaces one shown in the Declarations, you have to ask us to insure it within thirty days only if you wish Damage to Your Auto Coverage to apply to the replacing vehicle.

(c) Any **trailer** you own.

(d) Any auto or **trailer** you do not own while used as a temporary substitute for any other vehicle described in this definition which is out of normal use because of its breakdown, repair, servicing, loss or destruction.

"Family member" means a person related to you by blood, marriage or adoption who is a resident of your household, including a ward or foster child.

"Occupying" means in, upon, getting in, on, out or off.

"Trailer" means a vehicle designed to be pulled by a private passenger type auto. It also means a farm wagon or farm implement while towed by a private passenger type auto or a pick-up, sedan delivery or panel truck.

PART A

LIABILITY COVERAGE

We will pay damages for bodily injury or property damage for which any **covered person** becomes legally responsible because of an auto accident. We will settle or defend, as we consider appropriate, any claim or suit asking for these damages. Our duty to settle or defend ends when our limit of liability for this coverage has been exhausted.

"Covered person" as used in this Part means:

1. You or any **family member** for the ownership, maintenance or use of any auto or **trailer.**

2. Any person using **your covered auto.**

3. For **your covered auto,** any person or organization but only with respect to legal responsibility for acts or omissions of a person for whom coverage is afforded under this Part.

4. For any auto or **trailer,** other than **your covered auto,** any person or organization but only with respect to legal responsibility for acts or omissions of you or any **family member** for whom coverage is afforded under this Part. This provision applies only if the person or organization does not own or hire the auto or **trailer.**

SUPPLEMENTARY PAYMENTS

In addition to our limit of liability, we will pay on behalf of a **covered person:**

1. Up to $250 for the cost of bail bonds required because of an accident, including related traffic law violations, resulting in bodily injury or property damage covered under this policy.

2. Premiums on appeal bonds and bonds to release attachments in any suit we defend.

3. Interest accruing after a judgment is entered in any suit we defend. Our duty to pay interest ends when we offer to pay that part of the judgment which does not exceed our limit of liability for this coverage.

4. Up to $50 a day for loss of earnings, but not other income, because of attendance at hearings or trials at our request.

5. Other reasonable expenses incurred at our request.

EXCLUSIONS

We do not provide Liability Coverage:

1. For any person who intentionally causes bodily injury or property damage.

2. For any person for damage to property owned or being transported by that person.

3. For any person for damage to property rented to, used by, or in the care of that person. This exclusion does not apply to damage to a residence or private garage. It also does not apply to damage to any of the following type vehicles not owned by or furnished or available for the regular use of you or any **family member:**

   a. private passenger autos;

   b. **trailers;** or

   c. pick-up, sedan delivery or panel trucks.

4. For any person for bodily injury to an employee of that person during the course of employment. This exclusion does not apply to bodily injury to a domestic employee unless workers' or workmen's compensation benefits are required or available for that domestic employee.

5. For any person's liability arising out of the ownership or operation of a vehicle while it is being used to carry persons or property for a fee. This exclusion does not apply to a share-the-expense car pool.

6. For any person while employed or otherwise engaged in the business or occupation of selling, repairing, servicing, storing or parking of vehicles designed for use mainly on public highways, including road testing and delivery. This exclusion does not apply to the ownership, maintenance or use of **your covered auto** by you, any **family member,** or any partner, agent or employee of you or any **family member.**

7. For any person maintaining or using any vehicle while that person is employed or otherwise engaged in any business or occupation not described in Exclusion 6. This exclusion does not apply to the maintenance or use of a private passenger type auto. It also does not apply to the maintenance or use of a pick-up, sedan delivery or panel truck that you own.

8. For the ownership, maintenance, or use of a motorcycle or any other self-propelled vehicle having less than four wheels.

9. For the ownership, maintenance or use of any vehicle, other than **your covered auto,** which is owned by you or furnished or available for your regular use.

10. For the ownership, maintenance or use of any vehicle, other than **your covered auto,** which is owned by or furnished or available for the regular use of any **family member.** However, this exclusion does not apply to you.

11. For any person using a vehicle without a reasonable belief that the person is entitled to do so.

12. For any person for bodily injury or property damage for which that person is an insured under a nuclear energy liability policy or would be an insured but for its termination upon exhaustion of its limit of liability. A nuclear energy liability policy is a policy issued by Nuclear Energy Liability Insurance Association, Mutual Atomic Energy Liability Underwriters, Nuclear Insurance Association of Canada, or any of their successors.

LIMIT OF LIABILITY

The limit of liability shown in the Declarations for this coverage is our maximum limit of liability for all damages resulting from any one auto accident. This is the most we will pay regardless of the number of **covered persons,** claims made, vehicles or premiums shown in the Declarations, or vehicles involved in the auto accident.

We will apply the limit of liability to provide any separate limits required by law for bodily injury and property damage liability. However, this provision will not change our total limit of liability.

OUT OF STATE COVERAGE

If an auto accident to which this policy applies occurs in any state or province other than the one in which **your covered auto** is principally garaged, we will interpret your policy for that accident as follows:

1. If the state or province has a financial responsibility or similar law specifying limits of liability for bodily injury or property damage higher than the limit shown in the Declarations, your policy will provide the higher specified limit;

2. If the state or province has a compulsory insurance or similar law requiring a nonresident to maintain insurance whenever the nonresident uses a vehicle in that state or province, your policy will provide the required minimum amounts and types of coverage.

No one will be entitled to duplicate payments for the same elements of loss as a result of the application of this provision.

FINANCIAL RESPONSIBILITY REQUIRED

If we certify this policy as proof of financial responsibility for the future under any financial responsibility law, this policy shall comply with the provisions of the law to the extent of the coverage required.

OTHER INSURANCE

If there is other applicable liability insurance we will pay only our share. Our share is the proportion that our limit of liability bears to the total of all applicable limits. However, any insurance we provide for a vehicle you do not own shall be excess over any other collectible insurance.

PART B

MEDICAL PAYMENTS COVERAGE

We will pay reasonable expenses incurred for necessary medical and funeral services because of bodily injury caused by accident and sustained by a **covered person.** We will pay only those expenses incurred within three years from the date of the accident.

"Covered person" as used in this Part means:

1. You or any **family member** while **occupying,** or as a pedestrian when struck by, a motor vehicle designed for use mainly on public roads or by a trailer of any type.

2. Any other person while **occupying your covered auto.**

EXCLUSIONS

We do not provide Medical Payments Coverage for any person:

1. For bodily injury sustained while **occupying** a motorcycle.

2. For bodily injury sustained while **occupying your covered auto** when it is being used to carry persons or property for a fee. This exclusion does not apply to a share-the-expense car pool.

3. For bodily injury sustained while **occupying** any vehicle located for use as a residence or premises.

4. For bodily injury occurring during the course of employment if workers' or workmen's compensation benefits are required or available for the bodily injury.

5. For bodily injury sustained while **occupying** or, when struck by, any vehicle (other than **your covered auto**) which is owned by you or furnished or available for your regular use.

6. For bodily injury sustained while **occupying** or, when struck by, any vehicle (other than **your covered auto**) which is owned by or furnished or available for the regular use of any **family member**. However, this exclusion does not apply to you.

7. For bodily injury sustained while **occupying** a vehicle without a reasonable belief that the person is entitled to do so.

8. For bodily injury sustained while **occupying** a vehicle when it is being used in the business or occupation of a **covered person**. This exclusion does not apply to bodily injury sustained while **occupying** a private passenger type auto. It also does not apply to bodily injury sustained while **occupying** a pick-up, sedan delivery or panel truck that you own.

9. For bodily injury caused by discharge of a nuclear weapon (even if accidental), war (declared or undeclared), civil war, insurrection, rebellion or revolution or any consequence of any of these.

10. For bodily injury from any nuclear reaction, radiation or radioactive contamination, all whether controlled or uncontrolled or however caused, or any consequence of any of these.

LIMIT OF LIABILITY

The limit of liability shown in the Declarations for this coverage is our maximum limit of liability for each person injured in any one accident. This is the most we will pay regardless of the number of **covered persons,** claims made, vehicles or premiums shown in the Declarations, or vehicles involved in the accident.

Any amounts otherwise payable for expenses under this coverage shall be reduced by any amounts paid or payable for the same expenses under any Auto Liability or Uninsured Motorists Coverage provided by this policy.

No payment will be made under this coverage unless the injured person or his legal representative agrees in writing that any payment shall be applied toward any settlement or judgment that person receives under any Auto Liability or Uninsured Motorists Coverage provided by this policy.

OTHER INSURANCE

If there is other applicable auto medical payments insurance we will pay only our share. Our share is the proportion that our limit of liability bears to the total of all applicable limits. However, any insurance we provide with respect to a vehicle you do not own shall be excess over any other collectible auto insurance providing payments for medical or funeral expenses.

PART C

UNINSURED MOTORISTS COVERAGE

We will pay damages which a **covered person** is legally entitled to recover from the owner or operator of an **uninsured motor vehicle** because of bodily injury sustained by a **covered person** and caused by an accident. The owner's or operator's liability for these damages must arise out of the ownership, maintenance or use of the **uninsured motor vehicle.**

Any judgment for damages arising out of a suit brought without our written consent is not binding on us.

"Covered person" as used in this Part means:

1. You or any **family member.**
2. Any other person **occupying your covered auto.**
3. Any person for damages that person is entitled to recover because of bodily injury to which this coverage applies sustained by a person described in 1. or 2. above.

"**Uninsured motor vehicle**" means a land motor vehicle or trailer of any type:

1. To which no bodily injury liability bond or policy applies at the time of the accident.

2. To which a bodily injury liability bond or policy applies at the time of the accident but its limit for bodily injury liability is less than the minimum limit for bodily injury liability specified by the financial responsibility law of the state in which **your covered auto** is principally garaged.

3. Which is a hit and run vehicle whose operator or owner cannot be identified and which hits:
   a. you or any **family member;**
   b. a vehicle which you or any **family member** are **occupying;** or
   c. **your covered auto.**

4. To which a bodily injury liability bond or policy applies at the time of the accident, but the bonding or insuring company denies coverage or is or becomes insolvent.

However, "**uninsured motor vehicle**" does not include any vehicle:

1. Owned by or furnished or available for the regular use of you or any **family member.**

2. Owned or operated by a self-insurer under any applicable motor vehicle law.

3. Owned by any governmental unit or agency.

4. Operated on rails or crawler treads.

5. Which is a farm type tractor or equipment designed mainly for use off public roads while not on public roads.

6. While located for use as a residence or premises.

EXCLUSIONS

A. We do not provide Uninsured Motorists Coverage for bodily injury sustained by any person:

1. While **occupying,** or when struck by, any motor vehicle or trailer of any type owned by you or any **family member** which is not insured for this coverage under this policy.

2. If that person or the legal representative settles the bodily injury claim without our consent.

3. While **occupying your covered auto** when it is being used to carry persons or property for a fee. This exclusion does not apply to a share-the-expense car pool.

4. Using a vehicle without a reasonable belief that the person is entitled to do so.

B. This coverage shall not apply directly or indirectly to benefit any insurer or self-insurer under any workers' or workmen's compensation, disability benefits or similar law.

LIMIT OF LIABILITY

The limit of liability shown in the Declarations for this coverage is our maximum limit of liability for all damages resulting from any one accident. This is the most we will pay regardless of the number of **covered persons,** claims made, vehicles or premiums shown in the Declarations, or vehicles involved in the accident.

Any amounts otherwise payable for damages under this coverage shall be reduced by:

1. all sums paid because of the bodily injury by or on behalf of persons or organizations who may be legally responsible. This includes all sums paid under the Liability Coverage of this policy, and

2. all sums paid or payable because of the bodily injury under any workers' or workmen's compensation, disability benefits law or any similar law.

Any payment under this coverage to or for a **covered person** will reduce any amount that person is entitled to recover under the Liability Coverage of this policy.

OTHER INSURANCE

If there is other applicable similar insurance we will pay only our share. Our share is the proportion that our limit of liability bears to the total of all applicable limits. However, any insurance we provide with respect to a vehicle you do not own shall be excess over any other collectible insurance.

ARBITRATION

If we and a **covered person** disagree whether that person is legally entitled to recover damages from the owner or operator of an **uninsured motor vehicle** or do not agree as to the amount of damages, either party may make a written demand for arbitration. In this event, each party will select an arbitrator. The two arbitrators will select a third. If they cannot agree within 30 days, either may request that selection be made by a judge of a court having jurisdiction. Each party will pay the expenses it incurs, and bear the expenses of the third arbitrator equally.

Unless both parties agree otherwise, arbitration will take place in the county and state in which the **covered person** lives. Local rules of law as to procedure and evidence will apply. A decision agreed to by two of the arbitrators will be binding.

PART D

COVERAGE FOR DAMAGE TO YOUR AUTO

We will pay for direct and accidental loss to **your covered auto**, including its equipment, minus any applicable deductible shown in the Declarations. However, we will pay for loss caused by **collision** only if the Declarations indicate that Collision Coverage is afforded.

"**Collision**" means the upset, or collision with another object of **your covered auto**. However, the following are not considered "collision":

Loss caused by missiles, falling objects, fire, theft or larceny, explosion, earthquake, windstorm, hail, water, flood, malicious mischief or vandalism, riot or civil commotion, contact with bird or animal or breakage of glass. If breakage of glass is caused by a **collision**, you may elect to have it considered a loss caused by **collision**.

TRANSPORTATION EXPENSES

In addition, we will pay up to $10 per day, to a maximum of $300, for transportation expenses incurred by you because of the total theft of **your covered auto**. We will pay only transportation expenses incurred during the period beginning 48 hours after the theft and ending when **your covered auto** is returned to use or we pay for its loss.

EXCLUSIONS

We will not pay for:

1. Loss to **your covered auto** which occurs while it is used to carry persons or property for a fee. This exclusion does not apply to a share-the-expense car pool.

2. Damage due and confined to wear and tear, freezing, mechanical or electrical breakdown or failure or road damage to tires. This exclusion does not apply if the damage results from the total theft of **your covered auto**.

3. Loss due to radioactive contamination.

4. Loss due to discharge of any nuclear weapon (even if accidental), war (declared or undeclared), civil war, insurrection, rebellion or revolution, or any consequence of any of these.

5. Loss to equipment designed for the reproduction of sound, unless the equipment is permanently installed in **your covered auto**.

6. Loss to tapes, records or other devices for use with equipment designed for the reproduction of sound.

7. Loss to a camper body or **trailer** not shown in the Declarations. This exclusion does not apply to a camper body or **trailer** of which you acquire ownership during the policy period if you ask us to insure it within thirty days after you become the owner.

8. Loss to any vehicle while used as a temporary substitute for a vehicle you own which is out of normal use because of its breakdown, repair, servicing, loss or destruction.

9. Loss to TV antennas, awnings, cabanas or equipment designed to create additional living facilities.

10. Loss to any sound receiving or sound receiving and transmitting equipment designed for use as a citizens band radio, two-way mobile radio, telephone, or scanning monitor receiver, or their accessories or antennas.

LIMIT OF LIABILITY

Our limit of liability for loss will be the lesser of:

1. The actual cash value of the stolen or damaged property, or

2. The amount necessary to repair or replace the property.

PAYMENT OF LOSS

We may pay for loss in money or repair or replace the damaged or stolen property. We may, at our expense, return any stolen property to you or to the address shown in this policy. If we return stolen property we will pay for any damage resulting from the theft. We may keep all or part of the property at an agreed or appraised value.

NO BENEFIT TO BAILEE

This insurance shall not directly or indirectly benefit any carrier or other bailee.

OTHER INSURANCE

If other insurance also covers the loss we will pay only our share. Our share is the proportion that our limit of liability bears to the total of all applicable limits.

PART E

DUTIES AFTER AN ACCIDENT OR LOSS

We must be notified promptly of how, when and where the accident or loss happened. Notice should also include the names and addresses of any injured persons and of any witnesses.

A person seeking any coverage must:

1. Cooperate with us in the investigation, settlement or defense of any claim or suit.

2. Promptly send us copies of any notices or legal papers received in connection with the accident or loss.

3. Submit, at our expense and as often as we reasonably require, to physical examinations by physicians we select.

4. Authorize us to obtain medical reports and other pertinent records.

5. Submit a proof of loss when required by us.

A person seeking Uninsured Motorist Coverage must also:

1. Promptly notify the police if a hit-and-run driver is involved.

2. Promptly send us copies of the legal papers if a suit is brought.

A person seeking Coverage for Damage to Your Auto must also:

1. Take reasonable steps after loss, at our expense, to protect **your covered auto** and its equipment from further loss.

2. Promptly notify the police if **your covered auto** is stolen.

3. Permit us to inspect and appraise the damaged property before its repair or disposal.

PART F

GENERAL PROVISIONS

1. **POLICY PERIOD AND TERRITORY**

This policy applies only to accidents and losses which occur during the policy period as shown in the Declarations, and within the policy territory.

The policy territory is the United States of America, its territories or possessions, or Canada. This policy also applies to loss to, or accidents involving, **your covered auto** while being transported between their ports.

2. **CHANGES**

This policy contains all the agreements between you and us. Its terms may not be changed or waived except by endorsement issued by us. If a change requires a premium adjustment, we will adjust the premium as of the effective date of change. If we revise this policy form to provide more coverage without additional premium charge, your policy will automatically provide the additional coverage as of the day the revision is effective in your state.

3. **LEGAL ACTION AGAINST US**

No legal action may be brought against us until there has been full compliance with all the terms of this policy. In addition, under the Liability Coverage, no legal action may be brought against us until we agree in writing that the **covered person** has an obligation to pay or until the amount of that obligation has been finally determined by judgment after trial. No person or organization has any right under this policy to bring us into any action to determine the liability of a **covered person.**

4. **TRANSFER OF YOUR INTEREST IN THIS POLICY**

Your rights and duties under this policy may not be assigned without our written consent. However, if a named insured shown in the Declarations dies, coverage will be provided until the end of the policy period for:

(a) The surviving spouse if resident in the same household at the time of death, as if a named insured shown in the Declarations;

(b) The legal representative of the deceased person as if a named insured shown in the Declarations. This applies only with respect to the representative's legal responsibility for the maintenance or use of **your covered auto.**

5. **OUR RIGHT TO RECOVER PAYMENT**

A. If we make a payment under this policy and the person to or for whom payment was made has a right to recover damages from another we shall be subrogated to that right. That person shall do whatever is necessary to enable us to exercise our rights and shall do nothing after loss to prejudice them.

B. If we make a payment under this policy and the person to or for whom payment is made recovers damages from another, that person shall hold in trust for us the proceeds of the recovery and shall reimburse us to the extent of our payment.

6. **TERMINATION**

A. Cancellation. This policy may be cancelled during the policy period as follows:

1. The named insured shown in the Declarations may cancel by returning this policy to us or by giving us advance written notice of the date cancellation is to take effect.

2. We may cancel by mailing to the named insured shown in the Declarations at the address shown in this policy,

(a) at least 10 days notice

    (1) if cancellation is for nonpayment of premium; or

    (2) if notice is mailed during the first 60 days this policy is in effect and this is not a renewal or continuation policy;

(b) at least 20 days notice in all other cases.

3. After this policy is in effect for 60 days and this is not a renewal or continuation policy, we will cancel only:

(a) for nonpayment of premium; or

(b) if your driver's license or that of any other driver who lives with you or customarily uses **your covered auto** has been suspended or revoked during the policy period; or if the policy period is other than one year, since the last anniversary of the original effective date.

B. Nonrenewal. If we decide not to renew or continue this policy we will mail notice to the named insured shown in the Declarations at the address shown in this policy at least 20 days before the end of the policy period. However, if the policy period is other than one year, we will have the right not to renew or continue it only at each anniversary of its original effective date.

C. Automatic Termination. If we offer to renew or continue and you or your representative do not. accept, this policy will automatically terminate at the end of the current policy period. Failure to pay the required renewal or continuation premium when due shall mean that you have not accepted our offer.

If you obtain other insurance on **your covered auto,** any similar insurance provided by this policy will terminate as to that auto on the effective date of the other insurance.

D. Other Termination Provisions.

1. If the law in effect in your state at the time this policy is issued, renewed or continued, requires any longer notice period or any special form of or procedure for giving notice, or modifies any of the stated termination reasons, we will comply with those requirements.

2. We may deliver any notice instead of mailing it. Proof of mailing of any notice shall be sufficient proof of notice.

3. If this policy is cancelled, you may be entitled to a premium refund. If so, we will send you the refund. However, making or offering to make the refund is not a condition of cancellation.

4. The effective date of cancellation stated in the notice shall become the end of the policy period.

7. **TWO OR MORE AUTO POLICIES**

If this policy and any other auto insurance policy issued to you by us apply to the same accident, the maximum limit of our liability under all the policies shall not exceed the highest applicable limit of liability under any one policy.

8. **BANKRUPTCY**

Bankruptcy or insolvency of the **covered person** shall not relieve us of any obligations under this policy.

APPENDIX C
HOMEOWNERS POLICY

NAME OF COMPANY

**HOMEOWNERS POLICY
DECLARATIONS**

RENEWAL OF NUMBER

No. H
Named Insured and Mailing Address (No., Street, Apt., Town or City, County, State, Zip Code)

Policy Period: Years From: To: 12:01 A.M. Standard Time at the **residence premises**.

The **residence premises** covered by this policy is located at the above address unless otherwise stated: (No., Street, Apt., Town or City, County, State, Zip Code)

Coverage is provided where a premium or limit of liability is shown for the coverage.

Coverages and Limit of Liability	Section I Coverages				Section II Coverages	
	A. Dwelling	B. Other Structures	C. Personal Property	D. Loss of Use	E. Personal Liability Each occurrence	F. Medical Payments to Others Each person
	$	$	$	$	$	$

Premium	Basic Policy Premium	Additional Premiums			Total Prepaid Premium	Premium if paid in installments	Payable: At each At subsequent Inception (and) anniversary	
	$	$	$	$	$	$	$	$

	Premium for Scheduled Personal Property	$	$	$	$
Form and Endorsements made part of this Policy at time of issue: Form HO-	Combined Premium	$	$	$	$

Endorsement(s) HO-

Insert Number(s) and Edition Date(s)

DEDUCT-IBLE	SECTION I $	OTHER $	In case of a loss under Section I, we cover only that part of the loss over the deductible stated.

Section II **Other insured locations:** (No., Street, Apt., Town or City, County, State, Zip Code)

Special State Provisions	South Carolina: Valuation Clause (Cov. A) $	Minnesota: Insurable Value (Cov. A) $	New York: Coinsurance Clause Applies ☐ Yes ☐ No

Mortgagee (Name and address)

Countersigned:

By_____
                                      Authorized Representative

RATING INFORMATION

NUMBER OF FAMILIES	Not Town/rowhouse— Number of Families				Town/rowhouse— Family units in Fire Div.			HO-4 HO-6 Self-Rating		HO-4 and HO-6 Not rented to others		If YES Number of Families—		HO-6 Rented to others				If NO Number of Families	Annual Fire E.C. Rate	Year of Constr.	
	1	2	3	4	3-4	5-8	9 over	Code	No Yes	1-4	5-10	11-40	over 40	1-4	5-10	11-40	over 40			Year	Code
Code	(1)	(3)	(6)	(8)	(2)	(4)	(9)		(9)	(1)	(2)	(3)	(4)	(5)	(6)	(7)	(8)				

CON-STRUC-TION	Brick, Stone or Masonry (2)		Brick, Stone or (3)		Approved Roof		Frame with Aluminum or (5) Plastic Siding		Fire Resistive	Mobile Homes (4) enclosed Foundation	Mobile Homes Not enclosed (7) Foundation	Modular Homes rated (9) as Frame	Specifically Rated—Not (8) Fire Resistive	Unapproved Roof
	Frame (1)	Veneer	Stone (3)	Masonry		Roof			Resistive					

PROTEC-TION	Code	Not more than feet from hydrant	Not more than miles from Fire Dept.	South-ern:	Inside City limits	Inside Protected Suburb	Inside Fire District	Fire District or Town ( )

ZONE	Code	PREMIUM GR. NO.	DEDUCTIBLE: Type Code Size Code	Section I $	Other $

STATISTICAL REPORTING INFORMATION Codes: No. Type Classif. Cov. E Cov. F   Premium: Prepaid; If paid in Installments; Payable at: Inception   Each Anniversary

		Premium	Inception	Each Anniversary
Snowmobiles	( ) (—) ( ) ( ) ( )	$	$	$	$
Watercraft	( ) ((2)) ( ) ( ) ( )	$	$	$	$
Outboard Motor	( ) ((1)) ( ) ( ) ( )	$	$	$	$
ALL OTHER PREMIUMS (except Scheduled Personal Property)		$	$	$	$

(a) The **residence premises** is not seasonal; (b) no **business** pursuits are conducted on the **residence premises**; (c) the **residence premises** is the only premises where the Named Insured or spouse maintains a residence other than business or farm properties; (d) the **Insured** has no full time **residence employee(s)**; (e) the **Insured** has no outboard motor(s) or watercraft otherwise excluded under this policy for which coverage is desired. Exception, if any, to (a), (b), (c), (d) or (e)*.

* Absence of an entry means "no exceptions".

THIS DECLARATIONS PAGE, WITH POLICY JACKET, HOMEOWNERS POLICY FORM, AND ENDORSEMENTS IF ANY, ISSUED TO FORM A PART THEREOF, COMPLETES THE ABOVE NUMBERED HOMEOWNERS POLICY.

JDL 1776-0 (Ed. 7-75)

Homeowners 2
Broad Form
Ed. 7-77

AGREEMENT

We will provide the insurance described in this policy in return for the premium and compliance with all applicable provisions of this policy.

DEFINITIONS

Throughout this policy, "you" and "your" refer to the "named insured" shown in the Declarations and the spouse if a resident of the same household, and "we", "us" and "our" refer to the Company providing this insurance. In addition, certain words and phrases are defined as follows:

1. **"bodily injury"** means bodily harm, sickness or disease, including required care, loss of services and death resulting therefrom.

2. **"business"** includes trade, profession or occupation.

3. **"insured"** means you and the following residents of your household:

   a. your relatives;

   b. any other person under the age of 21 who is in the care of any person named above.

   Under Section II, **"insured"** also means:

   c. with respect to animals or watercraft to which this policy applies, any person or organization legally responsible for these animals or watercraft which are owned by you or any person included in 3a or 3b. A person or organization using or having custody of these animals or watercraft in the course of any **business**, or without permission of the owner is not an **insured;**

   d. with respect to any vehicle to which this policy applies, any person while engaged in your employment or the employment of any person included in 3a or 3b.

4. **"insured location"** means:

   a. the **residence premises;**

   b. the part of any other premises, other structures, and grounds, used by you as a residence and which is shown in the Declarations or which is acquired by you during the policy period for your use as a residence;

   c. any premises used by you in connection with the premises included in 4a or 4b;

   d. any part of a premises not owned by any **insured** but where any **insured** is temporarily residing;

   e. vacant land owned by or rented to any **insured** other than farm land;

   f. land owned by or rented to any **insured** on which a one or two family dwelling is being constructed as a residence for any **insured;**

   g. individual or family cemetery plots or burial vaults of any **insured;**

   h. any part of a premises occasionally rented to any **insured** for other than **business** purposes.

5. **"motor vehicle"** means:

   a. a motorized land vehicle designed for travel on public roads or subject to motor vehicle registration. A motorized land vehicle in dead storage on an **insured location** is not a **motor vehicle.**

   b. a trailer or semi-trailer designed for travel on public roads and subject to motor vehicle registration. A boat, camp, home or utility trailer not being towed by or carried on a vehicle included in 5a is not a **motor vehicle;**

   c. a motorized golf cart, snowmobile, or other motorized land vehicle owned by any **insured** and designed for recreational use off public roads, while off an **insured location.** A motorized golf cart while used for golfing purposes is not a **motor vehicle;**

   d. any vehicle while being towed by or carried on a vehicle included in 5a, 5b or 5c.

6. **"property damage"** means physical injury to or destruction of tangible property, including loss of use of this property.

7. "**residence employee**" means an employee of any **insured** who performs duties in connection with the maintenance or use of the **residence premises,** including household or domestic services, or who performs duties elsewhere of a similar nature not in connection with the **business** of any **insured.**

8. "**residence premises**" means the one or two family dwelling, other structures, and grounds or that part of any other building where you reside and which is shown as the "residence premises" in the Declarations.

SECTION I—COVERAGES

COVERAGE A
DWELLING

We cover:

a. the dwelling on the **residence premises** shown in the Declarations used principally as a private residence, including structures attached to the dwelling; and

b. materials and supplies located on or adjacent to the **residence premises** for use in the construction, alteration or repair of the dwelling or other structures on the **residence premises.**

COVERAGE B
OTHER
STRUCTURES

We cover other structures on the **residence premises,** separated from the dwelling by clear space. Structures connected to the dwelling by only a fence, utility line, or similar connection are considered to be other structures.

We do not cover other structures:

a. used in whole or in part for **business** purposes; or

b. rented or held for rental to any person not a tenant of the dwelling, unless used solely as a private garage.

COVERAGE C
PERSONAL
PROPERTY

We cover personal property owned or used by any **insured** while it is anywhere in the world. At your request, we will cover personal property owned by others while the property is on the part of the **residence premises** occupied by any **insured.** In addition, we will cover at your request, personal property owned by a guest or a **residence employee,** while the property is in any residence occupied by any **insured.**

Our limit of liability for personal property usually situated at any **insured's** residence, other than the **residence premises,** is 10% of the limit of liability for Coverage C, or $1000, whichever is greater. Personal property in a newly acquired principal residence is not subject to this limitation for the 30 days immediately after you begin to move the property there.

Special Limits of Liability. These limits do not increase the Coverage C limit of liability. The special limit for each following numbered category is the total limit for each occurrence for all property in that numbered category.

1. $100 on money, bank notes, bullion, gold other than goldware, silver other than silverware, platinum, coins and medals.

2. $500 on securities, accounts, deeds, evidences of debt, letters of credit, notes other than bank notes, manuscripts, passports, tickets and stamps.

3. $500 on watercraft, including their trailers, furnishings, equipment and outboard motors.

4. $500 on trailers not used with watercraft.

5. $500 on grave markers.

6. $500 for loss by theft of jewelry, watches, furs, precious and semi-precious stones.

7. $1000 for loss by theft of silverware, silver-plated ware, goldware, gold-plated ware and pewterware.

8. $1000 for loss by theft of guns.

Property Not Covered. We do not cover:

1. articles separately described and specifically insured in this or any other insurance;

2. animals, birds or fish;

3. motorized land vehicles except those used to service an **insured's** residence which are not licensed for road use;

4. any device or instrument, including any accessories or antennas, for the transmitting, recording, receiving or reproduction of sound which is operated by power from the electrical system of a **motor vehicle,** or any tape, wire, record, disc or other medium for use with any such device or instrument while any of this property is in or upon a **motor vehicle;**

5. aircraft and parts;

6. property of roomers, boarders and other tenants, except property of roomers and boarders related to any **insured;**

7. property contained in an apartment regularly rented or held for rental to others by any **insured;**

8. property rented or held for rental to others away from the **residence premises;**

9. **business** property in storage or held as a sample or for sale or delivery after sale;

10. **business** property pertaining to a **business** actually conducted on the **residence premises;**

11. **business** property away from the **residence premises.**

COVERAGE D
LOSS OF USE

The limit of liability for Coverage D is the total limit for all the following coverages.

1. **Additional Living Expense.** If a loss covered under this Section makes the **residence premises** uninhabitable, we cover any necessary increase in living expenses incurred by you so that your household can maintain its normal standard of living. Payment shall be for the shortest time required to repair or replace the premises or, if you permanently relocate, the shortest time required for your household to settle elsewhere. This period of time is not limited by expiration of this policy.

2. **Fair Rental Value.** If a loss covered under this Section makes that part of the **residence premises** rented to others or held for rental by you uninhabitable, we cover its fair rental value. Payment shall be for the shortest time required to repair or replace the part of the premises rented or held for rental. This period of time is not limited by expiration of this policy. Fair rental value shall not include any expense that does not continue while that part of the **residence premises** rented or held for rental is uninhabitable.

3. **Prohibited Use.** If a civil authority prohibits you from use of the **residence premises** as a result of direct damage to neighboring premises by a Peril Insured Against in this policy, we cover any resulting Additional Living Expense and Fair Rental Value loss for a period not exceeding two weeks during which use is prohibited.

We do not cover loss or expense due to cancellation of a lease or agreement.

ADDITIONAL
COVERAGES

1. **Debris Removal.** We will pay the reasonable expense incurred by you in the removal of debris of covered property provided coverage is afforded for the peril causing the loss. Debris removal expense is included in the limit of liability applying to the damaged property. When the amount payable for the actual damage to the property plus the expense for debris removal exceeds the limit of liability for the damaged property, an additional 5% of that limit of liability will be available to cover debris removal expense.

2. **Reasonable Repairs.** We will pay the reasonable cost incurred by you for necessary repairs made solely to protect covered property from further damage provided coverage is afforded for the peril causing the loss. This coverage does not increase the limit of liability applying to the property being repaired.

3. **Trees, Shrubs and Other Plants.** We cover trees, shrubs, plants or lawns, on the **residence premises,** for loss caused by the following Perils Insured Against: Fire or lightning, Explosion, Riot or civil commotion, Aircraft, Vehicles not owned or operated by a resident of the **residence premises,** Vandalism or malicious mischief or Theft. The limit of liability for this coverage shall not exceed 5% of the limit of liability that applies to the dwelling for all trees, shrubs, plants and lawns nor more than $500 for any one tree, shrub or plant. We do not cover property grown for **business** purposes.

4. **Fire Department Service Charge.** We will pay up to $250 for your liability assumed by contract or agreement for fire department charges incurred when the fire department is called to save or protect covered property from a Peril Insured Against. No deductible applies to this coverage.

5. **Property Removed.** Covered property while being removed from a premises endangered by a Peril Insured Against and for not more than 30 days while removed is covered for direct loss from any cause. This coverage does not change the limit of liability applying to the property being removed.

6. Credit Card, Forgery and Counterfeit Money. We will pay up to $500 for:

a. the legal obligation of any **insured** to pay because of the theft or unauthorized use of credit cards issued to or registered in any **insured's** name.

We do not cover use by a resident of your household, a person who has been entrusted with the credit card, or any person if any **insured** has not complied with all terms and conditions under which the credit card is issued.

b. loss to any **insured** caused by forgery or alteration of any check or negotiable instrument; and

c. loss to any **insured** through acceptance in good faith of counterfeit United States or Canadian paper currency.

We do not cover loss arising out of **business** pursuits or dishonesty of any **insured.**

No deductible applies to this coverage.

Defense:

a. We may make any investigation and settle any claim or suit that we decide is appropriate. Our obligation to defend any claim or suit ends when the amount we pay for the loss equals our limit of liability.

b. If a claim is made or a suit is brought against any **insured** for liability under the Credit Card coverage, we will provide a defense at our expense by counsel of our choice.

c. We have the option to defend at our expense any **insured** or any **insured's** bank against any suit for the enforcement of payment under the Forgery coverage.

SECTION I—PERILS INSURED AGAINST

We insure for direct loss to the property described in Coverages A, B and C caused by:

1. Fire or lightning.

2. Windstorm or hail.

This peril does not include loss to the interior of a building or the property contained in a building caused by rain, snow, sleet, sand or dust unless the direct force of wind or hail damages the building causing an opening in a roof or wall and the rain, snow, sleet, sand or dust enters through this opening.

This peril includes loss to watercraft and their trailers, furnishings, equipment, and outboard motors, only while inside a fully enclosed building.

3. Explosion.

4. Riot or civil commotion.

5. Aircraft, including self-propelled missiles and spacecraft.

6. Vehicles.

This peril does not include loss to a fence, driveway or walk caused by a vehicle owned or operated by a resident of the **residence premises.**

7. Smoke, meaning sudden and accidental damage from smoke.

This peril does not include loss caused by smoke from agricultural smudging or industrial operations.

8. Vandalism or malicious mischief.

This peril does not include loss to property on the **residence premises** if the dwelling has been vacant for more than 30 consecutive days immediately before the loss. A dwelling being constructed is not considered vacant.

9. Theft, including attempted theft and loss of property from a known location when it is likely that the property has been stolen.

This peril does not include loss caused by theft:

a. committed by any **insured;**

b. in or to a dwelling under construction, or of materials and supplies for use in the construction until the dwelling is completed and occupied; or

c. from any part of a **residence premises** rented by an **insured** to other than an **insured.**

This peril does not include loss caused by theft that occurs away from the **residence premises** of:

a. property while at any other residence owned, rented to, or occupied by any **insured,** except while any **insured** is temporarily residing there. Property of a student who is an **insured** is covered while at a residence away from home if the student has been there at any time during the 45 days immediately before the loss;

b. unattended property in or on any **motor vehicle** or trailer, other than a public conveyance, unless there is forcible entry into the vehicle while all its doors, windows and other openings are closed and locked and there are visible marks of the forcible entry; or the vehicle is stolen and not recovered within 30 days. Property is not unattended when the **insured** has entrusted the keys of the vehicle to a custodian;

c. watercraft, including its furnishings, equipment and outboard motors. Other property in or on any private watercraft is covered if the loss results from forcible entry into a securely locked compartment and there are visible marks of the forcible entry; or

d. trailers and campers.

10. Breakage of glass or safety glazing material which is part of a building, storm door or storm window.

This peril does not include loss on the **residence premises** if the dwelling has been vacant for more than 30 consecutive days immediately before the loss. A dwelling being constructed is not considered vacant.

11. Falling objects.

This peril does not include loss to the interior of a building or property contained in the building unless the roof or an exterior wall of the building is first damaged by a falling object. Damage to the falling object itself is not included.

12. Weight of ice, snow or sleet which causes damage to a building or property contained in the building.

This peril does not include loss to an awning, fence, patio, pavement, swimming pool, foundation, retaining wall, bulkhead, pier, wharf, or dock.

13. Collapse of a building or any part of a building.

This peril does not include loss to an awning, fence, patio, pavement, swimming pool, underground pipe, flue, drain, cesspool, septic tank, foundation, retaining wall, bulkhead, pier, wharf or dock unless the loss is a direct result of the collapse of a building. Collapse does not include settling, cracking, shrinking, bulging or expansion..

14. Accidental discharge or overflow of water or steam from within a plumbing, heating or air conditioning system or from within a household appliance. We also pay for tearing out and replacing any part of the building on the **residence premises** necessary to repair the system or appliance from which the water or steam escaped.

This peril does not include loss:

a. to a building caused by continuous or repeated seepage or leakage;

b. on the **residence premises,** if the dwelling has been vacant for more than 30 consecutive days immediately before the loss. A dwelling being constructed is not considered vacant;

c. to the system or appliance from which the water or steam escaped;

d. caused by or resulting from freezing; or

e. on the **residence premises** caused by accidental discharge or overflow which occurs off the **residence premises.**

15. Sudden and accidental tearing apart, cracking, burning or bulging of a steam or hot water heating system, an air conditioning system, or an appliance for heating water.

We do not cover loss caused by or resulting from freezing under this peril.

16. Freezing of a plumbing, heating or air conditioning system or of a household appliance.

This peril does not include loss on the **residence premises** while the dwelling is vacant, unoccupied or being constructed, unless you have used reasonable care to:

a. maintain heat in the building; or

b. shut off the water supply and drain the system and appliances of water.

17. Sudden and accidental damage from artificially generated electrical current.

This peril does not include loss to a tube, transistor or similar electronic components.

SECTION I—EXCLUSIONS

We do not cover loss resulting directly or indirectly from:

1. Ordinance or Law, meaning enforcement of any ordinance or law regulating the construction, repair, or demolition of a building or other structure, unless specifically provided under this policy.

2. Earth Movement. Direct loss by fire, explosion, theft, or breakage of glass or safety glazing materials resulting from earth movement is covered.

3. Water Damage, meaning:

a. flood, surface water, waves, tidal water, overflow of a body of water, or spray from any of these, whether or not driven by wind;

b. water which backs up through sewers or drains; or

c. water below the surface of the ground, including water which exerts pressure on, or seeps or leaks through a building, sidewalk, driveway, foundation, swimming pool or other structure.

Direct loss by fire, explosion or theft resulting from water damage is covered.

4. Power Interruption, meaning the interruption of power or other utility service if the interruption takes place away from the **residence premises.** If a Peril Insured Against ensues on the **residence premises,** we will pay only for loss caused by the ensuing peril.

5. Neglect, meaning neglect of the **insured** to use all reasonable means to save and preserve property at and after the time of a loss, or when property is endangered by a Peril Insured Against.

6. War, including undeclared war, civil war, insurrection, rebellion, revolution, warlike act by a military force or military personnel, destruction or seizure or use for a military purpose, and including any consequence of any of these. Discharge of a nuclear weapon shall be deemed a warlike act even if accidental.

7. Nuclear Hazard, to the extent set forth in the Nuclear Hazard Clause of Section I—Conditions.

SECTION I—CONDITIONS

1. Insurable Interest and Limit of Liability. Even if more than one person has an insurable interest in the property covered, we shall not be liable:

a. to the **insured** for an amount greater than the **insured's** interest; nor

b. for more than the applicable limit of liability.

2. Your Duties After Loss. In case of a loss to which this insurance may apply, you shall see that the following duties are performed:

a. give immediate notice to us or our agent, and in case of theft also to the police. In case of loss under the Credit Card coverage also notify the credit card company;

b. protect the property from further damage, make reasonable and necessary repairs required to protect the property, and keep an accurate record of repair expenditures;

c. prepare an inventory of damaged personal property showing in detail, the quantity, description, actual cash value and amount of loss. Attach to the inventory all bills, receipts and related documents that substantiate the figures in the inventory;

d. exhibit the damaged property as often as we reasonably require and submit to examination under oath;

e. submit to us, within 60 days after we request, your signed, sworn statement of loss which sets forth, to the best of your knowledge and belief:

(1) the time and cause of loss;

(2) interest of the **insured** and all others in the property involved and all encumbrances on the property;

(3) other insurance which may cover the loss;

(4) changes in title or occupancy of the property during the term of the policy;

(5) specifications of any damaged building and detailed estimates for repair of the damage;

(6) an inventory of damaged personal property described in 2c;

(7) receipts for additional living expenses incurred and records supporting the fair rental value loss;

(8) evidence or affidavit supporting a claim under the Credit Card, Forgery and Counterfeit Money coverage, stating the amount and cause of loss.

3. Loss Settlement. Covered property losses are settled as follows:

a. Personal property and structures that are not buildings at actual cash value at the time of loss but not exceeding the amount necessary to repair or replace;

b. Carpeting, domestic appliances, awnings, outdoor antennas and outdoor equipment, whether or not attached to buildings, at actual cash value at the time of loss but not exceeding the amount necessary to repair or replace;

c. Buildings under Coverage A or B at replacement cost without deduction for depreciation, subject to the following:

(1) If at the time of loss the amount of insurance in this policy on the damaged building is 80% or more of the full replacement cost of the building immediately prior to the loss, we will pay the cost of repair or replacement, without deduction for depreciation, but not exceeding the smallest of the following amounts:

(a) the limit of liability under this policy applying to the building;

(b) the replacement cost of that part of the building damaged for equivalent construction and use on the same premises; or

(c) the amount actually and necessarily spent to repair or replace the damaged building.

(2) If at the time of loss the amount of insurance in this policy on the damaged building is less than 80% of the full replacement cost of the building immediately prior to the loss, we will pay the larger of the following amounts, but not exceeding the limit of liability under this policy applying to the building:

(a) the actual cash value of that part of the building damaged; or

(b) that proportion of the cost to repair or replace, without deduction for depreciation, of that part of the building damaged, which the total amount of insurance in this policy on the damaged building bears to 80% of the replacement cost of the building.

(3) In determining the amount of insurance required to equal 80% of the full replacement cost of the building immediately prior to the loss, you shall disregard the value of excavations, foundations, piers and other supports which are below the undersurface of the lowest basement floor or, where there is no basement, which are below the surface of the ground inside the foundation walls, and underground flues, pipes, wiring and drains.

(4) When the cost to repair or replace the damage is more than $1000 or more than 5% of the amount of insurance in this policy on the building, whichever is less, we will pay no more than the actual cash value of the damage until actual repair or replacement is completed.

(5) You may disregard the replacement cost loss settlement provisions and make claim under this policy for loss or damage to buildings on an actual cash value basis and then make claim within 180 days after loss for any additional liability on a replacement cost basis.

4. Loss to a Pair or Set. In case of loss to a pair or set we may elect to:

a. repair or replace any part to restore the pair or set to its value before the loss; or

b. pay the difference between actual cash value of the property before and after the loss.

5. Glass Replacement. Loss for damage to glass caused by a Peril Insured Against shall be settled on the basis of replacement with safety glazing materials when required by ordinance or law.

6. Appraisal. If you and we fail to agree on the amount of loss, either one can demand that the amount of the loss be set by appraisal. If either makes a written demand for appraisal, each shall select a competent, independent appraiser and notify the other of the appraiser's identity within 20 days of receipt of the written demand. The two appraisers shall then select a competent, impartial umpire. If the two appraisers are unable to agree upon an umpire within 15 days, you or we can ask a judge of a court of record in the state where the **residence premises** is located to select an umpire. The appraisers shall then set the amount of the loss. If the appraisers submit a written report of an agreement to us, the amount agreed upon shall be the amount of the loss. If the appraisers fail to agree within a reasonable time, they shall submit their differences to the umpire. Written agreement signed by any two of these three shall set the amount of the loss. Each appraiser shall be paid by the party selecting that appraiser. Other expenses of the appraisal and the compensation of the umpire shall be paid equally by you and us.

7. Other Insurance. If a loss covered by this policy is also covered by other insurance, we will pay only the proportion of the loss that the limit of liability that applies under this policy bears to the total amount of insurance covering the loss.

8. Suit Against Us. No action shall be brought unless there has been compliance with the policy provisions and the action is started within one year after the occurrence causing loss or damage.

9. Our Option. If we give you written notice within 30 days after we receive your signed, sworn statement of loss, we may repair or replace any part of the property damaged with equivalent property.

10. Loss Payment. We will adjust all losses with you. We will pay you unless some other person is named in the policy to receive payment. Payment for loss will be made within 30 days after we reach agreement with you, entry of a final judgment, or the filing of an appraisal award with us.

11. Abandonment of Property. We need not accept any property abandoned by any **insured.**

12. Mortgage Clause.

The word "mortgagee" includes trustee.

If a mortgagee is named in this policy, any loss payable under Coverage A or B shall be paid to the mortgagee and you, as interests appear. If more than one mortgagee is named, the order of payment shall be the same as the order or precedence of the mortgages.

If we deny your claim, that denial shall not apply to a valid claim of the mortgagee, if the mortgagee:

a. notifies us of any change in ownership, occupancy or substantial change in risk of which the mortgagee is aware;

b. pays any premium due under this policy on demand if you have neglected to pay the premium;

c. submits a signed, sworn statement of loss within 60 days after receiving notice from us of your failure to do so. Policy conditions relating to Appraisal, Suit Against Us and Loss Payment apply to the mortgagee.

If the policy is cancelled by us, the mortgagee shall be notified at least 10 days before the date cancellation takes effect.

If we pay the mortgagee for any loss and deny payment to you:

a. we are subrogated to all the rights of the mortgagee granted under the mortgage on the property; or

b. at our option, we may pay to the mortgagee the whole principal on the mortgage plus any accrued interest. In this event, we shall receive a full assignment and transfer of the mortgage and all securities held as collateral to the mortgage debt.

Subrogation shall not impair the right of the mortgagee to recover the full amount of the mortgagee's claim.

13. No Benefit to Bailee. We will not recognize any assignment or grant any coverage for the benefit of any person or organization holding, storing or transporting property for a fee regardless of any other provision of this policy.

14. Nuclear Hazard Clause.

a. "Nuclear Hazard" means any nuclear reaction, radiation, or radioactive contamination, all whether controlled or uncontrolled or however caused, or any consequence of any of these.

b. Loss caused by the nuclear hazard shall not be considered loss caused by fire, explosion, or smoke, whether these perils are specifically named in or otherwise included within the Perils Insured Against in Section I.

c. This policy does not apply under Section I to loss caused directly or indirectly by nuclear hazard, except that direct loss by fire resulting from the nuclear hazard is covered.

SECTION II—LIABILITY COVERAGES

COVERAGE E PERSONAL LIABILITY

If a claim is made or a suit is brought against any **insured** for damages because of **bodily injury** or **property damage** to which this coverage applies, we will:

a. pay up to our limit of liability for the damages for which the **insured** is legally liable; and

b. provide a defense at our expense by counsel of our choice. We may make any investigation and settle any claim or suit that we decide is appropriate. Our obligation to defend any claim or suit ends when the amount we pay for damages resulting from the occurrence equals our limit of liability.

COVERAGE F MEDICAL PAYMENTS TO OTHERS

We will pay the necessary medical expenses incurred or medically ascertained within three years from the date of an accident causing **bodily injury.** Medical expenses means reasonable charges for medical, surgical, x-ray, dental, ambulance, hospital, professional nursing, prosthetic devices and funeral services. This coverage does not apply to you or regular residents of your household other than **residence employees.** As to others, this coverage applies only:

a. to a person on the **insured location** with the permission of any **insured; or**

b. to a person off the **insured location,** if the **bodily injury:**
   (1) arises out of a condition in the **insured location** or the ways immediately adjoining;
   (2) is caused by the activities of any **insured;**
   (3) is caused by a **residence employee** in the course of the **residence employee's** employment by any **insured; or**
   (4) is caused by an animal owned by or in the care of any **insured.**

SECTION II—EXCLUSIONS

1. **Coverage E—Personal Liability and Coverage F—Medical Payments to Others** do not apply to **bodily injury** or **property damage:**

a. which is expected or intended by the **insured;**

b. arising out of **business** pursuits of any **insured** or the rental or holding for rental of any part of any premises by any **insured.**

This exclusion does not apply to:

   (1) activities which are ordinarily incident to non-**business** pursuits; or
   (2) the rental or holding for rental of a residence of yours:
      (a) on an occasional basis for the exclusive use as a residence;
      (b) in part, unless intended for use as a residence by more than two roomers or boarders; or
      (c) in part, as an office, school, studio or private garage;

c. arising out of the rendering or failing to render professional services;

d. arising out of any premises owned or rented to any **insured** which is not an **insured location;**

e. arising out of the ownership, maintenance, use, loading or unloading of:

   (1) an aircraft;
   (2) a **motor vehicle** owned or operated by, or rented or loaned to any **insured; or**
   (3) a watercraft;
      (a) owned by or rented to any **insured** if the watercraft has inboard or inboard-outdrive motor power of more than 50 horsepower or is a sailing vessel, with or without auxiliary power, 26 feet or more in overall length; or
      (b) powered by one or more outboard motors with more than 25 total horsepower, owned by any **insured** at the inception of this policy. If you report in writing to us within 45 days after acquisition, an intention to insure any outboard motors acquired prior to the policy period, coverage will apply.

f. caused directly or indirectly by war, including undeclared war, civil war, insurrection, rebellion, revolution, warlike act by a military force or military personnel, destruction or seizure or use for a military purpose, and including any consequence of any of these. Discharge of a nuclear weapon shall be deemed a warlike act even if accidental.

Exclusion e(3) does not apply while the watercraft is stored and exclusions d and e do not apply to **bodily injury** to any **residence employee** arising out of and in the course of the **residence employee's** employment by any **insured.**

2. **Coverage E—Personal Liability,** does not apply to:
    a. liability assumed under any unwritten contract or agreement, or by contract or agreement in connection with any **business** of the **insured;**
    b. **property damage** to property owned by the **insured;**
    c. **property damage** to property rented to, occupied or used by or in the care of the **insured.** This exclusion does not apply to **property damage** caused by fire, smoke or explosion;
    d. **bodily injury** to any person eligible to receive any benefits required to be provided or voluntarily provided by the **insured** under any worker's or workmen's compensation, non-occupational disability, or occupational disease law; or
    e. **bodily injury** or **property damage** for which any **insured** under this policy is also an insured under a nuclear energy liability policy or would be an insured but for its termination upon exhaustion of its limit of liability. A nuclear energy liability policy is a policy issued by Nuclear Energy Liability Insurance Association, Mutual Atomic Energy Liability Underwriters, Nuclear Insurance Association of Canada, or any of their successors.

3. **Coverage F—Medical Payments to Others,** does not apply to **bodily injury:**
    a. to a **residence employee** if it occurs off the **insured location** and does not arise out of or in the course of the **residence employee's** employment by any **insured;**
    b. to any person, eligible to receive any benefits required to be provided or voluntarily provided under any worker's or workmen's compensation, non-occupational disability or occupational disease law;
    c. from any nuclear reaction, radiation or radioactive contamination, all whether controlled or uncontrolled or however caused, or any consequence of any of these.

SECTION II—ADDITIONAL COVERAGES

We cover the following in addition to the limits of liability:

1. **Claim Expenses.** We pay:
    a. expenses incurred by us and costs taxed against any **insured** in any suit we defend;
    b. premiums on bonds required in a suit defended by us, but not for bond amounts greater than the limit of liability for Coverage E. We are not obligated to apply for or furnish any bond;
    c. reasonable expenses incurred by any **insured** at our request, including actual loss of earnings (but not loss of other income) up to $50 per day for assisting us in the investigation or defense of any claim or suit;
    d. interest on the entire judgment which accrues after entry of the judgment and before we pay or tender, or deposit in court that part of the judgment which does not exceed the limit of liability that applies.

2. **First Aid Expenses.** We will pay expenses for first aid to others incurred by any **insured** for **bodily injury** covered under this policy. We will not pay for first aid to you or any other **insured.**

3. **Damage to Property of Others.** We will pay up to $250 per occurrence for **property damage** to property of others caused by any **insured.**

We will not pay for **property damage:**
    a. to property covered under Section I of this policy;
    b. caused intentionally by any **insured** who is 13 years of age or older;
    c. to property owned by or rented to any **insured,** a tenant of any **insured,** or a resident in your household; or
    d. arising out of:
    (1) **business** pursuits;
    (2) any act or omission in connection with a premises owned, rented or controlled by any **insured,** other than the **insured location;** or
    (3) the ownership, maintenance, or use of a **motor vehicle,** aircraft or watercraft.

SECTION II—CONDITIONS

1. Limit of Liability. Regardless of the number of **insureds,** claims made or persons injured, our total liability under Coverage E stated in this policy for all damages resulting from any one occurrence shall not exceed the limit of liability for Coverage E stated in the Declarations. All **bodily injury** and **property damage** resulting from any one accident or from continuous or repeated exposure to substantially the same general conditions shall be considered to be the result of one occurrence.

Our total liability under Coverage F for all medical expense payable for **bodily injury** to one person as the result of one accident shall not exceed the limit of liability for Coverage F stated in the Declarations.

2. Severability of Insurance. This insurance applies separately to each **insured.** This condition shall not increase our limit of liability for any one occurrence.

3. Duties After Loss. In case of an accident or occurrence, the **insured** shall perform the following duties that apply. You shall cooperate with us in seeing that these duties are performed:

a. give written notice to us or our agent as soon as practicable, which sets forth:

(1) the identity of the policy and **insured;**

(2) reasonably available information on the time, place and circumstances of the accident or occurrence; and

(3) names and addresses of any claimants and available witnesses;

b. forward to us every notice, demand, summons or other process relating to the accident or occurrence;

c. at our request, assist in:

(1) making settlement;

(2) the enforcement of any right of contribution or indemnity against any person or organization who may be liable to any **insured;**

(3) the conduct of suits and attend hearings and trials;

(4) securing and giving evidence and obtaining the attendance of witnesses;

d. under the coverage—Damage to the Property of Others—submit to us within 60 days after the loss, a sworn statement of loss and exhibit the damaged property, if within the **insured's** control;

e. the **insured** shall not, except at the **insured's** own cost, voluntarily make any payment, assume any obligation or incur any expense other than for first aid to others at the time of the **bodily injury.**

4. Duties of an Injured Person—Coverage F—Medical Payments to Others. The injured person or someone acting on behalf of the injured person shall:

a. give us written proof of claim, under oath if required, as soon as practicable;

b. execute authorization to allow us to obtain copies of medical reports and records; and

c. the injured person shall submit to physical examination by a physician selected by us when and as often as we reasonably require.

5. Payment of Claim—Coverage F—Medical Payments to Others. Payment under this coverage is not an admission of liability by any **insured** or us.

6. Suit Against Us. No action shall be brought against us unless there has been compliance with the policy provisions.

No one shall have any right to join us as a party to any action against any **insured.** Further, no action with respect to Coverage E shall be brought against us until the obligation of the **insured** has been determined by final judgment or agreement signed by us.

7. Bankruptcy of any Insured. Bankruptcy or insolvency of any **insured** shall not relieve us of any of our obligations under this policy.

8. Other Insurance—Coverage E—Personal Liability. This insurance is excess over any other valid and collectible insurance except insurance written specifically to cover as excess over the limits of liability that apply in this policy.

SECTION I AND SECTION II—CONDITIONS

1. Policy Period. This policy applies only to loss under Section I or **bodily injury** or **property damage** under Section II, which occurs during the policy period.

2. Concealment or Fraud. We do not provide coverage for any **insured** who has intentionally concealed or misrepresented any material fact or circumstance relating to this insurance.

3. Liberalization Clause. If we adopt any revision which would broaden the coverage under this policy without additional premium within 60 days prior to or during the policy period, the broadened coverage will immediately apply to this policy.

4. Waiver or Change of Policy Provisions. A waiver or change of any provision of this policy must be in writing by us to be valid. Our request for an appraisal or examination shall not waive any of our rights.

5. Cancellation.

a. You may cancel this policy at any time by returning it to us or by notifying us in writing of the date cancellation is to take effect.

b. We may cancel this policy only for the reasons stated in this condition by notifying you in writing of the date cancellation takes effect. This cancellation notice may be delivered to you. or mailed to you at your mailing address shown in the Declarations. Proof of mailing shall be sufficient proof of notice.

(1) When you have not paid the premium. whether payable to us or to our agent or under any finance or credit plan. we may cancel at any time by notifying you at least 10 days before the date cancellation takes effect.

(2) When this policy has been in effect for less than 60 days and is not a renewal with us. we may cancel for any reason by notifying you at least 10 days before the date cancellation takes effect.

(3) When this policy has been in effect for 60 days or more. or at any time if it is a renewal with us. we may cancel if there has been a material misrepresentation of fact which if known to us would have caused us not to issue the policy or if the risk has changed substantially since the policy was issued. This can be done by notifying you at least 30 days before the date cancellation takes effect.

(4) When this policy is written for a period longer than one year. we may cancel for any reason at anniversary by notifying you at least 30 days before the date cancellation takes effect.

c. When this policy is cancelled. the premium for the period from the date of cancellation to the expiration date will be refunded. When you request cancellation. the return premium will be based on our short rate table. When we cancel. the return premium will be pro rata.

d. If the return premium is not refunded with the notice of cancellation or when this policy is returned to us. we will refund it within a reasonable time after the date cancellation takes effect.

6. Non-Renewal. We may elect not to renew this policy. We may do so by delivery to you. or mailing to you at your mailing address shown in the Declarations. written notice at least 30 days before the expiration date of this policy. Proof of mailing shall be sufficient proof of notice.

7. Assignment. Assignment of this policy shall not be valid unless we give our written consent.

8. Subrogation. Any **insured** may waive in writing before a loss all rights of recovery against any person. If not waived. we may require an assignment of rights of recovery for a loss to the extent that payment is made by us.

If an assignment is sought. any **insured** shall sign and deliver all related papers and cooperate with us in any reasonable manner.

Subrogation does not apply under Section II to Medical Payments to Others or Damage to Property of Others.

9. Death. If any person named in the Declarations or the spouse. if a resident of the same household. dies:

a. we insure the legal representative of the deceased but only with respect to the premises and property of the deceased covered under the policy at the time of death;

b. **insured** includes:

(1) any member of your household who is an **insured** at the time of your death. but only while a resident of the **residence premises; and**

(2) with respect to your property. the person having proper temporary custody of the property until appointment and qualification of a legal representative.

INDEX

DATE DUE

OCT 28 '80	OCT 20 '90		
NOV 19 '81	DEC 2 '81		
DEC 10 '81	DEC 7 '81		
DE 7 '83	JAN 27 '84		
DE 05 '86	DEC 9 '86		
FE 04 '87	FEB 20 '87		
NO 2 '87	NOV 2 '87		
MR 01 '88	MAR 23 '88		
OC 17 '90	NOV 30 '90		
SEP. 26 1991	SEP 18 '91		